GENDER AND JIM CROW

The University of

North Carolina Press

Chapel Hill & London

gender

AND JIM CROW

WOMEN AND THE POLITICS OF WHITE SUPREMACY

IN NORTH CAROLINA, 1896–1920

GLENDA ELIZABETH GILMORE

Library of Congress Cataloging-in-Publication Data

Gilmore, Glenda Elizabeth.   Gender and Jim

Crow : women and the politics of white supremacy

in North Carolina, 1896–1920 / by Glenda

Elizabeth Gilmore.

p.   cm. — (Gender & American culture)   Includes

bibliographical references (p.   ) and index.

ISBN 0-8078-2287-6 (cloth : alk. paper)

ISBN 0-8078-4596-5 (pbk. : alk. paper)

1. Afro-American women—North Carolina—

Political activity.   2. Afro-American women—

North Carolina—History.   3. Afro-Americans—

Suffrage—North Carolina.   4. North Carolina—

Race relations.   5. North Carolina—Politics and

government—1865–1950.   I. Title.   II. Series.

E185.93.N6.G55   1996   96-10259

324'.089'960730756—dc20   CIP

The paper in this book meets the guidelines for

permanence and durability of the Committee on

Production Guidelines for Book Longevity of the

Council on Library Resources.

cloth   06 05 04 03 02   5 4 3 2 1

paper   06 05 04 03   8 7 6 5

Publication of this work was aided by a generous

grant from the Z. Smith Reynolds Foundation.

TO MILES

and in memory of my grandmother, Candy Lovin Welborn,

who saved me with stories

contents

illustrations

acknowledgments

The institutional support I have received for this book has been astonishing. Some of it enabled me to do research; some of it enabled me to write; all of it enabled me to keep faith in my ability to tell this story. A college fellowship from the National Endowment for the Humanities gave me a writing year; the history department of Yale University allowed me to accept it. Receiving the Lerner-Scott dissertation award from the Organization of American Historians encouraged me when I despaired of ever turning my dissertation into a book. Sympathetic colleagues and administrators at Queens College in Charlotte, North Carolina, allowed me to rearrange my teaching schedule so that I could work on the book; a Queens Faculty Development Grant sent me to the Rockefeller Archive Center in North Tarrytown, New York. At the dissertation stage, I received a research grant in women's studies from the Woodrow Wilson Foundation, an Albert J. Beveridge Research Award from the American Historical Association, an Archie K. Davis Award from the North Caroliniana Society, the Graduate Student Award given by the Coordinating Committee on Women in the Historical Profession and the Conference Group on Women's History (CCWHP/CGWH), and a teaching fellowship from the University of North Carolina at Chapel Hill. An article from the dissertation, "Gender and Jim Crow: Sarah Dudley Pettey's Vision of the New South," received the R. D. W. Connor Award from the Historical Society of North Carolina and the Letitia Woods Brown Memorial Publication Prize for Articles from the Association of Black Women Historians.

The commentators on the fourteen conference papers that emerged from this project shaped my thinking and repeatedly enabled me to correct my course. They are a distinguished group: James Anderson, Kathy Berkeley, Julia Blackwelder, Elsa Barkley Brown, Thavolia Glymph, Beverly Guy-Sheftall, Wanda Hendricks, Thomas Holt, Michael Hucles, Tera Hunter, Earl Lewis, Nancy MacLean, Jacqueline Rouse, Arnold Taylor, Liz Turner, and Lillian Williams. They will find abundant evidence of the influence of their insightful suggestions in these pages. The scholarly convention of paper presentation worked for me exactly as it should have. Through giving papers, I tested ideas, sharpened my thinking, received the wisdom of the leading people in my field, and learned from the audiences. I am grateful for those opportunities.

Kate Douglas Torrey of the University of North Carolina Press evidenced an early interest in publishing the work and has remained steadfast in her support. Edward Ayers, Jane Dailey, Laura Edwards, Bruce Fort, and Kate Torrey all read a late draft of the manuscript, and their hard work and thoughtful suggestions showed me ways to rethink important points and clarify confusing sections. Nancy Hewitt, serving as a reader for the University of North Carolina Press, helped me turn the dissertation into a book draft, and then her meticulous rereading vastly improved the book. Robert Johnston of Yale University and his students Andrew Hayek, Benjamin Heber Johnson, and Gus Kallergis saved me from making numerous errors and helped me tighten my arguments.

Two of my students at Queens College, Shelley Thompson and Scott Holmes, were the best work-study students anyone could have. They accepted their transformation into research assistants with grace and good humor. Once unleashed on newspapers on microfilm, clippings on microfiche, or interlibrary loan quests, they were indefatigable and energetic. Queens student Robin Morris conscientiously retraced my steps in examining the *Star of Zion* and pushed my work forward with her own keen research sense. I could depend on her to find my errors and correct them. And she accomplished all of this as a freshperson—she will be a great historian some day.

One of the best parts of becoming a scholar has been gaining a circle of smart friends who love to argue. My dissertation-writing group—Bruce Kalk, Sarah Wilkerson-Freeman, Leah Hagedorn, Karen Leathem, and Karl Campbell—both supported and criticized my ideas and compelled me to return to graduate school after a year-long illness. Leah Hagedorn and Karl Campbell read every word of the dissertation and argued every point exhaustively. Karen Leathem lived with scores of drafts over a seven-year period and cheerfully treated my work as her own. Her unparalleled editing skills and her deep knowledge of the South—actual and historiographical—

have left deep impressions on the book. Laura Edwards and I attended our first seminar on the South together. Her unmatched research skills, analytical mind, and commitment to exposing an alternative South have pushed me to rethink my arguments at every turn. Other friends and critics who have shaped this work include Leah Arroyo, Ruth Ben-Ghiat, Pamela Dean, David Godshalk, Steve Kantrowitz, Valinda Littlefield, Bryant Simon, and Marjorie Wheeler. Visiting the Rockefeller Archive Center with Valinda Littlefield and James Anderson enabled me to squeeze a month of work into a week.

While I was still browsing through history courses, at a time when becoming a scholar was the last thing on my mind, Paul Escott, David Goldfield, and Julia Blackwelder convinced me to take my study of history seriously. They made it seem as if getting a Ph.D. would be fun. Paul Escott steered me to the rich history of turn-of-the-century North Carolina and taught me to do primary research when he directed my master's thesis. Donald Mathews helped me structure the project at its inception, aimed me in the direction of the black church, and read various parts of the manuscript. His comments were invariably helpful. Harry Watson made career counseling a calming and supportive experience for graduate students at Chapel Hill.

My dissertation committee at Chapel Hill was a historian's dream team: William E. Leuchtenburg, James Leloudis, Joel Williamson, Jacquelyn Dowd Hall, and Nell Irvin Painter. They shaped me and my work, not just individually but collectively. Professor Leuchtenburg not only shared his encyclopedic knowledge of political history but also helped me develop a balanced perspective on the interconnected events of the twentieth century. Jim Leloudis saved me from making embarrassing errors in North Carolina history and at the same time helped me build theoretical approaches to the Progressive Era in the South. Joel Williamson shared his vast knowledge about the South, about writing, and about the scholar's role in his or her native land. He also gave me an invaluable gift—the ability to see history as art.

No deft turn of phrase can express my enormous debts to Jacquelyn Hall and Nell Painter. If I had never known them but only their work, I would have found many of the explanations for which I searched during my many years outside the academy. Working with them has done more than bring out the best in me; their friendship and counsel have transformed my life.

My years as Professor Hall's research assistant and our subsequent collaboration revealed to me the phenomenal commitment one must make to be a scholar. I am not sure I will ever live up to her example, but it may be enough to try. Professor Hall read every draft of the manuscript and all fourteen conference papers with unflagging attention, as if she was approaching the topic for the first time. She always found ways to push my thinking and my writing forward, to consider the implications of my arguments at deeper levels, and to shape the narrative so that people would want to continue reading it. Best of all, she is never boring. Her engagement with ideas makes being a historian seem breathlessly exciting. Being her friend lights up everyday life.

Professor Painter suggested this topic to me in the last seminar of my graduate career, and she continued to direct my dissertation after moving to Princeton University. Her approach to African American history—that it is central to the American experience—shaped the construction of the manuscript at every turn. She never suggested that I think like anyone else and always seemed to assume that I would be able to contradict the traditional southern narrative and live to tell about it. She has provided a wise professional role model on countless occasions. She has listened avidly to me give papers she just finished editing and, most importantly, helped me keep my faith in the importance of my topic. She is the consummate dissertation director and the best sort of friend.

Many years ago, Lu Leake of Wake Forest College made it possible for me to finish my undergraduate education. Without her interest in my situation, my life would have been very different. Later, Sherry Smith, my business partner, encouraged me to return to school. She took up the threads of our joint commitment and created a secure base that gave me the courage to change my career. During the course of this project, my parents, Mack and Lois MacKenzie, became the world's best grandparents. Their support of my family and their respect for my work have been invaluable.

My husband, Charles Johnson, taught me to ask questions, to work hard at writing, and to care about social justice. After fifteen years, each day I find new strengths to admire in him. He is a great dad, too. This book is dedicated to our son, Miles Aaron Johnson, whose past is in these pages and who gives the future its hope.

introduction

"There is an old adage, nevertheless a true one, that 'justice slumbers but never sleeps.' ... Ofttimes in slumbering, merit lies unrewarded for a time." Sarah Dudley Pettey was twenty-seven years old, the wife of a bishop in the African Methodist Episcopal Zion Church, when she began her "Woman's Column" with these words in August 1896. Writing from her home in New Bern, North Carolina, Dudley Pettey vowed to devote her forum in the *Star of Zion* not only to issues within "the limited confines of womanhood" but also to "the elevation of oppressed humanity." She understood that women's concerns were not simply private matters; they were public matters as well. African American families suffered, she told her readers, because the "American Eagle" protected "beneath his mighty wings all of his white children: while with his talons he ruthlessly claws all who are poor and especially those who trace their lineage to ebony hued parentage." Although Dudley Pettey promised to sprinkle her space with "fashion notes" and "household receipts," she knew that her female readers' interests stretched far beyond their own "hearthstones" to their "neighborhood ... town or city ... and the affairs of State."[1]

Before the turn of the century, Dudley Pettey and her peers saw themselves not as a marginalized group but as the vanguard of their race and sex. As members of the small but rapidly growing black middle class in the South, they were prepared for leadership by their educations, professional positions, and voluntary work. They did not call themselves feminists, but equality for women grounded their thinking as they championed strategies to benefit all African Americans. Although they could not vote, they took seriously their responsibilities as citizens.

I initially encountered this group of black middle-class women while investigating the 1920 election in North Carolina, the first in which women voted. Leading black women organized a registration campaign in African American sections of urban areas across the state. Discovering black women's presence at the polls, which complicated the received wisdom on southern politics and race relations, inspired me to explore the political culture of women, beginning in 1896 before black men lost their right to vote at the turn of the century. That investigation of women's political culture soon doubled back on itself as I realized that gender and race were no less intertwined in men's politics than they were in women's.

The result is a study of North Carolina politics with black women at its center. Some will argue that telling the story from their angle of vision distorts the southern political narrative as a whole. I would reply that historical re-vision is long overdue. The subfields of the discipline—African American history, women's history, social history, southern history, political history—are drawn by and for historians. Analyses that separate these subfields misrepresent the way people actually lived their lives. Re-visioning southern politics must take into account the plethora of new sources on African American and women's history, grapple with the theoretical insight that gender and race are socially constructed, and test new ideas about the junctures of public and private space in political culture.

In attempting that rewriting, I discovered—or created—a place quite different from the one I thought I knew as a native North Carolinian. Historian Robert Rosenstone wrote of one of his projects: "In no way was my purpose to write fiction; that is to make up evidence about the past."[2] Although I did not "make up" evidence, the "made-up" quality of white accounts in archives had to be my starting point. In the segregated South, whites invented a past for posterity by making up on a daily basis a multitude of justifications and rationalizations for racial oppression. Growing up there as a white girl in the 1950s, I lived that fiction. The subsequent separation of self from lies consumed much of my postadolescent, post–civil rights movement life, as I painfully peeled away a tissue of falsehoods and cut through many connections to my upbringing in the segregated South. After that, I believed no truth and took no evidence at face value. Fiction in the archives? What else? Basing southern political history on white archival sources has rendered African Americans as passive recipients of whites' actions. Black middle-class men have appeared as exceptions in the narrative, while black women have disappeared altogether.

Historians have begun only recently to reclaim the world that Sarah Dudley Pettey represented, and their work has prompted tantalizing ques-

tions about North Carolina history during the dramatic period from disfranchisement to woman suffrage. Two dissertations helped me define
the topic: Rosalyn Terborg-Penn's "Afro-Americans in the Struggle for
Woman Suffrage" and Evelyn Brooks Higginbotham's "Women's Movement in the Black Baptist Church, 1880–1920." By depicting complicated
and flexible political cultures among black women, these works caused me
to rethink the standard categories of race, gender, class, and politics. As I
completed the manuscript, Higginbotham's *Righteous Discontent: The Wom-
en's Movement in the Black Baptist Church, 1880–1920* appeared. Her sophisticated theoretical approaches to class and intraracial gender issues reinforced my analysis of the North Carolina case and helped me articulate
many points. Throughout my research and writing, unpublished papers
and published articles by Elsa Barkley Brown on black women's politics in
Richmond, Virginia, spurred me to think harder, to look at evidence in a
new light, and to make connections between the private and the public in
new ways. Almost twenty years ago, Jacquelyn Dowd Hall's *Revolt against
Chivalry: Jessie Daniel Ames and the Women's Campaign against Lynching* posed
questions regarding the nature of interracial cooperation and the importance of local context to women's politics that historians are just beginning
to answer. In many ways, *Gender and Jim Crow* could be subtitled "The Road
to Memphis" since I set out to find out how and why black and white
women came together in the interracial movement launched in the 1920s.[3]

My attempt to discover black women's place in politics built upon scholarship that recaptured white women's experiences and race relations among
men in the South. Anne Firor Scott's work on women's politics and voluntary societies and Marjorie Spruill Wheeler's chronicle of southern suffrage
leaders recaptured the past of southern white women. Suzanne Lebsock's
article on woman suffrage in Virginia shored up my argument. *Gender and
Jim Crow* also draws on careful depictions of North Carolina's politics from
whites' points of view. In those works, to a greater extent than in scholarship on other southern states, African Americans appear occasionally as
political actors. I took Eric Anderson's *Race and Politics in North Carolina,
1872–1901: The Black Second* as a model for centering the black political experience, and its documentation of black men's roles in that earlier period
gave me a basis for understanding black women's political heritage. Joel
Williamson's *Crucible of Race: Black-White Relations in the American South since
Emancipation* served as my first introduction to the Wilmington race riot
and Thomas Dixon, Jr., and has remained an inspiration.[4]

Ideas of public and private spheres as articulated by Jurgen Habermas
and modified by Nancy Fraser and other feminist theorists suggested questions about how political sites and boundaries changed as black men lost
the right to vote, as the state institutionalized segregation, and as women

gained the ballot. Barbara Fields's work on race as a social construction and Thomas Holt's study of concepts of manhood, citizenship, and liberty in Jamaica gave me ways to think about the making and remaking of race in connection with civil liberties and civil rights. David Roediger's articulation of the wages of whiteness under quite different circumstances helped explain why poor white men and women in North Carolina could work and vote against their own self-interest for so long.[5]

James Anderson richly portrayed the world of black education in the South, furnishing a framework for exploring the educational experiences of North Carolina's African American women. Other historians, most notably Cynthia Neverdon-Morton and Jacqueline Rouse, wrote about black women and reform in other southern settings, posing questions I could ask of my sources. Rich community studies including Earl Lewis's on Norfolk, George Wright's on Louisville, and Joe William Trotter's on southern West Virginia provided useful models. Robin D. G. Kelley's study of black communists in Alabama taught me never to doubt the complexity of the lives of African Americans who endured severely circumscribed conditions.[6]

Even as these historians and others recaptured the African American experience in the South, they posed new questions about class to complicate the narrative. Seeing through the scrim of the civil rights movement, historians who began writing African American history in the 1970s and 1980s often expected to find the "black community" united against oppression in the past. But just two decades earlier, the sociologist E. Franklin Frazier had condemned the black bourgeoisie as stultifying impediments to change. These oppositional treatments of class among African Americans serve as warnings against either mythologizing African American solidarity or applying notions of class formation based on white experience. Both overstatements reflect the fact that we know very little about the history of class in African American life, despite a century of broad generalizations on the subject. Others have gotten at class issues through memoirs—a valuable exercise but one that by necessity lacks context and the reach of historical research.[7] Moreover, historical scholarship on class among African Americans has tended to focus on a narrow stratum at the top of black society: W. E. B. Du Bois's "talented tenth." Most recently, historian Willard Gatewood has documented the close network of "aristocrats of color" across the country at the turn of the century.[8] The educated, middling black men and women who lived out their lives as good citizens in small North Carolina towns do not belong in either group.

Not surprisingly, the meanings of class among African Americans have changed considerably over the past century, and it is a mistake to assume that class constructions that exist now existed in the past. This book chronicles, indeed it celebrates, the black middle class in the years prior to 1920. The people in these pages were men and women who had forgotten neither their families' enslavement nor their own struggles for an education. They unabashedly believed that they were setting the best example for other African Americans to follow, and they aimed to help the less fortunate along. These middle-class black men and women saw themselves as ambassadors to the white power structure. Their skills at self-presentation and at interpreting whites' meanings convinced them that they should lead.

The concept of a middle class, as historians use it, seems too rigid to describe this group of leading black men and women. It is a term they never used; instead, they called themselves the "better" classes and understood their adoption of Victorian values as an application of their own Christian principles. Black men and women practiced middle-class habits— temperance, frugality, and hard work—as useful tools for living. Whites constantly denied them recognition as equals, but educated African Americans were confident that they could prove they belonged among the Best Men and Best Women, regardless of color. Certainly, my focus on black leaders often slights the black working-class point of view. That neglect underscores the point that this is only one story of African American resistance; others remain to be told.

The white men in these pages are a self-selected lot: those who publicly oppressed African Americans. They include leading Democratic politicians, rowdy white supremacists, and calculating disfranchisers, but they do not represent the racial views of all white men. The leaders depicted here wielded an inordinate amount of power to structure a discriminatory society and to influence other white men's racial ideologies. Missing here, for the most part, are the white men who became interracialists and tried to mitigate the worst of white supremacy or those who simply disapproved of white violence and tried to practice individual acts of kindness. I did not deliberately count them out; they simply did not have much influence on the racial climate and politics of the state from 1896 to 1920.

White women move in and out of the spotlight as their politics intersect with and diverge from black women's strategies. Most of the white women I introduce are middle-class leaders. Some actively worked for black disfranchisement; others tentatively began to foster interracial cooperation in the years before woman suffrage. Occasionally, the same woman did both. White women were overwhelmingly complicitous in shoring up white supremacy in 1898, yet they were at the vanguard of the movement for interracial cooperation by 1920. As feminist historians rewrite the past to reveal women's agency, we should retain a cautionary approach that takes into account the limits of the possible. Most white women simply could not overcome the racial contexts in which they lived, even if they had thought to try. A very few changed over time, broke with white men, and responded to black women's efforts.

Rewriting southern politics from Sarah Dudley Pettey's viewpoint means that everything looks different: the reasons for disfranchisement, its immediate effects on black political life, and its legacy. The first three chapters of this study argue that racial repression at the turn of the century did not simply institutionalize the prevailing trend in race relations; rather, it profoundly reordered society. These chapters explore relations of race and gender prior to disfranchisement. Chapter 1 traces the economic strategies, political ideologies, educational opportunities, and interracial experiences of a single family over four generations. The Dudley/Pettey family saga illustrates the contingencies of politics, the fruits of education, and the ebb and flow of interracial relations in the last half of the nineteenth century. Chapter 2 explores the education and civic work of African American women, focusing on how the intersections of race and gender affected their actions and ideologies. The third chapter examines constructions of race, class, and manhood among North Carolina's men, black and white, prior to disfranchisement and analyzes the deployment of those constructions in politics. At one level, this work is a collective biography: many of the people introduced in the first chapters figure in the subsequent accounts of the next two decades.

Chapters 4 and 5 explore the ways in which white Democrats crafted and deployed a gender-based version of white supremacy in the violent election campaign of 1898 and their subsequent disfranchisement of African American men in 1900. This is an oft-told tale, but most versions have probed white men's motivations and actions, accepted the common notions of white women's passivity and black men's criminality, and ignored black women altogether. Chapter 4 argues that the white supremacists responded to growing assertiveness among white women, to urban and industrial social pressures, and to spectacular African American successes. It also reveals the central roles black and white women played in the campaigns, both as actors and as objects. Chapter 5 then turns to the removal of African American men from the public sphere, begun with disfranchisement, exacerbated by the restructuring of the Republican Party and the growing reticence of the black church, and culminating in whites' demonization of the black family. Throughout, these chapters record African American resistance to the rising tide of white supremacy, revealing a black political milieu infinitely more varied than the binary construction of black resistance around the oppositional poles of Booker T. Washington and W. E. B. Du Bois.

The final three chapters argue that after disfranchisement of black men, black women became diplomats to the white community, just as southern progressivism flowered. Whites designed their progressive programs to exclude African Americans, but black women built social service and civic structures that wrested some recognition and meager services from the expanding welfare state. Ironically, as black men were forced from the political, the political underwent a redefinition, opening new space for black women. Contact between black and white women increased, and woman suffrage became an issue that forced activist white women to examine their racial ideology. Chapter 8 provides an analysis of black women's campaign to register and vote in 1920, white women's racial strategies during the woman suffrage struggle, and the effect of the black woman voter on white supremacy. Woman suffrage forever altered white supremacy's style and cleared a narrow path for black men to return to electoral politics.

The sources that undergird this account were written by African Americans. Expecting to find a dearth of black sources when I began this study, I soon found myself submerged under a deluge. My first day in the archives, I set up a random reel of *Star of Zion* microfilm, closed my eyes, and hit the forward button. I looked up to see Sarah Dudley Pettey's first "Woman's Column" fill the screen. And so we began together. In the pages of the *Star*, I soon met other women like her—women who had classical educations and read Latin and Greek; women who argued about politics and theology; women who founded a statewide African American Woman's Christian Temperance Union in the 1880s. Their names and impressive accomplishments had disappeared completely from the historical record. Since the *Star* has been published continuously since the early 1880s, I could trace these women over long periods of time. Once I identified leaders, I began the painstaking task of retrieving their lives. Turning first to the manuscript census, I built genealogies, traced residence patterns, and discovered the births of children. Then scattered sources, particularly school histories and church convention minutes, placed the women within their communities. North Carolina black women led cosmopolitan lives. Their papers and correspondence are scattered in archives in Boston, New York City, Washington, D.C., Evanston, New Orleans, and Atlanta.

Because of the central role Sarah Dudley Pettey plays in the early pages of my work, I was determined to find her descendants. After placing plaintive classified ads and making embarrassing telephone calls to strangers across the state, I finally located Dudley family members by contacting ministers of African American churches in New Bern. With Pettey's nephew, grand-

niece, and granddaughter contributing family papers and scrapbooks, I traced the Dudleys and the Petteys back to the Revolutionary War. Through similarly circuitous routes, I found descendants of the other women about whom I write. Only once did my determination falter. One day, while reading church records stored in a closet at a historically black college in Salisbury, I happened upon Sarah Dudley Pettey's obituary and discovered information that even her family did not know: that she had died in 1906 when she was only thirty-seven. I already knew, of course, that she was dead. So far, however, her writing had beckoned me on, led me to sources, and reassured me as I followed its trail. I mourned for my guide, stunned that I must now learn things she never knew. Later that day, rummaging in a hundred-year-old bookcase, I found the minutes of the Salisbury Colored Women's Civic League. These minutes, a meeting-by-meeting account of black women's civic activism from 1913 to 1920, are among only a handful of such documents in the entire South. Probably unread since they were placed in the bookcase in the 1920s, they revealed that black women entered politics long before they ever voted.

Once I was immersed in "black" sources, I learned to read "white" texts in new ways. Using the *Star* and other black newspapers in conjunction with white newspapers, I discovered two versions of white supremacy that revealed a great deal about the writers' points of view. Within rich local contexts, white writers responded to African American actions and ideas, sometimes directly, sometimes in coded messages. Material on white women was readily available, and many collections preserve the world views of privileged white women in North Carolina. Yet white women often hid their thoughts on race and erased interracial encounters reported by black women, leaving a scattering of partial truths behind.

Few of the black women in these pages ever became well known, yet they crafted a tradition of political activism that deserves celebration and emulation. Their lives remind us that white supremacy entailed more than violence and the denial of economic opportunities and political rights. It forced African Americans to endure an excruciating assault on their hopes and dreams. But what is most important about white supremacy remains least documented: African American resistance. The black men and women in these pages fought back, even though history has not registered battles won so slowly and victories so flawed. Justice slumbered throughout Sarah Dudley Pettey's life and beyond, and merit lay unrewarded for a longer time than she ever dreamed possible.

— Thesis
of book

GENDER AND JIM CROW

one

PLACE AND POSSIBILITY

"Some would say that woman is good [*is*]
in her place. This reminds me of what some white people say of the Negro:
that 'He is good in his place.' "[1] Sarah Dudley Pettey challenged the idea of
"place," not simply through words such as these but also through her acts.
She was an African American woman, the daughter of slaves, who lived in
obscurity in a small North Carolina town. In 1896, when she wrote these
words, Dudley Pettey thought she saw the day coming when a person's
place would depend not on sex or color but on energy and ability.

Since historians enter a story at its end, they sometimes forget that what
is past to them was future to their subjects. Too often, what they lose in the
telling is what made their subjects' lives worth living: hope. This is a book — *Topic*
about hope, about African American women such as Dudley Pettey whose
alternative visions of the future included the equity in society they had
learned to expect in their families, schools, and marriages.[2] Their progres- — *Thesis*
sive visions, if realized, would have ended white supremacy. These were
lives on the cusp of change.

With a less prosperous white elite than Virginia or South Carolina, a fast-
growing, but ferociously struggling, middling group of people of all hues,
and some chance for two-party government, North Carolina's people con-

tested power—economic, social, and political—more openly and more heatedly than many other southerners. In the western mountains, this upper South state resembled its neighbor eastern Tennessee, with pockets of bitter Unionists, an entrenched Republican Party, and a sparse African American population. In the east, where plantations produced cotton and tobacco, black majorities voted in the 1880s and 1890s, and rough port cities could only aspire to the grandeur of Charleston or Savannah. Inhabitants of the crossroad Piedmont hamlets, where whites barely outnumbered a growing black urban population, struggled to turn their locations into a reason for existence and then, as now, looked toward Atlanta with a mixture of envy and disgust.[3] North Carolina's geographical, economic, and historical diversity resulted in close gubernatorial and national elections and a legislature bristling with Republican representatives, not to mention the odd Prohibitionist or Silverite. Shared power among political parties meant that legal segregation came late to the state—not until 1899 did the state legislature demand that railroads provide Jim Crow cars—and that disfranchisement trailed the 1890 Mississippi law by a decade.[4]

Black North Carolinians realized the precariousness of their position even as they imagined the future. North Carolinian Charles Chesnutt, a child genius whose precocity and fair complexion often led whites to draw him into conversation, learned, along with his daily lessons in German and Latin, the depths of southern white prejudice. In his teenage years in the 1870s, before whites perfected Jim Crow institutions, Chesnutt confided to his diary the absurdity of walking around in a place where the color line moved under his feet. Later, after he had left North Carolina and became a renowned novelist, Chesnutt borrowed from mythology to describe his memories of the limited social space assigned African Americans in his home state. He compared white North Carolinians to Procrustes, the innkeeper at Attica, who indulged his fetish that each guest be made to fit his bed perfectly. If one was too short, Procrustes stretched him to new dimensions. If another was too tall, Procrustes simply cut off his legs so that he fit just right.[5] According to Chesnutt, African Americans in North Carolina slept each night in similarly circumscribed spots. "It was a veritable bed of Procrustes, this standard which the whites had set for the Negroes," Chesnutt commented. "Those who grew above it must have their heads cut off, figuratively speaking—must be forced back to the level assigned to their race." On the other side, the lynch rope swayed. "Those who fell beneath the standard set had their necks stretched, literally enough, as the ghastly record in the daily papers gave conclusive evidence."[6] There would be little rest for African Americans as the century drew to a close.

Nonetheless, even as black North Carolinians saw repression creeping across the South in the 1890s, they hoped to turn the tide in their own state.

Reading their story from beginning to end, rather than teleologically, we can see—as they did—that North Carolina could have been the pivot upon which national race relations turned. If people like Sarah Dudley Pettey and Charles Calvin Pettey had been able to hold their ground in the last decade of the nineteenth century, the trend toward disfranchisement and segregation might have been reversed and the history of the twentieth century rewritten. Certainly, black men and women in the state were equal to the task. Many enjoyed fine educations, economic success, and political power, and they saw clearly the danger that awaited them. They tried everything possible to save themselves. Their counterstrategies lay bare two lost worlds: one actual, the other woven from hope.

African Americans hoped that their success would offer testimony to convince whites to recognize class similarities across racial divides; they hoped to prove to whites that they could be Best Men and Best Women. Instead of undermining white supremacy, however, postbellum black progress shored it up. White men reordered southern society through segregation and disfranchisement in the 1890s because they realized that African American success not only meant competition in the marketplace and the sharing of political influence but also entailed a challenge to fundamental social hierarchies that depended nearly as much upon fixed gender roles as they did on the privileges of whiteness. Black progress threatened what southerners called "place."

Place assembled the current concepts of class and race into a stiff-sided box where southern whites expected African Americans to dwell. Southerners lived under a caste system in which skin color, class, and gender dictated the pattern of every daily interaction. For example, African Americans riding in carriages irritated white North Carolinians because such luxury challenged the connections of race, class, and place. How could whites maintain the idea that African Americans were lowly due to laziness if some African Americans worked hard enough to purchase carriages?[7] By embracing a constellation of Victorian middle-class values—temperance, thrift, hard work, piety, learning—African Americans believed that they could carve out space for dignified and successful lives and that their examples would wear away prejudice.[8] As African Americans moved to North Carolina's hamlets and cities to pursue professions and commerce, urban African Americans of the middling sort became increasingly visible at a time when most whites worked diligently to consign blacks to the preindustrial role of agrarian peasants. In one generation, African Americans moved from field hands to teachers, from carpenters to construction bosses. Freedpeople equipped themselves to compete with whites in business, the professions, and politics. Often education, buttressed by strong religious beliefs, made the difference. Black men and women embraced

Christian ideals, filtered through Victorian sensibilities, as standards of equity and morality in an effort to break the southern caste system.[9]

African American women helped make those accomplishments revolutionary. Women were integral components of economic gain, generational change, and ultimately civic participation. Educated black women believed progress would flow logically from predictions they had first heard from parents, black ministers, and northern missionary teachers. They expected advancement on three fronts: in living standards, in opportunities for women of both races, and in white attitudes toward African Americans. Raised by ex-slave mothers and grandmothers, the first and second generations of freedwomen saw racial progress as inclusive, not exclusive, of those less fortunate.[10] In a racially charged atmosphere, black women knew that private acts and family-based decisions could be used against them. They carefully considered each move, since a fleeting whim, if acted upon, could furnish whites "proof" of the capability or deficiency of an entire race.[11]

Charles and Sarah Pettey represent the extraordinary potential of ordinary African Americans in the first three decades of freedom. If we begin the story by adopting one family as a guide, we can trace hope's meaning as it beams through slavery's vicissitudes and Reconstruction's raw light to the moment of possibility before disfranchisement. The marriage of Sarah Dudley and Charles Calvin Pettey brought together two people convinced that race and gender discrimination were vestiges of the past, anachronistic feudalisms that would melt like snow under the rays of an upcoming age of reason. An examination of their lives reveals the ideals and hopes that made up their vision of a New South never to be born. Their story provides an opening wedge for understanding a group of men and women who saw themselves as the future of their race but who have virtually disappeared from the historical record.

Beginning with a close look at one family is bound to prompt questions concerning typicality. A historian can rescue a woman from oblivion, painstakingly reconstruct her life and her ancestors' lives, and finally make modest claims for her experience, only to face the charge that if the subject is *that* interesting or important, then she must be unrepresentative. However, a hierarchical presumption lurks in the typicality argument: average people are simply average; only their leaders are exceptional. Therefore, if the subject is interesting, she must be atypical. This study operates from a different premise: that every story would be interesting if we could recapture it and that each one has something to teach us. Writing history by grinding away the nuances of each person's experience produces the typical; in real life, we see individuality more readily. The world in these pages belonged to many women; here it is articulated by a few whose voices, by pluck or by chance, happened to survive.

Historians have used generational models to explain the dynamics of immigrant families, and the rage for genealogy testifies to the explanatory power of family narrative in many people's lives. Slavery, however, waged a war on the institution of the family, and the rupture between slavery and freedom cleft historical memory, often separating historians of African Americans from evidence of powerful family strategies over time. Yet what might be lost to documentation often loomed large in individual consciousness. Sarah Dudley Pettey is a case in point. The first member of her family to be born in freedom, her optimism and outspokenness sprang from the hopes and fortitude of three generations that came before her. To understand her, one must understand them.

Edmund Pasteur, Sarah Dudley Pettey's paternal great-grandfather, was born around the time of the American Revolution. John Carruthers Stanly of New Bern, North Carolina, the largest black slaveholder in the South, bought Pasteur sometime before the War of 1812. Stanly had himself been born a slave. His slave-trading father, a white man, had purchased his mother, an African Ibo woman, and impregnated her during the middle passage. The Stanly family later freed the son, who bore his father's name. Edmund Pasteur's African heritage remains unknown, but it may have been quite recent to him, given North Carolina's slave-trading patterns. His mother, or even Edmund Pasteur himself, might have been born in Africa, or his ancestors might have been enslaved in the Caribbean for a generation or more.[12]

It is impossible to know what kind of master Stanly proved to be, but at least he allowed Edmund Pasteur to hire himself out in the busy port city of New Bern. By 1815, Pasteur had saved enough money to buy his freedom, an action Stanly supported. Then, after three years of freedom, Edmund Pasteur had saved $750 to purchase a mulatto woman and her thirteen-month-old baby—his wife, Dinah, and his daughter, Sarah—from his original owner. Dinah, who was thirty-nine at the time, may have been her owner's daughter and had been married to Edmund for at least fourteen years. Despite Edmund Pasteur's manumission, her owner had allowed her to continue their relationship. However, the slaveholder's decision to sell Dinah and Sarah clearly owed more to avarice than to kindness since the $750 bought only a middle-aged woman and a suckling baby, not Richard, Edmund and Dinah's fourteen-year-old son, who remained enslaved.[13]

One word hints at Edmund Pasteur's thoughts on slavery and his family's condition. Pasteur later recounted that he had finally "ransomed" Richard, just as the boy was about to be sold into "slavery in remote countries."[14] Edmund never thought of himself, Dinah, Richard, and Sarah as property or as members of a degraded class of people who belonged in slavery. They were people who had been kidnapped, had lived through it, and now had ransomed themselves. Through his incredible efforts, Edmund Pasteur came to own his entire family, but they remained his slaves. In 1827, he petitioned the court to manumit Dinah, now fifty years old, Richard, twenty-two, and Sarah, nine. In this last and crucial effort, it seems that Edmund Pasteur failed.[15]

Thirteen years later, in 1840, Sarah Pasteur, by that time a young woman of twenty-two, gave birth to a baby boy, Edward Richard Dudley, Jr., named for his father, who was most likely a mixed-race free man.[16] Although Edward Dudley is listed in the census as a white man, the large Dudley family included many light-skinned people of African descent who married whites. Roughly one of every four "blacks" in New Bern was free in 1860, and free people of color made up 12 percent of the total population.[17] These astounding figures suggest a community teeming with complex racial interactions, a place where "black" and "white" were fluid, not frozen, categories. The port city on the Trent and Neuse rivers provided both wage labor and the opportunity to live off the fruits of the sea, advantages that attracted freed and runaway slaves and landless whites. Edward Dudley supported himself as a fisherman.[18] Pasteur and Dudley may have lived together openly, or their relationship may have been more clandestine. Even though Sarah Pasteur belonged to her father, as a slave she could not marry. Three years later, in 1843, Sarah and Edward had a second son, James.

The curse of slavery under which Sarah Pasteur had lived for twenty-five years struck now with the death of her father, just when she was most vulnerable. In the years after the Pasteurs' manumission attempt failed, slavery's institutional shell had hardened as white southerners grew to fear abolitionism and insurrection. In the 1830s, those few slaveholders who chose to emancipate their slaves encountered greater difficulties, and it must have been nearly impossible for a black man to free his slave family.[19] In 1843, after Dinah had died and Richard had vanished, Sarah, with a three-year-old and a baby, had cared for her father to the end in the small house that he owned. After her father's death, her lover Edward Dudley either could not or would not help but only watched as Sarah and his two children were sold as slaves.

Edmund Pasteur had paid dearly for his loved ones, but the white court-appointed executor of his estate sold Sarah and her two children cheaply, for $377 on credit, to Richard N. Taylor of New Bern, who owned a cotton mill and a fleet of schooners.[20] Being appointed executor was literally a license to steal: the proceeds of Pasteur's "property"—the house, Sarah, and the two children—went to the executor since Pasteur had no legally free heirs. The oldest boy, Edward Richard Dudley, Jr., was three, the youngest, James Dudley, only a few months old. Six years later, it appears that the boys' free father married a white woman and had a son, to whom he gave the same name as one of his slave sons: James. To Sarah, this must have been the unkindest cut of all.[21]

In the two decades of her family's enslavement, Sarah Pasteur secretly taught her children to read and write, and she must have provided great love and great hope. After secession, Sarah probably had a pipeline to the latest news by eavesdropping on meetings of the Confederate Soldiers Relief Society, over which her owner's wife presided during 1861. Confederate soldiers' relief in New Bern was short-lived, however, as whites scrambled to evacuate the city in January 1862 with the approach of Union troops. The Taylors fled with their slaves and spent the Civil War in Salisbury well to the west, where they put Edward to work in a tobacco factory. Salisbury stubbornly clung to the Confederacy even after Lee surrendered. A week later, General George Stoneman burned down the city. Finally, the period of the Pasteurs' captivity ended. Sarah Pasteur was forty-eight at the time, twenty-two years a slave. Her kidnapped boys emerged as free men, and they headed for home.[22]

The oldest, Edward Dudley, was twenty-five. He could read and write and was soon practicing a lucrative trade in New Bern as a cooper, which he probably learned in the tobacco factory. Dudley quickly assumed a leadership role amid the chaos of the Federal-occupied town. He joined a Masonic lodge and served on the police force.[23] A pillar of Saint Peters, the first African Methodist Episcopal (AME) Zion church in the South, Dudley headed the statewide Grand Lodge of Colored Good Templars, the first black branch of an international temperance order.[24] Sometime between 1862 and 1868, Dudley married a biracial woman named Caroline, who, like him, had learned to read and write in slavery. She joined her husband as a Good Templar.[25] The Dudleys taught their children to take pride in their African American roots and to take their places among the best people, regardless of race. Edward Dudley's place was in politics.

Dudley's experience as a black man serving as a lesser official in the Reconstruction South—a good citizen doing his duty—complements portraits of famous black Reconstruction leaders and counters white fictions about boisterous black swindlers taking over state legislatures. His daughter, Sarah, born in 1869, learned her political lessons at her father's knee. Members of Sarah's generation of African Americans were raised to expect full civil rights, a generational experience repeated only by those who came of age after the Voting Rights Act of 1965.

African Americans' continuous involvement after Reconstruction in

Thought by her great-great grandchildren to be a portrait of Sarah Pasteur, this is more likely a photograph of her daughter-in-law Caroline Dudley, taken in the late 1860s. Courtesy of Allene Dudley Bundy, New Bern, North Carolina.

eastern North Carolina local politics—through campaigning, voting, appointment, and election—meant that the violence and legal codification of segregation in the late 1890s represented cataclysmic ruptures in the fabric of black civil rights, not simply the institutionalization of repression.[26] If historians later took Jim Crow's career to be strange, African Americans at the time found it unbelievable. They expected reverses, even pitched battles, but they never expected to be counted out of the electoral process completely. The careers of Dudley and his daughter illustrate the ebb and flow of black political life throughout the second half of the nineteenth century and prove that it was not over until it was over: that is, until the 1900 constitutional amendment disfranchising African Americans.

This is not to say that some times were not better than others. The period from 1888 to 1894 seemed particularly bleak, even though African Americans continued to serve in the state legislature throughout the period.[27] In 1877 the legislature had seized the power to appoint local officials to counter black votes in the eastern part of the state. For two years, the legislators appointed justices of the peace, who in turn appointed other

8   PLACE AND POSSIBILITY

local officers; from 1879 until 1894, the justices of the peace appointed county commissioners, who then dished up the remaining slices of pie.[28] Black and poor white officeholders persisted, however. After 1888, the state legislature tightened its control on local offices by forcing officials to post high bonds that might prevent poor men from serving.[29] Raleigh's control proved onerous to both poor whites and African Americans, and "home rule" became an issue that crossed racial lines.[30] As they attempted to prevent African Americans from holding local offices, legislators trailed the boundaries of the Second Congressional District around eastern North Carolina in an attempt to contain black voting strength in national elections. Craven County fell within the borders of the "Black Second," and the Dudleys' neighbor, African American George White, became their congressman.

In many of the state's cities and eastern rural areas, African Americans took an active part in local politics, despite the obstacles the legislature placed in their paths. Edward Dudley served on New Bern's common council and was a city marshal. He won election to the state house of representatives in 1870, when seventeen other African Americans gained seats in the house and three in the senate. Two years later, he returned for another term.[31] Even more significant than Dudley's elections was his appointment as justice of the peace in New Bern from 1880 to 1884 since by appointing Dudley the legislature acknowledged his political power in state and national politics through the Republican Party. Dudley's tenure points up the system's flexibility and hints at a lack of resolve among all whites to exclude African Americans from politics.[32] The white *New Bern Weekly Journal* acknowledged as much in 1886 when it pitched the Democratic Party to African Americans: "Drawing the color line is wrong in principle. . . . Why seek to array one race against another? The negroes are citizens, and have the right of suffrage."[33] They might not have been happy about it, but white men had to reckon with black votes. Democratic appeals for African American votes resulted in few converts, however, and use of such a strategy abated in the early 1890s.

Tentative interracial alliances characterized politics in the century's last two decades. Dudley, for instance, forged a close alliance with white congressman Orlando Hubbs, and he maintained his loyalty to Hubbs when Hubbs battled African American James O'Hara for the nomination to the Second Congressional District seat in 1882. Dudley's opposition to O'Hara ran deeper than simply repaying any political debts to Hubbs. As statewide leader of the black Good Templars, Dudley despised O'Hara because he had attended an antiprohibition convention when the issue came up in the state in 1881.[34] Hubbs lost his fight for the nomination, and O'Hara relieved Dudley of his post as deputy collector of federal revenues. Dudley cemented the breach forever by calling O'Hara a "creature of the mob, organized for the sole purpose of 'sending a Negro to congress.' " "Thank God," Dudley concluded, his own principles counted for more than race and he had "never worshipped at the shrine of color." Dudley's hatred of O'Hara led him to support another white man, Furnifold Simmons, to replace him in Congress in 1886. When Simmons took the seat—he won Craven County by only forty-five votes—he recognized his debt to the district's African Americans.[35]

African Americans also knew they had carried Simmons's election. As one put it, O'Hara "got bit by his own dog."[36] Two years later, however, Simmons's own dog bit him, as white voters accused Simmons of being too responsive to black constituents. Simmons attributed his 1888 defeat to his failure to draw the color line, a lesson he would never forget.[37] Ironically, Dudley, who "never worshipped at the shrine of color," helped launch the career of the man who at the century's end would disfranchise him on account of color. African American votes counted until then.

If politics was a part-time passion for Edward Dudley, his family was a full-time one. His brother James also lived in New Bern, and his mother lived with him and Caroline. When the couple had a daughter in 1869, they named her Sarah, for her grandmother. Baby Sarah was the first member of the Pasteur-Dudley family born in freedom, even though more than a half century had elapsed since Edmund Pasteur ransomed himself. The year after Sarah's birth, Edward Dudley was elected to the legislature, after which he returned home most months to farm and to teach school.[38] Two boys and five girls followed Sarah. Edward Dudley's farm was worth $600 in 1870, and he approached farming as he did everything else, with high-spirited competition. He won prizes for his produce, including an eggplant two feet wide and pumpkins five feet tall.[39]

Sarah Pasteur and Caroline Dudley taught Sarah Dudley to read and write before the little girl was six. Literacy was the most valuable gift Pasteur had to give, first to her sons in slavery, then to her granddaughter in freedom. The family certainly needed no coaxing to enter the schoolroom after American Missionary Association teachers flocked to New Bern in the late 1860s and established at least five private schools, which supplemented the short public school year. Education had given hope to the Dudleys in slavery, had provided them with an advantage in Reconstruction, and would propel them into the future. By the time Sarah Dudley entered the classroom, New Bern's black public schools were graded, a northern innovation still unknown in white southern schools, and the teaching force included local African Americans.[40] Temperance societies dominated extracurricular life at each school.[41] After she completed the six grades the school system offered, Sarah Dudley attended the coeducational

New Bern State Colored Normal School, a state-funded teacher-training school that combined high school work with pedagogy courses.

One year later, thirteen-year-old Sarah left home for Scotia Seminary, a Presbyterian school for women in Concord, North Carolina, 200 miles to the west. There the biracial faculty oversaw a curriculum calculated to give students the knowledge, social consciousness, and sensibilities of New England ladies, with a strong dose of Boston egalitarianism sprinkled in. Mary McLeod, who followed Sarah Dudley to Scotia five years later, recalled that her northern white teachers there taught her that "the color of a person's skin has nothing to do with his brains, and that color, caste, or class distinctions are an evil thing."[42] Scotia's white founder, Luke Dorland, modeled the school on Mount Holyoke. He intended it to be a place where students learned to do as well as to think. Dorland believed that "skilled hands must be directed by a sound mind in a sound body, motivated by a zeal to serve others."[43] The cooking, music, and needlework that students learned along with their Latin was to be employed to their own ends, not in domestic service for white people. A Scotia woman would "make a good housewife as well as a good school teacher," and the cornerstone of Sarah's dormitory bore the words, "Head, Heart, and Hands."[44] When Sarah arrived, she joined 139 other young women students, who ate, lived, and studied with a faculty of white and black women teachers.[45] Her roommate was Lula Pickenpack, a slightly older girl from Charlotte who already had a serious suitor, Charles Calvin Pettey.

Sarah Dudley graduated with distinction from Scotia in 1883 and returned to New Bern as an assistant principal of the black graded public school. During her first teaching year, the average monthly salary of the state's 700 black teachers was $22, a little less than that of white teachers but the highest salary a black woman could earn anywhere.[46] Each school term lasted only four months, and in the summer, Dudley attended a month-long teacher-training session at the New Bern State Colored Normal School. The next year, she moved up to vice principal in the public school system and associate principal of the summer normal school under George White, who would soon become her congressman.[47]

Sarah Dudley kept in touch with Lula Pickenpack and Charles Pettey, who were now married.[48] Pettey stood 5 feet 8 inches tall, "with short arms and legs, a long body, a prominent receding forehead, cheeks indicative of Indian descent, complexion of an Indian . . . his black hair nearly straight."[49] Pettey had a piercing, direct gaze, a dashing mustache, and a beautiful singing voice. Despite his probable triracial mix, Pettey's racial identity was always African American, and he had been born in slavery in Wilkes County in the northwestern section of the state in 1849.[50] After the Civil War, Pettey farmed during the day and worked as a cobbler and basketmaker at night. He traded his handicrafts, along with ferry rides across the Yadkin River, to white people for reading lessons. After he could read, he hoarded every penny. Finally, in 1872, at age twenty-three, he put on a pair of shoes he had made, dressed himself in a suit sewn from fabric he had spun, pocketed $95 in savings, and walked ninety miles to Charlotte to enroll in college.[51]

The college, Presbyterian-supported Biddle Memorial Institute, offered classical training for men who wanted to be teachers or ministers, and there Pettey learned to read Latin and Greek. The institute did not insist on denominational fealty, and Pettey remained a member of the AME Zion Church. On weekends, he began preaching in the countryside, making "appointments," first at one crossroad and then another. Starting out on a Friday night, he would walk more than fifty miles in forty-eight hours. Pettey worked barely four months after graduation as head of a black public school in Charlotte when he became an elder in the AME Zion Church and discovered he would have to move to South Carolina to assume his new post. From his South Carolina base, Pettey established a normal school, built a national name for himself in the church, and with John Dancy, a prominent churchman, contributed to the *Star of Zion*, a denominational newspaper that soon became one of the twelve most important black newspapers in the nation.[52]

Sometime after 1881, Charles and Lula Pettey departed on a great adventure. Along with Alexander Walters, who would later help found the National Association for the Advancement of Colored People (NAACP), Pettey led a band of black colonists to California. They settled near San Francisco, founded a community named Petteyville, and spread out to establish AME Zion churches. Pettey became pastor of the downtown Stockton Street church.[53] Lula and Charles had two daughters, the first of whom they named Sarah. Lula died in 1887, and Charles was left with the two young girls.[54] He soon became bishop with responsibility for Texas, and in 1888 a conference brought him back to North Carolina and a reunion with Sarah Dudley. Within a year, they married and set up their home in New Bern.[55]

The recovered bits of the Petteys' life together confound notions of the South as an isolated, parochial place where African Americans existed as shadows, bent wraiths who shuffled subserviently along wooden sidewalks. Like many other successful black families in North Carolina's urban areas, the Petteys lived a deliberately conspicuous life. "There are plenty of carriages in New Bern," noted the black-owned *Raleigh Gazette*, "owned principally" by African Americans. Sarah Dudley Pettey rode around town in a black carriage drawn by a high-stepping mare. Charles Pettey sported silk top hats. At her table, Dudley Pettey served roast bear, lobster cutlets, and

Russian salad with sauce tartare and provided finger bowls.[56] The trappings of the Petteys' lives particularly annoyed white New Bernians, who termed the Petteys' society "colored swelldom." But "colored swelldom" had room to exist in New Bern, to rent reception rooms at the town's best "white" hotel, to shop in the best stores, and to host white townspeople at special programs in Saint Peter's AME Zion Church.[57]

The Petteys' group of affluent African Americans in New Bern contrasted with the population of James City, a virtually all-black town of 2,500 across the river. A comparison of the two reveals class differences, some of which can be traced back to the moment of freedom. James City represented the vestiges of a contraband encampment during the Civil War. African Americans who had fled there as slaves during the Federal occupation twenty-five years earlier had, of course, come with nothing. Across the river in New Bern, newly emancipated African Americans like Edward Dudley had advantages over them. Dudley knew the local people, he could read, and his barrels were in demand. John Stanly, the black slaveholder, had moved to Ohio, but his remaining New Bern relatives were even better off than Dudley. These initial differences carried over into the next generation: John's daughter, Sara, went to Oberlin College and Sarah Dudley went to Scotia Seminary, but in James City, young women went to work.[58]

Black people, whether they lived in New Bern or James City, certainly recognized variations in economic and educational standing; the important question is what those differences meant to them. Was class position the result of heredity? Were such gradations permanent? Should those who had become successful close ranks in order to exclude others?

Many southern whites would have answered "yes" to all of the above questions. Within that group of mostly backward-looking heirs of southern planters, class position was a matter of breeding—blood would tell. To maintain one's standing, one simply chose a marriage partner wisely. Amid the poverty of the postbellum economy, some southern whites tried to engineer their class system to run on heredity rather than on the economy. They remained tied to the land, and some managed to retain a degree of political power—though in North Carolina fewer did so than in the lower South. Their constrictive family bonds grew thick and tangled as the century progressed, and a part of white society froze looking back over its shoulder at a mythical antebellum romance. By the end of the century, some influential southerners, for example, Thomas Dixon, Jr., grafted the vines of hereditary class privilege onto pseudo-Darwinism to produce a mutant class system dependent upon fixed racial and gender categories. Who you were, more than what you did, mattered to these white southerners.[59]

But a growing group of white southerners would have answered "no" to each of these gatekeeping questions. This nucleus saw social position not as hereditary and inflexible but as broachable, if not exactly fluid. For the most part descendants of antebellum yeoman farmers and petty slaveholders who had emerged impoverished after the war, these young southerners grew restless as the Bourbons who "redeemed" the state in the 1870s held it in limbo for the next two decades by painting change as anathema to the southern way of life. Middle-class white men in the 1870s began to prepare for occupations that would lift them out of rural poverty and to lobby the state to educate its white citizens. To these men and women, merit mattered; the best men should lead, regardless of their birth.[60]

As white men recast class by arguing for the capability of educated and industrious people, African Americans furnished living proof of their theories. Because education represented the key to class mobility, African Americans came to see it as nothing less than sacred, a spiritual duty that fell more heavily on women because of motherhood. Dudley Pettey connected class, gender, and education directly when she argued, "In the civilization and enlightenment of the Negro race its educated women must be the potent factors." Clearly "civilization" represented *her* version of manners and morals, those middle-class values that she learned from her family, church, and Reconstruction teachers. Yet she also foresaw class aspirations brokered by educational achievement as inclusive: "Ere long Ethiopia's sons and daughters, led by pious, educated women, will be elevated among the enlightened races of the world."[61]

In Reconstruction schools, middle-class identity, then, was something to be learned and, in turn, taught. Girls like Sarah Dudley attended Scotia Seminary with girls who were dirt-poor orphans and with others who were simply dirt-poor, like Mary McLeod, the fifteenth child of slave parents. McLeod's home was so humble that when she arrived at Scotia, she had never climbed a flight of stairs or used a knife or fork.[62] Yet she learned skills of self-presentation that ultimately gained her a federal post and Eleanor Roosevelt's friendship. Although Sarah had been born free to a prestigious black politician, her husband, her father, and her beloved grandmother, like her James City neighbors, had been born slaves. Only a very few "aristocrats of color" used heredity to signify class standing.[63]

Differences in color might have mattered to some but not to most educated black North Carolinians setting out to prove their race's ability. Light-skinned people married darker people, politicians came in all hues, and the black press bragged most loudly about the intellectual achievements of very dark men such as Joseph Charles Price, the founder of the AME Zion Livingstone College.[64] Sarah Dudley Pettey, obviously of black and white heritage, attributed her success to her family's love and her education, not to her light skin. Sarah and Elizabeth Delany, born to educators at Saint Augustine's College in Raleigh in the 1890s, described their light-skinned mother's choice of their brilliant dark-skinned father this way: "Some colored women who were as light as Mama would not have gotten involved with a dark-skinned man, but Mama didn't care. She said he was the cream of the crop, a man of the highest quality."[65]

Upon the founding of the National Association of Colored Women's Clubs in 1896, Sarah Dudley Pettey lauded the organization's mission while deploring its use of the word "colored." She attributed its origin to the "softening" of the word "nigger" to "you colored people" in the antebellum South. All people are colored, she argued, "from the fairest blonde to the darkest hue of humanity." Far better to use the term "Afro-American . . . as it designates both the races and countries from whence we, the amalgamated race, came." It was typical of her to speak forthrightly of racial mixing; on another occasion, she argued that the word "Negro" was useless because it denoted "one type of the African race without mixture." By clinging to "Afro," she showed her pride in her African heritage; by linking it with "American," she held whites accountable for both slavery and miscegenation. When an African American writer proposed "affirming we are 'Americans, pure and simple,'" Dudley Pettey retorted that if "we [were] Americans, pure and simple," there "would be no class legislation against us; there would be no need of separate schools and churches."[66] To Dudley Pettey, race prejudice worked like class prejudice: it created false divisions among worthy human beings.

Black writers in the late nineteenth century regularly referred to racial segregation as "class legislation," and they saw race as one marker among many. Thus, to consider class among African Americans apart from the racial caste system in which they lived is to take too myopic a view. In real life, race, class, and gender never sorted themselves into convenient categories of analysis. Moreover, as Charles Chesnutt reminds us by invoking Procrustes, how African Americans viewed class differences among themselves mattered less in determining their wider opportunities than how whites saw those differences since it was whites who allotted the social space available.[67]

Whites tried to order the world to prevent African Americans from rising. When some blacks nevertheless achieved success, whites set off alarms. Whites preferred the Uncle Remus of the farm to the "colored swelldom" of the cities, and it was in the state's cities that black success showed most. After 1879, the percentage of black-owned urban property in the state increased at a time when the value of farms decreased and town lots grew more valuable. Wilmington ranked second in the South in black property ownership among cities with populations of 10,000 to 25,000. Only 5.6 percent of North Carolina's African Americans owned homes in 1870; by 1910, the figure had risen to 26 percent.[68] It must have seemed as if

Sarah Dudley Pettey, circa
1900. Courtesy of Corine
Pettey, New York,
New York.

African Americans were cornering the real estate market in North Carolina's towns and cities. In Wilmington, for example, many African Americans lived in "fine" houses with "pianos and servants and lace curtains to
their windows."[69]

Because her husband served as bishop of the Texas, Alabama, and Louisiana district, Sarah Dudley Pettey spent little time looking through her lace
curtains. Their honeymoon took them to Europe, California, and Mexico.
In England, the archbishop of Canterbury received them and U.S. minister
Robert Lincoln presented them at the Court of St. James. Their visit to
rural Ireland prompted Charles to write an article comparing the South's
racial situation to Ireland's ethnic strife caused by British home rule.[70] After
Pettey became bishop of the Allegheny-Ohio Conference in 1896, they
spent several months each year in Ohio, Pennsylvania, Delaware, Maryland, Kentucky, and the District of Columbia.[71]

Their five children—two boys and three girls—were born at two-year
intervals, and Pettey's two daughters lived with them in New Bern as well.
Traveling extensively, serving as her husband's secretary, and, beginning in

Bishop Charles Calvin Pettey, circa 1895. From the *Star of Zion*, 13 Dec. 1900.

August 1896, writing a bimonthly column for the *Star of Zion*, Sarah Dudley Pettey had to employ the organization of a field marshal. One of Sarah's sisters and one of Charles's cousins shared their household to help care for the children, and Sarah's brother, George, lived next door with his own growing family.[72]

Charles and Sarah made each other happy, and their devotion to one another spilled over into public life. He was extraordinarily proud of her, saw her as his equal, and bragged about her to his colleagues. Once, in an editorial in which Charles was bowing out of a long theological debate with readers of the *Star of Zion*, he promised, "Madam Pettey, who has been reviewing ... the Greek testament scriptures ... will remain at my desk; ... I am quite confident that she will be able to keep off all intruders."[73] She certainly was able, it turned out, since she subsequently accused a bumptious theological adversary of misrepresenting Charles's position just to vent "the great drops of gall escaping from the puncture in his swelling spleen."[74] Sarah and Charles made a formidable team.

The Dudley-Pettey marriage suggests mutual cooperation and equal partnership. Sarah and her peers understood marriage as a duty, the site of "civil enterprise" for the post-Reconstruction black generation. Analyzing the domestic fiction of black women writers of the period, novels that Sarah Dudley Pettey most certainly read, Claudia Tate has argued that the ideal marriage for these black women was an "industrious partnership" rather than a passionate dive into abandon.[75] The Dudley-Pettey union certainly qualified as an industrious partnership, even as it managed to convey, on occasion, just a hint of passionate abandon. Among African Americans, marriage itself was political, a testimony to capability as piercing white eyes peered through domesticity, searching for degeneracy.

Black male voters often saw themselves as representing their wives, not as patriarchs who assumed that their wives' interests coincided with their own but as family delegates to the electoral sphere. Although there is evidence of this delegate-husband model among some whites in the North, such as members of the Society of Friends, such evidence is rare in the nineteenth century, especially among white southern ladies and their patriarchal husbands. Eventually white women educated in the 1890s reshaped white marriage relationships, but southern black women were a generation ahead of them in forging companionate partnerships.[76] The pervasive white gaze, contact with earnest northern white and black women missionaries, strong ex-slave grandmothers and mothers, and a keen sense of fairness forged in the fires of discrimination all contributed to black women's construction of the ideal marriage, as did their coeducational experiences.

The fact that they saw their husbands as familial delegates to the political world did not mean, however, that some women did not seek self-representation. Charles encouraged Sarah to go forward, even on his own ground. Sarah traveled with Charles to churches in his district, where they both gave remarkable performances. First the bishop would preach, then the bishop's wife would take the pulpit and deliver a speech on woman's rights, either "Woman the Equal of Man" or "Woman's Suffrage." One of her male listeners called her "a power with the pen, clearly demonstrating the possibilities of a woman."[77] Dudley Pettey regularly reported in the *Star of Zion* on women's accomplishments that she believed would "be of historic interest a century from now." "What position is there," she asked rhetorically, "that woman cannot fill?"[78]

Dudley Pettey's belief in woman's equality was not an aberration in her church, but it may have been a minority opinion. In 1867 church leaders deleted the word "male" in the description of church officers' qualifications, at a time when other denominations argued that women had no place "teaching or preaching."[79] Thirty years later, Mary Small, a bishop's wife and recent deacon who had taught Sunday school in Fayetteville with

Charles Chesnutt, sought ordination as an elder. Bishop Charles Pettey created a huge controversy when he ordained her in 1898. Sarah was delighted. She opined that before the word "male" was struck, AME Zion women's "usefulness was limited to a certain narrow and prescribed sentimental boundary." That was no longer the case, she gloated, since the church had kept "pace with the advanced ideas of to-day." "To-day, to the called female church-worker there is no majestic Shasta looming up before her, with sexual prejudicial peaks and impregnable sentimental buttes saying 'thus far shalt thou come and no farther.' "[80]

To Sarah Dudley Pettey and Mary Small, it was no longer enough for AME Zion women to experience spirituality individually. A woman who experienced a calling could not hold it within; she must follow where it led, even if the road seemed steep. Evelyn Brooks Higginbotham has argued that in the African American tradition, personal testimony was seen as a political stand.[81] In slavery, the body was indeed the body politic. If a slave witnessed, his or her thoughts escaped bondage and entered a free market of ideas, a potentially revolutionary act that could liberate or endanger not just the speaker but also other slaves. Thus, once given voice, personal belief both embodied and mandated public action. As a result, if God called on a woman and filled her with the spirit, she should speak it aloud; she was responsible not simply for saving her own soul but for saving others' as well.

Mary Small's ordination as an elder, which seems to have been the first ordination of a woman in any denominational body in the United States, set off a firestorm of controversy in the AME Zion Church.[82] One minister devoted his column, "Red Hot Cannon Ball," to warnings of a "petticoat ministry," arguing that "women's work in the church from the earliest dawn till now has been in subordination to man." Since it could not have been God who turned this hierarchy upside down, women must be bearing false witness. The minister concluded, "I as much doubt a woman's call to the ministry as I do my ability to fly."[83] Such nay-saying merely propelled Sarah Dudley Pettey to greater rhetorical heights. Small was an "eloquent, pathetic and forcible preacher," Dudley Pettey argued.[84] If the clamor did not subside, she threatened, "I have almost gotten in the notion of being ordained myself."[85]

Oppression, whether on account of race or on account of sex, was all of a piece to Sarah Dudley Pettey since it sprang from the same sin: a hierarchical mind-set that violated Christian teachings. She linked race and sex discrimination closely: "Those persons who are disposed to criticise the advanced woman reason from the same analogy as that class of Anglo-Saxons who believe Anglo-Africans should be educated only for manual labor." It was wrong to "put a limit to the capabilities and possibilities of certain classes of humanity," she wrote.[86] Her feminism was not just a response to patriarchy but a response to racial oppression as well.

By contrast, a white woman's radicalizing experience generally came at the moment in which she found her "capabilities and possibilities" limited on account of her sex. Such an incident shaped self-identity because it sparked the recognition of exclusion and, therefore, of oppression. A black woman's radicalizing experience almost always occurred at the moment she realized that racial exclusion precluded possibility. By the time black female children first encountered sexism, they were armed with an ideological paradigm: racism is wrong; therefore sexism is wrong. The limitation of one's possibility might have mattered less if ambition represented self-indulgence, but God had given everyone work to do.[87] Women, Sarah Dudley Pettey argued, stood poised to enter "every door of usefulness." Slamming those doors shut was simply wrong.[88]

Together Charles and Sarah created a world in which, it seemed, anything could happen. Their own happiness surely colored their optimism, but as they looked around themselves prior to 1898, the Petteys saw racial and gender progress everywhere. Dudley Pettey wrote romantic, exhortatory, and relentlessly progressive columns in the *Star of Zion*. "This is . . . an age of evolution, an age of development, an age of restlessness and commotion," she commented approvingly. "The day is past when the world will bow to any one man's theory." Although some took issue with her controversial columns on economics, politics, and woman's place, no one challenged Sarah Dudley Pettey's right to be heard, and some male readers stepped up to champion her. She even inspired poetry:

> We've many brilliant women,
> With intellectual life—
> Just take for example,
> Our Bishop Pettey's wife.[89]

From the remove of New Bern and the cocoon of their love, the Petteys put the best possible face on the ominous stirrings of segregation and federal abdication of their rights. They saw the 1890 Mississippi election reform laws and the 1896 Supreme Court decision in *Plessy v. Ferguson* as temporary setbacks. Despite "frowns in the highest courts of the land," Charles Pettey argued, "we as a race are enjoying the brightest rays of Christian civilization. . . . The evils we are enduring are more than compensated for through God's providence by placing us within the touch of the greatest intellectual battery the world has ever witnessed."[90]

The Petteys could testify to the immediate dividends African Americans gained from investment in the great "intellectual battery." In the 1890s, educated African American professionals began to compete with whites for business and to earn more than many of their competitors in North Carolina. African Americans practiced medicine and law, taught and preached, and established mortuaries, pharmacies, and benevolent societies under the noses of, and in competition with, whites in the same professions. Leonard Medical School opened in 1881 at Shaw University in Raleigh to train black physicians, and Shaw inaugurated a pharmacy school nine years later.[91] By 1890, forty-six African Americans practiced medicine in the state. Although this figure hardly constitutes a black takeover of the medical profession, the numbers grew each year.[92] In a speech at Leonard's first commencement, graduating senior Lawson Andrew Scruggs linked racial uplift and professional training: "The colored man must go forward, he must harness himself for the battle, and we who stand before you tonight, are pioneers of the medical profession of our race."[93] Black women as well threatened white doctors' monopoly. In 1894, Lucy Hughes Brown, an orphan who had attended Scotia Seminary with Sarah Dudley Pettey, returned to North Carolina after attending medical college in Philadelphia. Along with two white women, she passed the state medical exam and opened a practice in Wilmington.[94]

Shaw University also pioneered black legal education in the state in 1888 after its white president determined that African Americans were being "taken advantage of" by white lawyers. The ranks of black lawyers grew rapidly; only fourteen practiced in the state in 1890, but by 1908 an additional forty-three had graduated from Shaw.[95] Others read law with practicing attorneys, according to the custom of the day.[96]

To whites, the important thing was not how *many* African Americans rose, but that *any* did. If, in the shambles of Reconstruction, some whites began to believe that merit and hard work mattered more than family background, old definitions of racial place might be changed. If accomplishments counted for something, African Americans could proceed accordingly. When John Leary, a black attorney in Charlotte, got thirsty, he drank from the dipper designated for bar members at the courthouse.[97] As a living testament to capability, successful African Americans' lives provided a perpetual affront to whites. The black lawyer, doctor, preacher, or teacher represented someone out of his or her place. The danger lay not in their numbers, but in the aspirations they inspired in their fellow African Americans and the proof they gave to the white lie of inherent African inferiority. Warnings began to sound in North Carolina's towns. As one African American newspaper put it, "The Negro has not said one word about rule, but his steady move in the wake of wealth, education and thrift is telling its own tale and causing alarm."[98]

Sarah Dudley Pettey knew that not all African Americans could be doctors and lawyers, and she believed that the future of the New South lay in an integrated industrial workforce. Traveling in Pennsylvania, she visited the Homestead steel mill and recalled with pride how black workers had come to be in the mills after a famous 1892 strike: "Hundreds of Afro-Americans . . . were sent for and employed. Some of these men retain their positions until to-day and many of the strikers were never more employed in the mills of Carnegie." Her comments on black strikebreakers shed light on the agonizing problem of the relationship between African Americans and white unions. Dudley Pettey came from a place where blacks were rapidly being excluded from industry, she pointed with pride to the strike-breakers for the most basic reasons: to prove to southern whites that African Americans were equal to and ready for the most difficult industrial work. Her strategy—to secure a toehold for African Americans through strikebreaking and to use their subsequent performance as evidence of their capabilities—later became a method by which both the Urban League and the NAACP sought to counteract union segregation after their efforts to gain the cooperation of organized labor had failed.[99] As she traveled in the North, Dudley Pettey noted that African Americans were losing jobs to "foreigners," who, she pointed out, "hardly lisp good English" before they seek to disfranchise black Americans.[100] Working-class solidarity meant little to people excluded from working at all.

In the South, African Americans faced competition for industrial jobs not from immigrants but from native-born poor whites pushed off their farms by the crop-lien system. African Americans pondering the future of the workforce could point to precedents for black industry in skilled trades and rudimentary factories. In the late 1880s, over 2,000 African Americans participated in segregated Knights of Labor chapters in the state, and blacks and whites held joint conventions.[101] Five and a half percent of North Carolina's African Americans worked in saw mills, in brick factories, as carpenters, or as stone and marble cutters.[102] The largest factory in Wilmington, the Sprunt Cotton Compress, employed several hundred African American workers, virtually all male.[103] The Ashley and Bailey silk factory in Fayetteville, a branch of a northern company, ran smoothly with a workforce of black women and children.[104]

Since northern capitalists could scarcely overlook such a numerous and cheap workforce, Charles Pettey reasoned that the future of the South would depend upon whether the "manufactories growing up in the South by the help of Northern capital employ . . . black labor."[105] African American slaves had furnished the primary labor force in some antebellum mills, and some southern capitalists mixed the races and the sexes in the new industries that developed after the war. Black and white men and women worked in the tobacco industry before mechanization, and African Americans remained in lower-paying jobs after the move to factories.[106] Black and white women worked side by side in commercial laundries.[107] It was vital that African Americans follow their work as it moved indoors. As Charles Pettey put it, "The washerwoman would now like to enter the steam laundry. The blacksmith would like to enter the foundry, where they are now molding the plow shares he made with the hammer."[108]

Much of the state's industrial growth, however, involved building cotton mills, and segregated cotton mills grew rapidly. By 1900, more than 30,000 white North Carolinians labored in cotton and knitting mills, more operatives than in any state except Massachusetts. Most workers were women, and 31 percent were under sixteen.[109] White mill promoters argued that employing African Americans presented a peculiar problem for two reasons: white women and children comprised the bulk of the workforce and needed to be protected from race mixing, and owners located the mills in isolated areas where they had to provide segregated housing. The rising tide of racial segregation washed over this new industry as owners invented job categories and designated particular jobs as suitable for men or women, for whites or blacks. Only a few of the dirtiest outdoor jobs fell to African Americans.

But rigid segregation in the cotton mills did not merely reflect the status quo; it was also a tool promoters used to tap growing white supremacist feelings and to offer racial exclusion as an employee benefit.[110] Cotton mill managers could dangle before poor white families something they lacked on the farm, giving them a glimpse of what increasingly defined white ladyhood: distance from all African Americans, with its implied protection from black men. A mill owners' apologist assured white workers: "The working of negroes, particularly negro men, beside white women within walls would not be tolerated. . . . The experience of the South with the 'unspeakable crime' has been bitter."[111] But, of course, integration was tolerated in many existing commercial and artisanal establishments. Moreover, poor white farm families neither worked within walls nor toiled in fields of racial purity. They often picked cotton, cured tobacco, and harvested squash side by side with African Americans and counted themselves lucky for the help. The cotton mill's promise of racial separation to poor white women represented new, pathetic bait in a Faustian bargain.

Once owners decided that only whites would work in southern cotton mills, they had to make the decision appear to be the only logical one. In order to suggest that the decision was natural, southern whites concocted notions that generally revolved around the idea that quick, crafty, Scotch-Irish mountaineers made good mill operatives whereas sluggish, crude African American cotton pickers did not. Anyone who gave a mill job to an African American jeopardized this fiction, and often during the late 1890s, reports cropped up of African Americans working in cotton mills. The manager of Vesta Mills, a Charleston, South Carolina, knitting factory, was frustrated by high turnover in his white female workforce and appealed to black ministers to recommend women to replace them. After recruiting this new workforce, he fired 300 white women and hired black women and a black male supervisor. The white women's male relatives subsequently demanded their jobs back in a widely published petition that condemned the black supervisor. The mill manager, they argued, "should preclude him from competing with our mothers, wives, sons, and daughters in light pursuits of the country." The petitioners worried "that he must be put in dangerous proximity with our maidens or they be deprived of opportunities for his benefit." By ignoring the black women mill workers and focusing on their male supervisor, the petitioners sexualized what was actually an economic threat. White men wanted to put their female relatives to work, and they wanted black women out of the way.[112]

The *Atlanta Constitution* reflected white people's hopes that African Americans would prove biologically incapable of cotton mill work when it ran a story on Vesta Mills in 1900, replete with four screaming headlines. "Negro Labor in Cotton Mills," the lead warned. "Experiment at Charleston Is Being Watched," cautioned the second headline. "Not Such a Great Success," opined the next. "Black People Do Not Seem to Take to the Work—Takes Long Time to Instruct Them—Then Suddenly Leave Their Jobs," confided the last. The story failed to mention that the black women had been called in when white women's turnover rate became too high to run the mill.[113]

If white-owned mills came under pressure for employing African Americans, then black-owned mills might prove that they made good workers and create competition to boot.[114] Warren G. Coleman, a wealthy black man in Concord, set out to raise black capital, hire black overseers, train black operatives, and start a mill.[115] The Dudleys and the Petteys had been friends of Coleman's for years—when Edward Dudley walked away with a ribbon for his five-foot-tall pumpkin, Warren Coleman claimed another for his thirty-five-pound cantaloupe.[116] Sarah Dudley Pettey called Coleman Mill the best "monument yet erected to Negro thrift, industry and energy." To Dudley Pettey, the mill represented "the closing event of the nineteenth century, and the crowning effort of Negro aspirations, capabilities and manhood."[117] Coleman sent salespeople like Lulu Jenkins, a Concord teacher, throughout the state to sell stock in his new venture.[118] Jenkins visited the Petteys as she traveled in the eastern part of the state, initially taking pledges to buy stock and then returning to collect increments of 10 percent from subscribers.[119] Among the mill's incorporators were many friends of the Petteys, including Lawson Andrew Scruggs, now a teacher at Leonard Medical School; E. A. Johnson, a Raleigh attorney whose sister married Sarah's brother Edward Richard Dudley III; and John Dancy, an AME Zion churchman who, with Charles Pettey, had built the *Star of Zion*.[120] Even with such prestigious backing and strong sales efforts, the mill remained undercapitalized. Apparently $50,000 to $100,000 was pledged, but only $23,000 was actually collected.[121]

Although Sarah Dudley Pettey believed that the industrialization she saw around her meant progress for blacks, it did not. She could not know at the time that automation and centralization of work in factories solidified economic differences between the races and built a new power structure that denied African Americans even the small chance a more agrarian economy had afforded them. After it took six years to build the Coleman Mill, it operated for only two years until Coleman's death in 1904. Coleman apparently spent his fortune and borrowed heavily from the Dukes of Durham to keep it afloat.[122]

Given white attempts to exclude African Americans from participation in the South's industrial awakening, Booker T. Washington's speech at the 1895 Cotton States and International Exposition in Atlanta takes on new meaning. Washington took the stage in the midst of the commercial carnival. Through the exposition, the South, with slightly more than 10 percent of the nation's wealth, sought to shake off the recession of 1893, to trumpet its capabilities, and to prove to northern investors that the southern "Negro problem" would not be a bar to progress.[123]

Whites and blacks heard Washington say two different things that day. Washington's white auditors emphasized his abdication of classical education for African Americans and his acceptance of a separate black place in the agrarian South. Yet blacks heard his argument for the inclusion, not the exclusion, of African Americans in the urban industrial order. Washington challenged his audience: "It is in the South that the Negro is given a man's chance in the commercial world." Speaking in Atlanta, one of the South's most unionized cities in 1895, Washington, like Sarah Dudley Pettey in Homestead, sought to remind whites that blacks had worked "without strikes and labor wars."[124] Washington foresaw the impending industrialization of the region, but his solution—vocational education—replicated the world of the past instead of predicting that of the future.[125] That day in Atlanta, Washington faced white captains of industry and asked for a job; blacks will "run your factories," he predicted. Unfortunately, when he gave up claims to a classical education, he relinquished a right upon which the growth of the black middle class depended. Certainly the Petteys had learned useful skills at Scotia Seminary and Biddle Memorial Institute—Sarah's dormitory's cornerstone read "Head, Heart, and Hands," after all—but they had also learned Latin. The grateful fervor with which whites embraced Washington's exposition speech soon made clear the one-sided nature of the Atlanta "Compromise."

Southern African Americans mounted vigorous opposition to the foreclosure of classical educations, the abdication of political power, and segregation.[126] Although the Atlanta Exposition is remembered primarily for Washington's speech, several discordant African American voices arose there, including Charles Pettey's and, oddly enough, Margaret Murray Washington's. Pettey answered Washington at the Negro Exhibition Hall, where it is doubtful that many, if any, white people heard him. As he began, perhaps Pettey remembered the day thirteen years earlier when, at Washington's invitation, he had addressed Tuskegee Institute's first class. Now he would strain those ties.[127]

The text of Pettey's Atlanta speech is lost, but another that reportedly echoed it that was given a short time later at Mobile, Alabama, has survived. It seems crafted as an answer to Washington. Pettey argued that full participation in economic progress required a complete education. "I would be the last one to discourage classical training," he said pointedly. Whereas Washington had recommended that African Americans narrow their horizons to succeed, Pettey exhorted his audience to "soar high, far beyond the cloudy pathway of all present astronomers and there blaze like the sun."[128] Only by receiving higher educations comparable to those of whites could African Americans have the chance to enter scientific fields. "Gentlemen, let the lamp of twenty five years experience be our guide," Pettey cautioned. "God forbid my saying one word against the Negro going to the topmost round of intellectual manhood."[129] Pettey held onto every shred of possibility and raised the stakes. He recommended no casting down of one's bucket where one stood, no settling for the right to work while bargaining away the right to vote. In exchange for Washington's clay-mired boots, Pettey offered wings.

Booker T. Washington's wife, Margaret Murray Washington, attended the Atlanta Exposition in her capacity as first vice president of the National Colored Woman's Congress, an event organized by the Woman's Auxiliary of the Negro Exhibition Hall. Lucy Hughes Brown, Sarah's old schoolmate, came as a delegate, as did many of the northern editors of the *Woman's Era*, the voice of the fledgling black club women's movement. The Woman's Congress issued a strongly worded set of resolutions on the state of southern race relations. Its resolves differ in principle from Washington's exposition address on at least one point. The women called "upon the Southern legislators, in the name of the common womanhood, to adopt a first and second class fare [on trains and streetcars], so that the womanhood of the race may be protected from every outrage and insult." Protesting Jim Crow cars by advocating that riders be separated on class lines rather than race lines runs counter to the image that the Wizard hoped to convey. Moreover, there is a striking difference in style between Washington's remarks and the women's resolutions. Whereas he was vague, they were specific. Whereas he seemed to accept subordination, they struck out at injustice.[130]

Perhaps the Petteys and Booker T. Washington saw things differently because of the profound differences between North Carolina and Alabama. If Washington's homiletic concessions represented canny strategies in the deep South, that simply points up the absurdity of whites anointing him the only spokesperson for African Americans. A look around New Bern through the Petteys' eyes underscores the dramatic differences between the upper and lower South in the 1890s, differences that African Americans in North Carolina recognized and cherished.[131] Shortly after Washington's speech, a black newspaperman found himself on a New Bern–bound train among several elderly black men and women who had just experienced six years of debt peonage in Mississippi. They had left North Carolina for the promise of a better life in the deep South, but they quickly discovered to their horror that "escape" was the only route out of sharecropping in "those bottoms." Even then "they will hunt you, catch you and bring you back and give you a good thrashing, just as they used to do in slavery times," said one sharecropper. One old woman, Mrs. P. E. Sutton, "looked real pitiful" and told of being whipped until her "back was as raw as a piece of raw beef." The returning emigrants concluded, "We had no rights, not even the right to vote." The dismayed correspondent, unlike Booker T. Washington, saw compelling connections between political, economic, and civil rights: "We colored people in North Carolina have a right to feel proud that we escaped at the last election such laws as the Democrats have in Mississippi."[132] As the grizzled sharecroppers traveled by train to New Bern in 1895, no Jim Crow law assigned their seats after they crossed the North Carolina line.

Debt peonage, disfranchisement, and segregation laws enacted outside the state hung over black North Carolinians in the 1890s like the sword of Damocles, evoking relief at escaping disaster thus far. In the summer of 1893, black North Carolina college student William Fonvielle tossed a few clothes and a volume of Shakespeare into his valise and departed on a train trip through the lower South to experience these curiosities firsthand. Operating from the premise that there was "as much difference in North Carolina and her sisters south of her as there is in North Carolina and Massachusetts," he poked his head out of the window in the hopes of glimpsing a "native" when the train crossed the South Carolina line. Spotting a one-gallused white man plowing behind an ox, Fonvielle "sat there and wondered if this tiller of the soil, this specimen of South Carolina manhood, had ever helped lynch anybody." He encountered "colored" and "white" waiting rooms for the first time in Spartanburg and pronounced Atlanta "a mean hole . . . chained down with prejudice." When he crossed the Georgia-Alabama line, he was forced to ride in his first Jim Crow car, which he dubbed a "pig-stye arrangement." As Fonvielle returned home through Tennessee, Jim Crow enforcement became spotty; some lines required it, but on others African Americans could "ride decently." Fonvielle's journey is like a snapshot from the eye of a hurricane: a calm view of segregation-in-progress. For William Fonvielle, at least, disfranchisement and Jim Crow represented anything but foregone conclusions in North Carolina.[133]

Other black North Carolinians, including Fonvielle's friend Sarah Dudley Pettey, cast anxious glances southward toward the stain of repression creeping in their direction. Two years after Fonvielle's journey, she condemned the owners of Atlanta's streetcar company for their "indiscreet and ungentlemanly execution of the power vested in them by a biased and prejudiced legislature"—in other words, for segregating the cars. Dudley Pettey endorsed a protest among black Atlanta women and urged them to go even further and boycott the lines.[134] Most black North Carolinians believed, however, that such repression could not happen in their state; they had progressed too far to turn back now. When the unfortunate Mississippi refugees finally walked freely along New Bern's streets, reassuring sights of black progress must have given them a feeling of relief akin to the relief Fonvielle experienced upon his homecoming. In the years just before and after Washington's speech, all eight barbers in New Bern were black, as were three butchers, two carpenters, and two general merchants. Three black lawyers practiced in the city, and eight black leaders organized the Mutual Aid Banking Company, the first black private bank in the state. School funds were distributed "pro rata per capita" to whites and blacks, and 4,293 black compared to 2,788 white children attended New Bern's public schools.

The Eastern North Carolina Industrial Stock and Fruit Fair, established in 1890 and staged annually by Craven County black leaders, prompted a white paper to comment, "It is to the credit of the colored citizens that the best of order was preserved everywhere," and the fair's secretary encouraged whites to attend in order to see members of the "colored race who are struggling to do something and be something." Besides watching the goat race and the alligator-wrestling competition, Sarah Dudley Pettey cheered as her children, sisters, and father took top honors for their paintings. Surely doing something and being something would count for something, and North Carolina would be the dam that held back the rising tide of white supremacy.[135]

The week after the fair, through the agency of a white lawyer, the Petteys purchased a resort in rural Alexander County, North Carolina, across the mountain from the Wilkes County homeplace where Charles Pettey was born in slavery in 1849.[136] Amid gently rolling hills, with springs and creeks lacing the land, sat a fine two-story hotel. On the other side of the road sprawled a gazebo and dining hall.[137] The Petteys now owned All Healing Spring, one of the premier "Health Resort[s] and Pleasure Retreat[s]" in western North Carolina. The resort's patrons had always been and would remain white—always.

Photographs of All Healing Spring during the period capture the fairest flowers of white womanhood lounging on the hotel's veranda, and accounts of summer parties and dances abound in the oral tradition.[138] The surrounding community discovered that the Petteys were the new owners in short order. A local white woman dutifully recorded each of the spring's proprietors in her scrapbook from 1892 until 1912. Next to Charles Pettey's name, she wrote "(Col.)." What was clear to contemporaries became shrouded in legend in subsequent years, and local folklore transformed Pettey from an African American into a white Confederate colonel.[139] Now innkeepers themselves, Charles and Sarah Pettey had quite outgrown their assigned spots in Procrustes's bed. So had many of their peers, the women apace with the men.

two

RACE AND WOMANHOOD

"Women are ... crowding the avenues once open only to men; they are entering the struggle and competing on equal terms," asserted Tena Nichols, a black Raleigh teacher, on a spring day in 1892. Nichols boasted to her listeners that women could be found "doing the actual work of the world ... taking an active, intelligent, resolute part in the march and progress of humanity." She spoke that day on "higher education for women"—a "God-given privilege," as she put it. Educating women would prove to be a wise investment for everyone, she reassured the skeptical among her audience, and its yield included "virtue preserved, social ills remedied ... and humanity blessed."[1] Higher education prepared black women for the world's work, not simply by showing them better ways to work but by showing them a better world. Women left seminaries, normal schools, and colleges with much more than a finite body of knowledge or a set of skills; they departed imbued with a reformist zeal for racial "uplift" and armed with a full quiver of intellectual weapons to aim at poverty and discrimination.[2] Moreover, most black women and men attended school together, and the coeducational experience influenced gender relations among educated African Americans by encouraging more equitable domestic partnerships and an active place for women in public life. Higher education produced strong female soldiers for the race. Soon, Nichols predicted, "young women of color will march to the front in one long unbroken line."

Upon graduation, black women teachers and activists shaped and reshaped strategies to outmaneuver the daily manifestations of racism they encountered on their way to the front. White supremacy has lasted so long because of its ability to make and remake itself. Black women tried to get out in front of racism, to anticipate an opportunity for interracial cooperation here, protest exclusion there, or, chameleonlike, to become invisible to whites and get on with things surreptitiously. Sometimes they fought straightforwardly, sometimes covertly, the open, ugly faces of segregation, racial violence, and economic exclusion, and they tried to peel away white supremacy's thousand disguises as well. Racism rolls along so smoothly because it seems to be impermeable. It is, however, a tightly wound tangle of individual strands, and black women set about unraveling them wherever they could. The Woman's Christian Temperance Union (WCTU) is a case in point. Because of a famous conflict between race leader Ida B. Wells and Union president Frances Willard, historians dismiss the WCTU as "racist." But that analysis overlooks the importance of the WCTU to southern black women and fails to recognize how its racial politics compared to racial politics in other organizations at home and abroad. It does not impart a sympathetic understanding of why, for a time, many of North Carolina's black women saw the WCTU as their best hope for building strong communities and securing interracial cooperation. Black women first forged their ideas of gender and race equity within their families; then their educational experiences and voluntary activities tested and refined those beliefs. Their concepts of woman's place were far from monolithic, but all were marked by the experience of exclusion and the challenge of meeting adversity.

Tena Nichols spoke at a singular moment. It was as if black southern educators, students, and parents were pausing in 1892 to consider their course. Several tributaries came together to produce this watershed: an educated generation had emerged with firsthand experience against which they weighed educational theories; black schools had produced a competent and increasingly female teaching force; African Americans now sought new funding sources since Reconstruction Era philanthropic aid had dwindled and southern whites stirred up frequent debates over the extent of state responsibility for black public education; African Americans argued over the future of coeducation; and curriculum disputes grew more intense as the decade wore on.

At the most fundamental level, the first generation of educated African

Americans born in freedom had completed college and had developed their own ideas about what an education should be. Rather than accepting uncritically northern missionaries' curricula and pedagogical methods, they could begin to retain what worked, reject what failed, and add new courses. Twenty years earlier, at the age of twenty-three, self-taught ex-slave Charles Pettey had entered a classroom for the first time and had taken his seat alongside city-schooled Charlotte boys of twelve or thirteen. His free-born wife Sarah had matriculated within a more regimented system: grade school, normal school, and seminary. From the 1880s until the tide of vocational training swamped them after 1900, African Americans began to formulate educational models based on their own postbellum experiences. Black men and women who went beyond grade school generally chose from among three courses of study: a classical curriculum that offered Latin and the humanities; a normal school program that included literature, history, math, basic science, and pedagogy; and a sprinkling of vocational courses to equip the student to pursue a profession, earn pin money, or simply provide for his or her family. In addition, black men could pursue a theological degree at church-supported schools, a separate course of study that included the Bible, exhortation, and Greek.

By 1892, most people knew some young woman from their own neighborhood, once a barefoot girl, perhaps the daughter of a freedwoman who could not read or write, who shone in the local school and then, through ingenuity, gumption, and luck, left home to pursue higher education.[3] These larger-than-life role models never made it look easy, but they placed education within the realm of the possible for the girls they left behind. Julia Sadgwar was a student at Gregory Normal Institute in Wilmington when her father suddenly died, and she eventually went on to Fisk University. Sadgwar recalled, "I found that I could not always wear whole shoes or dresses as some other girls did; . . . there were days when I would have only bread or perhaps a potato . . . but nothing stopped me."[4]

Sadgwar returned to North Carolina as a teacher, along with other women students, many transformed beyond recognition, who went back to their homes to fill the crying need for teachers in the fast-growing public school system. By the end of the 1890s, it became clear that women would dominate the teaching force. When Sarah Dudley went home to teach in New Bern in 1884, there were 2,231 black teachers in the state, of whom 731 were women. By 1890, black male teachers numbered 1,370 and female teachers 988; ten years later, as many women were teaching as men.[5] At the same time, African American men and women replaced whites as normal, seminary, and college professors in black institutions. To be sure, some elderly white women and men, veterans of Reconstruction, taught on, but an increasing number of black women and men joined them.

Financial support from Reconstruction Era constituencies faded in the early 1890s, and philanthropies with vocationally oriented agendas such as the General Education Board, the Anna T. Jeanes Fund, and the Rosenwald Foundation had not yet stepped in to fill the need, much less call the dance, as they ultimately would.[6] The Hampton Institute model of vocational training was merely one among many in 1892. It would be three years before Booker T. Washington successfully began to impose his personal experience and vision on his entire race, and almost a decade before northern white vocational philanthropists tightened their grip on southern black education into a choke hold.[7] It was not that African Americans did not want to learn useful skills; they did. But they also wanted to follow intellectual curiosity where it led. One only has to glance at the German drills in adolescent Charles Chesnutt's journals and read his accompanying self-admonishments to study harder to see how important classical education was to his sense of accomplishment and to understand how learning shaped his self-concept.[8] Nothing in Tena Nichols's speech decries learning practical pursuits, but it is doubtful that laundry classes came to mind when Nichols dreamed of her "God-given privilege."

The school "year" was fluid, lasting from four months at state expense to eight months with private supplementation. As poor as it was, the public school system in North Carolina outdistanced those of many other southern states.[9] Many whites hated paying a nickel for African American schooling. Perennially, African Americans would mount a court challenge to some white county functionary's decision to allocate tax dollars to schools separately on the basis of each race's local tax payments. An 1886 North Carolina Supreme Court ruling found these attempts to starve black education unconstitutional, which slowed the schemes a bit until after disfranchisement. Grudgingly, North Carolina's white majority helped fund black education, theoretically allocating dollars on a per-pupil basis and paying black teachers as much as whites until the late 1890s. This system—racially fair on its face—seldom proved equal in its execution. In a precariously balanced political climate, however, lip service counted for something.[10]

Even "equal" support was meager. Teacher Susie Rhone's rural one-room school accommodated pupils "rang[ing] from little tots of five years to great big folks of nineteen and twenty," sometimes seventy at once. Learning competed with farming, and many rural students attended only sporadically. Louise Dorr noted in late May 1886 that strawberry picking had kept students away for the past month. She struggled to lift her spirits even though sometimes it seemed "like trying to make tracks in the water to try to make impressions" on her students. The rewards of this attempt to walk on water could tide a teacher over for a term, however. Annie Day captured the exhilaration of teaching—any time, any place—when she wrote, "I forget everything while I am there, but the eager questioning faces and what I would teach them."[11]

Accounts of the summer subscription schools are the stuff of legend: Charles Chesnutt organized one at fifteen; far from his Fisk University dorm room, the green schoolteacher Willie Du Bois lost his virginity to his summer landlady; teenaged Anna Julia Haywood launched her eighty-year teaching career at a Chatham County subscription school.[12] As soon as their own terms ended, African American normal and college students scoured the countryside to scare up parents who might pass the hat and combine the proceeds with any unspent tax money to fund a summer school. The young teachers lived with their students' families. Chesnutt, who had taught in the Charlotte graded city school during the regular term, described the haphazard process of organizing a summer school in 1874. On a "dull" Fourth of July, Chesnutt went "up town to look around and see the country folks about a school. Got on the track of one." He tracked down Charles Pettey, who he thought operated a school nearby, where he was preaching to get the names of the committeemen in charge of school funding. Pettey informed Chesnutt that "he had lost his school, that there was but $89.93 in the treasury for that school and that they were going to build a school-house with it, and that there was but $20.00 for the school I was on the track of." After walking twenty-three miles on another day attempting to find support for a school, Chesnutt called it quits and went home to live with his parents for the summer.[13]

Summer schools encouraged cultural exchanges between citified teachers and countrified students. Teenager Anna Julia Haywood, a student at Saint Augustine's College in bustling Raleigh, traveled to nearby, but profoundly rural, Chatham County to teach. She inspired one country boy, Simon Atkins, to come back with her to Saint Augustine's to launch his own educational career, one that culminated in a college presidency.[14] Du Bois's students' daily struggles for survival moved him to mourn in *The Souls of Black Folk*, "How hard a thing life is to the lowly!"[15] Charles Chesnutt's discovery that his wards at a South Carolina summer school and their parents believed in ghosts added another mile to the yawning distance between him and his rural African American pupils: "Well! uneducated people, are the most bigoted, superstitious, hardest headed people in the world! . . . All the eloquence of a Demosthenes, the logic of a Plato, the demonstrations of the most learned men in this world couldn't convince them of the falsity, the absurdity, the utter impossibility and unreasonableness of such things. Verily, education is a great thing."[16]

Seven American Missionary Association (AMA) schools, more than in any other state, were located strategically throughout North Carolina.[17] Many more had existed in the early days of Reconstruction, serving as the only schools in many places, but by the 1890s, these institutions functioned mainly to extend the public school year and the number of grades. Some AMA schools operated for months after the public school year ended; others added grades to the public schools to make them high schools and normal schools. Entire families attended. Eula Wellmon Dunlap remembered that when her father heard about Lincoln Academy in Kings Mountain, he picked up everything and moved, building a house with his own hands at the edge of campus. She was three and her sister was five at the time: "For a while Father, Mother, sister, and I all went to school. . . . I spent most of my time marking on paper and playing with blocks. Several married couples went to school." She eventually completed high school there. Her father had to drop out to support the family but studied at night and became a teacher himself.[18]

At a time when mother, father, and toddlers learned in the same classroom, the southern white norm of single-sex institutions was out of the question. Even if it had been possible to make such a choice, it is doubtful that most African Americans would have chosen to separate the sexes in school. The idea of keeping ex-slave women in bondage to ignorance seemed wrongheaded to most freed people and to their northern champions, and women wanted to learn what men were taught. Moreover, by 1880, most African Americans realized that black women would probably work outside the home for a lifetime or at least temporarily. Equipping a woman with an education armed her for the wage-earning battle. Trades such as carpentry represented a relatively high-paying and semiautonomous alternative for black men that did not exist for black women. An uneducated black woman could support herself only as a domestic; an educated black woman might become a teacher.

Thus, although prescriptive literature and white northern teachers counseled a version of separate spheres for African American women and men, it was not the cult of southern ladyhood they advocated but rather an evangelically driven ethos of "usefulness." Pursuit of "usefulness" gave women a middle space between the spheres into which they might venture on the business of the race. At the same time, white southerners never extended the privileges of ladyhood to black women, forcing them to negotiate public space without the cloak of chivalry.[19] All of these factors meant that African Americans of both sexes entered Reconstruction valuing strength, initiative, and practicality among black women and that the system of higher education they constructed reflected those ideals, though sometimes more brightly than other times.[20]

As a result, African American college and teacher training in North Carolina took place mostly at coeducational institutions, giving black students academic experiences quite different from those of southern whites.

Even women like Sarah Dudley Pettey who attended single-sex seminaries first studied at coeducational normal schools where adult men and women sat side by side. Young men and women found themselves together on the same playing field, albeit under unequal conditions. Once together, men and women openly questioned southern white patriarchal norms. In addition, coeducation gave substantial numbers of black women access to a kind of learning that remained rare among white women in the South.

The contrast between black coeducational institutions of higher learning and southern white female academies in the 1870s and 1880s could not have been more stark.[21] Most upper-class white women's institutions kept young men, even brothers, at bay and offered primarily art, music, a smattering of literature, and "ornamental" languages, such as French. The occasional woman's college included a classical curriculum, but such offerings were rare in North Carolina until the late 1890s. Although it is tempting to minimize the importance of the two decades of lead time African American women enjoyed in acquiring higher education, it made a terrific difference. During that period, the state provided no opportunities for higher learning for poor or middling white women, apart from summer normal schools, which they could not attend without some private education past grade school. In the mountain counties, a small number of missionary schools admitted white women. A few smaller denominations, notably the Quakers, the Lutherans, and the Associated Reformed Presbyterian Church, began in the 1880s to allow a few female coreligionists to enter their schools. The white private colleges supported by mainstream denominations and the state university excluded women altogether. White North Carolinians opposed coeducation so vociferously that one educator noted in 1888, "No one would dare propose, with any hope of success, that [white] women be admitted to the University and leading denominational colleges of the state."[22]

Exclusion of women from white men's colleges meant more than separation from men; it also generally meant exclusion from classical educations, the core of traditional training for leadership. Mastery of the classical curriculum demonstrated intellectual equality with white men, by implication suggesting entitlement to power and prestige. Keeping it away from white women was the pedagogical equivalent of foot binding.[23] In 1892, after a long fight, the state funded a full-term normal school for white women in Greensboro. Soon, white women at the state's Normal and Industrial College began to see themselves as "New Women."[24]

By that time, as Tena Nichols's words remind us, African American women had been "New Women" since 1877, when a reluctant state legislature, wary of black voting strength and white legislators' fears of forced integration, had established a state-supported normal school in Fayette-

turn to pg. 218

ville for African Americans, the first such school in the country. The state did not limit the black school to a few months in the summer as it did the white normal schools but allowed it to continue for up to nine months as long as funding held out.[25] Apparently, the legislature neglected explicitly to approve women's admission to Fayetteville Colored Normal School. Surprised when women made up the majority of the first class, some befuddled legislators apparently protested against using state funds to educate black women. Fayetteville's African American principal answered the naysayers: "The presence of females has a refining influence on the manners of males and their reciting together in the same classes creates lively interest." Fayetteville's women students were its "brightest students and most promising teachers," he argued.[26] It was here that Charles Chesnutt matriculated; later, he became principal. The Fayetteville model held, and by the 1890s, the state operated seven coeducational, two-term, residential normal schools for African Americans. Whites in the cities where the schools were located welcomed the institutions since they conducted elementary practice schools that replaced locally supported public schools.

In addition to the normal schools, one state-supported and six denominational black colleges sprang up. In 1890, when Congress threatened to cut off funds to any state that failed to provide agricultural education to blacks, legislators scrambled to establish a state-supported African American college since they hoped to channel additional federal funds to a new agricultural school for whites. Unlike the new white school in Raleigh, the African American North Carolina Agricultural and Mechanical College (later the North Carolina Agricultural and Technical College) accepted women students.[27] All six denominational colleges predated the Agricultural and Mechanical College, and only the Presbyterians separated men and women, sending men to Biddle Memorial Institute and women to Scotia Seminary.[28] During their early years, most functioned as secondary schools, adding college courses as the student body became ready for advanced work, at which time they divided the preparatory, normal, classical, and theological departments.

Since few southern models existed, the schools' approaches to integrating women into classrooms and extracurricular activities were individualized. The resulting quandaries resembled those confronted by northern and western colleges that introduced coeducation around the same time, but they were played out in a quite different context and with quite different social ramifications. The issues involved not only gender relations but also race and class relations. The question of how best to educate black women hung in the air, hashed out at church programs such as Tena Nichols's, discussed in heated debates at black colleges, and, most famously, recorded in the pages of *A Voice from the South*, a book published in 1892 by Anna Julia

Haywood Cooper, a Saint Augustine's graduate, who, like Tena Nichols, had once taught in Raleigh. Although Cooper herself was an extraordinary person, black women across the South shared the complaints she enumerated in *A Voice from the South*.[29] Her work captured the zeitgeist so well, she might have named it *Voices from the South*. Nichols's speech serves as a case in point; it predated *A Voice from the South* by a few months and examined many of the same issues in Cooper's own hometown.

Allowing women on campus was only a beginning, Cooper insisted. The first generation of women students at coeducational colleges fought difficult battles to gain equal treatment. Entering the preparatory department of coeducational Saint Augustine's at the age of nine, Cooper grew up resenting the school's unequal treatment of women. She remembered feeling "(as I suppose many an ambitious girl has felt) a thumping from within unanswered by any beckoning from without."[30] She particularly disdained the attention lavished on the male theological department. For instance, Saint Augustine's offered a Greek class designed for budding male ministers that was normally off-limits to women, but when Cooper insisted, the professor made an exception and allowed her to join. She summarized her complaints: "A boy, however meager his equipment and shallow his pretensions, had only to declare a floating intention to study theology and he could get all the support, encouragement and stimulus he needed." On the other hand, "a self-supporting girl had to struggle . . . against positive discouragements."[31] We know from Cooper's description that coeducational colleges were no utopias for women, but her comments hint at the opportunities open to black women who fought to get ahead. Cooper ultimately did manage to take Greek and found teaching positions in the summer to send herself through school. In *A Voice from the South*, she advocated an absolutely equal education for black women, a visionary proposition that Cooper could articulate only because she had caught a glimpse of men's opportunities. Coeducation gave her a chance to peek into their lives.

By the time Cooper published *A Voice from the South*, a second generation of black women had entered college under the tutelage of professors who created an explicit rationale for women's training in a coeducational context. Livingstone College in Salisbury was an institution that realized many women's hopes, probably because pioneering black women had educated many of its faculty members. Simon Atkins, one of Livingstone's most influential professors in its early years, began as Anna Julia Haywood Cooper's star pupil and became her coteacher in summer schools.[32]

One of two colleges in the state controlled and financed by an independent African American denomination—in Livingstone's case, the African Methodist Episcopal (AME) Zion Church—Livingstone College did not

The entire student body of Livingstone College in Salisbury assembled on the porches of Huntington Hall, circa 1890. Courtesy of the College Archives, Carnegie Library, Livingstone College, Salisbury, North Carolina.

have to cater to whites, either in the form of northern supporters or local coreligionists. Livingstone's founders based their policies on their notions of fairness and equality, which presupposed a public role for black women that was at odds with southern white gender norms. When it opened in 1880, Livingstone defined its mission as equipping young men and women for religious and educational work in the South and in Africa. As Joseph Price, the first president, put it, that goal necessitated training "of the Head, Hand, and Heart"—intellectual, practical, and spiritual.[33] The school included theological, classical, normal, and preparatory departments, and the college's first student was a woman. From the start, African American men and women taught together. Victoria Richardson, who had been teaching with Charles Chesnutt in Charlotte, was one of four original faculty members.[34] The first group of students graduated with bachelor of arts degrees from the classical department in 1888. Two women marched with eight men, the first black women to earn the bachelor's degree in the state.[35]

The Livingstone model did not go unchallenged among African Americans. Some advocated the adoption of white gender norms and the limitation of woman's sphere.[36] Those AME Zion parents who felt that Living-

Classical graduating class of Livingstone College, 1914. Courtesy of the College Archives, Carnegie Library, Livingstone College, Salisbury, North Carolina.

stone went too far in educating women like men sent their daughters instead to single-sex Presbyterian Scotia Seminary. One AME Zion father charged, "We do not believe in the coeducation of the sexes after they attain a certain age." Separation would be far "better and safer" and more in keeping with white gender norms, since, he pointed out, southern whites did not "mix" the sexes. He suggested that the AME Zion Church open a female seminary instead of forcing members who preferred single-sex education to send their daughters to Scotia, where they often married Presbyterian ministers and converted, "sapp[ing] [the AME Zion Church] of its very life—our best educated women."[37] The irritated father proffered two practical benefits to soothe the tempers of the Livingstone women he would exclude. If they left and went to a female academy, he told them, they could save money on clothes and spend less time "writing notes [to boys] and in socials."[38]

Socializing between men and women students took place under conditions much more stringent than this AME Zion father implied. For example, Livingstone College professors knew that dancing students drew the ire of Methodist parents, so for recreation, students assembled in single-sex formations, paired up, and marched around the room to music, without touching—or actually "dancing."[39] Scrutiny at Lincoln Academy may have been even more pervasive. "We would march, play games, but you didn't get a chance to sit and talk to a boy. The teachers would keep you moving," Eula Dunlap recalled. Students socialized with members of the opposite sex only on one day of the year—Thanksgiving, "a great day"—when boys and girls lined up strategically and their teachers marched them up Kings Mountain two by two. "Then," Dunlap confided, "you would know who liked who, but there would be teachers in front, a few couples, then teachers, and so on."[40]

Fittingly, it was Cooper's protégé, Simon Atkins, who defended Livingstone against the move to purge its women.[41] Atkins and the forces he marshaled among his colleagues supported coeducation not by default but with a clear sense of purpose. They intended to produce women leaders. After the female seminary debate died down, the editor of the *Star of Zion* boasted, "Livingstone College is doing for women what no other institution is doing, bringing her up to be the equal of her eternal antagonist, man, in debate, in public spirit, in morals and thought; and side by side with him she determines to help solve the problems of human life."[42]

On Livingstone's campus, students redefined gender and self-consciously grappled with the implications of that redefinition. Women excelled academically and competed openly with men. Esther Carthey, at the top of the 1888 classical class, gave the valedictory in Latin as required, and through the 1890s, women continued to earn bachelor's degrees.[43] At commencement, female normal school graduates gave addresses entitled, "The Reformatory Movements of the Age," "Frivolous Society," and "How to Make a Living."[44] Lula Pettigrew earned the title "most voracious reader" in the college because she consumed every tome on the shelves, from *Lovers Once but Strangers Now* to *Natural Law in the Spiritual World*.[45] By the end of Ada Battle's first year, she had polished off all of the women in the composition competition and had earned a spot in the coeducational debate finals.[46] Women took leadership roles in single-sex and coeducational campus groups. For instance, an editorial staff of one man and two women founded the campus magazine, the *Living-Stone*.[47]

The seriousness with which Livingstone students debated gender roles indicates the importance they attached to working out their own models of manhood and womanhood. In the pages of the *Living-Stone*, students revealed their ideals of manly men and womanly women. Debater Ada Battle opened the discussion in an article she wrote on well-mannered men. Outspoken in an intellectual argument, Battle appreciated "the attentive glance, the quiet cordial bow, and the sweet disposition" in male students.[48] Cale Struggles responded by describing his ideal woman: "I like a modest, sweet tempered girl—one whom you can depend upon."[49] Although both sexes prized modesty and calm temperament, women students disagreed even among themselves on women's place after graduation. Charlotte Jordan found it unseemly for women to become lawyers, doctors, lecturers, and "politicians of the gentler sex" rather than wielding their influence through male family members.[50] But Maggie Hood had the final word when she suggested that someone as outstanding as Anna Cooper should represent the entire race, not just its women.[51] Tongue in cheek, she forgave men for holding women back: "This keeping woman in a state of degradation, is not to be attributed to the heartlessness of men, for their hearts are generally tender and soft; but it is to be charged to the faults of their heads (which are also soft)."[52]

William Fonvielle, the Livingstone student who toured the South in search of Jim Crow, later counted the marriages among his classmates and remarked with pride, "Livingstone men make husbands; Livingstone women make wives."[53] Unlike white women of the period, black women did not usually have to choose between higher education and marriage or between teaching and marrying. White women risked passing prime marriageable age in single-sex schools. One-half of the white women in the new state normal school's 1896 graduating class never wed.[54] African American women often taught after marriage, whereas most public school committeemen would not allow married white women to teach.[55]

Moreover, the prevailing image of middle- and upper-class white southern womanhood in the postbellum period devalued scholarship and outspokenness among young women, whereas many African American men and women prized a different ideal.[56] For example, Maggie Hood's quick wit did not stand in the way of her popularity. When Sarah Dudley Pettey attended Hood's wedding, she described her as "a classical graduate of Livingstone College, a young lady of rare attainments, and a brilliant society belle." Hood's classical education had not crippled her for daily life, Dudley Pettey continued, since she was also "thoroughly conversant with domestic economy." Maggie Hood represented an example to be emulated, Dudley Pettey told her readers, using her coverage of Hood's wedding to inject this plug: "The church of to-day needs educated women as well as men in every city to formulate, regulate, and direct the trend of society."[57]

Hood's ability to combine intellectual pursuits, domestic life, and romance proved more the rule than the exception for black college women. As Fonvielle recalled, "Most of the young women I learned to respect and admire [at Livingstone] are wives and mothers now."[58] Anna Julia Haywood Cooper argued in 1892 that a black woman had "as many resources as men, as many activities beckon her on." The solution to making marriage an attractive choice among those activities lay not in the woman asking, "How shall I so cramp, stunt, simplify and nullify myself as to make me eligible to the honor of being swallowed up into some little man?" Rather it depended upon the man's ability to direct his own efforts into "the noblest, grandest and best achievements of which he is capable."[59]

By admonishing men to fulfill their potentials, Cooper executed an end run around patriarchy. Ideal patriarchy should not limit women; it only did so when the man in question was stunted. In fact, men could take women's striving as a useful early warning sign to encourage them to exercise patriarchy more strenuously. If women were gaining in the race of life, Cooper chided, men should run faster. Cooper never addressed the problem that her reasoning created—that is, if patriarchy ceases to limit women, is it still patriarchy?—by calling the hand of the patriarch. Allowing women to grow should push men to even loftier heights; they were, after all, capable of greatness, were they not? Educated black women sought to establish partnerships that maximized the potential and efficiency of both members, and they tended to do that by avoiding hierarchical ideas of male dominance and female subordination. Men and women were different, but they had complementary work to do; once trained for that work, women were anxious to establish domestic relationships that allowed them to get on with the job.

Southern white women would seek such marriages in growing numbers beginning in the Progressive Era, but they were still rare in the nineteenth century. This arrangement seems to resemble the much-chronicled sort of partnerships that a small group of well-educated northern white women formed, but its roots and stakes, and therefore its significance, differ markedly. Springing from slavery, poverty, religion, and black women's daily contact with men rather than distance from them, this civic partnership played out in a society that rested on the subordination of black men as well as black women. In this case, the stakes had something to do with the question of "woman's sphere" but much more to do with the day-to-day survival of every southern African American, male and female.[60]

Anna Julia Haywood found love as well as adversity at Saint Augustine's. At least one male faculty member valued smart women: Haywood married her Greek professor, George Cooper. When he died shortly after their marriage, she faced the world as a twenty-one-year-old widow. She went on to Oberlin College and upon graduation in 1886 landed a teaching position back at Saint Augustine's. Throughout her first year, administrators praised her work, but two days before graduation, they fired her due to "incompatibility of temperament." The fragmentary record offers no clues, but Cooper must have spoken out in a way that displeased the administration. Cooper went out fighting, unsuccessfully demanding a hearing and reporting the story to the press. Her supporters lamented her termination, insisting that the "fair name of Mrs. Cooper, her brilliant attainment, her superior skill as a teacher, cannot be dimmed."[61] At once, she landed a position at the M Street School in Washington, D.C., and set about writing *A Voice from the South*. Despite challenges such as those Anna Julia Cooper met,

if men are so great...

black women flourished amid the rich mix of encouragement and adversity that coeducational colleges provided.

All of the preparation in the world, however, could not have readied black women for the realities of dealing with white women after graduation. Some had experienced close contact with white women teachers; Bennett College in Greensboro, Saint Augustine's College and Shaw University in Raleigh, and Scotia Seminary in Concord all had integrated faculties through the 1880s. Other students, such as those at Livingstone College, nestled on a campus that spared them much contact with whites. Neither model resembled the world at large. The white women who taught at black institutions represented anomalies in the South, often excluded from the rest of white society. They generally saw themselves as missionaries, and although they fervently maintained that "God's soul diamond in a black casket is as precious in His sight as the one in a white casket,"[62] many did not necessarily think their living students were yet their equals. Some thought they never would be.

Along with their diplomas, black women graduates marched off the stage flying class markers recognizable to whites. Their dress, deportment, piety, literacy, and concern for social progress matched similar characteristics of a tiny but growing group of white women. Educated black women expected whites to recognize class similarities across racial lines, and they sought forums that would bring them together with white women.

The Woman's Christian Temperance Union joined women of both races who sought to impose new values on southern life. Drawing heavily from the ranks of Methodists and Baptists, the WCTU at last gave evangelical women an outlet to act on the ideals their mothers had embraced during the Second Great Awakening of the 1830s and 1840s. At that time, the southern slave system had worked against social reform, although some manifestations of new sensibilities had appeared in North Carolina. Interracial temperance societies sprang up across the state in the 1830s, temperance groups held mixed male/female meetings, and Wesleyan and Quaker ministers traveled across the state preaching abolition at the risk of losing their lives.[63] After the war, the WCTU tapped those evangelical values.

The roots of the organized African American temperance movement in the state went back to Reconstruction, when several black temperance clubs joined the Independent Order of Good Templars (IOGT), an international organization for both men and women. Headquartered in Great Britain, the IOGT already had active white chapters in North Carolina. When the newly formed black chapters petitioned the state organization for official recognition, however, the white members refused to grant them a charter and would not even divulge the secret Templar password. Stung by this exclusion, the black Templars forged ahead and formed lasting ties with other white and black chapters throughout the world.[64] Black men and women joined the Templars in great numbers; the Raleigh chapter boasted 200 members.[65] In 1873, Sarah Dudley Pettey's father, Edward, presided over the statewide organization, and her mother, Caroline, joined the New Bern chapter.[66] The African American Templars recruited women as full members, elected them to office, and applauded their speeches at meetings. At a black IOGT meeting in Fayetteville in 1875, the keynote speaker recognized "the power of the females, and their duty in exercising it" within the organization.[67] Black women gained experience and self-confidence through their work in the Templars, and men came to admire their forcefulness and courage. When Sarah McLaurin gave a rousing speech to the Cape Fear lodge on New Year's Day in 1888, a male listener reported that "she addressed the house with as much bravery as did some of our modern heroes."[68]

While black men and women worked together as Templars, the monumental statewide prohibition referendum of 1881 set the stage for the WCTU's entry into the state.[69] In the midst of the 1881 prohibition campaign, Frances Willard visited Wilmington to mobilize women and encourage them to join the WCTU.[70] Willard worried about how southern white women would receive a northern woman, but her nervousness did not prevent her from advocating temperance work among African Americans. To Willard's surprise, southern white women embraced her suggestion with enthusiasm.[71] She observed: "Everywhere the Southern white people desired me to speak to the colored."[72] Willard was not the only white woman reaching out to black women; for example, when a "ladies' prohibition club" met at the Methodist church in Concord, the white women reported that "the galleries of the church were set apart for our colored friends."[73] Black men's votes and black women's political influence mattered in the temperance election.

Statewide prohibition failed in North Carolina in 1881, and many whites blamed blacks, despite the nearly unanimous endorsement of prohibition by the black press. Reports from across the state declared that African Americans had voted overwhelmingly in favor of whiskey, probably because many blacks kept small shops in which liquor sold briskly.[74] White prohibitionists, mostly Democrats, charged that liquor interests bought black votes to tip the election.[75] After 1881, temperance strategy centered on local-option elections, and the WCTU attempted to win prohibition town by town, county by county.[76] To that end, the white women began to organize and support black WCTU chapters throughout the state that reported to the white statewide officers.

The Woman's Christian Temperance Union mattered so much to southern black women reformers of the late nineteenth century because it promoted a working model of finer womanhood that meshed with their own ideals.[77] The union joined black women's religious and class values to their activism, even as it provided a safe forum for agitation. Black women welcomed its legitimation of a public role for women, a role they knew would be necessary for racial uplift. Through the telescope of the WCTU, southern African Americans could gaze upward past vacuous white southern belles to solid white women such as Frances Willard, WCTU national president. For example, a black man who cited Sarah Dudley Pettey as an example of "womanly womanhood," capable of galvanizing mixed male and female audiences with her suffrage speeches, seized upon this comparison: "Mrs. Dudley Pettey is a brilliant Frances E. Willard."[78]

For black women and a growing number of educated white women from poor families, class identity was a lesson to be learned and one they bore a responsibility to teach, and the WCTU facilitated that task. Black women reformers tried to impose upon uneducated women and men sobriety, thrift, purity, and a love for learning; if a woman embraced those values, they embraced her, regardless of the trappings of her life or her origins. Abna Aggrey Lancaster, whose mother and father taught at Livingstone College, recalled that it was not money that made a difference between people—"we were all poor"—but "training."[79] Mary Lynch, who trained Lancaster in temperance, herself learned and taught class standing. Born just after Reconstruction to poor parents, Lynch attended Scotia Seminary and began teaching at Livingstone in 1891. One hundred years later, a male Livingstone student recalled her from the 1920s as the professor of "finer womanhood." Teaching and learning "finer womanhood" became a strategy black women deployed to counter white supremacy.

On the other hand, many southern white women initially found the WCTU's public duties a challenge to their sense of propriety. The WCTU asked its members to step beyond the pale of southern white ladyhood. It encouraged them not only to visit jails but to break bread with the prisoners, black and white; to spend Thanksgiving at the county poor farm with its biracial conglomeration of demented alcoholics, lice-ridden wayward girls, and toothless, tobacco-spitting old women; to throw up a beribboned gauntlet at that most raucous of masculine preserves, the polling place, buttonhole voters who tried to elbow past, and glare at them while they voted.[80] Once white women overcame their fears, WCTU work probably changed their lives a great deal more than they changed the lives of the recipients of their beneficence. One reflected on her lunch with two white and six black men in the Winston-Salem jail: "The power of the Holy Spirit rested upon all. . . . It was a melting time."[81]

In the 1880s and 1890s, the North Carolina WCTU undertook a novel experiment in interracial contact. Black women hoped to find common

Mary Lynch, circa 1895. Courtesy of the College Archives, Carnegie Library, Livingstone College, Salisbury, North Carolina.

ground with white women in the WCTU to construct a cooperative venture joined by class and gender ties, one capable of withstanding the winds of white supremacist rhetoric. For several years in the 1880s, women worked as members of separate black and white chapters within a single statewide structure, the first postbellum statewide biracial voluntary organization in North Carolina.[82] Under the heat of temperance fever, racial boundaries softened ever so slightly.

Historians have argued that the WCTU's chief attraction for women was its critique of the drunken father and husband and that its activism sprang from belief in "feminine moral superiority."[83] White female temperance activists linked drinking with male profligacy, domestic physical abuse, and women's economic dependence. They drew on the doctrine of separate spheres to confer on women moral authority in family matters, even if the exercise of that power necessitated a temporary foray into the public sphere. Thus, among whites, temperance became increasingly a woman's issue, an expression of "female consciousness."[84] Black women's participation in the WCTU, however, meant something more than "home protection."[85] Although domestic issues certainly mattered to southern African American women, participation in the WCTU also folded into the cause of racial uplift.[86]

To counteract whites' blindness to the realities of middle-class black life, African American women used the WCTU to point up black dignity, industriousness, and good citizenship. Since many whites predicted that the absence of the "civilizing" influence of slavery would result in the extinction of African Americans, occasions of black drunkenness generated self-satisfied notice among whites. When white southern tobacco farmers came to town to tie one on, no one suggested that their drinking sprees foretold the racial degeneracy of the Anglo-Saxon "race."[87] But a drunken black man staggering home from a saloon might inspire an "I-told-you-so" editorial in the local white newspaper replete with Darwinistic predictions of the extinction of the black race in a single generation.[88] Thus, black women temperance activists worried not just about the pernicious effects of alcohol on the family but also about the progress of the entire race, and temperance activities bolstered African Americans' contested claims to full membership in the polity.

Moreover, black women saw in the WCTU a chance to build a Christian community that could serve as a model of interracial cooperation on other fronts. If, through white women's recognition of common womanhood and shared class goals, black women could forge a structure that encouraged racial interaction, they might later build on that structure. The WCTU represented a place where women might see past skin color to recognize each other's humanity. One source of black women's optimism sprang from Frances Willard's family background. As a child, her abolitionist parents opened their home as a stop on the Underground Railway, and her father was a Free-Soiler. Willard had the confidence of Frederick Douglass and William Lloyd Garrison, both members of an older generation of abolitionists.[89]

White women, however, envisioned interracial cooperation as a partnership in which the women they referred to as "our sisters in black" were junior partners, participating in a segregated structure that reported to white women. They believed the power relations of a biracial WCTU should mirror the racial hierarchy of society at large. Nonetheless, founding a biracial organization, even one separated internally, required courage and a vision of the future that differed from the white male perspective. By organizing black WCTU chapters, white women recognized gender and class as binding forces that mitigated racial differences.

In the late nineteenth century, African Americans and whites used the term "interracial cooperation" to signify working across racial lines to solve common problems. Black women undertook interracial cooperation without illusions of sisterhood because they believed racial progress depended on it as long as whites controlled southern institutions. Nothing about the term implied a common commitment to civil rights, to racial equality, to working together cheerfully, or even to working together with civility. There was never a point in the two decades of interracial cooperation within the WCTU when white women could not be characterized according to today's standards as "racist." Yet such a characterization reveals little about actual practice and obscures a more important truth: racism is never a static phenomenon. It waxes and wanes in response to a larger social context, sometimes perniciously defining the contours of daily life, sometimes receding as behavior and speech challenge the boundaries of racial constructs.[90]

It was black political power that convinced white women to work with African American women, whose support they needed in local-option campaigns. In 1883, Frances Willard returned to North Carolina, where she spoke again to black audiences, including one at Livingstone College, and brought the existing WCTU chapters into a statewide organization.[91] Within the state structure, "Work amongst the Colored People" became one of six departments, and all black chapters were subordinated to the white female department head.[92] Despite the separate chapters and the reporting structure, the biracial WCTU was a dramatic departure from the past. For a brief period, black and white women in the WCTU circumvented the racial conventions of their time.

Most of the white women who volunteered to organize black WCTU chapters were already involved in interracial educational or religious work. Rosa Steele, the wife of Wilbur Steele, the white president of Bennett College, an institution for African Americans, headed the statewide "Work amongst the Colored People" department. Steele bridged two worlds, and she had already earned a reputation among blacks as a "zealous" woman.[93] A Methodist and native New Englander, Rosa Steele lived in the college community surrounding Bennett. The Steeles regularly dined with African American friends, causing the white press to dub Wilbur "Social Equality Steele."[94] Rosa Steele found support among other white women connected with African American educational institutions. In Concord, for example, she turned to the wife of the white president of Presbyterian Scotia Seminary, which trained black women. Soon Scotia organized campus temperance activities as well as an African American WCTU chapter in the town.[95]

White women like Steele saw temperance work among African Americans as missionary labor, uplifting for the white women as well as the black women. Clearly Steele used the WCTU to promote her own agenda: "uplifting" the black race under white direction. The fact that black women continued to work for temperance without the supervision of white women worried her. "They have many workers of their own and many teachers doing this temperance work among them," Steele noted, but she added that white women must take the lead by supervising chapters. She advised white women to attend "each meeting to keep the organization on its proper line of work."[96] Although her belief in the superiority of white leadership indicated the distance she perceived between herself and blacks, Steele's racial attitudes represented those of the most liberal white women in the South. Southern white communities generally ostracized white women who promoted black education, but the WCTU accepted and used their talents in order to achieve its goals.[97]

African American women drew upon their long experience in temperance, and they chafed at the patronizing missionary approach of whites. Steele's exhortations inspired white women who had never attempted interracial work to try to organize black WCTU chapters in their hometowns. They often complained that when they approached African American women, "they were looked upon suspiciously by those whom they desired to help."[98] The racial dynamics baffled white women, who could not fathom black women's reactions. The white women who wanted to bring African Americans to the temperance cause were not able to recognize black women's capabilities. The black women were understandably resentful, and the gap between them loomed large. To make matters worse, most white women approached black women only during local-option elections, neglecting the work the rest of the time. Steele admonished white women not to view African Americans opportunistically or to cultivate them just for political purposes. Temperance would succeed only if whites showed a "real live interest in the colored man, not born of a disire [sic] to win his vote at election time," she argued.[99]

In many cities and towns, however, no white women came forward to head the "Work amongst the Colored People," and black women organized their own WCTU chapters. The experience of Mary Lynch and the Charlotte chapter illustrates how African American women came to the temperance cause and built their own statewide organization. A student at Scotia Seminary in Concord during the prohibition campaign of 1881, Lynch was caught up in the fever of the biracial ladies' temperance meetings and influenced by her teachers' participation in the WCTU.[100] Upon graduation, she moved to Charlotte to teach in the graded school, where she joined a sixty-member black WCTU chapter that formed in 1886.[101] That year, the Charlotte chapter sent delegates to the state convention who addressed the assembled white women.[102]

Once a town had black and white chapters, WCTU women occasionally launched joint ventures in community welfare that proved the WCTU's cooperative potential. For example, in the final months of 1886, white and black women united to build a hospital for African Americans in Charlotte. The white chapter held an art exhibition to raise funds for the cause, and the black chapter passed the hat at community meetings.[103] At the hospital's opening, the president of the white WCTU acknowledged, "We greatly appreciate the work of the (colored) W.C.T.U. in their co-operation with the White W.C.T.U."[104] The Charlotte white women realized the importance of black management of the hospital, and they pledged that African Americans would retain control of the work. Despite everyone's good intentions, funds ran out quickly, and both chapters struggled to support the hospital.[105] Ultimately, the cooperative hospital failed, and a separate group of white women, with funding from the Northern Episcopal Church, opened a larger facility for blacks under white women's management.[106]

In 1888, after five years of appealing to white women to organize black temperance chapters, Rosa Steele tried a new tactic that produced extraordinary results: she invited Sarah Jane Woodson Early, the African American superintendent of "Colored Work for the South" for the national WCTU, to North Carolina. Early spent five weeks in the state.[107] She entered the local prohibition battles raging in Raleigh and Concord and encouraged African American women to join the campaign.[108] One African American woman from Concord wrote that she had lobbied hard for black male votes and felt sure that "Christians will vote as they pray."[109] Early's African American audiences financed her trip, and by the time she left the state, fourteen black WCTU chapters stood on solid ground.[110]

The next year, building on Early's organizing campaign, African American WCTU leaders seceded from the state organization. Ultimately, black women found the racial hierarchy embedded in the WCTU structure contradictory on its face. If all WCTU members were temperance women, they must be equally worthy, sisters in the family of God. Because their temperance work involved multiple goals, African American women refused to trade equality for interaction. With secession, they rejected their status as a subordinate department under white direction. The black women made this clear when they named their organization the WCTU No. 2 and announced, "We cautiously avoided using the word colored . . . for we believe all men equal."[111] The white "Colored Work" committeewomen reported to their organization that the African Americans "desire to attain their full development and think this can best be done in an independent organization . . . with the department work under their own control." The new African American WCTU reported directly to the national WCTU and achieved organizational status equal to the white group, holding separate statewide conventions in 1890 and 1891.[112]

As North Carolina's black women organized the WCTU No. 2, black women across the South replicated their experience. Prior to the organization of the National Association of Colored Women's Clubs in 1896, the WCTU represented the principal interdenominational voluntary association among black women. Black WCTU organizations flourished in the North and the West, and black women in five southern states managed statewide unions. Southern African American women traveled to national and international temperance conferences, published newspapers, and learned skills of self-presentation that they took back to their churches and women's clubs.[113]

Throughout the 1890s in North Carolina, the WCTU No. 2 continued under the direction of African American women. In 1891, when Mary Lynch became a professor at Livingstone College, she found the campus branch of the Young Woman's Christian Temperance Union (YWCTU) languishing. Lynch immediately revitalized it and invited Anna Julia Haywood Cooper to speak to the group.[114] From her post at Livingstone, Lynch threw herself into temperance work; within five years, she formed connections with the nation's leading African American women and became president of the WCTU No. 2. Meanwhile, the group that Lynch oversaw at Livingstone flourished. One of Lynch's protégées was Annie Kimball, a student in the classical department. Kimball led the union in early-morning Sunday prayer meetings. Peer pressure to join must have been strong, for an observer reported, "Every girl, without an exception, [who was a] boarder in the school . . . has signed the pledge and become a member." Each year, the group visited the almshouse, bringing box lunches, tracts, hymn books, and Bibles. Livingstone chronicler William Fonvielle marveled, "Young women who at first were too embarrassed to lead a prayer meeting can do so now with all of the earnestness necessary."[115]

Kimball brought both racial and female consciousness to temperance work. She argued eloquently that where whites found black degeneracy, she found hope. The only trait becoming extinct among African Americans, she charged, was "the spirit of unmanly and unwomanly servility and fawning." Kimball exhorted her female classmates to lift "the banner of purity . . . around every home," and she predicted that the "dram-shop and all other places of ill-repute" would soon fall to "school houses, and churches of the living God." Then, she predicted, those whites who "maligned and slandered" blacks would be "utterly put down by a more enlightened and healthy public sentiment."[116] On a May day in 1894, Annie Kimball graduated as salutatorian of her class, gave the commencement address in Latin, and, that afternoon, married an AME Zion minister, George Clinton, whom Charles Pettey had taught thirty years earlier in South Carolina. The Clintons made their home in Charlotte, where she became state president of the YWCTU.[117]

After Annie Kimball Clinton moved to Charlotte, she joined a statewide network of African American women who had been active in the cause for over a decade. She could have attended any of several small WCTU group meetings in the city each week. In a single week in September 1897, one group met at the Congregational church, another at the Seventh Street Presbyterian Church, and the chapter at the Grace AME Zion Church kicked off its annual oratorical contest.[118] A "bicycle entertainment" raised almost $100 for "caring for the sick and needy and burying the dead."[119] To coordinate the separate groups, the citywide officers of the union met every Monday afternoon at a private home. Chapter activities included contemplative meetings, fund-raising, and outreach work among the intemperate at the jail and the hospital.[120] Annie Blackwell, a Charlotte public school teacher and wife of an AME Zion minister, edited the union's newspaper, the *W.C.T.U. Tidings*, which took as its motto, "The Lord giveth the word. The women that publish the tidings are a great host."[121]

When the WCTU No. 2 seceded, the white organization initially realized they should replace their outreach to African Americans with cooperation with the African American chapters. They appointed a committee to work with the black leaders, whom they called "genuine W.C.T.U. women."[122] But after a year, the whites again formed a committee on "Colored Work" that haltingly described its mission as "continu[ing] to work to assist in completing the work of organizing" African Americans. Two years later, the white superintendent entitled her report, "Home and Foreign Missionary Work among and through Afro-Americans." Did the switch to "Afro-Americans" indicate increased sensitivity, or was it a marketing ploy white organizers used to compete with the WCTU No. 2? Had "among and through" resulted from some sort of committee fight over whether to recognize black leaders by working "through" them? Whatever promise the new name held, "through" and "Afro-American" soon disappeared, and the white women returned to their work "amongst" the "colored people."[123]

White women knew about black women's activities, but apparently they refused to recognize black women's authority and competed with them to organize new African American WCTU chapters under local white control.[124] White women cryptically reported in 1895 that the "'sisters in black' have an Independent Union in Charlotte, well officered and doing good work."[125] The new white state superintendent noted, "Naturally we look for co-operation among the colored women under auspices of Unions controlled by them and this gives us an open door of helpfulness in many ways."[126] Black women must have resented white women who sought "co-operation" while assuming they knew best. The white women's efforts found some success among African American youth, in schools or prisons, all captive audiences, but only rarely did they form an organization of adult black women under white control after secession.[127]

Why did white women continue to try to establish black chapters even as they acknowledged the autonomy of the WCTU No. 2? There are at least two reasons. Except for a few leaders like Rosa Steele, most white women knew very little about, and discounted the abilities of, educated black women. Hence, they presumed that a black union would do better work under white leadership. Most importantly, however, the white women wanted very much to control the politics of the black temperance workers. They were not altogether sure that African Americans, because of their political allegiance to the Republican Party, could be trusted to vote for prohibition. Moreover, they believed that blacks proved easy prey for corrupt politicians and sinister forces. For example, after the formation of the WCTU No. 2, a white temperance worker announced an imminent Catholic peril among African Americans. She reported that Catholics, the archnemeses of prohibitionists, had spread out "propagating Catholicism among the *blacks* of the *South*." She asked, "Is it to *save souls* this new movement is made to Catholicise the negroes, or is it that he has a *vote* and now, that he is free, can aid in extending papal dominion in the United States?" (emphasis in original). White women reasoned that, left on their own, black women might not serve as political allies in local prohibition elections. Indeed, a primary duty of the white superintendents after secession was to distribute white ribbons signifying prohibition support to black women when a local-option election seemed threatening.[128]

Conflicts of race and politics surfaced in the national and international WCTU as well, and unraveling them reveals the importance of context in understanding women's divergent visions. The national WCTU's racial Armageddon began exactly where the North Carolina WCTU's secession crisis began: with the Good Templars' more perfect vision of equality. Predating the WCTU, the British Independent Order of Good Templars believed that "there are no classes or races, but one human brotherhood." African Americans like Edward Dudley became enthusiastic organizers. Across the South, white Templars, for their part, followed the North Carolina example and flatly refused to allow integrated lodges or biracial state organizations. The question split the international organization. One British faction would not abide individual segregated lodges, and some northern white and southern black U.S. chapters joined that group. Others affiliated with the rival sect, including some southern black lodges whose members concluded that temperance was worth the price of segregation. The two factions reconciled in 1886, and, amid tremendous controversy, the Good Templars decided to tolerate segregated lodges.[129]

The compromise crushed Catherine Impey, a British Good Templar who had stood up for complete integration. Two years later, after talking with Frederick Douglass about conditions in the South, Impey founded the magazine *Anti-Caste*.[130] On the other side of the world, North Carolina black female Good Templars shared her vision of sex and race equality, but their reality differed greatly from hers. She could hold out for a radical future; they lived in an oppressive present. Therefore, many black IOGT women joined the WCTU, worked to enlarge its vision, and, when they were not allowed to do that as equals, withdrew to manage their own affairs while pursuing interracial cooperation locally and using the national WCTU structure to meet their own ends.

The vast distance between Catherine Impey and Mary Lynch left room for a figure between them, Ida B. Wells. Ida Wells resembled many other black women leaders in North Carolina: born in slavery, educated at Rust College, she was a teacher and journalist like Sarah Dudley Pettey. After the lynching of three black men in Memphis, Wells wrote editorials in her newspaper, *Free Speech*, that exploded the myth that lynching always punished the crime of rape, even as it suggested that all interracial liaisons between white women and black men were not necessarily rape. As a result, Wells became a woman without a country. She was visiting New York City on business when a white Memphis paper printed a condemnation of her writing, after which she could not return to Memphis without risking death. The horror of the lynchings and her permanent exile dictated her strategy henceforth: unable to work from within the South, where she might measure initiative by response and edge forward by degrees, she would attack the entire structure of southern white supremacy by focusing on its most barbaric manifestation, lynching. Catherine Impey met Wells through Frederick Douglass and arranged for her to visit Britain in 1893 and 1894 to speak against the rising tide of lynching in the United States.[131]

Ida B. Wells attacked Frances Willard for being soft on lynching precisely because Willard had a reputation for interracial cooperation, not because she was the worst example of white women's racism Wells could find. The controversy started when an audience member asked, "Well what about people we know to be Christian, such as Dwight Moody and Frances Willard? How do they strike back at lynching and segregation?" Dwight Moody, a traveling evangelist, operated a northern divinity school that accepted white and black, male and female students; Mary McLeod went there after she graduated from Scotia Seminary. Wells replied that both Moody and Willard tolerated segregation—Moody at his southern engagements and Willard in her southern WCTU chapters. The controversy grew. On the next trip, Wells tried to push Willard into a public condemnation of lynching, partly because she knew Willard would be a powerful ally and partly because she had abandoned change by degree. She demanded justice, which, in her mind, could never be partial.[132]

Willard badly mishandled the situation by granting an interview in which she tried to condemn lynching while implying that it resulted from black-on-white rape. Willard would have done better simply to restate the national WCTU's 1893 resolution against lynching. She might have found it more difficult to respond to Wells's other criticism: "There is not a single colored woman admitted to the Southern WCTU, but still Miss Willard blames the Negro for the defeat of prohibition in the South." Any statement Willard could make about separate chapters but cojoined statewide unions, about the self-imposed secession of the WCTU No. 2, or about the value of delegate exchanges between white and black unions would have seemed limp indeed among the British radicals whose patronage both she and Wells courted. In the South, however, those seemingly conservative arguments would have been fodder for the cannons of white supremacists who waited to point out one by one the dangers of interracial cooperation.[133]

The controversy put southern black women like Mary Lynch in a very difficult position.[134] It was true that the 1893 national WCTU convention had condemned lynching, but at the same convention's main banquet, "a separate table had been assigned by the caterer, or somebody in higher authority, for the colored members." The black women refused to take the separate seats and sat down where they pleased. After someone asked them to go back to their table, "they got up and went out in a body; but their sisters had enough good sense and Christianity to call them back and treat them like sisters."[135] The informant in this account, published in an AME Zion journal from Salisbury, must have been Mary Lynch. Her analysis of the situation reveals a brilliant strategy well tailored to fit the limits of the possible. She laid the blame on the caterer or some addled functionary. No true WCTU woman could make such a mistake, she implies, even though she knew quite well this was not the case. "Someone" (no blame affixed here) tried to herd them to back to their seats. But the black women won, and Lynch concludes by reminding white women of their sisterhood, a sisterhood that she never neglected the opportunity to invoke, whether white women liked it or not.

The ideal of Christian sisterhood represented for Lynch a gender lifeline that she reached for even as a tide of white supremacy began to wash over the South in the 1890s.[136] Unlike Wells, Lynch swallowed her anger and sought balm in private for her pain, giving herself up to the WCTU because she thought it was the best chance she had to help her people. When she wrote to white WCTU national officials, she signed herself, "Yours for the cause." And she was theirs—partly. When Frances Willard died in 1898, Mary Lynch sent flowers, and her loyalty to the WCTU lasted a lifetime.[137]

If part of her belonged to the "white" WCTU, another part, adept at walking the wavy line of contradiction in the South, belonged to intraracial black women's activism. Lynch's internal struggle repeated itself in black women's national forums. "History is made of little things, after all," a *Woman's Era* reporter noted as she painted a dramatic scene of Ida B. Wells-Barnett "gracefully" giving "her approval" to a resolution offered by national WCTU organizer Lucy Thurman that endorsed the WCTU at the founding meeting of the National Association of Colored Women's Clubs (NACWC) in 1896. Lynch must have breathed a sigh of relief when she heard that peace had been declared, and the next year she attended the national NACWC convention to deliver the address, "Temperance Reform in the Twentieth Century."[138]

Meanwhile, flawed but significant interracial contacts continued between black and white WCTU women in North Carolina. As a result of Wells-Barnett's antilynching crusade, North Carolina's white WCTU convention condemned lynching in 1896, a symbolic but nonetheless important gesture, particularly considering that more than twenty years would elapse before southern white women moved again in an organized way against lynching.[139] Delegate exchanges continued between the black and white WCTUs as well. For example, when the black women met in state-wide convention in Salisbury in 1896, white WCTU delegates attended a session. That year, black women renamed their union the Lucy Thurman WCTU, honoring the black national organizer, and elected Mary Lynch state president. In 1897, Lynch presided over thirteen unions, attended the white state convention, and spoke at the national meeting, following Anthony Comstock and Anna Shaw.[140] The next year, she gave the opening prayer at the national WCTU convention marking the organization's twenty-fifth anniversary.[141]

In 1896, a black-supported coalition of Republicans and Populists won control of state government, giving African Americans their greatest political voice since Reconstruction and reordering the politics of temperance work. That year, Belle Kearney, a white Mississippian with North Carolina roots, delivered an address to the North Carolina white WCTU convention, the same one that condemned lynching, entitled, "Why the Wheels Are Clogged." Mary Lynch sat in the audience as a delegate from the Lucy Thurman WCTU and listened to Kearney tell the delegates that prohibition would never pass while 250,000 blacks voted in the South.[142] Quickly white women's local temperance strategies shifted to complement the Democratic Party's white supremacist platform. WCTU women helped organize mock elections limited to whites to demonstrate that prohibition would pass if blacks could not vote in temperance elections.[143] In 1898, the white WCTU ceased its work among African Americans forever, and delegate exchanges between the two WCTUs ended abruptly.[144] For the next few years, temperance, which had once held such promise for interracial understanding, would serve white supremacy.

It was a force beyond the control of women—party politics—that obliterated interracial contact within North Carolina's WCTU. Temperance was above all a political issue, and the WCTU solicited prohibition votes. As Democrats began to seek to exclude African Americans from the electoral process, white women were no longer concerned with black temperance and readily recast their former allies as part of the "Negro problem." Although the experience of the WCTU points up the difficulty of transcending difference, it also shows that as long as African Americans had political rights, women's interaction continued because black votes mattered. (Electoral politics, then, had a powerful impact upon the lives of those normally cast as the group with the least direct involvement in the process—women.) By the end of the decade, the political winds gathered strength until they swept through every corner of black women's lives, leaving few spaces untouched.

three

RACE AND MANHOOD

Rudyard Kipling thought he knew a man when he saw one. From his post in colonial India, he worked feverishly to explain why Indian men needed ruling and why the British were the men for the job. In the end, it all came down to self-control in the service of moderation. Unlike the darker races of the world, the Anglo-Saxon peoples had evolved far enough to bear up to adversity without crumbling; at the same time, they could handle success without resorting to excess. Darker people too often fell victim to their emotions; they were at best childlike and at worst animalistic, like Kipling's character Mowgli in *The Jungle Book*. In his instantly successful 1899 poem, "The White Man's Burden," Kipling described nonwhites as "fluttered folk and wild / . . . Half devil and half child."[1]

Halfway around the world, in North Carolina, white men and boys read Kipling's poetry as an endorsement of their own ideas of manhood and racial order. No one, they thought, had borne the "white man's burden" longer or more stoically than they. Suddenly the world was turning to their way of thinking. In the 1890s, southern middle-class white men embraced the racialization of manhood—so international, so scientific, so modern—and put it to work in their own backyards.[2] As one Charlottean, calling himself "Anglo-Saxon," put it, "Why should any man think that North Carolina is destined to prove an exception to Herbert Spencer's law of the 'Survival of the Fittest.' . . . It is all tommy-rot . . . to charge that prejudice, on account of color, is the foundation upon which is predicated white men's objections to negro domination." To "Anglo-Saxon," white supremacy was more than skin deep. Race was not simply much ado about a silly thing like color; the order of the universe depended on race, and "white" and "black" were outward manifestations of inner constitution.[3]

Thirty years earlier, during Reconstruction, the fathers of the men now reading Kipling and Spencer had faced the exigencies of organizing a biracial society in the wake of defeat. Black enfranchisement and federal scrutiny had forced the men of that generation to reckon with black political power, even as they tried to limit it through violence, fraud, gerrymandering, and poll taxes. Along with those pernicious methods, however, they grudgingly employed a meritorious concept—the ideology of the Best Man—to reduce the number of black voters and officeholders. According to this paradigm, only the Best Men should hold office, the men who, by faith and by works, exhibited benevolence, fair-mindedness, and gentility. Southern white men's belief in their own superiority gave them confidence that they could effectively manipulate the Best Man criteria to exclude most African Americans from officeholding, and the threat of federal oversight limited their choices in any event. Although it was inevitable that a few black men would be elected, the Best Man ideal could be used to hold them to the strictest of standards. Of course, not all white men who held office lived up to the model. The Best Man was not real but a theoretical device that worked to limit democracy by invoking the language of merit.

Although African Americans most often reasoned from a political ideology of natural rights, they seized upon the Best Man figure because it offered their only path to power. At the same time, it resonated with many educated African Americans' own religious beliefs and ideas of merit. The Best Man pursued higher education, married a pious woman, and fathered accomplished children. He participated in religious activities, embraced prohibition, and extended benevolence to the less fortunate. He could collaborate on social issues across racial lines, as the women of the WCTU did. He could hold a modest number of political offices. Edward Dudley certainly qualified as a Best Man in the eyes of African Americans, and his political career attests to the way in which the ideology could successfully be put into practice with a lifetime of careful calculation.[5] Such a steep path to power might prove arduous, but it constituted the only way African Americans could hope to gain a political hearing from whites.

Black Best Men believed that in order to continue to enjoy "manhood's rights," as they referred to the franchise and officeholding, they must con-

RACE AND MANHOOD

form to middle-class whites' definitions of manhood.[6] African Americans recognized the elusiveness of the Best Man definition and its dependence on whites' inclinations to privilege class status over racial lines. Reliance on the Best Man ideal meant that African Americans constantly had to prove their manhood in order to maintain civil rights, even if they could never prove it to whites' satisfaction.[7] If a certain black man led an exemplary life, whites still held him accountable for the conduct of his entire race. (His Best Man status was measured not just by his own behavior but also by that of any random stranger who happened to be African American.)

To the young white men whose fathers had forged the Best Man compromise, two events in the last decade of the nineteenth century underscored its current undesirability. First, an interracial coalition of Populists and Republicans gained control of the state legislature and moved to return many local offices to a popular vote. As a result, the number of black officeholders and appointees increased dramatically. Then, the Spanish-American/Cuban War forced ideologies of imperialism, race, and manhood to stand out in sharp relief as Afro-Cubans took the lead in their country's revolution. Black men rushed to prove their manhood and patriotism by enlisting in the Third North Carolina Regiment, the first in U.S. history commanded entirely by black officers.

As young white Democrats searched for ways to exclude African Americans from politics and power once and for all, international circumstances produced rhetoric that offered them a fresh rationale for white supremacy at the same time that it licensed their actions. After the Spanish-American/Cuban War, empire presented democracy with vexing representational problems. The closing of the frontier, a growing mass of impoverished wage workers, and increasing immigration shook many Americans' confidence in the broad extension of the franchise. Evolutionary theories exported wholesale from biology to society convinced many that progress was inevitable, though hard-won. Races, governments, and economies all moved forward in orderly, unavoidable "stages." It was up to those at the top to guide those below. These events and ideas gave rise to a new social language that implicitly authorized white supremacy in the South, while a modern international image of self-restrained, yet virile, white manhood lent urgency to the white supremacists' task.[8]

Seizing upon the language of empire, a new generation of white men—educated, urban, and bourgeois—used it in their effort to eclipse the possibility of the rise of a black Best Man. They plotted to replace the white Democrats of their fathers' generation within the party structure and to recapture power from the Populist/Republican coalition. Then the young white men would clean up the urban disorderliness and racial confusion in the state, chaos that demonstrated the need for firmer male control. They openly disavowed the lip service their fathers had paid to black political participation and argued that only one kind of man was fit for politics, the New White Man.[9] The South's New White Man stated bluntly that the prerogatives of manhood—voting, sexual choice, freedom of public space—should be reserved for him alone. To claim his proper place, he must toss out black men completely and nudge his father aside.[10]

Thus, as North Carolina's New White Men read Kipling, they fancied that they saw themselves between the lines. If they liked Kipling's description of darker men, they loved his model of manhood illustrating ideals of self-restraint for a new generation of southern white men. Kipling's poem "If" serves as an example:

> If you can keep your head when all about you
> Are losing theirs and blaming it on you,
>
> .   .   .   .
>
> If you can talk with crowds and keep your virtue
> Or walk with Kings—nor lose the common touch,
> If neither foes nor loving friends can hurt you,
> If all men count with you, but none too much;
> If you can fill the unforgiving minute
> With sixty seconds' worth of distance run,
> Yours is the Earth and everything that's in it,
> And—which is more—you'll be a Man, my son![11]

Evolution rendered black men "half devil and half child" and inscribed on white men alone a tendency toward the "golden mean."[12] This biological balance meant that because of their constitutional forbearance only white men were capable of political participation and governance. Obviously, they must regain control of politics and then disfranchise black men for their own good and everyone else's.

Southern white men who came of age after the Civil War inherited by default their fathers' conflicting models of manhood. Evangelical religion had swept Piedmont North Carolina before the war, calling many yeomen to lives of temperance, moderation, hard work, and fear for their immortal souls. There, Quakers lived in peace in several counties among fervent Methodists and Baptists and alongside dour Presbyterians.[13] In the east, where plantations abounded, the ideal of self-restraint touched the antebellum white image of manliness less directly, and Episcopalians dominated. There men believed they should be chivalrous to women and avoid horrible cruelty to slaves, but reputation mattered more than character. Reputation was made through the display of wealth, the exercise of patriarchy, and the passionate protection of one's honor. In eastern North Carolina, however, planters—who were poorer, had fewer slaves, and lived closer to towns—rarely ruled with the impunity of their lower South counterparts. In the west, the rugged mountains, sparsely populated with Scotch-Irish sometimes intermarried with Cherokees, nurtured a masculine culture that stressed agrarian self-sufficiency and rugged individualism.[14] These competing visions of manhood and honor contributed to North Carolina's reluctance to secede and, after the war, opened space for the Best Man compromise. There was no abrupt end to black officeholding with the departure of Federal troops, and the Republican Party remained viable. White men who had served the Confederacy sat in the state legislature with black representatives through the 1880s.

These men's sons, born in the 1850s and 1860s, lived their lives in a long denouement, their every act diminished by the climax of the Civil War. Their veneration of the war and disappointment at missing that ultimate test of manhood have been well documented, but their resentment of their fathers' generation has been less examined. Stirring stories of Stonewall Jackson had little tangible worth to the young white man trying to eke out a living in the rubble of the New South. Certainly it occurred to him that his father's recklessness had wrought catastrophe and humiliation. If victorious and sober Yankee men questioned their own masculinity in a rapidly industrializing and urbanizing culture, southern white men added a loser's shame and degrading poverty to that burden.

Despite the New White Man's eagerness to be on top—to rise economically by exercising self-mastery—his talk was democratic. He might have been a bit of a rube, but he was a smart one. He might have started in a humble home and traveled far, but he never forgot his origins. His road, however, led only one way: to town. The New White Man proposed to meet backward-looking agrarian unrest with forward-looking urban remedies. He sprang from North Carolina's failing farms, but he cast his lot with the state's rapidly growing cities.[15] As the price of a bale of cotton fell from ten cents in 1887 to five cents in 1894, many poor white people abandoned their land.[16] Cities remained small by national standards, but the rapidity of urbanization is still astonishing. From 1870 until 1900, the population of Greensboro grew from 497 to 10,035. Charlotte held the lead as the state's largest city throughout the thirty-year period, its population expanding from 4,473 to 18,091.[17]

Poor white families who abandoned their land in the 1890s discovered that they had arrived in town late. The New White Men had already been there a decade, hustling to make a living as lawyers, teaching in the graded schools, publishing newspapers, or subscribing stock to capitalize cotton mills. The latecomers' experiences ran counter to the language of prosperity that the New White Men broadcast like fertilizer, hoping that factories would spring up. New White Man Josephus Daniels, editor of the

Raleigh *News and Observer*, crowed about "Raleigh's Solid Boom . . . Not Noisy . . . But Sure." Everywhere he went in 1887, Daniels saw reason for optimism, and he concluded, "Raleigh is not over-modest and talks enough about itself, I reckon, but if there had been as much substantial progress in many other places I could name . . . the cry of 'booming' would go up to the clouds."[18] The same day, agrarian booster Leonidus Polk lamented in the *Progressive Farmer*, "If the towns, railroads, manufacturers, banks and all speculative enterprises flourish . . . and agriculture languishes under the same laws . . . something is radically wrong."[19] After the *Charlotte News* reported a "tremendous rain," the *Progressive Farmer*'s editor sniffed, "We can't recollect when Charlotte had anything that was not tremendous."[20] If things were bad for rural people in 1890, when one out of three white North Carolinians was sharecropping, conditions would grow progressively worse.[21]

If, in North Carolina, Josephus Daniels became the New White Man's mouth, future senator Furnifold Simmons became his brain, future governor Charles Brantley Aycock his heart, and author Thomas Dixon, Jr., his libido. Descended from modest farm stock rather than from planter families, men like Daniels, Aycock, and Dixon cultivated down-home manners and democratic rhetoric to reassure the folks back on the farm that they remained immune to the wiles of the white-cuffed railroad lawyers with whom they occasionally shared a whiskey in Raleigh. It was said that Charles Aycock "was born so close to the people that he could say whatsoever he liked . . . without giving offense."[22]

These supremely self-conscious young white men believed that the white-bearded Redeemers who controlled the state's Democratic Party spent most of their days in a catatonic stupor, growing progressively deaf to the cries of downwardly mobile whites. Convinced that the state would never attract industry under such leadership, they banded together in 1883 to form Raleigh's Watauga Club. At that precipitate moment in their lives—no man in the club was over thirty years old—the precocious Wataugans foreshadowed the methods of New White Men who would mature fifteen years later. They chose "Watauga," a name of Native American origins, because it sounded wholesome and rural and disguised the group's true purpose: to industrialize the state. Josephus Daniels joined, as did a young state legislator, Thomas Dixon, Jr. Walter Hines Page led the Wataugans until he left to launch a dazzling publishing career in New York City. From that distance, he sent home his famous "mummy" editorial in which he blasted the state's entrenched white leadership, declaring that "the world must have some corner in it where men sleep and sleep and dream and dream and North Carolina is as good a spot for that as any."[23] Charles Aycock, practicing law in Goldsboro with Daniels's older brother Frank, praised Page's plain speaking, but many North Carolinians expressed their outrage at his cheekiness.[24]

The New White Man's carefully cultivated modernity sprang mainly from his economic aspirations, but his disappointment in his father and his bitterness about his mother's stunted life contributed to his rage for change. Although he would never have said so straightforwardly, when the New White Man cataloged his region's ills, he recognized his father's failings. New White Men could blame their fathers for losing the Civil War, retarding industry, neglecting public education, tolerating African Americans in politics, and creating a bottleneck in the Democratic Party. They had ample evidence that the older generation of men had mistreated white women by failing to provide for them after the Civil War. Charles Aycock remembered that his mother ran the farm while his father dabbled in politics. Even though she managed the family's affairs, Serena Aycock signed legal papers with an "X." Her son Charles vowed to build a better public school system to educate the state's poor white women.[25] Josephus Daniels's father died during the war, and his mother's life was no tale of moonlight and magnolias. She worked as the postmistress in Wilson, serving a biracial public from her front parlor.[26] Wataugan Thomas Dixon, Jr., nursed a grievance over his mother's treatment at his father's hands that drove him to write and rewrite the New White Man's (auto)biography.

Walter Hines Page's company published Dixon's *The Leopard's Spots: A Romance of the White Man's Burden, 1865–1900* and his sequel, *The Clansman: An Historical Romance of the Ku Klux Klan*, which became the film, *The Birth of a Nation*. Northern and southern readers believed Dixon's accounts to be the inside—and true—story of Reconstruction and Thomas Dixon to be the ideal southern man. Dixon saw himself as the latest link in the evolution of a superman who, because of his personal racial purity, his experience in managing African Americans, and his triumph of will, could unify the nation.[27]

Born in 1864 nine miles north of Shelby, Dixon watched his parents give up on farming and move to town to wring a living out of operating a general store while his father preached at several poor Baptist churches. At sixteen, Dixon left home for Wake Forest College. In the fall of 1883, he entered graduate school at Johns Hopkins University to study political science and history.[28] Alongside classmate Woodrow Wilson, Dixon studied under Herbert Baxter Adams, whom he recalled as a "genius of the highest order."[29] Professor Adams combined the latest in evolutionary science with Victorian romanticism to construct his Teutonic germ theory. Adams believed that democracy sprang from the intellectual equivalent of a gene that made its way from German forests to Britain and then to colonial America. Moving only through pure bloodlines, it predisposed some men for self-government. Adams's theory crested around the time Dixon entered Johns Hopkins.[30] The Teutonic germ theory lent Dixon an explanatory system that anointed the Reconstruction racism of his youth with scientific balm: because African Americans lacked the Teutonic germ, their voting and officeholding amounted to a cruel hoax. The earlier generation of white men should have limited African Americans' political participation more strictly.

Dixon's preoccupation with interracial sex demonstrates how closely the personal and political were linked for southern white men of his generation. For Dixon, the fathers' racial sins ran deep, even into the blood. In *The Crucible of Race*, historian Joel Williamson constructed an intricate analysis of Dixon's sensationalization of miscegenation.[31] Building a new understanding of Dixon's family life, Williamson notes that Dixon's mother married when she was thirteen and thus became "a curiosity." Dixon's internal personal struggle, according to Williamson, centered around his inability to come to grips with white women's sexuality, especially that of his mother. Dixon projected his own insecurity about the sexual penetration of the impenetrable southern white woman onto black men, whom he routinely portrayed as rapists. At the same time, Dixon never overtly resented his father, whom he portrays in his autobiography, *Southern Horizons*, as a tower of strength.[32]

A close reading of Dixon's little-known later work, *The Sins of the Father*, suggests that his fears of miscegenation sprang not only from his father's role in his mother's early sexual initiation but also from other sins of his father. After the publication of *The Leopard's Spots*, a biracial man who lived in New York City began to claim publicly and often that he was Thomas Dixon's half brother, the son of Baptist preacher Thomas Dixon, Sr. When confronted with this allegation, Thomas, Jr., replied, "Yes I know that darky, he is always getting himself into trouble and I have helped him a number of times. His mother was a cook in our family in N.C." Although African Americans circulated accounts of Dixon's purported half brother, whites buried the information.[33] Whites' treatment of the claim reflects the conspiracy of silence that obscured biracial people of the time from their white contemporaries and from the historical record. Biracial children were almost always the progeny of white men and black women. Yet in the 1890s, respectable whites would admit no such thing. Miscegenation presented an acute problem for the generation that came of age amid Darwinian science and the rhetoric of imperialism. Dixon filled a real cultural need for whites when he emphasized the menace of black men raping white women and predicted that a "mongrel breed" threatened the social order. Through this fiction, he explained away the biracial people abounding in the South and erased from historical memory white men's sexual liaisons with and rape of black women. Whether in so doing he also deleted his personal memory of an intimate relationship between his father and the family cook will probably never be known.

Only once, in *The Sins of the Father*, did Dixon admit that most biracial people in the South resulted from white men's sexual exploitation of black women. *Sins* attempts to excuse white men of his father's generation for the part they played in miscegenation. In its pages, a promising young white man, Major Daniel Norton, returns from the Civil War, marries, and has a son. Life should be sweet, but his wife, whom he calls "little mother," suffers a wound in her throat, near her jugular vein, from thrashing about during the pain of childbirth. The wound threatens to erupt at any time, and if it does, little mother will bleed to death.[34] For a while, under the watchful eye of little mother's black Mammy, the family is happy. Then a servant, the octoroon Cleo, infiltrates the Nortons' home. Cleo tried to seduce Norton at his office, but he summoned the fortitude to fire her, so she slips into his house to help little mother after Mammy suffers a chill. One night Norton returns home to find little mother and Cleo playing with the baby. In the presence of both women, Norton is aroused only by Cleo. Cleo's "cheeks were flushed, eyes sparkling and red hair flying in waves of fiery beauty over her exquisite shoulders, every change of attitude a new picture of graceful abandon, every movement of her body a throb of savage music from a strange seductive orchestra hidden in the deep woods!" Norton later succumbs and has sex with Cleo.[35]

Little mother discovers the act and collapses, but others are quick to tell her not to blame Norton. The physician whom Norton calls to treat his hysterical wife exonerates him: "With that young animal playing at your feet in physical touch with your soul and body in the intimacies of your home, you never had a chance."[36] Even little mother shares responsibility because, like the "foolish wife" in the biblical story of Sarah and Hagar, she "brought a beautiful girl into her husband's house and then repented of her folly."[37] Little mother learns that her own father died in the arms of his mulatto mistress, and her mother urges her to understand Norton: "He isn't bad. He carried in his blood the inheritance of hundreds of years of lawless passion."[38] Little mother manages to forgive Norton but suffers a relapse and bleeds to death, asking only that he "rear our boy free from the curse."[39]

Cleo then bears her and Norton's daughter in secret. Now there is no escape from Norton's nightmare. He sends the daughter away, but because his motherless son loves Cleo so much, Norton allows her to become a house servant. For two decades, Norton and Cleo live together in blazing hatred; then Cleo entices the daughter to visit Norton's home in his absence. Young Thomas falls in love with her, not knowing she is black and his half sister. As Major Norton tours North Carolina campaigning to disfranchise African Americans, his son and daughter secretly marry. Distraught at the news of his children's marriage—and as frantic about racial purity as he is about incest—Norton confesses all to his son Tom, and they carry out a suicide pact.[40] The major succeeds, but Tom clings to life, ultimately saved by Cleo's last-minute disclosure that Norton's real daughter died at birth, whereupon she substituted a white foundling. Tom Norton's new wife is neither his sister, nor black; thus, the marriage is saved.

Sins can be read as an apologia for a generation of white men who had sex with black women, perhaps an apologia for Dixon's own father's sins, and as a brief for segregation and disfranchisement. Dixon explains Norton's temptation and fall in the most sympathetic terms. As for Norton's simultaneous hatred for the African American race and attraction to Cleo: "The history of the South and the history of slavery made such a paradox inevitable. The long association with the individual negro in the intimacy of home life had broken down barriers of personal race repugnance."[41] While Norton's lust is natural, Cleo's is supernatural, "the sinister purpose of a mad love that had leaped full grown from the deeps of her powerful animal nature."[42] To absolve southern white men, Dixon had to make black women Jezebels. In fiction, Dixon dealt with the troubling reality of the family cook's biracial son by absolving Thomas Dixon, Sr., from his sins, real or imagined. But even as Dixon offered forgiveness to the father in *Sins*, he made him pay for it by subjecting him to a hellish existence from which suicide offered the only escape. Never able consciously to hold his real father responsible, Dixon created a fictional father who kills himself. Norton's death freed his son Tom from the taint of racial impurity and made him a born-again white man.

Secret interracial liaisons between white men and black women before the turn of the century may have been less dramatic in real life than in Dixon's fiction, but perhaps just barely. African Americans hated hypocritical white men who surreptitiously kept black mistresses or who frequented the houses of black prostitutes. David Fulton, a black writer who grew up in Wilmington, remembered, "When I was boy in the south, the most popular Negro woman (among the whites) of my town was the courtesan." Fulton deplored the fact that some houses of prostitution run by black women catered only to white men and that the houses' madams could "enter any store and receive more attention than the wife of a Negro legislator."[43] Likewise, Fulton berated the African American woman who secretly accepted a white man as her lover. Black women must avoid "the man of a race that seeks her only under cover of darkness, to bask in her smiles, flatter her into sin; or in public places shun her as a viper."[44]

Black Best Men tried to patrol interracial sex. In Concord, home of the

Coleman Cotton Mill and Scotia Seminary, a group of African American men and boys formed a vigilante group to put an end to such secret liaisons. They roamed the streets with whips. When they found a white man "in company" with a black woman, they flogged them both. For some time, the whippings occurred nightly.[45] Such direct action was extremely risky and relatively rare. Most black critics wrote and preached against clandestine affairs rather than intervening in them, whip in hand.

Among the Reconstruction generation, whites and blacks alike overlooked the occasional white man and black woman who lived openly in a long-term domestic arrangement. These couples could not marry since interracial marriage remained illegal in North Carolina. In Wilmington, Robert H. Bunting, a white man who served as U.S. commissioner, lived with his African American companion in peace until 1898. In New Bern, E. W. Carpenter lived for many years with an African American woman and their large family. Only when he ran for clerk of the superior court did whites complain.[46] Cohabitation between white men and black women presented problems for African Americans as well since black men felt that such arrangements exploited black women. They were more likely than whites, however, to accept them as common-law marriages. Elsewhere, African Americans worked to overturn state bans on interracial marriages, a move quickly swamped by a growing pro-eugenics movement. At the 1898 meeting of the Afro-American Council in New York City, delegates proposed uniform laws across the nation allowing interracial marriage. When news of the Afro-American Council's proposal filtered back to North Carolina, whites seized upon the fact that one of the state's most outstanding black men, John Dancy, collector at the port of Wilmington, had attended the meeting. Here was proof of black Best Men's aspirations. Whites argued that they proposed such laws in order to marry white women themselves rather than to legitimate existing relationships between white men and black women.[47]

Intimate interracial relationships, tolerated through the 1880s, became intolerable to New White Men because interracial sex violated evolutionary principles and demonstrated an appalling lack of self-control among white men that could ultimately jeopardize political power. No longer was a white man who slept with a black woman demonstrating his strength; instead, he was proving his weakness. Such liaisons resulted in mixed-race progeny who slipped back and forth across the color line and defied social control. Thomas Dixon put this speech in the mouth of a leading character in *The Leopard's Spots*: "The future American must be an Anglo-Saxon or a Mulatto! We are now deciding which it shall be. . . . This Republic can have no future if racial lines are broken, and its proud citizenship sinks to the level of a mongrel breed."[48]

If New White Men wanted to regulate whiteness in public and private social relations, they would have to put force behind their haphazard efforts to police poor white women's sexuality. White men had always excluded black women from definitions of purity and spoke in rapturous terms of southern white women, generally ignoring "unruly" poor white women.[49] Now, however, New White Men set out to naturalize white women's purity, just as they naturalized black men's impurity. White women should now be chaste, regardless of their class, manners, or living conditions. The assumption of purity must be implicit, essential to all white women. Such purity was central to Aycock's definition of progress: "I would have all our people believe in the possibilities of North Carolina; in the strength of her men and the purity of her women."[50]

Eventually, the assumption of poor white women's purity would constitute more than just a tool for racial solidarity; it would become an integral part of an exchange for poor men's votes. If their men put race over class at the polling place, the Democrats promised, poor white women could be boosted up to the pedestal. At the same time, assuming white women's purity made it easy to draw clear lines in rape cases involving black men and white women. Henceforth, there could be no consensual interracial sex between white women and black men. White women would be incapable of it.

Despite the urgency of their task, New White Men had chosen an inauspicious moment to insist on poor white women's purity. Poverty, rapid urbanization, and industrialization exposed working women to new social codes and opportunities, broke the ties of patriarchal authority, and made poor white women more visible than ever before.[51] Southern towns had always harbored white prostitutes, but they had long remained out of sight and unspoken of by whites. Much of our evidence of them comes from African Americans such as Rose Leary Love, whose father John Leary practiced law in Charlotte. Love recalled the white prostitutes who took up residence in the best black residential district. "They were always dressed in expensive negligees or some other fancy dress." In addition to heavy makeup on their "very pretty" faces, "nearly all of them had a white poodle dog trailing along."[52] Locating white prostitutes in black neighborhoods served two purposes: it hid them from other white women, and it blackened the prostitutes, reading them out of the white race. If they were metaphorically black, white men could visit them without guilt and white women need not care about their reformation.

As North Carolina's towns grew, however, it became more difficult to overlook the white prostitutes, wayward girls, and drunken women who elbowed their way down the sidewalk beside the dignified white maidens and matrons. Although white southerners rarely left records of poor southern white women's departures from ladylike decorum, northerners were often struck by their habits. One transplanted northerner commented on the crowd at a dance: "All the men drunk and all the women dipping snuff or chewing tobacco."[53] Early in 1898, a northern woman visiting New Bern published a piece in a national magazine entitled, "Poor White Women of Our Southern Cities." She urged that northern charity be redirected from freedmen and mountain whites to the debauched poor white women of southern towns. "They are not an attractive or hopeful class," she wrote, but "feeble of body . . . weak of mind, sodden with snuff . . . not only utterly illiterate, but untrained . . . entirely without that romantic charm . . . dull, uninviting, thankless . . . material." Prostitution represented the only occupation open to these women "too sluggish and dull witted for factory work."[54]

It was fortunate for this writer that she returned North before her article appeared because her words had an explosive effect in New Bern. Certain that nothing could remedy the harm she had already done, New Bernians condemned her as "either totally depraved herself or . . . of unsound mind" and "not a southern woman." Moreover, they argued that no southern white woman would be so deranged as to take up prostitution simply to starve to death since such a "boundless state of immorality . . . does not and could not possibly exist in the South." At the next city council meeting, members accused the author of libel. More telling, at the same meeting, the council approved this ordinance: "Any lewd woman who shall be found on the streets or alleys soliciting male persons, drinking, sitting on the streets in front of or lounging about bar rooms, or conducting herself in a forward or improper manner shall be deemed guilty of a nuisance . . . and fined."[55]

The difficulty of patrolling white women's sexuality in public went hand in glove with other urban problems. Not only had the white fathers failed to uphold racial purity in their personal lives, but also they had tolerated racial impurity and social chaos in public life. In the 1890s, questions of racial segregation remained unsettled in North Carolina's towns.[56] Although New Bern residents sometimes observed the color line, it wavered in certain places: the station waiting room, the post office, and the revenue department, for example. Moreover, racial boundaries faded at periodic public attractions ranging from circuses to church services. Black and white New Bernians congregated to see Mille Christine, billed as "the two headed girl" but actually cojoined African American twins.[57] When Nora Clarette Avery, the "colored girl preacher," came to Sarah Dudley Pettey's church, whites sat on the right and blacks on the left, and the white section stayed packed throughout her revival.[58] Just as whites attended functions hosted by African Americans, African Americans joined whites at citywide functions. A photograph of the 1897 New Bern Fish, Oyster, and Game Fair reveals a knot of white women chatting with each other, while a few feet away, a black teenager stares at the camera in wonder. Nearby, Charles Pettey, in a silk top hat, stands beside his carriage.[59]

Increasingly in the 1890s, the growing commercial class of white men took such urban disorder to indicate a failure of manhood, and they worried about how such chaos looked to investors. When a Baltimore lawyer and a Swedish industrialist toured the state, looking to invest and relocate, what they saw appalled them. In Weldon, they sniffed "something rotten under the surface" and thought the town seemed "20 years behind the times." The problem, it seemed, was "Negro rule." The "old darkey" who served their dinner served as well on the city council. The train ride to Wilmington revealed a land "desolate" and "lying idle"; a "great desert with a few scrubby pines" just waiting for good Teutons—"thrifty German and Scandinavian families"—to transform it into a Garden of Eden. Finally, in Wilmington, they saw a plethora of black policemen and listened to whites bemoaning disorder in the streets. Alas, the visitors' "dream of a Florida at the mouth of the Cape Fear" must be deferred as long as "negroes guid[e] your Legislature and municipal bodies."[60] The idea of losing a "Florida at the mouth of the Cape Fear" must have been unbearable for the state's New White Men.

Such interracial proximity meant that social relations had to be negotiated and renegotiated each time a person walked down the street. Since Reconstruction, African Americans had strongly contested any attempt to limit their claims to manhood and womanhood in public. In 1882, when who would count as a man or woman in Charlotte was anyone's guess, two African American teenagers, Laura Lomax and her suitor, Jim Harris, set out on a stroll. A cultured and educated young woman, the daughter of an AME Zion bishop, Laura was her brothers' pride. On a narrow sidewalk, the couple brushed past old Doc Jones, a white herb doctor. Jones turned back and "insulted and struck" Laura Lomax. Jim Harris ran into a nearby barber shop, borrowed a gun, and pistol-whipped the offending white man. Despite the fact that Jones claimed the incident resulted from his affliction with "St. Vitus' dance," that night, a dozen young black men, including two of Laura Lomax's brothers, broke into Doc Jones's house and beat him up a second time. In their eagerness to avenge the insult, the men made no attempt to disguise their identities. Quickly police hauled Harris and Jones before a magistrate. Harris paid a twenty-five dollar fine for carrying a gun, but the magistrate made no ruling on the assault. The Lomax brothers stood trial and went free for payment of court costs. Even though her boyfriend and brothers had by now thoroughly pulverized Doc Jones,

Laura Lomax pressed the issue and ultimately won a verdict against him for assault.[61]

In addition to the free-flowing urban turbulence this tale reveals, it points up the fact that some African Americans, those who saw themselves as Best Men and Best Women, demanded that class serve as a marker of manhood and womanhood. When the editor of a white newspaper referred to Laura Lomax as Harris's "sweetheart" and "a colored girl," the editor of the black newspaper was quick to take exception: "We will remind [the white editor] that she is a respectable young lady, whose family is more prominent and wealthy than his." Then he invoked the Best Man bargain: "We want our ladies respected. . . . White men make us respect white ladies, and they must make white men respect ours. . . . They must not look upon us *all* as boys and wenches."[62] This threat, not so thinly veiled, depends on class recognition across racial lines. A translation: if you want us to use our influence on the "boys and wenches" among our race to protect *your* ladies, then you'd better use your influence on the crackers among your race to protect *our* ladies.[63]

Many black Best Men who lived in those rowdy towns and cities watched the growing disorder around them with great concern. An integral piece of the Best Man compromise was the requirement that leading African Americans influence for the better the behavior of poor blacks. For that reason, and because of their own embrace of Victorian manners and morals, middle-class black men and women worried constantly about poor black people's public activities. Urban avenues provided a stage upon which African Americans acted out the rituals of courtship while exercising the freedom and enjoying the relative anonymity that city life conferred. African American leaders of both sexes fretted, despaired, and condemned the unfolding tableau. Fifteen years after the Lomax affair, an African American in Charlotte glanced out of his office window to see a group of black men and women flirting, laughing, and eating ice cream on the corner. He castigated the men, calling them "corner-loafers and suckers who strut like a peacock, assume the air of a turkey gobbler, have the cunning of a fox, the grin of a possum, the cowardice of a cat, and are the boss liars of town."[64]

Black women's behavior gave race leaders pause as well. The novelty of urban amusements lured black women away from home and church and into danger, sometimes in interracial settings. In addition to generating negative images that middle-class black women and men wanted to keep out of whites' sight, these rambunctious women jeopardized racial politics when they put themselves beyond male protection.[65] One black man condemned the "thousands of young girls and women who are daily going down to degradation . . . in peanut galleries in theatres." The man who commented on the "boss liars" meted out strong words to the women on the corner as well. Only "soft women" stood around eating ice cream, he scolded, and "giddy-head girls" who gave their "money to these street dudes in order to have them keep their company" would earn only sorrow as interest on their investment. Two weeks later, he fumed at seeing "a young mulatto woman and two white women . . . smoking cigars on the streets." "What next?" he gasped.[66]

Middle-class African Americans worried not just about poor people but also about young people, many of them educated and from good homes, who seemed deliberately to tweak Victorian sensibilities. "Puck," a young African American man in Charlotte, offered a rare view of his teenage peers' style. He comically described the "masher," who "hangs about on street corners," the "vapid" young man "who parts his hair in the middle and cultivates about fifteen hairs on his upper lip," and the "boaster."[67] Most often, in youthful cultural signification, the provocateur does not completely understand the implications of the provocation, but black elders thought *they* did, and they did not like what they saw. Getting a clear view of these young people from the distance of a century is extremely difficult, partly because the black middle class controlled the African American press and wanted to present a united front of purpose and dignity, and partly because what grated on adults was youths' "attitude," a quality rarely recovered in archives. One place to look for "attitude" is in white complaints about blacks, which rose to a crescendo in the 1890s. "The Negro," whites sighed, is not what he or she used to be. These observations complemented explanations of racial degeneracy that contributed to the redefinition of manhood as white.[68]

What whites were seeing, of course, was not biological degeneracy but a rising African American youth culture that proffered a competing image of manhood. The black "community"—even the African American middle class—was not monolithic. A new assertive generation of middle-class African Americans believed that the only way to guarantee rights was to exercise them in daily actions. Some in the rising generation demanded instantly the same level of respect that the Best Men had so carefully earned over a lifetime. While black Best Men screened their private lives behind lace curtains, young African Americans were public men: "corner-loafers" and "street dudes." Whites would have to take them into account if only because they loomed so large. Black middle-class elders wanted to sweep away this masculine counterimage because they believed such men wildly miscalculated the power dynamic. To black Best Men, the vote was the wellspring of all possibility. Exercising the franchise carefully would bring about a time when African American manhood would no longer have to prove itself. They could not understand or abide young black men who believed that African American manhood did not have to prove itself to whites at all.

African American men could not know how chimerical their claims to manhood would prove in the closing years of the nineteenth century. The New White Men sought to remove black men from politics altogether and to reorder the public and private social landscape. To succeed, they would have to take control of the Democratic Party from their fathers' generation. Politics had begun to unravel for the old Redeemers in 1890 when Leonidus Polk, president of the state Farmers' Alliance, pressured the Democratic Party to endorse the farmers' ideals hammered out in a series of platforms at national Alliance conventions. The legislature of 1891, known as the "farmers' legislature," authorized a railroad commission, funded the full-year normal school for white women, and increased the school tax, but the battles these reforms sparked deepened the rifts in the party.[69] The national Democratic endorsement of the gold standard exacerbated the state Democratic leadership's problems with farmers, and even New Bern's Furnifold Simmons, the 1892 state party chairman, supported free silver that year.[70] Fed up with the "Old Stagers" who tightly grasped power, Polk, who described himself as a "young man's man," was ready to revolt.[71] On Simmons's watch and much to his distress, Polk's state party liaison Marion Butler led Alliance members out of the Democratic Party and formed a vigorous third party in the state.[72] Polk died suddenly just before the national Populist Party convention in Omaha, Nebraska, leaving North Carolina Populists to campaign for the party's national ticket without their native son at its head.[73]

A delicate power balance existed between the Democrats and Republicans, and a third party would surely tip the scales. Since Reconstruction, the Democrats had monopolized the governor's seat, but the margins of victory in those races ranged from 6,000 to 20,000 votes in a pool of 250,000 registered voters.[74] Alert to the danger, the leading Democratic newspaper immediately condemned the Populist Party as a "bastard political interloper" and predicted that its policies would "paralize [sic] business and . . . black the wheels of progress."[75] Charles Aycock hit the road to deliver fiery speeches for the Democrats. The party narrowly averted a disaster, held onto the governor's office, and sent a majority to the legislature. But two years later, in the midst of the 1894 depression, Simmons no longer headed the executive committee, and the situation looked grim. The ranking U.S. senator, fossilized Matthew Ransom, asleep up in Washington, D.C., did nothing.[76]

The election of 1894 was an utter disaster for the Democrats, whom

Daniels described as "thunderstruck."[77] For the first time since 1876, the North Carolina state senate lacked a Democratic majority, and Populists and Republicans could combine to outnumber the Democrats in the house. Worse yet, the legislature elected Populist Marion Butler and Republican Jeter B. Pritchard to the U.S. Senate.[78] Then the representatives struck the provision that required the legislature to appoint local officers and returned to home rule, resulting in the election in 1896 of numerous African Americans, particularly in sixteen eastern counties where black voters were in the majority.[79] A white New Bern man recalled that, as a result, Craven County had twenty-seven black justices of the peace, three black deputies, black school committeemen, a black register of deeds, black constables, and a black city attorney. African Americans also won election to the board of aldermen and the county commission.[80] One of the school committeemen was Edward R. Dudley.[81] What whites deplored, African Americans celebrated. Charles Pettey, commenting on this situation, bragged, "We have had colored coroners and State's attorneys elected by a majority of white votes. Our representative in Congress is a colored man, George H. White, my neighbor. Throughout the State there are over 100 petty magistracies filled by colored men."[82]

In statewide elections in 1896, the Republicans and Populists formally "fused" and together steamrolled the Democratic house and senate candidates. Out of 169 legislative seats, the Democrats won only 45.[83] Republican Daniel Russell captured the governor's seat. Charles Aycock despaired that his party "seemed on the eve of disintegration."[84] The Democratic Old Stagers found themselves buried in the debris as the New White Men dismantled the party hierarchy, and Furnifold Simmons ascended for a second time to the chairmanship of the state executive committee. As tensions with Spain over Cuba occupied white and black North Carolinians, Simmons and Aycock holed up in New Bern's Chatawka Hotel to plot their next step.[85]

North Carolina's black men saw the Spanish-American/Cuban War as an opportunity to prove their manhood by mobilizing black troops commanded totally by black officers. Two months after the United States entered the war in April 1898, the *Star of Zion* triumphantly proclaimed, "Cuba will be a Negro Republic," thus reordering the stakes of the war to give its African American readers reason to support the cause.[86] Some African Americans were quick to celebrate Afro-Cuban leaders in the conflict, to call Cubans "Negroes," and to depict their struggle as that of a vibrant, young race of darker men, burning to be free from hierarchical, dissipated Spain. If Cuba succeeded as a "Negro Republic," its democratic example would remind nearby southern states that African American men had the "genius" for self-government as well. Sarah Dudley Pettey recognized the stakes as early as 1896 and termed the insurgents "brave and patriotic" in the face of "beast-like brutality." She cheered, "*Vivant insurgents! Vivant Cuba!*" Once the United States entered the fray and white Americans died overseas to guarantee dark Cubans' political liberation, it would become more difficult for those at home to deny dark Americans' rights.[87] Finally, the war represented a chance to prove African American manhood through heroism in the heat of battle. Spain, the *Star of Zion*'s editor predicted, will "fight like a coward. . . . That she will lose Cuba the civilized world regards . . . as certain."[88] This African American Best Man, at least, stood squarely on the side of the brave, the civilized, world.

Others doubted that even heroism could arrest the theft of manhood already under way. A Kentucky black man reproved such jingoism with the admonition: "Don't rush to war. . . . [The African American] has nothing to fight for. . . . The white man says to him to-day, 'You are not a man, sir, and you are to serve and take such punishment as I see fit to give you.'" "Where is the Negro's head?" he asked. "Let the Negro stop and think and not rush too fast into battle unless he sees he is going to be treated better after it is over."[89] But others labeled such men "shoestring fellows" and predicted confidently that when the military needed real men, "They will call us."[90]

As he called up troops, President William McKinley sought to mitigate fears of the regular army's power and to raise support on the home front by commissioning existing state volunteer militias. By involving the civilian populace in the war, McKinley could offer upward career mobility and perhaps even extend federal benefits to state political figures. Thus, McKinley asked each governor for large numbers of troops, more than he expected to need. The issue of black volunteers came up immediately because even in southern states some militias included pre-existing black companies. Upon hearing of the declaration of war, other black men also rushed to form volunteer companies.[91]

In North Carolina, the Charlotte Light Infantry Company constituted the only black company in the state militia. Commissioned by a Democratic governor in 1887, the company by 1898 was led by C. S. L. A. Taylor and members carried state-issued guns at their mostly ceremonial functions. For example, they marched proudly past the reviewing stand on the occasion of Republican governor Daniel Russell's inauguration in Raleigh in 1896 and, a year later, paraded each day at the Negro State Fair.[92] Following the declaration of war, other black men around the state quickly organized companies of neighbors. The newly formed New Berne Riflemen, Colored, elected James Dudley, Sarah Dudley Pettey's uncle, as their captain.[93] When the state adjutant general telegraphed Dudley to ask whether he could raise eighty men to report to duty at a week's notice, Dudley fired back, "The Riflemen are all earnest men and show by their behavior that they mean business and are prepared to go to the war when called."[94]

Republican governor Daniel Russell's political debts to African Americans ran deep and wide, and he wanted to include black volunteer troops in the state's mobilization quotas.[95] Russell lobbied Washington, D.C., for authorization to create a black battalion under his primary black adviser, James H. Young. Permission was granted, and the black battalion became the second in the country commanded by black officers.[96] By June, Russell's political machinations in Washington, D.C., generated another call for troops, and the battalion grew to the Third North Carolina Volunteer Regiment. Young, promoted to colonel, commanded, and C. S. L. A. Taylor backed him up at the rank of lieutenant colonel. Kansas, Illinois, and Virginia also formed black regiments under black officers at a time when only one black officer served in the entire regular army.[97]

North Carolina black men clamored to enlist. Nine hundred recruits joined ten companies and boarded trains headed for Fort Macon, a fortification dating back to the 1820s located on a barren island off Morehead City.[98] Volunteers assembled by the first of June, then spent the summer marching up and down dunes in the blistering heat, swatting sand fleas, and picking sandspurs out of their flesh. At first, whites supported this African American rush to arms. "The reports that the colored man is weakening about enlisting, up country, is [sic] not seen here," boasted the *New Berne Journal*. As cars full of black men streamed toward Fort Macon, "All the men seemed in good spirits and showed no signs of not wanting to go to war."[99] Sarah Dudley Pettey, Charles Pettey, and Edward Dudley traveled to Fort Macon at that time and sent back glowing reports. At the center of camp life, a Young Men's Christian Association tent provided games and stationery along with daily prayers. The men, she thought, were in a high state of readiness.[100]

By August, the troops still sat, pickling in the thick, briny air. Their spirits lifted when they shipped out to Knoxville, Tennessee, to await mobilization to the Pacific. There, at Fort Poland, they found themselves with the Sixth Virginia Regiment, which had black officers under a white colonel. When the white colonel fired all of his black officers and replaced them with whites, the Sixth refused to obey them and courts-martial followed. Then the short war ended, and after spending three months in Tennessee, both black regiments deployed to Fort Haskell outside of Macon, Georgia, to await further orders. Georgia whites could not abide the idea of black soldiers with guns under the command of black officers. North Carolina black men, unused to Jim Crow laws, could not abide Macon's streetcar segregation. Trouble started whenever black soldiers went into Macon. In separate incidents, local whites killed four black North Carolinians. Juries acquitted all four murderers.[101] The entire fall, the black troops continued to hope they would be posted to Cuba, even for garrison duty.[102] From Georgia, shocking tales of racial injustice traveled home to North Carolina with furloughed soldiers.

Back home, Democrats had to counter the image of uniformed black soldiers that inconveniently belied their propaganda that African American men in power threatened the polity. To invert the patriotic symbolism of a black man in uniform, the Democrats portrayed the black troops as impostors, as sheep in wolves' clothing. Press coverage of black soldiers across the state shifted enormously between April, when local white editors praised blacks' enlistment, and October, when the white supremacy campaign centralized the party line and asserted that blacks were incapable of voting and officeholding.

The Democrats tailored the international language of racialized manhood to fit situations in their own backyards. Whites infantilized the soldiers on the one hand and portrayed them as animals on the other. To invoke the trope of the African American as evolutionary child, whites argued that dressing up black men in uniforms only served to point up the absurdity of their manly posturing, much like dressing up children in cowboy costumes. Suddenly, the soldiers were not men but Russell's "pets." They did not drill, they "frolicked." Newspapers began putting "soldiers" in quotation marks whenever they mentioned black troops. Complaining that the soldiers on trains "stood in the aisles, occupied two seats each, and took off their shoes," whites recommended that these "creatures" be transported in "cattle cars."[103]

When black soldiers came to town on leave, they carried themselves with confidence and brimmed with happiness at being home, irritating whites even further. To transform black soldiers from home protectors into sexual predators, whites portrayed them as swaggering phallic symbols. Furloughed black troops were "conspicuous by their important walk, the puffing of big cigars, and gallantry to the opposite sex of the Negro race."[104] This chivalrous treatment had a pernicious effect on black women, in turn unleashing their excesses: "These 'soldiers' were met by crowds of their female friends. . . . [The women] were so important at having their acquaintances in uniform that some of them felt entitled in making themselves offensive to the white people in the waiting rooms."[105] Everyone was out of place in this picture, whites thought, and they yearned to put black men and women back where they belonged. "Cotton will soon be ready to pick, sweet potatoes are growing in the hills, these are their duties," one white man complained. If the black troops would only come home, then "the white manhood of North Carolina . . . would stand at the head of the sisterhood of states in responding to the call of duty."[106]

Traveling by rail exposed black troops to white gangs who boarded the trains when they stopped. In collusion with the trainmen, who wired ahead that they should "do up the niggers" at the next stop, local whites would jump on the trains, start fistfights, and, if the going got tough, signal to pull out so that they could jump off and make their escape.[107] After finally being mustered out of the army in February 1899, the Third North Carolina had a particularly difficult time getting home from Macon. When they disembarked in Atlanta, members of the regiment were met by police who "very promptly clubbed [them] into submission." Whites lauded the action, saying the troops had "displayed the same ruffianism and brutality that characterized [them] while in service."[108]

The state's black Best Men and the troops themselves were heartbroken. Back in Knoxville, when the Third learned that the war had ended, they "wept like babies" at losing the chance to prove themselves in battle.[109] Edward A. Johnson, a Raleigh alderman whose sister married Sarah Dudley Pettey's brother, rushed to press with a laudatory history of black troops' wartime activities to refute the libel and slander that flew about them.[110] But many soldiers seemed numbed, like Early Hicks of Company D, the Third North Carolina Volunteers, who wrote home from Macon shortly before the troops were mustered out. Hicks said he knew that white supremacists such as Ben Tillman of South Carolina and Rebecca Latimer Felton of Georgia had captured the imaginations of "poor, blinded creatures" back home, but he placed his faith in the triumph of good over evil: "The ideal and truly great man and great woman are they who try to write their names in deeds of love and sympathy in the hearts and lives of mankind."[111] Deeds of love and sympathy would be in short supply as North Carolina's New White Men jockeyed for power.[112]

In the gendered complexities exacerbated by rapid industrialization and urbanization, Simmons, Daniels, and Aycock found the glue to join the black Best Men to street dudes, the brave soldiers to rapists. In 1898, the Democrats chose Furnifold Simmons to orchestrate the campaign to recapture a majority in the state legislature. Simmons knew that he must find an overarching issue to insure Democratic success in widely scattered races that often turned on local personalities and issues. He chose to make protection of white women the centerpiece of the campaign. By emphasizing sexuality, the Democrats placed race over class and spun a yarn in which white women of all classes highly prized their chastity and black men of all classes barely controlled their sexuality. By positing lust for white women as a universal trait in black men, whites explained away black Best Men's good behavior by arguing that they sought success simply to get close to white women. Likewise, when a poor black man stood accused of rape, the New White Men argued that the rapist had been stimulated by the black Best Man's elevated position. Black progress of any sort meant a move toward social equality, a code word for sexual equality.[113] Josephus Daniels demonstrated a gift for turning black men's good intentions into rape metaphors. For example, Daniels's newspaper depicted black Colonel James H. Young discharging his duties as director of the School for the Blind by peeping into a white blind girl's room.[114]

No matter what black Best Men did, their accomplishments constituted the brief for their prosecution. When the *New Berne Journal* argued that black officeholders sought "social equality with the Caucasian," Charles Pettey replied that since white men were "not accustomed to recogniz[ing] Negro manhood," they had no inkling of black men's motivations. As for penetrating the "social" barrier, Pettey stated bluntly, "More ill-bred white men have crossed this barrier to demoralize society than Negroes." African Americans wanted civil and political rights, not social equality, Pettey argued.[115] Nonetheless, whites continued to maintain that black elected officials hoped to "be brought into the social sphere of the higher classes."[116] The New White Men tucked all black men into Procrustes's bed, where they were damned if they stretched and damned if they shrank.

To drive black Best Men from politics and corral white Populist strays, Simmons, Aycock, and Daniels in 1898 created a local black-on-white rape scare, taking their cue from similar sensationalized reporting across the South. By the time they finished, they had racialized the definition of manhood and substituted race for class, the New White Man for the Best Man. Rhetorically, if not literally, Democrats embraced poor whites across class lines and politicized poor white men's personal lives, destroying the fragile black/white political alliance that had emerged with the Populist Party. The political machine exaggerated a series of sex crimes and allegations in order to strike terror into the hearts of white voters. It is difficult to determine how many of these incidents were actual crimes and how many sprang from collective fantasies inspired by Josephus Daniels's powerful manipulation of the media. The evidence suggests that the Democratic propaganda planted seeds of hysteria that ripened in the minds of an economically threatened people. From newspaper accounts across the state, eight instances emerge in which a black man stood accused of raping a white woman in the years 1897 and 1898. Juries sentenced four of the accused black men to death. One black man was lynched in 1897, and two more in 1898.[117] The Democrats reported every rape or attempted rape as if the crime had not existed prior to fusion rule.[118]

The hysteria began in August 1897 near Asheville when Kittie Henderson, a twenty-year-old handicapped woman, accused Bob Brackett of raping her as she made her way to church. Brackett was black, Henderson, white. The sheriff captured Brackett in short order and, accompanied by a mob, took him to Henderson for identification. Upon seeing Bob, she screamed, "You may hang him or burn him." The sheriff managed to get him to the jail but could only hold him one night before men broke in, freed the other prisoners, and seized Brackett. The kidnappers rode around for a while with Brackett, making him repeatedly describe the rape's details to them. Then they picked up Kittie Henderson and she watched him hang.[119] Quickly, North Carolinians found themselves caught up in the moral panic sweeping the region. "There has been of late a perfect epidemic of the crime of assault upon white women by negroes. Various states have suffered from it. . . . Is this to be the only one, or is it the beginning of more of the same nature in North Carolina?" the *New Berne Journal* asked after the Asheville lynching.[120]

A few days later, the Vance County sheriff arrested George Brodie, a local black man, for the rape of Nannie Catlett, a white woman. A white eyewitness at the trial reported that the African American spectators "stood stolid, rather vengeful to my eye, during the whole heart-rending recital of Brodie's victim." "These negroes cannot see the heinousness of the crime," he opined. Moreover, they could not understand Anglo-Saxon law: "Punishment by hanging . . . leaves them with the sting of imagined injustice." He recommended lynching instead of due process since it left a "sense of shock upon the race which even then seems to receive it all too dully."[121] A jury that included three African Americans quickly sentenced Brodie to hang, and the state militia whisked him out of town to prevent a lynching. Brodie was executed less than a month later.[122]

The same week that thousands watched Brodie die, 8,000 people gathered in Snow Hill, a small community in the Piedmont, to witness the public hanging of African American Dock Black for raping an elderly white woman. As blacks and whites jostled for position, pistols and knives flashed. Many spectators carried clubs. Twice the African Americans rushed the gallows, only to be driven back by whites brandishing guns in their faces. Dock Black announced from the platform that he had committed the crime; tempers ran so high that the whites drove the blacks from town.[123]

In early December, John Evans, a newcomer to Rockingham, found himself accused of the rape of a white girl. At first she identified her rapist as a white man or "a very bright mulatto," but after several lineups, she fingered Evans, a dark-skinned African American.[124] Evans had an alibi that witnesses of both races corroborated, but the jury convicted him. The Republican sheriff of Richmond County saved Evans from lynching, and Governor Russell put off his hanging, hoping that new evidence would surface.[125] The Democratic Executive Committee, meeting a few days after Evans's temporary reprieve, shamelessly decided to exploit the rape reports. Simmons chose as the central metaphorical figure of the upcoming campaign the incubus—a winged demon that has sexual intercourse with women while they sleep. The Democrats charged that while white men slumbered, the incubus of black power visited their beds. They summed up their platform as "safety of the home."[126] Democratic rule would "restore to the white women of the state the security they felt under the twenty years of democracy inaugurated by the immortal Vance."[127]

Zebulon Vance, now dead several years, had been among the original Redeemers, a figure adored by white farmers and townspeople alike. As they condemned black men, the Democrats used Vance as a convenient symbol to convince poor white Populists that they had failed to uphold manhood's duties when they put economic interests over racial interests in their alliance with black Republicans. However, in contrast to their broadside attacks on black elites, the Democrats granted the white Populists the defense of ignorance and left room for Populist face-saving. An observer reported that everywhere Populists heard Aycock's speeches linking rape reports to fusion rule, they "arose as one with a frenzy of repentance . . . [and as the] call to manhood seemed to increase in force and intensity . . . [they felt] a painful sense of guilt and degradation."[128]

The violence continued as the campaign heated up. In February, a mob tried to lynch Gus Harmon, a black man whom Missie Cuthbertson accused of assaulting her in Marion, a small town in the western part of the state.[129] Then, in the summer of 1898, as tensions rose over the upcoming election, the most symbolic case of all occurred in Concord, the center of African American progress and home of the black-owned Coleman Cotton Mill and Scotia Seminary. A twelve-year-old girl was raped and murdered while her family attended church services. A mob rounded up African Americans Joe Kizer and Tom Johnstone, obtained confessions, and took them to jail. That evening, men overpowered the sheriff and took the suspects to the edge of town, where they hung them and then riddled their bodies with bullets. Journalists converged on Concord to speculate wildly about the causes of the crime. One linked the grisly murder to the breakdown of racial deference inspired by the Coleman Cotton Mill's success. Another blamed the familiarity between white female teachers at Scotia Seminary and their African American women students.[130] Finally, just before the November elections, a Brunswick County jury sentenced a black man to death for the rape of a white woman.[131]

Seven cases of rape in which African American men stood accused in two years probably did not represent any real increase in the crime of black-on-white rape. For the previous two years, 1895 and 1896, the attorney general had counted twenty-eight rapes statewide. Neither he nor his successors specified the race of the rapists. They did, however, list the race of those lynched and executed. In 1895 and 1896, one black man was lynched for attempted rape, and none executed. If we can assume that any black man accused of raping a white woman would have been either lynched or executed, that leaves twenty-seven cases that did not involve black-on-white rape. Many of those twenty-seven convicted rapists must have been white men who raped white women since black men's rapes of black women were less likely to be prosecuted and white men's rapes of black women rarely resulted in convictions.[132] During the next two-year period, roughly July 1896 through July 1898—the first two years of fusion rule—the number of rapes rose to forty-two.

Historians have used the attorney general's figures documenting the rise in rape cases from twenty-eight to forty-two as proof of a raping rampage by black men.[133] In fact, the attorney general identified only three of those forty-two cases as ones in which black men raped white women. The newspaper accounts push the number to seven. Thirty-five cases remain. They might have involved black men who raped black women, or white men who raped black women, but white men who raped white women must have accounted for a large part of the rape increase.[134] These numbers suggest several possibilities: perhaps the fusionist judges and magistrates held white men more stringently accountable for rape; the rape scare may have increased reporting of the crime in general; or perhaps the white supremacy folk pornography unleashed some sort of white beast rapist who has escaped historians' notice. Interestingly, the number of "assault with intent to rape" cases, a crime that could have increased dramatically because of the rape scare propaganda, stayed relatively constant throughout the period.[135]

Despite the swift punishment of black men accused of rape in 1897 and 1898, rumors circulated that black rapists went unpunished by Republican and Populist officials. Alfred M. Waddell, a Wilmington Old Stager whose imagination was so captured by the rape scare that he summoned up the energy for a political rebirth, "remembered": "Crimes of all sorts increased alarmingly, and went unpunished. Negro jurors who sat in every case that was tried refused, in the face of the most overwhelming and undisputed evidence, to convict Negro criminals guilty of outrageous offenses."[136]

Contrary to Waddell's rendition, in each rape or attempted rape reported in 1897 and 1898, punishment came swiftly and lawfully, except in the Asheville and Concord cases, in which whites broke the law. In some of the counties in which rapists were punished, Republicans controlled the sheriff's office, and in many, African Americans held political power.[137] Governor Daniel Russell, politically boneheaded as usual, played right into the Democrats' hands when, after the Concord lynchings, he declared: "They deserved what they got. The provocation was so great that the act of killing these brutes, although not permissible in law, was almost excusable in morals and in justice."[138]

In addition to blaming the black Best Men for the alleged outbreak of rape, whites tried to make them responsible for stopping it. An integral part of black Best Men's contract for sharing power with white men had been African Americans' responsibility for the poor of their race, and now Democratic propaganda accused black Best Men of deliberate inaction. "It is time for those who stand in authority among the colored people to pronounce in no uncertain terms against these assaults," one white man asserted. "The cure for this crime lies largely, if not altogether with the colored leaders, and upon their heads must the blame be placed, if they do not attempt to act."[139]

African American men walked a fine line as they tried to condemn rape without condoning lynching and condemn lynching without condoning rape.[140] Before the 1898 rape panic, many North Carolina black men spoke bluntly about lynching: "Red-handed lynchers [are] butchering the Negro for almost any offense. . . . There are bad, worthless Negroes in the South, and there are bad, worthless white men who commit grievous crimes." White men should remember that "the Negro race with bodies and feelings like other races will not always submit tamely to this cruelty and bloodshed."[141] Black Best Men knew that accusations of rape were often false. White women's accounts had always been difficult to counter, but now that poor white women's purity must go unquestioned, defense became impossible.[142] On the national level, the Afro-American Council, with Charles Pettey's friend Alexander Walters at its head, condemned lynching in 1897, as did the Negro Protective Association, with the support of North Carolina delegate John Dancy. At the same time, the National Association of Colored Women met in Chicago and passed resolutions against both lynching and the "despoiler of homes and the degraders of womanhood, be he white or black." With a delegation of leading African Americans, Charles Pettey visited William McKinley during his reelection campaign. The group tried to extract a strong pledge from McKinley to speak out against lynching. Instead, he mouthed platitudes designed to reassure them of their Best

Man status: "Your race has made . . . progress in all that goes to make men better . . . better citizenship, better husbands, better fathers, better men."[143]

After the Asheville lynching, African American ministers ascended their pulpits to condemn both rape and lynching and to assume leadership in the crisis, just as whites had suggested. James Young offered a resolution concerning rapists at the Wake County Colored Baptist Association meeting that stated, "We as pastors will assist in bringing to justice such lawless characters."[144] A Presbyterian minister in New Bern, more than 250 miles from Asheville, organized a community meeting on "lynching and its prime cause" and invited "the lawyers, school-teachers, ministers, politicians, and business men of the city."[145] R. S. Rives, pastor of Sarah Dudley Pettey's church, responded to the assertion that blame for such crimes lay upon black leaders' heads by agreeing that rape was a "heinous" crime but declaring that "if lynching is the proper remedy white men ought to be lynched for assault upon colored women, and the fact that white men do perpetrate this meanest of all crimes upon my race cannot be denied." Then he reminded whites of the Best Man compromise: "There are at least two grades of society into which each of our races may be classified, and as a better remedy than lynching, I suggest a . . . combination of sentiment and purpose between the best elements of both races." Rives closed his letter, "Yours for the greatest good to the greatest number and the defence and safety of our womanhood."[146] The New White Man, however, did not want Rives's help in safeguarding "our womanhood." The black Best Man was dead.

In order to make protection of white womanhood the centerpiece of the legislative elections of 1898, the New White Men had launched a coldly calculated effort to defame black men. The sensationalization of rape and allegations of rape represented the worst, but not the only, aspect of their media blitz. As Furnifold Simmons kicked off the campaign, his cohort Josephus Daniels used the Raleigh News and Observer to spread wildly exaggerated accounts of interracial clashes between average citizens on the streets of eastern North Carolina cities. Simmons recalled later that they "filled the papers . . . with portraits of Negro officers and candidates. . . . The newspapers carried numerous exposures of Negro insolence and violence." At first, some eastern North Carolinians laughed openly at the tactic. The New Berne Journal quipped: "The 'outrage' editor of the News and Observer is getting 'slow.' He has not reported a case in Craven County in three days." Simmons collected hefty monetary contributions from industrialists across the state to reprint Daniels's newspaper articles as broadsides and send them to county Democratic leaders to distribute to voters. At first, many white political bosses saw Simmons's salacious propaganda for what it was and refused to distribute it or threatened to burn it. As Simmons leaned on his county bosses, however, they slowly straightened up, and he saw in the party and the press "a change of mind, a getting into step."[147] The manner in which gender and politics interacted after the white Democrats got "into step" is the subject of the next chapter.

four

SEX AND VIOLENCE IN

PROCRUSTES'S BED

Getting into step with Furnifold Simmons's 1898 effort to regain Democratic control of the legislature meant using the rape scare to generate heat and then watching steam build across the state. Simmons dispatched his agents everywhere.[1] They founded White Government Leagues, embellished local accounts of African American "outrages" for statewide broadcast, and reincarnated falsehoods in every Democratic rag. They even tried their hand at song:

Rise, ye sons of Carolina!
Proud Caucasians, one and all;
Be not deaf to Love's appealing—
Hear your wives and daughters call,
See their blanched and anxious faces,
Note their frail, but lovely forms
Rise, defend their spotless virtue
With your strong and manly arms.[2]

Legends of atrocities sprouted like mushrooms, but the stories were hard to pin down. They echoed each other, swept the state, and turned back again. If the situation appeared calm locally, reports circulated that the white people in the next town had suffered outrages. If conditions in that town looked sleepy enough when one arrived, news came that trouble had broken out farther down the road. With the now avid collaboration of local correspondents, Simmons and Daniels concentrated on fabricating and exaggerating stories about black majority counties to feed to the Piedmont, where white Democrats had voted Populist, and to the west, where whites had voted Republican. It was a brilliant strategy. The Populist white man who had valued his farm above his race discovered with a shock that he had opened the gates of hell for some distant white woman. The Democrats' pressure swelled white men's egos and honed their indignation. An explosion seemed imminent.[3]

That it finally came two days *after* the election testifies to the inexorability of hatred unleashed. Historians have treated the Wilmington slaughter as a riot, a coup, or a massacre and have scoured the archives to locate minutia of municipal politics to explain the violence. It is usually a tale told from the top down narrowly. Repeating it from the perpetrators' point of view, however, inadvertently serves to reify their version.[4] Giving voice to the roles of white women, black women, and black men draws back the curtain to reveal a highly contested stage. It also serves to remind us that what happened in Wilmington was about more than party politics or economic jealousy or even racism. It was about how political rhetoric can license people to do evil in the name of good. It reminds us that murder's best work is done after the fact, when terror lives on in memory.[5]

Instead of tracing one-by-one the steps white men took, it is helpful to shift the focus onto others: white and black women and black men. The very name historians give to the race wars of the 1890s—white supremacy campaigns—assumes that all of the choices fell to the white supremacists. Granting agency to everyone involved yields a more nuanced view of southern history and reveals that white power was contingent, the master of a thousand subtle and not so subtle disguises.

The political culture of women, white and black, in the white supremacy campaigns has commanded little scholarly attention.[6] White women at the turn of the century have most often been portrayed in southern history as either homebound or venturing into public space on a progressive mission.[7] Certainly some white women stayed home and some white women went out to do good, but others eagerly abetted the repression of African Americans. Furnifold Simmons, Charles Aycock, Josephus Daniels, and their red-shirted allies sought to persuade white women that fusion rule endangered them so that they would actively try to influence their husbands' votes even as they served the campaign as symbols of purity.

The Democrats' campaign depended in large part upon white women's cooperation. On the one hand, it objectified women and portrayed them as

helpless; on the other, it celebrated their involvement. If a white woman
rejected "protection" and went about her business in an integrated setting
or refused to make her husband a red shirt with a butterfly collar to wear to
the White Government League meeting, the entire Democratic project
suffered. When the Democrats made "safety of the home" central to the
campaign, they invited white women into politics. Once there, some white
women seized upon their victimization—the attention that the rape scare
focused upon them—to move into public roles and to wield political influence. They tried to turn their objectification into empowerment.

Some white women, on the other hand, rejected the tainted bait. De-
ploying their own language of domesticity, they reminded the white supremacists that African Americans did not threaten white home life but
instead strengthened it by providing domestic labor. Sometimes, through
all of the rhetoric, the heart still spoke. Some white women paid no attention at all to the New White Man's warnings and went on loving black men.
A white woman did harm enough by rejecting victimization; if she eloped
with a black man, she utterly betrayed the Democrats.

Black women's agency in the white supremacy campaign remains even
more elusive, partly because both historical language and method obscure
black women's political culture. In placing black women outside the political, in fashioning explanations for their actions entirely from ill-fitting
historical constructions based on white women's experiences, in overlook-
ing location as central to world view, historians have often missed the
complexity and contingency of African American women's politics.[8] Re-
defining the political and shedding completely the white middle-class construct of "separate spheres" remove obstacles to viewing black women's
activism on its own terms.[9]

When black women *are* included in southern history, the narrative most
often posits their self-sacrificing community activism rolling inexorably
toward the civil rights movement.[10] Although, in fact, black women did
cleave to a common political culture, one that privileged communitarianism over individualism, their tactics—how they voiced their beliefs and the
forums in which they chose to act—depended on their class, their age, and
the centrality of gender to their thinking.

Finally, it is at this moment that African American men vanish from
accounts of southern political history. This treatment creates an artificial
vacuum, an eerie silence that hollows out a cavern where the New White
Man's voice resounds too loudly. African Americans did not fall silent;
rather, they filled the air with a cacophony of spirited and dispirited arguments. Nor did the New White Man herald the new era with total as-
surance. He whispered aloud that his victory might be temporary if the
Supreme Court got wise to his tricks.

We can test these arguments in several settings. First, a close examination of New Bern, familiar terrain, finds white supremacist tactics agitating the citizens of that formerly peaceful city, while scattered incidents throughout the state as a whole reveal bubbling turmoil. Then Wilmington, the site of the racial massacre, takes center stage. Finally, statewide and national African American reactions to the events of 1898 belie the notion of black passivity.

Sarah Dudley Pettey did not get out on the streets of New Bern as much as usual in the summer and fall of 1898 since her fifth child, Theophytra, was born in March. But what she did see in her hometown disturbed her, although it was hard to judge the significance of the events. The preceding December, members of the Democratic Executive Committee met downtown at the Chatawka Hotel and determined to exploit "home protection" as their primary political strategy.[11] Then, two months later, the New Bern Ladies' Memorial Association became an official chapter of the United Daughters of the Confederacy.[12] Three days after Theophytra's birth, the white men in the town formed a Young Men's Democratic League, an organization dedicated to the "overthrow of Russellism and restoring to decent ways the good old state." They chose as secretary a very young white man, Romulus Armistead Nunn. Fresh out of the University of North Carolina at Chapel Hill, Nunn read law with Furnifold Simmons.[13] During the winter and spring, the rape reportage aroused some controversy, but the press continued to publish African American responses and sustained a certain civility when writing about black officeholders in the city.

This general calm prevailed until August 1898, when Charles Brantley Aycock hit town. He orated; he hobnobbed; he promised patronage. Wherever he went, "he [gave] inspiration to . . . white men favoring the cause of good government in the state."[14] Suddenly the local paper seized upon Simmons's incubus metaphor and the threat to white women's purity. At once, the campaign's goal became "white man's rights [and] safety of the home." White men were admonished to stop their selfishness and remember "those whose interest they represent."[15] Their neglect of unfranchised white women became a major theme in Aycock's soon-to-be-famous white men's "guilt and degradation" speech, which he honed that August in New Bern and subsequently gave across the state.[16] New Bern's white men conspicuously lacked that sense of guilt and degradation prior to Aycock's arrival. By the time he ended his visit, white men realized "how vital" the 1898 election was to the state's white women: "For them it is everything whether negro supremacy is to continue."[17]

There is a certain element of truth in the statement that it mattered to white women if African Americans participated in public affairs. The New White Men pushed for more stringent segregation just as southern white women sought a larger role in civic and commercial affairs. Combining higher standards of segregation with higher standards of female purity effectively constricted the space in which white women could move. To protect their virtue, white women must now be physically separated from black men. The idea of Josephus Daniels's mother serving black and white postal patrons from her front parlor had become unthinkable.

Despite New White Men's narrow demarcation of their paths, white women of all stations poured into public space, unsettling male confidence and demanding that everyone accommodate their presence. In ever-increasing numbers, they went to work outside of the home. In 1892, fewer than 1,000 women worked in the state's cotton mills. By 1900, 13,973 women were cotton mill workers, of whom only 1,474 were married. Of course, many of these single women lived under their fathers' roofs; even so, a young woman's ability to support herself threatened patriarchal authority.[18] Many mills operated in isolated company villages, but others flourished in urban areas, attracting women who lived outside of male "protection" altogether in boardinghouses or female-headed households.[19] At the same time, white women with a bit of education moved into teaching careers, newly regendered and rapidly expanding.[20] White women teachers imbued with missionary zeal poured out of the new state normal school to enlighten a benighted populace.[21]

While white women who worked whittled at patriarchy's veneer by gaining a modicum of independence, others who did not have to support themselves flocked to clubs and charitable organizations through which they entered public affairs.[22] Some among this group embraced and embellished the cult of the Confederacy, measuring the New White Man against his dead father's shadow and leading to the rapid growth of the United Daughters of the Confederacy in the 1890s.[23] The middle- and upper-class white women of the United Daughters of the Confederacy fictionalized the antebellum period as a time when white women had more of everything: more power, more money, more love, more protection. Just as modern blacks were not what their fathers had been as slaves, modern white men were not what their fathers had been as masters. If antebellum white men were giants, postbellum white men were pygmies. At a time when New White Men politely rejected their fathers' leadership, their wives and daughters came to idolize it.[24] The wages of the fantasy served as psychic compensation for the South's dire poverty. As twisted as this thinking was, southern white women used it to great effect. White women criticized modern men for impoverishing their families, for giving politics over to the rough and rowdy, for tolerating disorder in the streets, and for waffling before liquor interests—all conditions the New White Men also deplored but blamed on others.[25]

Thus, even without the Democrats' impetus, it suited many middle-class white women to push African Americans out of their way. Whites poured into urban areas at greater rates than blacks, yet some whites felt threatened by African American visibility in urban space. With rural migration to urban areas, social relations transformed as people of both races encountered strangers for the first time in their lives.[26] White women delighted in the new freedom this public space allowed, but many expected to wear the private sphere's protective cocoon out onto busy city streets. Since many urban white women began their lives in rural communities or small towns, smugly confident of their status, they cloaked themselves in the certainty of being known. A lady, they reasoned, should be recognized as one wherever she went. She should be able to participate robustly in public life without losing her delicacy, to throw one leg over a bicycle seat and peddle away as black onlookers cleared a path with downcast eyes.

When white men created and exaggerated the danger of black rapists, they underscored white women's dependency on white men, a tactic that put both black men and white women in their places. White men invoked danger and restriction just when white women sought pleasure and freedom. Thus, as the white supremacy campaign reasserted the New White Man's power over black men, domination of white women became a by-product. Yet the rhetoric that worked to limit white women's public mobility by predicating their dependency also conferred on women a perverted sense of power. Now white women could demand certain behavior from white men, out loud and in a political forum where they might finally be heard.[27]

Given these circumstances, any interaction between African Americans and white women in the late 1890s was fraught with racial pitfalls. For example, when a young white woman arrived to pick up her shoes from a black New Bern cobbler, he charged her twenty-five cents for the repair. That was too much, she protested, insisting repeatedly that the last time the bill amounted to ten cents. Finally the exasperated cobbler retorted, "You are an infernal liar." The white woman ran crying from the store.[28] In a racially charged society, African Americans found it difficult to set and collect fair prices. One might read between the lines of this account and find a white woman accustomed to cheating her black cobbler. The cobbler, perhaps incensed by the white supremacists' inflammatory accounts of black insolence, decided her carping was the last straw. Whatever the "truth" might have been, Simmons's minions pounced on such incidents with delight and wrote them large.

At any point where white women's activities intersected with the government, they might meet an African American official, especially after the Republican/Populist successes of 1896. At the New Bern post office, the black mail clerk called out, "Good morning," from behind the counter. If a white woman dropped by the courthouse to check on her taxes, she found "seven . . . negroes in a row making out the tax list."[29] On her way out, she might have to step over "one of these darkies stretched at full length upon the steps, sound asleep." She awakened such a "loafer" at her own peril since these men were "by no means choice in their language." Whites knew where to lay the blame for these daily annoyances: on fusion rule. When Democrats were in charge, black men were not found sleeping on the steps of public buildings.[30]

If a white New Bern woman ran afoul of the law, she had to deal with Sheriff Joseph Hahn, "a great fat white man" surrounded by four African American deputies.[31] The deputies realized the precarious position they assumed when they tried to enforce their authority over white women. For example, when African American deputy Jesse Godette ventured out to the Hooker farm to repossess a foreclosed timber cart, Mrs. Hooker faced him down with a double-barreled shotgun. Godette returned to town empty-handed.[32] White supremacists used the incident to ridicule Godette as a coward and, conversely, as a dangerous man when given authority over white women.

Craven County had a number of African American magistrates, and white women's cases inevitably came before them. Mrs. Habicht's dilemma illustrates how whites collapsed class distinctions in the 1898 campaign to elevate white women of low status above black men of high rank—in this case constable John Stanly and magistrate Frederick Douglass. Mrs. Habicht, a newcomer, was married to a bartender at a saloon owned by a white Republican. The Habichts lived above the saloon and soon got into a brouhaha with their landlord and employer. After the Republican swore out a warrant on Mrs. Habicht for disturbing the peace, Stanly picked her up and Douglass bound her over for trial. Since she was unable to post bond, Stanly and Douglass escorted her to jail. On the way there, some white men saw them, became outraged, and put up the woman's bond.[33]

Similar situations must have abounded in the years preceding this incident, and incarcerated white women were no rarity in county jails. The same month, another white woman appeared before black magistrates in New Bern. Most whites had always resented any authority a black man exercised over a white woman, but Aycock's speeches and the white supremacy literature licensed average white people to voice their complaints at the same time that they provided a language for their expression. Moreover, the white supremacists imbued individual encounters with great meaning by linking personal incidents to politics at its highest level. Journalists clamored to file stories on the "horrors of Negro rule." The Charlotte paper dispatched a reporter to New Bern to get the scoop. Josephus Daniels's *News and Observer* seized upon incidents such as the Habicht affair, printing the same story repeatedly, embroidering it more each time. After a while, flourishes abounded, and new details made shopworn tales fresh again.[34]

Populists derided the tactic, but they were whistling in the dark when they confidently vowed that their voters would never be swayed by such coverage. The Democrats "have jumped on the 'nigger' and are trying to ride into office on him," one Populist paper complained. Democrats' past treatment of poor white men was "only a foretaste" of what they would do if they regained power, Populists warned. "They . . . expect to overcome you by presenting negro, negro, all the time." If you "surrender your manhood" to the Democrats, you will "deserve all that you receive," another Populist cautioned.[35] But the Democrats' barrage of threats and insults drowned out Populist rebuttals. Populist senator Marion Butler took his life in his hands if he traveled in the eastern part of the state. The Democrats ridiculed the Populists as "impotent" and often referred to Marion Butler as "Mary Ann," a slang name for male homosexuals.[36] The paralyzed party floundered as its constituents flocked to Democratic clubs for repentant "Pops."[37]

Even as the white supremacy campaign inflamed Populist passions by posing white women as sexual prey of black men, it beckoned white women to an expanded forum. Women glided by in political parades, fashioned banners, peppered editors with letters, and decried "Negro rule" to mixed audiences at party rallies.[38] Their very presence counted. "The women are as deeply interested as the men," Democrats bragged, describing women as a "potent factor" in the campaign.[39] The White Government Leagues recruited male and female members, perhaps in an explicit attempt to compete with the Populist movement's culture. Both men and women had flocked to Populist rallies, day-long events consciously designed to commit the entire family to the cause by stressing the cooperative structure of rural life across gender and age boundaries.[40] The high level of female participation in White Government Leagues demonstrates women's key role in eroding Populist loyalty.

Organized by the Democrats in the spring of 1898, the White Government Leagues declared themselves open to all white men and women who believed in the superiority of their race. Charles Aycock's college buddy, Francis Winston, headed the group and called the leagues a haven for the "home loving." Winston constantly bowed to the women and boasted that "the white good women in North Carolina are unusually aroused."[41] Taking a fashion cue from Ben Tillman, the South Carolina governor who toured North Carolina at Simmons's invitation to speak for white supremacy, league members donned red shirts.[42] Organizers traveled to eve county to set up chapters and stage rallies, using "an odd combination of modern appliances with oldtime southern ideas, for some of the red shirters came on bicycles and the telephone was used to hasten backward delegations." Terrorism had come a long way since "the Kuklux had no telephones and wheels."[43]

White women accompanied these men into public space, arguing that they did so only because they wished to be safe in their homes. At a meeting in Laurinburg, for example, "a large number of ladies graced the occasion with their presence and the men were attired in red shirts."[44] At a subsequent Red Shirt rally, Rebecca Strowd, "a highly intelligent and cultured young lady" who was unmarried and presumably virginal, addressed the assembly. Although the reporter took care to mention that she spoke with "womanly grace and modesty," her language was direct and provocative. As never before, Strowd said, "white men are called upon in the names of their wives and daughters . . . to speak out and let the world know where they stand." "There is a black vampire hovering over our beloved old North Carolina," she declared. To vanquish it, all white men must vote Democratic. If the men wavered, "the ladies are not only willing but stand ready to perform their part of this noble work." Rebecca Strowd capped her speech by unfurling a banner made by women league members. The day after the election, it would be given to the precinct that brought in the most Democratic votes.[45]

Strowd's image of the African American political presence as a "black vampire" recalls the supernatural power Furnifold Simmons invoked when he used the term "incubus." Democratic rhetoric endowed African Americans with a mythical force that, Democrats argued, warranted extraordinarily repressive methods. Shortly after Rebecca Strowd's speech, Daniels's cartoonist drew a black hand holding white Republican politicians in its grip. Long, sharp claws replaced human nails, and hair covered the back of the hand.[46] In speeches such as Strowd's, white women wondered aloud if their men could prove equal to doing battle with such a force.

Although many white women took an active role in the campaign, that role was to demonstrate their passivity. To be present at all, they first declared themselves incapable of standing alone. As wives, mothers, sisters, and daughters of white men, they observed patriarchy firsthand, and their relation to privilege made them "collaborators" in its exercise, even as they remained subordinate to it.[47]

As some white women reveled in their newfound political role, many black women brought to the fray a finely honed political culture. White southern politicians responded to black women's challenges, sometimes overtly but more often by defining the limits of the possible, in ways that capitalized on local isolation and manipulated divisions among African Americans. The North Carolina white supremacy campaign and the Wilmington massacre are no exceptions. Even in white press accounts, political black women are ubiquitous.

The sources of black women's politics at the turn of the century go back to the antebellum period. Freedom, justice, and rights are relative concepts, and context conditions their meaning. Insightful historical interpretations of the slave community and the meaning of freedom upon emancipation indicate that the practice and perfection of government carried particular meanings for people such as Sarah Dudley Pettey.[48] Freedpeople used their prior experiences with power to craft ideals of community order, drawing on African institutions and their race's kidnapping, slavery, and deliverance with emancipation. In slavery, no one ever acted alone; any movement tugged at the entire web of enslavement. Furthermore, the slave market schooled African Americans in political economy.[49] Lockean liberalism posed "the preservation of their property" as "the great and chief end ... of men's uniting into commonwealths and putting themselves under government," but such talk is nonsense to people who *themselves* had been property. Drawing from their own experiences, freedpeople could more easily envision a commonwealth as a cooperative venture coalescing around property interests.[50]

To their lived experiences in slavery African Americans added a powerful New Testament vision of the ideal community.[51] The idea of what they called the "brotherhood of man" especially gripped middle-class African American men and women who rose within denominational hierarchies and dedicated themselves to home missionary work, and it sustained them in their belief that they should act for the entire race. They saw themselves as shepherds responsible for their flocks' votes as well as for their flocks' souls.[52]

Certain freedpeople, of course, embraced bourgeois individualism, even as certain communitarians were more successful than others in acting out cooperative values.[53] In addition, growing differences in African Americans' material circumstances after emancipation gradually weakened the cooperative ideology. By 1900, a laundress, as a second-generation freedperson, might see Sarah Dudley Pettey's upward climb as class distance—as part of the problem—rather than as her own lifeline out of oppression. But even if she did, whites increasingly privileged "race" over all else and reminded her daily that she and Dudley Pettey rowed the same boat. Whites sharpened such reminders for Dudley Pettey's benefit, of course, rather than for the laundress's benefit. Whatever their purpose, whites' declassing of upwardly mobile African Americans reinforced black cooperative civic culture.

Sarah Dudley Pettey believed that woman's place was in politics and that the middle class should lead the working classes to the benefit of all. She praised both strategies directly when black women protested the segregation of streetcars by an Atlanta rail company. "The Afro-American women of Atlanta, Ga., covered themselves with honor and glory when they met *en masse* and passed resolutions denouncing the action of the Atlanta Traction R.R.," she declared. A "biased and prejudiced legislature" had opened the door to such action, she declared, heaping praise upon the protesters: "These patriotic, liberty-loving women have sounded the proper keynote. . . . They have endeared themselves to the hearts of their fellow country-women by their bold and courageous stand." To break the back of the car company, she proposed "that the better class of Afro-Americans in Atlanta . . . make sacrifices and walk to and from their places of business."[54]

Dudley Pettey borrowed her language from the personification of patriarchy—those white men we call the "Founders"—but her definitions of honor, glory, patriotism, liberty, and courage would never have matched theirs. The truehearted citizens in her rendering were not Georgia's white male voters but her "fellow country-women," African American women without equal protection under the law or the franchise. At the moment that whites sought to impose segregation by law in the South, her words and actions offer a glimpse of African American women's civic strategies, which involved a delicate balance of gender relations, ever-adaptive interracial tactics shaped by place and circumstance, and an array of weapons sheathed in quivers bound by class position.

For most black women, politics began at home, blending the public and the private. Many African Americans worked to build domestic partnerships that allowed women to do race work outside the home, but their marriages played out in a society that rested on the subordination of black men as well as black women. Moreover, white society recognized no private sphere for black women and wanted them all to be available to serve whites' needs. In this case, the stakes of gender politics—being free to do race work in the home and in the world—had something to do with empowering women but much more to do with group progress.[55]

Because black women realized the practical importance of the group over the individual, whether black *men* could vote constituted the single most important variable in southern middle-class black women's political strategies, making theories borrowed from white women's suffrage experiences of little relevance. Prior to disfranchisement, the issue of woman suffrage hinged upon how black women prioritized issues of gender equity. Many women who cherished their right to vote in church conferences and temperance organizations believed that since whites had preempted electoral politics as a male preserve, the most important thing was that they be represented there by a strong voice. Others, such as Sarah Dudley Pettey, fervently worked for woman suffrage.[56] In any case, being without the vote was not equivalent to being without political influence. As a black male North Carolinian put it in 1897, "The women of our race, though denied the suffrage, [are] a prime factor in the Republican party."[57]

Even though they might disagree on the importance of women's direct electoral participation, most middle-class black women agreed that they should speak to, and often for, the uneducated women of their race. "The new woman," Sarah Dudley Pettey commented approvingly in the 1896 election, "has enlisted as a thorough-going political campaigner. She and aid-de-camps dress as unpretentiously as possible and . . . select the crowded tenements and flats where the laboring classes dwell. . . . They bring important issues before the wives, sisters, and mothers, then urge them to influence their husbands, brothers, and sons."[58] Her rendering of black women's political culture assumes that middle-class women should take the lead, even as it assumes the activity's utility: that poor women had influence with their husbands, brothers, and sons.[59]

Educated black women tried to control the political tactics of two groups: poor, uneducated black women and young African Americans of all classes.[60] Convinced that they worked for the good of the race, middle-class black women saw uneducated women as dangerously unprepared to articulate their politics to a white power structure. At the same time, middle-class African Americans fretted about how whites might garner political currency from young African Americans' actions. They shuddered when Josephus Daniels fired off yet another story of African American "insolence."

How did young African Americans and uneducated black women exercise their rights and express their politics? Such an analysis can be spun only from the flimsiest strands of evidence given by the most unreliable of sources: whites' complaints about African American women's and girls' street behavior during the bombastic 1898 campaign.[61] The white press used these stories to demonstrate how African American political success translated into personal ordeals for white women in the hopes that white men would forsake interracial political coalitions. We can use them differently: as indications of young girls' and poor women's politics. In the midst of rhetoric that disparaged them and their families, anonymous black women and girls did not wait for middle-class women to represent them. They struck back in the language of the streets.

Four altercations serve as representative examples. In New Bern, the daughter of a prominent white family set out on a leisurely stroll down

Middle Street. She soon met two black girls, probably teenagers. According to the white press, they were "young and ignorant and therefore impudent [and] had heard of the 'rights' of their race." As the white woman approached, the young girls locked arms and forced her to step off the high sidewalk and into the street as they passed.[62] On another occasion, an altercation in New Bern became more "pointed." One sweltering afternoon, an example "of the loveliest of southern womanhood . . . dressed in white" walked out to get some air on a bridge. As she ambled across, she met a black laundress who thrust "the point of her umbrella into her side." The white woman kept walking, but as she turned to go back across the bridge, she saw the black woman coming toward her again. This time, the laundress poked her harder with the umbrella and shouted, "Oh, you think you are fine!"[63]

An incident in Wilmington involved both sidewalks and umbrellas. When several white women encountered a black woman deliberately standing in their way on the sidewalk, one of them "caught hold of the negress to shove her aside to prevent the intended collision, and the negro viciously attacked her with an umbrella." A black male bystander shouted encouragement: "That's right; damn it, give it to her."[64] Finally, two white Winston-Salem women were riding bicycles near the R. J. Reynolds stemmery when the shift ended and African American women were pouring into the streets. The cyclists "turned into a narrow path to avoid meeting" the crowd but ran smack into a knot of black women pedestrians. Instead of slowing down, the white woman in front sped up and "so brushed past." Then, according to Josephus Daniels, "one of the wenches . . . got right in the middle of the path, and [the second cyclist] had to dismount from her wheel and roll it around the impudent negro wench; and all the impudent wenches laughed loudly and clapped their hands." "Such exasperating occurrences," he moralized, "would not happen but for the fact that the negro party is in power in North Carolina."[65]

What is going on here? There are at least three possibilities. First, the stories may be completely or partially fabricated, urban legends on the order of poisoned wells intended to arouse white male voters. Second, the white women, inspired by the white supremacy campaign, may have been reporting incidents that heretofore had been commonplace but unreported. Third, the sidewalk altercations may represent a departure from normal interaction; the stories may be at least partially true, and the laughter, poking, and physical isolation of white women by black women may constitute political actions using "weapons of the weak."[66]

If we accept the premise that the stories contain a grain of truth, then in order to uncover that truth, we must retell them without approbation and invective. That means removing the angelic white dresses, the demure manners, and the purported reluctance of the white women to cause a scene, all subjective attributes added by the newswriters. That done, we meet white women out in public space, getting into fights with black women. If we eliminate the subjectivity of the reportage on black women—the impudence, ignorance, and viciousness—they emerge standing up for their rights and abandoning deference. The African Americans in the stories are either young girls or working women going home with the laundry or leaving the tobacco factory. The white women are shopping, sashaying out for air, or riding bicycles. In almost every encounter, the black women comment—with either words or actions—on white women's freedom to pursue leisure in public while they have to work, even as they puncture the white women's superior demeanor.

Black and white women had met each other on the streets day in and day out since emancipation. What was different now? For one thing, the white women probably *were* putting on airs since the white supremacy campaign depicted them daily as virginal treasures under assault from "Negro domination" in politics. The black women understood these "airs" to result from the political winds. At the same time, the black women *were* more militant. In the months before the election of 1898, white editors slandered African American women openly, calling them wenches whenever possible, and concocted a bogus rape epidemic that implied that black men raped white women in part because black women were both ugly and immoral. Sarah Dudley Pettey's hometown white newspaper reported that a local black man had opined to his white New Bern neighbor that he looked forward to the legalization of interracial marriage because "we colored men can get white wives" but "it will not be so easy for white men to get good looking colored women."[67] In the streets, black women championed their right to hold political opinions and their husbands' right to vote, but they also struck back at a white supremacy campaign that made the political personal by encouraging white women to treat them shabbily in public and by defaming black women's morality and their husbands' characters. So, in a way, Josephus Daniels was right to blame black women's actions on "the negro party . . . in power."

These personal confrontations were just the sorts of incidents middle-class black women hoped to avoid by controlling the public actions of poor women and bumptious youths. In 1898, most educated black women thought their function as interpreters between the "folk" and the white supremacists had never been more critical since they hoped to hold on to what they deemed the race's most important right: the male franchise. Middle-class black women followed national and regional politics, understood lynching to be a political tool rather than random violence, and believed that one false move could destroy their chances to maintain male suffrage. They knew that whites made political hay from any conduct other than appropriate Victorian behavior and grafted it onto pseudo-Darwinian prognostications. Middle-class black women saw street altercations as fuel for the fires of race prejudice.[68]

By October, the white supremacy campaign's focus had moved to the streets of Wilmington. Since Wilmington was a port city with a large black middle class and many African American officials, its white citizens were sitting ducks for Simmons's white supremacy rhetoric. After the Republicans and Populists won control of the state legislature in 1894, they returned county and local offices to "home rule." As a result, African Americans, white Republicans, and Populists won election to local posts previously held by Democrats appointed at the state level. In Wilmington's 1897 election, Republicans claimed the majority on the board of aldermen, and they chose one of their own as mayor. White Democrats promptly protested the method by which Wilmington had regained home rule, and the defeated board and mayor refused to yield city hall. Before it was over, yet a third board of aldermen constituted itself and elected yet another mayor. The case went to the state supreme court, which decided in favor of the duly elected Republicans.[69] If the situation was tense in 1897, it grew even more so in 1898.

In August, Alexander Manly printed an editorial on interracial liaisons in his newspaper, the *Daily Record*.[70] The *Record* was the only African American daily in the state, and Manly enjoyed a reputation for "aggressiveness in battling for race." He held a minor patronage position under the Republican town ring.[71] Manly took offense when the white *Wilmington Messenger* resuscitated a year-old speech that Rebecca Latimer Felton had given at a Georgia farmers' convention.[72] Felton blamed white men for the grinding poverty in which most rural white women lived. In her attempt to shame them into providing for their families, she declared white farmers to be soft on the rape of white women by black men. Neglectful white men had let things deteriorate to the point that lynching of black rapists was the only remedy, according to Felton.[73] She glorified the antebellum white man, denigrated the postbellum white man, and used the modern black man to goad all concerned. The white supremacists recognized that her speech would serve their "guilt and degradation" campaign and resurrected it.

To answer Felton, Manly fought fire with fire. First, he argued that at least half the time white women lied about being raped. Then he pointed out that white men both raped and seduced black women. Why was it worse for a black man to be intimate with a white woman than for a white man to be intimate with a black woman, he wondered. African Americans had made such arguments before, but Manly added an indictment of white men's neglect of white women that built upon Felton's. "We suggest that the whites guard their women more closely, as Mrs. Felton says, thus giving no opportunity for the human fiend, be he white or black," Manly chided. "You leave your goods out of doors and then complain because they are taken away. Poor white men are careless in the manner of protecting their women." Thus, he accused white men of failing to live up to the demands of patriarchy, an accusation that Felton might make with impunity but that Manly made at considerable peril.

In the eyes of whites, Manly's great folly was his challenge to the mono-lithic purity of white women. When he suggested that poor white women often welcomed the attentions of black men, he played into the hands of Democrats who sought to win back poor rural Populist voters. Manly ventured, "The morals of the poor white people are on a par with their colored neighbors of like conditions." White women were not "any more particular in the matter of clandestine meetings with colored men, than are the white men with colored women." Manly spoke as a Best Man, as a member of the middle class discussing morality among poor people of both races. When he commented on white women's morality, he was not breaking new ground; Ida B. Wells-Barnett, for example, had been saying the same thing for years.[74]

It was the recontextualized political climate that gave Manly's words their explosive effect. Manly dared to equate the morals of poor white and poor black people. For Manly, class trumped race; poor white women were no better than poor black women. Before and after the Civil War, many interracial couples, including white women and black men, formed liai-sons, some of which became the equivalent of common-law marriages.[75] Now, as Democrats sought to strengthen white purity for political pur-poses, such arrangements revealed white weakness and thus could not be admitted openly. Manly's best-aimed blow was the suggestion that some white women freely chose black men as lovers, which shook the new construction of whiteness. All white women were pure. All black men were animals or children. Therefore, no white woman could prefer a black man over a white man.

Reaction to the August editorial came swiftly. White newspapers re-printed the statement each day until the election, often as the lead-in for a new "outrage" report. Manly, very handsome himself, had commented that some black men were "sufficiently attractive for white girls of culture and refinement to fall in love with." To this whites added, "Here he tells of his own experience, and he has been holding 'clandestine meetings' with poor white women, wives of white men." Manly's editorial became a "dirty defamation," a "sweeping insult to all respectable white women who are poor," and a "great slur."[76]

Sarah Dudley Pettey and her husband were friendly with Manly, and her silence at this moment speaks volumes. Dudley Pettey knew that when Ida B. Wells-Barnett had criticized the lynching of three Memphis men, she had been permanently exiled from the South for fear of her life. Dudley Pettey uncharacteristically restrained herself, but there are two hints of the Petteys' involvement behind the scenes. Parts of Manly's editorial echo Charles Pettey's response to an editorial in the *New Berne Journal* entitled "Mistakes of the Negro," in which he stated that white men crossed racial lines for sex. Later came Manly's cryptic statement: "Many of the points upon which the *Record* built its large success . . . were furnished to us by Bishop Pettey, who has ever shown himself to be one of our warmest friends and supporters." Manly added hastily, "Mrs. Pettey is no less distinguished than her renowned husband."[77]

The black Wilmington Ministerial Union helped Manly relocate his press after his white landlord evicted him. The Wilmington District Conference and Sunday School Convention endorsed his right to speak out, although it withheld explicit support for the editorial.[78] Tensions ran high as rumors circulated that whites were plotting to burn Manly's press.

Just before the election, "An Organization of Colored Ladies" delivered this threat: "Every negro who refuses to register his name next Saturday that he may vote, we shall make it our business to deal with him in a way that will not be pleasant. He shall be branded a white-livered coward who would sell his liberty." Whatever happened, these women would "teach our children to love the party of manhood's rights." The women published their resolution in Manly's paper, "the one medium that stood up for our rights when others have forsaken us."[79] The "Organization of Colored Ladies" was an example of what the *Washington Post* called Wilmington's "negro women republican aid societies," groups of black women who recognized that the white supremacy campaign threatened their rights.[80] Although Democrats considered white women's participation crucial, they expressed outrage that "negro women pass[ed] resolutions of ostracism against negroes who vote the democratic ticket." The Democrats used black women's participation in politics to goad white men for good measure, to point up that fusion had turned the world completely upside down. Black women, whom white men had always seen as powerless over even their own sexuality, were now fighting back. Just before the election, Democrats circulated the rumor that Congressman George White's wife had received a shipment of rifles and that his daughter was circulating a petition to convince black women to abandon their positions as servants in white homes.[81]

In addition to the street incidents and the Organization of Colored Ladies' manifesto, other hints suggest that black women played active roles in Wilmington politics. One cause of tension, a white apologist argued, arose from "the audacious Negro grudge developing against the streetcar conductors because they did not help black women on and off the conveyance as they did white women."[82] Not only were African Americans riding in unsegregated streetcars, but black women were angry that the white drivers did not assist them in boarding and disembarking. As black women's outrage mounted, white men felt increasingly pressed to counter their demands. Wilmington's white men formed an organization of "Minute-Men" and vowed to put an end to three things: rising crime, poor policing, and "negro women parad[ing] the streets and insult[ing] men and ladies." Invoking Manassas and Chancellorsville, they armed themselves and let it be known that they "would welcome a little unpleasantness."[83]

Black women's involvement in these street incidents, their support of the *Daily Record*, and their demand for chivalry from streetcar operators all hint that African American women questioned their assigned place and that white men deplored their rebellion. Yet the white supremacists either minimized black women's agency, ignored them, or ridiculed them. While white supremacists argued that black men's bad behavior reflected evolutionary laggardness, they also asserted that defective African American homes contributed to the problem. It was in the Democrats' best interests, however, to avoid entirely a discourse on black women or to portray them as incapable of making good homes since the campaign focused on black men's lack of restraint. Moreover, since the campaign sought to arouse white women, questions of gender interests across racial lines had to be avoided. On that count, the white supremacists succeeded spectacularly with some white women and failed miserably with others.

The white women in Alfred Moore Waddell's family collaborated avidly in the white supremacy campaign, and from them he drew strength to lead a racial massacre. The tensions of the era—tensions created by changing gender roles, the hopelessness of southern poverty, and the challenge of African American success—came together in the Waddell family. A Confederate colonel and a moderate in race relations as a Reconstruction politician, Alfred Moore Waddell's political fortunes had ebbed for more than a decade when he emerged to lead Wilmington's White Government League in 1898. A cross-class alliance of white men, the group seized upon Manly's editorial as proof of the social ramifications of African American political and economic success.[84] Armed to the teeth, the White Government League and its allies had been threatening the city's African Americans for weeks prior to the election. The inner circle of Democratic strategists had excluded Waddell, probably because of his age and his record for relative racial fairness during Reconstruction. One recalled, "The boys did not seem to want him to help. . . . They did not think he was of any value."[85] Determined to earn a place among the New White Men, Waddell began making speeches. He electrified his audiences with his reckless words: "We are going to protect our firesides and our loved ones or die in the attempt." He and his men would drive Manly and black politicians from Wilmington, Waddell promised, even if he had to "chok[e] the Cape Fear with the bodies of negroes."[86]

How did the women at Waddell's fireside feel about his words? At first they were surprised, then proud, then afraid. But they supported his strong stand. Waddell's wife, Gabrielle De Rosset, came from one of Wilmington's most distinguished families but had led a most difficult life. Her young parents took her to England during the Civil War, where her father appears to have been a profiteer and her mother played the gay southern belle. After Gabrielle's mother died from a self-administered opium overdose, her father sent her home to live with his parents and sisters, including the aunt whom she would call "Mother," Kate Meares. After the war, her father went to New York City, failed in business, and ended up as a grocery clerk in a one-horse Piedmont town, where he soon died. Gabrielle, forced to earn her living, became a governess in New England, quitting only when the family needed her to nurse her grandfather, whose face was being eaten away by cancer. After several months of horrific nursing duty, Gabrielle suffered a nervous breakdown and returned to Wilmington. She was now an old maid of thirty-two who had to support herself.[87]

The next year, she married Alfred Moore Waddell, already known around town as "old man Waddell."[88] He was a never-married Civil War veteran of sixty-two, and his promising career in politics had ended while Gabrielle was still a child. By the 1890s, Waddell could only cling to the shadow of his former glory, and his life at that point was a metaphor for the weakness white women saw in southern men at the turn of the century. The marriage seems to have been the last resort for an orphan past marriageable age whose only relatives were elderly. She always called him "colonel," even in her diary, and she often notes that the colonel was out late, after midnight. Waddell never mentioned his marriage in his autobiography.[89] The couple had no children. They were poor enough that Gabrielle had to teach music every day.

Gabrielle had made the best bargain she could for damaged goods.

Something was wrong with Alfred Waddell, but what was it? Archival material in the papers of the De Rosset and Waddell families offers no clue, but David Fulton does. Fulton was an African American from Wilmington who wrote a novel so factual that it barely qualifies as fiction. He tells us that Waddell drank and gambled to excess. In the years before he married Gabrielle, he lost his "palatial" home and moved to a humble house.[90] The marriage represented a second chance for both of them. For Alfred Waddell, the hypermasculine trappings of the white supremacy campaign provided an opportunity to act out his redemption upon a public stage.

Aunt Kate Meares described the impact Waddell's initial speech had on the family as "a surprise to me as to everybody else." They could scarcely believe the manly vigor that now gripped the old colonel. Meares feared that Waddell was now a "marked man" and reported to relatives that she implored Gabrielle to leave the city with her. "But she positively refuses to leave him—though he is really anxious for her to go," Meares worried. As for other white Wilmington families, "many believe there will be no trouble. . . . Others are sending their families in every direction. . . . One thing is sure the men [are] all thoroughly prepared for the worst—but so are the negroes, and the least spark may kindle a flame that will cost many lives before the thing is through."[91]

In the Piedmont, Waddell's cousin Rebecca Cameron gloried in the new role the white supremacy campaign extended to women. She wrote to Alfred on Church Periodical Club stationery to applaud his speech and to urge him to follow through on his threat to murder African Americans. "Where are the white men and the shotguns!" she exclaimed. "It is time for the oft quoted shotgun to play a part, and an active one, in the elections," Cameron told Waddell. She continued, "It has reached the point where blood letting is needed for the hearts of the common man and when the depletion commences *let it be thorough!* Solomon says, 'There is a Time to Kill.' " Finally, Cameron described the mood of the white women of Hillsboro: "We are aflame with anger here. . . . I wish you could see Anna. She is fairly impatient and blood thirsty. These blond women are terrible when their fighting blood is up."[92]

Waddell took Cameron's advice to heart. "What is the matter with us?" he queried white men at a Red Shirt rally. Waddell decided they were "afflicted with an excess of the virtue of forbearance." He alluded to the alleged rape epidemic as proof of "the ultimate ambition of the more aspiring members of that race." He condemned the "Organization of Colored Ladies" for calling whites who discharged black workers "demons."[93] The day before the election, he told a crowd, "You are Anglo-Saxons. You are armed and prepared, and you will do your duty. . . . Go to the polls tomorrow, and if you find the negro out voting, tell him to leave the polls, and if he refuses, kill him." Waddell agreed with Cameron that it was time "for the shotgun to play a part" in the election: "We shall win to-morrow, if we have to do it with guns."[94] Waddell's threats were especially absurd since white businessmen had blackmailed Governor Russell into withdrawing Republican candidates for local Wilmington spots open in the election. Across the state, Democrats swept into office and took control of the legislature, effectively hamstringing Republican governor Daniel Russell for the two remaining years of his term. In Wilmington, Republicans now held only the offices of mayor and alderman, positions voted on in odd years.[95]

Waddell had talked awfully big. Now what was he to do? The day after the 8 November election, white Democrats called a mass meeting. The meeting's purpose eluded Waddell since he was out of the loop, but he used the younger Democratic plotters' organization just as they had used his bombast. The meeting ran away with its conveners, and the thousand men present clamored for Waddell to mount the stage. Then they demanded that a committee draw up a white declaration of independence. "We do hereby declare that we . . . will never again be ruled by men of African origin," the document began. It urged employers to fire black help and ordered Alexander Manly out of the city. Then whites demanded resignations from the chief of police and the Republican mayor, who had another year to serve.[96]

Manly had already escaped the city, but Waddell and the committee issued an ultimatum to black civic leaders to respond to the declaration by the next morning or else. Through a series of bumbling misadventures on both sides, the answer did not come, and the deadline inched closer. On the morning of 10 November, they had to make good on their threats. They were ready. Wilmington "businessmen" had purchased a Colt rapid-firing gun, and the office of the *Wilmington Messenger* resembled "a veritable arsenal."[97]

With Waddell in the lead, an army of men rampaged around the city. The mob burned Alexander Manly's press, then hunted down prominent black leaders and either shot them or ran them out of town. "What have we done, what have we done?" one African American man screamed. A white man, who moments before had telephoned to have the rapid-firing gun sent over, found himself unable to answer since "they had done nothing." The Wilmington Light Infantry joined the rioting legions. Company K of the infantry was fresh from mobilization in the Spanish-American/Cuban War, in which Wilmington's black soldiers still served.[98] The infantry substituted military "discipline" for raging individual mayhem and added two cannons to the fray. At the end of the day, more than ten African Americans lay dead in the streets, and Alfred Waddell seized the mayor's office.[99]

Gabrielle Waddell was an eyewitness to the riot, yet she oddly distanced herself from it. Her account in her diary reads: "Day of rioting and dangers. armed men shut down Record press. Col at head and feeding people from Brooklyn refuging at Baptist church. . . . Telegrams and phones Col elected mayor. he out all night. I didn't undress." And the next day, "We home at 6 a.m. all day receiving congratulations feeding men at Armory. . . . Col out till after midnight."[100] Brooklyn was the African American neighborhood devastated by the fighting and the subsequent house-to-house searches. While her husband was in Brooklyn killing people, apparently Gabrielle was at the Baptist church feeding those fortunate enough to have escaped his reign of terror.[101]

Living with such ambiguity could only be accomplished by someone as practiced at contradiction as Gabrielle Waddell. The child of failed, though distinguished, parents, raised in a poor but proud family, the young bride of a remote old man, she did the Lord's work even as her husband did the devil's. What did she think of the events of that day? We have a few clues, but like Gabrielle herself, they are contradictory. The white supremacy campaign propelled Gabrielle De Rosset Waddell into public life, but that public life was as contradictory as her role in the 1898 riot. She became the state president of the United Daughters of the Confederacy, and in 1920, she was one of the North Carolina white women who attended the first southern women's meeting for interracial cooperation.[102]

Not every white woman believed the white supremacists' propaganda. Jane Cronly, like Gabrielle De Rosset the daughter of a prominent Wilmington family, surreptitiously tried to publish her own account of the riot. "My conscience has reproached me ever since [the riot] for not [telling] the truth," Cronly wrote in an editorial that she apparently never submitted for publication. "What spirit of evil entered into some of our best citizens that day, we can not conceive," Cronly continued. As African Americans recounted to her the events of the day, she came to believe that those who were killed had been "shot down like dogs."[103] She argued that Waddell's reasoning was absurd. Homes and families had not been in danger from African Americans; if that were true, why would they "have entrusted to them the care of their little children"?[104] Cronly argued that whites had wanted to follow Waddell's advice and mow down black voters at the polls with the Colt rapid-firing gun but that lawyers had advised separating the violence from election day so that their district would not lose its congressman as punishment. Cronly aptly observed that the murders' purpose was to teach African Americans an "object lesson" so that they would never vote again. Moreover, she pointed out that the attack came against people who owned property. But Jane Cronly must have been in the minority among the state's white women, for she reported ruefully that when whites talked about the violence against blacks that day, "females even . . . laugh over their sufferings."[105]

Wilmington's African American citizens fled the city. Those with horses sped to other towns to board trains headed North. Even then, getting away proved difficult. In New Bern, whites climbed up the railroad water tower so they could spot African Americans fleeing into town and shoot them.[106] Wilmington's poor black people, including more than 400 women and children, ran into the woods, where they lived for several days.[107] Survivors had no way of knowing whether more violence awaited them. Once they summoned the courage to return to their homes, it was difficult to know where the missing were: had they been driven away or killed?

Three days after the Wilmington massacre, an anonymous black woman sent a letter to President William McKinley begging for help. Why had he not sent troops; why had he left Wilmington's African Americans unprotected to "die like rats in a trap"? "We are loyal, we go where duty calls," she said, noting that many of Wilmington's young black men still served in the Third North Carolina Regiment. Now, with the damage done, McKinley could at least send a ship for the survivors, perhaps working out a way to take them to Africa, where "a number of us will gladly go." Then she hurled the rhetoric of patriotism back at the president of the United States: "Is this the land of the free and the home of the brave? How can the Negro sing my country tis of thee?" But to her heartbreaking complaint she added these words, equally heartbreaking: "The Negroes that have been banished are all property owners. . . . Had they been worthless Negroes, we would not care." Her cost accounting springs from the pathos of her predicament, so hopeless that we can scarcely imagine it. Is she less—or more—human for adding those class-biased words? She closed, "Today we are mourners in a strange land with no protection near. God help us. . . . I cannot sign my name and live."[108]

Black women had no forum and little recourse other than anonymous appeals to authorities outside the state, and no protection came. McKinley directed the U.S. attorney for the Eastern District of North Carolina to look into the affair, but the investigation bogged down. For his part, McKinley ignored a desperate Christmas Eve appeal from former Wilmingtonians R. H. Bunting and John R. Melton, white men who had been U.S. commissioner and police chief, respectively. Democrats especially hated Bunting because his common-law wife was black. The two begged McKinley for an audience and told of their banishment and the published death threat that hung over their heads.[109] Alfred Waddell settled in as mayor and began to be mentioned as a contender for the upcoming Senate seat. John

Dancy, the Petteys' friend who had been collector of the port of Wilmington, escaped to Salisbury.[110] Within a month after the riot, 1,400 African Americans left Wilmington. Six months later, prosperous African Americans were still departing by the scores in special rented cars attached to regular passenger trains going north and west.[111] Upon their departure, whites confiscated their property for unpaid taxes. The system worked so well that whites continued to fire black employees and hire whites, thus lending continuing momentum to the exodus.[112] Finally, the Third North Carolina Regiment returned home. From the North, Alexander Manly commented, "While the North Carolina negro troops were away fighting for the flag, the white man in the South rose up to drive the colored from the ballot box."[113]

Amid the turmoil of election week and the violence of the race riot, few people noticed an incident that recalled Alexander Manly's assertion that some rural white women freely loved black men. A week before the election, Mrs. Milton G. Brewer, the twenty-eight-year-old wife of a white farmer and the mother of four, ran away with Manly McCauley, a black day laborer who worked on her farm near Chapel Hill. Brewer and McCauley must have been madly in love and amazingly naive. They set out while her husband was away visiting a neighbor's farm. They spent four days together before a posse captured them less than sixty miles from home and took her to her father's house. Nothing was heard of McCauley's fate until his body was found four days later hanging from a tree beside a road.

Both Brewer's husband and her father were Republicans, apparently liberal on racial issues in politics. Whites concluded that Brewer's father had "reaped what he sowed" because years earlier he had confronted a mob chasing a black man accused of rape. In these parts, he had told the vigilantes, you could not tell about the white women; it might be rape or it might be love.[114] Josephus Daniels decided that this was one interracial incident best left unexploited. He held the story until after the election, and his coverage of it was brief. By the time the passion that Brewer and McCauley shared overwhelmed them, Alexander Manly had fled the state.[115]

The slaughter in Wilmington raised a storm of protest among African Americans across the nation as well as those in North Carolina. As soon as he heard of the massacre, author Charles Chesnutt wrote to publisher Walter Hines Page. By 1898 Chesnutt was an expatriate black North Carolinian living in Ohio; Page was an expatriate white North Carolinian living in New York City. Chesnutt poured out his anger: "It is an outbreak of pure, malignant and altogether indefensible race prejudice, which makes me feel personally humiliated, and ashamed for the country and the state."[116] When Page's next letter arrived twelve days later, the publisher chose not to mention the recent events or respond to Chesnutt's outpouring.[117] Three years later, Chesnutt published a fictional account of the riot, remarkably true-to-life, complete with miscegenation, murder, ignorant whites, and strong black women. His contrapuntal themes reflect the conflicting political cultures of an educated black doctor who urges caution and a black stevedore who calls for militant resistance.[118]

Fears of another violent outbreak and rumors of impending disfranchisement challenged African Americans who remained in the state. Democrats repeatedly had promised illiterate whites that once in power they would *not* limit the franchise by imposing a literacy test.[119] Now disfranchisement headed their agenda. Josephus Daniels visited Louisiana to study that state's disfranchising amendment and returned full of enthusiasm for the project.[120] Republican Daniel Russell sat impotent in the governor's mansion for two more years.

In the aftermath of the Wilmington violence, everyone looked to black congressman George White, who had won reelection from the "Black Second," to bring national scrutiny to bear on events in North Carolina.[121] People hoped that President William McKinley might condemn the violence in his December address before Congress, but he did not.[122] When Congress reconvened, White stood on the floor of the House, recounted the recent events in his state, and begged for "justice—simple justice."[123] The National Afro-American Council met in Washington, D.C., after Christmas. Council officers included Wilmington escapee John Dancy and Charlotte's George Clinton, still mourning the recent death of his young wife, Woman's Christian Temperance Union leader Annie Kimball Clinton. Ida B. Wells-Barnett gave a speech condemning the recent violence in Wilmington, and the council met with McKinley to beg him to speak out. Still McKinley remained silent and ignored his political debt to black Republicans.[124] With no word from McKinley to keep them in line, white Republicans at home panicked. Several called for a "lily-white" party at once, an action that African Americans characterized as the "blackest ingratitude."[125]

As these national political strategies came to naught, African Americans searched their own souls for explanations. Many black men blamed themselves for failing to live up to the requirements of being a Best Man, and their acceptance of that patriarchal ideal undercut their ability to mount an effective self-defense. John Dancy condemned Alexander Manly in the northern press for breaching manly standards. White men had reacted so strongly to Manly's editorial, Dancy argued, because they "will not permit their woman-hood to be slandered." Furthermore, Dancy said black leaders respected white men's protection of women and that chivalry worked to African Americans' advantage because "the better sentiment in the white race commends an attitude of defense of our womanhood." Then, in a comment that many interpreted as supportive of the Wilmington murderers, Dancy concluded, "The manhood of a race that will not defend its womanhood is unworthy of the respect of that womanhood."[126] Among African Americans, northerners generally felt Dancy's denunciation to be cowardly, but southerners tended to agree with him.[127]

Some previously outspoken black men in the state sought cover from white wrath. The editor of the *Star of Zion*, which had long bristled with political news and opinions, asked a white childhood friend to vouch for him in an open letter to the *Charlotte Daily Observer*. The editor's white friend testified to his sterling character and apolitical nature: "He has kept the line of making his paper distinctly religious, and has eschewed all matter of the Manly type."[128]

For others, it was not simply a matter of failing in politics but a matter of failing God. Many African Americans made little distinction between the world beyond and the world at hand. Rather than seeing the church merely as a convenient structure for political mobilization, they believed that God literally determined the outcome of elections. God had delivered them from slavery, and until this moment, many African Americans had clung to their high hopes for earthly progress. Like Puritan newcomers to Massachusetts, African Americans who came of age during Reconstruction felt that the world and God watched their every move. Thus, black spirituality in politics cut two ways: it gave African Americans the courage of their convictions, but it also made many assume the blame for events out of their control. They saw electoral politics as an aspect of spiritual striving, not as a secular, profane activity. Ballots were tools for building an ideal community on earth. The church was a political structure, and politics was a practical means to a religious end. To fail one was to fail the other.[129]

Some black ministers mounted jeremiads to remind their congregations that God's will was all-powerful and in so doing created guilt where none was warranted. God had sanctioned such horror to teach African Americans "a plain object lesson" through "suffering." They were like the "children of Israel. . . . When . . . that people pleased the Lord, He made them to triumph over all difficulties; but they fell before their enemies when they turned their backs upon his services."[130] African Americans were "passing through a calamitous ordeal, and there must be a cause." Since "God still lives and reigns supreme," the recent events must have been punishment for African American "ingratitude, sinfulness, [or] wayward lives."[131]

How had black North Carolinians displeased God? First, one minister argued, when African Americans helped vote down prohibition almost two decades earlier in 1881, they had lost their last chance to forge alliances with "the best white people." The alliance with the Populist Party had been "another great blunder." Inferior men had risen to the front, "irreligious, ignorant, and immoral political leaders." If they had united with the right kind of white men, those whites would "not have forsaken us when they could no longer use us."[132] Another commented, "What adds bitterness to our cup of woe is the sad fact that we brought it on ourselves"; "the Negro has been departing from God; Now God has departed from the Negro."[133] Their lament reveals both the empowerment and the bewilderment that come from believing that God is all-powerful.

What was left to do? Their strategy to seek the protection of the better class of whites had failed. Politics had failed. African Americans made one last direct appeal to God. The National Afro-American Council, with the support of leading ministers, declared a nationwide day of fasting, "a sincere, earnest probing of our own hearts, to see if there be any wicked way in us, a hearty confession of our own sins." After denouncing the evils of Jim Crow, disfranchisement, and lynching, the council appealed to "the operations of Providence to awaken us from our lethargy and bestir us to more manly endeavors as a people and as a race."[134] Charles Pettey signed the proclamation. Proud, political, and usually outspoken, the Petteys remained strangely silent after the Wilmington violence. Charles Pettey began to be ill more and more often. Congressman George White spoke for men like Pettey when he said, "I can no longer live in North Carolina and be a man."[135]

The white supremacy campaign taught many lessons even as it guaranteed white men their customary place at the top of the hierarchy. Middle- and upper-class white women learned that they would not be able to move into public space without the protection of white men. The New White Woman would act under the auspices of the New White Man, who promised her a role in state building as long as she pledged racial solidarity in return. White working-class men and women learned to pursue their racial rather than their class interests. Henceforth, they would have to live according to middle-class standards of propriety. If they failed to meet those expectations, the ever more intrusive power of the state would seek them out and shape them up.

African Americans learned that the new state would be biracial rather than interracial and that they would have to accept substandard and separate institutions. Black Best Men would have to leave North Carolina or outwardly conform to a place in society that was less than "manly." No government institutions remained that recognized class differences between African Americans, and the new Jim Crow laws deliberately obliterated class prerogatives.

Finally, there is a lesson for historians. Examining the race wars of the 1890s exclusively through the eyes of white supremacists does more than neglect the African American experience, it distorts the campaign's meaning by ignoring its context. What white men did and thought is important because they held the preponderance of power and used it so brutally. White men knew, however, what historians are discovering: that they did not act with impunity in a lily-white male world; rather, they reacted strategically in a racially and sexually mixed location. Moreover, the victories they won were not ordained or complete but began as precariously balanced compromises that papered over deep fissures in southern life. In fact, even the most committed leaders questioned what they had wrought. Charles Aycock acknowledged that the white supremacists had won a "glorious victory" but admitted that "the very extent of it frightens me."[136] In the end, white men may have constituted only half of the story. White women's support was crucial, as were the sophisticated political ideology, the complicated class and gender dynamics, and the rising resistance of African Americans. North Carolina's "white supremacy campaign" responded to black power even as it capitalized on black weakness.

five

NO MIDDLE GROUND

Political repression did more than alter black men's voting rights; it began to push African American men from the interracial public sphere. As citizens and as voters, African American men had represented their families in political and civic discourse. Silencing black men in public life changed their relationships with their families and their neighbors, with the Republican Party, with their churches, and with each other. Taking up the cause of disfranchisement after the violence of 1898, whites sought to impose a civil death sentence on both black men and black women. Once successful, whites came to see black men's disfranchisement as evidence of their unfitness for public life rather than as the cause of their exclusion from it. Precluded from participating in a rapidly changing "democratic" system, African Americans could no longer gain experience in self-government. After disfranchisement, whites could argue that it might be generations before African Americans acquired the requisite skills to become full citizens and thus "manly" men.

Concurrently, the Republican Party in North Carolina forcibly ejected African Americans from its ranks, snatching away their best weapon in the fight against the disfranchising amendment's effects. Their loss of party organization disrupted the core of black men's associational life. Since expulsion from electoral politics and expulsion from party politics occurred simultaneously, African Americans not only lost the vote but also lost the best way to regain it.

African Americans realized at once that disfranchisement would mean more than exclusion from elections. One black North Carolinian, James E. Shepard, characterized the limbo that African Americans faced this way: "We recognize the fact that there can be no middle ground between freedom and slavery. We cannot see that the best way to make a good man is to unman him."[1] After the disfranchisement campaign of 1900, African Americans began searching for that middle ground, for a place to stand after the earth and sky fell away. The varieties of black response underscore the ways in which limiting analysis to the electoral sphere impoverishes political history and creates a false dichotomy between the public and the private spheres.[2] Contestation over how best to maintain civic personhood produced new leaders and marginalized old ones as black men and women tried to invent a politics that decentered polls and parties. African American political culture survived, and black men and women began to shape strategies to meet the challenges of the new regime.

The new Democratic state legislature began crafting the disfranchising amendment early in 1899. Under the law, in order to vote, all men would be required to pay a poll tax and, except for those whose ancestors had been eligible to vote prior to 1 January 1867, to pass a literacy test. The amendment would take effect on 1 July 1902, but white men (whose ancestors could have voted) would not have to take the literacy test until 1908. This exemption—the grandfather clause—inflicted the greatest insult on black voters, even as it fostered their greatest hope. It was insulting because it meant that illiterate white men could vote unchallenged for six years, whereas college-educated African Americans must pass a literacy examination. At the same time, it sparked hope because African Americans thought it unconstitutional.[3] The U.S. Supreme Court had upheld poll taxes and literacy requirements in *Williams v. Mississippi* in 1898, but the constitutionality of the grandfather clause remained moot.[4] If the clause was the Achilles' heel of the amendment, its inclusion might lead the Court to expunge the entire law. Unlike other states that had disfranchised through a special constitutional convention, North Carolina scheduled a special popular election on the amendment for August 1900, largely because Democratic gubernatorial candidate Charles Aycock insisted that the people vote on it.[5]

To highlight the unfairness of the grandfather clause, some African Americans acknowledged the value of equitably administered literacy tests or property qualifications but declared that ancestral privilege as a voting qualification violated the Fifteenth Amendment. One black man remarked that it was "not the fault of the older class of voting Negroes that they are ignorant" since laws had forbidden their education under slavery. If the polity wanted the right kind of voters—those with good hearts and Christian intentions—he suggested, the legislature should enact a grandfather clause to disfranchise the descendants of those white slaveholders who had deliberately kept slaves illiterate.[6]

White Populists opposed the amendment on the grounds that one-fifth of the white voters of any party stripe could not read or write. Populist leaders were quick to point out that if the Court found the grandfather clause unconstitutional but let the literacy test stand, illiterate white men would lose the vote. It was a compelling argument, and it caused Furnifold Simmons to worry by the spring of 1900 that "the tide began to set alarmingly against us." The Democrats scrambled to call a special session of the legislature.[7] The solution they formulated was of dubious legal merit: the legislators announced that they intended to link the literacy test and the grandfather clause, come what may. They must "stand or fall together." In this way, the legislators tried to make clear their intentions so that if the federal judiciary struck the grandfather clause, it would have to strike the literacy test as well.[8] The effort might have meant little in a court test, but illiterate whites found it comforting and began to temper their opposition. In practice, it was the grandfather clause's short life—six years—that saved it. The clause would probably expire before the Supreme Court ruled on it. The six-year time limit also lent immediacy to Charles Aycock's proposed educational crusade for whites.[9] He later used the looming deadline as legislative blackmail to increase appropriations for public schooling. During the debates that produced the amendment, a few Democrats tried to extend the 1908 deadline to 1928, but when Aycock threatened to decline the party's nomination for governor if they did, talk of the extension died.[10]

When northerners questioned North Carolina's disfranchising amendment, the Democrats responded in reasoned tones that evoked good government and the integrity of the ballot.[11] With poor illiterate white men back home, however, the Democrats struck the same old note. To hell with constitutional issues, shouted Alfred Moore Waddell, stirring the embers of the 1898 conflagration. "The only issue is are you a white man or are you a negro?" he challenged the crowds. Waddell even conceded that North Carolina had violated the Fifteenth Amendment. That mattered little, he gloated, for "there aren't enough soldiers in the U.S. Army to make whites give up the vote."[12]

Aycock, the man with the common touch, left Waddell to rant in the east while he traveled to the west to gain support for the August referendum. In

a region where few African Americans lived and illiterate white mountaineers held civil rights dear, race baiting left Democratic traps empty. But
Aycock had a deal up his sleeve. As he described it later, "I promised the
illiterate poor man . . . that life should be brighter for him and the partner of
his sorrows and joys. I pledged the wealth of the State to the education of
his children."[13] The entire enterprise was a tough sell, east or west. One
white man remarked that it seemed as if the Wilmington race riot had been
started to "give old man Waddell bread and meat." According to his reasoning, the amendment fight was simply Waddell's dessert.[14]

Senator Marion Butler tried to defeat the amendment by pitting poor
white Populists against middle-class black Republicans, a spectacularly unsuccessful strategy. "What class of negroes would be left to vote?" he
inquired of the farmers who followed him. It would be "the trifling town
negro . . . who talks loud and takes up all of the sidewalk" who passed the
literacy test, not the good agrarian African American. Moreover, he reminded Populists that their whiteness went cheap; it bought only six years
under the grandfather clause. Those white boys under twelve who could
not learn to read and write would then be "put on a plane lower than the
town darkey with his eye glasses and cocked hat," Butler predicted.[15]

African Americans tried to make common cause with poor white voters,
especially Republicans in the western part of the state. They warned illiterate whites not to believe the Democrats' guarantees that disfranchisement
would not exclude them. If whites wanted proof of Simmons's lack of
trustworthiness, they might recall his 1898 promise not to disfranchise African Americans. One black writer taunted Simmons with the prospect that
whites would soon realize that "if you will fool the illiterate Negroes . . . you
will fool them also."[16]

Despite scattered efforts, African Americans could not mount an effective campaign against the amendment. Unfortunately, with the collapse
of fusion and the 1898 terror, black leadership fell into disarray.[17] In 1899,
only three African Americans served in the state legislature. The most
outspoken was Isaac Smith, a flamboyant, hot-tempered, and often irra-
tional New Bernian whom George White, the Dudleys, and the Petteys
detested.[18] Smith led a black delegation to testify before the legislature,
where they made matters worse. One delegate simply professed his wistful
confidence in white men's wisdom. Another reported that of the 125,000
African Americans who voted in the state, perhaps 25,000 had the education to pass the literacy test. Therefore, the legislature should disfranchise
the 100,000 and stop short of "persecution" of the other 25,000. When reports of the testimony surfaced, one black man complained, "They would
have done . . . more good to have stayed at home and kept their mouths

shut." Such hypocritical men led African Americans "to political martyr-dom with the wool over their eyes." If blacks had to "perish politically," he ventured, they should die "with their eyes open."[19] Horrified at the black delegates' testimony before the legislature, the *Star of Zion* promised to "make it warm for every Negro . . . that goes to Raleigh to misrepresent his race. This is not a time for Negro apologists."[20]

The major reason why North Carolina's African American leaders failed to mount effective opposition to the amendment, however, was that the Republican Party discouraged them from doing so.[21] When the amend-ment finally went to the people for a vote in August 1900, white Republi-cans advised African Americans to let them handle the opposition cam-paign. Republican governor Daniel Russell admitted that a Democratic "reign of terror" had targeted African Americans and that they remained "helpless" to register and vote down the amendment. He believed ratifica-tion was inevitable but held out hope that the courts would find the law unconstitutional.[22] Republican senator Jeter C. Pritchard, closely allied to black leaders, lay decidedly low.[23] He cautioned that any African American activism would spur a reaction that might retard their civil rights for a century.[24]

Part of the problem was the Republican Party's own lack of cohesion. White Republicans in western North Carolina and black Republicans in eastern North Carolina had reluctantly boarded the same party boat, and now whites tried to beat African Americans to the life rafts. Western Re-publicans saw the literacy requirement as Democratic revenge for their affiliation with eastern African Americans. The sooner the campaign was over the better. With the black man out of politics, they reasoned, whites in the rapidly industrializing Piedmont would begin to vote Republican. Across the west, Republican newspapers urged the party to expel black members.[25] In the east, the white party hierarchy, closely allied with black voters, feared that open African American opposition would increase west-ern white Republicans' resolve.[26] In the end, many African Americans decided to stay out of it in the hope that enough whites would vote against the amendment in their own self-interest.[27] National reaction to disfran-chisement was muted, partly because the federal government wanted to restrict suffrage in Hawaii and the Philippines. In fact, the national white press generally complimented North Carolina on its progressive attempt to revise suffrage.[28] No national African American organization existed that could challenge the amendment in the federal courts.[29]

The Democrats, however, left nothing to chance.[30] For weeks before the election, they armed New Bern whites to the hilt. The Naval Reserves drilled every night and concluded each evening by firing a volley at 11:00

P.M. During the day and early evening, random shots frequently rang out across the city. White republican William E. Clarke reported, "They had the negroes scared to death. I found it almost impossible to get anyone to distribute our tickets." On election day, in addition to armed intimidation, some registrars would allow only Democrats, not Republicans, to approach the polls. Boxes in some precincts were poorly labeled; in others, voters had to hand their ballots to a poll worker who put them into whichever box he chose. After the polls closed, a restless group of African Americans milled about the courthouse. Panicky Democratic election officials reported that the group "threatened to kill them unless they count[ed] their vote." Nonetheless, the registrars threw out three Republican precincts, making the crowd "cursing mad." When the results were in, the amendment triumphed in New Bern by 1,600 votes. Clarke commented sardonically that since the election was rigged anyway, the margin might have "been 16,000; but they had consciences. . . . It was a mockery from start to finish."[31]

Similar reports poured into Republican and Populist headquarters across the state. In Wilmington, for example, only 30 of 3,000 eligible African Americans registered to vote, and when their votes were "counted," only two had been cast against the amendment.[32] If African Americans had been allowed to vote in any numbers in the east, the amendment might have failed since it passed with only 59 percent of the votes statewide.[33] In New Bern, Clarke concluded that he could "not blame the negroes for not voting" since their votes would go uncounted anyway and the price of voting might be death. He held New Bern native Furnifold Simmons personally responsible for the "perfect farce of an election" and uttered disfranchisement's benediction: God will "exact a strict account of [Simmons] and he will have to pay it to the last penny."[34]

Awaiting the deferred retribution of a just God offered scant solace to African Americans, however, and they sought support outside the state. North Carolina's most prominent black leader, Congressman George White, announced that unless the Supreme Court quickly found the amendment unconstitutional, he would follow Moses's example and lead 50,000 of the state's African Americans to the North.[35] For White, who had started his career as the principal of the New Bern normal school with Sarah Dudley as his assistant, migration represented the only alternative to disfranchisement. He told the House, "They have spoken of my people as a thing to be managed. . . . Can they manage us like oxen?" he asked. "I want them to understand that, removed as we are thirty-five years from slavery, we are to day as you are, men."[36]

Even though white men discounted African American appeals to shared manhood, white women might still recognize similar entreaties to shared womanhood, but only if they considered them outside the sphere of electoral politics. Just after the amendment passed, Mary Lynch addressed the international WCTU convention in Edinburgh, Scotland.[37] No longer able to work with white women in her hometown of Salisbury, Lynch had to travel across the Atlantic Ocean in order to discuss shared concerns. Lynch's journey is a metaphor for the problem of knitting gender and class ties across racial lines. Race had one meaning in Salisbury, where organizing for temperance brought up issues of political power and black voting, and another in Edinburgh, where white women could recognize Lynch as a missionary working fervently for women's issues.

Locally, few strategies emerged to combat disfranchisement. The black women of Edenton formed the Woman's Prayer and Consecration Society of America and planned to pray for "the poor colored man in his mighty struggle for his political rights."[38] Some tried direct intervention at the ballot box. In Lexington, a black attorney fell into an argument with a white registrar when he accompanied a group of black men to register for the November election. When the registrar began asking questions such as, "Have you been in the penitentiary?," the black attorney intervened and accused him of deliberately slowing down the process to prevent registration. A white Democratic "poll watcher" slugged the attorney on the spot and later hunted him down and murdered him.[39] After the murder, the regular November election passed quietly, Charles Aycock went to the governor's mansion in January 1901 with a solidly Democratic legislature behind him, and Furnifold Simmons left for the U.S. Senate. William Clarke in New Bern counted the Republicans lucky that they had been cheated out of only 1,000 votes in that election.[40] African Americans stopped patronizing white-owned stores when they could buy from black merchants, leading some black businessmen to conclude sardonically that "oppression has it[s] virtues."[41]

After the amendment took effect in 1902, the *News and Observer* crowed that only 4.6 percent of North Carolina's African Americans remained registered to vote. Josephus Daniels had every reason, however, to minimize the number of black voters to underscore the success of the amendment.[42] African Americans seemed to believe that their voting strength remained stronger. Indeed, they wanted to maximize the number of black voters to retain the illusion of political power. An editorial in the *Star of Zion* estimated that 65,000 North Carolina African Americans were literate and could retain the vote.[43] This guess was not far from the truth, since census figures later showed 59,597 literate blacks of voting age.[44] Fraud, violence, and fear prevented them from voting. No official records indicate the actual numbers of blacks who managed to register in 1902, but the few surviving voter registration books reveal that the black voter was rare in that election and the next.[45]

As they watched the political turmoil climax in their hometown and state, the Petteys endured personal tragedy. In July, just as the amendment campaign heated up, Sarah Dudley Pettey and three of her children came down with a fever, and Charles fell ill a few weeks later. By November, ten family members had been stricken with the malady, diagnosed as malaria but probably yellow fever.[46] Despite their illnesses, both Charles and Sarah went north to the African Methodist Episcopal (AME) Zion conference in September. For the first time during their travels in North Carolina, the Petteys rode on a Jim Crow car, the result of the 1899 legislature's segregation of the railroads.[47] At the conference, Sarah vanquished strong opposition to her reelection as secretary of the Woman's Home and Foreign Missionary Society, the post through which she wrote her "Woman's Column." Most likely opposition to her reelection centered on the content of her columns, which everyone considered "spicy."[48] Charles fought a battle to increase the number of bishops within the church, lost, and left bitterly disappointed.[49]

Shortly after they returned home, Charles Pettey suffered a relapse. Yet, strangely, early in December he and Sarah insisted on traveling to a conference in his new South Carolina territory. AME Zion members assembled in Clio, the quietest place on earth. Although Clio was named for history's muse, history had forgotten Clio. It was just a road, really, where a few streets branched off unimaginatively at right angles and petered out in flat, sandy fields. Clio's black and white people separated themselves lackadaisically, simply by choosing opposite ends of the settlement. Down one of those short streets stood a white clapboard church surrounded by live oaks trailing wispy Spanish moss.

Arriving for the conference, Charles Pettey entered the packed church slowly, from the back, and made his way toward the main altar looming in front of him. His step faltered as he walked down the aisle with one hand on Sarah's arm. His other hand gripped the backs of the wooden pews. His skin was yellow. His bones were visible through his suit. People began to cry at the sight of him. Finally seated at the front, Pettey rested some moments, then leaned on Sarah's shoulder and pulled himself up out of his pew. In a weak voice, one that "did not even faintly resemble the trumpet voice" of which he had been so proud, Charles Pettey began to sing his favorite hymn. "Strong men wept like children" as he sang "When I am in my grave, weep not for me." Quickly, some men in the congregation swept

Sarah Dudley Pettey and her children, circa 1900. *Clockwise from left:* Theophytra, Charles, stepdaughters Sarah and Mamie, Calvin, Elveta, and Ethel. Courtesy of Corine Pettey, New York, New York.

him up and took him to a nearby house, where he lingered near death. Sarah Dudley Pettey took his place at the conference table, assigning ministers to new churches throughout the state. Slipping in and out of consciousness, Pettey called for George W. Clinton, the young Charlotte bishop who was his protégé, but Clinton arrived too late for Pettey to recognize him. Finally, on 8 December, Pettey struggled to sit up. Then he said clearly, "I will lay down here and put up my tools, believing that God doeth all things for the best. God bless my wife. God bless my dear wife and children." Then he fell back dead.[50]

Sarah was "almost frantic" on the long train ride back to New Bern with Charles's body. Two thousand people attended the funeral, where she and the children were "bathed in tears." The AME Zion Church declared thirty days of mourning, and across the nation, congregations gave freewill offerings for the widow and her seven children.[51] Some suggested that Sarah Dudley Pettey had earned a paying position in the church, perhaps that of financial secretary. Surely she was competent, and the church would be proving that it was "able to appreciate . . . intelligence and worth, whether in a woman or man, by thus honoring this accomplished woman."[52] But Sarah Dudley Pettey was not offered a position in the AME Zion Church. In fact, four years after her husband's death, she still had not received all of the back pay due to him.[53] She took the cash that she had and commissioned a large tombstone to mark Charles Pettey's grave. On it, she had carved these words: "Look up on high and remember that I am here when I am gone."[54]

If history were fiction, it would be tempting to draw a parallel between the political death of African Americans in North Carolina and the physical death of Charles Pettey. The novelist would surely create Pettey to represent the courage of the freedpeople, the embodiment of black patriotism, African American trust in democracy, and black Christians' belief in the sanctity of natural rights. If the novelist invented disfranchisement, she would have to write Pettey's death since such a figure could not live under those conditions. But the historian must limit her speculations to a more concrete sphere, one in which metaphorical leaps are fettered by the ropes of evidence. Still, it *is* difficult to imagine Charles Pettey living in the world the disfranchisers made. His death spared him that. From the mountains of postbellum North Carolina where he exchanged ferry rides to learn his letters, to the California settlement he pioneered in the 1880s, to Atlanta, where he answered Booker T. Washington, Charles Pettey had acted with courage and a sense of fairness. Now courage could bring death at a registrar's table and distorted standards of fairness excluded him. But if the waves of white supremacy crashed in to fill the void that Pettey's passing left in the public sphere, nothing could fill his place at home. Sarah mourned his death profoundly, and she envisioned him in a "land of delight where no storm clouds rise, to disturb or distress a sainted one," far away from turbulent North Carolina.[55]

Postdisfranchisement North Carolina was turbulent. When black leaders looked to the Republican Party, it looked away. Two black Best Men, John Dancy, collector of the port of Wilmington, and James Young, commander of the Third North Carolina Regiment, arrived at the state Republican Executive Committee's 1901 meeting. Both men had served previously on the committee and had shepherded votes and dispensed patronage across the state, but Senator Pritchard had failed to invite them to the meeting. When they arrived uninvited, he jumped up and locked them out of the room.[56] Pritchard declared the Republican Party "lily-white" and called on all black federal officeholders in the state to resign their posts at once.[57] The next year, when duly-elected black delegates arrived at the 1902 convention, whites ejected them. As the dejected black men left the convention hall, the band played and the white delegates sang, "Coon, coon, coon, I wish my color would fade. . . . Morning, night or noon, It's better to be a white man, Than a coon, coon, coon."[58] Such actions prompted George White to blast Pritchard as "an evil one . . . whom I have helped to elevate from obscurity from the mountain crags of western North Carolina to his present position. . . . Truly a wolf in sheep's clothing."[59] Somehow, Pritchard and John Dancy came to terms since Dancy became Washington, D.C.'s, recorder of deeds, an ascent that needed Pritchard's propulsion.[60]

While Pritchard purged black voters, President Theodore Roosevelt promised Booker T. Washington that there would be no lily-white Republicanism. To add insult to injury, Pritchard traveled to Alabama, Washington's home ground, to extol the virtues of expelling African Americans from the party. Washington fired off a letter to John Dancy warning that Pritchard "has done a great deal of harm in this state" and wondering why Dancy had not led a ground swell of indignation against him in North Carolina. Washington considered it Dancy's responsibility to stop Pritchard, even if Dancy's "relations with Senator Pritchard" put him in "an awkward position." In his vaguely menacing way, Washington ordered Dancy to act "for your sake as well as for that of the race."[61] No fool, Dancy acted. He arranged a meeting between the president and Bishops George W. Clinton and Alexander Walters. Roosevelt promised them that black Republicans could attend southern conventions and retain federal offices.[62] Just ten days after Washington wrote to Dancy, black Raleigh Republicans brandished a letter from one of Roosevelt's top aides condemning Pritchard's lily-white policy.[63] After the 1902 elections, Roosevelt castigated lily-white

Republicanism more strongly and purged many of its supporters. He tried to force Pritchard to recant, but the senator hedged a bit, arguing that he could not support federal appointments of black officials over his constituents' protests. At the same time, he pledged all of North Carolina's Republican electors to Roosevelt's 1904 candidacy.[64]

Despite their banishment from the Republican Party, some African Americans tried to give the impression that blacks remained a political factor in the state. W. B. Crittendon of Salisbury formed the Colored Voters' League of North Carolina and proposed that blacks vote on issues across party lines. The *Star of Zion* crowed that African Americans' Democratic votes in the 1902 election would tip the balance of power against the Republicans, surely an exaggerated claim.[65] After Roosevelt's election in 1904, black Republicans suggested that he appoint a state executive committee of "true Republicans" and declare the lily-white organization a fraud.[66]

If the Republicans had not acted so quickly to exclude African Americans, they might have mitigated the effects of disfranchisement. One black leader compared disfranchisement to the "shock of an earthquake," arguing that the black man did not "know to what extent he is hurt.... Some are only waiting to see just how greatly they are damaged, before making a move."[67] As African Americans were trying to assess the damage, the organizing institution of black political life, the Republican Party, ousted them. Counterfactual analysis is a risky business, but it is useful to imagine how sustained black participation in the Republican Party might have affected the amendment's administration. The party had been a viable alternative in North Carolina for two generations, and almost half of the African American men of voting age were literate. Republican pressure might have mandated fair administration of the literacy test, resulting in black registration.[68] Continued black voting would have increased the chances of appointing Republican registrars, especially in places like New Bern, where there was a long history of interracial cooperation between the two parties.[69] Moreover, as Republicans, African Americans would have maintained political ties to national leaders and a venue for political debate.

African Americans took the Republicans' action as hard as they had taken the amendment's passage. William F. Fonvielle, roving correspondent for the *Star of Zion*, interviewed the man on the street after the 1902 convention. He approached black men throughout Greensboro, notebook in hand. Some were afraid to respond. One said, "Please say for me that I am more hurt than astounded." At the corner of Nile and Egypt streets, Fonvielle encountered a street musician strumming a guitar, a hat two sizes too small perched on his head. The musician opined that he tried to ignore politics and enigmatically sung, "I'm gwine live until I die," in answer to

Fonvielle's questions. At the train station, as Fonvielle watched the north-bound train pull out, the black porter swung out of the car door and called back, "It's not my funeral, I live in Jersey."[70]

As it turned out, living in "Jersey" became the most attractive alternative to thousands of the state's African Americans. George White made good on his promise and founded a settlement in southern New Jersey known as Whitesboro.[71] Although historians have tended to consider black migra-tion from the South during and after World War I as the "Great Migration," Carter Godwin Woodson, writing in 1918, dated the "Migration of the Talented Tenth" prior to that time.[72] Woodson argued that it was "the intelligent laboring class" that made up most of this early migration.[73] Woodson's periodization aptly characterizes the North Carolina situation. Between 1900 and 1910, 27,827 African Americans left the state, 14,792 men and 13,035 women. In the following decade, 1910 to 1920, 29,162 African Americans emigrated. Even with the upheaval and opportunity that World War I brought, the increase in black migration in the second decade of the century was less than 2,000 people. More men left the state in the first decade than in the second.[74] George White's words, "I cannot live in North Carolina and be a man," resonated for many other African Ameri-can Best Men in the state.[75] Certainly economic factors and kinship net-works affected emigration, but to many, the answer to the question, "Why are hundreds of the best Negroes . . . leaving this State?," was plain and simple. "It is because of the institution of jim crow cars, the passage of the disfranchise amendment, and the bitter political campaigns of 1898 and 1900," the *Star of Zion* responded.[76]

Those who were the first to leave were probably the best educated. In 1917, in an address to the Southern Sociological Congress, a white lawyer and racial philosopher from Winston-Salem noted the rapid black exodus from the state. He observed, however, that by that time the number of "young, collegebred negro men and women going north . . . is probably not as great, proportionately, as it was a decade ago." He attributed the de-crease in the flow to the "constant insistence" of schools modeled upon Washingtonian ideas that "the south is the best section for the negro."[77] Indeed, Washington doggedly insisted that blacks could be more success-ful in the South, despite political and personal persecution. In a letter to W. E. B. Du Bois in 1910, Charles Chesnutt scoffed at Washington and termed him "a professional optimist." Chesnutt, the former North Caro-linian, confided, "Personally, I have not been any farther South than Wash-ington but once in twenty-seven years."[78]

It would be impossible to generalize about 27,827 individual decisions to leave home, but a debate on a hot summer night in 1901 revealed the tensions over the issue among African Americans in Charlotte. Two young women, Addie Sagers and Laura Arnold, squared off on the topic, "Is the South the Best Home for the Negro?," at the Price Lyceum, a Chautauqua-style summer lecture series for African Americans. The issue engaged the entire community, including those who would ultimately stay behind, and women participated actively in the debate over the decision to move.

Sagers took the Washingtonian position. She pointed out that the only employment open to blacks in the North was as a "bell boy, waiter, a cook or a house maid. Even the drudgery work is done by foreigners." Few African Americans could hold professional positions in the North. For example, in Chicago, she claimed, there were only eleven black teachers. Unions also excluded African Americans, she argued. She might have used North Carolina expatriate Alexander Manly's plight as evidence, since he was forced to attempt to pass for white to find work as a painter in unionized Philadelphia.[79] Sagers pointed to the black-owned Richmond bank and Coleman Cotton Mill as enterprises that would have been impossible to build in the North. Then she tried to diffuse her opposition: "My opponents no doubt will say the Negro is being disfranchised in the South. I heartily cooperate with that law, because the Negroes see clearly the necessity of educating their children."[80]

Sagers's opponent, Laura Arnold, devastated her. "The South may be a 'land of flowers' for the Anglo-Saxon, but for the Negro—at his touch, the flowers fold their petals and wither away, and he finds himself, with bleeding hands grasping the prickly thorns," Arnold countered. She had little patience for the argument that blacks owned more land in the South since they could not enjoy security on that land. "Displease by look, word, or deed a white man," Arnold reminded her audience, "and if he so desires, before nightfall, your property is likely to be reduced to ashes, and the owner a mangled corpse." Lynching and segregation had increased while educational and employment opportunities had decreased, and the ultimate symbol of southern degradation was disfranchisement. The black southerner's "judges of his illiteracy are his enemies, one of whom recently said, no Negro could explain a clause of the Constitution to *his* satisfaction." If lucky enough to register, African Americans risked their lives to cast votes that went uncounted, Arnold noted.

Move North at once, Arnold urged, escape impending doom! She acknowledged that the unknown was frightening but argued that if the Puritans could cross the ocean in small boats, surely North Carolina's African Americans could board northbound trains. Even if God had intended that living in the South serve as a test of black faith, he never meant for things to go this far. The South was now a "crucible . . . [where] many of us . . . will be burned to cinders." She concluded, "My friends! You sleep over a volcano, which may erupt at any moment, and only your lifeless bodies will attest that you believed the South to be the best home for the Negro." Arnold's masterpiece received more points than any other speech that night. Two weeks later, Arnold, who had been employed as the printer's "angel" at the *Star of Zion*, took her own advice and moved to Washington, D.C.[81]

Facing such emotionally charged issues without the traditional support of a party structure, North Carolina's black men and women cast about for new leaders with fresh styles. The glare of Booker T. Washington's immense personal power has eclipsed other black southern leaders and obscured his followers' understanding and practice of his philosophy.[82] The North Carolina case suggests that Washington secured his iron grip on southern African Americans partially by default. Black Best Men such as George White and Alexander Manly who were passionate about politics and functioned as the ideological counterweight to Washingtonianism left the South after disfranchisement.[83] At the same time, Reconstruction Era activists such as Charles Pettey passed from the scene. Certainly the lack of access to the formal electoral process diverted the attention of many who remained behind away from the political sphere and toward business development and religion.[84] For example, the pages of the *Star of Zion*, once packed with political news and opinion, became almost exclusively devoted to church affairs. The editorial page, a former hearth for fire-eating pundits, adopted a new masthead with a drawing of an open Bible.[85]

It is probable, however, that the silence in print provided white noise for a ferocious face-to-face debate. Many of those who remained went underground. As for the changes in the *Star of Zion*, a telling clue exists. John Dancy, writing from his safe post in Washington, D.C., passionately responded to an attempt to ban political discourse in the AME Zion Church. In the denominational magazine, he reminded his readers, "All we have and are, came through politics, and it is too late in the day to try to curry favor with somebody by declaring the opposite of a recognized truth." Dancy revealed what his church meant to him and to people like Charles Pettey: "Zion Church is and always has been an organized protest against religious, political and manhood inequality and injustice."[86]

As one might suspect, Sarah Dudley Pettey did not fit well into the postdisfranchisement, externally apolitical church. Since Charles died just after a quadrennial AME Zion conference, Sarah retained her editorship of the "Woman's Column" until 1904, but she wrote infrequently. She went north for some time to live with her friend Mary Small.[87] The church owed Pettey's estate more than $3,000, and Dudley Pettey now faced the difficulty of supporting her large family. She sold All Healing Spring and traveled throughout the country speaking to churches for the money that could be collected from the congregation.[88] In 1904, Sarah spent part of Christmas with *Star* editor J. W. Smith's family, and he appealed to the bishops to approve a pension for "this struggling widow."[89] At the next conference in 1904, the activist women in the church adroitly allowed Dudley Pettey to remain in her unpaid position but added another secretary's seat that would encompass editorship of the "Woman's Column." That spot went to Annie Blackwell, who had edited the *WCTU Tidings*.[90]

In 1906, Sarah became quite ill and died in a matter of a few weeks. She was only thirty-seven years old. John Dancy recalled in her obituary that he had known her since she was a little girl. He lamented, "Mrs. Pettey has never been quite herself since [Pettey's] sudden demise. . . . They were quite wedded to each other, and their ambitions and hopes ran along the same channels." The Petteys, he continued, "were public spirited, yea high spirited. . . . They cared for money only as a means to provide their comforts and aid them in gratifying their ambitions." With her husband's death, Dancy added cryptically, "Mrs. Pettey realized fully her great loss, and was never entirely herself again."[91]

How could Sarah Dudley Pettey have remained "herself" amid the shambles of her dreams? In the space of a few years, she had gone from lecturing on woman suffrage and African Americans' civil rights at the side of her powerful husband to being alone in a world in which black men could not vote. Her dreams—her *self*—had died in 1900 with the death of Charles Pettey and the passage of disfranchisement. There is no tombstone beside Charles Pettey's to mark Sarah's grave—the money was gone by then—and we have no record of her last words as we do of his. But Sarah wrote her own valedictory in the bleak period after her husband's death: "Strive to live long; if not in years, live in manly acts and noble deeds, remembering ever that knowledge truly is life."[92] Dudley Pettey's noble deeds died with her, and she vanished from the written record—into a vortex of silence.

Disfranchisement and party expulsion abruptly whisked a people with a well-developed political heritage out of "politics" as traditionally defined. Did that mean that they ceased to act politically? In fact, it meant that their political activity increased. Artificially excluded from the electoral realm, African Americans found that the rest of life took on a more political cast. Disfranchisement seemed to spur whites to vilify the African American family, putting the "private" sphere in the middle of public life. As African Americans lost their own public voices, whites' cacophonous reports of their lives and culture arose from the South to fill the vacuum. In a period when northern imaginations thrived on accounts of barbarity in the new territories and northern muscle flexed at the prospect of shouldering the "white man's burden" while counting the profits from pineapple and sugar plantations, white southerners breathed a sigh of relief at their intellectual redemption. Now all fair Americans of northern European heritage shared a common instructional task—uplifting darker peoples from barbarity. White southerners might even teach their countrymen a thing or two about it.[93]

But first the South had to establish its credentials on the subject. White southerners had to prove that black southerners had been and remained barbarians and that the South had dealt with this situation extremely well, given its limited resources and misguided northern interference at every turn. Perfecting this rationalization required that southern whites draw attention away from African American accomplishments and toward black shortcomings.[94] A ground swell of literature emerged to argue these points.

No one made the argument better than North Carolinian Thomas Dixon, Jr.[95] Living in New York, haunted by the black family cook's son's claims of kinship, in 1902 Dixon drew inspiration from the Wilmington massacre and the amendment campaign to write *The Leopard's Spots: A Romance of the White Man's Burden, 1865–1900*. Three years later, he followed up with *The Clansman: An Historical Romance of the Ku Klux Klan*.[96] To write "fiction," Dixon had only to read the propaganda Furnifold Simmons had disseminated in the white supremacy and disfranchisement campaigns. What made Dixon's work so pernicious was that he told the truth—half-way—by appropriating pieces of reality. But he reversed the power dynamics and outcomes to make heroes villains, villains heroes, and lies truth.

As easily as he borrowed historical events, Dixon appropriated characters. In *The Leopard's Spots*, he simply changed the names of North Carolina political figures. His hero, Charlie Gaston, is Charles Aycock with a fictionalized love life, but he metamorphoses into Alfred Moore Waddell for a few pages to lead the Wilmington race riot. The rape and murder of little Flora Camp closely parallel the 1898 Concord rape and murder that Simmons's machine spent as political capital. Alexander Manly is in the pages, as are the women's sidewalk altercations and Lincoln Academy, the American Missionary Association school a few miles from Dixon's family home. Even Mrs. Habicht, the bartender's wife brought before New Bern's black magistrate for disturbing the peace, makes an appearance.[97]

Since many of the events actually occurred, readers could not separate fiction from fact and were unaware that Dixon had reversed the outcomes to make African Americans seem powerful and abusive. Dixon portrays 500 rioting black soldiers from the Third North Carolina Regiment invading Wilmington. There *was* violence between whites and black North Carolinians in uniform, but it was African Americans who bore the brunt of it. There *was* a riot in Wilmington, but Alfred Moore Waddell benefited from it, whereas Charles Gaston, his fictional counterpart, was a victim of it. When it was over, Waddell went to the mayor's office, not to the jail where Dixon imprisons the beleaguered and lovelorn Gaston.

When Dixon links North Carolina's racial "problem" with that facing the rest of the nation after the Spanish-American/Cuban War, he explicitly makes Simmons's point, with the new territories in mind. "Hear me, men of my race, Norman and Celt, Angle and Saxon, Dane and Frank, Huguenot and German martyr blood!" shouts Gaston/Aycock from the stump. "It took Spain eight hundred years to expel the Moors. When the time comes the Anglo-Saxon can do in one century what the Spaniard did in eight." Then Dixon resurrects poor, drunken Mrs. Habicht: "Shall we longer tolerate the arrest of white women by negro officers and their trial before negro magistrates? Let the manhood of the Aryan race with its four thousand years of authentic history answer that question!"[98]

Thomas Dixon fictionalized Furnifold Simmons's and Alfred Moore Waddell's political rhetoric and rearranged the power relations to make the white man the underdog. Dixon bragged that his old friend from Watauga Club days, publisher Walter Hines Page, found *The Leopard's Spots* so engrossing that he could not take his eyes off the manuscript long enough to cross a New York City street and walked into the path of a streetcar. Page did indeed find the work's gossip about his North Carolina acquaintances fascinating, but Dixon fabricated Page's collision with the streetcar.[99] Dixon, who was too pugnacious to fear libel, admitted himself that he wrote from reality and called himself a historian.[100] In a letter to Gabrielle De Rosset Waddell, Dixon wrote that he was an "ardent admirer" of Waddell and that the "Wilmington revolutionists did a very important work in the preservation of our civilization."[101] Dixon explored the same themes in *The Clansman*, the book that spawned the film *The Birth of a Nation*.

African Americans in North Carolina condemned *The Leopard's Spots* as "one of the meanest books."[102] Many white and black southerners saw it as a shameless attempt to capitalize on the recent political violence. Charles Chesnutt wrote to a congressman who admired the book, telling him that although Dixon drew on North Carolina's racial politics, he had gotten things backward. Dixon was right, Chesnutt acknowledged, in claiming that a great deal of "intermingling" of white and black blood had taken place, but it had "been done with the entire consent and cheerful cooperation of the white race."[103] Of course, African Americans offered Dixon's black alleged half brother as their prime example.[104]

At first, southern whites realized that Dixon had duped them also. In

1905, when a play adapted from *The Clansman* toured in the upper South, the press condemned the author for misrepresenting southern life and stirring up animosity. In Columbia, South Carolina, the audience hissed Dixon when he appeared on the stage, and "many prominent young [white] men" went to his hotel to call him out to fight. Everywhere people feared violence. Even in Wilmington, the press predicted that Dixon would be subjected to worse than hissing if the play continued to tour the South, and others thought that "innocent blood" might be shed as a result of it. The minister of a large Atlanta Baptist church called it a disgrace and begged Dixon to "give the negro a rest from abuse and incendiarism!" African Americans applauded this reaction and took it to mean that "hope is revived" and that the "Dixon stripe" was fading among whites.[105] To their dismay, however, in Atlanta life followed "art," and the city erupted into a vicious race riot shortly after *The Clansman* played there.[106]

Dixon quelled opposition to his play by soliciting the attendance of politicians who had a stake in the audiences' acceptance of the narrative as truth. He toured state capitols and sought the endorsement of governors. In Raleigh, Aycock's successor, Robert B. Glenn, called the play "great historical truth"; in Atlanta, Governor Joseph M. Terrell stood and applauded loudly at its conclusion.[107] These men, riding the white supremacy wave to power, needed to reconstruct Reconstruction in order to justify their own recent actions.

Dixon used the same strategy—preempting criticism by getting elected officials to endorse his work—when *The Clansman* became the film, *The Birth of a Nation*. He scheduled a showing at the White House for southerner and former Johns Hopkins classmate Woodrow Wilson. Dixon later recalled an audience of Supreme Court justices and congressmen watching a preliminary screening, and his mind reeled at their emotional and uncritical reactions. Dixon reported that he "realized for the first time . . . that we had not only discovered a new universal language of man, but that [the film] would be equally resistless to an audience of chauffeurs or a gathering of a thousand college professors."[108]

The Birth of a Nation became an overnight sensation, the highest grossing film to that date. The National Association for the Advancement of Colored People organized boycotts against it in many cities, and municipal censors often found it incendiary.[109] When New York City censors tried to close *The Birth of a Nation* before its world premiere, Dixon's attorney argued that it had been shown in the White House; a hurried telephone call there answered by Woodrow Wilson's daughter verified that fact.[110] As it swept the nation in 1914, white audiences wept and cheered the story, and the film spurred the growth of the second Ku Klux Klan.[111] In fifteen years, white southerners had gone from pariahs to patriots in the national imagination, and white northerners had taken up the "white man's burden." Dixon's blistering spotlight on North Carolina's past scorched the historical landscape beyond recognition.

Across the nation, African Americans lacked a forum to counteract such propaganda, and they found that whites listened only when racial portrayals fit racist stereotypes of debasement. Even well-meaning whites began to advocate the betterment of African American homes to turn back the supposed tide of black debauchery. Mary Helm, a southern white woman dedicated to missionary work among southern African Americans, argued that if disfranchisement "turned the Negro from politics to home-building it was a blessing to him as well as to the country."[112]

Whites argued that the purpose of black education should be to produce better homes. One white educator told the North Carolina legislature in 1901 that the state must appropriate money for elementary black education out of self-protection: "No two races live in peace together when one is enlightened and the other is semi-barbarous."[113] North Carolina's white superintendent of public instruction announced in 1902 that the "great and generous Anglo-Saxon race" now realized its error in educating the "child-race." "We have too often flung him the part of the money that the Constitution required us to give, and then left him without direction to waste it at his will," he declared.[114] Now whites would control black education.

There is a direct link between the fabricated discourse on black barbarity and the industrial education movement. As white writers crafted the image of debased black home life, they also embraced Booker T. Washington's popularization of the industrial education ideal.[115] The drive for home improvement featured the Hampton Institute industrial model of training and helped convert northern philanthropists to the cause. For almost four decades, many African Americans had rejected the Hampton model as oppressive, funding and attending colleges that offered classical curricula instead.[116] But after disfranchisement, those graduates watched as philanthropists tried to turn their alma maters into industrial training schools or set up new trade schools that drained contributions away from them. Black classical colleges declined after 1900 as dollars flowed to vocational schools.[117]

The industrial education ideal and reports of black debauchery were mutually reinforcing. When appropriations from northern philanthropists became contingent upon industrial education, educators increased their public condemnation of black home life to attract money. To obtain funding, educators of African Americans began to point out their students' deficiencies rather than their accomplishments. Some black educators even began to emphasize their pupils' lack of basic living skills. Scotia Seminary in Concord now stressed its "domestic arts"; Saint Augustine's College in Raleigh boasted of new classes in printing, carpentry, and bricklaying. Shaw University, the home of law and medical schools, stated, "We do not teach trades, and make no pretensions to doing it, for we have no desire to inaugurate a trade school, but we do pretend to carry on industrial work along educational lines, and this work will be extended more and more as fast as financial means are obtained."[118]

Whereas previously they had extolled their students' proficiency in Latin and Greek as proof of African Americans' capability, now black colleges downplayed the fact that they offered classical courses. Charles Pettey's alma mater, Biddle University, made much of its rule that every student in preparatory and normal school spend at least an hour a day in required industrial courses.[119] It did not publicize the fact that Hebrew remained a requirement for future ministers. But white educators, often agents of northern philanthropists, actually patrolled black campuses. One white critic suggested that Biddle drop Hebrew and substitute instead "the languages of the Congo Valley and of Timbuctoo."[120] Many black schools invited white supremacists to give campus talks, and students made a big show of welcoming them. For example, just after the disfranchising amendment passed, Charles Aycock spoke at Shaw's medical and law school commencement, at which he warned graduates to stay out of politics and "was applauded to the echo." Little wonder that Edward A. Johnson, dean of the law school, left shortly for New York City to launch his political career from Harlem.[121]

Established black institutions found themselves competing with overnight wonders set up to attract philanthropists' dollars. James E. Shepard, who had complained that disfranchisement left "no middle ground" between slavery and freedom and that the best way to make a good man was not to "unman him," quickly reinvented himself. By 1903, he was saying that the black man "came to this country a slave and faithfully served his years of bondage, as all races before him had to do." Now he was "learning the lesson[s] of manhood: when these are acquired he will stand forth in power and glory."[122] Shepard's astonishing amnesia helped him forget the manhood he had so recently claimed, and within five years, he established a "National Religious Training School . . . devoted to the practical training of the Negro in Morals and Religion." He asked the "evil one," former senator Jeter Pritchard, to serve as president of the school's board. Shepard explained the advantages of wedding the industrial school and the religious school: "It awakens the sluggish, dormant energies of the individual. . . . It lessens crime, reduces idleness, stops violence and teaches lessons of self-restraint."[123] Shepard found his middle ground by retreating behind a landscape of accommodation.

At Livingstone College, wholly supported by the AME Zion Church, students and professors realized the danger to their tradition at once. One professor argued that all of North Carolina's leaders, white and black, had classical training, and he recalled founder Joseph Price's description of education's purpose: teaching "the Head, Hand, and Heart."[124] On another occasion, Livingstone alumni rushed the stage at an Afro-American Council meeting when the organizers displayed a likeness of Booker T. Washington. They would not budge until a portrait of Joseph Price hung beside that of the Wizard of Tuskegee.[125]

They fought a losing battle, however, and quickly realized that if they wanted to survive, they would have to solicit northern dollars like their competitors. In 1902, Bishop Hood wrote to a representative of the Rockefeller-funded General Education Board asking for help: "The moral and intellectual training [at Livingstone] is not excelled by any," but "we have not been able to do what we have desired on industrial lines, because we have not had the means."[126] A Rockefeller agent visited the school and noted that Livingstone was "entitled to respect and sympathy," despite the fact that it suffered from the "misdirected efforts of negro churches to provide educational advantages."[127] Livingstone College merged with East Tennessee Industrial School in 1903 and quickly notified philanthropists of the move.[128] Future correspondence included photographs of the women in the "cooking department." When an agent of the General Education Board visited Livingstone, he found the entire female student body in the laundry, scrubbing away.[129] Yet Livingstone continued to graduate men and women who went on to be doctors, lawyers, teachers, and business leaders. Behind footlights that focused on industrial courses, the normal, classical, and theological schools continued to attract the overwhelming majority of students.[130]

Since home improvement must start with black women, the industrial education movement included the subtext of female moral reform. In 1900, William Hannibal Thomas, an African American, published a book that described unbridled immorality among black women.[131] Even though some white educators of African Americans condemned Thomas's premise, they attached caveats. The white president of Scotia Seminary defended his women pupils, describing them as "living virtuous lives," but he noted that many of the girls' mothers said to him, "I know I am not what I ought to be, but I don't want her to be like me." At least he added that immorality existed among the "uncared for masses . . . not because they are Negroes, but because they are uncared for." A Saint Augustine's professor called Thomas's charge of unchecked morality an exaggeration but acknowledged that there was a grain of truth in it.[132] In this perverse way, black women now shouldered the blame for disfranchisement, which whites argued had been necessary because of the barbarity black mothers fostered by not teaching their sons right from wrong.

"Industrial" education for black women meant training to be servants since all industries except commercial laundries and tobacco factories remained closed to black women. In practice, such curricula directed philanthropists' dollars into courses for men, which required more expensive equipment; for example, printing presses cost considerably more than lye. Moreover, women's laundry, nursing, and cooking classes saved the schools money since students' uncompensated schoolwork replaced women's wage labor. Resourceful women students worked the system to accomplish their own goals. In the summer, many female students at industrial schools parlayed their training into relatively high-paying domestic jobs in northern cities. Others used their dressmaking or millinery skills at home to earn money for tuition. They made sure that class barriers remained fluid enough to allow a woman who worked her way through college as a summer domestic to become a teacher upon graduation.[133]

Despite black women's clever use of industrial education, the overall system was gendered in ways that disadvantaged women. It reinforced differences in men's and women's curricula after black women had battled for years for equal consideration in coeducation, and it drew money away from women's teacher-training programs. In North Carolina, whites closed four black state normal schools and diverted the money to establish industrial programs for men at the remaining three schools. The move displaced women students who had been in the majority at the closed institutions and reallocated scarce funds from teacher preparation to male students' manual training at the remaining schools.

The story of the end of coeducation at the state-supported North Carolina Agricultural and Mechanical College (A & M) illustrates how the industrial model could work against women. In 1900, the school's white trustees voted to exclude women in order to open up dormitory space for men. Defending their action, they argued, "It was doubtful [that the college] was even intended for women any more than white A. and M. college was intended for white girls." But a scarcity of dorm rooms was not the only reason for expelling the women, the trustees revealed. Governing the school had become difficult since "neither the girls or boys wanted to engage in the harder kinds of manual labor in the presence of the other sex, but would strive to dress up in fine clothes to impress the other."[134] This rhetoric about sacrificing the women to save the school came from A & M's staunchest white supporters. Its white enemies employed a sexualized style to try to close the school completely. They alleged that coeducation had given rise to unbridled immorality at A & M, making it necessary to expel all of the students, women and men.[135]

No white person connected with A & M, friend or enemy, spoke for the excluded black women. They had to speak for themselves. The women of the African American teachers association pleaded with white officials that "special attention . . . be paid to our girls." It was a matter of fairness, the teachers pointed out: "The boys have the A. and M. college; the whites have the Normal and Industrial School for girls. . . . No provision has been made [for] . . . Negro girls."[136] Their protests fell on deaf ears, but for all of their mindful and unmindful attempts to eviscerate black women's education, whites had acted too late. The genie—love of knowledge—was out of the bottle. Two generations of African American women drew on their educations to resist racism and poured into the state's black public schools to train the next generation.[137]

Occasionally the talk of barbarity, immorality, and ignorance simply became unbearable, and African Americans struck back at their detractors, especially if the defamer was African American and close at hand. One such incident occurred in New Bern, where African Americans had attended public schools for forty years when A. L. E. Weeks came to town. A Shaw graduate and Baptist minister, Weeks started the New Bern Collegiate Industrial Institute.[138] He wasted no time in contacting the General Education Board, but the board remained unimpressed, calling him a "persistent beggar." Weeks *was* persistent, and he wrote to white Baptist ministers nationwide to describe alleged intolerable conditions among North Carolina's African Americans and to seek donations.[139]

A Seattle, Washington, minister passed the letter along to a reporter who used it as the basis for an article entitled, "N.C. Negroes Barbarous." Weeks claimed the city had no library or Young Men's Christian Association. He described Craven County as the most backward place in the "black belt" and said that he had discovered "within forty miles of this place an altar upon which burnt offerings are offered for sin." The sanctification wave had struck eastern North Carolina, and "more than three hundred thousand negroes are being more or less carried away by ignorant ideas of worship." Moreover, he continued, New Bernians were "doing absolutely nothing for the development of the negroes in changing these conditions industrially." Then he appealed for money.[140]

False news of their hometown's benightedness rankled some African Americans who had migrated from New Bern to the Pacific Northwest, and they sent clippings home. Black New Bernians called a protest meeting at once. Weeks was denounced as "an ingrate of the blackest dye, [who] has attempted to disrupt the peace and posture of this state." New Bern's African Americans pointed to their forty years of graded public schools, their three private high schools, their rate of homeownership—the highest in the state—and added, "as for culture, refinement and moral standing, our citizens will compare favorably with any in the country."[141] They wrote to the editor of the *Seattle Times* and even penned a poem to express their outrage:

What savages! So very green,
That almost cane-grass can be seen,
Twisting its roots around the brain,
Enough to make us all insane.

. . . .

Send with a sympathetic tear,
Six thousand dollars in my care;
Your confidence in me will bring
A change among this heathen ring.[142]

The outrage of New Bern's black men could not compare to that of New Bern's black women. A "Committee of 50 Ladies in the So Called Black Belt" demanded that Weeks retract his statement, or "we will not be responsible for [what] your punishment will be." They mocked his use of the term "black belt" and compared him to a "black ball rolling in our midst loaded with slander and insults." They wanted an accounting of any money sent by "your northern friends" for "these poor little barefoot savages whose mothers are practicing heathen rites." They threatened, "We are not men we are the ribs and won't allow such insults."[143]

The reaction of New Bern's black women reflects a crafty use of their position in the political order. "We are not men we are the ribs and won't allow such insults" reveals their perception of the special place they held in civic life. Weary of being blamed for barbarity while they struggled to maintain Christian homes, they traded on their peculiar status as women. A man should refrain from insulting womanhood, and if he would not, the women planned to use informal power to convince him of the errors of his ways. The pressure worked, and Weeks spent two weeks apologizing and trying to clarify his letter.[144] Finally they forgave him, and he sighed, "Hell came open and I came out."[145]

Within a decade, the white supremacy campaign and disfranchisement had erased the image of the black middle class from the minds of white North Carolinians. What began as improbable political rhetoric became the dominant version of of North Carolina culture as far away as London. In 1910, a British author just back from North Carolina reported that although white people paid taxes for schools, they were afraid to let their daughters "stir away from home unprotected" for fear of black rapists and therefore educated them at home, a patent absurdity.[146] African Americans had no platform from which to combat such lies. Black men no longer voted, participated in the Republican Party, or spoke out on issues, nor could they openly receive "white" educations. Black women stood accused of gross immorality and failing to provide comfortable homes that could produce law-abiding citizens.

An incident in 1906 in Salisbury, the home of Livingstone College, serves as a parable for the entire decade. Murderers broke into the home of a prosperous white farm family and killed Isaac Lyerly, his wife, and two of their children, then set their beds on fire. Apparently unaware that two daughters, Addie and Maggie, slept upstairs, the murderers left. Addie Lyerly found her family chopped to pieces downstairs, the fire in the beds only smoldering since it had been doused by blood. The baby was still alive. The two girls ran through the woods for help, past the house of their black tenants, the Dillinghams. The Dillinghams and another black tenant family, the Gillespies, had been feuding with the Lyerlys. Isaac had ordered them to sow wheat and they had refused. Isaac's wife had argued with Della Dillingham over Della's borrowing the washtubs and returning them dirty.[147]

Quickly the sheriff rounded up the Dillinghams and the Gillespies and threw them in jail, a structure beside the courthouse that was originally a private home.[148] The governor asked the sheriff if he could defend the jail in case of an attack, and the sheriff said he felt confident that he could and refused assistance. The next evening, a mob overwhelmed about twenty deputies, who fought back, even shooting a would-be lyncher in the buttocks. The guards did not, however, shoot to kill. When the mob broke through, the sheriff shouted, "They have got the prisoners and you men of property in Salisbury will suffer for it."[149]

The mob took three male prisoners from the jail, hung them, and then riddled their bodies with "thousands" of bullets. They then went to fetch Addie and Maggie Lyerly to see the bodies. Early reports of the lynching included the news that "women of this section of the State are thoroughly aroused and many approve of the lynching." In the carnage that followed the lynching, "one prominent woman who visited the scene . . . cut off an ear from one of the victims."[150] After the lynchings, the mob turned its fury toward Livingstone College, and cries of "Now let us go and burn up the nigger college!" went up. Only after cooler heads remembered the kindness of certain Livingstone professors to the community in the past did the crowd turn away from that mission.[151]

The governor sent troops, and a local grand jury charged the leaders of the mob, George Hall, a bootlegger, and G. H. Gentle, occupation unknown, both strangers to Salisbury, with murder. Local men who were arrested but not tried included Bud Bullabough, alias Bully Boy, alias Billy McConeyhead; John Cauble; Francis J. Cress, a drayman; and Henry Goodman, a clerk.[152] The two out-of-towners went to prison for their roles in the lynching, but Cress and Goodman continued to work in Salisbury for many years.[153] Bully Boy disappeared without a trace.

The white elite—the press, the governor, and most law enforcement officials—condemned the lynching, called it humiliating, and demanded that the lynchers be brought to justice.[154] They wondered out loud, "Who are lynchers in North Carolina?" "What class of citizens take the execution of criminals into their own hands in the face of the practically unanimous censure of the press and the condemnation of the governor, the officers and the best citizenship of the state?" They placed the lynchers in that class of whites who had been poor tenant farmers and were now earning good livings in the state's industries. "The sudden transition of North Carolina from a purely agricultural state . . . to a prosperous industrial state has lifted these people from penury and subservience into comfort and independence. They had not been prepared for this change." This class of white people could not be expected to have the "requisite finer sensibilities and nicer distinctions—reverence for law, respect for the rights of others . . . do not spring into being in a day." The problem was that "these people have been catered to by politicians, but they have not been led to think." To solve the problem, the "true manhood of this state [should] set itself to the task of uplifting and improving those unappreciative of our laws."[155]

This analysis—that lynching was the work of the lower class of whites, a class that needed to be controlled by more educated whites, or "true manhood"—became the accepted wisdom across the South. Racism among lower-class whites, so the story went, raged so virulently that the white middle class could barely contain it.[156] But it was poor whites who, as Populists, had united with African Americans ten years earlier in a fusion government to increase educational appropriations and make local government more responsive to its citizens; it was poor whites who had voted against the amendment. Then white farm families found themselves forced to work at cotton mills by the failure of the biracial agrarian and governmental reform they had supported as fusionists. The perpetrators of mob violence might have been hotheaded men like Bully Boy, but the lynchers merely acted out the logical extension of Furnifold Simmons's rhetoric.

In the 1898 white supremacy campaign, poor white Populists had accepted the white supremacist logic that their racial interests overrode their class interests. They did so to prove their manhood by protecting their women, but now new class barriers within their race barred their claim to manliness. The fact that elite whites blamed the violence on poor white men and called for more control over their behavior recalls the prediction African Americans made about Simmons and illiterate whites: "If [he] will fool the illiterate Negroes . . . [he] will fool them also." North Carolina's impoverished white men traded their economic future for "manhood," only to find themselves forever consigned to the ranks of the good ol' boys.

A few days after the lynchings and violence in Salisbury, Jack McClay, an eleven-year-old white boy, appeared before the local magistrate in faraway Asheville. He was charged with looping a rope around his white playmate's neck, flinging it over a beam, and leaving the playmate dangling. The six-year-old thus hanged managed to free himself and ran home howling with angry red welts around his neck. The boys told the judge they had just been playing a game—a game they called "Salisbury."[157]

six

DIPLOMATIC WOMEN

After disfranchisement, "the Negro," white supremacists were fond of saying, was removed from politics. But even as African American men lost their rights, the political underwent a transformation. As state and local governments began to provide social services, an embryonic welfare state emerged. Henceforth, securing teeter-totters and playgrounds, fighting pellagra, or replacing a dusty neighborhood track with an oil-coated road would require political influence. Thus, at the same time that whites restricted the number of voters by excluding African Americans, the state created a new public role: that of the client who drew on its services.[1] Contemporaries and historians named this paradoxical period the Progressive Era.

From the debris of disfranchisement, black women discovered fresh approaches to serving their communities and crafted new tactics designed to dull the blade of white supremacy. The result was a greater role for black women in the interracial public sphere. As long as they could vote, it was black men who had most often brokered official state power and made interracial political contacts. After disfranchisement, however, the political culture black women had created through thirty years of work in temperance organizations, Republican Party aid societies, and churches furnished both an ideological basis and an organizational structure from which black women could take on those tasks. After black men's banishment from politics, North Carolina's black women added a network of women's groups that crossed denominational—and later party—lines and took a multi-issue approach to civic action. In a nonpolitical guise, black women became the black community's diplomats to the white community.

In the first twenty years of the century, the state, counties, and municipalities began to intervene in affairs that had been private in the past. Now, government representatives killed rabid dogs and decided where traffic should stop. They forced bakers to put screens on their windows and made druggists stop selling morphine. They told parents when their children could work and when their children must go to school. As they regulated, they also dispensed. Public health departments were formed, welfare agencies turned charity into a science, and juvenile court systems began to separate youthful offenders of both sexes from seasoned criminals. Public education expanded exponentially and became increasingly uniform across the state. The intersection of government and individual expanded from the polling place to the street corner, from the party committee meeting to the sickbed.

Black women might not be voters, but they could be clients, and in that role they could become spokespeople for and motivators of black citizens. They could claim a distinctly female moral authority and pretend to eschew any political motivation. The deep camouflage of their leadership style—their womanhood—helped them remain invisible as they worked toward political ends. At the same time, they could deliver not votes but hands and hearts through community organization: willing workers in city cleanup campaigns, orderly children who complied with state educational requirements, and hookworm-infested people eager for treatment at public health fairs.

Southerners at the time called themselves "progressives," but historians have been loath to allow that name to stick. For those who championed a static history of the region, the "Progressive Era" ran counter to their continuity arguments. Moreover, those who found the roots of northern progressivism twining amid urban growth and rapid immigration saw only a stunted transplant on southern soil that remained comparatively rural and isolated. Finally, southern progressive solutions seemed a pale imitation of those in the North. If southerners reformed at all, historians judged their programs to be too little, too late.[2]

Even for those who claimed to locate a southern Progressive Era, the juxtaposition of African Americans losing ground and whites "progressing" remained problematic. In a period when the country moved from an administrative government that maximized free enterprise toward an interventionist state, the white South busily invented and embellished segregation and drove black men away from the polls. White southern Democrats applied a pernicious ingenuity to the task of expanding state services in a society divided by the color line, and they allocated government money in increasingly unequal racial divides. C. Vann Woodward termed it "Progressivism—for Whites Only." J. Morgan Kousser went further, attaching an additional caveat: "Progressivism—for Middle Class Whites Only."[3] Southern progressivism lived but, according to these readings, without the participation of blacks, poor whites, or women.

After Woodward, Anne Firor Scott, searching for southern progressivism, discovered white women at its center. Social reform enabled women to claim a privileged knowledge in civic affairs and to exercise power prior to suffrage, even in the South, where middle-class white women faced a stereotype of helpless gentility. White women fought child labor, ran settlement houses, and assumed responsibility for municipal housekeeping in growing New South cities.[4] Working-class southern white women used progressive ideas and programs to shake the South's confidence in its grossly unfair wage system and to condemn its anti-union virulence, thus challenging the familiar notion that social control was the raison d'être for reform.[5]

But even if southern progressivism included women, was it reserved for whites? The answer is that whites intended for it to be, and it would have been even more racist, more exclusive, and more oppressive if there had been no black women progressives. Black women fought back after disfranchisement by adapting progressive programs to their own purposes, even while they chose tactics that left them invisible in the political process.[6] As southern African American women began this task, they were further away from southern white women than ever before. Since black men could not vote, white women dropped appeals to black women to influence their male family members. Many white women had chosen race over gender in the white supremacy campaigns and had gained their first electoral experience under a racist banner.

Given the distance between white and black women, the point is not that black women simply contributed to progressive welfare work and the domestication of politics, although, of course, they did. In comparing black women's progressivism to white women's progressivism, one must be cautious at every turn because black and white women had vastly different relationships to power. To cite just one example, white middle-class women lobbied to obtain services *from* their husbands, brothers, and sons; black women lobbied to obtain services *for* their husbands, brothers, and sons.

Black women's task was to try to force those white women who plunged into welfare efforts to recognize class and gender similarities across racial lines. To that end, they surveyed progressive white women's welfare initiatives and political style and found that both afforded black women a chance to enter the political. They had two purposes in mind. First, they would try to hold a place for African Americans in the ever-lengthening queue forming to garner state services. Second, they would begin to clear a path for the return of African Americans to the ballot box.

As confused and obfuscating as the term "progressive" is, one might wonder if it even applies to black women activists at all.[7] Considering black women as progressives, however, demonstrates how gender and race as tools of historical analysis can enrich traditional political history. In this case, they lead us to rethink progressivism's periodization, roots, and results. Certainly, one can only apply the term "progressive" to this time and in these circumstances with a profound sense of irony. But it is important to make an explicit attempt to reclaim "progressivism," to stroll among the dismembered corpses of other historians' definitions and gather up some limbs, a hank of hair here, a piece of bone there. Then, like Dr. Frankenstein, perhaps we might build a new progressivism, this one a little less monstrous than some of those other hulks that still walk among us.

Given the expansion of the public sphere and whites' attempts to exclude African Americans from new state and municipal programs, black women's religious work took on new meaning. In the wake of disfranchisement, African American men and women turned to their churches for solace and for political advice.[8] Yet many black men now feared the potentially explosive mixture of politics and religion in turbulent times.[9] Ministers of all denominations began to circumscribe their own discourse and to monitor their flocks' debate. A Baptist minister declared that such "perilous times" made even "preaching of the pure gospel embarrassing, if not dangerous."[10]

Using women's church organizations to press for community improvement incurred less risk than preaching inflammatory sermons on civil rights. The church remained, in the words of John Dancy, "an organized protest," but the nature of that protest transformed itself from arguments at Republican conventions and good turnouts at the ballot box into a flanking movement. While white political leaders kept their eyes on black men's electoral-political presence and absence, black women organized and plotted an attack just outside of their field of vision. They began by transforming church missionary societies into social service agencies.

This is not to say that the political intentions of denominational women's groups were apparent to insiders or even omnipresent in the beginning. Initially, the groups did three things: they focused church attention away from spiritual debate and toward social conditions; they taught women to be organized managers; and they offered a slim ray of hope for community improvement in the midst of political disaster. Henry Cheatham, who had been recorder of deeds in Washington, D.C., prior to Dancy's assumption of the post, deplored African Americans' "political misfortunes" and gloomily predicted that civil rights might be lost forever. Cheatham argued that the "one thing" that remained for African Americans was the work women did in Sunday schools to build better homes, to educate the children, and to improve the community in general.[11] In effect, he implored North Carolina Baptist women to use church work as a parapolitical tool.

African American women needed little urging. They understood their new role in community life and their unique ability to execute it. One Baptist home missionary, Sallie Mial of Raleigh, put it this way: "We have a peculiar work to do. We can go where you can not afford to go."[12] Mial's "peculiar work" was social welfare reform. The tasks of black women's home missionary societies read like a Progressive Era primer. They organized mothers' clubs and community cleanup days. They built playgrounds and worked for public health and temperance. Marshaling arguments from the social purity and social hygiene movements, they spoke on sexual dangers outside of marriage. To achieve their goals, southern black women entered political space, appearing before local officials and interacting with white bureaucrats.

Even as they undertook this "peculiar work," black women knew that they must avoid charges of political interference. As a black woman, Mial could go where black men could no longer afford to go—into public space—for two reasons. First, her presence could not be misconstrued as a bid for sexual access to white women, as the Democrats so cunningly characterized black men's exercise of citizenship. Second, Mial could enter the realm of politics as a client, as an interpreter of social needs for families whom she represented to a state that had pledged something to her. Mial and thousands of other southern black women set about expanding on the state's amorphous promise, even as the growing bureaucracy tried to find practical ways to exclude African Americans from its largesse.

Sallie Mial would have never openly characterized her work as political, even though she may have understood it to be. Indeed, her success depended upon remaining invisible in the political process, a posture that contributes to historians' difficulties in recovering her experience. Taking a lesson from the high price of black men's former public presence, capitalizing on the divisions among whites over the allocation of new services to African Americans, and concerned about gender politics among African Americans, black women reformers depended on not being seen at all by whites who would thwart their programs and not being seen as political by whites who would aid them. They used their invisibility to construct a web of social service and civic institutions that remained hidden from and therefore unthreatening to whites.

Women's organizations within religious bodies were not new, but they became more important, expanded, and reordered their priorities after disfranchisement. For example, the Women's Baptist Home Mission Convention of North Carolina began in 1884, primarily as an arm for evangelical work. At the turn of the century, the group employed Mial as a full-time missionary in the state. In this capacity, she organized local women's groups and founded Sunshine Bands and What-I-Can Circles for girls.[13] Mial explained her work to the African American Baptist men this way: "We teach the women to love their husbands, to be better wives and mothers, to make the homes better."[14] At the same time, church workers taught Baptist women lobbying and administrative skills. One woman remembered, "From this organization we learn[ed] what is meant to be united."[15] Another observed, "Many of our women are being strengthened for the Master's use." Along the way, the organization began calling itself the Baptist State Educational Missionary Convention.[16]

Making "the homes better" covered a wide range of community activities. Good homes rhetoric was, of course, promulgated by whites to justify white supremacy; southern educational reformers used depictions of debasement, for example, to justify industrial education.[17] Black women could use this discourse for their own purposes, and they grasped the opportunity it gave them to bargain for the state services that were beginning to improve whites' lives but were denied to African Americans. As Margaret Murray Washington put it, "Where the homes of colored people are comfortable and clean, there is less disease, less sickness, less death, and less danger to others [that is, whites]." Good homes, however, required good government. "We are not likely to [build good homes] if we know that the pavements will be built just within a door of ours and suddenly stop," Washington warned.[18] Turning from the ballot box to the home as the hope of the future was canny political strategy that meshed nicely with the new welfare role of the state, and it explicitly increased women's importance at a time when women across the nation campaigned to extend their influence through volunteer activities and the professionalization of social work.[19]

The elevation of the home to the centerpiece of African American life sprang from several sources. Certainly it resonated with a nationwide Progressive Era movement for better homes, particularly among immigrant enclaves in crowded northern cities. But among North Carolina's African Americans, the movement's roots reached closer to home. Religious convictions that had inspired nineteenth-century black women who did church work continued to serve as moral imperatives to bring families to godly lives. African American women tried to eliminate grist for the white supremacy mill by abolishing the images of the immoral black woman and the barbaric black home. Moreover, now that voting required literacy, education was political, and it began at home. Able to tap into the larger context of rhetoric on better homes and the importance of literacy, black women expanded their roles, first in the church, then in the community as a whole.[20]

Some men felt threatened by this new activity, even though most women made it clear that their goal was not to preach or to rise within the formal church hierarchy, as, for example, Mary Small had done in the African Methodist Episcopal (AME) Zion Church in the 1890s. William F. Fonvielle, a supporter of coeducation at Livingstone College, had called repeatedly on women to work for racial uplift. But in 1900, he complained that there were too many women delegates at the AME Zion general conference. He came away from the experience completely opposed to women representatives, even though "some of them are good friends of mine. . . . It looks like a bad precedent."[21] Many black Baptist men questioned the expenditures for home missions.[22] When Baptist women implored men to "Give us a push," the men wondered if they should not push the women out of the limelight altogether. Unlike the AME Zion convention, by 1900 Baptist men and women met separately, and women often found themselves fending off attempts to abolish the Baptist Educational and Missionary Convention. Even those who did not want to sweep away the women's structure were determined to insure its control by men. They advocated solving the problem "by appointing an advisory committee each year to attend the Women's Convention and to advise with them in their deliberations, and [send] . . . an annual report to this body."[23]

Women did their best to reassure men by stressing their solidarity with them. "We are your sisters, your wives, your mothers. We have not outgrown you. We have been given to you to help you. We dare not leave you. You have opened your hearts, and given us increased privileges in the churches," Sallie Mial told the men's Baptist convention. Roberta Bunn, another paid missionary, said that the women's relationship with the men's convention was "indestructible" but that women had an important place to fill that men could not. She quoted Scripture: "I sought for a man among them that should make up the hedge, and stand in the gap before me." She reminded the brothers that when God could find no man to fill the gap, two women stood in.[24] Over the years, the debate over the power of women's organizations among North Carolina Baptists escalated. By 1917, women insisted that "it behooves us to think of and discuss the great questions confronting us as citizens of this great nation," while the men reiterated that the women needed "intelligent supervision" and directed them to turn their funds over to the men's convention.[25]

The growth of women's organizations in the AME Zion Church demonstrates women's desire to carve out a distinct space for themselves within the denomination. After the turn of the century, AME Zion women created a formal, hierarchical, and separate women's structure and changed the thrust of their work from evangelism to education and social service. When Sarah Dudley Pettey served as treasurer and then secretary of the Woman's Home and Foreign Missionary Society, the organization's primary activity was fund-raising for African missions. She began the "Woman's Column" in the *Star of Zion* during her term as secretary, and her writing revealed her personal concerns more than it represented the society. In the 1890s, society officers met only once every four years at the regular convention, and all were wives of bishops.[26]

The structure of the Woman's Home and Foreign Missionary Society changed radically between 1900 and 1915, and the women moved from integration with the men to performing separate functions within the church. In 1901, while Dudley Pettey still edited the "Woman's Column," the society persuaded the *Star of Zion* to allow Marie Clay Clinton, George Clinton's new wife, to write a "missionary" column.[27] That column eventually grew into a separate women's newspaper, the *Missionary Seer*.[28] At the 1904 convention, Woman's Christian Temperance Union (WCTU) activist Annie Blackwell demanded that women operate the Woman's Home and Foreign Missionary Society autonomously, and a women's convention began meeting the next year.[29] An independent executive board oversaw the society's business, and by 1912, the board dealt with the issue of bishops' wives monopolizing the board by making them nonvoting members.[30] The women's convention began electing the *Star*'s "Woman's Column" editor in 1912.[31] The term "missions" came to be broadly interpreted to mean social service work among African American neighbors.

Two North Carolina women, Marie Clinton and Victoria Richardson, founded youth educational departments within the society. Clinton had arrived in Charlotte in 1901 when she married widower George Clinton, and by the following year, she became fast friends with Victoria Richardson of Livingstone College.[32] Richardson's uncles were the famous Harris brothers who had founded the Fayetteville graded school during Reconstruction. Legend had it that Victoria's parents sent her from Ohio to North Carolina to save her from making an unsuitable early marriage. After a brief stint as Charles Chesnutt's colleague at the Charlotte graded school in the 1870s, Richardson went to teach at Livingstone College when it opened in 1880. She stayed a lifetime, teaching music and building the library. With her warm friend Mary Lynch, Richardson set an example of

Victoria Richardson, circa 1900. Courtesy of the College Archives, Carnegie Library, Livingstone College, Salisbury, North Carolina.

"finer womanhood" for Livingstone's women students.[33] "Saved" from love, Victoria Richardson never married.

In 1904, Marie Clinton established the Buds of Promise within the Woman's Home and Foreign Missionary Society. "Blooming All for Jesus," the Buds functioned as an educational service club for AME Zion children aged three to twelve.[34] In 1909, Victoria Richardson began the Young Woman's Home and Foreign Missionary Society for teenaged girls. The group took on social service work, nursed the sick, visited the elderly, and presented public health programs.[35] By 1912, the officers of the Woman's Home and Foreign Missionary Society had years of social service experience behind them and an organization that could channel women's energies from the cradle to the grave. Annie Blackwell served as corresponding secretary, and elder Mary Small presided.[36]

These African American women's denominational groups created a vast network throughout the South, virtually invisible to whites. It is helpful to see the groups as cells through which information and ideas could pass quickly. The invisibility of black women's work suited them. They did not want to antagonize their husbands by making a power play within their denominations—the men in the church were already uneasy about their activities. They did not want to endanger their families by drawing attention to themselves. They did not want to risk interference from whites by being overtly political. Better to call social work "missionary work"; better to gather 100,000 Baptist women in a movement to produce good homes. If such activities resulted in organizing the community to lobby for better schools, swamp drainage, or tuberculosis control, no white could accuse them of meddling in politics.

From these bases, women forged interdenominational links. North Carolinian Anna Julia Cooper, by then living in Washington, D.C., was present at the creation of the National Association of Colored Women's Clubs in 1896. Delegates to that first meeting represented a wide range of women's denominational organizations, interdenominational unions such as the WCTU and the King's Daughters, and secular civic leagues. In her capacity as North Carolina's state WCTU president, Mary Lynch attended the first national convention in 1897; she became national corresponding secretary at the second. The Biddle University Club of Charlotte was a charter member.[37] North Carolina black women founded a statewide federation of clubs in 1909 and elected Marie Clinton president.[38]

In addition to the women's clubs, the WCTU survived as an organizational home for black women after the white WCTU women found their work overtaken by the male Anti-Saloon League. By 1901, the national organization was paying a state organizer, and Lucy Thurman, national superintendent of "Colored Work," visited North Carolina regularly.[39] Marie Clinton was an active member, and she helped direct WCTU work toward efforts to help children. Victoria Richardson served as state president of the Loyal Temperance League, an organization that encouraged youngsters to sign the temperance pledge and sponsored oratorical contests denouncing strong drink. Their work left telling memories. At eighty-four, Abna Aggrey Lancaster recalled her excitement on the day in 1914 when Mary Lynch visited her Sunday school class. Seven-year-old Lancaster returned home for Sunday dinner proudly boasting that she would never allow alcohol or tobacco to touch her lips.[40] Decades later, George Lincoln Blackwell, Annie Blackwell's nephew, still savored his victory in a Loyal Temperance League oratorical contest as one of the proudest moments of his childhood.[41] Almost every large city in the state had a WCTU chapter. Lynch marveled at the organization's progress: "It seems a long time since that sultry day in July when in Salisbury we launched our little bark upon the waves of opposition."[42]

Activist black women also met at frequent regional sociological conferences. The Progressive Era trend toward organization, discussion, and investigation blossomed in these huge confabulations. Mary Lynch went to the Negro Young People's Christian and Educational Congress in Atlanta in 1902, where she delivered the address, "The Woman's Part in the Battle against Drink."[43] There she met Charlotte Hawkins, a young Boston student who had just moved to Sedalia, North Carolina, and banker Maggie L. Walker of Richmond. She also renewed ties with Lucy Thurman of the national WCTU and Josephine Silone-Yates, president of the National Association of Colored Women's Clubs.[44] The Woman's Day theme was "No race can rise higher than its women."[45]

As women were building vast voluntary networks, public school teaching was becoming an increasingly feminized profession. In 1902, the number of black women teachers and black men teachers was almost the same: 1,325 women and 1,190 men. The percentage of black women teachers exactly matched that of white women teachers: 52 percent.[46] By 1919, 78 percent of black teachers were women, and 83 percent of the white teachers were women.[47] The growing number of black women teachers did not escape notice. At the 1903 meeting of the Negro State Teachers Association, more than half of the delegates were women, including Sarah Dudley Pettey's sisters, Nannie and Catherine. Men had abandoned the profession, one speaker complained, because "they cannot compete with [women] teachers who are willing to work for low wages."[48]

But that analysis leaves black women taking the rap for the white supremacists. White women flocked to public teaching at the same time as black women, yet their salaries rose because politics determined educational allocations on the state level. It was black men's exclusion from the political sphere, not black women's willingness to work for low wages, that caused African American teachers to be poorly compensated. In some counties, salaries for black teachers actually declined after the fusion government ended.[49] Generally, however, throughout the state in the first two decades of the century, black teachers' wages crept upward, even as they continued to fall further behind white teachers' salaries. The statewide average salary in 1905 was $156 for whites and $107 for African Americans. Fourteen years later, whites averaged $353 and blacks $197.[50] The increasing number of black women teachers was a result, not a cause, of declining wages. In addition to driving black men from the profession, low wages contributed to a difference in the marital status of white and black women teachers. White women teachers were almost always single. Many black women teachers were married women who remained partially dependent upon their husbands' income.

The most staggering statistic was the growth in the number of white teachers: from a total of 5,472 in 1902 to 11,730 in 1919, a 214 percent increase. During the same period, the number of black teachers rose from 2,515 to 3,511, a 139 percent increase.[51] White teachers' numbers grew at the expense of black education. The white North Carolina Normal and Industrial College at Greensboro graduated large numbers of white women teachers at the same time that the state eliminated four black normal schools and banned women from the North Carolina Agricultural and Technical College.[52] Black women had a much harder time than white women formally preparing to teach, and fewer jobs awaited them after they graduated.[53]

Those who did succeed were likely to be active members of church women's organizations, involved in the WCTU, and participants in their city's literary societies and civic leagues. The black woman teacher had to withstand the scrutiny of white superintendents on the lookout for moral failings at the same time that she had to vanquish intense competition among dozens of aspirants for a single position. She had to be so unselfish, so dedicated, and so above reproach that no gossip could touch her.[54] Teachers' organizational connections protected and nurtured them. Conversely, they took their organizations' goals into their classrooms.

Even without their own progressive agenda, African American women teachers would have found schools to be an increasingly politicized setting. After 1900, the importance of literacy for voting and the movement toward industrial education commanded the attention of both the black and white community, and perennial battles over allocating taxes for education turned the black schoolhouse into a lightning rod, propelling female teachers into the political sphere, for better or for worse. The disfranchisers split among themselves over black public education after the amendment passed. Alfred Moore Waddell, ever the bumbling misanthrope, once chose a commencement address as a platform for condemning universal education: "There are thousands of enlightened persons who do not subscribe to the belief . . . that in popular education alone is to be found the panacea for all social political evils." Waddell added that education is even less useful when "applied to both races indiscriminately."[55] But other whites, notably Charles B. Aycock, saw universal education as the South's salvation. As far as they were concerned, even African Americans could participate in the forthcoming redemption, though not in equal measure.[56] Charles D. McIver, president of the North Carolina Normal and Industrial College for white women, tried to convince African Americans that disfranchisement would boost black education by encouraging parents to send their children to school, stating that "temporary disfranchisement . . . is a much less evil than permanent ignorance."[57] Aycock, who had threatened to refuse the Democratic Party's gubernatorial nomination if the time limit on the grandfather clause was extended, later threatened to resign the governorship if the state legislature allowed whites to tax themselves separately for the benefit of their own children.[58] His threat sprang partly from compassion—"Let us not be the first state . . . to make the weak man helpless"—but partly from his concern that such a move would encourage the U.S. Supreme Court to find the amendment unconstitutional.[59]

The racial inequities of school funding have been well documented, but the efforts of black students and teachers to keep their schools from starving cannot be celebrated enough. Even in the best black schools, for example, the Charlotte graded school, there were few desks and "two and sometimes three small pupils sat crowded in a wide seat." The state gave so little—inadequate furniture, a meager library—but teachers made so little go so far. "There was much blackboard space in a room which was a good thing," Rose Leary Love recalled. "At the time, blackboards were not termed visual aids, but they really were the most important available ones." The teachers used them to explain lessons; the pupils used them in lieu of paper. In the state's eyes, African Americans were not training to be full citizens; they needed no civics classes, no maps, no copy of the Constitution, no charts on "How a Bill Becomes a Law." That left teachers on their own to define citizenship. Somehow they did. Teachers chose talented students to "draw the National Flag or the State Flag on the blackboard," Love remembered. "These flags were assigned a place of honor on the board and they became a permanent fixture in the room for the year. Pupils were careful not to erase the flags when they cleaned the blackboards."[60] Despite whites' efforts to rob African Americans of their country, black teachers taught each day under the flag.

A centralized state bureaucracy grew to oversee the curriculum in African American schools. In 1905, Charles L. Coon, a white man who had recently been superintendent of Salisbury's schools and secretary of the General Education Board, accepted the newly created position of superintendent of the state colored normal schools.[61] According to his boss, Coon's oversight would "send out into the counties each a larger number of negro teachers, equipped with the knowledge and the training, and filled with the right ideals necessary for the . . . most practical, sensible and useful education of the negro race."[62] By putting African American normal schools under the control of a white man, the state hoped to produce teachers who embraced industrial education and to force the private African American normal schools out of business.

Ironically, state oversight created controversy rather than quelling it primarily because of Coon's independent personality. An amateur statistician who often challenged authority, Coon created a furor by proving that the state spent less on African American education than the taxes blacks paid in. In fact, Coon produced figures to prove that black tax dollars educated white children. Coon's boss, James Y. Joyner, distanced himself from Coon's argument and decried him to Josephus Daniels.[63] But Aycock admitted that Coon spoke the truth, and one white lawyer observed, "Our attempts to oppress the negro's mind are enslaving us just as bad as slavery did."[64]

By the time Coon addressed the predominately female Negro State Teachers Association in 1909, his trial by fire had turned him into a political agitator. He argued that the tide had turned against white supremacy. "I do not believe we need to spend much more time upon that species of the white race who would doom any other race to mental slavery," he commented, "anymore than we should spend time fighting over again the battles of whether a man has the right to hold in bodily servitude another man of another race." He suggested that the teachers unite to work for better instruction, longer school terms, and improved school facilities in the next decade. Furthermore, he recommended that blacks "interest the white people in your schools. . . . Then get your churches, lodges, and societies to help. . . . We must see to it that we interest the local communities, white and black."[65] Coon's prescription for African American education fit perfectly into black women's organizational missions and pointed up the political nature of black women teachers' jobs.

Whites quarreled a great deal more over funding black education than they did over its content, which white educators overwhelmingly agreed should be based on the Hampton model. Very little industrial training could begin, however, without spending dollars on equipment and tools. Ironically, it proved more expensive to build a bookcase than to explain an algebra problem on a broken piece of slate. Outside help would be critical. As a few dollars began to trickle down, black women teachers learned to exploit whites' support of industrial education. The Negro State Teachers Association recognized in 1903 that "the industrial and manual idea . . . is a much felt need in our public and private schools, since the development of negro womanhood is one of its immediate results." At the same time that black women recognized the potential of industrial education to improve home life, they began to clamor for a greater voice in its administration. When officials from the Rockefeller-funded General Education Board and local white educators met with black teachers in 1913, Charlotte Hawkins Brown told the group flatly that since women made up the majority of rural teachers, industrial education would fail unless philanthropists and white educators listened more closely to black women's suggestions and rewarded them for their efforts.[66] African American women's tilting of the industrial education ideology was slight but important. While paying lip service to the ideal of producing servants for white people, black women quietly turned the philosophy into a self-help endeavor and the public schools into institutions resembling social settlement houses. Cooking courses became not only vocational classes but also nutrition courses where students could eat hot meals. Sewing classes may have turned out some dressmakers and cobbling classes some cobblers, but they had the added advantage of clothing poor pupils so that they could attend school more regularly.

The Negro Rural School Fund, a philanthropy administered by the Rockefeller Foundation's General Education Board, gave the state's black women teachers the basic tools they needed to incorporate social work into the public school system. Begun in 1909 as the Anna T. Jeanes Fund, it paid more than half of the salary of one industrial supervising teacher on the county level. County boards of education paid the rest.[67] The Jeanes supervisor traveled to all of the African American schools in a county, ostensibly to teach industrial education. In 1913, the General Education Board offered to pay the salary of a state supervisor of rural elementary schools in North Carolina to oversee the thirteen Jeanes teachers already in place and to expand the work to other counties. In naming the supervisor, the board had a hidden agenda: northern philanthropists did not trust southern state administrators to allocate and spend their grants wisely. They wanted a white man loyal to them in state government, a professional who could walk the tightwire of interracial relations, placating obstreperous legislators at the same time that he kept a keen eye on black industrial curricula. They found their man in Nathan C. Newbold, who had been superintendent of public schools in Washington, North Carolina.[68]

In his first report, Newbold displayed his facility for straddling the color line. He condemned white injustice to African Americans at the same time that he explained it away as a reasonable vestige of the past, now, fortunately, antiquated. "The average negro rural schoolhouse is really a disgrace to an independent, civilized people," Newbold wrote as he surveyed his new field. "To one who does not know our history, these schoolhouses, though mute, would tell in unmistaken terms a story of injustice, inhumanity and neglect on the part of our white people," he observed. If someone unfamiliar with the South's history stumbled upon such buildings, the newcomer would surely think North Carolina's whites "unchristian." But the stranger would be wrong, he explained, since the black schools were no worse than white schools had been twenty-five years ago. Now that whites had remedied their own situation, he was sure they would eagerly set about improving black schools. Newbold always offered whites a face-saving excuse for past inaction at the same time that he spurred them to action.[69]

Nonconfrontational and optimistic, as state agent for the Negro Rural School Fund Newbold became an extraordinary voice for African American education. He quickly persuaded more county boards of education to fund half of a Jeanes teacher's salary at the same time that he forged strong alliances with the incumbent Jeanes teachers. By the end of his first year, twenty-two counties employed Jeanes teachers, who found themselves in the often awkward position of having to report to both Newbold and the county superintendent.[70] Newbold appointed a black woman, Annie Wealthy Holland, as his assistant.[71] The Jeanes board's initial expenditure of $2,144 in the state in 1909 grew to $12,728 by 1921.[72]

Most women who became Jeanes teachers came to social service work through their own organizations. For example, the Jeanes teacher in Rowan County was Rose Douglass Aggrey, a Shaw University graduate, poet, and classical scholar. Her husband, J. E. Kwegyir Aggrey, was born in the Gold Coast, Africa, was educated by British missionaries, and came to the United States to attend Livingstone College. He taught at Livingstone until the Phelps-Stokes Association sent him back to Africa as a missionary in 1920.[73] Staying behind in Salisbury, Rose Aggrey was active in the Woman's Home and Foreign Missionary Society of the AME Zion Church, forging close friendships with Mary Lynch and Victoria Richardson. Aggrey later became president of the statewide federation of black women's clubs.[74] Aggrey's daughter remembered that her mother often appeared before the school board and the county commissioners to plead for money for school improvements, to lobby for a longer school year, or to facilitate consolidation of one-room schools into graded structures.[75] Aggrey was extremely well connected within the Jeanes structure; in 1919, her friend Marie Clinton's husband, George, served on the national board of the Negro Rural School Fund.[76]

Faced with local white administrators' neglect, Jeanes teachers had an enormous amount of responsibility. Sarah Delany, the Jeanes supervisor in Wake County, recalled, "I was just supposed to be in charge of domestic science, but they made me do the county superintendent's work. So, I ended up actually in charge of all the colored schools in Wake County, North Carolina, although they didn't pay me to do that or give me any credit."[77] Delany, raised as a "child of privilege" on the Saint Augustine's College campus, stayed overnight with parents in rural areas, where she encountered not just a lack of indoor plumbing but a condition even more appalling to a citified house guest: no outhouse. Delany went to her pupils' homes to teach their parents how to "cook, clean, [and] eat properly," and when General Education Board officials visited North Carolina in 1913, she agreed to serve on the statewide committee to establish a cooking curriculum. She painted schoolrooms, taught children to bake cakes, raised money to improve buildings, and organized Parent Unions.[78] Jeanes teachers also transformed their students into entrepreneurs.[79] In 1915, their Home-Makers Clubs, Corn Clubs, and Pig Clubs involved over 4,000 boys and girls and 2,000 adults in 32 counties. The clubs were intended to teach farming, of course, but they also enabled poor rural African Americans to

Rose Aggrey, circa 1915. Courtesy of the College Archives, Carnegie Library, Livingstone College, Salisbury, North Carolina.

make money on their produce. The students raised more than $6,000 selling fruits and vegetables that year.[80]

Jeanes teachers saw themselves as agents of progressivism, and they combined public health work with their visits to schools and homes. Unlike Rose Aggrey and Sarah Delany, Carrie Battle, the Jeanes supervisor in Edgecombe County, had grown up desperately poor. Her mother worked at two domestic jobs and Battle went hungry to save money for tuition at Elizabeth City State Normal School. After she began teaching, Battle visited the homes of pupils across the county to organize a Modern Health Crusade against tuberculosis in the schools. Moving from school to school with a set of scales, she would not weigh ill-groomed boys and girls, nor would she weigh anyone in a dirty schoolroom. She made the children promise to clean up the room, bathe, use individual drinking cups, and sleep with the windows open. One boy reported, "Pa said that was too foolish—I would catch cold and die if I slept with the windows up." Another outmaneuvered his father by waiting to raise the window until the man was snoring. Soon Battle had established Modern Health Clubs in every school and a total of 4,029 children enrolled as Crusaders. Her work attracted attention from the white community, and she began to cooperate with the white Red Cross nurse to produce public health programs. Many of Battle's students had never been farther than ten miles from their homes. She brought the world to them through regularly scheduled visits of the "Moving Picture Car," a truck equipped with projection equipment used to screen films on health education.[81]

Jeanes teachers also built schools across the state—schools for which the state took credit and of which the counties took possession. Weary of asking for their fair share of tax dollars, black communities simply built their own schools and gave them to the county. For example, in the academic year 1915–16, thirty-two black schools were built and thirty improved at a total cost of $29,000. African Americans contributed over $21,000 of the total: $15,293 in cash and the equivalent of $5,856 in labor.[82] The school at Chadbourn represents a typical case. Local African Americans deeded to the county "a large building nearly completed to contain four class rooms, and nine acres of land." Moreover, they pledged more than $850 the next year to pay additional teachers and make further improvements to the building.[83] In Mecklenburg County, the white chairman of the school board told African Americans that the board was "willing to help those people who would help themselves" and that if African Americans "could pay half of the expense in as far as the board was able it would pay the other half." Amazingly, the black community was "encouraged" by this offer, built six schools, and forced the board to make good on its promise.[84]

The next year, the Julius Rosenwald Committee, a Chicago-based philanthropy, appropriated $6,000 to stimulate public school building in rural areas of North Carolina. Although this amount was a great deal less than African Americans were already raising annually to build their own schools, Rosenwald grants often embarrassed state and county officials into contributing funds for building black schools. The Rosenwald grants would provide a third of the cost of schools, local African American communities would raise a third, and tax dollars would account for a third. The Jeanes teachers organized teachers, parents, and students to support school-building projects by raffling box lunches, setting aside part of a field to grow a crop for the school, or providing the building materials for the structure from their own lands.[85] Their efforts made the Rosenwald seed money flower. For example, the first "Rosenwald" school built in North Carolina cost $1,473, of which the fund contributed $300.[86] By 1917, Jeanes teachers saw to it that the state's twenty-one Rosenwald schools teemed with activity night and day. Parent Unions met there, and teachers returned in the evenings to conduct "moonlight schools" where adults could learn to read.[87]

The unique role of the Jeanes teacher points up the distinctiveness of southern progressivism and provides clues to the reasons for historians' difficulties in finding and understanding it. The Jeanes teacher had no counterpart in the North. She did social work on the fly, leaving neither permanent settlement houses nor case files behind through which one might capture her experience. She understood the latest public health measures and passed them along even in the most remote areas. She fought to obtain Rosenwald school money to build schools that were airy and modern, then turned them into clubhouses in the evenings. By establishing Parent Unions, she provided a new organizational center for black communities. She lobbied school boards and county commissions for supplies and support. And she accomplished all of this while trying to remain invisible to the white community at large. To locate the progressive South, one must not just visit New South booster Henry Grady in Atlanta but find as well a schoolroom full of cleanly scrubbed Modern Health Crusaders, lined up for hot cereal cooked by the older girls in Rosenwald kitchens, each Crusader clutching the jelly jar that served as his or her very own glass.

By 1910, African American women in the state realized the need to create a united front to lobby local governmental officials and to improve civic life. Connected on the state level through the North Carolina Association of Colored Women's Clubs, these organizations would have to bring together on the local level denominational women's groups, interface with public school programs, and marshal all of the experience and resources that women had acquired in the past decade. The Salisbury Colored Women's Civic League exemplifies such an organization, and it brought together women who have appeared often in these pages: Mary Lynch, Victoria Richardson, and Rose Aggrey.

It took a strong leader to inspire such accomplished women, and the Civic League found such a leader in its president, Lula Spaulding Kelsey, the daughter of Lucy Sampson and John Spaulding. Lucy, a Lumbee Indian, had met John when he came to teach her class at the State Croatan Normal School in Pembroke. Both of their families were "freeish," the eastern North Carolina term for those blacks and mixed-race people whose ancestors had never been slaves.[88] Their daughter Lula attended normal school in Wilmington and then went on to Scotia Seminary for two more years. Upon graduation from Scotia, Lula Spaulding began teaching there, probably in home economics since her son recalls that she taught "finer womanhood." About the time that Lula began teaching in Concord, her father, a cousin of C. C. Spaulding, founder of North Carolina Mutual Life Insurance Company, moved to nearby Salisbury to establish an office of North Carolina Mutual.[89] Lula visited her family often and soon became friendly with Rose Aggrey.[90] Sometime around 1909, her mother's health

Livingstone College students, circa 1905. William "Billy" Kelsey is standing second from the right. Courtesy of the College Archives, Carnegie Library, Livingstone College, Salisbury, North Carolina.

failed and her father began to go blind. The young teacher determined that she had no choice but to move to Salisbury and take over her father's business.

The North Carolina Mutual agent held a privileged place in black communities, and the job involved traveling around the county every week "managing the debit": collecting money from customers for premiums. It was so rare for a woman to do this job that the incumbent was known as the "debit man." Lula Spaulding became the debit man in Salisbury. She took over her father's office and went about supporting herself and her parents. Soon she attracted the attention of William Kelsey, the strikingly handsome barber who owned the shop below her office. William, much older than Lula, began courting her with rides in his buggy and promises to build a house for her mother and father beside the house that would be theirs. After their marriage in 1911, Lula always honored William not only for marrying her but also for taking on support of her sick mother and blind father. Repaying this symbolic debt may have been one reason that Lula Kelsey was driven to work so hard as the years went by.

A decade before their marriage, William Kelsey had started a funeral business with Stephen Noble, who had a team of horses and a wagon. Noble was contracting to carry African American bodies for the white funeral home, and Kelsey saw the potential of keeping the business within the black community if he and Noble joined to bury the dead. When Kelsey and Noble began, there was no embalming. Relatives laid out the deceased on a "cooling board," the barber "dressed" the body, and the burial took place the same afternoon or the next morning, with the dead wrapped in a cloth. Eula Dunlap recalled that the first metal coffin she ever saw at Lincoln Academy in Kings Mountain was brought there by "Billy" Kelsey for burying his sister around 1910.[91]

William Kelsey enjoyed barbering and wanted to maintain the undertaking business as a sideline. But Lula Kelsey realized that funeral homes represented the wave of the future, especially since a 1909 law required filing an official death certificate within three days of death, a requirement that prevented families from burying their own dead relatives.[92] Shortly after her marriage, Lula Kelsey went to Raleigh to embalming school and became one of the first licensed female morticians in the state. Thereafter, Lula, not William, went with Noble in his wagon to the homes of the deceased, where she made an incision under the corpse's arm, drained all the blood from the body, and injected embalming fluid in the vein. She brought cosmetics, clothing, and tables on which to display the body. If the minister did not show up at graveside, she preached the funeral. By 1923, Lula Kelsey purchased a large building for the Kelsey and Noble Funeral Home and drove a big black Dodge hearse.[93] Her insurance background led her to found the Kelsey Mutual Burial Association, in which she served as an agent for a fire insurance company and sold life insurance and bonding services through another. She became a notary public in 1917, and later in life, she founded two other funeral homes in nearby towns. William Kelsey helped in the funeral home, but Lula Kelsey ran it, and he kept his barbering business. On Saturday nights when the barber shop got crowded, Lula would come down from her office and commandeer the system, rotating clients through the chairs more quickly by lathering one while William cut and shaved another.

Throughout all of this activity, William and Lula Kelsey loved one another. Kelsey was proud of his wife's entrepreneurial spirit and progressive attitudes. His job, as he saw it, was to let her "go ahead." They had eight children, most born during the first decade of their marriage, seven of whom lived, and they raised a foster child. Lula and William Kelsey managed their household with the same organization that they applied to their businesses and kept their children busy with chores. At home, Lula Kelsey depended upon Lillie Boger, who served as cook and nanny, and at work upon her lifelong secretary, Annie Hauser.[94]

No woman or man in Salisbury had been in as many homes as Lula Kelsey in her roles as debit man and embalmer. She saw cases of need firsthand, and she knew everyone. Moreover, in both of her occupations, she functioned completely independently of whites. Unlike a public school teacher or even a tradesperson with a biracial clientele, Lula Kelsey did not have to calculate white reaction to her every move. At the same time, she did not have to worry about what African American men thought of her. Her husband supported her career completely, and as one of the city's leading businesspeople, she could not be accused of sticking her nose into men's domain when she proposed reforms. To these advantages Lula Kelsey added supreme self-confidence, organizational genius, enormous energy, and faith in the future. In the middle of this frenetic activity, Lula Kelsey founded the Salisbury Colored Women's Civic League in 1913. She presided over the group for at least two decades, throughout the birth of her eight children and the growth of her companies. The league's constitution stated that "its object shall be the general civic interest of our people." Group goals included increased homeownership, better education, and improved public health. It aimed also to "stimulate a desire for the beautiful" by promoting public cleanup campaigns. Membership was open to any woman who met those challenges and paid ten cents a month. Forty to fifty women regularly attended monthly meetings.[95]

Women from all walks of life joined the Civic League. As Rose Aggrey's daughter recalled, "There wasn't poor and rich . . . not a rigid difference between people. The difference between people was those who had training and those who didn't."[96] Her mother, an active Civic Leaguer, had a knack for getting "women of all backgrounds together." The league's rolls included the wife of an AME Zion bishop, a dressmaker, a teacher, a laundress, a domestic worker, and a woman "from the other side of town— not trained, whose husband was in trouble, but a fine Christian woman."[97] Members embraced a wide range of religious denominations—Mrs. A. Croom was a Baptist minister's wife, Lizzie Crittendon an Episcopalian, Lucy Spaulding a Presbyterian, and Mary Lynch and Victoria Richardson members of the AME Zion Church—and they put the agendas of their women's missionary societies into action in the Civic League.[98] Those with "training" dominated the officers' ranks. Kelsey served as president, Mary Lynch and Victoria Richardson as vice presidents, and Kelsey's business secretary, Annie Hauser, as secretary. In addition to the general officers, the league divided the city into four sections, each of which had a female ward boss.[99] In turn, ward bosses chose block chairwomen and held them responsible for organizing every household.[100]

Many of the Civic League's projects involved interaction with white women. In fact, the impetus for the league's formation appears to have been an interracial community cleanup day, a project initiated by white club women throughout the state. Whites had tried to organize cleanup efforts before 1913, but "the most vigorous urging failed to stir the Negroes to action." It was not until they recruited Lula Kelsey to meet with a white male civic leader that plans for a joint cleanup day went forward. White Salisbury citizens finally realized that they could not coerce civic action among African Americans and that "without a Negro leader it is probable that the movement would have been a flat failure."[101] The city donated twelve barrels of lime, a disinfectant, and the Civic League supervised its distribution. The city's two African American doctors spoke to the women on sanitation and disease.[102]

Cleanup days evoked images of African Americans in the traditional role of servants, but they also put white people to work at servants' tasks: raking yards, whitewashing fences, carting trash, and improving housing. This made them a perfect place for black women to launch interracial forays. Moreover, on cleanup days, the entire community expected white landlords to improve their rental houses in black neighborhoods. As segregation rigidified, even the most prosperous black families found it difficult to buy decent housing, and they often had to tolerate living in neglected white-owned rental housing at close quarters. In the absence of building standards and housing laws, community cleanup days focused white attention on slumlords while also organizing black neighbors around a positive self-help project.[103]

As knowledge of disease transmission grew, whites initiated cleanup days to protect themselves from the peril they imagined they were in due to their poor black neighbors' lack of sanitary measures. Typhoid spread by flies and tuberculosis by uncleanliness, and both represented public health emergencies in the South in the 1910s. It is difficult to imagine just how prevalent and problematic flies were in urban areas with poor sanitation or how thoroughly they invaded homes before screening. In a sketch entitled, "You better eat before you read this," Eula Dunlap recalled that people sold the contents of their privies for fertilizer, and it was spread on fields and gardens, with dire consequences. The flies were so thick inside homes that if someone was sick in the summer, a family member had to fan constantly. Babies wore fly netting draped around them as they played outdoors in the summertime.[104] The death rate during "fly season" soared dramatically in the black community and increased modestly in the white community.[105] In reality, germs traveled to both communities, but better health care for whites limited their mortality rate.

The fly carried more than disease; it also carried the germ of interracial cooperation. Since flies knew nothing about the color line, they flew back and forth across it with no regard for class standing or race. As white interracialist Lily Hammond put it in her essay, "The Democracy of the Microbe," "The [white] club women came upon Christian principles of racial adjustment without realizing that they were dealing with racial problems at all. They simply started out with common sense as their guide and cleanliness as their goal."[106] In order to eradicate flies, one had to pick up garbage and extend sanitary sewage treatment to both the white and the black community. Such a cause fit perfectly into African American women's better homes movement.

As we have seen, interracial contact between women had existed since Reconstruction. The chief vehicle in the 1880s and 1890s was the WCTU. Religious white women from the North consistently worked as social service missionaries to the black community—women such as Lillian Cathcart, the American Missionary Association teacher who headed Lincoln Academy. By the turn of the century, southern white women occasionally worked in charitable causes directed at aiding African Americans. For example, Mary De Bardeleben, a Southern Methodist woman, began the black settlement houses known as Bethlehem Houses that flourished by 1914.[107] A group of white Episcopal women had managed Charlotte's Good Samaritan Hospital for African Americans since the 1890s.[108] Among North Carolina Baptists, white women spent the year of 1906 exploring "Daybreak in the Dark Continent, a Study of Africa" and gave "short but pointed talks" at the black women's missionary societies. White women took up collections for African American home mission work within the state, and at church conferences, black women heard "how the dear white ladies denied themselves to help us."[109] These contacts, well meaning as they were, were fraught with white ignorance about black life and exuded white superiority and privilege.

Interracial cooperation in public health campaigns coupled this missionary tradition with Progressive Era confidence in science and efficiency. No doubt some white women actually cared about African Americans' well-being, but most did not set out to eliminate flies in order to convert the heathen or to forge the ties of interracial cooperation or even to improve the health of the black community. They perceived their domestic servants as sources of disease and saw cleanup days as an attempt to solve this problem by enlisting the aid of black women leaders. As progressive public health campaigns made it apparent that germs spread throughout the entire community, African Americans seized upon white fears as a way to turn attention to their neighborhoods. George Clinton warned, "I am very much afraid that the average [white] Church member knows a great deal more about China than he does of the section of his city where the colored people live; his good wife can tell you more about the children of India than she can about the children of the woman who washes her clothes. In all conscience there can be no apology for this kind of ignorance."[110] In Clinton's Charlotte, when white women heard a program entitled, "Preventable Diseases: Where Does Your Servant Live?," they immediately hatched plans for a citywide cleanup day.[111] When they called a meeting with the mayor and city health officers to launch the work, they invited "the women of the colored missionary societies" to be present.[112] The white Charlotte women included black women not out of a spirit of interracial concern but out of a drive for self-preservation. Still, they were doing something controversial.

The minutes of the Charlotte Woman's Club do not record black women's attendance at the meeting that kicked off the cleanup day. The white women did not want their efforts publicized, and they used coded phrases and silence within their internal records as safeguards. White women operated in the civic sphere without the protection of the ballot and crossing racial lines could fuel the argument that introducing white women to politics would undermine racial segregation. Yet from these feeble beginnings, white women eventually grew bolder as they coupled their original narrow self-interest with a growing concern for the general social welfare. By 1920, the white Charlotte Woman's Club had set up clinics that employed black and white nurses, whose salaries were partly paid by the club.[113] Slowly, a pattern of contact emerged from public health campaigns that led to the institutionalization of interracial work within the social welfare context.[114]

The minutes of the Salisbury Civic League indicate that in Salisbury, as in Charlotte, public health work led to increased interracial contact. Mary Lynch headed a committee that visited "some of the white civic league ladies" and reported that the black women delegates had been cordially treated.[115] This initial visit prompted continuing contact. White women made cash donations and distributed flower seeds and plants to the Civic League, and the two groups cooperated each year in the cleanup campaigns.[116]

These efforts, begun through voluntary club work, aided the institutionalization of charity after 1910. In the following decade, large cities in North Carolina established Associated Charities branches to formalize and coordinate social service casework. In cities that were large enough, as in Charlotte, African Americans formed auxiliaries of the Associated Charities, presided over by leading black club women.[117] In Salisbury, the relationship was more informal, and Lula Kelsey became an unpaid social worker for the Associated Charities. The Civic League joined the Associated Charities in 1917. Soon Civic Leaguers passed out pledge cards for the Associated Charities' annual fund-raising campaign throughout the African American community.[118] Thereafter, when a needy case came to the attention of the Civic League, they referred it to the Associated Charities.[119] The Associated Charities used the league to determine whether a person seeking help really needed it and asked Kelsey to perform home studies on applicants. Kelsey's son recalled that whenever an African American came for help to the Associated Charities office, the white social worker there would telephone Lula Kelsey before she acted.[120]

With disfranchisement, African American women became diplomats to the white community, and contact with white women represented a vital, though difficult, part of that mission. As white women gained more power in social service organizations and public education during the first two decades of the century, they began to exercise growing influence in the public sector.[121] Contact between black and white women came about not because the two groups felt gender solidarity but because white women controlled the resources that black women needed to improve their communities. What interracial contact meant to white club women is more confusing, as it must have been to the white club women themselves. Just as their mothers had met educated, middle-class black women for the first time in the 1880s in the Woman's Christian Temperance Union, after the white supremacy campaign, many white club women got their first glimpse of organized African American women when they planned cleanup days together. Such meetings may have been the first time a white woman had ever spoken to black woman who was not a servant. From these contacts, a handful of white and black women formed cooperative working partnerships to further mutual goals, as did Lula Kelsey and the white Associated Charities social worker. But those partnerships were rare. To some, they represented a necessary step toward accomplishing their own civic goals; to others, they offered some fulfillment of religious imperatives. Beyond that, most white women probably did not give much thought to the meaning of their contacts with black women.

Yet however sporadic and confusing women's interracial contacts were, they represented a crack in the mortar of the foundation of white supremacy. White club women came to know more about the black community and its women leaders and became less pliant in the hands of male politicians who attempted to manipulate them to further the gendered rhetoric of white supremacy. The same process had taken place in the 1880s when white temperance women ignored the dire warnings of men and planned local-option campaigns together with black women. But imperialist rhetoric, scientific racism, the Democrats' white supremacy campaign, and women's lack of direct access to the political process had ended those contacts. This time, things would be different. This time, the local contacts between black and white club women had a chance to take root and grow.

In addition to fostering useful contact between women of both races, community cleanup work earned certain black women power within their neighborhoods and brought them into contact with city officials. The Civic League did not just hold cleanup days; it inspected homes afterward, counseled residents who did not follow sanitary practices, and reported them to the city if they did not comply with sanitary guidelines.[122] The membership card of the Civic League required the bearer to pledge to "improve the sanitary condition of the home in which I live" and to use "lime to disinfect and whitewash." Upon presentation, the bearer of the card could claim one gallon of lime, "Given by City; distributed by COLORED WOMEN'S CIVIC LEAGUE."[123] This public/private partnership across racial lines was a shaky one, but organized African American women quickly capitalized on it.

White men in local government came to know Lula Kelsey, Rose Aggrey, Mary Lynch, and the other leaguers as spokespeople for the black community—as women who could get things done. The women proceeded as if the city owed them a fair hearing in return for their civic work. Shortly after the first cleanup day, the league voted to send a representative to speak with the city administration about "helping with the cemetery," and by the next month, Lula Kelsey announced to the group that she had met with the mayor and he had "promised that it would be taken care of better in the future."[124] When a disorderly woman came to the attention of the leaguers, a mysterious blind white girl who apparently disturbed the peace of the community, Kelsey reported that she had "discussed her with the mayor and he says that he 'will take her in hand.' "[125]

In the first few months of league activism, contacts with city officials seemed to be limited to Lula Kelsey's privileged relationship with the mayor, but by the next year, the league had appointed a committee to appear before the board of aldermen to urge the passage of an ordinance requiring "sanitary privies" in the city.[126] The city lacked a public playground for its African American children, and the Civic League lobbied city officials to provide one. The league's attempts to win support from local government did not always succeed. Victoria Richardson suggested that a committee appear before the county commissioners to request permission to use the public schools "to give lessons on different subjects" in the evenings.[127] Apparently the commissioners tied African American adult education to literacy and voting and denied the league use of the buildings, but "moonlight schools" began meeting the next month in Lula Kelsey's living room. Within a short time, the moonlight school teachers reported that two men had made "wonderful progress."[128]

The league's projects read like a checklist for Progressive Era reform. Its work to establish playgrounds, for example, reflected two concerns: to provide supervision for children's play and move it from "the neighbor's back yard" to venues where sanitation and activities could be controlled. Both goals meshed with the "play movement" that swept the nation at the turn of the century.[129] Likewise, the women participated in "maternalist politics" by sponsoring "baby day," when mothers could bring their babies to a meeting for a doctor's advice.[130] Civic League women centered much of their effort around the public schools. They held fairs and paper drives to raise money for the industrial department of the graded schools, and a teacher who was a member of the league organized a Junior Civic League at her school.[131] The women visited the city jail regularly, ministered to a chain gang, and began an outreach program at the county home for the indigent.[132]

By 1917, Salisbury's African American women had two mechanisms in place to gain a hearing before both private and public manifestations of the state. First, contacts with white club women provided entry into the growing private social welfare system. Since black club women had met the white club women involved in social service, the Civic League could join the Associated Charities and then use that membership to direct the flow of aid to the African American community. Second, with husbands and brothers virtually disfranchised, diplomatic women could go in their places to the mayor and county commissioners to lobby for city services and, once there, cast their mission in female-coded, and unthreatening, terms.

As much as southern whites plotted to reserve progressivism for themselves, and as much as they schemed to alter the ill-fitting northern version accordingly, they failed. African American women embraced southern white progressivism, reshaped it, and sent back a new model that included black power brokers and grass roots activists. Evidence of southern African American progressivism is not to be found in public laws, electoral politics, or the establishment of mothers' aid programs at the state level. It rarely appears in documents that white progressives, male or female, left behind. Since black men could not speak out in politics and black women did not want to be seen, it has remained invisible in virtually every discussion of southern progressivism. Nonetheless, southern black women initiated every progressive reform that southern white women initiated, a feat they accomplished without financial resources, without the civic protection of their husbands, and without publicity.

At the same time that black women used progressivism to reshape black life and race relations, an organizational approach slowly began to replace racial "paternalism." The black community in Salisbury would not listen to influential whites who told them to clean up their communities. Nothing happened until whites recognized black women leaders, met with them publicly, and gave them authority. Then the city was "completely transformed."[133] Despite whites' extensive efforts to undermine black education by imposing a nineteenth-century version of industrial education, black women's progressive ideas made industrial education modern and useful by linking it to the sanitary science movement. Contacts between white and black women with progressive agendas set the groundwork for inclusion of African Americans in formal social service structures. Her desire to help solve civic problems gave Lula Kelsey the right to appear before city officials during a period when black men risked their lives if they registered to vote for those officials.

This is certainly not to argue that disfranchisement was a positive good or that African Americans were better off with limited social services than they would have been with full civil rights. It means that black women were given straw and they made bricks. Outward cooperation with an agenda designed to oppress them masked a subversive twist. Black women capitalized upon the new role of the state to capture a share of the meager resources and proceeded to effect real social change with tools designed to maintain the status quo.

seven

FORGING INTERRACIAL LINKS

As a few black and white women came together in their hometowns to tackle mutual problems, they simultaneously deepened their ties to statewide and national voluntary organizations, building networks that institutionalized their dialogue.[1] In the decade before woman suffrage, white and black North Carolina women structured statewide federations of local women's clubs that clarified their members' reform impulses and coordinated their activities.[2] Many of these same women worked together locally to found branches of the Young Women's Christian Association (YWCA). The state boards and national offices that supported the women's clubs and YWCAs gave women the opportunity to view interracial work from a distance. This remove provided space to lift interracial civic concerns out of complicated and personalized local contexts and facilitated the search for structural solutions. Moreover, the national networks allowed white women to see past the parochial racism that surrounded them at the same time that they afforded black women opportunities to orchestrate regional strategies to fight Jim Crow.

Although far-flung networks might routinize interracial dialogue, getting results depended on personal connections between individual black and white women close to home. Charlotte Hawkins Brown, who led the statewide Association of Colored Women's Clubs, often counted on Lula Martin McIver, the wife of the president of Greensboro's state-supported white women's normal school, to represent her interests before white civic activists. In Charlotte, Mary McCrorey enlisted the city's most powerful white woman, Ida McDonald Hook, in her efforts to found one of the first African American YWCAs in the South. When North Carolina's women confronted the crisis of World War I, the value of these limited interracial contacts became apparent to all. Throughout the state, leading women of both races conducted nationally mandated fund-raising drives and conservation programs in concert with one another. Then, as the nation recovered from war in 1919, North Carolina women's wartime experiences nourished the regional movement to plant Commissions on Interracial Cooperation throughout the South.

The term "interracial cooperation" came into common usage as African Americans and whites began to meet in more formalized settings to tackle social problems.[3] It is easier to know what it did not mean to whites than to understand what it did mean. Neither black nor white women believed that the results of an interracial project would benefit both races in equal measure. Nor were white interracialists integrationists. White women rarely followed their own reasoning to its logical conclusion. They began to identify with black women's efforts as wives, mothers, and community leaders to better their race, but they never advocated abolishing segregation, even if a tiny number of white women began to realize that Jim Crow caused substandard conditions for both blacks and whites. By the end of World War I, white women's mission was to refine Jim Crow, to make it work better. Segregation was so embedded in their worldview that it was as natural as the sunrise.[4] Black women wanted to end segregation and reverse political powerlessness, but they did not speak of these goals to white women. Instead, they set their shoulders, fixed their facial expressions, watched their language, and undertook interracial work without illusion because they knew that racial progress depended upon it.

As president of the North Carolina Association of Colored Women's Clubs, Charlotte Hawkins Brown began to direct African American women's formal civic experiences in the state in 1912 and continued to do so for twenty-five years. In keeping with the tradition among whites of anointing a visible leader as spokesperson for the entire race, in time Brown came to take both the blame and the credit for the health of race relations in North Carolina. She stepped into the vacuum created when male leaders such as George White and John Dancy left the state and the rank-and-file black voter left politics. No black man could claim prominence to equal hers in the state during the period. Brown's work and racialist ideologies illustrate that the decade before woman suffrage constituted a critical period in defining the boundaries of race relations that would remain in place until the post–World War II era.

Charlotte Hawkins Brown's life also provides a parable of the possibilities and the personal costs of interracial cooperation. Her story is so interwoven with myth—fiction that she fashioned to outmaneuver racism—that it is difficult to separate the reality of her experience from the result of her self-creation. The difference between her lived life and her public persona reveals a great deal about her perception of southern whites' racial ideologies and the points at which she saw possibility. Charlotte Hawkins Brown invented herself, repeatedly and with brilliance, but at great personal cost. Called "the twig bender of Sedalia," Brown might well have been called its wizard.[5] Her covert style contrasts sharply with Sarah Dudley Pettey's forthrightness. Although part of that difference might be individual, most is generational and situational. Pettey forged her political strategies to meet the opportunities she thought she saw. Brown crafted hers to circumvent the obstacles she knew she faced.

Brown related an invented life story through biographical entries, news releases, and fund-raising brochures. According to her account, she was born in Henderson, North Carolina, in 1883 to Caroline Frances Hawkins, the daughter of Rebecca and Mingo Hawkins. Her father was Edmund H. Hight, from "whom fate separated me at birth" and who "belonged to a family that had grown up on the adjoining plantation."[6] Brown characterized her grandmother, Rebecca Hawkins, as a "fair" woman "with blue eyes," the African American sister of her white master, "a great railroad captain whose vision and foresight built up the great Southern Railroad." Brown cast the white master as the Hawkins family's "protector."[7] "About the time of my birth, colored people in large numbers were leaving for parts north," she remembered. Charlotte moved with her mother and brother to Cambridge, Massachusetts, where her mother remarried and the family lived in a large, handsome house near Harvard University.[8] Caroline Hawkins managed a hand laundry in the basement, and Charlotte attended the public schools of Cambridge. Whisked away from the South at an early age, Charlotte was "not conscious of the difference in color and took part in all the activities of my class."[9] She acquired a New England accent, which she kept all of her life.

Charlotte Hawkins's family insisted that she get a practical education and sent her to Massachusetts State Normal School in Salem. Alice Freeman Palmer, the wife of a Harvard professor and the first female president of Wellesley College, was a member of the state board of education that oversaw the school. One day a few months before she entered the normal school, as Charlotte Hawkins was pushing a baby carriage while reading a high school Latin textbook, she chanced to meet Palmer on the street. Hawkins was babysitting to raise money for a silk slip to wear under her new organdy graduation dress, but Palmer assumed that she was an impoverished student, overcoming all odds to get an education. Palmer mentioned Hawkins favorably to the principal of her high school when they next met, and the incident ended. Now, when Hawkins realized that Palmer was an overseer of her normal school, she wrote to her and reminded her of their chance meeting. Palmer responded by paying Hawkins's tuition.[10]

Several months before graduation, Charlotte Hawkins met a supervisor from the American Missionary Association (AMA) on a train. The AMA representative impressed upon Hawkins the needs of the South, and Hawkins left school to accept a position at a one-teacher school in Sedalia, North Carolina, near Greensboro in 1901.[11] The AMA funded the school for two years, then withdrew support. For a year, Hawkins drew no salary, and she and the students survived on what they grew, the produce their parents donated, and a $100 county appropriation. Charlotte Hawkins returned to Cambridge and approached Alice Freeman Palmer for financial help, which Palmer promised to consider when she returned from Europe some months later. Palmer died in Europe, however, and Hawkins decided to name the school in her memory. With continuing county support and private contributions, Palmer Memorial Institute taught practical vocational skills to its students, and Hawkins became active in the North Carolina Teachers Association and in women's club work. In 1911, Hawkins married Edward S. Brown, "a Harvard man," and he moved with her to Sedalia to work at Palmer. But the marriage lasted only a few months since Edward said he could not remain in Sedalia and be "Miss Hawkins's husband."[12]

In the South, Brown tells us, she demanded the respect of whites and received it from the "quality people." She insisted upon being addressed as "Miss," "Mrs.," or, after she gained honorary degrees, "Doctor."[13] She refused to be Jim Crowed and reported that several times she was "put out of Pullman berths and seats during all hours of the night." But the incidents ended happily, Brown remembered, because "stranger than fiction is the fact that each time my southern lawyer, taking no percent of the recovery, sued and won."[14] By 1920, with the support of prominent Greensboro whites, Brown built Palmer Memorial Institute into a sprawling complex. She was proud that the most powerful whites in Greensboro served on the Palmer board, including Lula McIver and Julius Cone, head of the huge Cone Mills.[15]

As Brown rendered it, the theme of her life story is challenge met through interracial cooperation. Brown shaped the narrative in two critical

Charlotte Hawkins Brown in her wedding dress, 1911. Courtesy of the North Carolina Division of Archives and History.

ways: she minimized the restrictions of race in her daily life and exaggerated whites' helpfulness at every critical juncture. She obscured the fact that she was illegitimate by making it seem as if her father, Edmund Hight, was separated from the family by slavery. Brown was born in 1883 and had an older brother, demonstrating that her mother had a long-term relationship with Hight. The Hight family continued to live near Henderson throughout the twentieth century. Brown's grandmother, Rebecca Hawkins, may have been the sister of railroad magnate Captain John Hawkins, Jr., but, far from acting as the family's protector, he retained no contact with his black relatives and was a Democrat of the white supremacist persuasion.[16]

Brown mythologized her birth to remind southern whites of slavery's legacy: their shared kinship with African Americans. At the same time, she drew whites as sympathetic figures, the "protectors" of their African American relatives. Such circumstances did exist in the South; they just did not happen to exist within Charlotte's immediate family. As whites created the fictional "good darky" who treasured the interpersonal relationships that sprang from the close association of whites and blacks during slavery, Brown created a fictional "good master" who realized the responsibilities of miscegenation and loved his family, white and black. She used this good master to assuage whites' guilt about slavery and to argue that even slaves and masters achieved interracial understanding. She did not have to fight whites who melded ancestral ties to romantic class mythologies; she could simply join them. She shared their aristocratic roots.

Brown had moved to Cambridge not "about the time of my birth" but at the age of six. Yet she claimed to have no memory of her early life in North Carolina, no firsthand recollection of discrimination against blacks in the South, indeed no racial consciousness while growing up, even though she spent a great deal of time in the South during her childhood, even entire summers. Brown remade herself as a New Englander. When asked how her name should appear on her high school diploma, she instantly dropped her North Carolina name—Lottie Hawkins—for the more genteel sounding "Charlotte Eugenia Hawkins," which she made up on the spot. She spoke in a manner that "combine[d] the mellow tones of the southern Negro and the quick clipped qualities of New England—people turn[ed] around to see who [was] speaking."[17]

By casting herself as a New Englander, Brown attempted to remain above the southern racial structure. In Greensboro, she occupied a place much like that of African diplomats to the United States—she was an exotic but North Carolina's own exotic. If whites accused her of being an outside agitator, Brown could fall back on her North Carolina roots. Then she presented herself as native stock, a female, black Ulysses who fought her way back to the South and to her own people, where she belonged.

The story of the AMA's dispatch of Charlotte Hawkins to the South to save her people competes with another, more complicated parable that Brown merely hinted at and may have consciously avoided dwelling upon. Rather than seeing herself as a New England missionary to a foreign place, Brown may have construed her return to North Carolina as coming to terms with the realities of race in her own life. One night at a Cambridge meeting, she watched magic lantern slides of the race work being done by African Americans in the South. She was particularly struck by two educators, Joseph Price, the founder of Livingstone College, and Lucy Laney, the founder of Haines Institute in Augusta, Georgia. She noted that both Price and Laney were, like herself, very dark skinned. Price and Laney were also brilliant, and their faces on the screen moved Brown to feel that there was a place where she might belong: the South.[18] Brown never acknowledged publicly that she had any personal reason for wanting to leave New England, choosing rather to emphasize the missionary aspect of her return.

As the years passed, accounts of the relationship between Alice Freeman Palmer and Brown made it seem as if Palmer had sent Brown to the South to found the school and that they had enjoyed a close friendship. One writer described their relationship as one between "mentor and student."[19] The introduction to an address Brown delivered on a national radio program in 1940 stated: "While a schoolgirl [in Cambridge], she won the friendship of Mrs. Alice Freeman Palmer, former President of Wellesley College, through whom she was privileged to know the Eliots, Cabots, Lowells, and other distinguished people."[20] Contemporary newspaper accounts, which relied on Brown's own promotional material, reported that Palmer's "efforts" had made the school possible and "until her death she was an ardent supporter of her namesake."[21]

Although Brown did not actually lie about Palmer's interest in her and the school, she embroidered the truth. Brown and Palmer spent less than fifteen minutes together in their lifetimes, and Palmer never promised that she would personally contribute to the school. Instead, Palmer had told Brown upon their second meeting that she was too busy at the moment but that after her return from Europe she would contact friends in Boston to encourage them to support the school. Why, then, when Palmer never returned, did Brown name the school Palmer Memorial Institute? Actually, Brown originally named the school Alice Freeman Palmer Settlement in order to gain support from Palmer's friends in Boston.[22] Palmer, after a brilliant career, had died at a young age and was mourned by her friends, and a memorial to her could prompt contributions. Brown exaggerated Palmer's interest in her project in order to capitalize upon her death. She purchased the Boston Blue Book and the telephone directory and wrote letters to people in Boston who might have known Palmer. She portrayed her school as a settlement, a concept that Palmer's associates would be sure to understand and support.

Around 1910, Brown cannily began to play southern pride against northern dollars when she inspired white leaders in Greensboro to challenge their community to take over the financial support of Palmer.[23] In soliciting southern white support, Brown never mentioned the word "settlement" and most often called the school Sedalia rather than Palmer. For example, Brown named the group of students who sang African American spirituals the Sedalia Singers.[24] She understood the white southerners' sense of place, and since her school was the only thing in the crossroads of Sedalia, she did not encroach upon white territory in appropriating the name. The location of Palmer at Sedalia facilitated support from Greensboro whites. It was ten miles outside of the city, surrounded by sparsely populated farmland. Brown never permitted Palmer students to travel alone to Greensboro but instead brought them as a group, with the boys clad in coats and ties and the girls wearing hats and white gloves. Once in the city, they did not mingle with Greensboro's African Americans; rather, Brown negotiated special seating sections for her students at public events.[25]

Although Brown cloaked the curriculum at Palmer in vocational disguises and portrayed it to the press as an industrial school until the late 1930s, the institute offered mostly academic courses from its inception.[26] Booker T. Washington met Brown on a trip to Boston while she was still a student there and pronounced her "the only convert that he made in New England." If he believed her to be a convert, she outfoxed the Wizard himself.[27] To facilitate fund-raising, Brown invited one of Washington's agents, Monroe Work, to the school in 1911 to give his seal of approval to the vocational curriculum. Work did not like what he saw, however. "Increase your enrollment," he wrote. "All your literary and industrial teaching needs to be made more practical and especially does the literary teaching need to be correlated with the industrial teaching."[28] Brown never embraced Washington's vocational philosophy past the point of providing for the school's basic needs, but she portrayed the school as industrial, detailing "farm yields" in fund-raising letters.[29] An unidentified Palmer teacher explained the ruse this way: "[Brown] always had a college preparatory class . . . a cultural academic school. All the Negroes had to have that in order to get along in the South." Even though this teacher believed, along with Brown, that African Americans profited most from classical knowledge coupled with reinforcement of middle-class values, support for that sort of training did not exist. So Brown and her teachers positioned Palmer as a "vocational" school. Funding for industrial education "could always get through," the teacher recalled. Despite the vocational exterior, she continued, "you could teach anything you wanted when you got in your school. You came inside your class room and you taught them Latin and French and all the things you knew."[30] Although initially Brown's students were the poor children of the neighborhood, by 1920, Palmer functioned as an academic boarding school that drew students from counties across the state and included secondary grades.[31]

Notwithstanding her vocational cover, at times Brown argued that her approach to "cultural" instruction benefited whites as well as African Americans. She explained, "Recognizing the need of a cultural approach to life, believing absolutely in education through racial contacts, I have devoted my whole life to establish for Negro youth something superior to Jim Crowism." She tried to accomplish this "by bringing the two races together under the highest cultural environment that will increase race pride, mutual respect, confidence, sympathetic understanding, and inter-racial goodwill."[32]

Brown tried to create a third space for herself and for her students, a space neither white nor black. She often told Greensboro whites that "I will be separated, but never segregated."[33] To Brown, the difference be-tween separation and segregation was based on whether racial distance was of one's own choosing. She sought to distance herself from common whites, never intrude on either race where she was not wanted, and ignore Jim Crow restrictions in the world at large. Her philosophy resulted in a bizarre set of racial rituals that Brown convinced Greensboro whites to participate in and accept. For example, when Brown visited her physician, her secretary called ahead to communicate Brown's estimated time of ar-rival. Then Brown entered the office, brushed through the white waiting room and past the one marked "colored," and seated herself in a vestibule off of the doctor's study.[34] When Brown visited her attorney, her strategy differed somewhat since he had only one waiting room, and whites sat there. The secretary telephoned, the receptionist buzzed the lawyer as Brown pushed open the outer office door, and the attorney sprang out, ushering Brown into his private office at once.[35]

Brown reported that she frequently pushed the color line to the limits, but she added a fanciful version of chivalrous white support of her efforts. Contrary to her account, Brown's attorney did not altruistically volunteer to litigate numerous cases against the railroad without charging a fee. Again, Brown embellished the reality—that in 1920 she had the nerve to risk white support for Palmer by suing the railroad over segregation on Pullman cars—with a version featuring beneficent whites that represented only a partial truth. The attorney actually told Brown to bear up, advised her not to sue, cheekily suggested that she adopt Booker T. Washington as her role model, and demanded 50 percent of any recovery. Brown responded that Washington was a wise man "for his generation, but conditions have changed considerably for both races." She also reminded the attorney that their original bargain included a contingency fee of only 33 percent.[36]

Why did Brown repeatedly overdraw white understanding and support and minimize the restrictions that her color placed on her? Throughout her life, she operated by a simple rule: it is better to overestimate possibility than to underestimate it. Charlotte Hawkins Brown created a fictional mirror of civility in race relations and held it up to whites as a reflection of their better selves. From slavery, she drew compassion; from the loneliness of Cambridge, racial liberality among her schoolmates; from Alice Free-man Palmer's deferral, a legacy; and from frightened, pinched southern whites, chivalry of a sort. Brown was a political genius, especially suited for interracial work. Her renderings served her own purposes, but she did not delude herself into thinking that they were true. Immune to her own romantic stories, Brown was the consummate pragmatist. So convinced was she of her mission and of her opponent's rigid character, that she could risk the heartbreak of gilding the lily. She expected nothing, received little, and turned that pittance into bounty.

But Charlotte Hawkins Brown was a double agent. When she refused to turn her head toward the "colored" waiting room, she must have felt the stares of its patrons burn into her consciousness. In the decade preceding 1920, Brown immersed herself in social welfare projects and political activity that she kept hidden from whites. After 1920, Brown acquired a national reputation for her interracial work and landed official positions in interracial organizations, success that brought her activities under public scrutiny. Until then, and thereafter when she could, Brown generally said one thing to whites and then did another if it suited her purposes.

Brown's double life left its mark on her. A friend once described her as "ofttimes uncontrolled in the high temper which years of disillusion and strain naturally produced—keen disappointment in people and things." Brown might be consumed by "an ungovernable rage" over a small incident but when faced with a major crisis always remained "calm and calculating."[37] Living her life as a diplomat to the white community, Brown could never be just Lottie Hawkins. African American women who chose to take up interracial work walked a tightrope that required them to be forever careful, tense, and calculating. One slip would end their careers; they worked without nets.

In Lula Martin McIver, Brown found an exception to her belief that the southern white woman stood at the center of the race "problem." Their first meeting represents a classic case of the Brown treatment. Constantly seeking funds for Palmer Memorial Institute, Brown decided in the spring of 1905 that she must approach prominent white men in Greensboro for support. In Greensboro, Brown had no magic key such as Alice Freeman Palmer's name. Sedalia was a crossroads, Palmer Institute tiny, and Brown unknown. She had no historic connections to white North Carolinians there, no reputation in the black community, no denominational bridge since she had converted to Congregationalism, a faith rare in the South among either African Americans or whites. She had only herself—the New England persona she so carefully cultivated—and courage.

In 1904, she had written a poignant letter to Charles McIver, president of the white women's normal college in Greensboro. It began, "This letter may come to you from a strange source, but it comes from one whose heart is in the educational and moral uplift of our people." It concluded by begging McIver to come to Palmer for a visit. A year later, Brown was still imploring him to the same end, touting the ease of the train ride and signing herself "Very Anxiously Yours."[38] Still McIver did not come. One morning Brown dressed carefully in her customary ankle-length dress, hat, and white gloves and set out to call on him in Greensboro. She had no appointment. Most often Brown did not write or telephone ahead and risk refusal from those she wished to meet but simply appeared on their doorstep. That morning she knocked on the front door of the president's residence and found that he was away. His wife, Lula Martin McIver, invited Brown in, an unusual act in itself. Lula McIver was stunned by Brown's appearance at the door. "Her daring, her enthusiasm, her faith intrigued me," McIver recalled. The two women talked for over an hour and warmed toward each other. Soon, McIver was advising Brown on "the best way to win friends" and on how to raise money among the Greensboro elite for the school.[39]

When Lula McIver opened the door, Brown chanced upon a valuable connection that would prove enduring. Brown sat in the parlor of the state's foremost white female educational advocate. Graduated from the Moravian academy in Salem, Lula Martin had longed to become a doctor like her father. After she learned that the profession was virtually closed to women, she became an outspoken feminist. As an adolescent, she abandoned the Moravians for the Methodists upon reading that the early Moravian settlers chose wives by lottery. In 1885, strong-willed Lula Martin met Charles Duncan McIver, a dedicated young teacher, who supported her feminist ideas and called her a "most sensible" woman. They married in a ceremony that omitted the word "obey," and Lula refused a wedding ring, which she regarded as a "badge of slavery."[40]

The McIvers worked to build North Carolina's white public educational system one school at a time. While Charles traveled throughout the state promoting graded school education, Lula served as his advance team, preceding him to scrub courthouse venues speckled with tobacco juice, to set up chairs, to post flyers, and to raise a crowd. She was delighted when Charles became first president of the state-supported normal school for white women since both felt that educating women would be the key to building an effective public school system. She helped to found the Woman's Association for the Betterment of Public School Houses, and after Charles's death, she accepted a paying position as its field secretary.[41]

The subtleties of Lula McIver's racial ideology are elusive, but at the center of her thinking about race lay the strongly held belief that African Americans deserved a good education. For nearly a half century after they met, McIver continually raised money for Palmer Memorial Institute. Lula McIver attended meetings of black women's clubs in Greensboro. After the early death of Charles McIver in 1909, and to the eternal perplexity of Greensboro whites, each semester Lula McIver invited a male African American student from nearby North Carolina Agricultural and Technical College to board in the president's residence where she lived until her death. There, surrounded by young white women students, Lula McIver offered an object lesson in race relations.[42]

Both Brown and McIver realized the restrictions on their relationship in the Jim Crow South. For starters, McIver was a woman and thus not powerful in her own right. Moreover, as the normal school's maternal figurehead, she had to act circumspectly since all of her actions reflected upon the school, which was still in the minds of some a dangerous experiment that wasted state money to educate women. Given these restrictions, McIver could do three concrete things for Brown: influence prominent white Greensboro men to support her, introduce leading club women to Palmer's mission, and raise money. She did another intangible and invaluable thing for Brown: Lula McIver publicly referred to Charlotte Hawkins Brown as her friend.[43]

It appears that Lula McIver realized that her husband's influence would be more valuable than her own, and she urged Charles to write an "open letter of endorsement" for Palmer Memorial Institute shortly after she met Brown. Since Charles McIver served on the Southern Education Board, his vote of confidence carried weight in the North as well as the South. The letter went out in June 1905, but Charles McIver admitted in it that he had never been to Palmer.[44] He died four years later. Long after that, Brown named Charles D. McIver as her "first friend" in North Carolina.[45] There is no record that McIver ever made the trip to Sedalia or that Brown ever met him. With Lula McIver's help, Brown appropriated the memory of Charles McIver as she had that of Alice Freeman Palmer.

Local support of Palmer flowered around 1914 when Lula McIver brought a delegation of white women from across the state to visit the school. A member of the delegation wrote an account of the visit that appeared in the *Greensboro Daily Record* and encouraged white women to take an interest in Brown's work. Brown struck just the right note in her solicitation letter: Palmer, she said, "has conducted its work for the past 13 years without seeking very much help from our southern friends." She claimed friendship and a debt come due in the same breath.[46] The 1914 campaign was the beginning of a steady stream of white visitors to the school and financial support from white North Carolinians.[47] In 1917, Lula McIver conducted some of Greensboro's leading white businessmen on a tour of the school. Many of the men who had ignored Brown's previous appeals converted after that visit. E. P. Wharton recalled that Charlotte Brown had called on him around 1903 to obtain support for Palmer and that he was "ashamed of [him]self for losing sight" of Brown's work. He subsequently served for decades as a Palmer trustee. By 1920, the board of Palmer Memorial Institute included a Greensboro attorney, a banker, and an industrial magnate.[48] McIver sought no publicity for a trip she made to Boston with Charlotte Hawkins Brown two years later. There McIver called upon prominent white women, vouched for Brown's success, and asked for contributions to Palmer. When northern white women visited Palmer, they would not spend the night at the black school but stayed instead with Lula McIver.[49]

In 1919, Charlotte Hawkins Brown, with the endorsement of Lula McIver, published a remarkable novel, *Mammy*. On its face, the appearance of *Mammy* places Brown squarely in the accommodationist camp of African Americans, currying favor from whites by invoking the ties of slavery. The story tells of a loving black woman who nurses a white family and raises its children. Then, when the woman becomes old and ill, the family provides no help beyond an occasional visit to her drafty log cabin. Ultimately, they stand by as Mammy goes to the county home. Brown dedicated the book to "my good friend, Mrs. Charles Duncan McIver." She continued, "It is with gratitude I acknowledge her personal interest in the colored members of her household."[50]

What could Brown have hoped to accomplish by the publication of *Mammy*? At the time, she served as president of the statewide Association of Colored Women's Clubs, refused Jim Crow seating, and was secretly organizing a campaign to interest the state's black women in woman suffrage. She had spent almost twenty years building her dignity in North Carolina. It was amazing that she would play the *Mammy* card now. A close reading of Brown's introduction and McIver's response to the dedication indicates that both saw *Mammy* as a tool to promote their agenda: interracial cooperation among women. Mammies represented the one point of contact between southern black and white women, and white women continually bragged about their love for their Mammies. But Brown's *Mammy* is not a tale of love rewarded; it is an indictment of white neglect of African Americans. Brown calls upon white women to remember their duty to black women and redefines that duty in new ways. It is no longer enough to be fond of ol' Mammy; white women must act on that affection.

McIver framed her endorsement of *Mammy* carefully. She said that today's white woman was not the person her mother was, for in her mother's day, there was "understanding and sympathy" between the races. The problem was the separation of the races since there could be no racial harmony without "knowledge of each other's problems and an active interest in solving them." McIver endorsed the concept of "racial integrity" but reminded white southerners that their "task [was the] training of the uncivilized African." Brown must have winced at that remark, but it preceded McIver's most important statement: "I verily believe that to the most intelligent southern white women we must look for leadership in keeping our 'ship of state' off the rocks of racial antagonism." She signed the piece, "Your friend, Lula Martin McIver."[51]

Interracial cooperation, association among black and white women to solve mutual problems, was the solution that *Mammy* endorsed. McIver did not propose that white women individually care for their mammies but that they enter the public sphere and provide leadership. Male sailors had steered the ship of state onto rocky racial shores. It was time for women to man the lifeboats and rescue government from the oppressive racial politics of the white supremacists. In the same month that *Mammy* appeared, the state's white and black women began to do just that by traveling to Memphis, Tennessee, for a formal interracial summit. The state associations of women's clubs and the YWCAs sent forth those first intrepid female navigators.

From 1910 to 1920, while Charlotte Hawkins Brown delicately developed contacts among whites, she directed most of her remaining energy to building the statewide Association of Colored Women's Clubs, formed in 1909.[52] Brown attended that organizational meeting and spoke at national conventions in 1910 and 1912.[53] Women brought to club work the skills they had learned the hard way in their church work. In order to placate men who worried about their entrance into public life and to minimize denominational jealousies, the association embarked on a public relations campaign, sending speakers to other African American organizations throughout the state.[54] Brown won the presidency of the state federation in 1912.[55] By 1916, she served on the national board of directors.[56] Her national prominence, like that of Mary Lynch and Marie Clinton before her, gave North Carolina club women a pipeline to the country's most dedicated women activists, and local clubs benefited from the connections. For example, when Elizabeth L. Davis, National Association of Colored Women's Clubs (NACWC) organizer, visited the Salisbury Colored Women's Civic League in 1915, she brought practical suggestions that had worked elsewhere. Davis advised the Salisbury women to pressure the natural gas company to equip modern kitchens in Rosenwald schools, a suggestion that the local club saw to fruition.[57] Mary B. Talbert, president of the NACWC and a native North Carolinian, met with state clubs in 1917.[58] Brown's connections guaranteed that African American women's clubs in small North Carolina towns heard the NACWC's national agenda and acted upon it. Although they benefited from these contacts at the national level, southern black club leaders recognized that they shared problems peculiar to the Jim Crow South. In 1920, they joined together to form the Southern Federation of Colored Women's Clubs, a regional lobby within the NACWC, to give their concerns greater weight at the national level. Charlotte Hawkins Brown became chair of the executive board.[59]

African American federated women met in statewide conventions each year. In 1914, Mary Lynch led twenty-one women from the Salisbury Civic League to the meeting. The delegates to the statewide conventions represented many individual clubs, with different interests, that had come together under citywide federations. In Salisbury, the Civic League provided the umbrella structure, and its members came from organizations as diverse as the Embroidery Club, the Mother's Club, the Book Club, and the Young Woman's Christian Temperance Union.[60] As hundreds of diverse women gathered each year, they opened with a song that gave voice to their mutual purpose:

> Rise, ye daughter of Carolina,
> For our mission is sublime.
> Listen to our clarion watchword,
> "We are lifting as we climb."

As they sang the state song, delegates scanned an audience that included distinguished white women. In 1915, one of the few women doctors in the state, Delia Dixon-Carroll, a physician at Meredith College, addressed the crowd. Her brother was Thomas Dixon, Jr. She spoke just one year after the film *The Birth of the Nation*, based on his novel, had opened to such admiring white crowds.[61] Her family connection was not lost on her African American audience. Mary Lynch reported that Dixon-Carroll was the sister of Thomas Dixon, whom she called "an enemy to the Negro race." After hearing Dixon-Carroll speak, Lynch metaphorically severed the relationship between the two Dixons, allowing a new sibling relationship to take shape. Lynch reported that Dixon-Carroll "unlike her brother is helping all she can to raise the race and proclaim herself a sister to them." After the formal speeches, black and white women formed small groups for round-table discussions on the interracial work of white women's clubs.[62]

While the black women's association reached out to white women, the white women's federation reciprocated in a more tentative manner. If the activities of the white Charlotte Woman's Club are any indication, the interracial contact within public health campaigns at the beginning of the decade had borne fruit. White women moved from the isolation of discussing racial issues with each other to interracial dialogue by 1919. That year, the Woman's Club embarked upon a course of study to better understand the "perplexing and disquieting" problem of race relations. The white women, cocooned within their upper-class sense of entitlement, kicked off the year by discussing the well-worn servant problem, but this time the lecture's title reveals a twist: "Service in the Home—Workers' Viewpoint."[63] In subsequent months, the white women read and discussed the works of Gilbert Stephenson and Thomas Page on race relations and debated an article entitled, "The Negro in Relation to Our Public Agencies and Institutions." The white women did not simply argue among themselves; they reserved time for discussion with "Negro Race Leaders."[64] This activity drew a mild reproach from the editors of the *Charlotte News*, who suggested that the real danger to society lay in the fact that black women could now find employment outside of white homes. Rather than spending time studying the larger sociological implications of race relations, white women needed to teach by individual example—mistress to servant—a solution that conveniently removed both white and black women from civic affairs and put them back in the home. White women did not respond; they had moved past the Mammy model upon which the editors drew.[65]

Several white Woman's Club members took the lead in promoting African American efforts to found a black YWCA. The club had founded the white YWCA in 1902 to provide housing, training, and recreation for women who poured into the city to work in textile mills and offices. By 1914, the white YWCA was a three-story brick edifice that straddled a city block.[66] When southern black women approached the national YWCA to organize branches, the national board determined that any African American branch in a southern city must be supervised by an existing "central" YWCA. "Central" meant "white." If black women wanted to start a YWCA, there must first be a white YWCA in the city and its board must agree to start a black YWCA, which would then be overseen by a management committee of three white women and two black women.[67]

Southern black women resented these hurdles, but they believed strongly in the YWCA's ability to reach young urban black women. In 1915, Charlotte newcomer Mary Jackson McCrorey became involved in the effort to found a black YWCA, and black women approached Woman's Club president Ida McDonald Hook.[68] McCrorey's timing was good. That year, an interracial conference of southern YWCA workers in Louisville, Kentucky, had promoted increased African American organization in the South, despite the caveats the national board had placed on such organization the year before.[69] Student YWCAs drew black college women into service at African American schools throughout the state, including a chapter at Livingstone College.[70] Colleges were turning out African American women with YWCA training, but there were no black city YWCAs in which they could put their experience and ideals to work. At the same time, the number of vulnerable young black women grew as rural-to-urban migration increased. Despite the strength of denominational youth groups, they reached primarily church members' daughters. YWCA work could fill a critical gap that the churches and woman's clubs could not. It could seek out the urban newcomer, who was most likely uneducated and living in substandard housing, and teach her to make her way in the city.

Throughout the country, the YWCA specialized in reaching wage-earning women, giving them support and guidance on workplace issues, and directing them to wholesome leisure after hours.[71] Black women worked for wages in far greater proportions than white women, making the YWCA even more important to them. As an alternative to juke joints, bars, and the emotionalism of fast-growing charismatic religion, the YWCA provided a forum where middle-class black women could demonstrate genteel leisure activities, teach domestic skills, and act as role models embodying the possibilities of the African American woman. Black southern YWCAs took over former residences, generally large grand dwellings. A few bedrooms were reserved upstairs for emergency transients, and black women filled the parlors and porches downstairs with classes and meetings. In the hyperdomestic setting of the YWCA, educated black women, numerically overwhelmed by a flood of new migrants, could defend the position they had worked so hard to capture as representative race women, as interpreters of black life to whites, and as power brokers within the black community. Poor country girls saw, perhaps for the first time, what a middle-class home should look like, while they learned practical skills. If black women had not considered YWCAs so important, they could not have endured the years of racial humiliation it took to organize them.[72]

Mary McCrorey burst on the Charlotte scene in 1915 when she married Dr. Henry Lawrence McCrorey, the president of Biddle University. Her parents, Alfred and Louise Jackson, had been slaves of a professor at the University of Georgia, and Mary was their eighth child, the first born in freedom in 1869. She graduated from Atlanta University and taught for several years before Lucy Laney, whose magic lantern image had inspired Charlotte Hawkins Brown in Cambridge, invited her to become assistant principal at the Haines Institute in Augusta, Georgia, in 1895. The Haines Institute was part educational facility, part social settlement, and renowned as the most successful private school in the South managed by African Americans. There, Jackson taught Greek and became Haines's most popular instructor.[73] Laney believed in the YWCA, and Mary Jackson McCrorey was determined to found an African American YWCA when she arrived in Charlotte. Two other black branches existed in the South: one established in 1896 in Baltimore and another in 1913 in Norfolk, Virginia.[74] Young Men's Christian Associations for African Americans flourished in almost every North Carolina city by this time, and women used their facilities on occasion.[75] McCrorey understood that in order to establish a black YWCA in Charlotte she would have to obtain the approval and cooperation of the white women who led the Charlotte YWCA, women who were also active in the Woman's Club.

The opening of the Phyllis Wheatley Branch of the YWCA in 1916 made McCrorey's dream come true, but at the same time, it placed certain constraints upon her. As chairperson of the board of the Wheatley Branch, McCrorey depended on the white women for funds and, with three white members on the five-member board, for approval of her plans. Soon, McCrorey found herself in the middle of an interracial battle shaping up between southern black women volunteers and official YWCA organizers. McCrorey's friend Lugenia Burns Hope fired the first shot in 1917, after her hopes for an Atlanta YWCA were dashed yet again. The YWCAs' slow pace of growth among southern African Americans was disgraceful, especially since large numbers of black women and girls were pouring into urban areas to answer the demand for war workers. Hope attributed the failure to white women's lack of interest and Adela Ruffin's ego. Ruffin, a black North Carolinian, was the southern field supervisor for the YWCA, the only link to the national YWCA board, and she felt that the YWCA should be a club for middle-class girls, not a way to reach the young women pouring into the slums. McCrorey agreed with Hope on the YWCAs' mission and chafed under the national YWCA's requirement that white women be in the majority on black branches' boards. However, her dependency on her own white-majority board put McCrorey in a difficult position. When McCrorey dared to criticize white control of the YWCA, Ruffin misrepresented that criticism to McCrorey's white board as a personal attack on their leadership. McCrorey told Hope the white women had paid her expenses to a meeting in Cleveland, Ohio. Once there, Ruffin tried to "put me completely 'out of commission,'" McCrorey lamented, by making it seem as if she resented the white women's efforts.[76] McCrorey did resent the structure that delayed African American YWCAs until white women saw fit to help, but she knew that she depended on good relations with Charlotte white women. Ultimately, Adela Ruffin forced McCrorey to respond to the statement, attributed to Hope, that "the Southern white woman does not understand us and therefore we ask that we be permitted to form independent organizations." McCrorey and the other African American board member found a way to answer without making any "comment on our women themselves."[77]

As pleased as McCrorey might have been with the white women on her board, the issue was one of white supremacy. "If we are segregated, then why can we not be represented by our own women in National bodies and why can not our leadership be recognized?" McCrorey asked Charlotte

Hawkins Brown. Finally, after repeated protests, black women won a place for an African American representative on the national YWCA board, a position that went to Brown.[78] The ordeal solidified the friendship of Brown, McCrorey, and Hope. McCrorey signed her letters to Brown "With Plenty of Love" and addressed her as "Lottie Dear," a rarity at a time when even close associates referred to each other as "Mrs." or "Miss" and since Brown allowed almost no one to call her "Lottie."[79] While McCrorey proceeded with the utmost care in the YWCA negotiations, she spoke forthrightly on most other occasions. One white woman commented after a meeting, "Mrs. McCrorey was less antagonistic than I have ever seen her"—a backhanded compliment indeed.[80]

Mobilization for the U.S. entry into World War I drew immediately upon women's interracial contacts. Organizational lines between women's groups of both races blurred when the Council of National Defense asked Laura Holmes Reilley to head the North Carolina Woman's Committee (NCWC). Reilley was a past president of both the white Charlotte Woman's Club and the state federation.[81] The NCWC's charge was to coordinate all war work of North Carolina women. Reilley set up an integrated structure of county councils that included leading African American and white women, carefully chosen to represent clubs, YWCAs, and denominational social service programs.[82] Several months later, a white member of the Council of National Defense suggested that states segregate their councils. The North Carolina group protested at once, arguing that "good results have been obtained by incorporation of negroes in county Councils. As the work of the two races lies together, their organization should be together."[83] Sometimes the pressure for separate organizations came from national African American women organizers who felt that black women deserved the recognition they would receive if they were allowed to operate their own state-level organization.[84] Although Reilley continued to oppose a separate organization for blacks, she met with national field representative Alice Dunbar-Nelson and threw her support to hiring a full-time African American worker in North Carolina.[85] Dunbar-Nelson reported after a visit to Charlotte that the black woman who headed war work there told her that "the colored people are simply aching to be put in touch in an official way with the situation."[86]

Even though official credit did not come their way, the state's African American women remained undeterred. A single meeting of the Salisbury Colored Women's Civic League found members filling "comfort bags for colored soldiers" and collecting money while they listened to a Greensboro woman speak on the Red Cross work done by that city's African American women.[87] Women in each county in the state duplicated the Salisbury effort. Washington County reported to Reilley that seven white and two black branches of the Red Cross produced countless comfort bags, bought an ambulance for the front, and put together first-aid kits.[88] Winston-Salem was proud of its new Red Cross auxiliaries, one white, one black, founded as the result of interracial cooperation between women.[89]

YWCA and YMCA work in Charlotte during the war centered on Camp Greene, close to the center of the city, where thousands of white and black troops were stationed, including a company of African American troops from Lowell, Massachusetts.[90] Two YMCAs, one for whites and the other for African Americans, set up tents at the camp.[91] Black and white women who had been active in the YWCAs ran separate Hostess Houses, social comfort stations that supervised limited mingling between the sexes and warned the troops of the evils of prostitutes, at the camp. Their task was formidable. The white director complained bitterly of the "notorious women who make the round of the camps," and her tales of actual encounters with them opened club women's eyes to the need for "cleaner moral towns and cities for the sake of the industrial army as well as the fighting force."[92] The white Charlotte Woman's Club furnished and staffed the white Hostess House, but the women found racial tensions so intense at the camp that they had to back away from the interracial style they had cultivated in town. Prejudice was so strong among the troops, most of them from elsewhere, that the white YWCA director met with the black YWCA director at her home because soldiers' racial tension bubbled over when the two talked to each other at the camp.[93]

The Liberty Bond campaign demonstrated once more the usefulness of integrated county councils. White women now knew individual black women to whom they could turn to organize the black community. White and black women acted in concert to sell bonds. An African American woman, Addie Dickerson, traveled across the state to address meetings arranged by the black women on the county councils. In Durham, the Liberty Loan coordinator reported, "I turned it over to our colored chairman . . . Martha Merrick. She and Mrs. W. Y. Pearson, chairman of the National Defense, will work up a big public meeting with musical program and are very enthusiastic over it."[94] The reference is typical: the white woman is referred to as "Mrs." with her husband's initials, the black woman's own name stands alone. White women's actions and their enthusiasm began to outstrip their language.

To suggest that interracial cooperation was the exclusive province of urban, well-educated women would neglect the wartime project that produced the most profound change in the lives of North Carolina women: the farm home demonstration agent program. Food production had to increase for the duration, and as men went to war, the country turned to women to cultivate the home garden and the small farm. The white, mostly urban, club women on the state council were at a loss concerning how to marshal rural forces. Laura Reilley wondered if the state home demonstration agent, Jane S. McKimmon, might "be able to reach people that the rest of us do not know."[95] By the time the war ended, Jane McKimmon had reached an entire group of people that she had not known previously: black women. The experience inspired her to launch a fight that integrated her agency staff.

Home demonstration work among whites started in 1911 as a function of the state agricultural extension service, with Jane S. McKimmon at the helm. Parallel to this structure for whites, Nathan Newbold, state agent for the Negro Rural School Fund, used the Jeanes teachers to disseminate home demonstration curricula. In 1915, Annie Wealthy Holland, a Virginian who had studied at Hampton Institute, became state home demonstration agent among African Americans under a program completely separate from the state agriculture department. The title cloaked her real job— supervisor of the Jeanes teachers—in a nonmanagerial guise that avoided raising whites' ire.[96]

When Laura Holmes Reilley asked Jane McKimmon to encourage rural farm women to produce food, Reilley tapped an administrator whose passion for her mission obscured racial difference. Born in Raleigh, McKimmon had been the first home demonstration agent in the state and had built North Carolina into one of five "pioneer" states in home demonstration work in the country.[97] McKimmon could not succeed in increasing food production and preservation without the help of North Carolina's rural black women, and the black women were ready to get started. McKimmon, in turn, responded to their enthusiasm. "The eager calls from the colored people have been attended to," she wrote. "In every organized county the [white] home demonstration agent has been glad to assist where she could," McKimmon reported. She continued, "Intelligent colored women and men have come out to the demonstrations and agreed to go back and instruct others of their race in the art."[98]

In 1917, McKimmon received federal emergency money to hire part-time "North Carolina Colored Assistant Emergency Home Demonstration Agents" in forty-one counties and two cities, Wilmington and New Bern. The women whom she hired were often Jeanes teachers, and they worked intensively during the critical summer months. For example, Rosa Hargrave, a Jeanes teacher and member of the Salisbury Colored Women's Civic League, held the post in Rowan County. Annie Holland received the title "Colored District Agent."[99]

The black agent reported to the white agent in each county, and their close association caused white women to begin to explore conditions in the black community. The white agent in Davidson County reported that her black assistant sought to establish community clubs in the far reaches of the county. "I believe with her energy, tact, and diplomacy that she is going to be able to handle them all without any trouble," she declared. The agent, Dazelle Foster, certainly had energy. After relating that in one week she had traveled "24 miles by rail, 26 by auto and 16 by team," Foster concluded, "the days and hours are not long enough for me to give the help called for."[100] In Wilmington, the white supervisor and two black assistants divided the city into districts and promoted home gardens and canning clubs.[101] From New Bern came an open letter from the black community that reported that "'Hooverism' has been our main thought, and 'Waste Not' our motto in all our work."[102] In counties where no black women worked as demonstration agents, white women addressed groups at black churches and worked with Annie Holland to plan mass meetings. They also invited black women to their demonstrations. In one county, black women repaid the favor by presenting the county agent with a watermelon.[103] In 1919, white and black home demonstration agents organized 202 girls clubs and 232 woman's clubs among black women in the state, involving over 12,000 people.[104] By the end of the war, home demonstration agents of both races represented the state as inspectors, educators, and welfare workers. They worked to eliminate malaria, hookworm, and typhoid fever. They demonstrated the fireless cooker and the sewing machine. They taught nutrition and soil conservation.

With the war's end, federal funds disappeared abruptly and the black women's home extension jobs vanished, even though N. C. Newbold had plotted to obtain peacetime funds to continue employment of Jeanes teachers in that capacity in the summers and to centralize home extension work under his management rather than McKimmon's.[105] For a while, the interracial links that black and white women forged remained, and the white state demonstration agents continued to work with the Jeanes teachers on a voluntary basis. When white agents received resources, literature, and instruction from the state, they called in their county Jeanes teachers and shared it with them. "I have given the colored [Jeanes teacher] in this county lessons and demonstrations in bread making, securing free yeast for her; also lessons in home millinery, and anything else that I stress in my white clubs, and she in turn demonstrates to the colored women," the Beaufort County white agent confessed. "While she is not paid by us, she is much interested in the uplift of her race and very often goes with me on trips and holds meetings for the colored women while I meet with the white." Reports from Robeson, Mecklenburg, and New Hanover counties indicated similar experiences.[106]

The alliances forged in an emergency held strong enough for black and white women to choose to continue to drive together down rutted roads, chatting about their work and their hopes for the future. Their shared purpose reminded them of their common womanhood. Nowhere is this better illustrated than in the actions of the white Robeson County demonstration agent who confided that she invited black teachers to her office for sessions on millinery work and gave them money to buy materials to teach their students the same skills. Twirling ribbons, making velvet flowers, and gluing feathers, these women ostensibly made hats, but they also trimmed the racial divide.[107]

When federal funds disappeared, McKimmon countered Newbold's plan with one of her own. She decided to make a stand to secure funding for black home demonstration agents in her department, a plan her white county agents supported completely. "There is not a Home Agent in Demonstration work who is not eager to see work for negro women and girls continued," McKimmon argued. She made hiring black agents her agency's priority, telling her superiors that "no better expenditure of funds could be made than that for the payment of negro assistants."[108] She won her battle, and within two years, her department hired full-time African American women agents in six counties.[109]

The successful response of white women to the emergency created by World War I gave them confidence in their managerial abilities and made them question the male model of race relations. For more than a year, white women had attended interracial meetings, planned mutual projects through clubs and state agencies, and forged personal friendships. As Jane McKimmon's testimony illustrates, they did not want to return to complete separation of the races; they wanted to work with black women on social problems. This does not mean that white women questioned or rejected the ideology of white supremacy. They changed their behavior first to respond to the crisis. Now at war's end, they were left with the more confusing business of sorting out their thoughts and developing a racial ideology that allowed room for continued racial interaction. Black women realized this to be an unprecedented opportunity and increased pressure for formal contacts with white women.

In May 1920, Charlotte Hawkins Brown reported with delight that Ida McDonald Hook, state president of the white federation, had invited her to speak at its convention.[110] But Hook gave a different version, reporting that Brown approached her and asked to speak.[111] Probably Mary McCrorey introduced the two women to each other, and their differing memories of the overture were simply nods to the separate audiences that watched them on the tightrope of interracial politics. In any event, Brown spoke in May 1920. She asked for three things: an end to lynching and mob violence, cooperation between the black and white federations to establish a home for delinquent African American girls, and "the right of the Negro woman to share equally the franchise which would soon be granted to the womanhood of the state."[112] Her assertive speech built upon the decade of contact between black and white women, but her introduction of the suffrage issue into women's voluntary activities departed from the past. In the spring of 1920, it appeared likely that Congress would send the Nineteenth Amendment to the states for ratification. Brown's uncharacteristic forthrightness on the topic represented a preemptive strike. She knew that race would figure in any ratification campaign in North Carolina, and she seized the occasion to persuade white club women that black club women might become their political allies.

Before the issue of woman suffrage could reach a climax in North Carolina, however, Brown and McCrorey journeyed to Tuskegee for the regular biennial meeting of the National Association of Colored Women. Whereas Mary Lynch represented an older generation of activists by presenting the topic, "Moral Education a Necessity," a new generation planned a private interracial summit. Along with Brown and McCrorey, Lugenia Hope, Lucy Laney, and Margaret Washington wanted to capitalize on the wartime contacts between white and black women and to create a women's organization to improve race relations. Hope invited to the meeting two white Methodist women, Carrie Parks Johnson and Sara Estelle Haskin. Johnson and Haskin were introduced to the entire convention and then met with southern leaders privately. The leaders hoped to convince the white women to help find a place for interracial women's work through the Commissions on Interracial Cooperation.[113] Addressing the two white women, Hope invoked the debt they incurred to black women during the war and flatly challenged them to "help us find a place in American life where we can be unashamed and unafraid." Carrie Johnson remembered that as she listened to the black women, years of schooling in southern racial conventions faded and "my heart broke." Emotion swept over toughened Mary McCrorey and she later recalled, "The spirit of that meeting will last me the remainder of my life."

As they left, the white women asked the black women to complete a list of suggestions for continuing discussion and to send some delegates to the white Woman's Missionary Convention meeting that fall in Memphis.[114] Carrie Johnson carefully chose the black delegates to Memphis. She wrote

Ida Hook asking for her critique of Brown's recent speech to the North Carolina white federation. Hook responded, "I do not think that you would make a mistake in having Charlotte Brown speak to your women. . . . I did not hear a single adverse criticism."[115] Hook's advice convinced Johnson. She issued an invitation to Brown to address the meeting.

On the train to Memphis, a group of white men pulled Brown out of the Pullman car and marched her past "southern white women passing for Christians" who were on their way to the Memphis meeting. The white women sat silent as the men forced Brown to the Jim Crow car.[116] Brown probably recognized among the fellow Memphis delegates North Carolina white women whom she had come to know over the past decade. Among them was the wife of the governor, Fanny Bickett. Another traveler who sped toward Memphis that night—a woman unlikely to be moved by pleas for interracial cooperation—was Gabrielle De Rosset Waddell, the wife of the leader of the Wilmington massacre, Alfred Waddell. Since Alfred's death, Gabrielle Waddell had become field secretary for the Woman's Auxiliary of the Protestant Episcopal Church.[117] Johnson invited white women to Memphis who were "influential in themselves . . . [and] in strategic positions in church circles and club life," not necessarily those who had expressed an interest in interracial work. It is likely that Bickett and Waddell did not completely understand the nature of the meeting they were attending until they arrived. Johnson had given the gathering no publicity since "the whole situation was too strange and too delicate."[118]

When Brown rose to address the white women, the frustration of a decade of interracial work erupted, and she shared the humiliation of being ousted from the Pullman car two nights before. She exhorted white women to fight lynching, to recognize the dignity of the African American woman, and to help black women. Brown ended on an ominous note: "You are going to reach out for the same hand that I am reaching out for but I know that the dear Lord will not receive it if you are crushing me beneath your feet."[119] Most of the white women were profoundly moved. If Gabrielle Waddell felt anything, regretted anything, or feared anything, her diary kept her secret. She noted that Brown "occupied" the morning of the meeting and that she spent the rest of the day lunching with Bickett and visiting friends.[120]

The Memphis meeting inspired blacks and whites in many states to found Women's Committees of the Commission on Interracial Cooperation. In North Carolina, Brown and McCrorey served on the board, which Bickett chaired.[121] But a full year later, the white and black women still had not issued a joint platform based on the list of black women's concerns begun at the Tuskegee meeting. Brown, McCrorey, and Hope favored a version that included the controversial demand for protection of African

American voting rights. Their language was blunt: "We believe that the ballot is the safe-guard of the Nation and that every citizen in the Nation should have the right to use it. We believe that if there is ever to be any justice before the law, the Negro must have the right to exercise the vote."[122] But the white women balked at the suffrage statement and the condemnation of lynching, both points "which the Negro women dared not leave out."[123] Whites suggested the wording, "We believe that the ballot is the safe-guard of the Nation, and that every *qualified* citizen in the Nation should have the right to use it."[124] Brown, McCrorey, and Hope found their strong stand for suffrage undercut by Margaret Murray Washington and Jennie Dee Moton. Ultimately, Washington and Moton refused to sign the strong suffrage statement, and Brown's friend Minnie Crosthwait of Fisk University expressed the more radical group's frustration: "I can not agree with them on this question, I fear ever, because I am so sick and tired of dodging and parleying over things I know to be right."[125]

Interracial cooperation led straight into politics. As black and white women inched toward cooperation on a grass roots level, they came face-to-face with larger political forces. With a decade of women's interracial experience behind them, many African American women believed that the time had come to take a firm stand on suffrage. When women gained the right to vote one month before the Memphis meeting, black women realized that they must recast the politics of interracial cooperation. Black women looked to their white allies to support their right to vote, a gesture that underscores the success of interracial cooperation. Yet white women's confusion over black women's suffrage reveals the limits of voluntary interracial work. Black and white women alike must have wondered how they could continue in the coming months to steer the "ship of state" away from the "rocks of racial antagonism" upon which turn-of-the-century men had foundered.

eight

WOMEN AND BALLOTS

The issue of race dominated the campaign to ratify the Nineteenth Amendment in North Carolina in 1920, and race became the centerpiece of the subsequent drive to register women voters. Since the beginning of World War I, white women involved in interracial social service projects had allowed their racial practices to outrun their racial ideologies. Now they must decide if they wanted the black women who had been their allies to vote. Those white women who held equal passions for woman suffrage and white supremacy had to balance their attraction to the ballot with the putative detraction of black women voters. Those white women who opposed their own enfranchisement took up race as a cudgel to attempt to win their fight. Before it was over, all white women—suffragists and antisuffragists alike—developed new political styles that took race into account.

Black women, heretofore circumspect about electoral politics in interracial circles, now found themselves forced to take a stand. Some began by speaking out before ratification; afterward, registering to vote required a public act. African American women had to weigh their chances of successfully registering, determine whether voting might endanger their hard-won contacts with white civic leaders, and guess how their presence at the polls might effect black men's opportunity to regain the vote. Organizations such as the Salisbury Colored Women's Civic League had spent almost a decade building ties to white power. Now every league member would have to judge how well those connections would hold if a showdown came at the polls.[1]

The story of woman suffrage in North Carolina calls into question the traditional historical treatment of the South within the national movement. Defining the northern suffrage experience as normative meant finding the southern suffrage experience deficient on three counts: southern suffragists came to the cause late, lacked grass roots support, and were, of course, racist.[2] Although all of this is partially true, it obscures rather than illuminates the racial politics of woman suffrage, particularly in the upper South. Recent work on southern suffragists and antisuffragists attempts to correct this interpretation. It reveals a broad suffrage constituency strategically divided over state recognition versus federal ratification of woman suffrage, and it exposes the ways in which antisuffragists used race as a weapon.[3]

These more nuanced views of woman suffrage in the South prompt new questions regarding the implications for the whole of southern politics. To win their fight, North Carolina's white suffragists deliberately forced an artificial separation between race and gender. When their opponents inflated race, suffragists deflated it. Their rhetorical aim was to neutralize the Democrats' favorite racial bugaboo—the menacing black male voter. Most white woman suffragists downplayed race because they knew that if it became central to the ratification discussion, they would lose.[4] Like Solomon's solution, however, their strategy cleaved an organic whole.

North Carolina's white suffragists created a southern political world that did not exist: one in which race did not matter. In truth, as the Nineteenth Amendment impended, race preoccupied everyone *except* the white suffragists: black men and black women, white antisuffragists of both sexes, and those white male politicians whose careers were monuments to whiteness. An analysis that draws in equal measure on race and gender steers the story of woman suffrage back into the deeper political currents. It introduces suffragists among southern African Americans, prompts questions regarding the importance of women's voting rights among the disfranchised, and calls for sharper demarcations between the white suffragists' and the white antisuffragists' racial politics. Centering race and regionally contextualizing the meaning of woman suffrage make the episode more, not less, critical to the master narrative of southern political history. In the fall of 1920, the suffrage strategies of African Americans and the racial strategies of whites collided as the North Carolina legislature considered woman suffrage, as Tennessee's ratification made the Nineteenth Amendment law, and as black and white women converged on registrars across the state. Women's politics forever changed racial politics in North Carolina.

Arriving in Raleigh in early August, 120 North Carolina state legislators found the capital city in an uproar over the Nineteenth Amendment, now just one state short of ratification. The antisuffragists, organized by Episcopalian Mary Hilliard Hinton as a chapter of the Southern Women's Rejection League, had emerged from nowhere a mere two months earlier and set up headquarters in the Raleigh Hotel. Over at the Yarborough Hotel, Gertrude Weil, a young, northern-educated Jewish woman from eastern North Carolina, captained the Equal Suffrage League, a chapter of the National American Woman Suffrage Association (NAWSA). Hinton had come to the work recently. Weil, a seasoned veteran, had presided over her chapter for a year.[5] Governor Thomas Bickett called the legislators into special session to consider taxation issues, but it was inevitable that ratification of the amendment would dominate the session. An apostate antisuffragist converted to ratification under national Democratic pressure, Bickett argued that the legislators must act from practical rather than ideological motives. They faced "a condition not a theory. . . . Woman Suffrage is at hand." Therefore, Bickett urged, the legislators should exhibit "wisdom and grace" by voting for ratification.[6]

A slim majority of the state's white male Democrats opposed woman suffrage. Still uneasy about their illegitimate grab for power through the disfranchising amendment, their use of the now outlawed grandfather clause, and their resorts to violence when "constitutional" measures failed, most Democrats had long feared any amendment to the federal Constitution that touched on voting rights. If the federal government opened the polls to women, could it not enforce the Fifteenth Amendment and open the polls to African Americans? Any interest federal officials evidenced in the state's elections could only hurt the Democrats.

Since their political religion was white supremacy, white Democrats began preaching it against woman suffrage, even though the old sermon scarcely fit the new sin. White supremacy's most powerful symbol—the puffed-up black male voter who conflated political and sexual power—shriveled when the threat was female. Because it was white women who clamored to vote, it took several leaps to put black men in the middle of the question. Politicians quickly made those links—white women voters would lead to black women voters followed by black male voters—but the entire exercise suffered from its attenuated nature. Moreover, woman suffrage might begin to free women from their fear of that old image of sexually dangerous black men lusting for political power. When women voted, white men would lose their privileged interpretive position in politics. They could no longer shake the apparition of black men at white women to scare them away from public life. When white women went to the polls and outvoted black men, male Democrats who brayed about the dangers of "Negro rule" would begin to seem absurd. Like Dorothy, woman suffragists were powerfully close to drawing open Oz's curtain, and many white male politicians could ill afford to be seen without racial mythology magnifying their powers.

The incoherence of the Democrats who opposed the Nineteenth Amendment represents their inability to carry on politics as usual without black men to serve as their whipping boys. U.S. senator Lee Overman, from Salisbury, stated flatly that the game would be over when woman suffrage passed: "The Woman's Suffrage Amendment . . . is a reaffirmation of the Fifteenth Amendment." But to rest his case on nullification of the federal Constitution left him too far out on a limb, and he struggled to find some other reason to oppose woman suffrage. The outcome of the amendment, he predicted, would be that "the illiterate colored woman . . . may vote and pair with the most intelligent woman of the Caucasian race."[7] He did not explain why the literacy test would fail to apply to black women. During an earlier debate on the issue in 1917, one state legislator argued that white women thought themselves too delicate to enter the rough-and-tumble world of politics, and as a result, "Why, my cook would vote while my wife would not."[8] Very awkwardly, these men attempted to crosscut racial issues by drawing class lines with talk of the "illiterate colored woman" and voting cooks. To white male Democrats, the introduction of black women into the political process brought up confusing issues of the interconnectedness of class and race that reminded them of the fusion challenge of 1896. With the huge growth in the numbers of female industrial workers, an interracial political alliance might be more successful this time around. If the cooks voted but the middle-class white wives did not, the balance of power could shift.

This class-biased race baiting lacked sufficient rhetorical punch to change minds already made up for suffrage. The image of the black cook going off to vote after fixing a white family's grits and buttermilk biscuits could not carry the same political freight as that of the lustful black male voter lurking around the courthouse. Making white people afraid of black women voters was problematic since it went straight to the heart of the southern peculiarities of racial intimacy and distance. White southerners did not actually know their servants as complete people, but they nonetheless liked to think they knew them, and their knowing was gendered. White women and black women lived and worked in close quarters. Cooking, cleaning, raising children, and nursing all involved intimate bodily functions. If a white woman did not want to do the cooking herself, she simply had to trust her cook on the most basic level, even if she did not grant her any political wisdom. This sort of relationship—though fraught with inequality—did not readily lend itself to the kind of demonization favored by Democratic politicians. Of course, interracial domestic intimacy cut both ways. The same white men who demonized black men often bragged about how well they understood African Americans because of their privileged relationships with their "old black mammies."[9]

In fact, the thought that their cooks might vote did not daunt many white woman suffragists. Lula McIver tried to persuade Lee Overman to convert to suffrage by describing the sorts of women she knew who were worthy of the ballot. The list included her eldest daughter, a self-supporting Vassar graduate; her youngest daughter, who bested two boys in the statewide high school debate finals; her sister-in-law, "a childless widow, a wage earner, a tax-payer"; and "my faithful colored cook." McIver's widowed cook had been left with "nothing but trouble and four small children," whom she had struggled to educate. Now the cook owned her own home and paid taxes. One daughter was a nurse and the other a graduate in home economics. The two sons, though "sober young men," had been less well educated. McIver unabashedly informed Overman: "She and her daughters want to vote and they are far better prepared to exercise the franchise intelligently than the sons are although both sons have been called to the colors." McIver was proud to be in such company herself: "*I want to vote.* I appeal to you as my representative to make it possible."[10]

It is important to remember who represented North Carolina exactly two decades after disfranchisement. The turn-of-the-century white supremacy campaign became a springboard to political success, and those who had failed to participate found it difficult to win any office. To run at all, a candidate had to prove that he had stood up for white men's "rights" to whip fusion in the late 1890s. Charles Aycock's name became sacred when he died while running for the U.S. Senate in 1912. Furnifold Simmons still held the Senate fiefdom he had seized as his reward for masterminding the campaign; if anything, he was more powerful than ever after twenty years in Washington, D.C. Josephus Daniels had ascended during World War I to become secretary of the navy.

Cameron Morrison, the Democratic candidate for governor in 1920, characterized himself as the last of the disfranchisers to redeem his reward. Indeed, Morrison remained true to his training: he made the issue of "colored women" voters the centerpiece of the Democratic primary.

Morrison's opponent was O. Max Gardner, an avowed woman suffragist. Morrison predicted that Gardner's suffrage support would open the polls to black women voters and prompt federal scrutiny. Poor Gardner was "kicked and cuffed all over . . . and abused for his suffrage views as though he had founded the negro race or written the Women's Bible." Pundits concluded that Gardner lost the primary to Morrison on the issue of woman suffrage alone.[11]

The state legislature divided deeply on ratification; a slight majority opposed it. Most urban legislators supported it, as did three of the state's leading newspapers.[12] Those from rural areas, including the heavily black eastern part of the state, remained opposed.[13] By the summer of 1920, the national Democratic leadership was putting considerable pressure on North Carolina's Democrats to ratify, and Bickett came around.[14] Northern Democrats considered woman suffrage certain and realized that their southern counterparts' opposition might drive their own future female constituents into the Republican ranks. The Democrats' track record so far was dismal: only six of the thirty-five states that had ratified by August were predominately Democratic. Stonewalling now did not bode well for future elections. Moreover, the League of Nations appeared to be in trouble, and Democrats expected women's votes to influence Congress in their favor on that issue.[15]

At Equal Suffrage League headquarters in Raleigh, Weil calculated that suffrage stood a 50–50 chance of passing: 60 legislators for, 60 against. Her guess was quite close. The day before they were due to vote, 63 North Carolina legislators sent an antisuffrage pact to the Tennessee legislature, also in session to consider ratification. The North Carolinians promised to withhold ratification if Tennessee would do the same, but Tennessee representatives wanted no part of the devilish deal. For Weil to win, she must move three legislators into her column. Then the tied vote would go before the lieutenant governor, who happened to be the bruised but unbowed suffrage supporter O. Max Gardner.[16]

Long before Weil realized how close she was, Hinton and the Southern Women's Rejection League set out to make race the central issue of the campaign. They used methods remarkably similar to those Simmons had perfected twenty years earlier—distortion, sexually suggestive rhetoric, and the manipulation of statistics—to argue that woman suffrage threatened white supremacy. For example, when the president of Virginia's Equal Suffrage League spoke in Raleigh, the antisuffragists twisted her words. The suffragist said, "There is already political equality for the negro wherever the negro possesses the necessary qualifications for a vote." But the antisuffragists put these words in her mouth: "We know that woman suf-

frage means political equality for the negro and his share of the offices."[17]
The antisuffragists invoked Simmons-like hyperbole to measure the manhood of the men who might vote for ratification: "God grant that North Carolina has enough men with the spirit of the old South left in them to go down with their backs to the wall."[18] The echo was no accident. Simmons's former propaganda chief, Romulus Nunn of New Bern, served on the executive committee of the men's States Rights Defense League, where he employed the tricks he learned as a young man under Simmons's tutelage. Gabrielle De Rosset Waddell joined him in the work as vice president of the North Carolina chapter of the Southern Women's Rejection League.[19]

While the antisuffragists depended on white supremacy's familiar stories, the suffragists countered with crisp, reasoned arguments very new to the state's racial politics. Weil calmly answered the major charges relating to woman suffrage and race. The highest-minded antisuffrage argument was that a federal suffrage amendment violated states' rights. Weil countered that even the antisuffragists could not reverse the events of the past century. North Carolina had ratified eighteen previous amendments, Weil reminded them, "Why object NOW to the same method?"[20] When the antisuffragists declared that woman suffrage threatened the use of the literacy test, Weil responded, " 'Equal suffrage' does not necessarily imply UNIVERSAL suffrage. . . . I myself am strongly in favor of demanding higher qualifications for voting than at present. . . . It is the only way to cope fairly and effectively with the negro problem, which is a difficult problem with or without the negro woman."[21]

Weil's response—that she, too, supported the literacy test and would even like to see it strengthened—seems to fall within white supremacy's ideological boundaries, but actually it lies a bit beyond white supremacy's practical margins. The antisuffragists did not want literate African Americans to vote any more than they wanted illiterate African Americans to vote. By 1920, the literacy test stood for all of the complicated chicanery, including violence, that kept African Americans away from the polls. But Weil posited a different sort of literacy test, perhaps a "fair" quiz, "effectively" administered by honest officials. The antisuffragists spoke in code, but Weil refused to recognize their shared language of whiteness. Instead, she spoke plainly and took a literacy test to mean a literacy test rather than a signifier of white supremacy.

The antisuffragists' third racial argument suggested that black women would find ways to vote that had previously eluded black men, implying—again in code—that it would be difficult to use violence against black women. Weil's answer to that charge is the most interesting of all. She could have countered that black women could be more easily intimidated than black men. In fact, woman suffrage could even refine violence: just a show of force might be enough to keep black women from the polls. But violence or the threat of it, heretofore mainstays of electoral politics in the state, had no place in the suffragists' arguments. Instead, they substituted a twisted version of fair play to maintain white supremacy. The Equal Suffrage League calculated that if all adults, black and white, male and female, voted in North Carolina, the effect of woman suffrage would be to add 392,000 white women to the rolls to vote against a total of 336,000 black men and women.[22] Concocting an argument that dared speak of the deployment of 336,000 African Americans to the polls represented a departure from political discourse of the past. For the past twenty years, the rhetoric of competitive racialism had virtually disappeared, along with the black voter.

The antisuffragists were correct: woman suffrage put the African American back in politics. Woman suffragists were the first group since the Populists to formulate a political critique that crossed regional lines and pushed aside race in the South to focus on a substantive issue. Some Democrats thought they were just as dangerous to their unchallenged rule as the Populists had been.

Being a part of a national movement gave North Carolina's white woman suffragists some courage of their convictions, but NAWSA's absolute refusal to address the race issue gave them more. Black woman suffragists such as Ida B. Wells-Barnett tried to force NAWSA to declare support for black women voters, but the white national leadership cleaved to single-issue politics and argued that winning the ballot for all women could not be deterred by addressing potential discrimination against some women. Their argument is one of those purely ideological stands that are undercut in every attempt at their application. As long as there were women who were African American, NAWSA's refusal to see race was absurd in practice. It was, however, a powerful theoretical tactic in the South, and it furnished North Carolina's white suffragists with the useful strategy of remaining above the antisuffragists' racial arguments. NAWSA leaders accepted the "equation of the Negro and the immigrant" in an attempt to win southern ratification, and they comfortably upheld suffrage restrictions in their "progressive" argument that women's votes would improve social conditions.[23]

The North Carolina legislature voted to table the issue, but the next day, the Tennessee legislature made woman suffrage law across the country.[24] Suddenly, North Carolina women were eligible to vote in the November election, a little over two months away. Registration books opened in North Carolina the first week in October, a few days before Gabrielle Waddell, Fanny Bickett, and Charlotte Hawkins Brown went to Memphis for the interracial meeting. They returned home to face an enormous controversy over black women's registration.

While white suffragists tried to subordinate race to gender, African Americans—suffragists and antisuffragists alike—melded the two categories. Among disfranchised African Americans in North Carolina, woman suffrage represented a weapon that could be used to hold the black community hostage or brandished to open up an escape route from political powerlessness. The issue split African Americans on the local level no less sharply than it did on the national level. Nationally, black suffragists argued from a philosophical base that NAWSA had ceased to highlight: that voting represented a natural right. Charles Chesnutt put it simply: "I believe that all persons of full age and sound mind should have a voice in the making of the laws by which they are governed." Drawing on the lesson he had learned so long ago in his home state, he noted that "the rights and interests of no class are safe so long as they are entirely in the hands of other social classes." Women, Chesnutt declared, "constitute a class."[25] Chesnutt's argument recalls Sarah Dudley Pettey's unwavering belief in human rights. W. E. B. Du Bois mounted the same argument but took it one step further to conclude that woman suffrage would benefit the entire race. "Even southern 'gentlemen,' as used as they are to the mistreatment of colored women, cannot in the blaze of present public opinion physically beat them away from the polls," Du Bois guessed. If black women could not be driven away from the polls, perhaps their presence would open space for black men. Fully aware of interracial work among women in the South, Du Bois predicted that southern white women would "learn political justice much more quickly than did their men."[26]

Other African Americans doubted that line of reasoning. Annie Blackwell had come to know North Carolina's white women well through her work in the Woman's Christian Temperance Union in the 1880s and 1890s. She saw the 1898 white supremacy campaign wrench temperance "sisters" apart. If woman suffrage became law, Blackwell worried that a "grandmother clause" might keep black women from voting. Once that happened, empowered white women would lend their votes to racial persecution. Blackwell mused, "We . . . realize the influence that [white] women exert without the ballot—what would it be with the ballot?" Blackwell saw no signs that woman suffrage would lead to a more just world. She argued, "If the women of the dominant race had a broader and clearer vision of the Fatherhood of God and the Brotherhood of man, they would exert that influence now in the legislative halls and criminal courts." When white women had proven that they would give black people a "fair chance, and equal opportunity," then and only then would Annie Blackwell endorse woman suffrage.[27]

Contrary to Du Bois's argument, some black leaders worried that black women's presence at the polls would bring back the violence of 1898 rather than obliterate it. At the most basic level, some argued that voting had brought nothing but trouble anyway. One black man reviewed the rigors and horrors black men had endured to vote and concluded, "Now if the colored man has did all of this and yet he is denied the ballot what does anybody want to get our women in the same hole for?"[28] James Dudley, the president of the state-supported black North Carolina Agricultural and Technical College since its founding, issued a warning to the state's black women after the ratification of the Nineteenth Amendment: "Your entrance now in the political field will add fresh fuel to the fires of race prejudice and political hate. . . . Prejudice is losing its grip. . . . Why prolong the struggle?"[29] Behind Dudley's concern for maintaining the status quo lurked a complicated fear concerning white women in public space. In the South, contact between white women and black men always spelled trouble. If white supremacy dictated that a white woman enjoyed white men's protection wherever she went, a black man might infer that her presence at the polls would depend upon his absence. Under a racial system so heavily dependent upon gender, the further white women advanced into public space, the less room there would be for black men since there could be no common ground. As upper- and middle-class white women sought to vote and to participate more fully in civic life, many black men shuddered. James Dudley hinted delicately that if white women voted, they would lose caste. He cautioned black women not to "imitate" the white suffragists' actions: "I do not believe the white women who are going to become politicians and partisans are setting the best example for you to follow."[30]

A growing number of black men and women, however, pointed out that things could get no worse, and they predicted that woman suffrage would in fact ease voting restrictions on black men. Protests against James Dudley's letter poured in from across the nation. W. E. B. Du Bois called him "the last of a pitiable group" in the Crisis, and the Baltimore Afro-American labeled him "truckling" and suggested that he bowed to the white state legislators who paid his salary.[31] Mary Ovington, the white secretary of the National Association for the Advancement of Colored People (NAACP), wrote to Dudley and demanded an explanation. Dudley hemmed and hawed, explaining on the one hand that he was not a puppet of whites and had not surrendered his "manhood" and asserting on the other hand that if Ovington understood southern politics she would realize that African Americans must maintain low profiles to keep the peace. Ovington ended the exchange stiffly by informing Dudley that she found his meandering apologia "fully unconvincing."[32]

The young editor of the *Star of Zion*, William Jacob Walls, condemned the letter and declared that he was "surprised and ashamed" that this kind of advice could come from an "assumed leader of our race."[33] Lucie Bragg Anthony, a physician from just over the border in South Carolina, soon wrote to second Walls's position. She first objected to Dudley's advice to "keep out of politics" and reminded him that she was a citizen and as such was already in politics. Therefore, she should have a right to vote. Women needed the vote to continue their work for the welfare of their race and their country, she argued. Anthony was particularly irate at Dudley for predicting that women would "add fuel to the fires of racial prejudice." The fires of race prejudice had been burning out of control for twenty years. She professed that it was just like a man to shirk responsibility for his own situation and turn around and place the blame for African American political problems on women. "We suppose if everything doesn't turn out right it will be a case of Adam and Eve. The woman gave me the apple, and I ate it," Anthony recounted. "Well, brother," she continued, "we are so used to being blamed for the forbidden fruit, we are now in a good fix to be blamed for the forbidden suffrage."[34]

Charlotte Hawkins Brown pleaded with Dudley "for the sake of the emancipation of the race from this political thralldom . . . to espouse woman suffrage, our only hope." Brown believed that African Americans might use woman suffrage as an entering wedge to regain a place in electoral politics.[35] Like Annie Blackwell, Brown held no illusions about pre-existing gender solidarity across racial lines, but she understood the gender-based system of white supremacy and wagered that it could be turned upside down. She realized, along with Du Bois, that white men justified violence at the polls by arguing that white women must be protected from sexual threats. Black women posed no such threat. She also knew that white women who were suffragists wanted to downplay, rather than exploit, the racial aspects of woman's suffrage since she had contact with the leading white female suffragists in her capacity as state president of the Association of Colored Women's Clubs. Brown had put herself at the center of suffrage's racial politics when she spoke to the white club women's state convention earlier in the year and told the assembled white delegates that black women expected to "share in the suffrage that will soon be granted the womanhood of our state."[36] White suffragists buried the statement, fearful that the race issue would hurt their cause, but the white antisuffragists apparently discovered and twisted Brown's remarks. The president of the white women's clubs, a suffragist, noted that the convention received Brown's remarks cordially but that the "Anti-Suffragists have made capital of it and are saying 'that she advocated equality and the Federation endorsed her.' This of course is absolutely untrue."[37]

When Brown returned from the Memphis meeting, she faced an even bigger controversy concocted to scare middle- and upper-class white women into registering as Democrats. A week before the registration books opened, a Greensboro newspaper issued "A Challenge to the White Men and Women of North Carolina." Purportedly reprinting a letter from the "Colored Women's Rights Association for Colored Women," the newspaper named Charlotte Hawkins Brown as the organization's president. Mailed from Greensboro supposedly by mistake to selected white women across the state, the "Colored Women's Letter," as it came to be known, urged black women to register and vote in a language quite alien to black women's suffrage rhetoric. "The time for the Negroes has come," the letter began. It went on to argue that if black women registered, they could join with white cotton mill operatives and control the industrial counties of the state. It gave instructions on how to register and urged black women to file suits in federal court if denied registration. "There are plenty of white Republicans that will help us," it continued. "The white women of North Carolina will not vote and while they sleep let the Negroes be up and doing. When we get in power we can demand what we wish and get it." The letter closed, "Keep this a secret—don't let it get into the hands of Democrats. Yours for Negro liberty."[38]

The white male writers who impersonated members of the "Colored Women's Rights Association for Colored Women" showed their race, class, and sex with every turn of phrase. The thoroughly middle-class Brown would have been appalled at the idea of joining white cotton mill workers; rather, her sympathies lay with reformist white middle-class women. She knew quite well that white women would not "sleep" while the "Negroes would be up and doing," a shopworn image that elite white supremacists often used to inspire the white masses to action. Brown also knew that there were not "plenty of white Republicans who will help us," and she never would have directed black women to their doors. There is even a hint of sexual innuendo: "We can demand what we wish and get it."

Just past the preposterous racial threat, however, another threat lurks. The letter had a dual purpose. In the alternative reading, the Colored Woman is merely a stand-in for the poor white mill worker. If the middle-class white women did not stir themselves to register and vote, working-class white women, aided by their Republican allies, would. In a political culture ideologically dependent on white solidarity, this was not an argument that could be uttered aloud, but it is embedded here. The letter's author automatically assumed that white women who worked in cotton mills would vote against his interests at their first opportunity.

Brown went straight to the white editor of a competing Greensboro newspaper and explained that she did not write the "Colored Women's Letter," that she was president of the North Carolina Association of Colored Women's Clubs, and that she was certain that if the "Colored Women's Rights Association for Colored Women" existed, she would have heard of it. The newspaper published her defense, including her speculation that she was "inclined to the opinion that the letters were written by some white person to cause trouble."[39]

That was certain, but which white person was it? The Greensboro postmark was meant to implicate Brown or the Republican State Executive Committee headquartered there. The chairperson of the Republican Party denied at once that the party had anything to do with the letter. He assured the "good [white] women of the state that the Republican party's politics will be to let the negro stay out of politics." Another Republican functionary suggested that the letter represented "a poor forgery perpetrated by Democrats. . . . It is following upon the methods adopted by the Simmons machine."[40] The Republicans had supported ratification all along and made their position on black women voters exceptionally clear. John J. Parker, an ardent supporter of woman suffrage, won the Republican nomination for governor and ran against antisuffragist Cameron Morrison. Parker advertised in the Equal Suffrage League newspaper that he "Heartily Favor[ed] Woman's Suffrage."[41] He generally followed this strong endorsement with a dismissal of black voters. Typical of Parker's remarks was, "The negro as a class does not desire to enter politics. The Republican Party of North Carolina does not desire him to do so."[42]

Simmons's protégé Cameron Morrison, in a gubernatorial race suddenly made unpredictable by the presence of women voters, probably bore at least indirect responsibility for the "Colored Women's Letter." In any case, sending the letter to white women was part of a general fear-mongering campaign mounted to induce them to register as Democrats. In the primary, Morrison had antagonized white women by using Gardner's advocacy of woman suffrage against him. Now Morrison had to convince women to come to the polls and cast their first vote for him. One white man summarized Morrison's problem this way: "He must have the women votes or perish, but he does not know how to go after them for he does not fit his platform or the age in which he lives."[43] Ultimately, a more facile way to win women's votes than the "Colored Women's Letter" emerged: freshly-minted Democratic women politicians pleaded Morrison's case for him.

After avoiding race during the ratification process, white woman suffragists reached for it now as their first political tool. Upon ratification of the

Nineteenth Amendment, white woman suffragists sought power in the party that recently had preferred to keep them powerless. It is worth asking why this was the case, if only because they must have realized how they could have confounded southern politics by registering Republican. In North Carolina, with its long tradition of close elections, 392,000 white women Republicans would have been in a better position than enfranchised African American men ever were to tilt the balance of power. Certainly many white women simply wanted to join their family's party—their father's party—because of class-based interest and tradition. Class and gender meshed for suffrage leaders; upper-class white southern women saw the Republicans as the party of rough-and-tumble masculinity and of the working class. But above all, registering Democratic was a vote for whiteness. The Democratic Party had been the White Man's Party. Now it would be the White Woman's Party as well, even if it had shunned that opportunity until now.

Two polished female speakers headed out across the state to rally white women for the Democrats: Fanny Bickett and Delia Dixon-Carroll. Bickett, wife of the lame-duck governor, had just returned from the interracial meeting in Memphis. Five years earlier, Dixon-Carroll had cast herself as a racial moderate when she addressed the convention of the North Carolina Association of Colored Women's Clubs.[44] As Bickett and Dixon-Carroll began their tour, the registration books opened in Virginia, a few days before registration was to begin in North Carolina. From Richmond came reports of 8,500 black women standing in the registration lines. Others recounted that fully 10 percent of the women who registered in Danville, a town on the North Carolina border, were African Americans.[45] On the stump, Bickett and Dixon-Carroll declared that the tide of black women's registration continued unabated in Virginia and would spill over into North Carolina as soon as the books opened.

Good white women must vote since "the ignorant and the vicious, the selfish and the sordid will not fail to register."[46] This description is raceless on its face, but it is an adroit attempt to link black women with poor white women. Dixon-Carroll and Bickett must have assumed that their listeners would place all black women in the "ignorant and the vicious" category, even though they themselves certainly knew better. The "selfish and the sordid" were another matter altogether. Not knowing whether poor white women would vote in great numbers, Democratic women began to build an immoral political image for them, similar to that of the rapacious black voter but on the other side of the color and gender line. The "selfish and the sordid" reference could evoke fears of fast-and-loose white women and their black female allies undermining the homes of charitable-and-pure white women.

Dixon-Carroll admitted, "The Democratic government of North Carolina did not give women suffrage. They had a wonderful opportunity and passed it up." But she excused them: "Suffrage women are sports. We will not hold this against them." She concluded by reminding her audiences that "White Supremacy rests in woman's hands."[47] At last, the suffragists' arguments meshed with those of their former archenemies, the antisuffragists. What had been for the antisuffragists a virtue prior to enfranchisement—the avoidance of public life—instantly became a fault since white women must register to outnumber black women. Even the former leader of the antisuffragists, Mary Hilliard Hinton, announced that she would make the ultimate sacrifice and register.[48]

As reprehensible as their speeches were, simply dismissing Bickett and Dixon-Carroll as racists obscures the difference between their political arguments and those of traditional male Democrats and antisuffragists. In keeping with the preratification argument that woman suffrage would bring more white women to the polls than black women, Bickett and Dixon-Carroll acknowledged that black women had a right to register and vote. Their language is that of competitive sport, bluntly repugnant to the modern ear because of the naked racial competition it champions. They urged their team of good white women to outnumber, overwhelm, and vanquish the black women who would go to the polls. They projected victory for white supremacy through electoral means rather than through political violence, chicanery at the polls, or diffuse cultural intimidation. This is a paradigmatic shift in southern political language—one that most white men had not made.

To encourage white women of the "right type" to register, Dixon-Carroll and Bickett portrayed registration sites and polling places as safe and friendly, making claims that white men would have to honor in the future. In Asheville, women held tea parties and invited registrars to come and bring their books.[49] But even if white women could register in parlors, they had to show up at the polls to cast their ballots. With white women present, it would be difficult to urge men to "go out to the polls tomorrow and if you find the negro out voting tell him to leave the polls and if he refuses, kill him, shoot him down in his tracks," as Gabrielle Waddell's husband had done two decades earlier.[50] W. E. B. Du Bois and Charlotte Hawkins Brown were right: in North Carolina, at least, southern "gentlemen" would not use violence against black women. But no moral injunction or fear of the "blaze of present public opinion" alone could have deterred white men from beating up black women. Rather, after 1920, electoral violence decreased in part because polling places underwent dramatic cultural changes to accommodate white women.[51] The feminization of that public space began in 1920; within the decade, the League of

Women Voters orchestrated election day just as efficiently as the Red Shirts had done in 1898.

As Dixon-Carroll and Bickett toured the state, the Democrats painted dire pictures of black women clamoring to vote. Just as they had lied twenty years earlier about the outrage of "Negro domination" in eastern North Carolina, now they exported whoppers about hordes of black women registering there. The chairperson of the Democratic Executive Committee, recalling Furnifold Simmons in 1898, issued the bogus alarm that in the state's so-called black belt, Republican registration swamped that of the Democrats and "negro women are registering rapidly." At the time he floated his falsehood, black women had not tried in large numbers to register anywhere in the state, and they never succeeded in doing so in the east. His remarks were meant to arouse white women in the heavily Republican west.[52] The Democrats deployed their black woman voter scare during the first two weeks of October, the month allotted to registration. On the four Saturdays of the month, the registrars took the books to a public place and long lines formed. During the week, a potential voter could seek out the registrar at his home or work. A few white women did register during the week, but the odd practice that dictated that the book travel with the registrar as he went about his business certainly had a chilling effect on black women's registration.

Since in order to register, black women would have to come before the full view of the community on a Saturday, it would be safer if they came as a group. The state Association of Colored Women's Clubs and the NAACP coordinated a registration drive for black women in the Piedmont and the west that took the Democrats by surprise, even as they cried wolf about large numbers of black women registering in the east. In disavowing the "Colored Women's Letter," Charlotte Hawkins Brown never said that black women did not want to vote. Even as she branded the letter a forgery, she was busy crafting a sophisticated campaign to register black women. Assailed by white people for something she did not do, she hatched a far more grandiose scheme that escaped their notice. By the end of September, she ordered masses of literature from the National Association of Colored Women's Clubs to be distributed in every city. Then she proceeded to mastermind black women's registration through the state association, working closely with chapters of the NAACP, by now established in North Carolina's urban areas.[53] Brown wrote to Dudley, who opposed her on the issue, "I have to admit I am in the fight up to my neck and I expect to win out in it because it is right."[54]

A close look at Salisbury reveals how the process worked. Even without the ballot, the Salisbury Colored Women's Civic League had been a political force since 1913, and suffrage had been on members' minds for a long time. Elizabeth Lindsey Davis spoke to the Salisbury club in 1915, two months before her endorsement of woman suffrage appeared in the NAACP's publication, the *Crisis*. A few meetings later, the league voted to study woman's suffrage in an organized fashion.[55] On 24 August 1920, the day before the North Carolina legislature tabled the Nineteenth Amendment and two days before the Tennessee legislature voted to make it law, the Salisbury Colored Women's Civic League changed its name to the Negro Women's Civic League and established a permanent suffrage department.[56] Before the registration books opened in October, Brown dispatched instructions to the Salisbury Civic League. Members should wait until the last two Saturdays in order to take the registrars by surprise. To urge women to register and educate them in the process, the Civic League asked ministers to discuss woman suffrage from their pulpits on Sunday. On Monday, women ward bosses, turning to the organizational structure they had built for cleanup days and Associated Charities drives, simultaneously held four citywide meetings. Afterward, black women fanned out across the city, meeting at churches on consecutive evenings during the week.[57]

On the next to the last Saturday of the registration period, African American women across the state marched together to the registrars. White Democrats, who had manipulated so cavalierly the threat of black women voters, stood by incredulously on that day as black women passed the literacy test and entered their names on the books. "The sudden appearance of negro women at the polling places came as a surprise to the Democrats," blurted white men in Asheville. "Saturday was the first day that the colored women of Greensboro have shown any marked inclination to have their names placed on the registration books," marveled the newspaper that had concocted the "Colored Women's Letter" scheme. "It appeared that some influence had been brought to bear upon the negro women, so great was the increase."[58]

The registrars, Democratic (and occasionally Republican) functionaries at the lowest level, apparently had not been forewarned about how to handle such an occasion. Without a plan, they pulled out the little-used literacy tests; the black women read them and registered. But by the next week— the fourth and last Saturday—the state Democratic Executive Committee had issued marching orders to the registrars. They made whites and African Americans form separate lines, took everyone in the white line first, spent inordinate amounts of time quizzing the black women, failed them whenever possible, and then turned away the hundreds left in line at the end of the day. A band of white men assaulted a registrar for registering a black woman at the same time that he registered a white woman, a gesture that implied their civic equality.[59]

In the first two weeks of the month, eight black women had managed to register in Salisbury. During the last two weeks, black women approached the registrars in great numbers. One white man in nearby Kannapolis happened upon a black woman from Salisbury escorting local black women to register. When he stopped her and asked her business, she informed him that a similar campaign had succeeded in registering 119 black women in her hometown. He investigated and found her claim to be true. Still, he could not fathom a homegrown activist African American woman and was sure that some northern Republican had paid her organizing expenses. He never mentioned the name of the suffrage organizer, but if she was not Lula Kelsey, she had probably been trained by Lula Kelsey. Such women were completely outside his experience.[60]

Across the South, black women organized campaigns similar to that of the Salisbury Civic League, and they reported their experiences to NAACP headquarters in Washington, D.C., which had long made it clear that it supported "the right to vote for both men and women."[61] The NAACP had grown quickly in North Carolina, and it seems to have done so in those early years without attracting a great deal of scrutiny from white people. The *Crisis*, no doubt, proved a vital organizing tool. Rose Aggrey read it as early as 1913, and she must have shared it with other members of the Salisbury Civic League.[62] W. E. B. Du Bois, editor of the *Crisis*, was the keynote speaker at an interracial meeting of educators in Durham in 1916. By 1918, there were seven NAACP branches in the state. Mary McCrorey invited W. E. B. Du Bois to speak in Charlotte that year, and he addressed a large audience in Raleigh on the same trip.[63]

From across the South in 1920, reports of black women's triumphs and humiliations poured into the NAACP. In Mobile, Alabama, registrars told black women that they must own property to vote, and when the black juvenile court officer challenged them, court officials fired her.[64] From Birmingham came the news that when a teacher attempted to register, the registrar "called her an ugly name and ordered her out." Another teacher "answered every question asked her—ex post facto law, habeas corpus proceedings, etc." The disgusted registrar still would not yield and "tore up her card and threw it in her face."[65] Ultimately, in Birmingham, 225 black women succeeded in registering, although 4,500 made the attempt.[66]

It is impossible to know how many black women became voters in North Carolina in 1920. The voter registration books supply the only notation of race in the electoral process, and the state did not require their preservation. In a few counties, scattered books survive. For example, in Salisbury, despite reports of 119 black women registrants, the patchy records list only 9 black women. They also reveal, for the first time in the century, that a large number of black men registered to vote.[67] In Greensboro, 2,678 African Americans were twenty-one, literate, and thus eligible to vote.[68] Redistricting in that city required many white men to reregister, and, of course, all women had to register for the first time. Registrations totaled 4,156. White women who registered numbered 1,735 and made up 45 percent of the total. Ninety-four black women registered, constituting 5 percent of the total number of women. Remarkably, 190 black men registered. The total number of African Americans who registered represented 11 percent of those eligible to do so.[69]

In Raleigh, black women had taken advantage of the August ratification to register in a special September school tax election, and they voted in greater proportions than white women in that election. In a special election, a majority of registered voters must participate to levy a tax. Black women turned out to vote for school taxes in large numbers. In one precinct, 19 black women registered, 17 voted, and 15 voted for the tax. Of the 16 white women registered in that precinct, only 8 voted.[70] In nearby Wilson, in the October registration for the general election, 819 white women and 383 white men registered, compared to 62 black women and 122 black men. Of 1,386 new registrants in Wilson, 13 percent were African American.[71]

The most dramatic story unfolded in Asheville in the heavily Republican western part of the state. On 16 October, hundreds of black women approached the registrars.[72] To generate this turnout, Asheville's African American women used strategies that resembled those of the Salisbury Civic League. They held scattered meetings for several weeks, culminating in a mass meeting at the community hall. Several black men instructed black women on where and how to register. In a single precinct, 100 black women came forward, but only 43 actually applied after watching others fail. Only 17 succeeded in registering, despite the fact that the local press argued, "It is entirely proper for colored women who are qualified to register to vote."[73] Since there was a two-party structure in the west, each party accused the other of bringing black women to the polls. The Republicans accused the Democrats of failing to administer the literacy test and denied playing any role in black women's registration. The Democratic chairman wagered, "I will give 100 dollars reward for any instance where a democratic registrar has registered a negro woman or a negro man without subjecting him or her to the educational test."[74] As October ended, it became clear that black women's appearance before the registrars had a galvanizing effect on white women. For example, over 6,000 white women registered in Asheville, roughly 75 percent of those eligible. An amazing total of 600 black women attempted to register there, but fewer than 75 succeeded. On that last Saturday, the registrars must have applied the test more deviously; in one precinct alone, more than 100 black women applied but only 2 passed.[75]

Black women met with more success in Charlotte. African Americans owned 80 percent of the property in the Second Ward, and the Johnson C. Smith University campus dominated the Tenth Ward. A new middle-class black suburb, Washington Heights, spread in the Eleventh Ward.[76] Over 168 black women registered in the Second and Tenth wards, and some of the 75 women who registered in the Eleventh Ward were probably African Americans. Of the 3,763 Charlotte women who registered, at least 4 percent were black women.[77]

Whether black women met with success or failure at the registration site depended not just on individual registrars but also on where they lived. Black women succeeded more often in the Piedmont and the west, in cities such as Charlotte or in large towns such as Salisbury. In the east, registration proved difficult, even in urban areas. In Wilmington, for example, 3,000 new female registrants included only 10 African American women.[78] Whites in nearby Kinston conducted "one of the most strenuous campaigns since the adoption of the white supremacy amendment." Amid rumors that black women planned to register, the registrars vowed publicly that none would succeed.[79] Over in Laurinburg, white men had to convince white women of their racial duty to register since local white women "didn't want" suffrage.[80]

Anna A. Clemmons's experiences in Southport, a small coastal village, recall the white supremacy campaign of two decades earlier and illustrate vividly the widening breach in political practice between the east and the rest of the state. Clemmons wrote in desperation to Emma Wold, secretary of the National Woman's Party (NWP), to ask for her advice on how Clemmons might register as an absentee voter, actually a brilliant strategy. She told Wold that she was "no agitator or race leader." She served as a private duty nurse for a prominent white surgeon, and during the flu epidemic of 1918, she had saved many white lives. The local Red Cross had recognized her valor by awarding her a certificate for "heroic services." Clemmons was a Methodist and a property owner.[81]

Wold expressed surprise that Clemmons had been refused and told her that black women were registering elsewhere in North Carolina. "Have you tried personally?" Wold inquired. "If not, will you try and let us know the result?" If Clemmons was refused, Wold promised, the NWP would "see what can be done about it."[82] In fact, Clemmons had tried personally, and she quickly wrote to describe her experience. After her seven brothers tried to register and failed, Clemmons presented herself before the registrar on 15 October. He refused her, saying she could not read and write to "suit" him. She noted, "All persons of colored origin in this whole county have been unable to suit the registrar." But Wold's promise of an inquiry frightened Clemmons, who cautioned Wold not to use her name in any ensuing investigation since there is "so much prejudice existing until I am most assured I will be a victim of a lawless mob."[83]

Wold implied to Clemmons that help was on the way. "We have been giving the situation in the south a great deal of thought," she wrote. The NWP would explore an "enabling act" to place "federal authorities over registrars and election officials in all the states."[84] The NWP, however, did not sponsor voting rights legislation. Instead, a controversy erupted in the party over black women's rights. Mary White Ovington, appalled by the reports flowing in to the NAACP from the South, urged NWP president Alice Paul to make black women's right to vote a major issue. Paul refused to consider African American concerns and insulted black delegates at the party's convention. Anna Clemmons never heard from Emma Wold again.[85]

Self-help proved the only recourse for black women in eastern North Carolina. Clara Mann's campaign illustrates the resounding effect of black women's registration attempts. Mann was among a group of black men and women who presented themselves before a New Bern registrar. He announced to the group that they would have to "read the entire constitution, commit it to memory by the one reading, and write the entire thing," Mann recalled. "I thought that if I tried he would see that I was determined and give in, but . . . he got cross and deliberately informed me that they were not going to register any colored men or women."[86] The registrar then told Mann: "If she was the President of Yale and Colored she could not register."[87]

Clara Mann was not the president of Yale University, but she was a Hampton Institute graduate, the local Jeanes teacher, and the wife of a doctor.[88] She went straight to a local black attorney, but he advised her not to pursue her case. That advice, she angrily informed him, amounted to a "trick for 'Mr. John,'" and she left vowing to take up the issue with "some of our *real men*."[89] Before she was through, she enlisted the aid of Walter White of the NAACP, Attorney General of the United States A. Mitchell Palmer, and the national secretary of the Republican Party.[90]

Through efforts such as Clara Mann's, reports of registration irregularities reached the federal government. Black women in Wilson, who had registered in considerable numbers, turned their regular NAACP meeting into a protest, calling for an investigation into the election. They acted openly; the white press proclaimed, "Negro Women Make Known [They] Want to Vote."[91] In Washington, D.C., the NAACP lobbied for a congressional investigation, but southern congressmen blocked the effort.[92]

Probably less than 1,000 black women registered across the state that fall.[93] To judge the success of black women's drive for suffrage, however, one must look not just at the few hundred who managed to register on two Saturdays in 1920 but at the example they set for those who followed. The number of black women who voted in 1920 may have been small, but their significance in the state's racial politics was large. For the first time since 1896, black voters approached the registrars en masse. They assembled as the result of a coordinated, subversive campaign, a gendered attack on gender-based white supremacy. By their presence at the polls, black women dared whites to use violence and won the dare. When turned away, African American women refused to keep quiet, enlisted outside help, and sought to inspire their communities to greater activism. Despite the immediate failure of some of these formal protests, black men and women registered in ever-increasing numbers throughout the 1920s. Existing registration books reveal a scattered few African American voters in 1918, but they record hundreds by 1928.[94] A decade after her first attempt, Clara Mann voted in New Bern.[95]

Black women voters altered the political style of white supremacy. White women did not appeal to men to protect them with shotguns as they went to the polls. Instead, they roused white women to outnumber black women—an unfortunate, but legal, method of winning elections. For all of their efforts, black women could not and did not end racism, although they found ways to increase their power within a system that aimed to render them powerless. Political violence and disfranchisement represent temporal manifestations of white supremacy. Diminishing those vulgar mechanisms resulted in new, more subtle provisions to sustain inequality in a state that became known for its comparative civility, even as it continued to resist African Americans' claims to full citizenship.[96]

In 1921, white supremacy still stood, but it was a new racism for a new order. For the next forty years, North Carolina whites would cultivate a "progressive mystique" dependent upon education, polite interracial forums, and the relative absence of violence. This new model of white supremacy effectively constricted African American life in the state for another generation. In Greensboro in 1960, over lunch at Woolworth's, white North Carolina's insidious racist artifice would meet another, equally indigenous heritage: the activism that North Carolina's African Americans so carefully crafted and nurtured during the darkest days of Jim Crow.

epilogue

When I began this work, some warned me that I would be writing a tragedy. It is a tragedy, but one mixed with triumph. In the span of Sarah Dudley Pettey's lifetime, optimism gave way to despair, civil rights vanished never to be regained, and economic opportunities constricted. Yet Charlotte Hawkins Brown, born only fifteen years after Dudley Pettey, lived to see African American students demand seats at a Woolworth's lunch counter in Greensboro in 1960. It must have especially pleased her that the sit-in leaders came from North Carolina Agricultural and Technical State University, the university that the accommodationist James B. Dudley had built. Three days after the protest began, white women students from Lula McIver's Woman's College joined the black men and women. The white and black protesters saw their actions as a radical departure from the past, but they drew on the tradition of activism that Brown and McIver had nurtured.[1]

Perhaps the measure of tragedy should not be a single lifetime but the length of time the white supremacists envisioned their reign would last: a millennium. When one recalls that the disfranchisers assumed that their new racial order would last a thousand years, the fault lines that black women found in its foundation seem miraculous and immediate. Those who explore the politics of the oppressed must ask themselves how much worse life might have been without their resistance. Without black women's efforts and white women's limited responses, the racial politics of the United States might have moved closer to the South African system. The people in these pages left tangible and intangible legacies. Many black interracialists lived to see the end of segregation and the restoration of voting rights. They realized their vision.

Many white interracialists clung to their vision of a benign segregated society long after their black counterparts disavowed their leadership. Nathan C. Newbold, who stood up for black education in the 1910s, became distraught at black calls for integration in the late 1940s. As the doctrine of "separate but equal" came under fire, Newbold argued for the equality of North Carolina's system of black public school education. He searched frantically for ways to prove that his separate system was worth saving. He favorably compared black and white school property, teachers' salaries, and pupil expenditures. Newbold's racial politics remained static throughout his life; it was the world that changed. Upon his retirement in 1950, an admirer noted that Newbold had been "a radical" in the first twenty years of his career. Many whites had come around to Newbold's point of view, but many African Americans had moved past it. A genteel interracialist, Newbold embodied North Carolina's progressive mystique. How can one judge those who mitigate horrific systems? Newbold helped many people even as he strengthened the segregationist structure that aimed to keep them helpless. His attempt in the final hours to "save" segregation represents the logical outcome of his life's work.[2]

John J. Parker, the pro–woman suffrage Republican candidate for governor who ran against Cameron Morrison, found that his perfunctory dismissal of black voters, so civil compared to that of the Democrats, cost him the greatest opportunity of his life. When Herbert Hoover nominated Parker to the U.S. Supreme Court in 1930, an NAACP staffer found a yellowed clipping in the vast files documenting discrimination against black voters in 1920. Parker's vow, "The negro as a class does not desire to enter politics. The Republican Party of North Carolina does not desire him to do so," became the petard with which the NAACP ousted Parker. It cost him the nomination, and Parker's misfortunes must have sounded like a fire bell in the night to other loquacious white supremacists who aspired to high federal office. The same year, Furnifold Simmons suffered defeat and relinquished his Senate seat. Simmons lost the first time North Carolina used the secret ballot, and he blamed his loss on voter fraud: a fitting democratic requiem for an old tyrant.[3]

Other legacies are not as direct or as easily measured. Such an inheritance involves how we know what we know—how history comes to us through each other, without the intrusion of professional historians—and how we make that knowledge a part of ourselves. As I discovered time after time, the long-dead women about whom I wrote lived in their students' memories. Three examples will suffice. Woman's Christian Temperance Union (WCTU) leader Mary Lynch began teaching shortly after Reconstruction; in the 1920s, Lula Kelsey's son was among her pupils. A. R. Kelsey became the first African American to run for office in Salisbury in the 1960s. By then, the Lynch-Kelsey connection spanned almost a century.[4]

Sometimes legacies are the stuff of legend. Mary McCrorey taught at Johnson C. Smith University for many years before she sought a seat on the all-white Charlotte School Board in 1937. Although McCrorey lost the race, she earned the distinction of being the first black woman candidate for public office in North Carolina. McCrorey later attributed her political opportunities directly to woman suffrage: "Since the passage of the 19th Amendment all adult citizens are recognized as equal in civil and political rights and must have an equal share in government."[5] To McCrorey, the Nineteenth Amendment represented more than votes for women; it meant that everyone, male and female, black and white, could claim their rights. Years later, Kat Crosby, an educator who helped lead the desegregation of the Charlotte-Mecklenburg schools, recalled that although by the time she attended Johnson C. Smith University, Mary McCrorey was dead, women students understood that McCrorey exemplified the woman they should strive to be. As Crosby put it, "The shadow of Ma Mac was on every door."[6]

When I finally located Sarah Dudley Pettey's nephew, Edward Richard Dudley III, who had an illustrious career as U.S. ambassador to Liberia and as the first African American state supreme court judge in New York, he immediately recalled of his aunt, "She was a woman suffragist in the 1890s." His memory was one of triumph. But when I reached Sarah Dudley Pettey's granddaughter, Corine Pettey, and she listened over the telephone as I related the story of the grandmother she never knew, she became quiet. Finally, she said, "When I was growing up, poor and black, in New York City, my Aunt Sadie used to come over to see my father. . . . They would start telling tales about their lives as children in the South—about riding around in horsedrawn carriages, and such things—and we children would try hard to keep a straight face, because we didn't dare laugh in front of Daddy. But when we got in the other room, we would laugh. We were sure that they were making it all up for our sakes."[7] So, I thought, a tragedy.

But when I met Corine Pettey in New York, I found that her life story was one of success and political activism. Now an elementary school principal, she had been president of the student chapter of the NAACP at Queens College. In the 1960s, she sought the office of Democratic district leader, running on an antiwar, antipoverty program. When I saw the photograph on her campaign poster, the years fell away and there before me was the image of Sarah Dudley Pettey with a microphone, as determined as ever.[8]

When white and black southerners search their pasts, they can find reason for hope amid a heritage of violence and racial oppression. The worst of southern politics, now visible on a national scale, has obscured the best of southern politics for too long.

NOTES

ABBREVIATIONS

The following abbreviations are used throughout the notes.

ARC	Amistad Research Center, Tilton Hall, Tulane University, New Orleans, La.
CPL	Robinson-Spangler Room, Charlotte Public Library, Charlotte, N.C.
DU	Manuscript Department, Perkins Library, Duke University, Durham, N.C.
FWML	Frances E. Willard Memorial Library for Alcohol Research, Evanston, Ill.
LC	Carnegie Library, Livingstone College, Salisbury, N.C.
MSRC	Moorland-Spingarn Research Center, Howard University, Washington, D.C.
NAACP Papers	National Association for the Advancement of Colored People Papers, Manuscript Division, Library of Congress, Washington, D.C.
NCC	North Carolina Collection, Wilson Library, University of North Carolina, Chapel Hill, N.C.
NCDAH	North Carolina Division of Archives and History, Raleigh, N.C.
RAC	Rockefeller Archive Center, North Tarrytown, N.Y.
SC	Schomburg Center for Research in Black Culture, New York Public Library, New York, N.Y.
SL	Arthur and Elizabeth Schlesinger Library on the History of Women in America, Radcliffe College, Cambridge, Mass.
SHC	Southern Historical Collection, Wilson Library, University of North Carolina, Chapel Hill, N.C.
WCJL	University Archives, Walter Clinton Jackson Library, University of North Carolina, Greensboro, N.C.

INTRODUCTION

1. Sarah Dudley Pettey, "Woman's Column," *Star of Zion*, 6 Aug. 1896. The *Star of Zion* did not number its pages until 23 June 1898.

2. Rosenstone, "Experiments in Writing the Past," 12.

3. Terborg-Penn, "Afro-Americans in the Struggle for Woman Suffrage"; Higginbotham, "Women's Movement in the Black Baptist Church" and *Righteous Discontent*; Elsa Barkley Brown, "African-American Women's Quilting," "Negotiating and Transforming the Public Sphere," " 'What Has Happened Here,' " and " 'Womanist Consciousness' "; Hall, *Revolt against Chivalry*.

4. Anne Firor Scott, *Southern Lady* and *Natural Allies*; Anne Firor Scott and Andrew M. Scott, *One Half the People*; Marjorie Spruill Wheeler, *New Women of the New South*; Lebsock, "Woman Suffrage and White Supremacy"; Eric Anderson, *Race and Politics*; Williamson, *Crucible of Race*.

5. Habermas, *Structural Transformation*; Nancy Fraser, *Unruly Practices*; Ryan, "Gender and Public Access"; Barbara Jeanne Fields, "Ideology and Race in American History"; Thomas C. Holt, *Problem of Freedom*; Roediger, *Wages of Whiteness*.

6. James D. Anderson, *Education of Blacks*; Neverdon-Morton, *Afro-American Women of the South*; Jacqueline Anne Rouse, *Lugenia Burns Hope*; Earl Lewis, *In Their Own Interests*; George C. Wright, *Life behind a Veil*; Trotter, *Coal, Class, and Color*; Kelley, *Hammer and Hoe*.

7. Frazier, *Black Bourgeoisie*. For a review of recent memoirs, see Pinckney, "Aristocrats."

8. Gatewood, *Aristocrats of Color*. On Du Bois's philosophy of the "talented tenth," see W. E. B. Du Bois, *Souls of Black Folk*, 132–39, and Daniel Levering Lewis, *W. E. B. Du Bois*, 73, 133, 165.

CHAPTER ONE

1. Sarah Dudley Pettey, "The Up-to-Date Woman," *Star of Zion*, 13 Aug. 1896.

2. According to Tate, *Domestic Allegories of Political Desire*, 194, domestic fiction by black women authors remained optimistic until 1900. I aspire, like many historians before me, to fulfill Herbert Gutman's charge: "The essential question of study is not what has been done to men and women but what men and women do with what is done to them" (Abelove, *Visions of History*, 203).

3. For an overview of North Carolina during this period and contestation over the state's future, see Escott, *Many Excellent People*. Wilmington was the only North Carolina city with a population of over 10,000. For urbanization in comparative perspective, see Larsen, *Rise of the Urban South*.

4. Delap[p] "Populist Party in North Carolina," 53, 57. On the separate coach law, see *News and Observer*, 2 Mar. 1899, 3. South Carolina passed a separate coach law in 1900, according to Tindall, *South Carolina Negroes*, 301–2. Virginia also passed such a law in 1900, according to Wynes, *Race Relations in Virginia*, 68–83, and Workers of the Writers' Project of the Works Progress Administration, *Negro in Virginia*, 237–43.

5. Charles W. Chesnutt, *Marrow of Tradition*, 61; *Compact Edition of the Oxford English Dictionary* (Oxford: Oxford University Press, 1989), 2:2313. Chesnutt's journal, which he kept as a teenager in Charlotte and Fayetteville, offers an invaluable view of North Carolina in the 1870s. See Brodhead, *Journals of Charles W. Chesnutt*. On Chesnutt, see Helen Chesnutt, *Charles Waddell Chesnutt*; Frances Richardson Keller, *American Crusade*; Andrews, *Literary Career of Charles W. Chesnutt*; Flusche, "On the Color Line"; Williamson, *Crucible of Race*, 61–70; and Pettis, "*Marrow of Tradition*."

6. Charles W. Chesnutt, *Marrow of Tradition*, 61.

7. On race as a social construction, see Barbara Jeanne Fields, "Ideology and Race in American History"; Higginbotham, "African-American Women's His-

tory"; Roediger, *Wages of Whiteness*; and "Abolish the White Race." On pathbreaking attempts to come to terms with the social construction of race, see Cox, *Caste, Class, and Race*, and Dollard, *Caste and Class*. For a current example, see Roediger, *Towards the Abolition of Whiteness*, 5–6.

8. Most of what we know about class formation is based on the study of people who lived under very different circumstances from those of black southerners. See, for example, E. P. Thompson, *Making of the English Working Class*, and Blumin, *Emergence of the Middle Class*. Works that deal with gender and class formation proved the most important to my thinking, even though many of them deal exclusively with white women. See Welter, *Dimity Convictions*; Stansell, *City of Women*; Ryan, *Cradle of the Middle Class*; Hewitt, *Women's Activism and Social Change*; Lerner, "The Lady and the Mill Girl"; and Smith-Rosenberg, "Beauty, the Beast, and the Militant Woman." On class formation in the South during this period, see Hahn, "Class and State in Postemancipation Societies." For class issues among whites in southern cities, see Doyle, *New Men, New Cities, New South*, 189–225. On the complexity of class in North Carolina, see Janiewski, *Sisterhood Denied*; Hall et al., *Like a Family*, esp. 114–80; Escott, *Many Excellent People*, 4–12; and Greenwood, *Bittersweet Legacy*. Willard B. Gatewood, *Aristocrats of Color*, explores the black upper class and makes clear that this group was part of a national network that grew large enough in the South to affect local class structure only in a few cities. Insightful new community studies of African Americans include George C. Wright, *Life behind a Veil*; Earl Lewis, *In Their Own Interests*; and Trotter, *Coal, Class, and Color*.

9. For black women's connection to Victorian culture, see Carlson, "Black Ideals of Womanhood."

10. The motto of the National Association of Colored Women's Clubs, "Lifting as we climb," embodies this impulse among educated women in North Carolina at the time. See Elizabeth L. Davis, *Lifting As They Climb*, and Wesley, *History of the National Association of Colored Women's Clubs*. Stephanie J. Shaw argues in "Black Club Women" that the founding of the National Association of Colored Women's Clubs was not a response to the oppression of Jim Crow but was the result of the development of a sense of community under slavery, an extension of self-help beyond the immediate family in the African tradition, and the progressive voluntarism that swept the country after the Civil War. The club work of black women is explored more thoroughly in Chapters 2, 6, and 7.

11. Higginbotham labels this strategy the "politics of respectability" (*Righteous Discontent*, 14–15). For a discussion of the family as the location of citizenship for black women in literature, see Tate, *Domestic Allegories of Political Desire*, 124–79.

12. On Stanly, see John Hope Franklin, *Free Negro in North Carolina*, 31–32; Schweninger, *Black Property Owners*, 49, 88, 108–10; and Vass, *History of the Presbyterian Church in New Bern*, 135–36.

13. "Edwd. Pasteur, 10 Sept. 1818," Craven County Deed Book 41, 40, NCDAH.

14. New Bern manumissions list only one slave named Edmund freed between 1775 and 1861. See Craven County Miscellaneous Records, Slaves and Free Negroes, 1775–1861, NCDAH. A fragment of the family's journey to freedom is recounted in scrapbooks (xerox copies), file 1833–79, box 13, Hunter Collection,

DU. In 1830, John Stanly owned roughly 163 slaves, "more than twice as many slaves as the second largest free Negro slave owner in the South," according to Schweninger, "Anomaly of Black Slaveholding," 178. See also Schweninger, *Black Property Owners*, 110. Stanly owned 32 city slaves, mostly servants and barbers. Pasteur must have been a city slave who had the opportunity to earn money. See "Petition of Edmund Pasteur, a Free Man of Colour, to Emancipate His Wife Dinah and Children," Spring Term, 1827, folder County Courts (Petitions and Bills of Complaint), box 6.24, Bryan Collection, P.C. 6.1, NCDAH.

15. In the 1820s in North Carolina, manumission bills filed by white slaveowners routinely met with success. On emancipation, see John Hope Franklin, *Free Negro in North Carolina*, 19–35. Since Sarah Pasteur was sold after Pasteur's death in 1843, the petition must have been unsuccessful or the family must have been reenslaved illegally. It is possible that the attorney, John Bryan, did not file the petition since it is among his papers rather than in the court records for the period. On the racial climate in the 1830s in North Carolina, see John Hope Franklin, "Slaves Virtually Free."

16. My thanks to Emily Miles of the Craven-Pamlico-Carteret Regional Library in New Bern and to the Reverend James Delemar who led me to Allene Dudley Bundy and Delores Dudley Humphrey, great-great-granddaughters of Sarah Pasteur. The Dudley Family Scrapbook in Bundy's possession contains a photograph of a beautiful young woman with the inscription on the back, "Grandpa Dudley's Mother—This is a picture of Allen's great-grandmother. (Name Unknown)." Allen was Allene Dudley Bundy's father; his father was George Dudley; George's father was Edward Richard Dudley, Jr.; and Edward's mother was Sarah Pasteur. Allene Bundy and I were skeptical that this woman (not over thirty-five) could have been Sarah Pasteur since her daguerreotype would have to have been made before her reenslavement in 1843. However, the photograph does not appear to be a daguerreotype, and the dress and hair style appear to be from after 1865. It is most likely a likeness of Caroline Dudley, not Sarah Pasteur.

17. In 1860, there were 2,360 whites, 2,383 slaves, and 689 free people of color in New Bern. In Craven County, there were 8,747 whites, 6,189 slaves, and 1,332 free people of color. See U.S. Bureau of the Census, *Population of the United States in 1860*, 349, 351, 355, 359. See also Boykin, *Negro in North Carolina*, 27–28, 31–32.

18. On the opportunities available to African Americans along North Carolina's coast, see Cecelski, "Shores of Freedom." On fishing, see Mark T. Taylor, "Seiners and Tongers." On Edward R. Dudley, see U.S. Bureau of the Census, Manuscript Census, 1850, New Bern, N.C., M432, reel 626, 284. It is possible that Sarah's lover was a slave since slaves are not listed by name in the census. White Sarah Dudley lived seven houses away from the Pasteurs and owned ten slaves, including adult male slaves who were listed as black, not mulattoes. I would discount this possibility since the naming of Pasteur's son—Edward Richard Dudley, Jr.—seems intended to establish patrimony and since Edward Richard Dudley, Jr., never mentioned his father and was (at least in the census takers' eyes) considerably lighter than his mother.

19. On the increasing difficulty of emancipation, see Rosser H. Taylor, *Free Negro in North Carolina*, 6–13. As emancipation was becoming more difficult, the legislature abolished free blacks' right to vote in 1835. It is possible that Edmund

Pasteur voted until then, since at least fifty free blacks voted in New Bern until a petition from New Bern whites to the legislature led to the 1835 action. If Edmund Pasteur was a voter, ironically, his descendants could have voted under the grandfather clause after disfranchisement in 1900. See John Hope Franklin, *Free Negro in North Carolina*, 107–8, 116, and Rosser H. Taylor, *Free Negro in North Carolina*, 14.

20. Estate of Edmund Pasteur, filed Nov. 1845, Craven County Estates Records, NCDAH. U.S. Bureau of the Census, Manuscript Census, 1850, New Bern, N.C., Schedule 2, Slave Inhabitants, 231, shows Sarah and two "mulatto" boys, ten and seven, enslaved to R. N. Taylor. The low price may reflect the cronyism between the executor and the buyer or the fact that the mother had a three-year-old boy and a months-old infant. On Richard N. Taylor, see Richard Edwards, *Statistical Gazetteer*, 571; Alan Watson, *History of New Bern*, 256–57, 263; and U.S. Bureau of the Census, Manuscript Census, 1850, New Bern, N.C., 286.

21. Only one Edward R. Dudley is listed in New Bern in the census, and he appears only once, in 1850. As a white twenty-five-year-old, he would have been only fifteen in 1840 and therefore could not have helped Sarah Pasteur. It is probable that he was a member of the mixed-race Dudley family. This family, headed by Oliver Dudley, included very light-skinned members who married whites. The Marriage Bonds show that Edward Dudley married a white woman, Caroline Calhoon, in 1849 and had a son, James, by 1850. He lived near the waterfront in a community of black and mixed-race people, next door to a family named Laughinghouse. Dudley disappeared from New Bern in the 1850s and may have joined the exodus of Dudleys, Laughinghouses, and other mixed-race families who moved to Ohio, where many of their descendants chose their own racial identities. See Groom Edward Dudley, #000025901, Craven County Marriage Bonds, NCDAH; U.S. Bureau of the Census, Manuscript Census, 1850, New Bern, N.C., M432, reel 626, 284; Elizabeth Marsh to author, 14 Apr. 1990, in author's possession; and Dudley Family Scrapbook, Craven-Pamlico-Carteret Regional Library, New Bern, N.C. Marsh's research for a white descendant of the Dudley family puzzled about his grandfather's silence unmasks "race" as a social construction.

22. "Mrs. Sarah E. C. Dudley Pettey," in Majors, *Noted Negro Women*, 57–58; Alan Watson, *History of New Bern*, 374; James S. Brawley, *Rowan County*, 90, 108; Raynor, *Rebels and Yankees*, 35–39, 62; *Salisbury Evening Post*, 29 Apr. 1975, 6–7.

23. Majors, *Noted Negro Women*, 58. Alan Watson, *History of New Bern*, 459, lists E. Dudley on a baseball team with white players (the Atlantics). For Dudley as a Mason, see *Daily Nut Shell*, 29 May 1875. *Charles Emerson and Co.'s New Bern Directory, 1880–'81*, 133, lists black Masonic lodges. For African Americans in New Bern during this period, see Mark Mitchell, "History of the Black Population of New Bern." New Bern became the center for black-owned business in the 1870s and 1880s. See *Beveridge and Co.'s North Carolina State Directory, 1877–1878*, 239–72, and *Chataigne's North Carolina State Directory and Gazetteer, 1883–1884*, 272–84. On race relations in New Bern at the time, see *The Radical* 1, no. 1 ([1867]), in uncataloged North Carolina material, [New] Addendum, American Missionary Association Archives, ARC.

24. "James Walker Hood," in Walls, *African Methodist Episcopal Zion Church*, 578; "James Walker Hood," in Lucas, Parramore, and Thorpe, *Paths toward Freedom*,

159; Harry Van Buren Richardson, *Dark Salvation*, 205; Alan Watson, *History of New Bern*, 413, 448–49. James Walker Hood was the minister of Saint Peter's when Dudley joined. On the Good Templars, see Chapter 2 and clipping from *New Bern Daily Times*, 12 June 1873, scrapbooks (xerox copies), file 1833–79, box 13, Hunter Collection, DU. For a general description of the Good Templar movement among African Americans in North Carolina, see Haley, *Charles N. Hunter*, 27–30.

25. Caroline Dudley's maiden name, which began with an "E," is unknown. A sketch probably written by her daughter hints that she was the child of her owner: "Mrs. Dudley as a slave enjoyed peculiar advantages and most favorable indeed in those poverty days of servitude." See Majors, *Noted Negro Women*, 58. Caroline Dudley died between 1880 and 1891, and Edward Dudley married Susie Blackwell, who had nine children of her own. See U.S. Bureau of the Census, Manuscript Census, 1880, Craven County, N.C., 8th Township, 2, and Manuscript Census, 1900, Craven County, N.C., Microcopy T-623, reel 1190, 132A.

26. The two sides of the change versus continuity argument are represented by C. Vann Woodward, who argues that the 1890s marked a disruption in southern history with the institutionalization of segregation laws, and Howard N. Rabinowitz, who argues that exclusion of African Americans was in place by 1890. See Woodward, *Origins of the New South* and *Strange Career of Jim Crow*, and Rabinowitz, *Race Relations in the Urban South*. For a continuation of this debate, see Thelen, Rabinowitz, and Woodward, "Perspectives." For recent cases similar to the one I describe here and contradictory to Rabinowitz's, see Graves, "Jim Crow in Arkansas," and Greenwood, *Bittersweet Legacy*.

27. According to Eric Anderson, after the legislatures in which Dudley served (1870 and 1872), the "legislatures of 1876, 1879, 1883, and 1887 each had fifteen or more black members" (*Race and Politics*, 248). Several African Americans were elected in 1896. See Edmonds, *Negro and Fusion Politics*, 104–5.

28. Edmonds, *Negro and Fusion Politics*, 67–71; Eric Anderson, *Race and Politics*, 248–51.

29. Eric Anderson, *Race and Politics*, 162; Edmonds, *Negro and Fusion Politics*, 41; Frenise A. Logan, *Negro in North Carolina*, 49–55.

30. Eric Anderson, *Race and Politics*, 214–15; Steelman, "Republican Party Strategists."

31. Balanoff, "Negro Legislators," 30; Hamilton, *Reconstruction in North Carolina*, 536; Alan Watson, *History of New Bern*, 437; *Turner's North Carolina Almanac, 1873*, 34. A similar law limited local government in Virginia. See Martin, *Negro Disfranchisement in Virginia*, 84–85.

32. *Charles Emerson and Co.'s New Bern Directory, 1880–'81*, 54, 127; *Branson's North Carolina Business Directory for 1884*, 238; Alan Watson, *History of New Bern*, 471.

33. *New Bern Weekly Journal*, 1886, quoted in Alan Watson, *History of New Bern*, 479.

34. Eric Anderson, *Race and Politics*, 97–112; *Messenger*, 23 Sept., 7 Oct. 1882.

35. Clipping from *Western Sentinel*, 8 Nov. 1883, scrapbooks, file 1880–86, box 13, Hunter Collection, DU; Frenise A. Logan, *Negro in North Carolina*, 33–37; Eric Anderson, *Race and Politics*, 135–40; Alan Watson, *History of New Bern*, 478–81. By the time Simmons wrote his memoirs, he no longer recognized his debt to African Americans. See Rippy, *F. M. Simmons*, 16–17.

36. *Messenger*, 26 Feb. 1887.

37. Eric Anderson, *Race and Politics*, 143–62; Alan Watson, *History of New Bern*, 483; Rippy, *F. M. Simmons*, 18.

38. For short biographical sketches of Sarah Dudley Pettey, see Majors, *Noted Negro Women*, 57–64 (which gives her year of birth as 1868), and Culp, *Twentieth Century Negro Literature*, 182 (which gives her year of birth as 1869). I compiled the Dudley family history from information supplied by the family's descendants as well as the U.S. Bureau of the Census, Manuscript Census, 1870, New Bern, N.C., 144 (which lists Sarah and her brother as born within two months of each other in 1870); Manuscript Census, 1880, Craven County, N.C., 8th Township, 2; and Manuscript Census, 1900, Craven County, N.C., 8th Township, Microcopy T623, reel 1190, 132A and 232A. A clipping from the 1940s in the Mollie Lee Collection, Richard B. Harrison Public Library, Raleigh, N.C., announcing the appointment of a Manhattan borough president named Edward Richard Dudley led me to Sarah Dudley Pettey's nephew, Edward Richard Dudley III of New York, former ambassador to Liberia and state supreme court judge. Through Judge Dudley, I located Corine Pettey of New York, Sarah's granddaughter.

39. Alan Watson, *History of New Bern*, 545. Dudley is listed as a "Principal Farmer" in *Branson's North Carolina Business Directory, 1896*, 212. For Dudley's worth, see U.S. Bureau of the Census, Manuscript Census, 1870, Craven County, N.C., Seventh Ward City, 144. For perspective on the financial condition of southern African Americans during Reconstruction, see Schweninger, "Prosperous Blacks in the South" and *Black Property Owners*, esp. 197–207.

40. Leloudis, " 'A More Certain Means of Grace,' " 11–14; Brodhead, *Journals of Charles W. Chesnutt*, 7–8.

41. On the earliest schools, see Goldhaber, "Mission Unfulfilled," and Joe M. Richardson, *Christian Reconstruction*, 29, 239. On schooling prior to disfranchisement, see Westin, "The State and Segregated Schools"; Hugh Victor Brown, *E-Qual-ity Education in North Carolina*, 24; Knight, *Public School Education*; M. C. S. Noble, *History of the Public Schools*; and Rabinowitz, "Half a Loaf." North Carolina seems to have been at the forefront of African American education in the South, partly through the efforts of James W. Hood, minister of Saint Peter's AME Zion Church, later bishop, who served as assistant superintendent of education in North Carolina's Reconstruction government in 1868. See Frazier, *Negro Church in America*, 48; "Bishop J. W. Hood," *Southwestern Christian Advocate*, 7 Nov. 1918, microfiche 400, Hampton University Newspaper Clipping Files; and Noble, *History of the Public Schools*, 319–20. On New Bern schools, see Alan Watson, *History of New Bern*, 570–74. On states that did not create such progressive school systems, see Lamon, *Black Tennesseans*, chaps. 3, 4, 5, and McMillen, *Dark Journey*, chap. 3.

42. Peare, *Mary McLeod Bethune*, 57; Newsome, "Mary McLeod Bethune," 89–90.

43. Newsome, "Mary McLeod Bethune," 75–76.

44. *Messenger*, 18 Nov. 1882. According to Newsome, although Scotia did not offer vocational training in home economics and nursing until after Sarah graduated, it was taught informally during her time there ("Mary McLeod Bethune," 77). The dormitory still stands.

45. *Messenger*, 18 Nov. 1882; "Special Issue of the Barber-Scotia Index" (Jan. 1967), NCC; Newsome, "Mary McLeod Bethune," 80.

46. Knight, *Public School Education*, 313–14.

47. For Dudley's attendance at normal school, see *Biennial Report of the Superintendent of Public Instruction of North Carolina for the Scholastic Years 1883–'84* (Raleigh: Ashe and Satting, [1884]), 185. *Branson's North Carolina Business Directory for 1884*, 242, notes that the normal school received $500 from the state and $200 from the Peabody Fund.

48. *Messenger*, 5 Feb. 1887; Hazel Williams, telephone interview with author, 7 Mar. 1990. Williams is Lula Pickenpack's granddaughter, whose mother, Mamie, was raised by Sarah Dudley Pettey.

49. *Star of Zion*, 13 May 1897.

50. Pettey was the slave of Benjamin F. Petty, one of the largest slaveholders in Wilkes County. Pettey's father was Jorden Pettey, born in 1816. Jorden was married to Fanny, born in 1820. In 1850, the year after Charles's birth, the census listed among Benjamin's slaves a one-year-old mulatto boy. The census did not list a mulatto woman of childbearing age on the farm or a mulatto man old enough to be Jorden Pettey. Moreover, Jorden and Fanny are identified in subsequent censuses as black. Petty owned one twenty-year-old mulatto male slave, and it is possible that he was Charles's father. It is also possible that Benjamin Petty fathered Charles, since it is unlikely that Benjamin would have purchased a one-year-old without owning the baby's mother. Benjamin Petty's wife, Cynthia, was six years older than her husband and had given birth to nine children at two-year intervals by 1850, but by then the youngest was five years old. Cynthia died a short time later. Charles Pettey loved and later provided for Jorden Pettey, and nothing in Charles's own rendering of his background accounts for his mulatto makeup. See Absher, *Heritage of Wilkes County*, 383; Hickerson, *Happy Valley*, 44–45; Simpson, *Heritage of Wilkes County*, 399–400, vi; U.S. Bureau of the Census, Manuscript Census, 1850, Wilkes County, N.C., M432, reel 656, Slave Schedule, 1111, and reel 649, 347; Manuscript Census, 1860, Wilkes County, N.C., Slave Schedule, M653, reel 927, 456; and Manuscript Census, 1870, Wilkes County, N.C., M593, reel 1165, 372. The 1870 census lists the following people in the household of Jorden and Fanny: George, twenty-four; Charles, twenty; Ann Horton, twenty-three; and Jane Isbelle, twenty-one. It is likely that Ann and Jane were also Fanny Pettey's children and had been sold to Petty relatives. Benjamin Petty's daughter, Lucinda, married Thomas Isbell in 1829. See Wilkes County Marriage Bonds, NCDAH. On Wilkes County whites' perceptions of Charles Pettey, see Crouch, *Historical Sketches of Wilkes County*, 74. For a biographical sketch of Pettey, see Walls, *African Methodist Episcopal Zion Church*, 580–81.

51. Sarah Dudley Pettey, "Bishop Charles Calvin Pettey," in Hood, *One Hundred Years*, 195–201; Walls, *African Methodist Episcopal Zion Church*, 580–81.

52. Walls, *African Methodist Episcopal Zion Church*, 319, 348. A desperate Charles Chesnutt, then sixteen years old, spent 5 July 1875 tracking down Charles Pettey at Moore's Sanctuary AME Zion Church, where he was preaching. Chesnutt was searching for a school where he could teach during the summer, but he discovered that Pettey had "lost his" own summer school and could not help him. See Brodhead, *Journals of Charles W. Chesnutt*, 42. On the Lancaster Normal and Indus-

trial Institute, see Hartshorn, *Era of Progress*, 296, and W. E. B. Du Bois, *Negro Common School*, 11. As early as 1874, there were 26,836 members of the AME Zion Church in North Carolina, according to the *Educator*, 19 Dec. 1874. The 1900 census counted 66,356 members in North Carolina and 184,542 nationwide; in 1916, these numbers had risen to 74,365 and 257,169, respectively. See U.S. Bureau of the Census, *Special Reports: Religious Bodies, 1906*, 458, and *Religious Bodies, 1916*, 503. I. Garland Penn lists the *Star of Zion* as a leading newspaper in *The Afro-American Press*, 197–98.

53. *Messenger*, 8 Oct., 26 Nov., 10 Dec. 1887, 2, 24, 31 Mar. 1888; Walls, *African Methodist Episcopal Zion Church*, 100; Harry Van Buren Richardson, *Dark Salvation*, 212; Beasley, *Negro Trail-Blazers*, 160. Petteyville no longer exists, and no record verifies its founding, according to John Gonzales, California State Library, to author, 16 Apr. 1990, in author's possession. The standard geographical reference, Hart, *Companion to California*, lists Allensworth as "the state's only settlement founded and governed by blacks" (9). On other western migrations of African Americans, see Painter, *Exodusters*, and Cohen, *At Freedom's Edge*, 251. For Walters and the NAACP, see Painter, *Standing at Armageddon*, 226. On black women in western migrations, see Sterling, *We Are Your Sisters*, 372–76.

54. *Messenger*, 5 Feb. 1887; Hazel Williams, telephone interview with author, 7 Mar. 1990.

55. Walls, *African Methodist Episcopal Zion Church*, 216–17; Culp, *Twentieth Century Negro Literature*, 182.

56. *Raleigh Gazette*, 21 Aug. 1897; "Last Will and Testament of Charles Calvin Pettey of Newberne, North Carolina," 21 Dec. 1900, Craven County Estates Records, NCDAH; *Star of Zion*, 4 Feb., 23 Sept. 1897.

57. *New Berne Journal*, 23 Nov. 1897.

58. Weisenfeld, "'Who Is Sufficient.'" John Stanly moved to Ohio in the late 1840s.

59. For a discussion of this sort of privileging of family bloodlines that extended to 1930, see Wyatt-Brown, *Southern Honor*, 119–21.

60. Steven Hahn recognizes the divide between planters and commercial/industrial leaders in the South and moves southern history beyond the continuity/change argument through a class analysis in "Class and State in Postemancipation Societies." The "middling sorts" who became New White Men will be discussed at length in Chapter 3. Escott makes this argument for North Carolina during Reconstruction in *Many Excellent People*, esp. 136–70.

61. Culp, *Twentieth Century Negro Literature*, 184–85.

62. Peare, *Mary McLeod Bethune*, 52–62.

63. In *Aristocrats of Color*, Gatewood positions this small class in urban areas, networked over vast distances by social, marriage, and business ties.

64. On Price, who attended the Dudleys' church in New Bern as a teenager, see Yandle, "Joseph Charles Price."

65. Delany and Delany, *Having Our Say*, 41.

66. *Star of Zion*, 10, 24 Sept. 1896. On the frankness with which other African American families in North Carolina at the time faced racial "mixing," see Delany and Delany, *Having Our Say*, 65–66.

67. Tate argues that Charles Chesnutt's novels *House behind the Cedars* and *Mar-*

row of Tradition demonstrate that "bourgeois individuation" was the defining force behind his class analysis. This, of course, fits with Chesnutt's life, in which every act represented an effort to transcend the boundaries of race through sheer force of will. See Brodhead, *Journals of Charles W. Chesnutt*, and Tate, *Domestic Allegories of Political Desire*, 139–40.

68. Schweninger, *Black Property Owners*, 144, 155, 176–84.

69. Edward A. Johnson, *Negro Soldiers in the Spanish-American War*, 140. For a detailed look at black urban Raleigh, see Carter, *Urban Negro in the South*, 37–82.

70. Majors, *Noted Negro Women*, 59–63; Culp, *Twentieth Century Negro Literature*, 182; *Star of Zion*, 4 Nov. 1897.

71. Walls, *African Methodist Episcopal Zion Church*, 224; Haley, *Charles N. Hunter*, 82.

72. U.S. Bureau of the Census, Manuscript Census, 1900, Craven County, N.C., 8th Township, Enumeration District 54, 232A.

73. *Star of Zion*, 21 Apr. 1898.

74. Ibid., 3 Aug. 1899, 1.

75. Tate, *Domestic Allegories of Political Desire*, 124–25; "Woman's Place," *Woman's Era* 1, no. 6 (Sept. 1894): 8.

76. On the difference between generations of white women leaders, see Marjorie Spruill Wheeler, *New Women of the New South*.

77. *Star of Zion*, 8, 22 July 1897. It certainly could not be argued that all or most black women supported woman suffrage in the 1890s, however. Prior to the disfranchisement of black men in the South, there appears to have been an open debate about woman suffrage on its own terms: arguments over its inherent fairness, for example. After disfranchisement, the debate shifted to include whether or not woman suffrage would aid black male suffrage. See "Colored Women and Suffrage," *Woman's Era* 2 (Nov. 1895): 11.

78. *Star of Zion*, 21 Oct. 1897.

79. Virginia Baptists, for example, claimed that the Bible expressly forbade women's "teaching and preaching." See *Woman's Era* 1, no. 6 (Sept. 1894): 8. This does not mean that women did not find work and power within the Baptist Church, as Higginbotham demonstrates (*Righteous Discontent*, 2). On eliminating sex discrimination in the AME Zion hierarchy, see Walls, *African Methodist Episcopal Zion Church*, 111.

80. *Star of Zion*, 23 June 1898.

81. Higginbotham, *Righteous Discontent*, 120–21.

82. Mary Small, wife of Bishop John B. Small, lived in Wilmington and Fayetteville during the 1880s and 1890s. She received her license to preach in 1892, and Bishop Alexander Walters named her a deacon in 1895. See John B. Small Diaries, LC; *Messenger*, 22 July 1882, 24 Nov. 1888; Bradley, *History of the A.M.E. Zion Church*, 393; Walls, *African Methodist Episcopal Zion Church*, 111–12; and *Star of Zion*, 7 July 1898, 1. The controversy over the ordination continued through 1899. Beverly Guy-Sheftall outlines a similar debate within the AME Church (in which women were not ordained) in the mid-1880s in *"Daughters of Sorrow,"* 150–51. Jualynne E. Dodson argues that women's ordination in black churches connected to white denominations would have been extremely difficult ("Power and Surrogate Leadership," 40). For women's activism in the Evangelical Church, see Gilkes, " 'To-

gether and in Harness.'" Two arguments Gilkes uses to prove greater freedom for women in the Sanctified Church apply to the AME Zion Church as well: that it emphasized education and independence from white control. Higginbotham's profound treatment enabled me to sort out why AME Zion women made these issues central to their lives. See Higginbotham, *Righteous Discontent*, 120–49.

83. Reverend S. A. Chambers, "Red Hot Cannon Ball," *Star of Zion*, 16 June 1898, 1.

84. Ibid., 23 June 1898, 5.

85. Ibid., 25 Aug. 1898, 4.

86. Ibid., 13 Aug. 1896.

87. Nancy F. Cott argues that not all women's activism may be equated with feminism, which she defines as a challenge to male supremacy. Cott outlines three sources of women's activism: female consciousness, communal consciousness, and feminism. Some of North Carolina's African American women avoided feminism, but for most, the imperative to action of female consciousness or communal consciousness put them in a position in which they had to oppose male domination also. See Cott, "What's in a Name?," 826. Patricia Hill Collins also defines feminism in *Black Feminist Thought*, 19–40. Collins argues that feminism cannot be defined narrowly by its conformity to the language of white middle-class women. Class shapes the way women express feminism. Because Sarah Dudley Pettey was highly educated and literary, she articulated her beliefs in a manner that would be recognized as feminist by whites and middle-class blacks of the time, and by historians later, but other women in her community might have held the same beliefs and expressed them through their everyday actions. bell hooks has deplored the "either/or" thinking that asks black feminists to rank the importance of race or gender and recommends that they not be seen as "two movements competing for first place." See hooks, *Feminist Theory* and *Talking Back*. Higginbotham argues, "The black Baptist women's advocacy of a new social order combined a progressive gendered and racialized representation of orthodoxy" that reached back into the antebellum period (*Righteous Discontent*, 123). For a discussion of the formation and articulation of Afrocentric and feminist values, see Patricia Hill Collins, "Social Construction of Black Feminist Thought"; Elsa Barkley Brown, "Womanist Consciousness"; Harley, "For the Good of Family and Race"; Dill, "Dialectics of Black Womanhood"; and Deborah K. King, "Multiple Jeopardy, Multiple Consciousness."

88. *Star of Zion*, 21 Oct. 1897. Katharine Du Pre Lumpkin, in *The Making of a Southerner*, 215, recalls the moment she realized that to African Americans, the "Negro problem" was a white problem. African Americans believed strongly that by rejecting race discrimination they moved closer to salvation than whites and that it was whites who were laggards.

89. *Star of Zion*, 14 Jan., 30 Sept. 1897.

90. Ibid., 3 June 1897.

91. Whitted, *History of Negro Baptists*, 158–59; Savitt, "Education of Black Physicians"; Carter, *Shaw's Universe*; "Commencement Program: Leonard Medical School and Pharmacy School," 28 Mar. 1894, Shaw Portfolio, NCC.

92. Savitt, "Education of Black Physicians," 161. Leonard graduated eighty-nine physicians in the last two decades of the nineteenth century.

93. Scruggs, "Medical Education," 3.

94. Scruggs, *Women of Distinction*, 166; Bowles, *Good Beginnings*, 39. Brown trained at the Woman's Medical College of Pennsylvania, one of the few schools that accepted women and was open to all races. Brown must have practiced in Wilmington no more than two years. Hine, *Black Women in White*, 54, notes that she became head of nurses' training at McClennan Hospital in Charleston, S.C. See "Librarian Finds First Woman Doctor," *News and Courier* (Charleston, S.C.), 12 Sept. 1977, 3A; "Hospital and Training School for Nurses, Charleston, S.C.," folder 1899, box 200, series 1, subseries 1, General Education Board Collection, RAC; *Woman's Medical College Alumnae Transcript* (1912), 36, and L. H. Brown, "Minutes of the Hospital Association," *Hospital Herald*, 25 Jan. 1899, both in Archives and Special Collections on Women in Medicine, Medical College of Pennsylvania, Philadelphia, Pa.; and Waring, *History of Medicine in South Carolina*, 183.

95. Harold R. Washington, "History and Role of Black Law Schools," 165–66; Whitted, *History of Negro Baptists*, 159; Frenise A. Logan, *Negro in North Carolina*, 108.

96. John Leary advertised during 1898 in the *Star of Zion* for men who might want to read law with him. Leary, the first dean of Shaw University Law School, had a brother, Louis, who died with John Brown at Harpers Ferry. On Leary, see William J. Simmons, *Men of Mark*, 432–35, and Love, "Plum Thickets and Field Daisies," CPL.

97. Love, "Plum Thickets and Field Daisies," CPL.

98. *Wilmington Sentinel*, quoted in *Raleigh Gazette*, 28 Nov. 1896.

99. *Star of Zion*, 1 July 1897. On black labor at Homestead in 1892, see Krause, *Battle for Homestead*, 346. For an excellent overview of African American strikebreaking, including at Homestead, see Whatley, "African-American Strikebreakers." For a glimpse of the thorny historiography of race and labor, see Roediger, *Towards the Abolition of Whiteness*, 21–38.

100. *Star of Zion*, 21 Jan. 1897.

101. *Messenger*, 21 Aug. 1886, 5 Feb., 9 July 1887; Philip Foner, *Organized Labor*, 49; Janiewski, *Sisterhood Denied*, 18–21; Frenise A. Logan, *Negro in North Carolina*, 102–4. Gerald David Jaynes argues convincingly that the "threat of black competition" shaped the labor force throughout the remainder of the century. See Jaynes, *Branches without Roots*, 273–75. My interpretation owes a debt to his larger argument, that there were "economic origins of the color line" (ibid., 253–316). The city in which African Americans were most integrated into the industrial workforce may have been Richmond, and Peter J. Rachleff brilliantly chronicles the possibilities of organizing across racial lines there in *Black Labor in the South*, 109–78.

102. Frenise A. Logan, *Negro in North Carolina*, 90.

103. Prather, *We Have Taken a City*, 115.

104. Ashley and Bailey Company auction brochure, *The Ten Successful and Modern Plants of the Ashley and Bailey Co.* (Lowell, Mass.: J. E. Conant, Sept. 1913), 10–13, 146–62, NCC; "Colored Mill Hands," *Independent*, 11 Nov. 1899, and "The Silk Mill a Success," n.p., microfiche 298, Hampton University Newspaper Clipping Files. The latter mentions that Gertrude Hood, daughter of Bishop Hood, was a

supervisor at the factory and describes Ashley and Bailey as a "well regulated school." However, "A Horrified Contemporary," *Richmond Dispatch*, 17 Nov. 1900, ibid., paints a terrible picture of the "lashing" of children in the mill. See also Holland Thompson, *From Cotton Field to Cotton Mill*, 252–53. Of the 135 women silk mill workers in North Carolina in 1900, 55 were black. See U.S. Bureau of the Census, *Occupations at the Twelfth Census*, 356.

105. *Raleigh Gazette*, 28 Aug. 1897. For an overview of southern industrialization, see Ayers, *Promise of the New South*, 104–31.

106. Janiewski, *Sisterhood Denied*, 95–105; Frenise A. Logan, *Negro in North Carolina*, 91–92.

107. Tompkins, *Cotton Mill, Commercial Features*, 109.

108. *Daily Charlotte Observer*, 16 Nov. 1895, 1.

109. U.S. Bureau of the Census, *Occupations at the Twelfth Census*, 354–56. *Annual Report of the North Carolina Bureau of Labor and Printing* (Raleigh: various publishers, 1889–1922) provides information on the growth of mills, but the bureau gained its information through voluntary, and often haphazard, surveys.

110. Ruth Milkman's works are useful in understanding racial segregation of job categories as well as sex segregation, particularly her argument that sex-typing is made to seem a " 'natural' and permanent feature of the labor process." See Milkman, *Gender at Work*, 26.

111. Holland Thompson, *From Cotton Field to Cotton Mill*, 248–49.

112. Broadus Mitchell, *Rise of Cotton Mills*, 216–21; Frenise A. Logan, *Negro in North Carolina*, 91; *Star of Zion*, 27 May 1897, 3. The following clippings all demonstrate the intense interest, in both North and South, in the use of black women's labor in the Vesta Mill: "Three Thousand Dollars," *Charleston Messenger*, 14 Apr. 1900; "The Negro in Cotton Mills," *New York Sun*, 27 June 1900; *State*, 25 Jan. 1901; "Negro Labor a Failure," *Boston Transcript*, 25 Jan. 1901; "Colored Labor in the South," *Baltimore Sun*, 26 Jan. 1901; *New Orleans Times-Democrat*, 29 Jan. 1901; "Negro Cotton Mill Labor," *Charlotte Observer*, 1 Feb. 1901; "The Cause of the Failure of the Vesta Mills," *Charleston Observer*, 1 Feb. 1901; "Negro Labor Unreliable," *Times Democrat*, 2 Feb. 1901; "Southern Factories and Negro Help," *Boston Transcript*, 6 Feb. 1901; "Negro Labor in the Mills," *New York Times*, reprinted in *Mobile Register*, 7 Feb. 1901; and *Atlanta Constitution*, 13 Feb. 1901, microfiche 298, Hampton University Newspaper Clipping Files.

113. "Negro Labor in Cotton Mills," *Atlanta Constitution*, 18 Aug. 1900, microfiche 298, Hampton University Newspaper Clipping Files.

114. In Jacob Elsas's Atlanta Fulton Bag and Cotton Mill, black women were hired in the folding department at lower wages than white women in 1897. After he observed that they did a good job at less pay than the workers they replaced, Elsas reduced the pay of the remaining white women. The white women struck, and the strike "caused a big flurry among the working classes of the South." See *Raleigh Gazette*, 14 Aug., 4 Sept. 1897; *Daily Charlotte Observer*, 5 Aug. 1897, 4; 6 Aug. 1897, 1; 7 Aug. 1897, 8; 8 Aug. 1897, 1; 10 Aug. 1897, 1; and Fink, *Fulton Bag and Cotton Mills Strike*, 40. The stakes accorded Coleman's effort are reflected in this headline on his venture: "Negro Object Lesson: Demonstration of Success of Work in Black Cotton Mill," n.p., n.d., microfiche 298, Hampton University Newspaper Clipping Files.

115. Burgess, "Tar Heel Blacks"; Robbins, "Blacks and Business," 77; J. K. Rouse, *Noble Experiment*; "Colored Mill Hands," *Independent*, 11 Nov. 1899, microfiche 298, Hampton University Newspaper Clipping Files.

116. Frenise A. Logan, *Negro in North Carolina*, 101; Burgess, "Tar Heel Blacks," 188–237.

117. *Star of Zion*, 24 Feb. 1898, 2.

118. Burgess, "Tar Heel Blacks," 269.

119. *New Berne Journal*, 29 Nov. 1897; *Raleigh Gazette*, 4 Sept., 11 Dec. 1897. *Star of Zion*, 9 Sept. 1897, places Sarah Dudley Pettey, George White, Lula Jenkins, and Warren Coleman at the New Bern Fair together.

120. Burgess, "Tar Heel Blacks," 188–237. On John Dancy, see "The Life of John Dancy," Dancy Collection (uncataloged), LC.

121. Broadus Mitchell, *Rise of Cotton Mills*, 215–16.

122. Burgess, "Tar Heel Blacks," 381–85; "Negro Ran Mill at a Loss," *New York Times*, 4 July 1904; "Only Cotton Mill Operated by Negroes," n.p., n.d.; "Negro's Cotton Mill Fails," *New York Times*, 29 June 1904; and "The Negro in Cotton Manufacturing," *New York Times*, 30 June 1904, microfiche 298, Hampton University Newspaper Clipping Files; Ayers, *Promise of the New South*, 105–7.

123. Mullis, "Extravaganza of the New South."

124. Booker T. Washington, "Atlanta Exposition Address (1895)," reprinted in *Up from Slavery*, 218–25. Rayford W. Logan analyzes the address in *Betrayal of the Negro*, 304. For the best discussion of Washington's "embryonic notion of capitalism's revolutionary potential," see Childs, "Concepts of Culture." See also Meier, *Negro Thought in America*, 97–118; Woodward, *Origins of the New South*, 365; Williamson, *Crucible of Race*, 72; and Harlan, *Booker T. Washington*, 215–28. On unionized Atlanta, see Mercer Griffin Evans, "History of the Organized Labor Movement," and Deaton, "Atlanta during the Progressive Era."

125. Woodward, *Origins of the New South*, 365. Joel Williamson argues that Washington's program "was designed for the agrarian order of the nineteenth century" (*Crucible of Race*, 72). I would add that Washington understood that the South's future was in industry.

126. Woodward, *Origins of the New South*, 367; Harlan, *Booker T. Washington*, 227. For discussions of alternatives to Washington's leadership, see Williamson, *Crucible of Race*, 40–70, and Ayers, *Promise of the New South*, 322–26.

127. Harlan, *Booker T. Washington*, 133.

128. The title of Pettey's speech at the exposition was "The Negro Question." The speech Pettey gave in Mobile is reprinted in part in *Star of Zion*, 13 May 1897. Other references to the speech include *Star of Zion*, 8 July 1897, 20 Jan. 1898, and "Colored Clerical Visitors," *Daily Register*, n.d., clipping in lateral files, Dancy Collection (uncataloged), LC, which refers to the "address at the exposition grounds" given by Pettey "several weeks ago."

129. *Star of Zion*, 13 May 1897.

130. "The National Colored Woman's Congress," *Woman's Era* 2, no. 9 (Jan. 1896): 2–6; Tate, *Domestic Allegories of Political Desire*, 128–31.

131. Schweninger, *Black Property Owners*, 200–207.

132. *Raleigh Gazette*, 19 Dec. 1895.

133. Fonvielle, "The South As I Saw It." Greenwood recounts an incident that

caused one railroad to provide separate waiting rooms in 1893, which would have been prior to Fonvielle's trip through Charlotte. He must have connected at another station, demonstrating the seeming randomness of Jim Crow to contemporaries. See Greenwood, *Bittersweet Legacy*, 150–51.

134. *Star of Zion*, 8 Oct. 1896.

135. *Business Directory of New Berne, N.C.*, 28, 71–73, 75; Alan Watson, *History of New Bern*, 542–43, 545–47.

136. I first discovered the All Healing Spring property in Pettey's will and then traced it to a location near Taylorsville, N.C. See "Last Will and Testament of Charles Calvin Pettey of Newberne, North Carolina," 21 Dec. 1900, Craven County Estates Records, NCDAH. The date of Pettey's purchase is from the Annie Watts Eckerd Scrapbook, in the possession of Opal Watts Harrington, Taylorsville, N.C. I am indebted to Opal Harrington for sharing her knowledge of Alexander County history with me.

137. "All Healing Spring, Alexander County, N.C." ([1887]), copy of broadside in the possession of Opal Watts Harrington, Taylorsville, N.C.; Opal Watts Harrington, telephone interview with author, 13 Jan. 1990; photograph at Mescimer's Auto Supply Company, Ellendale, N.C.

138. Mrs. W. B. Pittard, Jr., "Social Life Centered on Healing Springs," *Times* (Taylorsville, N.C.), [1960s], clipping in the possession of Opal Watts Harrington, Taylorsville, N.C.; Opal Watts Harrington, telephone interview with author, 13 Jan. 1990.

139. In "Social Life Centered on Healing Springs," Mrs. W. B. Pittard, Jr., refers to one of the proprietors as "a Mr. Pettey from the North." Opal Watts Harrington recalls that a man named Pettey, whom she believed to be from Wilmington and Philadelphia, owned the resort at the turn of the century. She suspected that Pettey was black because of the inscription in the Annie Watts Eckerd Scrapbook, in Harrington's possession, Taylorsville, N.C.: "Bishop Petty (Col.) bought All Healing Springs Sept. 1st, 1897. He was of Wilmington and formerly of Wilkes Co." Since the resort had always been segregated, however, she could not explain his ownership. (Opal Watts Harrington, telephone interview with author, 13 Jan. 1990.) I have found no clue suggesting what the Petteys planned to do with the resort, which continued to serve exclusively white patrons.

CHAPTER TWO

1. Tena M. Nichols, "Higher Education for Women," *Raleigh Gazette*, 12 May 1892, in file 1887–99, box 13, Hunter Collection, DU. Tena Nichols taught in the Raleigh black graded school. See clipping from *News and Observer*, 4 Nov. 1897, ibid.

2. On racial "uplift," see Higginbotham, "African-American Women's History," 271.

3. For this generational change in Georgia, see Bruce Fort, "Atlanta University and the Campaign for Black Literacy in Rural Georgia, 1869–1900," presented at the Southern Historical Association meeting, Nov. 1992, in author's possession. For an overview of education after slavery, see Angela Y. Davis, *Women, Race, and Class*, 99–109.

4. Julia A. Sadgwar, "Some Phases of an Important Problem," pamphlet in the uncataloged North Carolina material, [New] Addendum, 1869–1988, American Missionary Association Archives, ARC. On Gregory Normal Institute, see "Good Work at Wilmington," n.p., n.d., microfiche 98, Hampton University Newspaper Clipping Files.

5. Knight, *Public School Education*, 314; Scruggs, *Women of Distinction*, 313; *Biennial Report of the State Superintendent of Public Instruction for 1898–1899 and 1899–1900* (Raleigh: Edwards and Broughton, 1900), 296–97.

6. The American Missionary Association reduced its teaching force in the South as public elementary schools opened and focused instead on higher education. Contributions from individual white northerners, such as the scholarship that sent Mary McLeod to Scotia Seminary, shrunk, along with support from northern white women's church groups. See Westin, "The State and Segregated Schools," 11–15, and Leavell, "Trends of Philanthropy."

7. On the imposition of vocational education, see James D. Anderson, *Education of Blacks*. Its impact on black women in North Carolina will be discussed in Chapter 6.

8. See, for example, Brodhead, *Journals of Charles W. Chesnutt*, 58.

9. The state mandated four months of free education each year for all citizens between the ages of six and twenty-one, according to Westin, "The State and Segregated Schools," 20. Works that chronicle the history of African Americans in a single state usually include a chapter on education in that state, but no such monograph exists at this time for North Carolina. See Newby, *Black Carolinians*; McMillen, *Dark Journey*; Lamon, *Black Tennesseans*; Dittmer, *Black Georgia*; and Jacqueline Jones, *Soldiers of Light*. On North Carolina, see Knight, *Public School Education* and *Notes on Education*; Hugh Victor Brown, *E-Qual-ity Education* and *History of the Education of Negroes*; Kousser, "Progressivism"; Westin, "The State and Segregated Schools"; Leloudis, "'A More Certain Means of Grace'"; and Peek, *History of Education*. For overviews of the South, see James D. Anderson, *Education of Blacks*; Harlan, *Separate and Unequal*; Charles S. Johnson, *Negro College Graduate*; W. E. B. Du Bois, *College-Bred Negro*; and Guy-Sheftall, "Black Women and Higher Education."

10. Coon, "Beginnings of North Carolina City Schools" and "School Support"; Frenise A. Logan, "Legal Status of Public School Education." Louis R. Harlan, in *Separate and Unequal*, devotes a chapter to North Carolina in the 1880s and 1890s and demonstrates the ways white school committees circumvented equal distribution of funds (47). In Mississippi, Neil McMillen found that most whites completely opposed funding for black education (*Dark Journey*, 75).

11. Susie M. Rhone to Charles N. Hunter, 17 Mar. 1903, file 1901–3, box 1; Louise Dorr to Charles N. Hunter, 25 May 1886, file Jan.–Aug. 1886, box 1; and Annie W. Day to Charles N. Hunter, 18 Mar. 1887, file 1887–1900, box 2, all in Hunter Collection, DU. J. R. Hawkins, *The Educator: A Condensed Statement of the Department of Education of the African Methodist Episcopal Church* ([1900]), 27, NCC, refers to a "Miss Louisa Dorr, a faithful teacher from the North," as a founder of Kittrell College, an AME school. Although this suggests Dorr was white, many black northern women also came to the state to teach. Even city schools were crowded: one had 1,000 children and 15 teachers. See "Letter from a Graduate,"

Saint Augustine's Record 14 (Nov. 1908), microfiche 231, Hampton University Newspaper Clipping Files.

12. On Chesnutt, see Brodhead, *Journals of Charles W. Chesnutt*, 65–83. On Du Bois, see Daniel Levering Lewis, *W. E. B. Du Bois*, 68–71. On Anna Julia Haywood (later Cooper) in summer school, see Newbold, *Five North Carolina Negro Educators*, 5, and *Messenger*, 5 Aug. 1882.

13. Brodhead, *Journals of Charles W. Chesnutt*, 42–43.

14. Newbold, *Five North Carolina Negro Educators*, 5; *Messenger*, 5 Aug. 1882. Atkins went to Saint Augustine's in 1880, and in 1882, he and "Annie Haywood" (as Anna Julia Haywood Cooper was then known) returned to Chatham County to run a summer school.

15. W. E. B. Du Bois, *Souls of Black Folk*, 96–108. On the sadness that this "heroic futility" generated, see Daniel Levering Lewis, *W. E. B. Du Bois*, 70.

16. Brodhead, *Journals of Charles W. Chesnutt*, 81–82. For a perceptive analysis of the cultural function of summer schools, see Bruce Fort, "Atlanta University and the Campaign for Black Literacy in Rural Georgia, 1869–1900," presented at the Southern Historical Association meeting, Nov. 1992, in author's possession.

17. James W. Cooper, "From Beaufort to Blowing Rock, North Carolina: 'The Old North State'" ([1910]), 6, pamphlet in the uncataloged North Carolina material, American Missionary Association Archives, ARC. On the American Missionary Association, see Jacqueline Jones, *Soldiers of Light*, and Maxine Deloris Jones, "'A Glorious Work.'" For a firsthand account of the longest-lived of the American Missionary Association schools, Lincoln Academy in Kings Mountain, see Eula Wellmon Dunlap, "Reminiscences," Lincoln Academy Papers, American Missionary Association Archives, ARC.

18. Eula Wellmon Dunlap, "Reminiscences," and June Smith, "History of Negro School," *Gastonia Gazette*, [1957], both in Lincoln Academy Papers, American Missionary Association Archives, ARC.

19. In many southern cities—Atlanta, for example—school boards established separate public high schools for white boys and girls. Separate high schools were never built for black boys and girls. The first black high school in North Carolina was Charlotte's Second Ward High School, established in 1923, by which time many white high schools already existed. On sex segregation in public high schools, see Tyack and Hansot, *Learning Together*, 124–30.

20. David Tyack and Elisabeth Hansot, writing about common schools, point out that covert education of blacks during slavery involved both sexes and that northern teachers brought experience in coeducational common schools. Both factors probably contributed to coeducational higher education, but northern white teachers usually advocated the separation of the sexes after a certain age. See ibid., 54–56. On the importance of literacy and "education as the practice of freedom," see hooks, *Talking Back*, 62–63.

21. According to Solomon, *In the Company of Educated Women*, 53–54, by 1912, only seven southern white colleges were coeducational, none of which were North Carolina schools. Most of these accepted women only as day students in graduate, professional, or upper-division programs and provided no residential facilities or campus activities for women. The University of North Carolina admitted a few women under the above restrictions in 1897 but did not become fully

coeducational until 1972. See Dean, *Women on the Hill*, 16. On the development of white women's education and coeducational issues, see Woody, *History of Women's Education*; Horowitz, *Alma Mater*; Solomon, *In the Company of Educated Women*; Tyack and Hansot, *Learning Together*; Lynn D. Gordon, *Gender and Higher Education*; and Howe, *Myths of Coeducation*, 221–29. On the education of women in the South, see Anne Firor Scott, *Southern Lady* and "Historians Construct the Southern Woman"; Stringer and Thompson, *Stepping off the Pedestal*; McCandless, "Progressivism and the Higher Education of Southern Women"; Urban, "History of Education"; Dyer, "Higher Education in the South"; and Kett, "Women and the Progressive Impulse." For women in North Carolina, see Pope, "Preparation for Pedestals," and Farnham, *Education of the Southern Belle*. Farnham argues that southern women's education advanced relatively quickly in the antebellum period but failed to keep pace after the war. See also Dean, "Covert Curriculum." For a bibliographical essay on southern women's education, see Shadron et al., *Stepping off the Pedestal*, 145–68.

22. Smith, quoted in Woody, *History of Women's Education*, 269. Smith noted that North Carolina secondary schools were slowly accepting white girls and that women were clamoring to enter the university's normal department, established by the legislature to train the state's teachers. Since many women entered the teaching profession, he predicted that the university would eventually have to yield to them. Instead, the legislature appropriated money for a state normal school for white women. Among the missionary schools were Mars Hill in the far western part of the state and the forerunner of Pfeiffer College, then in Lenoir. New Garden Boarding School, a coeducational preparatory school for Quakers, became coeducational Guilford College in 1888, and in the 1880s, Lutheran Lenoir-Rhyne College in Hickory and Catawba College, founded by the Associated Reformed Presbyterian Church, accepted a few women. See Pope, "Preparation for Pedestals," 93, and Gilbert, *Guilford*, 13.

23. A 1911 survey found that only 4 of 140 southern women's institutions calling themselves colleges were accredited. See Colton, "Southern Colleges," "Standards of Southern Colleges," and "Improvement in Standards."

24. For the educational culture and self-perceptions of students at North Carolina's state-supported normal school for white women, see Dean, "Covert Curriculum," and "Learning to Be New Women."

25. Westin, "The State and Segregated Schools," 81–86.

26. Quoted in Hugh Victor Brown, *E-Qual-ity Education*, 42.

27. See Lamon, *Black Tennesseans*, 90, on the Morrill Act in Tennessee. On the founding of the North Carolina Agricultural and Mechanical College, see Frenise A. Logan, "Movement in North Carolina to Establish a State Supported College for Negroes"; Gibbs, *History of the North Carolina Agricultural and Technical College*, 3; and Hudson, "North Carolina Blacks," 55.

28. The American Baptist Home Mission Society founded Shaw University in Raleigh before 1870, and the Episcopal Church established Saint Augustine's College in 1867. Presbyterian Scotia Seminary in Concord functioned as a sister school to male-only Biddle Memorial Institute in nearby Charlotte, both founded in 1867. The Methodists started Bennett College as a coeducational school in 1873. The AME Zion Church began Livingstone College as Zion Wesley Institute

in 1880, and the AME Church opened Kittrell College in 1886. On these schools, see Carter, *Shaw's Universe*; C. S. Brown, "Negro Baptists of North Carolina"; Halliburton, *History of Saint Augustine's College*; Delany and Delany, *Having Our Say*, 39–60; Parker, *Biddle–Johnson C. Smith University*; Stowell, *Methodist Adventures*, 155–61 (Bennett College); and J. R. Hawkins, *The Educator: A Condensed Statement of the Department of Education of the African Methodist Episcopal Church* ([1900]), 27–43, and "Kittrell College Announcements," both in NCC. Other black schools in the state called themselves colleges or institutes, but they had much weaker claims to such titles than the seven schools above.

29. The best treatment of these issues in the North and West is Solomon, *In the Company of Educated Women*. There is little on Cooper's early life in North Carolina in Cooper Papers, MSRC. On Cooper, see Mary Helen Washington, "Introduction"; Hutchinson, *Anna J. Cooper*; Scruggs, *Women of Distinction*, 207–9; Dannett, *Profiles of Negro Womanhood*; and Harley, "Anna J. Cooper."

30. Anna Julia Cooper, *Voice from the South*, 76.

31. Ibid., 77.

32. Atkins joined Livingstone in 1884 as head of the preparatory department. He later became the president of Winston-Salem State Normal School. See *Messenger*, 5 Aug. 1882, and Newbold, *Five North Carolina Negro Educators*, 6–7. For Atkins's view of higher education for African Americans from 1865 to the 1890s, see Simon G. Atkins, " 'Lest We Forget'—An Appreciation," *Africo American Presbyterian* (Dec. 1919), microfiche 18, Hampton University Newspaper Clipping Files.

33. *Living-Stone* 17 (Mar. 1901): 15.

34. This account of the history of Livingstone College is taken from Yates, *He Spoke, Now They Speak*, iii–14; *Messenger*, 12 Mar. 1887; Walls, *Joseph Charles Price and African Methodist Episcopal Zion Church*, 307–10; Fonvielle, *Some Reminiscences*; *Catalogue of Livingstone College* ([1899, 1905]); and W. T. B. Williams, "Livingstone College: A Self-Help Negro Institution," folder 92, box 102, series 1, subseries 1, General Education Board Collection, RAC.

35. *Messenger*, 28 Apr. 1888. Black women also earned A.B.'s by 1888 at Atlanta University and Oberlin College in Ohio.

36. Linda Perkins, " 'Cult of True Womanhood.' "

37. *Messenger*, 5 May 1888.

38. Ibid., 27 Oct. 1888.

39. Abna Aggrey Lancaster, interview with author, Salisbury, N.C., 25 June 1991.

40. Eula Wellmon Dunlap, "Reminiscences," Lincoln Academy Papers, American Missionary Association Archives, ARC.

41. *Messenger*, 8 Dec. 1888. Although the *Messenger*'s editor wrote that there had been a fight over coeducation at Livingstone at the AME Zion conference in May 1888, the conference minutes do not bear him out, indicating that those in power in the church supported coeducation and did not allow the question of a female seminary to come to the floor. See *Daily Proceedings of the Eighteenth Quadrennial Session of the General Conference of the A.M.E. Zion Church*. The *Star of Zion* commented mildly after the conference that a female seminary might be "desirable, but not feasible" (13 Dec. 1888). The decision was deferred and never revisited.

42. *Star of Zion*, 9 June 1898, 1.

43. Fonvielle, *Some Reminiscences*, 61, 123–25, 127–28. Carthey became a missionary for the AME Zion Church in the South. For the first-year classical curriculum at Livingstone College, see W. E. B. Du Bois, *Negro in Business*, 19.

44. *Star of Zion*, 9 June 1898, 1; *Messenger*, 4 June 1887.

45. Fonvielle, *Some Reminiscences*, 29.

46. *Living-Stone* 2 (Oct. 1890): 46; Fonvielle, *Some Reminiscences*, 39.

47. Fonvielle, *Some Reminiscences*, 30–32. For an overview, see Little, "Extra-Curricular Activities."

48. *Living-Stone* 2 (Apr. 1890): 19.

49. Ibid. 2 (Jan. 1891): 97. Cale Struggles (spelled "Streggles" elsewhere) may have been a pseudonym of William Frank Fonvielle, who created fictional characters in the magazine who may have represented composites of actual students. See Fonvielle, *Some Reminiscences*, 107–11.

50. *Living-Stone* 2 (Feb.–Mar. 1891): 99.

51. Ibid. 8 (Jan. 1892): 145; 2 (Mar. 1890): 6.

52. Ibid. 3 (June 1891): 27–28.

53. Fonvielle, *Some Reminiscences*, 62.

54. Solomon, *In the Company of Educated Women*, 119–21, using statistics from northern schools, finds that roughly one-half of white college women married, though they did so later than white women who did not attend college. For women at North Carolina Normal and Industrial College in the classes of 1893 through 1911, the lifetime marriage rate averaged 68 percent. See Dean, "Covert Curriculum," 248.

55. I have found no rule prohibiting married women from teaching in the reports from the Department of Public Instruction during this period. The examples of married African American women teaching are countless, and often a woman taught in the school where her husband was the principal.

56. For expositions of the ideal marriage for southern white women, see Jean E. Friedman, *Enclosed Garden*, and for black women, see Tate, *Domestic Allegories of Political Desire*.

57. *Star of Zion*, 5 Nov. 1896.

58. Fonvielle, *Some Reminiscences*, 13.

59. Anna Julia Cooper, *Voice from the South*, 70–71.

60. Scores of studies on northern white women and separate spheres followed these three pathbreaking works: Welter, *Dimity Convictions*; Smith-Rosenberg, "Beauty, the Beast, and the Militant Woman"; and Lerner, "The Lady and the Mill Girl."

61. Clipping from *Outlook*, 24 June 1887, scrapbooks, file 1800–1886, box 13, Hunter Collection, DU. Cooper began teaching at the M Street School in September 1887. See Mary Helen Washington, "Introduction," xxxiii. Henry and Nanny Delany, then employed at Saint Augustine's, must have been on Anna Julia Cooper's side of the controversy, since in 1891 they named their daughter Annie Elizabeth (Bessie) after her. Cooper's first name often appears as "Annie" in clippings from the 1880s. See Delany and Delany, *Having Our Say*, 42.

62. Rosa Steele, white wife of the president of Bennett College and head of "Work amongst the Colored People," in *Anchor* 2 (May 1886): 6.

63. Whitener, *Prohibition in North Carolina*, 27–28; Ida C. Hinshaw, "Pleasant Hill Temperance Society" (1931), unpublished paper, uncataloged, FWML.

64. Templars material, file 1818–85, box 1, Hunter Collection, DU. For a discussion of the Good Templars and prohibition during this period, see Whitener, *Prohibition in North Carolina*, 56. For the IOGT and race, see Haley, *Charles N. Hunter*, 27–30. For a similar situation in Alabama in which whites seceded from the international IOGT organization, see Sellers, *Prohibition Movement in Alabama*, 45–47. See also Fahey, *Collected Writings of Jessie Forsyth*, and Walton and Taylor, "Blacks and the Southern Prohibition Movement." Some black women apparently continued to see the Good Templars as an alternative to the WCTU, according to *Woman's Era* 1 (24 Mar. 1894): 3: "There is a Lodge of Good Templars formed and governed entirely by women which has been in existence for many years."

65. Clipping from *Banner of Temperance*, n.d., file 1833–79, box 13, and "Temperance," n.p., 20 Nov. 1871, scrapbooks (xerox copies), file 1833–1902, box 13, Hunter Collection, DU.

66. Clipping from *New Bern Daily Times*, 12 June 1873, scrapbooks, file 1833–79, box 13, and "Fifth Anniversary of the Victor Fire Company," n.p., [1870], scrapbooks, file Mainly News and Editorials, box 16, both in Hunter Collection, DU.

67. *Educator*, 5 Feb. 1875. William A. Link finds the situation quite different within white male temperance societies, in which white men created a world "infused with the traditions of nineteenth-century male culture" (*Paradox of Southern Progressivism*, 35–36).

68. *Messenger*, 7 Jan. 1888; Fahey, *Collected Writings of Jessie Forsyth*.

69. Whitener, *Prohibition in North Carolina*, 60–80. On the racial politics of the 1881 election, see Helen Chesnutt, *Charles Waddell Chesnutt*, 29; Brodhead, *Journals of Charles W. Chesnutt*, 168–69; and Eric Anderson, *Race and Politics*, 96–98. On the election in Charlotte, see Greenwood, *Bittersweet Legacy*, 79–97, and clipping from *Daily Record*, 28 Apr. 1881, file 1880–86, box 13, Hunter Collection, DU.

70. Frances E. Willard Diary, 11, 12, 13, 14 Mar. 1881, and clippings from *Wilmington Morning Star*, 12 Mar. 1881, *News and Courier* (Charleston, S.C.), 15 Mar. 1881, and *Our Union*, May 1881, 10, all in Frances Willard Scrapbook, FWML; Ellen J. Y. Preyer to Mrs. Little, 11 Sept. 1939, in "Miss Frances Willard in North Carolina," uncataloged, FWML. My thanks to Alfred Epstein, librarian at the Frances E. Willard Memorial Library, for his invaluable assistance. See also Rogers, "W.C.T.U. in North Carolina."

71. On Willard's first southern trip, see Bordin, *Woman and Temperance*, 76–78; Frances E. Willard, *Glimpses of Fifty Years*, 373–74; and Slagell, "Good Woman Speaking Well," 292–314. On her visit to Georgia, see Ansley, *History of the Georgia Woman's Christian Temperance Union*.

72. Frances E. Willard, *Glimpses of Fifty Years*, 373.

73. *Temperance Herald*, 16 June 1881.

74. Every African American newspaper in the state, except for one, endorsed prohibition, according to the *Temperance Herald*, 16 June 1881. One-fourth of the liquor dealers attending a convention called to fight the referendum were African American, according to Whitener, *Prohibition in North Carolina*, 70. Municipal prohibition passed in Charlotte in 1881, and whites gave part of the credit to black

allies, according to Greenwood, *Bittersweet Legacy*, 96. For an overview of why temperance was so important to white men and women, see William A. Link, *Paradox of Southern Progressivism*, 42–48.

75. Whitener, *Prohibition in North Carolina*, 58, 61–80. For similar situations in nearby states, see Moore, "The Negro and Prohibition in Atlanta," and Pearson and Hendricks, *Liquor and Anti-Liquor*, 212–13, 217. Blacks in Alabama voted for prohibition, according to Sellers, *Prohibition Movement in Alabama*, 259.

76. Whitener, *Prohibition in North Carolina*, 81–101.

77. There has been little mention of black women's participation in the WCTU. An exception is Anne Firor Scott, *Natural Allies*, 99–103. Scattered references include the following: Jean E. Friedman, *Enclosed Garden*, 124; Salem, *To Better Our World*, 36–37; Neverdon-Morton, *Afro-American Women of the South*, 206–7; Guy-Sheftall, *"Daughters of Sorrow,"* 22; Mossell, *Work of the Afro-American Woman*, 177–78; and Wedell, *Elite Women*, 67–68, 92–93. Thanks to Leslie Dunlap of Northwestern University for graciously sharing her research and ideas with me at a critical stage in my writing.

78. *Star of Zion*, 23 July 1896.

79. Abna Aggrey Lancaster, interview with author, Salisbury, N.C., 25 June 1991. For the best explanation of the reasons for the difference between the white and black linkage of occupation and class, see Harley, " 'When Your Work Is Not Who You Are.' " On class differences between black activist women in the twentieth century, see Deborah Gray White, "Slippery Slope of Class."

80. Wolfe, *Look Homeward, Angel*, 255–57, describes this sort of temperance assault on the polls in Asheville. As white Baptist women and their children surrounded voters, the children "sang with piping empty violence: 'Think of sisters, wives, and mothers; Of helpless babes in some low slum; Think not of yourself, but others; Vote against Demon Rum.' " For a visit to a county almshouse, see *North Carolina White Ribbon* 4 (Nov. 1899): 5.

81. *Anchor* 2, no. 4 (July 1886): 5.

82. After the Civil War, no male or female voluntary organizations in North Carolina admitted blacks or held regular biracial conventions prior to the WCTU. The IOGT accepted separate black chapters in 1886, after the WCTU came to the state. The only organization of any type that held biracial conventions prior to the WCTU may have been the Knights of Labor, which had black members (male and female) in separate chapters, but it was not a voluntary organization. See Whitener, *Prohibition in North Carolina*, 55–56. On the context of temperance reform in the United States, see Blocker, *American Temperance Movements*, and Epstein, *Politics of Domesticity*. On women in early postbellum temperance movements, see Blocker, *"Give to the Winds Thy Fears."*

83. Sims, " 'Sword of the Spirit,' " 394. Epstein builds on female consciousness in *Politics of Domesticity*. See also Anne Firor Scott, *Natural Allies*, 94–96.

84. Black women in the WCTU acted from female and communal consciousness. See Cott, "What's in a Name?," 826–27.

85. My thinking on black women's activism and feminism owes a debt to the following works: Tate, *Domestic Allegories of Political Desire*; Elsa Barkley Brown, "Womanist Consciousness"; Patricia Hill Collins, "Social Construction of Black Feminist Thought"; hooks, *Feminist Theory*; Carby, *Reconstructing Womanhood*; Hull

et al., *All the Women Are White*; Giddings, *When and Where I Enter*; Sterling, *We Are Your Sisters*; Higginbotham, *Righteous Discontent*; Dill, "Dialectics of Black Woman-hood"; Hurtado, "Relating to Privilege"; and Terborg-Penn, "Discontented Black Feminists."

86. The term "uplift" represents the class presumptions inherent in educated black women's approach to community work. Black WCTU members used the term without question. See Higginbotham, "African-American Women's History," 271.

87. Sims, "'Sword of the Spirit.'" For discussions of the WCTU ideology, see Bordin, *Woman and Temperance* and *Frances Willard*; Frances E. Willard, *Glimpses of Fifty Years*; and Ansley, *History of the Georgia Woman's Christian Temperance Union*.

88. Woodward, *Origins of the New South*, 352; Williamson, *Crucible of Race*, 115–16, 120. Williamson fixes 1915 as the year by which whites became convinced that blacks were not dying out but actually increasing in numbers (ibid., 461). The progressive reformer Alexander McKelway of North Carolina insisted that alcohol had "annihilated other inferior races" and was doing the same to African Americans (quoted in William A. Link, *Paradox of Southern Progressivism*, 70–71).

89. "The Position of the National Woman's Christian Temperance Union of the United States in Relation to the Colored People," 6 Feb. 1895, uncataloged, FWML.

90. Simply calling white women "racist" does not help us, in David Roediger's words, "understand how historicized racial identities dramatically shaped what workers [or women] could do and dream in their lifetimes and how better deeds and dreams can be made possible in ours" (*Towards the Abolition of Whiteness*, 77). My analysis of the relationship among electoral politics, social practice, and the changing construct of "racism" was strengthened by Goodwyn, "Populist Dreams and Negro Rights"; Horton, "Testing the Limits of Class Politics"; and Jacquelyn Hall's reading of this section.

91. Sims, "'Sword of the Spirit'"; Bordin, *Woman and Temperance*, 78; Walls, *Joseph Charles Price*, 284.

92. Rogers, "W.C.T.U. in North Carolina," 22–23; Sims, "'Sword of the Spirit,'" 398.

93. *Messenger*, 24 June 1887. When the African American editor of the *Messenger* visited his daughter at Bennett College, he and his wife had dinner with Rosa and Wilbur Steele. Apparently Rosa Steele preached and prayed during the dinner, and he left very impressed with her piety and enthusiasm.

94. "Wilbur Daniel Steele," Clipping File through 1975, Biography, vol. 139, 711–12, NCC. Wilbur Daniel Steele was the son of Rosa and Wilbur Fletcher Steele, born in Greensboro in 1886 at the height of Rosa's WCTU organizing. For "Social Equality Steele," see Whitener, *Prohibition in North Carolina*, 85. On the Prohibition Party, of which Wilbur F. Steele was a member, see ibid., 82.

95. *[Minutes of the] Second Convention*, 16; *Anchor* 1, no. 8 (Nov. 1885): 6.

96. *Minutes of the . . . [Third] Annual Meeting*, 29–30; *Minutes of the Fifth Annual Convention*, 12.

97. *[Minutes of the] First Convention*, 14; *Anchor* 2, no. 4 (July 1886): 2. The first superintendent of "Colored Work" was Mrs. L. P. Rothwell of Wilmington. To understand the advances made in "interracial cooperation" in a few short years,

consider that Emma A. Unthank was one of the young girls in the Band of Hope organized by Steele in Greensboro. Unthank's father was the model for one of the black characters in Tourgee, *Fool's Errand*. See *Minutes of the Fourth Annual Convention*, 64.

98. *Minutes of the Fifth Annual Convention*, 51.

99. *Anchor* 2, no. 2 (May 1886): 6.

100. *Messenger*, 17 June 1882, 8 Apr. 1883. Frances Willard's assistant, Anna A. Gordon, listed "Miss Ainsworth, Teacher of Colored School" (Scotia Seminary) in Concord as a contact in North Carolina in 1881. Ainsworth possibly taught Mary Lynch and introduced her to the WCTU. See Anna A. Gordon, "Directory of Southern Addresses," uncataloged, FWML.

101. *Minutes of the Fifth Annual Convention*, 29; *Messenger*, 7, 14 Aug. 1886.

102. *Anchor* 2, no. 5 (Aug. 1886): 2; *Minutes of the Fourth Annual Convention*, 37, 63.

103. *Messenger*, 18 Dec. 1886, 19 Feb. 1887.

104. Ibid., 16 Apr. 1887.

105. Ibid., 7, 28 Apr. 1888.

106. Ibid., 19 May 1888; Greenwood, *Bittersweet Legacy*, 111–12. Jane Wilkes's papers and the annual reports of the hospital reveal that black women could not even form an auxiliary to support the hospital and that white women dictated all policies and hired all employees. See Wilkes Papers, CPL, and *Fifth Annual Report of the Good Samaritan Hospital for Colored People*, box 1, Good Samaritan Hospital Collection, NCDAH.

107. *Minutes of the Sixth Annual Convention*, 41. On Early, see Scruggs, *Women of Distinction*, 71–74, and Lawson, "Sarah Woodson Early."

108. *Minutes of the Sixth Annual Convention*, 41.

109. Annie L. Harrington to the editor, *Messenger*, 2 June 1888.

110. *Minutes of the Sixth Annual Convention*, 40.

111. *Union Signal*, 27 Nov. 1890, quoted in Sims, " 'Sword of the Spirit,' " 398.

112. *Minutes of the Seventh Annual Convention*, 17; *Minutes of the Ninth Annual Convention*, 17.

113. In 1898, black women organized southern unions in Georgia, North Carolina, Tennessee, Arkansas, and Texas. Unions in other states were organized at various times: Maryland in 1896; Washington, D.C., in 1897; Alabama (at least Tuskegee) in 1902; and Louisiana. See *Union Signal*, 24 Mar. 1898, 3; 3 Dec. 1896, 17; 25 Nov. 1897, 2; 25 Dec. 1902, 3; and Rowland, "Frances Joseph Gaudet."

114. *Living-Stone* 8, no. 3 (Sept. 1891): 44; no. 4 (Oct. 1891): 63; no. 6 (Dec. 1891); no. 7 (Jan. 1892): 145; Fonvielle, *Some Reminiscences*, 119. *Minutes of the Eighth Annual Convention*, 41, refers to the Charlotte WCTU No. 2.

115. Fonvielle, *Some Reminiscences*, 119–21.

116. *Living-Stone* 8, no. 1 (May 1891): 3.

117. *Star of Zion*, 15 June 1899, 1. Annie Kimball Clinton died six years after her marriage, and her husband became a bishop in the church.

118. Ibid., 9 Sept. 1897. The meetings at churches were not exclusively for church members and announcements stated, "Everyone Invited" or "Public Invited."

119. Ibid., 14 Apr. 1898, 26 Aug., 2, 23 Sept., 7, 21 Oct. 1897.

120. Ibid., 4 Mar. 1897.

121. On Annie Blackwell, see Walls, *African Methodist Episcopal Zion Church*, 409–10; *Star of Zion*, supplement, 15 July 1897, 2; 4 Nov. 1897, 3; 23 June 1898, 7; 18 Aug. 1898, 8; 5 Jan. 1899, 5; 16 Feb. 1899, 8; *Union Signal*, 11 Oct. 1900, 1.

122. *Minutes of the Seventh Annual Convention*, 17, 37.

123. In 1892, the national WCTU abolished the "Work amongst the Colored People" department and gave the black WCTU chapters equal organizational status. Mrs. J. E. Ray, the director of "Home and Foreign Missionary Work among and through Afro-Americans" for North Carolina, asked that the state's white WCTU retain this department as a "trial to local needs." Ray replaced Steele after she moved with her husband to Denver. Elizabeth Putnam Gordon, *Women Torch-Bearers*, 252, lists Mrs. J. E. Ray as the superintendent of "Work amongst the Colored People" for the entire nation, among black women like Frances E. Harper and Lucy Thurman. This seems unlikely. See "Continue to Assist," in *Minutes of the Eighth Annual Convention*, 21; *Minutes of the Tenth Annual Convention*, 4; *Minutes of the Eleventh Annual Convention*, 68–74; and *Minutes of the Twelfth Annual Convention*, 4.

124. *Minutes of the Eleventh Annual Convention*, 68; *Minutes of the Tenth Annual Convention*, 4.

125. *Minutes of the Thirteenth Annual Convention*, 71.

126. *Minutes of the Eleventh Annual Convention*, 71.

127. *Minutes of the Thirteenth Annual Convention*, 70–72.

128. *Minutes of the Eleventh Annual Convention*, 69, 73.

129. Fahey, *Collected Writings of Jessie Forsyth*, 35, 86–97, 127–31.

130. Ibid., 31, 365–70; Vron Ware, *Beyond the Pale*, 173–74, 184–87. Because Impey left no papers, Ware did not have access to information on her temperance background in trying to discover her early influences.

131. This account is drawn from Duster, *Crusade for Justice*. Gail Bederman brilliantly explores Wells's canny strategy of juxtaposing barbarism, "civilization," and manhood in Britain in " 'Civilization.' "

132. Duster, *Crusade for Justice*, 111–13, 151–52, 201–12; Vron Ware, *Beyond the Pale*, 198–215. Ware points out that Willard, champion of an end to the double standard, could never accept Wells's premise that white women voluntarily had sex with black men (ibid., 207).

133. Vron Ware, *Beyond the Pale*, 214.

134. The controversy also put northern black temperance leaders, male and female, in a difficult position. On Lucy Thurman's reaction, see *Woman's Era* 3 [Aug. 1896]: 10. On other reactions, see ibid. 2 (July 1895): 6–7, 12, and Frederick Douglas [*sic*], William Lloyd Garrison, Francis J. Garrison, Thomas Wentworth [*sic*] Higginson, Elizabeth Stuart Phelps-Ward, Herbert D. Ward, Julia Ward Howe, Ednah Cheney, Joseph Cook, and Lyman Abbott, "The Position of the National Woman's Christian Temperance Union of the United States in Relation to the Colored People" (Boston, 5 Feb. 1895), uncataloged, FWML.

135. *A.M.E. Zion Quarterly Review* 3 (Apr. 1893): 417.

136. Vron Ware, *Beyond the Pale*, combines analyses of racism, sexism, and imperialism in a way that emphasizes once again the connections between local and international politics. See also Timberlake, *Prohibition and the Progressive Movement*, 115–21.

137. *Union Signal*, 10 Mar. 1898, 13; 24 July 1899, 13.

138. Alice Ruth Moore (later Dunbar-Nelson), *Woman's Era* 3 [Aug. 1896]: 10; Wesley, *History of the National Association of Colored Women's Clubs*, 43, 45.

139. *Minutes of the Fourteenth Annual Convention*, 15–16; Hall, *Revolt against Chivalry*.

140. *Star of Zion*, 6 Aug. 1896; *Minutes of the Fourteenth Annual Convention*, 20; *Minutes of the Fifteenth Annual Convention*, 8; *Charlotte Daily News*, 28 Nov. 1897, 12. Lynch served until 1917, and at some later date, the Lucy Thurman WCTU changed its name to the Sojourner Truth WCTU, according to Tyler, *Where Prayer and Purpose Meet*, 208, 275. The WCTU No. 2 did not hold a statewide convention from 1891 to 1896 and was restructured under Lynch's leadership in 1896. See *Union Signal*, 6 Aug. 1896, 1; 3 Dec. 1896, 9, 17.

141. *Star of Zion*, 7 Sept. 1899, 5; *A.M.E. Zion Quarterly Review*, nos. 1–2 (1899): 100; *Minutes of the Ninth Annual Convention*, 17. On the location of the WCTU convention, see Elizabeth Putnam Gordon, *Women Torch-Bearers*, 253. On Lynch's prayer, see *Union Signal*, 3 Dec. 1898, 4.

142. *North Carolina White Ribbon* 6, no. 1 (1 July 1896).

143. Whitener, *Prohibition in North Carolina*, 121. Walton, "Another Force for Disfranchisement," makes a similar argument for Tennessee. After disfranchisement, whites attributed passage of local-option prohibition laws to the absence of black voters. See Timberlake, *Prohibition and the Progressive Movement*, 155.

144. The last listing of "Work amongst the Colored People" is *Minutes of the Fifteenth Annual Convention*, 24.

CHAPTER THREE

1. Rudyard Kipling, "The White Man's Burden" (1899), quoted in Painter, *Standing at Armageddon*, 153.

2. Edwards, " 'To Act Like Men,' " and *"Gendered Strife and Confusion."* Historian Gail Bederman argues, " 'Civilization' *naturalized* white male power by linking male dominance and white supremacy to human evolutionary development" (" 'Civilization,' " 7).

3. *Daily Charlotte Observer*, 30 Oct. 1898, 2.

4. The term "best man" appeared frequently in the press and probably developed from the term "better classes," used by both whites and blacks in lieu of "middle class." See Greenwood, *Bittersweet Legacy*.

5. Laura Edwards, "Politics of Manhood."

6. A plethora of books appeared beginning in the 1880s portraying black Best Men. For example, see William J. Simmons, *Men of Mark*; Dunbar, *Representative Negroes*; Kletzing and Crogman, *Progress of a Race*; Richings, *Evidences of Progress*; and Culp, *Twentieth Century Negro*.

7. On Best Men and the "better classes," see Greenwood, *Bittersweet Legacy*.

8. On this new image of masculinity, see Bederman, " 'Civilization,' " 7–8. See also Dubbert, "Progressivism and the Masculinity Crisis"; Filene, *Him/Her/Self*; Brod, *Making of Masculinities*; Vance, *Sinews of the Spirit*; Stearns, *Be a Man!*, 33–112; and Segal, *Slow Motion*. For comparative anthropological work on the creation of the imagery of manhood, see David D. Gilmore, *Manhood in the Making*.

9. Young white Democrats used the term "New Man" less than their fathers had used "Best Man," and they took for granted that the New Man would be white. See, for example, Daniels, *Tar Heel Editor*, 198–207. On northern influence in the creation of the New White Man, see Silber, *Romance of Reunion*. The intergenerational struggle of white men is recorded in Woodward, *Origins of the New South*, 142–74, and Ayers suggests the dichotomy between young and old white men in *Vengeance and Justice*, 235–65. Cell, *Highest Stage of White Supremacy*, 180, terms this group "New South Men." For other "New People," see Anne Firor Scott, "'New Woman' in the New South," and Locke, *New Negro*.

10. I argue, with Cell, *Highest Stage of White Supremacy*, that the men who instituted segregation and disfranchisement in North Carolina were forward-looking, not backward-looking. Unlike Cell, however, I do not believe that exclusion in North Carolina was the alternative to segregation, simply because the evidence of African American participation from 1890 to 1896 shows an increase in racial interaction—politically, socially, and economically—rather than a trend toward exclusion. The situation in North Carolina points up the importance of politics in forging "social" attitudes. Because large numbers of white Republicans contested elections, no consensus on exclusion grew. Cell's review of the literature on the origins of segregation and the change/continuity debate remains the clearest analysis of the writing on the question. Howard Rabinowitz, in *Race Relations in the Urban South*, argues that segregation in southern cities was a closed question by 1890 and represented an improvement over exclusion.

11. Rudyard Kipling, "If," reprinted in Joseph Morris and Adams, *It Can Be Done*, 4–5. My grandfather, born at the turn of the century on a North Carolina farm, left me this book, and this poem was one of his favorites.

12. In their introduction to "If" in *It Can Be Done*, Joseph Morris and St. Clair Adams tell us: "The central idea of this poem is that success comes from self-control. . . . In all things [a man] must hold to the golden mean. If he does, he will own the world, and even better, for his personal reward he will attain the full stature of manhood" (ibid., 4).

13. Jon Butler, *Awash in a Sea of Faith*, 275–82; Mathews, *Religion in the Old South*; Boles, *Great Revival*; Loveland, *Southern Evangelicals*; Bode, "Formation of Evangelical Communities."

14. As a whole, North Carolina simply did not conform to the model set out by Bertram Wyatt-Brown in *Southern Honor*. The differences in the economy in various parts of the state, in slaveholding patterns, and in the ethnic origins of the people meant that the antebellum ideal of masculinity was a great deal more complicated than the honor-driven patriarchy he describes. The sweep of evangelical religion into the state produced competing subcultures of masculine ideals between believers and nonbelievers, and the market economy of the Piedmont and seaport towns in the east produced a thriving group of petite bourgeoisie. The ideals of honor and manhood identified in Wyatt-Brown and Steven M. Stowe, *Intimacy and Power*, should not be overgeneralized in the case of North Carolina. Edward L. Ayers is alert to contingencies of time and place in his discussion of honor in *Vengeance and Justice*, 9–33. The west remained a profoundly rural frontier throughout most of this period. Rural men often have an independent vision of manhood in any time and place, and rural southern men probably continue in that

tradition. This ideal of manhood is discussed in Ownby, *Subduing Satan*. It is this rural man, not the planter's son, who became the "Rebel" and was, as Wilbur J. Cash put it, "techy" (*Mind of the South*, 73). For other discussions of antebellum masculinity, see Gorn, " 'Gouge and Bite' "; Greenberg, "The Nose, the Lie, and the Duel"; and McCurry, "Two Faces of Republicanism."

15. There is a great debate on the class origins of the disfranchisers. J. Morgan Kousser, in *Shaping of Southern Politics*, argues that the planter class provided more disfranchisers than the thoroughly bourgeois group C. Vann Woodward identified in *Origins of the New South*. Simmons was the only planter among North Carolina's masterminds, however, and he was a lawyer. In determining who brought about disfranchisement, it is as important to examine the course the disfranchisers took in young adulthood as it is to determine their birthplace, since it matters less where these men came from than where they prepared themselves to go. Moreover, arguing over planter versus bourgeois roots is a tautology since in the 1860s and 1870s there were so few bourgeois families from which to spring. Selling one's land is an act of self-embourgeoisement, as is going to the state university to prepare for a career. In North Carolina, at least, the great division in world view seemed to arise not between men born planters and those born small farmers, but between those who chose as young men to live in towns and those who remained on the farm. For a cogent discussion of this, see Cell, *Highest Stage of White Supremacy*, 119–20, 153–70. Cell also argues that the southern bourgeoisie began to grow in the 1890s and that cities had a disproportionate influence on the political economy (ibid., 96–99). Dwight B. Billings, Jr., in *Planters and the Making of a "New South,"* argues that the disfranchisers were an extension of the planter elite, "not new men to state politics" (196). He offers biographical backgrounds on Democrats in the 1899 state senate to prove that they were better educated than the average North Carolinian and that "the Democrats who entered the senate in 1899 were not new men" (ibid.). It might be more helpful to look at the backgrounds of state house members after disfranchisement rather than before. Contrary to Billings's findings on the rank and file, the leaders—Aycock, Daniels, and Winston, with Simmons the exception—were new men, not planters. He does not note if they were urban or rural, but 23 were lawyers, 6 were businessmen, and 5 were merchants, totaling 34 members with occupations dependent on commercial growth in urban areas of the 52 listed. Billings does allow that Aycock "was an upwardly mobile member of North Carolina's small middle class" (ibid., 198), but he argues that members of the middle class were in the pocket of the elites (ibid., 211). I would argue that the first was rising, the latter falling, and that the 1898 coalition represented a collision as they passed.

16. Lefler, *North Carolina History*, 372.

17. Woodward, *Origins of the New South*, 137.

18. *State Chronicle* (Raleigh, N.C.), 28 Apr. 1887.

19. *Progressive Farmer*, 28 Apr. 1887.

20. Ibid., 3 July 1894. Written one month after Polk's death, this comment indicates that the publication kept up his traditions. The same could be said of Charlotte a century later.

21. Nathans, *Quest for Progress*, 13. For an extensive analysis of class issues among whites during this period, see Escott, *Many Excellent People*.

22. Orr, *Charles Brantley Aycock*, 26; Connor and Poe, *Life and Speeches of Charles B. Aycock*; Robert W. Winston, "Aycock"; *Acceptance and Unveiling of the Statue of Charles Brantley Aycock*; *Presentation and Unveiling of Memorial Tablet, Charles Brantley Aycock*; Roper, "Charles Brantley Aycock." On Daniels, see Daniels, *Tar Heel Editor* and *Editor in Politics*, and Morrison, *Josephus Daniels Says* and *Josephus Daniels*. On Simmons, see Rippy, *F. M. Simmons*. Furnifold Simmons came from a landed family and lived in New Bern, an old port city. As an attorney, Simmons cast his lot with those promoting urban growth. Aycock was, in fact, a railroad attorney himself (Orr, *Charles Brantley Aycock*, 112), but that did not necessarily mean he had a steady income. The railroads dispensed their work as crumbs along with railroad passes to insure that all of the lawyers in the state were in their pockets and would have a conflict of interest that would prevent them from suing the railroad. James Leloudis discusses these men as students in " 'A More Certain Means of Grace,' " 94–114.

23. Daniels, *Tar Heel Editor*, 291–300; Morrison, *Josephus Daniels*, 13; Cooper, *Walter Hines Page*, 70; Walter Hines Page, in *State Chronicle*, 2 Feb. 1886, reprinted in Cooper, *Walter Hines Page*, 78.

24. Cooper, *Walter Hines Page*, 79. On Aycock's practice with Frank A. Daniels, see "Address by Judge Frank A. Daniels," in *Presentation and Unveiling of Memorial Tablet, Charles Brantley Aycock*, 14–15.

25. Aycock was the youngest of ten children, and he looked the most like his mother. Aycock's son-in-law and biographer said that Aycock's mother's "intellectual gifts made up in a large degree for her lack of education." See Connor and Poe, *Life and Speeches of Charles B. Aycock*, 7; Orr, *Charles Brantley Aycock*, 6; and "Address by Judge Frank H. Daniels," in *Presentation and Unveiling of Memorial Tablet, Charles Brantley Aycock*, 9–11.

26. Daniels's father chose to work in Federal-occupied New Bern, and he was killed by Confederate forces who fired on a ship trading between New Bern and Confederate lines. Morrison argues that Daniels's father was falsely accused of having Union sympathies, however he certainly avoided Confederate service and bet on a Union victory (*Josephus Daniels*, 4–5). His mother's position as postmistress became quite lucrative, but she lost it in a political patronage battle in 1882 (Daniels, *Tar Heel Editor*, 98).

27. Dixon, *Leopard's Spots*, "Historical Note."

28. Cook, *Fire from the Flint*, 35–38. Cook had access to Dixon's autobiography for a brief time before Dixon's widow reclaimed it and restricted its use. Through a dramatic series of events, it became available again in 1984 when M. Karen Crowe produced a critical edition of it. See Dixon, *Southern Horizons*, 167.

29. Dixon, *Southern Horizons*, 167.

30. Karina, " 'With Flaming Sword,' " 82; Novick, *That Noble Dream*, 87–88; Painter, *Standing at Armageddon*, 151.

31. On miscegenation and Dixon's influence on the theater, see Flynn, "Melting Plots," and Williamson, *Crucible of Race*, 158.

32. Williamson, *Crucible of Race*, 169; Dixon, *Southern Horizons*, 141–44.

33. John Edward Bruce, Bruce Grit Columns, microfilm reel 3, Bruce Collection, SC. The Bruce Grit columns ran in the *Star of Zion* and other black newspapers across the nation.

34. Dixon, *Sins of the Father*, 57. Bleeding and thrashing were Dixon's favorite activities for southern white women, apparently because as a child he had watched his mother almost die from hemorrhaging after childbirth. See Dixon, *Southern Horizons*, 141–44.

35. Dixon, *Sins of the Father*, 79–80.

36. Ibid., 123.

37. Ibid., 134.

38. Ibid., 137.

39. Ibid., 162.

40. I am grateful to Joel Williamson, author of a recent biography of William Faulkner, for pointing out that Dixon's tangled plot anticipates that of Faulkner's *Absalom, Absalom*.

41. Dixon, *Sins of the Father*, 36.

42. Ibid., 42.

43. Fulton, "Plea for Social Justice," 5.

44. Ibid., 11.

45. *Raleigh Gazette*, 5 Feb. 1898. The first white man whipped was not a "native southerner."

46. Daniels, *Editor in Politics*, 309; *New Berne Journal*, 15 Sept. 1898.

47. *New Berne Journal*, 25 Sept. 1898. *Raleigh Gazette*, 20 Mar. 1897, reported that black senator W. Lee Person introduced a bill "for the protection of the morals of our colored ladies," which was defeated. This bill, which would have made co-habitation illegal, was aimed at preventing white men and black women from living together without marriage. See *Journal of the Senate of the General Assembly* (1897), 356. Subsequently, the 1899 legislature tried to pass a "Jim-Crow bed law" to fine white men caught sleeping with black women, but the bill failed. See Orr, *Charles Brantley Aycock*, 138.

48. Dixon, *Leopard's Spots*, 198.

49. The case of Mary Bobbit is an example of the mild state involvement in biracial affairs during Reconstruction. Bobbit, a white woman, was arrested for "living with a negro man in open violation of law." Bobbit swore that she would "rather die than be separated from him." She was fined $50, which she did not have, and therefore she went temporarily to the county poorhouse. See *Daily Nut Shell*, 18 July 1878. During the antebellum period and Reconstruction, white women's chastity was not always assumed in rape trials in which black men were the accused. See Bardaglio, "Rape and Law"; Hodes, "Sex across the Color Line" and "Romantic Love across the Color Line"; Bynum, *Unruly Women*; Laura Edwards, "Sexual Violence"; and Berry, "Judging Morality."

50. *Presentation and Unveiling of Memorial Tablet, Charles Brantley Aycock*, 25.

51. For treatments of similar situations, involving similar pressures, in the North and Midwest at earlier times, see Stansell, *City of Women*, and Meyerowitz, *Women Adrift*. For the South, see Glenda E. Gilmore, "Militant Manhood in a New South City: The Men and Religion Forward Movement and Atlanta's Anti-Prostitution Crusade," paper presented at the American Historical Association, 1995, in author's possession.

52. Love, "Plum Thickets and Field Daisies," 168–70, CPL. When Anna Hagood, "an old white woman," died in "an unsavory part of the city" with $500

in gold in 1887, a black newspaper urged that the $500 be used to set up a "house of refuge for women, in which this woman had much to do with causing the need of" (*Messenger*, 1 Oct. 1887). The "negligees" were apparently "loose gowns" or "Mother Hubbards," precursors to the "artistic" dress adopted by avant-garde women in the 1880s. Prostitutes wore them when other women wore corsets and bustles. See Blanchard, "Boundaries and the Victorian Body," 30–31.

53. George Moulton to Mary Graves, 20 Jan. 1898, Clarke Papers, in the possession of Mary Moulton Barden, New Bern, N.C.

54. *New Berne Journal*, 11 June 1898.

55. Ibid.

56. On patterns of segregation, see Cell, *Highest Stage of White Supremacy*, 133–34. It seems clear that Rabinowitz and Woodward were correct in arguing that segregation spread from newer Piedmont cities to old eastern cities. In this case, that would mean that Charlotte segregated more quickly and to greater effect than New Bern. That seems to have been the case with residential segregation, but there was also plenty of urban interracial interaction in Charlotte, including amusements and revivals in Latta Park.

57. *New Berne Journal*, 23, 24 Nov. 1897. See also Mille Christine Collection, NCDAH.

58. *New Berne Journal*, 6, 10 July 1897.

59. The photograph is from John B. Green III, *New Bern Album*, 222. I have identified the man in the top hat as Charles Pettey, but it is difficult to be certain.

60. *Daily Charlotte Observer*, 14 Oct. 1898, 2.

61. *Messenger*, 19, 26 Aug., 25 Nov. 1882; *Daily Charlotte Observer*, 18, 19, 23, 25, 26 Aug. 1882.

62. *Messenger*, 19 Aug. 1882.

63. For background on Charlotte's black and white "better classes" and Laura Lomax's father, Bishop Thomas Henry Lomax, see Greenwood, *Bittersweet Legacy*, esp. 79, 86, 137, 139, 145.

64. *Star of Zion*, 12 Aug. 1897.

65. W. F. Fonvielle, "An Appeal to Women for Women," ibid., 16 Feb. 1899, 3.

66. Ibid., 12 Aug., 2 Sept. 1897, 16 Feb. 1899.

67. *Messenger*, 3 Feb. 1883.

68. "The Physical Degeneracy of the Modern Negro" by R. H. Johnson (*Star of Zion*, 30 Sept. 1897), an African American physician, is typical of the anecdotal writing on racial degeneracy. Johnson believed that the future of the black race was amalgamation, but as a reviewer pointed out, "The movement of the race is in the direction of the black type." On theories of racial degeneracy held by whites, see Williamson, *Crucible of Race*, 115–16, 119–20, 134–35, 141. The cult of the faithful old-timey black servant developed at this time. See Ayers, *Promise of the New South*, 340–43. An interesting place to witness this twisted nostalgia is in early films produced by whites. Thomas R. Cripps points out a rash of happy slave films, including *Old Mammy's Charge* (1914) and *A Slave's Devotion* (1913) ("African Americans on the Silver Screen," 113).

69. Steelman, "Progressive Era in North Carolina," 26.

70. Furnifold Simmons to editor, *Daily Charlotte Observer*, 27 Oct. 1900, Clipping File, Simmons Papers, DU.

71. L. L. Polk to E. A. Oldham, 30 Dec. 1882, Oldham Collection, DU.

72. W. R. Allen, "Turn on the Light," 10 Oct. 1900, broadside, Simmons Papers, DU; James L. Hunt, "Making of a Populist"; Ingle, "Southern Democrat"; Steelman, "Republican Party Strategists." On the Alliance and Populism in the South and North Carolina, see Delap[p], "Populist Party in North Carolina"; Goodwyn, *Populist Moment*; McMath, *Populist Vanguard*; Soloutos, *Farmer Movements*; Hicks, "Farmers' Alliance"; Schwartz, "Estimate of the Size of the Southern Farmers' Alliance," which estimates 78,000 Alliance members in North Carolina in 1890 (765); Theron P. Jones, "Gubernatorial Election of 1892"; and Muller, "New Populism." For an example of another biracial political coalition, see Horton, "Testing the Limits of Class Politics."

73. Noblin, *Leonidas LaFayette Polk*, 290–91.

74. Lefler and Newsome, *North Carolina*, 543–44.

75. *State Chronicle*, 6 July 1892.

76. Daniels remembered that Ransom "regarded himself as a sort of a feudal lord" (*Editor in Politics*, 45).

77. Daniels, *Editor in Politics*, 124.

78. Delap[p], "Populist Party in North Carolina," 57.

79. Edmonds, *Negro and Fusion Politics*, 38–41, 67–83.

80. Romulus A. Nunn, "Presentation of Portrait of Senator Furnifold McLendel Simmons," 13 May 1946, Nunn Collection, DU.

81. *New Berne Journal*, 6 July 1897; Phillip J. Weaver, "Gubernatorial Election of 1896."

82. *Raleigh Gazette*, 28 Aug. 1897. The total number of local black officials during this period is unknown but estimated in Edmonds, *Negro and Fusion Politics*, 117–35. Eric Anderson argues that Edmonds may have underestimated the number of black officeholders (*Race and Politics*, 247–51).

83. Delap[p], "Populist Party in North Carolina," 63.

84. Orr, *Charles Brantley Aycock*, 111.

85. *New Berne Journal*, 3 Dec. 1897.

86. *Star of Zion*, 2 June 1898, 3.

87. Ibid., 10 Sept., 15 Oct. 1896, 28 Jan. 1897. Historian Michael H. Hunt, in *Ideology and U.S. Foreign Policy*, depicts Americans' varying perceptions of Cubans, sometimes as light, sometimes as dark. Cubans' mixed racial heritage simply boggled the minds of many southern whites who thought of race as a bipolar "thing."

88. *Star of Zion*, 19 May 1898, 2. See also Gatewood, "North Carolina's Negro Regiment," 370.

89. *Star of Zion*, 9 June 1898.

90. Ibid., 16 June 1898.

91. See Glenda E. Gilmore, "Black Militia in the Spanish-American/Cuban War"; Steelman, *North Carolina's Role in the Spanish-American War*; Bond, "Negro in the Armed Forces"; Coston, *Spanish-American War Volunteer*; William H. Johnson, *Colored Volunteer Infantry of Virginia*; Steward, *Colored Regulars*; Lynk, *Black Troopers*; "Virginia's Colored Volunteers," *Southern Workman* 27 (July 1898): 132; Gatewood, "Alabama's Negro Soldier Experiment," "Black Americans and the Quest for Empire," "Kansas Negroes," "Negro Troops in Florida," and *"Smoked Yankees"*; Nalty, *Strength for the Fight*; Jack D. Foner, *Blacks and the Military*.

92. *Messenger*, 10 Dec. 1887; C. S. L. A. Taylor to Daniel Russell, 15 Dec. 1896, folder 19, Russell Papers, SHC; *Raleigh Gazette*, 28 Aug. 1897.

93. *New Berne Journal*, 26 Apr. 1898. Other groups formed in Wilmington, Asheville, and Raleigh, according to Gatewood, "North Carolina's Negro Regiment," 372.

94. *New Berne Journal*, 28 Apr. 1898.

95. Crow and Durden, *Maverick Republican*, 63–67.

96. At the time, Young was a member of the state house. See *Raleigh Gazette*, 20 Mar. 1897. The other black battalion was the Ninth Ohio. See Glenda E. Gilmore, "Black Militia in the Spanish-American/Cuban War," 53. Josephus Daniels of the *News and Observer* particularly hated James Young and attacked his appointment to the Board of Agriculture and the board of directors of the School for the Blind. See Morrison, *Josephus Daniels Says*, 101–2.

97. Gatewood, "North Carolina's Negro Regiment," 372–77. At the same time, Kansas created the Twenty-third Kansas Regiment, and Illinois the Eighth, both commanded by black officers. Virginia created the Sixth, which was led by black officers under a white commanding colonel. See Glenda E. Gilmore, "Black Militia in the Spanish-American/Cuban War," 53.

98. As in the Civil War, neighbors formed companies and stayed together throughout the term of enlistment. African American men in Raleigh, Wilmington, Charlotte, Greensboro, Asheville, Durham, and Fayetteville joined together. See *Roster of the North Carolina Volunteers*, 89–91, 95–123.

99. *New Berne Journal*, 1, 8 July 1898.

100. *Star of Zion*, 21 July 1898.

101. Gatewood, "North Carolina's Negro Regiment," 381–85; Glenda E. Gilmore, "Black Militia in the Spanish-American/Cuban War," 53–54.

102. *Star of Zion*, 10 Nov. 1898, 8, 9.

103. *New Berne Journal*, 14 Aug. 1898.

104. Ibid.

105. Ibid., 17 Aug. 1898.

106. Ibid.

107. Edward A. Johnson, *Negro Soldiers in the Spanish-American War*, 94.

108. Ibid., 108–9.

109. Newbold, *Five North Carolina Negro Educators*, 133.

110. Edward A. Johnson, *Negro Soldiers in the Spanish-American War*. Johnson graduated from Shaw University Law School and served as its dean for several years. After being twice elected alderman in Raleigh, he moved to New York City in 1906. Johnson became Harlem's representative to the state legislature, the first black man elected to that office, and had a long political career. He mentored his nephew, Edward Richard Dudley III, who moved to New York City to practice law and learn politics from his uncle. See "Harlem's Colored Voters' Victory," *New York World*, 30 Sept. 1917; "Negro Alderman and Assemblyman," *New York Sun*, 7 Nov. 1917; "Will Be First Negro to Sit in Assembly," *New York World*, 8 Nov. 1917; "Negro Assemblyman Will Speak in City," *Rochester, N.Y., [?]*, 5 Mar. 1918; "Negro Rights Bill up to Gov. Whitman," *New York Post*, 2 Apr. 1918; "Denunciation of Injustice Done to Colored Men," *Rochester, N.Y., Democrat*, 1 June 1918; and "Colored Citizens Have Legislator as Their Guest," *Rochester, N.Y., Times*, 1 June

1918, microfiche 381, Hampton University Newspaper Clipping Files. Johnson was in Harlem's "best society," a group that included W. E. B. Du Bois, James Weldon Johnson, and fellow Raleigh expatriate Hubert Delaney, according to Jervis Anderson, *This Was Harlem*, 335.

111. *Star of Zion*, 12 Jan. 1899, 3. Early Hicks was from Henderson. See *Roster of the North Carolina Volunteers*, 104.

112. Most southern states abolished black companies in their militias after the Spanish-American/Cuban War. See Herndon, "Phasing Out of the Savannah Negro Militia." The 1899 North Carolina legislature abolished the black company in the state militia, according to "James H. Young," in Lucas, Parramore, and Thorpe, *Paths toward Freedom*, 200.

113. Williamson, *Crucible of Race*, links white supremacy to white men's psychosexual impulses. For similar uses of sexual imagery during Reconstruction, see Hodes, "Sexualization of Reconstruction Politics."

114. Morrison, *Josephus Daniels Says*, 101–2; Daniels, *Tar Heel Editor*, 288.

115. *New Berne Journal*, 1 Aug. 1897; *Star of Zion*, 19 Aug. 1897.

116. *New Berne Journal*, 23 Sept. 1897.

117. Ray Stannard Baker, *Following the Color Line*, 175.

118. *News and Observer*, 27 Oct. 1898, 4.

119. *Daily Charlotte Observer*, 10 Aug. 1897, 4; 11 Aug. 1897, 1; 12 Aug. 1897, 1. The recounting of the rape is an example of the way southern white men used black-on-white rape stories as folk pornography. See Hall, " 'Mind That Burns.' "

120. *New Berne Journal*, 13 Aug. 1897.

121. *Raleigh Gazette*, 21, 28 Aug. 1897; W. E. Christian, in ibid., 6 Nov. 1897; *News and Observer*, 2 Sept. 1897, 1, 4.

122. *New Berne Journal*, 18 Aug. 1897; *Raleigh Gazette*, 21, 28 Aug. 1897.

123. *New Berne Journal*, 5 Sept. 1897; *News and Observer*, 2 Sept. 1897, 4.

124. *Star of Zion*, 9 Dec. 1897.

125. Ibid.; *Raleigh Gazette*, 5 Feb. 1898.

126. "An Incubus Must Be Removed," *New Berne Journal*, 10 Aug. 1898.

127. *New Berne Journal*, 3 Dec. 1897.

128. Romulus A. Nunn, "Presentation of Portrait of Senator Furnifold McLendel Simmons," 13 May 1946, Nunn Collection, DU.

129. *Raleigh Gazette*, 5 Feb. 1898.

130. Burgess, "Tar Heel Blacks," 331–34.

131. McKelway, "Race Problem in the South."

132. *Biennial Report of the Attorney-General of North Carolina, 1896* (Winston: M. I. and J. C. Stewart, 1896), 18, 25–27.

133. Orr, *Charles Brantley Aycock*, 109.

134. There were 19 rapes in 1896–97, 23 in 1897–98, and 14 in 1898–99. The Democratic legislature that took over in 1899 did not improve the situation; there were 21 rapes in 1899–1900 (the vast majority of which must have been white-on-white rapes). See *Biennial Report of the Attorney-General of the State of North Carolina, 1897–1898* (Raleigh: Guy V. Barnes, 1899), 71–72, 73, 96–97, and *Biennial Report of the Attorney-General of the State of North Carolina, 1899–1900* (Raleigh: Edwards and Broughton and E. M. Uzzell, 1901), 34–35, 37, 42, 60, 84, 85.

135. The number of "assaults with intent to rape" were 26 in 1893, 27 in 1894,

29 in 1895, 30 in 1896, 29 in 1897, 27 in 1898, 27 in 1899, and 37 in 1900. These figures indicate a huge increase in this crime *after* the Democrats regained power, perhaps reflecting a lag between the propaganda and its popular use. See *Report of the Attorney-General of North Carolina, 1894* (Raleigh: Josephus Daniels, State Printer and Binder, 1895), 34; *Biennial Report of the Attorney-General . . . 1896*, 25; *Biennial Report of the Attorney-General . . . 1897–1898*, 41, 57; and *Biennial Report of the Attorney-General . . . 1899–1900*, 48, 68.

136. Alfred Moore Waddell, in "Proceedings of the Society for the Study of Race Conditions and Problems in the South, 1900," quoted in McCord, *American Negro as a Dependent*, 63.

137. In western towns, such as Asheville and Marion, Republicans often held local offices. In Brunswick County, African Americans were in the majority.

138. *Daily Charlotte Observer*, 10 Sept. 1898, 3.

139. *New Berne Journal*, 13 Aug. 1897.

140. On lynching, see Ray Stannard Baker, *Following the Color Line*, 175–76; Chadbourn, *Lynching and the Law*; Raper, *Tragedy of Lynching*; Bederman, " 'Civilization' "; Ayers, *Vengeance and Justice*; Hall, *Revolt against Chivalry*, esp. 128–57; Williamson, *Crucible of Race*, 185–89; and Brundage, *Lynching in the New South*.

141. *Star of Zion*, 4 Feb. 1897. African Americans who advocated retaliatory violence most often lived in the North. See W. D. Clinton, "Get Guns for the Mob," and Editor, "His Mouth More Dangerous Than His Gun," ibid., 9 Sept. 1897.

142. On the contrast between community protection and the expectations of elite white women as well as other women, see Edwards, "Defiance and Protection."

143. *Star of Zion*, 24 June 1897; 9 Sept. 1897; Wesley, *History of the National Association of Colored Women's Clubs*, 56. Pettey joined Walters in California in the 1880s. On Pettey's visit to McKinley, see Walls, *African Methodist Episcopal Zion Church*, 558. Walters later became a founding member of the NAACP. See Walters, *My Life and My Work*; Painter, *Standing at Armaggedon*, 26; and Daniel Levering Lewis, *W. E. B. Du Bois*, 249–50.

144. *Star of Zion*, 26 Aug. 1897. See also *Proceedings of the Thirty-first Annual Session of the Baptist Educational and Missionary Convention*, 40, and *Raleigh Gazette*, 21 Aug. 1897.

145. *New Berne Journal*, 15 Aug. 1897.

146. Ibid., 17 Aug. 1897.

147. Ibid., 28 Oct. 1897; Rippy, *F. M. Simmons*, 26, 29. Simmons made a private deal with industrialists that Democrats would not raise taxes within the next two years if they were victorious in 1898 (ibid., 23). Apparently, he hid his promise, even from other Democratic leaders. Later a former Simmons associate called it "deep-sea stuff, which, coming to light many years later, had still lost none of its odor." See Brooks, *Southern Lawyer*, 51.

CHAPTER FOUR

1. Simmons used modern party organization and efficient clerical methods. He identified men who supported his cause in each county and asked them to refer

lists of Democratic sympathizers in each precinct. If someone failed to join his campaign, he had them replaced. People began to speak of the Simmons "machine." See Rippy, *F. M. Simmons*, 23–30.

2. "Rise, Ye Sons of Carolina!," *Wilmington Messenger*, 8 Nov. 1898, 1.

3. For example, the *Daily Charlotte Observer* sent H. E. C. Bryant to report on "Negro domination." Charlotte historian Janette Greenwood argues that the Democrats' white supremacy slogans "simply did not make much sense" there since the last black alderman had served in Charlotte in 1893 under Democratic rule (*Bittersweet Legacy*, 189–90). My conceptualization of the Democrats' use of power is based on Foucault's *History of Sexuality* and *Discipline and Punish*. The events of 1898 offer a good example of the convergence of two areas generally thought of as separate in our society—sexuality and politics—but which are not separate at all. See Padgug, "Sexual Matters." These events exemplify what Padgug describes as "the struggles which have occurred around [sexuality], both between and within classes," and the role sexuality "plays in legitimating contemporary society and class struggle" (ibid., 28).

4. The only accounts that decenter the white supremacists are Prather's *We Have Taken a City* and Edmonds's *Negro and Fusion Politics*. Prather includes evidence of black women's attitudes toward the riots. Works that cover the white supremacy campaign include Shapiro, *White Violence and Black Response*, 64–75; Mabry, *Negro in North Carolina Politics*, 43–56; Escott, *Many Excellent People*, 247–61; Crow and Durden, *Maverick Republican*; Kousser, *Shaping of Southern Politics*; Eric Anderson, *Race and Politics*; Steelman, "Progressive Era in North Carolina"; Wooley, "Race and Politics"; Higuchi, "White Supremacy on the Cape Fear"; McDuffie, "Politics in Wilmington"; and Kantrowitz, "'No Middle Ground.'" For fictional accounts, see Charles W. Chesnutt, *Marrow of Tradition*, and Fulton, *Hanover*. For contemporary descriptions, see "Race Troubles in the Carolinas"; Waddell, "Story of the Wilmington, N.C., Race Riots"; McKelway, "Race Problem in the South" and "Cause of the Troubles in North Carolina"; "North Carolina Race Conflict"; and Kelly Miller, "Race Problem in the South II."

5. A recent novel on the affair is Gerard, *Cape Fear Rising*.

6. For works by political scientists on political culture, see Ellis, *American Political Cultures*, viii–ix; Rogers M. Smith, "Beyond Tocqueville, Myrdal, and Hartz"; Richard W. Wilson, *Compliance Ideologies*, ix–x, 2–3; Almond, "Separate Tables"; and Rae, "Class and Culture." For historical accounts that offer useful ways of thinking about the political culture of women, though they exclude southern black women and therefore complicate the task of recovering their experience, see McGerr, "Political Style," and Ryan, "Gender and Public Access" and *Women in Public*. For an article that combines thinking about culture, politics, political culture, and historical context, see Thomas C. Holt, "Political Uses of Alienation."

7. The two contrasting views of southern white womanhood are exemplified by Jean E. Friedman, *Enclosed Garden*, and Anne Firor Scott, *Southern Lady*. Historians are beginning to recover women's conservative public presence. See, for example, MacLean, *Behind the Mask of Chivalry*.

8. On location as central to world view, see Hall, "Location, Location, Location." All too often, authors who write about white women's activism and discuss black women in a separate chapter or note their "contributions" distort black

women's history, just as writing white women into male-defined narratives did thirty years ago.

9. Scores of studies on northern white women and separate spheres followed these pathbreaking works, such as Cott, *Bonds of Womanhood*; Welter, *Dimity Convictions*; Smith-Rosenberg, "Beauty, the Beast, and the Militant Woman"; and Lerner, "The Lady and the Mill Girl."

10. The use of this image represents an important first step in recovering the story of black women's political activism. It does not, however, tell the entire story. For examples of works that emphasize the unity and self-sacrifice of black women's political action, see Glenda E. Gilmore, "'We Can Go Where You Cannot Afford to Go'"; Neverdon-Morton, *Afro-American Women of the South*; and Salem, *To Better Our World*. For a call to complicate the story, see Higginbotham, "Rethinking the Subject of African American Women's History."

11. *New Berne Journal*, 3 Dec. 1897.

12. Ibid., 15 Feb. 1898.

13. Ibid., 18 Mar. 1898; Alan Watson, *History of New Bern*, 567. See *Pocket Manual of North Carolina*, 282, for the Nunn family.

14. *New Berne Journal*, 11 Aug. 1898.

15. Ibid., 10 Aug. 1898.

16. Romulus A. Nunn, "Presentation of Portrait of Senator Furnifold McLendel Simmons," 13 May 1946, 22, Nunn Collection, DU.

17. *New Berne Journal*, 14 Aug. 1898.

18. U.S. Bureau of the Census, *Occupations at the Twelfth Census*, 356. *Fifth Annual Report of the Bureau of Labor Statistics*, 127, lists under 1,200 women mill operatives, and *Fifteenth Annual Report of the Bureau of Labor and Printing for 1901* (Raleigh: Edwards and Broughton and E. M. Uzzell, 1902), 195, sets the number of women in mills at 18,377 in 1901. For the beginning of the process, see Hall et al., *Like a Family*, 33–44.

19. On the revolutionary implications of this domestic arrangement, see Meyerowitz, *Women Adrift*, and Hall, "O. Delight Smith's Progressive Era." Unfortunately, figures for women "adrift" in North Carolina cities are unavailable since no city was large enough in 1900 to be analyzed separately. In 1910 Charlotte was the only city in the state to be broken out in the census abstract, but working women are not shown by racial category. Of 4,796 working women in Charlotte in 1910, the number of women who worked in the two principal occupations open to black women, laundress and servant, totaled 2,201. This would indicate that white women made up close to 50 percent of the women's workforce. The 592 women who worked in mills were probably white. See U.S. Bureau of the Census, *Thirteenth Census of the United States*, 4:215, 217, 219.

20. Whereas the number of teachers grew quickly, as documented in Chapter 5, few North Carolina women pursued commercial clerical careers in 1900 or even 1910. See U.S. Bureau of the Census, *Occupations at the Twelfth Census*, 356.

21. On the founding of the North Carolina Normal and Industrial School at Greensboro and its class implications, see Dean, "Covert Curriculum." In lobbying for the state normal school for white women, educators pointed out that African American normal schools had existed since Reconstruction and that white women of limited means had no way to train for occupations in order to

support themselves. Moreover, such women would be agents of the state, support compulsory public education, and raise literacy levels among poor whites. See Holder, *McIver of North Carolina*, 72–73.

22. For white women's activism outside of the suffrage movement across the nation, see Blair, *Clubwoman as Feminist*. For the best treatments of the changes among southern white women prior to the turn of the century, see Anne Firor Scott, *Southern Lady*, and Hall, "O. Delight Smith's Progressive Era" and *Revolt against Chivalry*. See also Anne Firor Scott, "'New Woman' in the New South" and "Women, Religion, and Social Change"; Marjorie Spruill Wheeler, *New Women of the New South*; McDowell, *Social Gospel in the South*; Walter J. Fraser, Jr., Saunders, and Wakelyn, *Web of Southern Social Relations*; Rosemary Skinner Keller, Queen, and Thomas, *Women in New Worlds*; Sims, "Power of Feminism"; Osborne, "Widening the Sphere"; Dean, "Covert Curriculum"; Roydhouse, "'Universal Sisterhood'"; Shadron, "Out of Our Homes"; and Roth, "Matronage."

23. Poppenheim, *United Daughters of the Confederacy*.

24. Charles Reagan Wilson, *Baptized in Blood*; Foster, *Ghosts of the Confederacy*. On women and the Lost Cause, see Whites, "Rebecca Latimer Felton and the Wife's Farm" and "Rebecca Latimer Felton and the Problem of 'Protection.'" Whites argues that Felton's lynching rhetoric was a tool for her main project: to shame white men into elevating the condition of rural white women. Felton unfavorably compared the men of the 1890s to those of the Old South.

25. For one white woman's castigation of white men, see Whites, "Rebecca Latimer Felton and the Wife's Farm," 354, and "Rebecca Latimer Felton and the Problem of 'Protection.'" The pages of North Carolina's white women's temperance newspapers, the *Anchor* and the *North Carolina White Ribbon*, and the minutes of state WCTU conventions are filled with admonitions that women must get involved in politics because men had shirked their duty, echoing the national WCTU discourse. However, southern white women could add the fiction of halcyon days under slavery when men were chivalrous and honored women to the WCTU condemnation of current men's failure to do their duty.

26. Whites moved to North Carolina's towns in greater percentages than blacks, particularly in the 1890s. Whites made up 52 percent of the state's urban population in 1890, 59 percent in 1900, and 64 percent in 1910. See U.S. Bureau of the Census, *Thirteenth Census of the United States*, vol. 3. These figures and historical trends were not apparent to people at the time, of course, and whites feared that African Americans were leaving the farms. For a contemporary analysis, see folder 25, box 2, Coon Papers, SHC.

27. Democrats suggested that white women were in sexual danger from white Republicans as well. Republican Robert Hancock, a close ally of Governor Russell and the appointed president of the Atlantic and North Carolina Railroad, was accused by his niece (who was apparently pregnant) of seduction, and her mother threatened to sue him. The newspapers had a field day. See G. L. Hardison to Marion Butler (and clipping), 11 Jan. 1898, and J. S. Basnight to Marion Butler, 13 Jan. 1898, both in file 1–14 Jan. 1898, J. S. Basnight to Marion Butler, 19 Jan. 1898, file 15–20 Jan. 1898, and G. L. Hardison to Marion Butler, 25 Jan. 1898, file 21–31 Jan. 1898, all in Butler Collection, SHC.

28. *New Berne Journal*, 30 Sept. 1898.

29. Ibid., 16 Sept. 1898.

30. Ibid., 3 Sept. 1898.

31. Ibid., 16 Sept. 1898; Alan Watson, *History of New Bern*, 490–91.

32. *New Berne Journal*, 4 Oct. 1898.

33. "Trial of White Women by Negroes," [1898], broadside, NCC.

34. Alan Watson, *History of New Bern*, 140. The *Daily Charlotte Observer* reporter was H. E. C. Bryant. The *News and Observer* published numerous reports of the same incidents, making it sound as if they were separate occurrences.

35. Despite the fact that North Carolina Populists had formed local pacts with black Republicans, they continued to be racist. However, their self-interest and rationality allowed them to cross racial lines momentarily, much like the white women in the WCTU had expanded their gender interests across racial lines a decade earlier. Their actions outdistanced their ideology. Left alone to govern in a biracial coalition, they might have changed their ideas to match their actions at a later date. They did not get that chance. See "Poor Man's Honor: Populists," *People's Paper*, 14 Oct. 1898. On the splits that the campaign caused between black Republicans and white Populists, see "The Negro Smith Scores Populist Johnson" ([1898]), broadside, NCC.

36. *Wilmington Messenger*, 3 Nov. 1898, 2, refers to "blear-eyed Mary Ann Butler." On the term "Mary Ann," see Blanchard, "Boundaries and the Victorian Body," 40 (n. 41).

37. Joseph King to Marion Butler, 25 Oct. 1898, file 21–31 Oct. 1898, Butler Collection, SHC; *Daily Charlotte Observer*, 5 Nov. 1898, 8; "Comments by the State Democratic Committee on the Hand Book Issued by the Peoples Party State Executive Committee" ([1898]) and "Five Lessons for North Carolina Voters" ([1898]), broadside, both in NCC.

38. Michael McGerr, in "Political Style," claims that political style eschewed popular demonstrations in the latter decades of the nineteenth century. Furthermore, he argues that women suffragists reclaimed a popular, direct political style that moved their cause forward. The campaign of 1898 in North Carolina does not fit with his analysis of the general trend in the male political style because it reflected a conscious decision among male Democrats to invoke popular styles such as the mass demonstration, the parade, the handbill, and the rally. In addition, white women's participation in such direct political activity was sanctioned when the cause was race, but ten years later, southern suffragists avoided such activities lest they antagonize southern men, contrary to the national trend and McGerr's argument. Perhaps McGerr's analysis of the demise of popular politics at the end of the century holds less value for the South than for the North.

39. *Wilmington Messenger*, 5 Nov. 1898, 1.

40. See Goodwyn, *Populist Moment*. For the best description of this sort of family rally, which moved from Alliance to Populist culture, see Theodore Mitchell, *Political Education*, 49–50.

41. *News and Observer*, 23 Aug. 1898, 6.

42. *Daily Charlotte Observer*, 5 Nov. 1898, 5.

43. *Wilmington Messenger*, 3 Nov. 1898, 4.

44. *News and Observer*, 5 Oct. 1898, 4.

45. Ibid., 9 Oct. 1898, 3.

46. Daniels sent cartoonist Norman E. Jennett to art school in New York City to train for the campaign. See Daniels, *Editor in Politics*, 148–50.

47. My argument here owes a great deal to Hurtado, "Relating to Privilege." The term "collaborator" is hers.

48. Some historians and scholars in critical legal studies are moving toward a historicized explanation of "freedom" and a clarification of the connection between the rhetoric of "natural rights" in property and the development of capitalism. For example, see Thomas C. Holt, *Problem of Freedom*, esp. 3–9, and "'Empire over the Mind'"; Barbara Jeanne Fields, "Advent of Capitalist Agriculture"; Schwalm, "Meaning of Freedom"; and Eric Foner, "Meaning of Freedom in the Age of Emancipation."

49. On the slave community and slave religion, see Levine, *Black Culture*; Gutman, *Black Family*; Genovese, *Roll, Jordan, Roll*; Blassingame, *Slave Community*; Rawick, *From Sundown to Sunup*; Joyner, *Down by the Riverside*; and Webber, *Deep Like the Rivers*. I find the above scholars convincing, primarily because without such explanations of cooperation, the communitarianism I find in early and late Reconstruction would be inexplicable. Richard J. Ellis argues that the concept of communitarianism in slavery was invented by 1960s historians and substitutes a political culture of "fatalism," which he uses to explain freedpeople's failure to embrace staple agriculture, wage labor, and a market economy (*American Political Cultures*, 120–39). In contrast, I find freedpeople incredibly hopeful in the face of overpowering reasons to be fatalistic.

50. As David Montgomery put it, "The former slaves' own conception of freedom . . . was above all a collective vision, rooted in generations of common experience in the United States" (*The American Civil War and the Meanings of Freedom: An Inaugural Lecture Delivered before the University of Oxford on 24 February 1987*, quoted in Elsa Barkley Brown, "To Catch the Vision of Freedom."

51. African Americans acted out their faith long before the Social Gospelers began to call for the same sort of ideal community on earth. See Curtis, *Consuming Faith*, and Luker, *Social Gospel in Black and White*.

52. For this ideal at work, see Higginbotham, *Righteous Discontent*.

53. For example, Charles W. Chesnutt struggled to equip himself for competition but ultimately left the South, where, he came to believe, his race would always blot out his merit. See Brodhead, *Journals of Charles W. Chesnutt*.

54. *Star of Zion*, 8 Oct. 1896.

55. Most of the white women who stepped out of the home and into politics were single, but a small cohort—for example, Alice Freeman Palmer and Carrie Chapman Catt—were married. The white concept of separate spheres did have some effect on black women, but probably less on those who remained in the South than on black women in the North. See, for example, Linda Perkins, "'Cult of True Womanhood.'"

56. Walls, *African Methodist Episcopal Zion Church*, 111. On voting in the Baptist Church, see Higginbotham, *Righteous Discontent*, 12. See also Jacqueline Jones, *Labor of Love*, 66. For national woman suffrage arguments during this period, see *Woman's Era* 1, no. 6 (Sept. 1894): 8; 2, no. 7 (Nov. 1895): 11.

57. *Raleigh Gazette*, 20 Mar. 1897.

58. *Star of Zion*, 15 Oct. 1896.

59. On "uplift," see Higginbotham, "Rethinking the Subject of African American Women's History," 68, and "African-American Women's History," 271.

60. The motto of the National Association of Colored Women's Clubs, "Lifting as we climb," puts the best spin on this impulse among educated North Carolina women at the time, but it brings up as many questions as it answers about class. See Elizabeth L. Davis, *Lifting As They Climb*; Wesley, *History of the National Association of Colored Women's Clubs*; and Stephanie J. Shaw, "Black Club Women."

61. Urbanization made street "etiquette" a matter of grave concern across the country in the second half of the nineteenth century. Moving from communities where almost everyone was immediately recognizable to those where one rarely saw a familiar face caused a crisis in how people greeted each other, where they looked as they walked, where they went, and when they went there. This dilemma occurred in North Carolina's rapidly growing towns, which attracted African Americans as well as whites. See Szuberla, "Ladies, Gentlemen." For a more recent treatment of the same subject by a southern white woman, see Pratt, "Identity." My interpretation of street behavior as political owes a debt to James C. Scott, *Domination*. African Americans also made use of the streets for parades and barbecues. See *Raleigh Gazette*, 5 Dec. 1896, for an account of a parade of 500 African Americans in Bethel "marching through and around the town." On this tradition in the North and whites' attempts to control it, see Shane White, "'It Was a Proud Day.'"

62. *New Berne Journal*, 30 Sept. 1898. The incidents involved not only black women and girls but also black men and boys. One of my favorite accounts follows: "Two of Wilmington's most prominent and respected businessmen were out driving, and a dozen little negro boys chased them and made vulgar remarks about the horse and the men." The specific comparison the boys made between horse and man is left to the imagination. See *Daily Charlotte Observer*, 7 Sept. 1898, 2. For an account of black boys slapping a white girl, see ibid., 10 Sept. 1898, 2.

63. *New Berne Journal*, 7 Sept. 1898.

64. *Wilmington Messenger* article, reprinted in *News and Observer*, 8 Sept. 1898, 4.

65. *Winston Free Press* article, reprinted in *News and Observer*, 22 Sept. 1898, 3.

66. James C. Scott, *Weapons of the Weak*.

67. *New Berne Journal*, 1 Oct. 1898.

68. For racial degeneracy arguments, see Williamson, *Crucible of Race*, 115–24.

69. The best account of these events is Prather, *We Have Taken a City*, 30–48.

70. Manly's editorial was reprinted in white newspapers across the state. It originally ran on 18 August 1898 in the African American Wilmington *Daily Record*, but no copy of this issue exists. The *Wilmington Morning Star* reprinted it on 25 August and the *New Berne Journal* and the Raleigh *News and Observer* on 26 August. The *Wilmington Messenger* seems to have reprinted it every day until the election, often as a preface for news of black "outrages" on white women. See, for example, *Wilmington Messenger*, 5 Nov. 1898, 6. Alexander L. Manly was a descendent of North Carolina governor Charles Manly, who served from 1849 to 1851. In addition to his white family, Charles Manly had a large black family by several women slaves. He freed his children and gave them land. I am also descended from Charles Manly. For Alexander Manly's background, see Prather, *We Have Taken a City*, 68–70. See also *Raleigh Gazette*, 12 Feb. 1898.

71. "Cape Fear Happenings," *Raleigh Gazette*, 19 Dec. 1897. Black Wilmington correspondent T. Johnson claimed that some people were "dissatisfied" with Manly's being named clerk in the Office of the Register of Deeds. The black columnist for the *Daily Charlotte Observer* called the *Daily Record* the "only Afro-American daily paper published in the world." See D. C. Covington, "Afro-American Interests," *Daily Charlotte Observer*, 17 Oct. 1897, 10.

72. Wooley, "Race and Politics," 186.

73. Whites, "Rebecca Latimer Felton and the Wife's Farm"; Kantrowitz, " 'No Middle Ground' "; Williamson, *Crucible of Race*, 124–30; Talmadge, *Rebecca Latimer Felton*; Floyd, "Rebecca Latimer Felton, Champion of Women's Rights," and "Rebecca Latimer Felton, Political Independent." Felton saved numerous clippings of the Manly affair and the Wilmington massacre. She repeated her famous "lynch 1,000 weekly" remark when notified by the press of Manly's editorial. See "Lynch 1,000 Weekly, Declares Mrs. Felton," n.p., n.d., "Newspaper Clippings," Mss. 81, Felton Collection, Hargrett Rare Book and Manuscript Library, University of Georgia, Athens, Ga. She commented on the editorial in a letter in *Literary Digest* 17, no. 22 (26 Nov. 1898), ibid. Felton wrote, "When the negro Manly attributed the crime of rape to the intimacy between negro men and white women of the South the slanderer should be made to fear a lyncher's rope rather than occupy a place in New York newspapers."

74. In 1894, for example, Wells said, "It is a sacred convention that white women can never feel passion of any sort, high or low, for a black man. Unfortunately facts don't always square with convention" (*Westminster Gazette*, 10 May 1894, quoted in Vron Ware, *Beyond the Pale*, 169). On Wells's involvement in the politics of the 1890s, see Bederman, " 'Civilization.' " See also Duster, *Crusade for Justice*.

75. For two early works on interracial relationships during this period, see Johnston, "Miscegenation in the Ante-Bellum South" and *Race Relations in Virginia*. Newer treatments include Hodes, "Sex across the Color Line" and "Sexualization of Reconstruction Politics," and Laura Edwards, "Politics of Manhood." Hodes and Edwards find evidence of interracial sex during the Reconstruction Era, including sex between white women and black men. See also Williamson, *New People*. Several accounts of relationships between white women and black men were reported in North Carolina, including the Brewer-Manly liaison discussed later in this chapter. Accounts abound in the black press of sex between white men and black women, including the incident discussed in Chapter 3 in which black men whipped the white lovers of black women in Concord and David Fulton's complaint regarding the power of black courtesans over white men in Wilmington. See Fulton, *Hanover*, 11. For the politics of racial superiority and sex, see Stoler, "Making Empire Respectable," and Hall, " 'Mind That Burns.' "

76. *Wilmington Messenger*, 1 Nov. 1898, 6.

77. *Star of Zion*, 6 Apr. 1899, 3.

78. *Wilmington Morning Star*, 26 Aug. 1898; Prather, *We Have Taken a City*, 74.

79. Proclamation in *Daily Record*, n.d., reprinted in *News and Observer*, 22 Oct. 1898, 2.

80. H. L. West, in *Washington Post*, quoted in *Wilmington Messenger*, 1 Nov. 1898, 2.

81. *Wilmington Messenger*, 5 Nov. 1898, 5; *News and Observer*, 1 Nov. 1898, 1.

82. McKelway, "Cause of the Troubles in North Carolina."

83. *Wilmington Messenger*, 5 Nov. 1898, 4.

84. Prather, *We Have Taken a City*, 63.

85. George Rountree, "Memorandum of My Personal Recollection of the Election of 1898," folder 41, box 3, Connor Papers, SHC.

86. Prather, *We Have Taken a City*, 89; *News and Observer*, 6 Nov. 1898, 10.

87. De Rosset Family Papers, collection description, SHC. On her nervous breakdown, see John Lord to Kate Meares, 2 Mar. 1895, folder 59, box 5, ibid.

88. Clipping, folder 20, vol. 6, Waddell Papers, SHC.

89. Waddell, *Some Memories*. Ray Stannard Baker, *Following the Color Line*, 166, quotes a 1907 editorial letter that stated, "If a man isolates himself from feminine society, the first and only conclusion reached is 'he has a woman of his own' in saddle, of a duskier shade. This conclusion is almost without exception true." The record is silent on why Waddell waited until he was sixty-two to marry.

90. Fulton, *Hanover*, 16.

91. Kate D. Meares to R. A. Meares, 29 Oct. 1898, folder 59, box 5, De Rosset Family Papers, SHC.

92. Rebecca Cameron to Alfred Moore Waddell, folder 2B, Waddell Papers, SHC. Although the worst violence broke out in Wilmington, white Democrats across the state were armed and threatened Republicans and Populists away from the polls. George Moulton, traveling the week before the election, found "shot gun frolics" and a battle raging in the swamps of Robeson County, where Croatans had come out for white supremacy. In Kittrell to the north, he found "politicks . . . in a terable mess . . . riffels and armes of all kinds" in the hands of Democrats, who swore a Republican's life was "not worth a straw." See George Moulton to Mary Graves, 23, 30 Oct., 6 Nov. 1898, Clarke Papers, in the possession of Mary Moulton Barden, New Bern, N.C. On the Croatans in the campaign, see *Wilmington Messenger*, 3 Nov. 1898, 1; 5 Nov. 1898, 1.

93. *News and Observer*, 6 Nov. 1898, 10.

94. Weldon, "North Carolina Race Conflict," 707.

95. Prather, *We Have Taken a City*, 106; *Wilmington Messenger*, 9 Nov. 1898, 3, 8. Apparently, they forced Russell to withdraw the Republican candidates by threatening to riot and then rioted anyway.

96. Copy of speech, 9 Nov. 1898, folder 2B, Waddell Papers, SHC; *Wilmington Messenger*, 10 Nov. 1898, 8. For an account of the "Secret Nine," the inner circle of Democratic leaders, see Prather, *We Have Taken a City*, 107–11.

97. *Wilmington Messenger*, 1 Nov. 1898, 4.

98. Ibid., 13 Sept. 1898, 4; 21 Sept. 1898, 4.

99. Prather, *We Have Taken a City*, 96–124; Thomas Clawson, "The Wilmington Race Riots in 1898," Clawson Papers, SHC; Weldon, "North Carolina Race Conflict"; George Rountree, "Memorandum of My Personal Recollection of the Election of 1898," folder 41, box 3, Connor Papers, SHC; *Wilmington Messenger*, 11 Nov. 1898, 1, 4. The most detailed discussion of the riot and the politics that led up to it is McDuffie, "Politics in Wilmington." It was not enough for Wilmington whites to kill their black rivals and turn white Republicans out of office; they desperately sought approval for their actions as well. The Wilmington papers printed complimentary accounts and refuted critical northern comments. See *Wilmington Messenger*, 17 Nov. 1898, 4; 19 Nov. 1898, 3.

100. Gabrielle De Rosset Waddell Diary, folder 91, box 7, vol. 13 (Nov. 1898), De Rosset Family Papers, SHC.

101. It is possible that the people she fed were white since residential segregation was never complete in eastern North Carolina cities. See *Wilmington Messenger*, 6 Nov. 1898, 5.

102. Gabrielle De Rosset Waddell Diary, folder 94, box 7, vol. 18 (Oct. 1920), De Rosset Family Papers, SHC. On the United Daughters of the Confederacy, see folder 5, box 60, ibid.

103. Account Book, 1889–92, File Account of the Race Riot in Wilmington, 1898, Cronly Family Papers, DU. The account was never published and possibly was never sent. It was addressed to "Editor Independant [*sic*]." The *Independent* had published other articles on the riot.

104. Ibid. Alexander J. McKelway reported that "nurses began to threaten the safety of their charges, and the cooks began to hint at poisoning," absurdities that would have resulted in the nurses and cooks being fired on the spot. Whites created a fantasy that blacks were arming to kill them. See McKelway, "Race Problem in the South," 1058, and *Daily Charlotte Observer*, 9 Oct. 1898, 2.

105. Account Book, 1889–92, File Account of the Race Riot in Wilmington, 1898, Cronly Family Papers, DU. Cronly had compassion for African Americans who had been victims of the riot, but she was certainly not a liberal on racial issues. She wrote terrible fiction depicting African Americans. In "Aunt Urbania's Colored Servant," which she wrote under the pen name Emmett Reid, Susan Sauls, the daughter of a black minister, moves north to work as a domestic. The story is a sort of Pygmalion account, but Sauls is hopelessly ignorant, unclean, and out of place in the North. Cronly seems to use the story to prove that African Americans are happier in the South, where whites accept them, shortcomings and all.

106. *New Berne Journal*, 13 Nov. 1898. New Bern whites had mobilized into a Red Shirt force and had appointed a "large number of democrats" as "special policemen on the day of the election." See *Wilmington Messenger*, 6 Nov. 1898, 6.

107. "Colored Citens [*sic*]" to President William McKinley, 15 Nov. 1898, file 17743–1898, Department of Justice, Record Group R660, National Archives, Washington, D.C.

108. Anonymous to William McKinley, 13 Nov. 1898, ibid.

109. C. M. Bernard to John W. Griggs, 5 Dec. 1898, 1 Apr. 1899, and R. H. Bunting and John R. Melton to William McKinley, 24 Dec. 1898, all in ibid.

110. Dancy Collection, uncataloged, LC; Dancy, *Sands against the Wind*.

111. *Star of Zion*, 15 Dec. 1898, 4; 4 May 1899, 4. Higuchi, "White Supremacy on the Cape Fear," 119, documents the out-migration of African Americans for several years after the massacre.

112. Prather, *We Have Taken a City*, 147–50.

113. "Demand Justice: Editor Manley Lectures on the Rights of the Colored Race to Citizenship," *Providence [?]*, [1898], microfiche 394, Hampton University Newspaper Clipping Files.

114. *Durham Daily Sun*, 29 Oct. 1898, 1; 2 Nov. 1898, 4; 4 Nov. 1898, 1; 7 Nov. 1898, 1; *Wilmington Messenger*, 6 Nov. 1898, 7. The white press felt compelled to explain the incident: "That a white woman could stoop so low as to elope with a

negro seems impossible. But the woman was born of a family who winked at social equality" (ibid., 10 Nov. 1898, 6).

115. The *Wilmington Messenger*, amazingly obtuse, published an account of the Brewer-McCauley escape next to its daily reprint of Alexander Manly's editorial (1 Nov. 1898, 6).

116. Charles Chesnutt to Walter Hines Page, 10 Nov. 1898, reprinted in Helen Chesnutt, *Charles Waddell Chesnutt*, 104.

117. Walter Hines Page to Charles W. Chesnutt, 22 Nov. 1898, reprinted in ibid., 105.

118. Charles W. Chesnutt, *Marrow of Tradition*. On the two conflicting strategies and on David B. Fulton's *Hanover*, see Gleason, "Voices at the Nadir."

119. Lefler and Newsome, *North Carolina*, 522.

120. Daniels, *Editor in Politics*, 324, 374–80.

121. *Star of Zion*, 17 Nov. 1898, 4; Eric Anderson, *Race and Politics*, 284–95.

122. *Star of Zion*, 8 Dec. 1898, 4.

123. Ibid., 9 Feb. 1899, 1.

124. Ibid., 5 Jan. 1899, 4.

125. Ibid., 15 Dec. 1898, 4.

126. *A.M.E. Zion Quarterly Review* 9, nos. 1–2 (Jan.–Apr. 1899): 76. Dancy was editor of the *Quarterly Review*; although the quotation is from an unsigned editorial, it is written in his authorial voice. Dancy was not without detractors, and his abandonment of Manly sparked a huge controversy across the nation. John E. Bruce (Bruce Grit) supported Dancy and blamed Manly for bringing on the riot. Bruce believed that Manly was reckless because he was a mulatto and said that peace might prevail if "these gentlemen with large Caucasian reinforcement would cease in their efforts to revolutionize the social order" (*Star of Zion*, 12 Jan. 1899). Bruce did support protest against the repression. See Indignation Meeting to John E. Bruce, 29 Nov. 1898, microfilm reel 3, 13–77, Bruce Collection, SC.

127. *Star of Zion*, 5 Jan. 1899, 4; John C. Dancy to John E. Bruce, 31 Jan. 1899, microfilm reel 1, 311, Bruce Collection, SC.

128. *Star of Zion*, 8 Dec. 1898, 4.

129. Historians have seen the black church as a force in politics at three junctures: slavery, Reconstruction, and the civil rights movement. I argue that the black church was directly involved in the politics of the 1890s and became a guerrilla force after disfranchisement. On slave religion as a radical force, see Levine, *Black Culture*; Gutman, *Black Family*; Blassingame, *Slave Community*; Rawick, *From Sundown to Sunup*; Raboteau, *Slave Religion*; and Stuckey, *Slave Culture*. Works that emphasize the otherworldliness of the church during slavery include Frazier, *Negro Church in America*, 9–25; Genovese, *Roll, Jordan, Roll*; and Patterson, *Slavery and Social Death*. On the church and Reconstruction, see Woodson, *History of the Negro Church*, 198–223; Clarence Earl Walker, *Rock in a Weary Land*; Montgomery, *Under Their Own Vine and Fig Tree*, 142–90; Frazier, *Negro Church in America*, 47–49; Harding, *There Is a River*, 324–32; and Marable, *How Capitalism Underdeveloped Black America*, 197. Most theoretical discussions of the church as a political force occur outside the historical discipline. See, for example, West, *Prophecy Deliverance!*; Reichley, *Religion in American Public Life*, 281–84; Paris, *Social Teaching of the Black*

Churches; Baer and Singer, *African-American Religion*; Harris, "Something Within"; Kenneth Hill, "Politics and Participation in the Black Church"; Marx, "Religion"; and Marable, "Religion and Black Protest Thought." Robin Kelley has pointed out that other than Vincent Harding and W. E. B. Du Bois, no historian has taken seriously the connection between African American spirituality and politics (" 'We Are Not What We Seem,' " 88).

130. *Star of Zion*, 12 Jan. 1899, 1. The opinion is that of Bishop J. B. Small, Mary Small's husband.

131. Ibid., 4 May 1899, 1.

132. Excerpts from Bishop J. W. Hood's annual address, in ibid., 15 Dec. 1898, 1.

133. Ibid., 22 Dec. 1898, 1.

134. Ibid., 11 May 1899, 1; "Afro-American Proclamation: Solemn and Extraordinary," n.p., 3 May 1899, John C. Dancy Scrapbook, Secular and Religious, Dancy Collection, LC.

135. George H. White, *Defense of the Negro Race*.

136. Charles B. Aycock to Henry G. Connor, 10 Nov. 1898, folder 40b, box 3, Connor Papers, SHC. Aycock also commented that he "greatly" regretted what happened in Wilmington.

CHAPTER FIVE

1. James E. Shepard, *Morning Post* (Raleigh, N.C.), 2 Jan. 1900, scrapbooks, 1903–14, file 1900–1902, box 14, Hunter Collection, DU.

2. Jurgen Habermas carefully historicized the changing idea of the European public sphere, and historians of the United States have begun to use his theories. We must beware of applying them wholesale, however, since Habermas's project was specific to the period and place he studied. Southern African American history during the institutionalization of segregation and the subsequent Jim Crow years is in large part about conceptualizations of space and sphere, mitigated by race, gender, and class. As historians of women in this country add to Habermas's theory, theoretical insights about gender and the public sphere must also be contingent upon race, place, and time. See Habermas, *Structural Transformation*; Calhoun, *Habermas and the Public Sphere*; Seidman, *Jurgen Habermas*; Nancy Fraser, *Unruly Practices*, 113–43, and "Rethinking the Public Sphere"; and Ryan, "Gender and Public Access."

3. *Star of Zion*, 19 July 1900, 4. On disfranchisement in North Carolina, see Mabry, *Negro in North Carolina Politics*, 57–81; Edmonds, *Negro and Fusion Politics*, 198–217; Kousser, *Shaping of Southern Politics*, 182–96; and Eric Anderson, *Race and Politics*, 296–312. On similar campaigns in other southern states, see Tindall, "Campaign for the Disfranchisement of Negroes" (South Carolina); Mabry, "Disfranchisement of the Negro" (Mississippi); and Martin, *Negro Disfranchisement* (Virginia).

4. Woodward, *Origins of the New South*, 321–23.

5. Kousser, *Shaping of Southern Politics*, 130–81; Orr, *Charles Brantley Aycock*, 149.

6. *Star of Zion*, 1 Jan. 1900, 4.

7. Quoted in Connor, *North Carolina*, 475.

8. "Opinion of about one hundred and seventy-five North Carolina lawyers that the Amendment is Constitutional, that the 4th and 5th sections will stand or fall together, and that no native-born white man will be disfranchised," [1900], broadside, NCC; Edmonds, *Negro and Fusion Politics*, 200–201.

9. John Hope Franklin, *From Slavery to Freedom*, 447; Charles B. Aycock, "Inaugural Address as Governor of North Carolina, January 15, 1901," in Connor and Poe, *Life and Speeches of Charles B. Aycock*, 233–38; "Letter to the Legislature," 1901, Governor's Letter Book #109, 141, Charles Brantley Aycock, Governor's Papers and Letter Books, NCDAH; Charles B. Aycock, "Address before the Democratic State Convention at Greensboro, June 23, 1904," in Connor and Poe, *Life and Speeches of Charles B. Aycock*, 258–60. By 1915, when the Supreme Court found the grandfather clause unconstitutional in *Guinn v. United States*, North Carolina's clause had expired.

10. For a portrait of Aycock that examines his conflicted personal feelings over the disfranchising amendment, see Robert W. Winston, "Aycock." On education during this period in North Carolina, see Leloudis, "'A More Certain Means of Grace.'"

11. Charles Aycock compared the situation in North Carolina to that in Hawaii. He quoted Senator Shelby M. Cullom's findings that native Hawaiians were not capable of self-government in his acceptance speech for the Democratic nomination for governor, 11 April 1900 (reprinted in Connor and Poe, *Life and Speeches of Charles B. Aycock*, 212). He also used this defense in a letter to Professor Harvey Lee Prescott. See Charles B. Aycock to Harvey Lee Prescott, 11 Feb. 1901, Governor's Letter Book #111, 94–95, Charles Brantley Aycock, Governor's Papers and Letter Books, NCDAH.

12. Clipping from [Greensboro, 1900], folder 20, vol. 6, Waddell Papers, SHC.

13. Aycock, "Inaugural Address," in Connor and Poe, *Life and Speeches of Charles B. Aycock*, 232.

14. Clipping from [Greensboro, 1900], folder 20, vol. 6, Waddell Papers, SHC.

15. Clipping from *Caucasian* (Raleigh, N.C.), 4 Jan. 1900, scrapbooks, file 1908–14, box 14, Hunter Collection, DU. North Carolina whites often used the image of African Americans wearing eyeglasses to play on the white supremacist emotions of their audiences. Since many poor whites could not afford glasses and could not read or write so had no need for them, the image elicited a wide range of resentments. Virginians used a similar argument when they warned that the educational provision would eliminate the "old time Negro" and favor "the gingercake [mulatto] school graduate—with a diploma of side whiskers and beaver hat, pocket pistols, brass knucks, and bicycles" (Martin, *Negro Disfranchisement*, 129).

16. *Star of Zion*, 26 July 1900, 5.

17. Eric Anderson, *Race and Politics*, 296–97.

18. Mabry, *Negro in North Carolina Politics*, 61–62; Edmonds, *Negro and Fusion Politics*, 106–12.

19. *Star of Zion*, 19 Jan. 1899, 4; 26 Jan. 1899, 1; *New Berne Journal*, 3 Mar. 1899; Alan Watson, *History of New Bern*, 495; Edmonds, *Negro and Fusion Politics*, 106–8; Mabry, *Negro in North Carolina Politics*, 60. All three black representatives spoke against the amendment, but to no avail. One of the delegates, J. O. Crosby, was playing up to the legislators in an effort to keep his Salisbury Normal School open.

See *Biennial Report of the State Superintendent of Public Instruction for 1898–1899 and 1899–1900* (Raleigh: Edwards and Broughton, 1900), 197–98.

20. Clipping from *Morning Post* (Raleigh, N.C.), 2 Jan. 1900, scrapbooks, file 1900–1902, box 17, Hunter Collection, DU; *Star of Zion*, 26 Jan. 1899, 1.

21. Eric Anderson, *Race and Politics*, 301–2. Governor Daniel Russell had feared for his life when he was forced to flee from a mob that marched on the governor's mansion in 1898 after the Wilmington insurrection. Russell sent out conflicting signals about the amendment. He argued that it was unconstitutional but also suggested in a speech that he might favor some limitation of African American suffrage rights. See Alice Sawyer Cooper, "Sarah Amanda Sanders Russell," folder 94, and Daniel L. Russell, "Republicanism in the South," folder 19, both in Russell Papers, SHC. See also Crow and Durden, *Maverick Republican*, 145–46.

22. Quoted in Edmonds, *Negro and Fusion Politics*, 203.

23. Pritchard and Butler tried early on to sponsor legislation in the Senate outlawing the grandfather clause. See Edmonds, *Negro and Fusion Politics*, 198.

24. Haley, *Charles N. Hunter*, 130.

25. *Press* (Hickory, N.C.), 24 Nov. 1898, and *Times* (Hendersonville, N.C.), n.d., both quoted in *Caucasian*, 24 Nov. 1898, quoted in Crow and Durden, *Maverick Republican*, 138–39; opinion of A. E. Holton, ex-chairman of the North Carolina Republican Executive Committee, reprinted in "Hurt by Negro Votes," *Washington Post*, 7 Sept. 1900, microfiche 364, Hampton University Newspaper Clipping Files. See also Gordon B. McKinney, "Southern Mountain Republicans."

26. Crow and Durden, *Maverick Republican*, 150–51; Mabry, *Negro in North Carolina Politics*, 75.

27. *Star of Zion*, 12 July 1900, 4.

28. See, for example, *Outlook* 62 (11 Aug. 1900): 1898–1900, which praises the bill's purpose and is lightly critical of the grandfather clause, and ibid. 65 (11 Apr. 1903): 847, which endorses the practical effects of the bill. For a critical piece that calls the amendment "plain discrimination against colored citizens," see *Chautauquan* 31 (Sept. 1900): 554. On suffrage restriction and racial attitudes regarding the Philippines and Cuba, see Michael H. Hunt, *Ideology and U.S. Foreign Policy*, 80–91, particularly the comparison to the situation in the South (80) and "Uncle Sam's New Class in the Art of Self-Government." See also Williamson, *Crucible of Race*, 337, and Painter, *Standing at Armageddon*, 228–29.

29. The successful challenge to the grandfather clause in *Guinn v. United States* resulted from the legal activism of the NAACP. See John Hope Franklin, *From Slavery to Freedom*, 447, and Daniel Levering Lewis, *W. E. B. Du Bois*, 483. The National Afro-American Council, a forerunner of the NAACP, met a few weeks after the election, and a large number of black North Carolinians attended, seeking advice and aid. The council could only use moral suasion and political influence, which was rapidly fading. See *Star of Zion*, 2 Aug. 1900, 1.

30. The *New Berne Journal* reported that white interest in the election was "intense, while the colored people took little interest" (quoted in Alan Watson, *History of New Bern*, 498). Since Isaac Smith represented New Bern in the legislature and was at the center of the suffrage debate, if the *New Berne Journal* found little interest among African Americans, they must have remained circumspect around whites.

31. William E. Clarke to George Moulton, 5 Aug. 1900, Clarke Papers, in the possession of Mary Moulton Barden, New Bern, N.C. See also Alan Watson, *History of New Bern*, 498.

32. *Outlook* 65 (11 Aug. 1900): 1898–1900; *Chautauquan* 31 (Sept. 1900): 554. For other instances of registration fraud and violence, see Eric Anderson, *Race and Politics*, 304–7.

33. Kousser, *Shaping of Southern Politics*, 193.

34. William E. Clarke to George Moulton, 5 Aug. 1900, Clarke Papers, in the possession of Mary Moulton Barden, New Bern, N.C.

35. *Star of Zion*, 7 Sept. 1900, 4.

36. Ibid., 24 Jan. 1901, 1. For a discussion of White's reaction to disfranchisement, see Eric Anderson, *Race and Politics*, 296–312.

37. Marcus H. Boulware to Mrs. M. J. Bahnsen, 12 May 1974, Clipping File, vol. 91, 725, NCC; *Union Signal*, 1 Nov. 1900, 13. On the international work of the WCTU, see Tyrrell, *Woman's World/ Woman's Empire*.

38. *Star of Zion*, 20 Sept. 1900, 6.

39. Ibid., 11 Oct. 1900, 4. Both parties still send poll watchers to the polls in predominately black precincts in North Carolina. The man who was murdered was R. C. O. Benjamin.

40. William E. Clarke to George Moulton, 13 Nov. 1900, Clarke Papers, in the possession of Mary Moulton Barden, New Bern, N.C. His numbers are about right. In 1896 in Craven County, the Republican candidate for governor received 2,867 votes and the Democratic candidate received 1,656 votes. In 1900, 932 people voted Republican and 2,611 voted for Aycock. See Edmonds, *Negro and Fusion Politics*, 230.

41. *Star of Zion*, 11 Oct. 1900, 2.

42. *News and Observer*, 4 Nov. 1902, 1. The percentage is based upon reports from Democratic registrars that Daniels called "estimates," "most of them official."

43. *Star of Zion*, 24 Oct. 1901, 4.

44. Edmonds, *Negro and Fusion Politics*, 229.

45. Rowan County is one of the few counties in the state in which scattered voter registration books are available to researchers. Although other counties might have such books, they are housed in closed warehouses. Since no complete set of registration books for any single precinct in Rowan County exists from 1890 to 1925, however, objective analysis is impossible. For example, even though these books reveal that many more blacks were registered to vote in 1916 than in 1904, one cannot be sure that all of the 1904 registration books still exist, and each precinct is missing books for several years at odd intervals. See Rowan County Voter Registration Books, Edith M. Clark History and Genealogical Room, Rowan County Public Library, Salisbury, N.C. The "Grandfather Book," which is a record of illiterate whites who appeared before a magistrate to swear that their ancestors voted before 1867, still exists in Rowan County at the Office of the Register of Deeds. William Mabry consulted Warren County voter registration books and found twelve blacks registered in Warrenton Township in 1902. See Mabry, *Negro in North Carolina Politics*, 77.

46. *Star of Zion*, 15 Nov. 1900, 1; 13 Dec. 1900, 1, 4, 5.

47. After the 1898 election, the imposition of a Jim Crow law was a foregone conclusion. See *Daily Charlotte Observer*, 2 Dec. 1898, 3, 4, and *News and Observer*, 4 Feb. 1899, 5; 2 Mar. 1899, 3. On creeping segregation, see Woodward, *Strange Career of Jim Crow*, 67–91. The legislature passed a law that required railroads to provide separate cars for blacks and whites in 1899, but streetcars remained unsegregated until a state law mandated segregation of the cars in 1907. For an explanation of the timing of these laws, see Campbell, "Corporate Hand," 119–38.

48. *Star of Zion*, 13 Sept. 1900, 5.

49. Ibid., 10 Jan. 1901, 2.

50. The description of Pettey's death suggests that he died of yellow fever, which begins with fever, causes hepatic congestion, and ends in renal failure. Physicians at the time were quite confused about yellow fever but achieved breakthroughs in its treatment and eradication within five years after his death. See Humphreys, *Yellow Fever*, 3–15. The account of Pettey's death is taken from various articles in the *Star of Zion*, 13 Dec. 1900, 1, 4, 5; 20 Dec. 1900, 1, 4, 5, 8; 3 Jan. 1901, 1, 2, 6, 7; 10 Jan. 1901, 2, 6; 31 Jan. 1901, 2, 5, 7. His last words were recorded in the 20 December 1900 issue by an eyewitness. The church was still in use when I visited it in the summer of 1994.

51. *Star of Zion*, 3 Jan. 1901, 1.

52. Ibid., 20 Dec. 1900, 1.

53. *Official Journal of the Twenty-second Quadrennial Session*, 254. The church owed Pettey $3,365 at his death. In 1904, it still owed Sarah Dudley Pettey $2,000.

54. I drove into Evergreen Cemetery at twilight, despairing of finding Pettey's grave among the hundreds of others, but I stopped beside it. Sitting on a slight rise, the monument still dominates the cemetery.

55. *Star of Zion*, 24 Jan. 1901, 5.

56. Roller, "Republican Party of North Carolina," 55.

57. *Star of Zion*, 17 Oct. 1901, 4.

58. *News and Observer*, 31 Aug., 29 Oct., 30 Nov. 1902; *Morning Post* (Raleigh, N.C.), 2, 30 Aug., 7 Oct. 1902, all quoted in Haley, *Charles N. Hunter*, 142. See also clippings from *Raleigh Liberator*, 18 Mar. 1905, and *[Morning] Post* ([Raleigh, N.C.]), 3 Jan. 1905, scrapbooks, file 1904–7, box 14, Hunter Collection, DU. "Coon, Coon, Coon" was widely popular.

59. George H. White to Booker T. Washington, 22 Jan. 1902, quoted in Reid, "Biography of George H. White," 187.

60. More African Americans held federal office under Theodore Roosevelt than under any other president to that time. Dancy's salary was $4,000 per year. See "National Capital Topics," *New York Age*, 2 Jan. 1902; "Negroes in Uncle Sam's Employ," ibid., [7 July 1905]; and "At the National Capital," *Freeman* (Indianapolis, Ind.), 2 Jan. 1909, microfiche 380, Hampton University Newspaper Clipping Files.

61. Booker T. Washington to John C. Dancey [*sic*], 7 Oct. 1902, Dancy Collection, uncataloged, LC. For a detailed discussion of Theodore Roosevelt's racial politics, see Williamson, *Crucible of Race*, 345–55, and Dyer, *Theodore Roosevelt and the Idea of Race*. Williamson notes that Washington discussed federal appointments with Roosevelt "early in 1902" and that Roosevelt appointed an African American in Alabama soon after Pritchard's visit (*Crucible of Race*, 351). Sometime shortly

after Washington's letter to Dancy, Washington visited Roosevelt's "spoilsman," James S. Clarkson, and got reassurance that African Americans would retain patronage positions. See Woodward, *Origins of the New South*, 463–64, and Harlan, *Booker T. Washington*, 3–7. This piece of political blackmail haunted Dancy. One paper reported, "We learn that . . . Dancy was a regular delegate in the Lilywhite State convention in North Carolina, and that he did not say a word in protest" (clipping from *New York Age*, 9 June 1904, microfiche 380, Hampton University Newspaper Clipping Files).

62. *Star of Zion*, 9 Oct. 1902, 4.

63. *New York Times*, 21 Oct. 1902; *Daily Charlotte Observer*, 23 Oct. 1902, quoted in Roller, "Republican Party of North Carolina," 100.

64. Eric Anderson, *Race and Politics*, 250; Roller, "Republican Party of North Carolina," 100–110. Roosevelt faced the issue again when he organized the Progressive Party in 1912, according to Arthur S. Link, "Progressive Party's 'Lily White' Policy."

65. *Star of Zion*, 25 Sept. 1902, 5; 18 Sept. 1902, 4. Crittendon is not listed in existing voting registers in Salisbury, but it is probable that he was a registered voter and that his precinct register is missing since other black men, including several professors at Livingstone College, maintained their registration but are also not listed in the existing books. See, for example, West Ward Election Precinct, Rowan County Voter Registration Books, Edith M. Clark History and Genealogical Room, Rowan County Public Library, Salisbury, N.C. For reports that African Americans throughout the nation were deserting the Republican Party, see "Negro Voters Restless," *Times*, n.p., 5 Aug. 1900, microfiche 364, Hampton University Newspaper Clipping Files.

66. Clipping from *Raleigh Liberator*, 18 Mar. 1905, scrapbooks, file 1904–7, box 14, and "The Negroes Discuss Their 'Grievances,'" n.p., [1905], scrapbooks, file 1904–7, box 14, Hunter Collection, DU.

67. Hood, "Enfranchisement of the Negro Race."

68. The literacy figure is from Helen Edmonds's analysis of the 1900 census in *Negro and Fusion Politics*, 228–29. In Craven and New Hanover counties, the locations of New Bern and Wilmington, respectively, more than half of the black men of voting age were literate, in the case of Wilmington, 63 percent. Most of the counties with large urban centers had more literate than illiterate black men over the age of twenty-one.

69. Sarah Dudley Pettey's father, Edward Dudley, lived to see the Republicans turn lily-white. But he must have experienced some satisfaction when his old friend and political ally Mayer Hahn walked out of the executive committee that voted to do so. See Roller, "Republican Party of North Carolina," 106.

70. *Star of Zion*, 6 Nov. 1902, 1.

71. Reid, "Biography of George H. White," 191–93.

72. Woodson, *Century of Negro Migration*, 147–66. Jack Temple Kirby dates the beginning of the black migration from the South at 1910. See Kirby, "Southern Exodus." James R. Grossman notes that in the upper South a large migration occurred before World War I. The only town in North Carolina with a large number of *Chicago Defender* subscribers was Asheville, with over 100 subscribers. See Grossman, *Land of Hope*, 33, 76–77.

73. Woodson, *Century of Negro Migration*, 147–66.

74. For valuable demographic studies, see Maslowski, "North Carolina Migration," 104, 107, 130–31; Marcus E. Jones, *Black Migration in the United States*, 38–50; T. Lynn Smith, "Redistribution of the Negro Population," 155–73; and Daniel M. Johnson and Campbell, *Black Migration in America*. The migration pattern of North Carolina's African Americans followed an east coast trail to Virginia, Pennsylvania, New York, and other northeastern states, according to Maslowski, "North Carolina Migration," 119. For broader treatments, see Grossman, *Land of Hope*; Marks, *Farewell*, 70–79; and Denoral Davis, "Socio-Historical and Demographic Portrait." Tolnay and Beck contend, as did Laura Arnold, that violence was an important factor in decisions to migrate ("Rethinking the Role of Racial Violence"). Joe W. Trotter argues that historians should examine more closely the southern roots of migration at the same time that they continue the relatively recent focus on the historical forces behind migration ("Introduction: Black Migration in Historical Perspective").

75. George White interview, in *Daily Charlotte Observer*, 28 Aug. 1900, quoted in Eric Anderson, *Race and Politics*, 308–9; "Southern Negro's Plaint," *New York Times*, 26 Aug. 1900, and "Congressman White's Break," *New York Age*, 13 Sept. 1900, microfiche 68, Hampton University Newspaper Clipping Files.

76. *Star of Zion*, 27 Sept. 1900, 4. Interestingly, "Jim Crow" is not capitalized in the original, perhaps because the editor refused to capitalize it at a time when the white press would not capitalize "Negro."

77. Gilbert T. Stephenson, "The Meaning of Negro Migration Northward," *News and Observer*, 5 Aug. 1917, 22.

78. Charles Waddell Chesnutt to W. E. B. Du Bois, 21 Nov. 1910, in Helen Chesnutt, *Charles Waddell Chesnutt*, 240–41.

79. Ray Stannard Baker, *Following the Color Line*, 160–61. Manly finally gave up trying to pass for white and took a job as a janitor so that he could live openly with his darker wife, who had been a Fisk Jubilee Singer, and their two children.

80. *Star of Zion*, 22 Aug. 1901, 1.

81. Ibid., 22 Aug. 1901, 1; 5 Sept. 1901, 8.

82. For the dynamics of this process, see James D. Anderson, *Education of Blacks*, 79–109.

83. John Dancy never returned to North Carolina after his appointment as recorder of deeds in Washington, D.C., and after a few years moved his family to Detroit, Michigan, where he became head of the Urban League. See Dancy, *Sands against the Wind*, and clippings in the John Dancy Scrapbook, Dancy Collection, LC.

84. C. Vann Woodward comments more extensively on this effect in *Origins of the New South*, 365–66.

85. The other AME Zion publication, the *Quarterly Review*, ran fewer articles on politics after 1902 and became primarily a magazine on church affairs.

86. *A.M.E. Zion Quarterly Review* (third quarter, July–Aug.–Sept. 1906): 106.

87. *Star of Zion*, 29 Aug. 1901, 1.

88. "Last Will and Testament of Charles Calvin Pettey of Newberne, North Carolina," 21 Dec. 1900, Craven County Estates Records, NCDAH; *Star of Zion*, 26 Sept. 1901, 3.

89. *Star of Zion*, 7 Jan. 1904, 4.

90. *Official Journal of the Twenty-second Quadrennial Session*, 254. The *Star of Zion* masthead continued to list Dudley Pettey as a contributing editor.

91. *A.M.E. Zion Quarterly Review* 6 (first quarter, 1907): 75–76.

92. *Star of Zion*, 30 May 1901, 5.

93. On the concept of the "white man's burden" and national reaction to it, see Painter, *Standing at Armageddon*, 141–69.

94. Rayford W. Logan, *Betrayal of the Negro*, 271–72; Woodward, *Strange Career of Jim Crow*, 72–74.

95. Williamson, *Crucible of Race*, 151.

96. Dixon, *Leopard's Spots*, "Historical Note."

97. Ibid., 350, 412, 436. On Dixon as a historian, see Davenport, "Thomas Dixon's Mythology of Southern History," and John Hope Franklin, "*The Birth of a Nation*."

98. Dixon, *Leopard's Spots*, 434–43.

99. Dixon, *Southern Horizons*, 264–65; Cook, *Fire from the Flint*, 109. On the untruthfulness of this account, see John Milton Cooper, *Walter Hines Page*, 168.

100. In a foreword Dixon wrote late in life for another book, he noted, "I have been compelled to use living men and women as important characters. If I have been unfair in treatment, they have the remedy under the law of libel" (quoted in Frank Smethurst, "America in Black, White and Red," *News and Observer*, 6 Aug. 1939, Clipping File through 1975, vol. 39, 731, NCC).

101. Thomas Dixon to Alfred Moore Waddell, 2 Apr. 1913, and Thomas Dixon to Gabrielle De Rosset Waddell, 7 Apr. 1913, both in folder 61, box 5, De Rosset Family Papers, SHC.

102. *Star of Zion*, 13 Nov. 1902, 1; 27 Nov. 1902, 1. See also Kelly Miller, "As to *The Leopard's Spots*." For Dixon's reply, see Cook, *Fire from the Flint*, 118. See also Bloomfield, "Dixon's *The Leopard's Spots*"; Josiah W. Bailey, "Thomas Dixon, Junior"; and Karina, "'With Flaming Sword.'"

103. Charles W. Chesnutt to F. D. Crumpacker, 9 May 1902, in Helen Chesnutt, *Charles Waddell Chesnutt*, 181.

104. John Edward Bruce, Bruce Grit Columns, microfilm reel 3, Bruce Collection, SC.

105. *The State* (Columbia, S.C.), quoted in *News and Courier* (Charleston, S.C.), 18 Oct. 1905, 3; 19 Oct. 1905, 7; and Len G. Broughton, minister of Atlanta's Baptist Tabernacle, in *Knoxville Journal and Tribune*, 9 Nov. 1905, all quoted in Cook, *Fire from the Flint*, 142–43. For the Wilmington account and the black reaction, see *A.M.E. Zion Quarterly Review* 4 (fourth quarter, 1905): 99–101. See also Inscoe, "*The Clansman* on Stage and Screen," 145–47, and Da Point, "The Greatest Play of the South."

106. Painter, *Standing at Armageddon*, 217.

107. Cook, *Fire from the Flint*, 141, 143.

108. Ibid., 173.

109. On the national reaction to *The Birth of a Nation*, see Williamson, *Crucible of Race*, 174–76; Daniel Levering Lewis, *W. E. B. Du Bois*, 506–9; and Rogin, "'The Sword Became a Flashing Vision.'"

110. Cook, *Fire from the Flint*, 173. Woodrow Wilson denied the rumor that he

compared *The Birth of a Nation* to "writing history with lightning." See John Hope Franklin, *"The Birth of a Nation,"* 16 (n. 12).

111. *The Birth of a Nation* opened in Atlanta in December 1914, packing the theater at $2.00 per person. See Dittmer, *Black Georgia*, 185.

112. Helm, *Upward Path*, 147. For an analysis of the rhetoric, see Newby, *Jim Crow's Defense*, 113–40.

113. *Star of Zion*, 28 Feb. 1901, 2.

114. J. A. Joyner, in *Biennial Report of the Superintendent of Public Instruction of North Carolina for the Scholastic Years 1900–1901 and 1901–1902* (Raleigh: Edwards and Broughton, 1902), vii–xi. There is a large body of literature on how disfranchisement affected the public schools in North Carolina. See Harlan, *Separate and Unequal*; Leloudis, "'A More Certain Means of Grace,'" 311–12; and Margo, *Disenfranchisement*.

115. James D. Anderson, in *Education of Blacks*, has proven that African Americans did not embrace the Washingtonian ideal of industrial education and cheerfully implement it in their institutions, but that northern white philanthropists and their "liberal" southern white allies in the education movement strangled support of any other type of African American education. He makes it clear that the white ideal of industrial education rarely remained intact, as African Americans subverted it in order to make it more useful to their purposes. He points out that African Americans often managed to hide academic courses behind the screen of industrial education, keeping alive what they had been taught earlier. His work and our discussions have given me the context to formulate these questions about gender and industrial education and to tie together the politics of industrial education and the politics of North Carolina.

116. Ibid., 102–10.

117. Ibid., 114–37; Leloudis, "'A More Certain Means of Grace,'" 243–48; Daniel Levering Lewis, *W. E. B. Du Bois*, 266–68.

118. Du Bois, *Negro Artisan*, 46, 54, 69.

119. Ibid., 48.

120. William E. Curtis, "Thinks Negroes Should Study Congo Dialects and Drop Hebrew," *St. Louis Times*, 21 Nov. 1907, microfiche 227-1, Hampton University Newspaper Clipping Files. Two years later, Biddle University offered a "purely English course" for the student whose training had been "partial." See "Biddle University," *Africo-American Presbyterian*, 18 Mar. 1909, microfiche 221-1, ibid.

121. "Aycock Cheered by Shaw's Students," *News and Observer*, 17 Mar. 1901, microfiche 261, Hampton University Newspaper Clipping Files; "Negro Must Face the Inevitable," *News and Observer*, 11 May 1900, scrapbooks, 1903–14, file 1900–1902, box 14, Hunter Collection, DU.

122. "The Negro As an American Citizen," *Morning Post* (Raleigh, N.C.), 6 Nov. 1903, microfiche 103, Hampton University Newspaper Clipping Files.

123. "School for Colored Race," *Nashville [?]*, 6 Aug. [1909], "Durham's Great Work," *Bee*, 7 Aug. 1909, "The National Religious Training School and Chautauqua at Durham," including endorsement from A. C. Dixon, Thomas Dixon's brother, *Daily Charlotte Observer*, n.d., and "A Useful Institution," *Daily Charlotte Observer*, Feb. 1911, microfiche 221, Hampton University Newspaper Clipping Files. See also other references in microfiche 103, ibid.

124. *Living-Stone* 17 (Mar. 1901): 15.

125. *Star of Zion*, 9 July 1903, 3.

126. Bishop J. W. Hood to Mr. Baldwin, president L.I.R.R. Co., 1 Apr. 1902, folder 920, box 102, series 1, subseries 1, General Education Board Collection, RAC.

127. [Wallace Buttrick] to Everett P. Wheeler, 6 Feb. 1904, folder 920, box 102, series 1, subseries 1, ibid.

128. *Sketch Book of Livingstone College and East Tennessee Industrial School*, 11; W. H. Goler to C. C. Clark, 15 Feb. 1904; J. [Troxell] to W. H. Goler, 15 Feb. 1904; and W. H. Goler to General Education Board, 12 Feb. 1904, all in folder 920, box 102, series 1, subseries 1, ibid.

129. Photographs in folder 920, box 102, series 1, subseries 1, ibid.

130. Advertisement in *Star of Zion*, 8 Oct. 1908, microfiche 188, Hampton University Newspaper Clipping Files; "Some of the Prominent Graduates of Livingstone College," 3 Nov. 1925, folder 920, box 102, series 1, subseries 1, General Education Board Collection, RAC.

131. *Star of Zion*, 14 Feb. 1901, 1.

132. Du Bois, *Negro Church*, 179.

133. For a good description of these strategies, see Mamie Garvin Fields, *Lemon Swamp*, 83–105, 141–58.

134. "Chairman Scales Defends the Colored A. and M. College," *Raleigh Post*, 25 Nov. 1902, file 1900–1902, box 14, Hunter Collection, DU.

135. Clipping from *News and Observer*, 29 Nov. 1902, file 1900–1902, box 14, ibid.

136. "Our Colored State Normal Schools," *School Record*, Mar.–Apr. 1903, 14–15, file 1903, box 14, ibid. For the participation of women at the highest levels of the teachers association, see *Star of Zion*, 1 July 1897. On the North Carolina Teachers Association, see Percy Murray, *North Carolina Teachers Association*.

137. By 1900, there were as many black women as black men teaching in the public schools. By 1910, women outnumbered men by more than two to one. See *Biennial Report of the State Superintendent of Public Instruction . . . 1898–1899 and 1899–1900*, 296–97, and *Biennial Report of the State Superintendent of Public Instruction for 1908–1909 and 1909–1910* (Raleigh: E. M. Uzzell, 1910), 213.

138. "The New Bern Collegiate Industrial Institute," n.p., n.d., microfiche 230, Hampton University Newspaper Clipping Files.

139. "Autobiography of Rev. Alfred Leonard Edward Weeks and Annie Elizabeth Cooke Weeks"; S. M. Brinson to Wallace Buttrick, 10 June 1902; Isaac Smith to Rev. W. H. Buttrick, 20 Jan. 1903; Wallace Buttrick to Isaac Smith, 26 Jan. 1903; A. L. E. Weeks to Wallace Buttrick, 23 Jan. 1909; A. L. E. Weeks to F. T. Gates, 11 Feb. 1909; and O. G. Villard to Wallace Buttrick, 5 Nov. 1909, all in folder 941, box 104, series 1, subseries 1, General Education Board Collection, RAC.

140. Weeks, *Victims of Circumstances*, 4–5.

141. Ibid., 11–13.

142. Ibid., 19–20.

143. Ibid., 32–33.

144. Ibid., 45.

145. Ibid.

146. William Archer, *Through Afro-America* (1910), quoted in Winfield Collins, *The Truth about Lynching*, 64–65.

147. Interview with Addie Lyerly, *Salisbury Post*, 14 July 1974.

148. W. G. Briggs, in clipping from *Raleigh Evening Times*, 11 Aug. 1906, scrapbooks, file 1904–7, box 14, Hunter Collection, DU.

149. Clipping, n.p., 14 Jan. 1952, and clippings from *News and Observer*, 8, 9 Aug. 1906, all in Lyerly File, vertical files, Edith M. Clark History and Genealogical Room, Rowan County Public Library, Salisbury, N.C.; Lockhart, "Lynching in North Carolina," 153.

150. Clipping from *News and Observer*, 9 Aug. 1906, scrapbooks, file 1904–7, box 14, Hunter Collection, DU; Williamson, *Crucible of Race*, 188.

151. J. E. Kwegyir Aggrey to Mr. Smoot, 10 July 1926, in Edwin W. Smith, *Aggrey of Africa*, 98.

152. Clipping from *News and Observer*, 10 Aug. 1906, scrapbooks, file 1904–7, box 14, Hunter Collection, DU. The reporter refers to Bud Bullabough, alias Bully Boy, alias Billy McConeyhead. More likely this man's name was Bullaboa, a family listed in the city directory, and he was related to the McConeyhead family. The two families lived close to each other, and the women were cotton mill operatives.

153. Williamson, *Crucible of Race*, 189. The *Salisbury-Spencer, North Carolina, City Directory II* lists Francis M. Cress as a driver for the lumberyard. Henry Goodman was a salesman at the Globe Department Store.

154. North Carolina governors at least tried to prevent lynchings from 1900 onward. See "Negro Brought Here to Prevent a Lynching," *Raleigh Post*, 15 Nov. 1903; "No Danger of Lynching," *Daily Charlotte Observer*, 17 July 1904; "Jail Is Stormed by Masked Mob and Negro Lynched," *New York Journal*, 27 Aug. 1905; "Pleaded with Angry Mob," n.p.; and "Lynching Imminent in North Carolina . . . Militia Called Out," *The State* (Columbia, S.C.), 14 Feb. 1908, microfiche 327, Hampton University Newspaper Clipping Files.

155. W. G. Briggs, "North Carolina Humiliated by Mob's Work at Salisbury," *Raleigh Evening Times*, 11 Aug. 1906, scrapbooks, file 1904–7, box 14, Hunter Collection, DU.

156. At the time, many people searched for the "causes" of lynching, disregarding the fact that the primary "cause" was that the lynchers could get away with it. Often these analyses argued that lower-class white men had not evolved as far as upper-class men and therefore used more barbarous methods to preserve "law and order." See Bishop, "Causes, Consequences, and Cure of Mob Violence"; Bassett, "Stirring Up the Fires of Race Antipathy"; Kilgo, "Inquiry Concerning Lynchings"; Chadbourn, *Lynching and the Law*, 4; Tindall, *Emergence of the New South*, 171–72; Williamson, *Crucible of Race*, 188; Hall, *Revolt against Chivalry*, 139–49, 207–8; and Ayers, *Vengeance and Justice*. Ida Wells-Barnett noted that the victim of lynching was generally the poor and uneducated black. See Wells-Barnett, "Lynching."

157. Clipping from *News and Observer*, 10 Aug. 1906, scrapbooks, file 1904–7, box 17, Hunter Collection, DU. For a discussion of children and lynching, see Brundage, *Lynching in the New South*, 2.

CHAPTER SIX

1. My conception of the expansion of the public sphere and the growth of an interactive state draws heavily on Jurgen Habermas's work and his redefinition of the term "citizen" and on Nancy Fraser's argument that this movement from citizen to state client was gendered, at least in the United States, since it brought the state into matters that were heretofore in the private, or woman's, sphere. See Habermas, *Structural Transformation*, and Nancy Fraser, "Rethinking the Public Sphere."

2. Richard L. Watson surveys the historiography of southern progressivism in his essay "From Populism through the New Deal."

3. Because of southern racial dynamics and arguments regarding change versus continuity, the southern progressive movement remains even less understood than the national progressive movement, if that is possible. For the latest word, see Hall, "O. Delight Smith's Progressive Era"; William A. Link, *Paradox of Southern Progressivism*; and Ayers, *Promise of the New South*. The classic treatments include Arthur S. Link, "Progressive Movement in the South"; Woodward, *Origins of the New South*, 369–95; Tindall, *Emergence of the New South*, 219–84; and Grantham, *Southern Progressivism*. For attention to race, see Woodward, *Origins of the New South*, 369–95; Kousser, "Progressivism"; Dittmer, *Black Georgia*; and Painter, *Standing at Armageddon*, 253–82. On southern white women and progressivism, see Anne Firor Scott, "'New Woman' in the New South" and *Southern Lady*. On North Carolina, see Leloudis, "School Reform," and Sims, "Power of Feminism." For a review of the literature on women and progressivism in the South, see Hall and Anne Firor Scott, "Women in the South," 488–95.

4. Anne Firor Scott, *Southern Lady*, pt. 2, and "'New Woman' in the New South." For the political dynamics on a national scale, see Paula Baker, "Domestication of Politics," and Chafe, "Women's History." For an argument that women's work in social welfare and politics did not "change the fundamental nature of the state itself or alter the character of the male-dominated polity," see Sklar, "Historical Foundations of Women's Power." My argument for much of the remainder of this book is that black women did alter the political manifestations of white supremacy. See also Boris, "Power of Motherhood."

5. Hall, "O. Delight Smith's Progressive Era."

6. Anne Firor Scott, in "Most Invisible of All," suggests that black club women participated in southern progressivism but that their past had been lost, hence they were invisible. I, of course, concur but would add that their invisibility was often deliberate. For a reconceptualization of black women's work in the context of progressivism, see Lasch-Quinn, *Black Neighbors*.

7. Authors of the three most recent works on African American women's voluntary activities during the period chose not to use the framework of progressivism. See Neverdon-Morton, *Afro-American Women of the South*; Jacqueline Anne Rouse, *Lugenia Burns Hope*; and Salem, *To Better Our World*.

8. Higginbotham, *Righteous Discontent*; Dodson, "Power and Surrogate Leadership"; Gilkes, "'Together and in Harness'"; McAfee, *History of the Woman's Missionary Society*.

9. *A.M.E. Zion Quarterly Review* (third quarter, July–Aug.–Sept. 1906): 106; Frazier, *Negro Church in America*, 47–49.

10. *Proceedings of the Thirty-sixth Annual Session of the Baptist Educational and Missionary Convention*, 11.

11. *Minutes of the Thirty-first Annual Session of the Halifax County Sunday School Convention*, 4.

12. *Proceedings of the Thirty-second Annual Session of the Baptist State Educational and Missionary Convention*, 17. This convention was held in New Bern in 1899, and Sarah Dudley and Charles Pettey attended as emissaries from the AME Zion Church (ibid., 9).

13. *Centennial Year, Woman's Baptist Home and Foreign Missionary Convention of North Carolina*.

14. *Proceedings of the Thirty-second Annual Session of the Baptist State Educational and Missionary Convention*, 17.

15. *Yearbook of the East Cedar Grove Missionary Baptist Association*, 9.

16. *Proceedings of the Thirty-second Annual Session of the Baptist State Educational and Missionary Convention*, 17.

17. Even the most sympathetic whites called for home improvement, as did Joanna Moore, a white woman and editor of the widely read journal *Hope*, when she spoke to black Baptist women. Ibid., 9.

18. Mrs. Booker T. Washington, "Negro Home."

19. On black women and welfare, see Linda Gordon, "Black and White Visions of Welfare"; Ross, *Black Heritage*; and Lerner, *Black Women in White America*, 437–520. On the professionalization of social work, see Fitzpatrick, *Endless Crusade*; Chambers, "Women in the Creation of the Profession of Social Work"; and Walkowitz, "The Making of a Feminine Professional Identity."

20. The argument that the literacy requirement for voting increased the importance of black women as teachers recalls Linda Kerber's argument regarding the importance of the American Revolution and the founding of the republic to women. See Kerber, "Republican Mother," and Norton, *Liberty's Daughters*, 272. The Progressive Era rhetoric on good homes drew on an older Victorian construction of the purity of the home and female moral authority. For a sensitive untangling of this language and its meaning, see Pascoe, *Relations of Rescue*, xiii.

21. *Star of Zion*, 18 Oct. 1900, 5.

22. Lassiter, *Mount Zion Woman's Missionary Union*, 7. For women's increasingly active role in the black Baptist Church and men's resistance, see Higginbotham, *Righteous Discontent*, 120–49.

23. *Proceedings of the Thirty-ninth Annual Session of the Baptist Educational and Missionary Convention*, 49.

24. *Proceedings of the Thirty-seventh Annual Session of the Baptist Educational and Missionary Convention*.

25. *Proceedings of the Third Annual Session of the Union Baptist State Convention*, 27, 55.

26. There were more than 500,000 AME Zion Church members in 1909, according to Helm, *Upward Path*, 243.

27. *Star of Zion*, 14 Feb. 1901, 4.

28. Only scattered issues of the *Missionary Seer* exist in the Carnegie Library, Livingstone College, Salisbury, N.C.

29. Mattie W. Taylor, *Celebrating One Hundred Ten Years*, 13.

30. Ibid., 15.

31. Ibid., 28.

32. Caldwell, *History of the American Negro*, 9–14; *Star of Zion*, 18 Sept. 1902, 8.

33. Mattie W. Taylor, *Celebrating One Hundred Ten Years*, 39; Victoria Richardson personnel folder, Trent Collection, LC; Wactor, *Miscellany*, 2; Fonvielle, *Some Reminiscences*, 45–46. The characterization of Richardson and Lynch as teaching Livingstone's women students "finer womanhood" is A. R. Kelsey's, a Livingstone student who knew them both (A. R. Kelsey, interview with author, Salisbury, N.C., 14 May 1991).

34. Mattie W. Taylor, *Celebrating One Hundred Ten Years*, 43.

35. Wactor, *Miscellany*, 3.

36. *Star of Zion*, 22 Aug. 1912, 7; Jacob W. Powell, *Bird's Eye View*; Bradley, *History of the A.M.E. Zion Church*, 237; Walls, *African Methodist Episcopal Zion Church*, 413–16.

37. *A History of the Club Movement among the Colored Women of the United States of America* ([1902]); "Minutes of the Conventions, Held in Boston, July 29, 30, 31, 1895, and of the National Federation of Afro-American Women, Held in Washington, D.C., July 20, 21, 22, 1896," 30, 31, 121; *Minutes of the National Association of Colored Women* ([1897]), 4; and *Minutes of the Second Convention of the National Association of Colored Women* ([1899]), all on microfilm in *Records of the National Association of Colored Women's Clubs, 1895–1992* (Bethesda, Md.: University Publications of America, 1993); *Woman's Era* 2 (July 1895): 13; 3 (July 1896): 1. For overviews of the beginnings of black women's clubs, see Elizabeth L. Davis, *Lifting As They Climb*; Wesley, *History of the National Association of Colored Women's Clubs*; Hunton, "Women's Clubs"; Maude Thomas Jenkins, "History of the Black Woman's Club Movement"; Lerner, "Community Work of Black Club Women"; Neverdon-Morton, *Afro-American Women of the South*, 190–201; Salem, *To Better Our World*, 29–63; and Stephanie J. Shaw, "Black Club Women."

38. At the eighth convention, Marie Clinton sang to the assembled delegates, Mary Lynch introduced a motion praising Madame C. J. Walker, and Charlotte Hawkins, now Brown, spoke on the "lone woman." See *National Association of Colored Women, Eighth Biennial Session* ([1912]) and *Seventh Biennial Convention of the National Association of Colored Women* ([1910]), both on microfilm in *Records of the National Association of Colored Women's Clubs*.

39. *Star of Zion*, 13 June 1901, 8; 2 Apr. 1903, 8; *Daily Charlotte Observer*, 17 June 1901, 8.

40. Abna Aggrey Lancaster, interview with author, Salisbury, N.C., 25 June 1991.

41. George Lincoln Blackwell, telephone interview with author, 13 Jan. 1991.

42. *Daily Charlotte Observer*, 17 June 1901, 8.

43. *Star of Zion*, 11 Sept. 1902, 5.

44. *Souvenir and Official Program*.

45. *Star of Zion*, 11 Sept. 1902, 5.

46. *Biennial Report of the Superintendent of Public Instruction of North Carolina for the Scholastic Years 1900–1901 and 1901–1902* (Raleigh: Edwards and Broughton, 1902), 111.

47. *Biennial Report of the Superintendent of Public Instruction of North Carolina for the Scholastic Years 1916–1917 and 1917–1918* (Raleigh: Edwards and Broughton, 1919), 42.

48. Clipping from *Morning Post* (Raleigh, N.C.), 14 June 1903, file 1903–14, box 14, Hunter Collection, DU.

49. In Wake County, for example, the average annual salary in 1899 for black men was $127; for black women, it was $107. But by 1910, black men's salaries averaged only $105, and black women's annual compensation fell to $90. The gap between white and black teachers' earnings, roughly $20 per year in 1899, increased to more than $200 by 1910. See clipping from *News and Observer*, 28 Oct. 1910, file 1903–14, box 14, ibid.

50. *Biennial Report of the Superintendent of Public Instruction of North Carolina for the Scholastic Years 1904–1905 and 1905–1906* (Raleigh: E. M. Uzzell, 1907), 243, and *Biennial Report of the Superintendent of Public Instruction of North Carolina for the Scholastic Years 1918–1919 and 1919–1920* (Raleigh: Edwards and Broughton, 1921), 97. Harlan, *Separate and Unequal*, paints a grim picture of the unfair allocation of resources for black education after Aycock's election, including teachers' salaries (106–10). Kousser, in "Progressivism," corroborates Harlan's evidence statistically and focuses on how the taxation system worked to privilege rich counties in the east.

51. *Biennial Report of the Superintendent of Public Instruction . . . 1900–1901 and 1901–1902*, 111, and *Biennial Report of the Superintendent of Public Instruction . . . 1916–1917 and 1917–1918*, 42.

52. On the mission of the Greensboro school, see Dean, "Covert Curriculum."

53. For an overview of teacher-training institutions in the state, see "Report and Recommendations of the 'Statewide Committee of Ten Superintendents'" ([1916]), folder 1038, box 115, series 1, subseries 1, General Education Board Collection, RAC.

54. Littlefield, "After Teacher Training, What?," notes the high number of married female teachers in a sample of applications of Durham public school teachers and explores the culture in which black women taught.

55. Clipping from *The State* (Columbia, S.C.), 15 June 1905, 6, and A. M. Waddell to E. A. Alderman, 31 Jan. 1903, both in folder 3, box 1, Coon Papers, SHC.

56. On the educational movement in North Carolina during this period and McIver and Aycock, see Leloudis, "'A More Certain Means of Grace.'" In addition to Harlan, *Separate and Unequal*, and Kousser, "Progressivism," see Prather, *Resurgent Politics*; M. C. S. Noble, *History of the Public Schools*; and Knight, *Public School Education*.

57. Charles Duncan McIver, "Disfranchisement and Education." At the time, North Carolina had no compulsory school attendance law.

58. Josiah W. Bailey, "Popular Education."

59. Charles B. Aycock, "Letter to the Legislature," 1901, Governor's Letter Book #109, 141, Charles Brantley Aycock, Governor's Papers and Letter Books, NCDAH.

60. Love, "Plum Thickets and Field Daisies," CPL.

61. Leloudis, "'A More Certain Means of Grace,'" 243; George-Anne Willard, "Charles L. Coon"; J. Y. Joyner to Charles L. Coon, [1904], folder 26, box 2, Coon Papers, SHC.

62. J. Y. Joyner to Charles L. Coon, [1904], folder 26, box 2, Coon Papers, SHC.

63. Summary of Coon's 1909 Atlanta speech for *World's Work*; J. Y. Joyner to Charles L. Coon, 27 Sept. 1909; F. S. Hargrave to Charles Coon, 28 Sept. 1909 (for black reaction); and R. D. W. Connor to Charles L. Coon, 29 Sept. 1909; W. T. Lyon to Charles L. Coon, 30 Sept. 1909; and Charles B. Aycock to Charles L. Coon, 28 Oct. 1909 (for white support), all in folder 28, box 2, ibid.

64. Thurston T. Hicks to Charles L. Coon, 17 Oct. 1909, folder 18, box 2, ibid.

65. Charles Lee Coon, "How to Better the Negro County Schools," folder 28, box 2, ibid.

66. Clipping from *Morning Post* (Raleigh, N.C.), 14 June 1903, file 1903–14, box 14, Hunter Collection, DU; "Minutes First North Carolina Conference for Negro Education," 5, folder 1042, box 115, series 1, subseries 1, General Education Board Collection, RAC.

67. N. C. Newbold, "Supervising Industrial Teachers: Some Things They Helped to Do Last School Year, 1916–1917," folder 1044, box 115, series 1, subseries 1, General Education Board Collection, RAC.

68. N. C. Newbold to Wallace Buttrick, 27 Feb. 1913, folder 1038, and "Report of N. C. Newbold, State Supervisor Negro Elementary Schools for North Carolina, for the Month of June 1913," folder 1042, both in box 115, ibid.

69. "Report of N. C. Newbold, . . . June 1913," 3, folder 1042, box 115, ibid.

70. Ibid., 15. On the work of other philanthropies and the growth of the Jeanes teaching force in the South, see General Education Board, *Report of the Secretary, 1914–1915*, 35–39, *Report of the Secretary, 1916–1917*, 41–44, *Report of the Secretary, 1917–1918*, 51–55, *Annual Report of the General Education Board, 1918–1919*, 53–56, and "North Carolina School Survey," in *Annual Report of the General Education Board, 1920–1921*, 39–42; Phelps-Stokes Fund, *Negro Status and Race Relations in the United States, 1911–1946*, 17–20; Lance G. E. Jones, *Jeanes Teacher*, 59; James D. Anderson, *Education of Blacks*, 135–47; and Hanchett, "Rosenwald Schools," 387–427. For an analysis of African American education in North Carolina during this period, see U.S. Department of the Interior, *Negro Education*, 55–83. For an overview of programs available, see Leavell, "Trends of Philanthropy," and William A. Link, *Paradox of Southern Progressivism*, 243–57.

71. Newbold, "Annie Wealthy Holland," in *Five North Carolina Negro Educators*, 61–85.

72. Arthur D. Wright, *Negro Rural School Fund*, 171.

73. For the extraordinary story of the Aggrey family, see Edwin W. Smith, *Aggrey of Africa*. On the Aggreys' courtship and marriage, see folder 7, box 147.2, and clipping from *Lodge Journal and Guide* (Norfolk-Portsmouth, Va.), 18 Nov. 1905, 1, folder 35, box 147.1, both in Aggrey Papers, MSRC. Aggrey spent most of the 1920s in Africa, returning to New York City in 1927 to defend his doctoral dissertation at Columbia University. He caught a fever and died before his defense. His daughter, Abna Aggrey Lancaster, recalls that the dissertation manuscript was never seen again.

74. Abna Aggrey Lancaster, interview with author, Salisbury, N.C., 25 June 1991; J. R. Larkins, "Testimonial in Honor of Mrs. Rose Douglass Aggrey," 15 Dec. 1957, in author's possession; "Noted Negro Teacher Retires," in author's possession; Rountree, *Brief Chronology of Black Salisbury-Rowan*, 16.

75. Abna Aggrey Lancaster, interview with author, Salisbury, N.C., 25 June 1991.

76. Arthur D. Wright, *Negro Rural School Fund*.

77. Delany and Delany, *Having Our Say*, 79–80.

78. Miss S. L. Delany, "Monthly Progress Letter for December 1913," in "Schedule of Educational Work and Progress Letter"; "Minutes First North Carolina Conference for Negro Education," 2; and "Reports of Progress for January, 1914," all in folder 1042, box 115, series 1, subseries 1, General Education Board Collection, RAC.

79. Lance G. E. Jones, *Jeanes Teacher*, 48–52; Neverdon-Morton, *Afro-American Women of the South*, 89–93; James D. Anderson, *Education of Blacks*, 135–47.

80. "Report of N. C. Newbold, . . . June 1913," 6, folder 1042, box 115; N. C. Newbold, "Supervising Industrial Teachers: Some Things They Helped to Do Last School Year, 1916–1917," 2, 6, folder 1044, box 115; and N. C. Newbold, *Summary of Reports of Home-Makers Club Agents, North Carolina, 1915*, folder 1048, box 116, all in series 1, subseries 1, General Education Board Collection, RAC.

81. Mrs. C. L. Battle, "The Effects of the Modern Health Crusade in the Rural Negro Schools of Edgecombe County," paper presented at the Second Annual Conference on Tuberculosis, Goldsboro, N.C., 3 Oct. 1922, reprinted in Pankey, "Life Histories of Rural Negro Teachers," 77–81. On Battle's background, see ibid., 28, 36–37, 41–42, 49, 58. For similar campaigns held in white schools, see George M. Cooper, "Medical Inspections." On motion pictures, see "The American Sociological Congress and Its Plan for the Extension Campaign," folder 909, box 87, series 3, Laura Spellman Rockefeller Collection, RAC.

82. "Summary of Reports of N. C. Newbold, State Agent Negro Rural Schools for North Carolina, July 1, 1915–June 30, 1916," 2, folder 1043, box 115, series 1, subseries 1, General Education Board Collection, RAC. Aycock reported with pride that during his administration (1901–5), 700 schools were built for whites and 100 for blacks. The figures on black contributions to school building cited above call into question whether the state built those 100 black schools or whether African Americans built them. See Harlan, *Separate and Unequal*, 102.

83. "Report of N. C. Newbold, State Supervisor Rural Schools for Negroes for North Carolina, for the Month of March, 1914," 3–4, folder 1042, box 115, series 1, subseries 1, General Education Board Collection, RAC.

84. "Colored Teachers Endorse the County Board of Education," *Charlotte Chronicle*, 6 May 1914, microfiche 255, Hampton University Newspaper Clipping Files.

85. N. C. Newbold, "Supervising Industrial Teachers: Some Things They Helped to Do Last School Year, 1916–1917," folder 1044, box 115, series 1, subseries 1, General Education Board Collection, RAC. On the campaign to build Rosenwald schools in North Carolina, see Hanchett, "Rosenwald Schools." Hanchett deals primarily with school building in the 1920s and 1930s.

86. "Summary of Reports of N. C. Newbold, State Agent Negro Rural Schools for North Carolina, July 1, 1915–June 30, 1916," 4, folder 1043, box 115, series 1, subseries 1, General Education Board Collection, RAC.

87. N. C. Newbold, "Supervising Industrial Teachers: Some Things They Helped to Do Last School Year, 1916–1917," folder 1044; "Summary of Reports

of N. C. Newbold, State Agent Negro Rural Schools for North Carolina, July 1, 1915–June 30, 1916," folder 1043; and "Summary of Reports of Mr. N. C. Newbold, State Agent for Negro Rural Schools of North Carolina, January 1, 1916, to December 31, 1916," folder 1044, all in box 115, series 1, subseries 1, General Education Board Collection, RAC.

88. Lumbee Indians and African Americans intermarried, and North Carolina folklore holds that the Lumbee are descendants of English members of the Lost Colony and Croatan Indians. John Spaulding was African American. The Spaulding family regarded themselves, in the words of their grandson, Aaron R. Kelsey, as "Negroes." Kelsey also called his family "freeish," a term that probably came from the expression "free issue" used to describe African Americans born free during slavery. See A. R. Kelsey, interview with author, Salisbury, N.C., 14 May 1991. I am indebted to Kelsey for sharing with me his memories of his mother, his encyclopedic knowledge of racial politics in Rowan County, and his keen sense of place and time.

89. On the founding and growth of the North Carolina Mutual Life Insurance Company, see Weare, *Black Business in the New South*.

90. L. M. Spaulding to Prof. and Mrs. J. E. Aggrey, 26 May 1906, folder 6, box 147.3, Aggrey Papers, MSRC.

91. Eula Wellmon Dunlap, "Reminiscences," Lincoln Academy Papers, ARC.

92. Mable Parker Massey, "Vital Statistics in North Carolina," 129.

93. A. R. Kelsey, interview with author, Salisbury, N.C., 14 May 1991.

94. Ibid.

95. Constitution, in Minutes of the Salisbury Colored Women's Civic League, LC. The league changed its name from "Colored" to "Negro" in 1920, although Mary Lynch began suggesting the name change in 1916. The information on members is taken from rolls and dues lists throughout the minutes.

96. Abna Aggrey Lancaster, interview with author, Salisbury, N.C., 25 June 1991.

97. Ibid.; A. R. Kelsey, interview with author, Salisbury, N.C., 14 May 1991. Lancaster and Kelsey went over the rolls and told me stories about the women they remembered from their childhood.

98. Lizzie Crittendon was the wife of W. B. Crittendon, who formed the Colored Voters' League of North Carolina.

99. Minutes of the Salisbury Colored Women's Civic League, 28 July 1913, 28 June 1916, LC.

100. *Outlook* 106 (4 Apr. 1914): 742.

101. Ibid.

102. Minutes of the Salisbury Colored Women's Civic League, 28 July 1913, LC.

103. For a description of housing problems, see "The Negro Problem." Black families began developing their own suburban neighborhoods in order to exclude white landlords and control housing standards. McCrorey Heights was such a neighborhood in Charlotte. See Mamie Garvin Fields, *Lemon Swamp*, 162–79, and Watson, *Colored Charlotte*.

104. Eula Wellmon Dunlap, "Reminiscences," Lincoln Academy Papers, ARC. Typhoid can be spread by flies, but tuberculosis cannot. William A. Link argues, "None of the southern social reforms of the Progressive Era were individually

more important or together more coherent than the modernization of public health and public education" ("Privies, Progressivism, and Public Schools").

105. Mable Parker Massey, "Vital Statistics in North Carolina," 131.

106. Hammond, *Southern Women and Racial Adjustment*, 16.

107. On Cathcart, see Eula Wellmon Dunlap, "Reminiscences," Lincoln Academy Papers, ARC. On De Bardeleben and the Bethlehem Houses, see Hall, *Revolt against Chivalry*, 71–77.

108. Good Samaritan Hospital Collection, NCDAH; Wilkes Papers, uncataloged, CPL.

109. *Minutes of the Fifteenth Annual Meeting of the Woman's Missionary Societies*, 62; *Minutes of the Twenty-third Annual Session of the Women's Baptist Home Mission Convention*, 5, 13. See also Helm, *From Darkness to Light*, 208, 211, 215, 217, and Hammond, *Southern Women and Racial Adjustment*, 7–13.

110. Clinton, "What Can the Church Do?"

111. Minutes of the Charlotte Woman's Club, 1910–11, 20, 21, Charlotte Woman's Club Papers, Special Collections, Atkins Library, University of North Carolina, Charlotte, N.C. On white women and the "servant problem," see Weatherford, *Negro Life in the South*, 37–38.

112. Hammond, *Southern Women and Racial Adjustment*, 16.

113. In Atlanta, the Anti-Tuberculosis Association was at the center of this type of work, but in North Carolina, the work seems to have been accomplished by the women's clubs. I found few records of the North Carolina Anti-Tuberculosis Association. The scarce North Carolina records reveal that the North Carolina Association for the Prevention of Tuberculosis began in 1906 with a board that included only male physicians. The work failed. During an undocumented period of the association's history, it appears that the board was interracial in 1910, including North Carolina Agricultural and Technical College president James Dudley and Charles McIver's widow, Lula McIver. See James B. Dudley to Charles N. Hunter, 22 Mar. 1910, file 1910–12, box 4, Hunter Collection, DU. By 1920, a new board, made up of white club women and one white male physician, had institutionalized the effort across the state. See *The First 50 Years* (N.p.: North Carolina Tuberculosis Association, [1956]), 4–6, pamphlet, American Lung Association of North Carolina Records, Raleigh, N.C. Despite the lack of documentation on the effort to eradicate tuberculosis, it is clear that in North Carolina, white club women seized the public health initiative and, working through state educational officials, solicited help from the Rockefeller Sanitary Commission to eradicate hookworm, build sanitary privies, and establish county health departments. See James Y. Joyner to F. T. Gates, 23 Dec. 1909, folder 114, box 5; [?] to Mrs. Eugene Reilley, president of the North Carolina Federation of Women's Clubs, 8 Feb. 1910, folder 114, box 5; Wickliffe Rose to Dr. John A. Ferrell, 17 Oct. 1910, folder 114, box 5; and John A. Ferrell to Wickliffe Rose, 12 Oct. 1919, folder 115, box 5, all in series 2, Rockefeller Sanitary Commission Collection, RAC. For the best account of public health reform, see William A. Link, *Paradox of Southern Progressivism*, 142–49.

114. The minutes of the Atlanta Anti-Tuberculosis Association emphasize interracial cooperation. See Mary Dickinson, "Report of Race Relationship as Illustrated by the Atlanta Anti-Tuberculosis Association—Presented at the Confer-

ence at the Southern Methodist Church at Memphis, Tenn., Oct. 6–7, 1920," and report of Rosa Lowe, Anti-Tuberculosis and Visiting Nurse Association, both in scrapbook, folder 21, box 8, Atlanta Lung Association Collection, Atlanta History Center, Atlanta, Ga.; Parsons, "White Plague"; Hunter, "Household Laborers"; Jacqueline Anne Rouse, *Lugenia Burns Hope*, 71–72, 80–82; and Shivery, "History of Organized Social Work."

115. Minutes of the Salisbury Colored Women's Civic League, 26 Aug. 1913, LC.

116. Ibid., 27 Jan. 1914, 24 Mar. 1913, 26 Jan. 1915.

117. In Charlotte, Mary Jackson McCrorey became president of the Associated Charities Auxiliary in 1916.

118. Minutes of the Salisbury Colored Women's Civic League, 7 Jan. 1917, and City-Wide Associated Charities Campaign Card in Minute Book, LC.

119. Ibid., 4 Sept. 1917.

120. A. R. Kelsey, interview with author, Salisbury, N.C., 14 May 1991. The social worker was Mrs. Linton.

121. Nancy Fraser, *Unruly Practices*, 144–60.

122. Minutes of the Salisbury Colored Women's Civic League, 30 Sept., 28 Oct. 1913, LC.

123. Membership card of the Salisbury Colored Women's Civic League, in ibid.

124. Ibid., 30 Sept., 28 Oct. 1913. The mayor was Walter H. Woodson, who served from 1913 to 1919. See *Salisbury Evening Post*, Bicentennial Edition, 29 Apr. 1975, 12.

125. Minutes of the Salisbury Colored Women's Civic League, 25 Nov. 1913, LC.

126. Ibid., 1 Sept. 1914.

127. Ibid., 28 Jan. 1916.

128. A. R. Kelsey, interview with author, Salisbury, N.C., 14 May 1991; Minutes of the Salisbury Colored Women's Civic League, 26 Feb., 11 Apr. 1916, LC.

129. Minutes of the Salisbury Colored Women's Civic League, 28 Apr., 29 Sept. 1914, 26 Feb., 8 Aug. 1916, LC. On directed play and controlled recreation, see Cavallo, *Muscles and Morals*; Kasson, *Amusing the Million*, 102–4; and Traywick, "Play Life of Negro Boys and Girls."

130. Minutes of the Salisbury Colored Women's Civic League, 30 Sept. 1913, LC. For mothers' aid and the welfare state, see Michel and Koven, "Womanly Duties."

131. Minutes of the Salisbury Colored Women's Civic League, 27 Jan., 30 June, 24 Nov. 1914, LC.

132. Ibid., 28 Mar. 1915, 3 Nov. 1914, 28 Jan. 1916.

133. *Outlook* 106 (4 Apr. 1914): 742.

CHAPTER SEVEN

1. This drive for order is discussed in Wiebe, *Search for Order*, and David W. Noble, *Progressive Mind*, 81–96.

2. Anastatia Sims documents in detail the growth of white women's clubs in North Carolina in "Power of Feminism."

3. The common usage of the term "interracial cooperation" was institutionalized in the name of the Commission on Interracial Cooperation. See Hall, *Revolt against Chivalry*.

4. An exception is Katharine Du Pre Lumpkin, who came to believe segregation was wrong (*Making of a Southerner*).

5. Ceci Jenkins, incomplete notes for "The Twig Bender of Sedalia" ([1946]), unpublished biography of Charlotte Hawkins Brown, reel 1, #12, Brown Collection, Manuscript Collection, SL. See also Birmingham, *Certain People*; Benjamin Brawley, *Negro Builders*; Brownlee, "She Did It"; Daniel, *Women Builders*, 133–63; Dannett, *Profiles of Negro Womanhood*, 2:59–63; Kathleen Thompson, "Charlotte Hawkins Brown"; Hall, *Revolt against Chivalry*; Hunter, " 'The Correct Thing' "; Marteena, *Lengthening Shadow*; Neverdon-Morton, *Afro-American Women of the South*; Jacqueline Anne Rouse, *Lugenia Burns Hope*; and Stewart, "Charlotte Eugenia Hawkins Brown." The North Carolina Division of Archives and History has designated Palmer Memorial Institute a historic site and has collected a plethora of material on Brown's life, some of which is accessible at the visitors' center. See Charles W. Wadelington site report, Research Report File, 1960–85, North Carolina Department of Cultural Resources, Division of Archives and History, Historic Sites Microfilm, reel 5, NCC.

6. "A Biography," reel 1, and "Some Incidents in the Life and Career of Charlotte Hawkins Brown Growing out of Racial Situations, at the Request of Dr. Ralph Bunche," reel 1, #2, both in Brown Collection, SL.

7. "Some Incidents," 1–2, reel 1, #2, ibid.

8. "A Biography," reel 1, ibid. The language of "A Biography" is closely echoed in Daniel, *Women Builders*, 133–63. It appears that Brown wrote "A Biography" for Daniel's book, and that Daniel used Brown's account of her early life extensively. A Victorian house that matches Brown's description of her house as "a large 12 room house of imposing appearance" still stands at 69 Dana Street. It is within walking distance of Harvard University but not next to Harvard Yard, as Brown sometimes described it. The address is from Jenkins, "Twig Bender of Sedalia," 13, reel 1, #7, Brown Collection, SL.

9. "A Biography," 13, reel 1, Brown Collection, SL.

10. Why Brown contacted Palmer remains a mystery. Since Brown's parents were already paying her tuition at Salem, Brown probably did not write to ask Palmer for tuition. Perhaps Palmer believed Brown to be impoverished and interpreted the letter as a request for financial support. It is possible that Palmer's position as a member of the state board of education enabled her to designate student scholarships and that instead of personally paying Brown's tuition, she made such a scholarship available to her. It seems unlikely that Palmer would have paid for Brown's education without exploring her circumstances after they had only passed on the street. On Palmer, see Bordin, *Alice Freeman Palmer*. On the Brown/Palmer relationship, see "A Biography," 16–18, reel 1, and Jenkins, "Twig Bender of Sedalia," reel 1, #7, both in Brown Collection, SL. The description of the Brown Manuscript Collection at the Schlesinger Library reads: "During her senior year of high school, Alice Freeman Palmer, formerly president of Wellesley College, encouraged her to attend the State Normal School at Salem and gave financial support." Sylvia Dannett reports that after Brown and Palmer met on the

street, "From that time, until Mrs. Palmer's death, Charlotte enjoyed the distinguished educator's friendship and patronage. . . . Mrs. Hawkins accorded her beloved patroness the highest honor within her power by naming her school the Alice Freeman Palmer Institute. That December, when Mrs. Palmer died in Paris, the word 'Memorial' was added to the name" (*Profiles of Negro Womanhood*, 60). All of these accounts are based on information Brown furnished about the relationship.

11. Daniel, *Women Builders*, 139; "A Biography," 19, reel 1, Brown Collection, SL.

12. Charlotte E. Hawkins to Dr. Buttrick, 31 Aug. 1904, folder 1005, box 111, series 1, subseries 1, General Education Board Collection, RAC. Brown's marriage remains an enigma, and I could find no record of a divorce, although Kathleen Thompson, in "Charlotte Hawkins Brown," claims she divorced her husband in 1915 (173). Hawkins apparently met Brown in the summer of 1910 when she returned to Cambridge. He must have proposed before she returned to North Carolina, and by February 1911, they announced their engagement. A Boston wedding followed on 12 June 1911, where friends filled the church with banks of flowers fifteen feet high. By August, the couple were in Sedalia, where Brown reported that her husband had become very involved in the school. Edward Brown stayed for just one school year and that summer left to teach school in Georgia. Charlotte Brown recalled that they separated "not because of unpleasantness but because he was unwilling to be called Miss Hawkins's husband." Apparently, Edward Brown also resented the fact that Charlotte did not give over to him management of the school. Once in Georgia, he refused to send her any support, but they remained in touch for a few years. Charlotte Brown toyed with the idea of joining her husband in Georgia, but he apparently never asked her to do so. After 1913, mention of him disappears from Charlotte Brown's correspondence. This profoundly sad experience left Brown with the cloak of married respectability and gave her a "ghost husband," typical of the marriages of many black women reformers who were Brown's contemporaries. The above account of Brown's marriage is based on the following correspondence: Mary Grinnell to Charlotte Hawkins Brown, 4 Oct. 1910, 8 Feb. 1911; H. F. Kimball to Charlotte Hawkins Brown, 12 June 1911; and J. G. Bright to Charlotte Hawkins Brown, 1 Aug. 1911, all on reel 2, #33; Mary T. Grinnell to Charlotte Hawkins Brown, 6 Aug. 1912, 17 Feb. 1913, reel 2, #34; and Charlotte Hawkins Brown Ebony Questionnaire, 16, reel 1, #11, all in Brown Collection, SL.

13. Brown wrote that it was a "big surprise" that the white people in the South refused to "use the term 'Miss'" when they addressed black women. She continued, "Naturally I was constantly being insulting and insulted which merited for me the name 'Yankee Huzzy.'" See "Some Incidents," 5, reel 1, #2, Brown Collection, SL. Leading whites in Greensboro referred to her as "Dr. Brown" after she received honorary degrees from Wilberforce, Lincoln, and Howard universities. See Junius Scales to Glenda Gilmore, 4 Jan. 1990, in author's possession.

14. "Some Incidents," 6, reel 1, #2, Brown Collection, SL.

15. Letterhead, Palmer Memorial Institute, C. Hawkins Brown to W. E. B. Dubois [*sic*], 10 June 1930, W. E. B. Du Bois Papers, reel 33, University of Massachusetts, Amherst.

16. Ruth Anita Hawkins Hughes, *Contributions of Vance County People of Color*,

360–63, 103, outlines these family histories, but her account does not identify Brown as a direct descendant of John Hawkins. Brown's oral family tradition establishes this link. Thanks to Andre Varr, a descendant of Brown, for sharing family history with me.

17. Jenkins, "Twig Bender of Sedalia," 1, reel 1, #7, Brown Collection, SL.

18. Ibid., insert B; "Some Incidents," 9, reel 1, #2, Brown Collection, SL.

19. Linda Simmons, *Heritage of Blacks*, 169.

20. Charlotte Hawkins Brown, *The Negro and the Social Graces* (Atlanta: Commission on Interracial Cooperation, n.d.), reprint of an address given on *Wings over Jordan*, broadcast by CBS, 10 Mar. 1940, folder 51, box 94-3, Spingarn Papers, MSRC.

21. Eva M. Young, "Palmer Memorial Institute Unique," *Charlotte Observer*, 10 Mar. 1940, folder 51, box 94-3, ibid.

22. Jenkins, "Twig Bender of Sedalia," E.F. 16, reel 1, #7, Brown Collection, SL.

23. Ibid., E.F. 16, E.F. 17; "Some Incidents," reel 1, #2, Brown Collection, SL.

24. For an example of the conflation of Sedalia and Palmer Institute, see *Palmer Memorial Institute*.

25. Brown sought to convince whites that her students were different from average Greensboro African Americans. The description here is from interviews and conversations with Dawn Gilmore, Brooks Gilmore, and Lois MacKenzie, the author's aunt, uncle, and mother, respectively. The author's grandfather, Clyde Manly Gilmore, was Brown's physician, and the author's mother, MacKenzie, was her attorney's secretary in the 1950s.

26. Brown transformed the institute in the late 1930s into a preparatory school for upper-class African Americans. By 1940, the school letterhead read: "The Charm School Idea of the Palmer Memorial Institute, Charlotte Hawkins Brown, President and Promoter." See C. Hawkins Brown to My Dear Friend, 20 Mar. 1940, folder 124, box 112-4, Washington Conservatory of Music Records, MSRC.

27. Jenkins, "Twig Bender of Sedalia," insert G, reel 1, #7, Brown Collection, SL.

28. Monroe Work to Charlotte Hawkins Brown, 22 May 1911, reel 2, #33, ibid.

29. Charlotte Hawkins Brown to Wallace Buttrick, 19 Dec. 1912, folder 1005, box 111, series 1, subseries 1, General Education Board Collection, RAC.

30. "Charlotte Hawkins Brown," Dannett Collection, uncataloged, LC. See also Dannett, *Profiles of Negro Womanhood*, 59–63. The notes for Dannett's biographical sketches often do not identify the interviewee and are fragmentary.

31. Map, "Palmer Memorial Institute—Sedalia—Enrol[l]ment—1920–1921," folder 1006, box 111, series 1, subseries 1, General Education Board Collection, RAC.

32. "Some Incidents," reel 1, #2, Brown Collection, SL.

33. Author's conversations with Dawn Gilmore.

34. Ibid.

35. Author's conversations with Lois MacKenzie.

36. F. P. Hobgood to Charlotte Hawkins Brown, 4 Oct. 1921, and Charlotte Hawkins Brown to F. P. Hobgood, 4 Oct. 1921, both in series 2, Correspondence, July–Dec. 1921, Brown Collection, SL.

37. Jenkins, "Twig Bender of Sedalia," reel 1, D, ibid.

38. Charlotte E. Hawkins to Dr. McIver, 21 May 1904, file Southern Education Board, 1904, Correspondence G–M, box 14, and C. E. Hawkins to Dr. McIver, 13 Apr. 1905, file Southern Education Board, 1905, Correspondence, E–L, box 15, both in Charles D. McIver Collection, WCJL.

39. Mrs. Charles D. McIver to editor of *Greensboro Daily News*, [ca. 1940], reel 1, #13, and Jenkins, "Twig Bender of Sedalia," reel 1, #7, both in Brown Collection, SL.

40. This account of Lula McIver's life is taken from Holder, *McIver of North Carolina*, 63–67. See also Virginia T. Lathrop, "Mrs. McIver Believes Greatness of the Past Holds State's Hope for Present and Future," *News and Observer*, 6 Oct. 1940, Clipping File, vol. 94, reel 24, 371–72, NCC.

41. On the McIvers, see Leloudis, "'A More Certain Means of Grace,'" and Dean, "Covert Curriculum." On the association, see Leloudis, "School Reform." See also Lula Martin McIver to Charles L. Coon, 4 Feb. 1909, folder 28, box 2, and Lula Martin McIver to Charles L. Coon, 25 Jan. 1910, folder 29, box 2, both in Coon Papers, SHC.

42. Sallie Waugh McBryan to Mrs. McIver, 22 Nov. 1913, file Correspondence, 1909–44, box 141, Lula Martin McIver Collection, WCJL; "Famous Landmark at WCUNC Razed," *Durham Morning Herald*, 26 Oct. 1952, Clipping File, vol. 94, reel 24, 343–44, NCC.

43. Since McIver raised money for Palmer Memorial Institute, traveled to New England with Brown, and took groups of women to Sedalia, she and Brown must have been in touch often. Yet neither woman's papers contain correspondence making the arrangements necessary to complete such elaborate projects; they merely contain snippets referring to the events after the fact. They must have telephoned each other a great deal and met in person. McIver drove her own car to Sedalia. See Lula Martin McIver to Charlotte Hawkins Brown, 6 Apr. 1920, reel 2, #41, Brown Collection, SL.

44. Charles D. McIver letter, 5 June 1905, reel 2, #30, Correspondence, 1902–6, ibid.

45. "Award Will Go to Dr. Brown," *Greensboro Daily News*, 10 Apr. 1947, Clipping File, vol. 18, reel 5, 239, NCC.

46. C. Hawkins Brown to My dear Sir [Professor Julius I. Foust], 25 May 1914, file General Correspondence, 1913–15, box 57, Foust Collection, WCJL.

47. Jenkins, "Twig Bender of Sedalia," 77, reel 1, #12, Brown Collection, SL. Mrs. Al Fairbrother, the story's author, was a leading club woman, a close friend of McIver's, who served with her on the board of the Children's Home Society, and that year a delegate to the national convention of white women's clubs. See Cotten, *North Carolina Federation of Women's Clubs*, 75.

48. E. P. Wharton to Charlotte Hawkins Brown, 12 Jan. 1917, reel 2, #37, Jan.–Apr. 1917; Mrs. Charles D. McIver to editor of *Greensboro Daily News*, n.d., reel 1, #13; and Jenkins, "Twig Bender of Sedalia," 78, reel 1, #12, all in Brown Collection, SL. Jenkins's list of trustees includes E. P. Wharton, L. Richardson of Vick's Chemical Company, C. H. Ireland, W. H. McLean, C. A. Warton, Mrs. C. D. McIver, J. H. Smith, and Lelia D. Yancey. Brown began seeking funding for the school from the General Education Board and the Rockefeller family in 1904 and continued to do so for more than fifty years. They never provided funding,

however, apparently because they thought that counties should assume responsibility for precollegiate schools and that direct foundation support to private schools relieved governments of their responsibilities. See, for example, Charlotte E. Hawkins to Dr. Buttrick, 31 Aug. 1904, folder 1005, box 111; W. T. B. Williams to Trustees of the John F. Slater Fund, 15 Feb. 1908, folder 1005, box 111; Charlotte E. Hawkins to Dr. Buttrick, 1 July 1909, folder 1005, box 111; Wallace Buttrick to John D. Rockefeller, Jr., 30 Mar. 1909, folder 1005, box 111; John D. Rockefeller, Jr., to Mrs. Bright, 20 Oct. 1911, folder 1005, box 111; Charlotte Hawkins Brown to Wallace Buttrick, 19 Dec. 1912, 8 Jan. 1913, folder 1005, box 111; N. C. Newbold to Dr. E. C. Sage, 20 Dec. 1916, folder 1005, box 111; "Visit of N. C. Newbold to Palmer Memorial Institute," 13 Feb. 1917, folder 1006, box 111; and Charlotte Hawkins Brown to John D. Rockefeller, 11 July 1917, folder 1006, box 111, all in series 1, subseries 1, General Education Board Collection, RAC. Brown continued to appeal to other northerners for financial help and named a building for one of her major benefactors, Galen Stone. See "Palmer Institute Doing Good Work in Rural North Carolina," *New York Age*, 14 Feb. 1920, microfiche 230, Hampton University Newspaper Clipping Files.

49. H. F. Kimball to Charlotte Hawkins Brown, 6 Nov. 1916, reel 2, #36, 1916, and "Notes," copy of notebook maintained by Charlotte Hawkins Brown, reel 1, #8, both in Brown Collection, SL; Annie L. Vickery to My Dear Mrs. McIver, 7 Mar. 1917, file Correspondence, 1909–44, box 141, Lula Martin McIver Collection, WCJL.

50. Charlotte Hawkins Brown, *Mammy*.

51. Lula Martin McIver to Charlotte Hawkins Brown, 6 Apr. 1920, reel 2, #41, Brown Collection, SL.

52. Wesley, *History of the National Association of Colored Women's Clubs*, 25, 32, 45, 51, 311, 315. For a good overview of the politics of both white and black women's clubs, see Anne Firor Scott, *Natural Allies*, 111–58.

53. Marteena, *Lengthening Shadow*, 77; *Seventh Biennial Convention of the National Association of Colored Women* ([1910]), *National Association of Colored Women, Eighth Biennial Session* ([1912]), and minutes of the 1914 meeting (cover missing), all in *Records of the National Association of Colored Women's Clubs*, microfilm 1108, reel 1, pt. 1. The minutes of the 1914 meeting list Marie Clinton as state president, but Brown always claimed to have won election in 1912. Brown, Clinton, Maud Brooks Cotton, and Adela Ruffin of the YWCA attended the 1914 convention (ibid., 26).

54. At the 1911 meeting of the North Carolina Teachers' Association, Adela Ruffin of Winston-Salem State Normal School delivered the address, "What Are the Women's Clubs Doing to Educate Our People?" See Hugh Victor Brown, *E-Qual-ity Education*, 186.

55. Wesley, *History of the National Association of Colored Women's Clubs*, 70–71; Gale, "N.A. Colored Women's Biennial."

56. *National Association of Colored Women, Tenth Biennial Session* ([1916]), in *Records of the National Association of Colored Women's Clubs*, microfilm 1108, reel 1, pt. 1.

57. Minutes of the Salisbury Colored Women's Civic League, 8, 29 June 1915, LC.

58. Ibid., 1 Mar. 1917.

59. "Form Southern Federation of Colored Women's Clubs," n.p., 13 Mar. 1920, microfiche 548, Hampton University Newspaper Clipping Files.

60. Minutes of the Salisbury Colored Women's Civic League, 28 Apr., 26 May 1914, 29 June 1915, LC.

61. Rogers, "Dr. Delia Dixon-Carroll," 8, 12. Thomas Dixon, Jr., was very proud of his sister's accomplishments, and they seem to have been quite close. See Dixon, *Southern Horizons*.

62. Minutes of the Salisbury Colored Women's Civic League, 8 June 1915, LC.

63. Program and Minutes of the Charlotte Woman's Club, 1919–20, 10, Charlotte Woman's Club Papers, Special Collections, Atkins Library, University of North Carolina, Charlotte, N.C.

64. Ibid., 16. Gilbert Stephenson was a Winston-Salem attorney, author of *Race Distinctions in American Law*. See Thomas Nelson Page, *The Negro*. The article, "The Negro in Relation to Our Public Agencies and Institutions," appeared in *American City* (Aug. 1918).

65. *Charlotte News*, 2 May 1919.

66. "75th Anniversary, 1902–1977," brochure of the annual meeting of the YWCA, 7 Feb. 1977, Charlotte Young Women's Christian Association File, vertical files, CPL; Busby, "Effect of Race and Class on the Development of the Charlotte Young Women's Christian Association." On the YWCA and race in a later period, see Lynn, *Progressive Women in Conservative Times*, 23–33, 43–67.

67. Hall, *Revolt against Chivalry*, 83; Neverdon-Morton, *Afro-American Women of the South*, 215–18; Jacqueline Anne Rouse, *Lugenia Burns Hope*, 92–94.

68. A newspaper account of the founding written in 1935 gives the founder as Elizabeth Preston Allen and the date as 1917, which is at least a year too late. McCrorey became a board member and quickly assumed leadership. On Hook, see Mrs. J. A. Yarbrough, "Women Builders of Charlotte," *Charlotte Observer*, [1933], Clipping File, vol. 70, reel 18, 463, NCC, and "Mrs. Charles C. Hook, Charlotte, 1919–1921," in Carraway, *Carolina Crusaders*, 52–55.

69. "The Young Women's Christian Association among Colored Girls and Women, 1928," Interracial/Negro/Committee on Colored Work, 1915–37, folder 6, box 40, Young Women's Christian Association Papers, Sophia Smith Collection, Smith College, Northampton, Mass.; Hall, *Revolt against Chivalry*, 83–86.

70. *Living-stone* 20, no. 6 (Mar. 1913): 13; 25, no. 4 (Feb. 1915): 17.

71. Clipping from *New York Tribune*, 23 Mar. 1919, microfiche 548, Hampton University Newspaper Clipping Files. This article on black women delegates to a Department of Labor conference in Washington, D.C., outlines the connections between the YWCA and working women.

72. Hall, *Revolt against Chivalry*, 84–86; Jacqueline Anne Rouse, *Lugenia Burns Hope*, 96–102.

73. "In Memoriam"; Hartshorn, *Era of Progress*, 443; "Mrs. Mary Jackson McCrorey"; "Editorial Comment in Memoriam Henry Lawrence McCrorey"; Fisher, "Biographical Sketch of Henry Lawrence McCrorey"; "Some Personalities Connected with the Establishment and Growth of Biddle University, Now Johnson C. Smith University," Charlotte Colleges and Universities File, Johnson C. Smith, vertical files, CPL; Parker, *Biddle–Johnson C. Smith University*, 23; Lucas, Parramore, and Thorpe, *Paths toward Freedom*, 172; Yenser, *Who's Who in Colored America, 1941–*

1944, 129. Mary McCrorey was Henry McCrorey's second wife, and both were over forty when they married. He had two daughters by his first marriage. On Lucy Laney, the Haines Institute, and Mary Jackson, see Daniel, *Women Builders*, 5, 18; McCrorey, "Lucy Laney"; and Patton, "Lucy Craft Laney."

74. Neverdon-Morton, *Afro-American Women of the South*, 209–18.

75. North Carolina produced one of the most prominent African American YMCA leaders, William Trent. Trent graduated from Livingstone College and managed the Young Men's Institute (YMI) in Asheville in the early 1890s. The YMI was a forerunner of the YMCA, built and funded by George Vanderbilt. Trent then served as head of the YMCA in Atlanta throughout the Progressive Era and, later in life, as president of Livingstone College, which houses his papers.

76. Adela Ruffin visited the Charlotte YWCA in November 1917. See Adela Ruffin to Helen Davis, 10 Nov. 1917, Interracial/Negro/World War I/Women, 1918–21, folder 13, box 42, Young Women's Christian Association Papers, Sophia Smith Collection, Smith College, Northampton, Mass.; Mary C. J. McCrorey to Mrs. Hope, 7 May 1920; "Mrs. Hope of the Cleveland Meeting," 29 May 1920; "What the Colored Women Are Asking of the Y.W.C.A."; "To the National Board of the Young Women's Christian Association"; Minutes of the Cleveland Meeting, 1920; "Minutes of the meeting held in the offices of the South Atlantic Field Committee, Richmond, Virginia, 3 July 1920"; and Mary J. McCrorey to Mrs. Hope, 27 Jan. 1921, all in box 5, NU 14-C-5, Y.W.C.A., Neighborhood Union Papers, Special Collections, Robert Woodruff Library, Atlanta University, Atlanta, Ga.

77. Mary C. J. McCrorey to Mrs. Hope, 24 Jan. 1921, box 5, NU 14-C-5, Y.W.C.A., Neighborhood Union Papers, Special Collections, Robert Woodruff Library, Atlanta University, Atlanta, Ga.

78. Mary J. McCrorey to Charlotte Hawkins Brown, 2 Apr. 1920, reel 2, #41, Brown Collection, SL; Mrs. Lewis H. Lapham to Charlotte Hawkins Brown, 21 June 1921, box 5, NU 14-C-5, Y.W.C.A., Neighborhood Union Papers, Special Collections, Robert Woodruff Library, Atlanta University, Atlanta, Ga.; Hall, *Revolt against Chivalry*, 86. The national board largely ignored Brown for several years, even failing to notify her of meetings. They saw her as outspoken. See "Bureau of Colored Work" and "Special," 6 Feb. 1923, both in Interracial/Negro/Committee on Colored Work, 1915–37, folder 6, box 40, Young Women's Christian Association Papers, Sophia Smith Collection, Smith College, Northampton, Mass. Brown later encountered the same racial misunderstandings over the founding of a YWCA in Greensboro. See Charlotte Hawkins Brown to My very dear Friend [Lula McIver], 17 Sept. 1926, file Correspondence, 1909–44, box 141, Lula Martin McIver Collection, WCJL.

79. Mary J. McCrorey to Charlotte Hawkins Brown, 2 Apr. 1920, reel 2, #41, Brown Collection, SL.

80. Mrs. W. A. Newell to Maude Palmer Henderson, 5 May 1927, folder 26, box 3, Ames Papers, SHC. On Bertha Payne Newell, a white leader in North Carolina's interracial movement, see Hall, *Revolt against Chivalry*, 343–44 (n. 38).

81. Mrs. J. A. Yarbrough, "Interesting Carolina People," *Charlotte Observer*, 10 Jan. 1937, Clipping File, vol. 122, reel 31, 510, NCC; Breen, "Southern Women in the War," 252–53.

82. Laura Holmes Reilley to D. H. Hill, 18 Oct. 1917, file Women's Committee,

box 39, North Carolina Council of Defense, World War I Papers, 1903–33, pt. 2, Military Collection, NCDAH.

83. Minutes of Executive Committee (Woman's Committee), 14 Feb. 1918, ibid. For an account of this incident, see Breen, "Southern Women in the War," 277–80. These campaigns were nationwide, and the NACWC and the NAACP helped organize them. See "Work Colored Women Are Doing for Loan," *New York Post*, 19 Oct. 1918, microfiche 548, Hampton University Newspaper Clipping Files.

84. Breen, "Southern Women in the War," 279–80; Hull, *Give Us Each Day*, 44–45.

85. Breen, "Black Women and the Great War," 426.

86. Ibid., 429.

87. Minutes of the Salisbury Colored Women's Civic League, 20 Nov. 1917, LC.

88. Lida T. Rodman, "Report to Mrs. Eugene Reilley," 5, file Woman's Council of National Defense, box 26, Rodman Papers, NCDAH.

89. "Community Service of Winston-Salem Women," file Women and the War Correspondence and Reports, box 17, World War I Papers, Miscellaneous, Military Collection, NCDAH.

90. *Star of Zion*, 23 Aug. 1917, 3.

91. Ibid., 29 Aug. 1918, 8.

92. "Minutes of the Executive Committee of the Woman's Committee of the Council of National Defense," file Woman's Committee, box 39, North Carolina Council of Defense, World War I Papers, 1903–33, pt. 2, Military Collection, NCDAH.

93. Laura Holmes Reilley to Mrs. Joseph R. Lamar, 18 July 1918, quoted in Breen, "Southern Women in the War," 278.

94. File Durham, box 3, Woman's Liberty Loan Committee Fourth Campaign, Liberty Loan Campaigns, World War I Papers, 1903–33, pt. 4, Military Collection, NCDAH. Men also took up interracial work connected to the war. In 1918, the white director of the War Savings Certificates and Thrift Stamp campaign called a meeting of black leaders in Winston-Salem, and afterward attendees organized almost every North Carolina county for the Liberty Loan campaign. See "Report of N. C. Newbold, State Agent Negro Rural Schools, for North Carolina, for Month of January, 1918," folder 1044, box 115, series 1, subseries 1, General Education Board Collection, RAC.

95. Laura H. Reilley to Dr. D. H. Hill, 6 July 1917, file Woman's Council, box 39, North Carolina Council of Defense, World War I Papers, 1903–33, pt. 2, Military Collection, NCDAH.

96. File 1911–12, box 1, McKimmon Papers, PC234, NCDAH; Newbold, "Annie Wealthy Holland," in *Five North Carolina Negro Educators*, 77; Rogers, "Jane Simpson McKimmon," in *Tar Heel Women*, 279–84.

97. Clipping from *Greensboro Daily News*, 9 Nov. 1919, Conceit Book, 1915–30, box 23, McKimmon Papers, NCDAH.

98. "Third Annual Report of Home Demonstration Work," 38, file 1917–18, box 1, ibid.

99. File 1919–20, box 1, ibid.

100. "Fifth Annual Report, Home Demonstration Work, 1919," 65, file 1919–20, box 1, ibid.

101. "Annual Report—1917," 4, file 1917, box 1, ibid.

102. "Report of North Carolina 1918 Home Demonstration Work," 5, file 1918–19, box 1, ibid.

103. Ibid., 5–6.

104. "Fifth Annual Report," 65, file 1919–20, box 1, ibid.

105. "Report of N. C. Newbold, State Agent Negro Rural Schools for North Carolina for Month of October, 1918," folder 1044, box 115, series 1, subseries 1, General Education Board Collection, RAC.

106. "Report of the Division of Home Demonstration Work," 26–27, file 1920–21, box 1, McKimmon Papers, NCDAH.

107. Ibid.

108. Ibid., 28.

109. "Eighth Annual Report, N.C. Agricultural Extension Service, Home Demonstration Work," file 1922–23, box 1, ibid.

110. Charlotte Hawkins Brown to James B. Dudley, 3 May 1920, reel 2, #41, Brown Collection, SL.

111. File Commission on Interracial Cooperation, 1920, box 1, Ames Papers, SHC.

112. "What the Negro Woman Asks of the White Women of North Carolina," Charlotte Hawkins Brown Speeches, 1920–29, reel 1, #14, and clipping of account of May 1920 meeting, n.p., n.d., reel 1, #29, both in Brown Collection, SL.

113. *Minutes of the Twelfth Biennial Convention of the National Association of Colored Women, July 12th to 16th, 1920*, 7, 37, in *Records of the National Association of Colored Women's Clubs*, reel 1, pt. 1.

114. Jacquelyn Dowd Hall rescued this meeting and the subsequent Memphis meeting from historical obscurity in *Revolt against Chivalry*, 87–95. The black women present were Brown, McCrorey, Hope, Laney, Washington, Fisk University registrar Minnie L. Crosthwait, Jennie Dee Moton of Tuskegee, and Marion B. Wilkinson, president of the South Carolina Federation of Colored Women, a close friend of Brown and McCrorey's. See "Statement from Negro Women," folder 1, box 1, Ames Papers, SHC.

115. Ida McDonald Hook to Carrie Parks Johnson, folder 1, box 1, Ames Papers, SHC.

116. Hall, *Revolt against Chivalry*, 93; "Some Incidents," reel 1, #2, Brown Collection, SL.

117. Folder 1, box 1, Ames Papers, and T. F. Darden to Mrs. Alfred Moore Waddell, 26 May 1922, folder 63, box 5, De Rosset Family Papers, both in SHC.

118. Folder 1, box 1, Ames Papers, SHC.

119. Brown address, folder 1, box 1, ibid.; Hall, *Revolt against Chivalry*, 93–94.

120. Gabrielle De Rosset Waddell Diary, folder 94, box 7, vol. 18 (Oct. 1920), De Rosset Papers, SHC.

121. Folder 1, box 1, Ames Papers, SHC.

122. "First Draft," section 2, folder 1, box 1, ibid.

123. "Statement of Negro Women in Session, Mar. 26, 1921," folder 1, box 1, ibid.

124. Folder 1, box 1, ibid. (emphasis added).

125. Minnie L. Crosthwait to Charlotte Hawkins Brown, 15 July 1921, file July–Dec. 1921, reel 3, #41, Brown Collection, SL. The women's approach was quite different from the men's. A year earlier, the white state superintendent of education had called "representative Negroes" together for a conference. Of the thirty-eight African Americans who attended, only two were women. At the conference, the superintendent warned the attendees that white people did not feel "safe" in the aftermath of the war and suggested that they adopt a statement deploring violence. The resulting declaration is accommodationist. The representatives condemned migration, lauded the state for being good to them, and insisted that lynching could not be addressed without eliminating rape. See "Declaration of Principles, by Representative Negroes of North Carolina, Raleigh, September 26, 1919," folder 1044, box 115, series 1, subseries 1, General Education Board Collection, RAC.

CHAPTER EIGHT

1. A pathbreaking survey of African American woman suffragists that remains unpublished is Terborg-Penn, "Afro-Americans in the Struggle for Woman Suffrage." An excellent national overview is Giddings, *When and Where I Enter*, 119–31, 159–70. See Adele Logan Alexander, "Adella Hunt Logan," for a detailed analysis of one woman's suffrage connections. Hall, *Revolt against Chivalry*, 42–47, deals will issues of race and suffrage, discusses black suffragists, and chronicles black women's efforts to persuade the Commission on Interracial Cooperation to include suffrage in its position paper (96). For an essay on black women and suffrage in Virginia that supports the argument in this chapter, see Lebsock, "Woman Suffrage and White Supremacy."

2. The first in-depth treatment of southern suffragists' racial politics was Kraditor, *Ideas of the Woman Suffrage Movement*, 163–218. Kraditor draws her conclusions regarding the politics of race and suffrage from an exploration of the racial rhetoric of Kate Gordon and Laura Clay, who opposed the ratification of the Nineteenth Amendment but favored woman suffrage. Gordon and Clay left the National American Woman Suffrage Association because of their position. Although these women had been suffrage leaders, their stand separated them from the thousands of southern white suffragists who sought to gain support for ratification of the amendment by minimizing the effect of the amendment upon racial issues. See also Flexnor, *Century of Struggle*, 319–23; O'Neill, *Everyone Was Brave*; Anne Firor Scott, *Southern Lady*, 181–83; Anne Firor Scott and Andrew M. Scott, *One Half the People*; Fuller, *Laura Clay*, 113–28; Morgan, *Suffragists and Democrats*, 92–99; and Kenneth R. Johnson, "Kate Gordon." For the details of the woman suffrage campaign in North Carolina, see Elizabeth A. Taylor, "Woman Suffrage Movement," and Catt and Shuler, *Woman Suffrage and Politics*, 476–80.

3. Marjorie Spruill Wheeler, *New Women of the New South* and "Mary Johnston." On African American suffragists, see Adele Logan Alexander, "How I Discovered My Grandmother" and "Adella Hunt Logan." On the antisuffragists in North Carolina, see Elna Green, "Those Opposed."

4. North Carolina's suffragists were typical of southern suffragists who sup-

ported ratification of the federal amendment. See Marjorie Spruill Wheeler, *New Women of the New South*, 127.

5. Elna Green, "Those Opposed," 318; Wilkerson-Freeman, "Emerging Political Consciousness of Gertrude Weil."

6. Catt and Shuler, *Woman Suffrage and Politics*, 478–79.

7. Ibid., 463–64. Overman opposed woman suffrage to the end, according to the *Salisbury Evening Post*, 29 Apr. 1975, 3P.

8. *News and Observer*, 28 Feb. 1917, 2.

9. For African American comment on white men embracing their black "mammies," see "Suffrage Again," *Newport News Star*, 12 July 1918, microfiche 375, Hampton University Newspaper Clipping Files.

10. Lula Martin McIver, untitled, file Miscellaneous Speeches, box 141, Lula Martin McIver Collection, WCJL (emphasis in original). Although this is filed as a speech, it seems to be a letter to Lee Overman.

11. W. T. Bost, in *Greensboro Daily News*, 12 Sept. 1920, 1; Morrison, *Governor O. Max Gardner*, 30–36.

12. W. T. Bost of the *Greensboro Daily News* was an avid suffragist. Josephus Daniels's support for woman suffrage is reflected in the *News and Observer*'s coverage. The *Charlotte Observer* also backed suffrage, even though it downplayed its support during favorite son Cameron Morrison's campaign. The *Charlotte Observer* discounted the effect of black women voting by arguing in 1915, "Experience so far has only tended to minimize capitalization of the negro influence on the fortunes of the suffrage cause" ("The Negro and Suffrage," *Charlotte Observer*, 3 Nov. 1915, microfiche 375, Hampton University Newspaper Clipping Files).

13. *News and Observer*, 8 Aug. 1920, 3.

14. Marjorie Spruill Wheeler, *New Women of the New South*, 34–35.

15. *News and Observer*, 17 Aug. 1920, 1. At the eleventh hour, Furnifold Simmons appealed to the legislature to ratify the amendment on the grounds of the expediency of protecting the South from northern Democrats' reprisals. See also Richard L. Watson, "Southern Democratic Primary," 29.

16. Suffrage Association Clipping File, box 56, Weil Papers, NCDAH; Elizabeth A. Taylor, "Woman Suffrage Movement," 185.

17. File Miscellaneous, box 56, North Carolina Equal Suffrage League Association, Weil Papers, and broadside, in file Political Campaign Material, Nunn Papers, PC 341, both in NCDAH.

18. *State's Defense*, 17 Aug. 1920, quoted in Elna Green, "Those Opposed," 327; Terborg-Penn, "Afro-Americans in the Struggle for Woman Suffrage," 290; Cott, *Grounding of Modern Feminism*, 32.

19. Elna Green, "Those Opposed," 322, 325.

20. File Miscellaneous, box 56, North Carolina Equal Suffrage League Association, Weil Papers, NCDAH. The major problem with this argument was, of course, the South's support of prohibition. This contradiction did not go unnoticed. See, for example, James W. Johnson, "Views and Reviews," *New York Age*, 28 Sept., 12 Oct. 1918, microfiche 82, Hampton University Newspaper Clipping Files.

21. Gertrude Weil to J. O. Carr, 8 July 1919, file North Carolina Equal Suffrage League Association Correspondence, 1915–20, box 54, Weil Papers, NCDAH.

22. File Miscellaneous, box 56, North Carolina Equal Suffrage League Association, ibid.

23. On Wells-Barnett and suffrage, see Schechter, "Feminism and the Color Line"; Sterling, *Black Foremothers*, 109–11; and Duster, *Crusade for Justice*.

24. Catt and Shuler, *Woman Suffrage and Politics*, 480–81.

25. Charles W. Chesnutt, "Women's Rights," 182. The issue of *Crisis* in which this article appears, *Crisis* 10 (Aug. 1915), contains a symposium on woman suffrage and demonstrates the widespread support it received among black intellectuals. See also Terborg-Penn, "Afro-Americans in the Struggle for Woman Suffrage," 100.

26. Du Bois, in *Crisis* 15 (Nov. 1917): 8; Daniel Levering Lewis, *W. E. B. Du Bois*, 417–19.

27. Annie Walker Blackwell, "The Responsibility and Opportunity of the Twentieth Century Woman," quoted in Guy-Sheftall, *"Daughters of Sorrow,"* 114, 116. Blackwell was serving as president of the AME Zion Woman's Home and Foreign Missionary Society at the time she made these remarks and was living in Pennsylvania. She had moved from North Carolina in 1900, after interracial WCTU work collapsed under the strain of the white supremacy campaign.

28. W. R. Parker, in *Charlotte Observer*, 2 Oct. 1920, 2.

29. Ibid., 4 Oct. 1920, 4. Dudley was president when women were banished from the North Carolina Agricultural and Technical College. On Dudley, see Spruill, *Great Recollections from Aggieland*, and Newbold, *Five North Carolina Negro Educators*, 36–59. James Dudley was not related to Sarah Dudley Pettey.

30. *Charlotte Observer*, 4 Oct. 1920, 4; *Greensboro Daily News*, 6 Oct. 1920, 4.

31. *Crisis* 21 (Mar. 1921): 200; *Afro-American*, 22 Oct. 1920, 10.

32. Mary White Ovington to James B. Dudley, 8 Oct. 1920, file Suffrage— Woman, 15 Mar.–11 Nov. 1920, C 407, and James B. Dudley to Mary White Ovington, 28 Oct. 1920, and Mary White Ovington to James B. Dudley, n.d., both in file Voting, 1–9 Nov. 1920, C 284, all in NAACP Papers. Two years later, Governor Cameron Morrison gave the commencement address at Dudley's North Carolina Agricultural and Technical College. He told the graduates, "Here [in North Carolina] you have justice and every opportunity but political power and an office, and if you must have it you had better move to other states where you can get those and nothing else. In North Carolina we are working out the best civilization on earth." James Dudley knew which side his bread was buttered on. See "Gov. Morrison Talks to A. & T. Graduates," *New York Age*, 3 June 1922, microfiche 227, Hampton University Newspaper Clipping Files.

33. *Star of Zion*, 7 Oct. 1920, 4.

34. Ibid., 21 Oct. 1920, 4. On Anthony, see *Messenger*, 8 Sept., 9 Oct. 1886, 1 Jan., 5 Nov. 1887, and Yenser, *Who's Who in Colored America, 1933–37*, 32. Anthony may have been a Jeanes teacher since she was once employed by the Sumter County schools. See Frank A. Bachman to N. C. Newbold, 18 Nov. 1919, folder 1039, box 115, series 1, subseries 1, General Education Board Collection, RAC.

35. Charlotte Hawkins Brown to James B. Dudley, 3 May 1920, reel 2, #41, Brown Collection, SL.

36. Brown reported to Dudley that she had argued for black women's suffrage rights in ibid. Of the speeches that remain, the one most likely to have been the

address to the white club women's convention does not include these points, but it is obviously incomplete. See "What the Negro Woman Asks of the White Women of North Carolina," Excerpts of Speeches, 1920–29, reel 1, #14, Brown Collection, SL. An undated clipping from an unknown newspaper includes the language quoted (Miscellaneous, reel 1, ibid.). See also "The North Carolina Federation of White Women's Clubs," 20 May 1920, reel 1, ibid. If Brown did not ask white women to support black women's right to vote, she certainly came to believe she had.

37. Ida M. Hook to Mrs. Luke G. Johnson, 2 Aug. 1920, quoted in "Background of Memphis Conference of October 1920," typescript, folder 1, box 1, Ames Papers, SHC.

38. *Greensboro Patriot*, 27 Sept. 1920, 1.

39. *Greensboro Daily News*, 28 Sept. 1920, 4.

40. Ibid., 26 Sept. 1920, 4; *Durham Morning Herald*, 22 Oct. 1920; North Carolina State Executive Committee of the Republican Party broadside, NCC.

41. *Everywoman's Magazine*, July–Aug. 1920, box 54, Weil Papers, NCDAH.

42. *Charlotte Observer*, 11 Oct. 1987, 4C; "Declares the Republican Party in North Carolina Does Not Want the Negro," file Voting, 21–31 Oct. 1920, C 284, NAACP Papers. The Republican Party in other southern border states accepted black women as delegates to caucuses and conventions. On Kentucky, see "Is First Woman Member of Race in South So Honored?," *Dallas Express*, 13 Mar. 1920, and on Texas, "Negro Women of Houston Register in Large Numbers," *Chronicle*, 8 July 1918, microfiche 548, Hampton University Newspaper Clipping Files.

43. *Greensboro Daily News*, 12 Sept. 1920, 1.

44. Gabrielle De Rosset Waddell Diary, folder 94, box 7, De Rosset Family Papers, SHC; Minutes of the Salisbury Colored Women's Civic League, 8 June 1915, LC.

45. *Charlotte Observer*, 6 Oct. 1920, 1; *Greensboro Daily News*, 1 Oct. 1920, 4. The Richmond report may well have been true since 2,410 black women succeeded in registering. See Lebsock, "Woman Suffrage and White Supremacy," 84–87.

46. *Greensboro Daily News*, 27 Sept. 1920, 2.

47. Ibid.

48. *News and Observer*, 8 Oct. 1920, 1.

49. *Asheville Citizen*, 17 Oct. 1920, 11.

50. Quoted in Weldon, "North Carolina Race Conflict," 707.

51. Lynching decreased at the same time. North Carolina appears to have been the least violent of the southern states in the 1920s since no lynchings occurred there from 1922 to 1929. See Wilbur J. Cash, *Mind of the South*, 300. Another reason electoral violence decreased was that the progressives sought to reform the process. Electoral reforms came late to North Carolina, however, in part because Furnifold Simmons, who controlled the party machinery, opposed them.

52. *Asheville Citizen*, 23 Oct. 1920, 3. The chairperson was Tom Warren.

53. Three sources undergird this analysis of the mechanisms of the campaign to register black women. Taken together, the Charlotte Hawkins Brown Collection, SL, and the NAACP Papers demonstrate that the campaign was coordinated through the clubs and the NAACP chapters, and the Minutes of the Salisbury

Colored Women's Civic League, LC, reveal its execution on a local level. I have found no "smoking gun" piece of documentation that proposed the campaign but have pieced together its workings by moving backward from its manifestations.

54. Charlotte Hawkins Brown to James B. Dudley, 3 May 1920, reel 2, #41, Brown Collection, SL.

55. Minutes of the Salisbury Colored Women's Civic League, 26 Feb. 1916, LC. Undoubtedly members of the league read the suffrage issue of *Crisis* 10 (Aug. 1915) in which Davis's piece appeared (191), along with Adella Hunt Logan, "Colored Women as Voters." The NACWC endorsed suffrage on 7 August 1914, and the Salisbury Colored Women's Civic League sent delegates to national meetings. On the endorsement, see Wesley, *History of the National Association of Colored Women's Clubs*, 77, and file Suffrage—Woman, 27 Nov. 1914–29 July 1915, C 407, NAACP Papers.

56. Minutes of the Salisbury Negro Women's Civic League, 14 Aug. 1920, LC.

57. Ibid., 28 Sept. 1920.

58. *Asheville Citizen*, 17 Oct. 1920, 1; *Greensboro Patriot*, 19 Oct. 1920, 1.

59. Charles H. Moore to James Weldon Johnson, 15 Nov. 1920, file General Correspondence, 15–30 Nov. 1920, C 6; William Sherman Turner to William Pickens, 30 Dec. 1920, file Voting, 1921, C 285; James A. Lowe to NAACP, 1 Jan. 1921, file Voting, 1921, C 285; Mrs. William Mann to Dear Sirs, 25 Oct. 1920, file 21–31 Oct. 1920, C 284; and Affidavit of Clara D. Mann, 23 Oct. 1920, file Voting, 1–9 Nov. 1920, C 284, all in NAACP Papers; *Western Sentinel*, 5 Oct. 1920; *Greensboro Patriot*, 4 Nov. 1920, 8.

60. *Greensboro Daily News*, 6 Oct. 1920, 6; *Charlotte Observer*, 18 Oct. 1920, 3.

61. Pamphlet, Annual Conference, National Association for the Advancement of Colored People, Washington, D.C., 16–17 May 1917, box 17, reel 22, John Hope and Lugenia Burns Hope Papers, Special Collections, Robert Woodruff Library, Atlanta University, Atlanta, Ga.; Daniel Levering Lewis, *W. E. B. Du Bois*, 417–19.

62. That year her husband, J. E. Kweygir Aggrey, wrote a "worshipful letter" to Du Bois in which he asked for a summer internship at the magazine. See Daniel Levering Lewis, *W. E. B. Du Bois*, 417.

63. File Lynching, Winston-Salem, N.C., 1918–26, C 383, NAACP Papers; "Educators Meet at Durham, N.C.," American Press Association, [1916], microfiche 103, Hampton University Newspaper Clipping Files; *Star of Zion*, 2 May 1918, 8; clipping from *News and Observer*, 11 May 1918, scrapbooks, file 1915–18, Hunter Collection, DU. Du Bois made this tour during World War I, just before he wrote his famous "Close Ranks" editorial for the *Crisis*. See Daniel Levering Lewis, *W. E. B. Du Bois*, 552–55. By 1920, Du Bois had become anathema to North Carolina whites. See "The Pay of Negro Teachers," *Greensboro Daily News*, 4 May 1920, microfiche 255, Hampton University Newspaper Clipping Files.

64. W. E. Morton to NAACP, file Voting, 10–30 Nov. 1920, C 284, NAACP Papers.

65. H. M. Kingsley to NAACP, 9 Nov. 1920, file Voting, 1–9 Nov. 1920, C 284, ibid.

66. Charles McPerson to NAACP, file Voting, 1–9 Nov. 1920, C 284, ibid. For a summary of reports from across the South, see "Disfranchisement of Colored

Americans in the Presidential Election of 1920" ([1920]), file Voting, Dec. 1920, C 284, ibid.

67. Black men continued to vote in Salisbury in very small numbers after disfranchisement, but a marked increase occurred after 1920. The precinct books for the area surrounding Livingstone College are missing. See East Ward Election Precinct, 1918–24, and Hellig's Mill Election Precinct, 1902–20, Rowan County Voter Registration Books, Edith M. Clark History and Genealogical Room, Rowan County Public Library, Salisbury, N.C.

68. Lewinson, *Race, Class, and Party*, 218.

69. *Greensboro Patriot*, 25 Oct. 1920, 1. The sources for these figures are registrars' counts reported to the press. Most of the black registration was in two precincts. In the Northeast precinct, out of 1,013 registered voters, 75 were black men and 40 were black women. At Eagle Hose Company, 1,000 people registered, including 114 black men and 44 black women. Black registration in other precincts amounted to 4 or 5 people per precinct. *Greensboro Daily News*, 24 Oct. 1920, 8, gives the number of black men who registered to vote as 92.

70. *News and Observer*, 3 Oct. 1920, 1.

71. Ibid., 25 Oct. 1920, 8.

72. *Asheville Citizen*, 17 Oct. 1920, 11.

73. Ibid., 4, 11.

74. Ibid., 22 Oct. 1920, 14.

75. Ibid., 24 Oct. 1920, 14.

76. Burke, *Brooklyn Story*; *Charlotte City Directory*, 21–22.

77. The press reported that a majority of women who registered in the Second and Tenth wards were African American; 188 women registered in the Second Ward and 149 in the Tenth Ward. See *Charlotte Observer*, 24 Oct. 1920, 1, and *Greensboro Daily News*, 24 Oct. 1920, 8.

78. *Wilmington Morning Star*, 24 Oct. 1920, 1.

79. *News and Observer*, 20 Oct. 1920, 5; *Wilmington Morning Star*, 21 Oct. 1.

80. *News and Observer*, 19 Oct. 1920, 13.

81. Anna A. Clemmons to secretary of the National Woman's Party, 10 Oct. 1920, file Correspondence, 1920, reel 5, National Woman's Party Papers.

82. Emma Wold to Anna A. Clemmons, 20 Oct. 1920, file Correspondence, 1920, reel 5, ibid.

83. Anna A. Clemmons to Emma Wold, 24 Oct. 1920, file Correspondence, 1920, reel 5, ibid.

84. Emma Wold to Anna A. Clemmons, 2 Nov. 1920, file Correspondence, 1920, reel 5, ibid.

85. Mary White Ovington to Elizabeth Green Kalb, 9 Oct. 1920, file Suffrage—Woman, 15 Mar.–11 Nov. 1920, C 407, and Alice Paul, National Woman's Party Press Release, file Suffrage—Woman, 18 Feb.–15 May 1919, C 407, both in NAACP Papers; Mary White Ovington to Harriot Stanton Blatch, 3 Dec. 1920, and Harriot Stanton Blatch to Alice Paul, 20 Dec. 1920, both in file Correspondence, 1920, reel 5, National Woman's Party Papers. See also Terborg-Penn, "Discontented Black Feminists" and "Discrimination against Afro-American Women"; Ella Rush Murray, "Woman's Party"; "White Woman's Burden"; Zimmerman, "Alice Paul"; Ellen Carol Du Bois, "Working Women"; Cott, "Feminist

Politics" and *Grounding of Modern Feminism*, 68–72; and Irwin, *Story of the Woman's Party*.

86. Mrs. William Mann to Dear Sirs, 25 Oct. 1920, file Suffrage, 21–31 Oct. 1920, C 284, NAACP Papers.

87. Affidavit of Clara D. Mann, 6 Nov. 1920, file Suffrage, 21–31 Oct. 1920, C 284, ibid.

88. Marjorie Mann Stuart, daughter of Clara D. Mann, telephone interview with author, 10 Apr. 1990. I located Stuart through the help of Allene Dudley Bundy, great-niece of Sarah Dudley Pettey.

89. Mrs. William Mann to Walter White, file Voting, 1–9 Nov. 1920, C 284, NAACP Papers.

90. Walter White to Mrs. William Mann, 28 Oct. 1920, file Voting, 21–31 Oct. 1920, C 284, ibid. On the petition to the national secretary of the Republican Party, see Mrs. William Mann to Walter White, file Voting, 1–9 Nov. 1920, C 284, ibid. On the appeal to A. Mitchell Palmer, see Walter White to Mrs. William Mann, 3 Nov. 1920, file Voting, 1–9 Nov. 1920, C 284, and Mrs. William Mann to NAACP, 5 Nov. 1920, file Voting, 1–9 Nov. 1920, C 284, both in ibid.

91. Charles H. Moore to James Weldon Johnson, 15 Nov. 1920, file General Correspondence, 15–30 Nov. 1920, C 6; William Sherman Turner to William Pickens, 30 Dec. 1920, file Voting, 1921, C 285; James A. Lowe to NAACP, 1 Jan. 1921, file Voting, 1921, C 285; and *Times* (Wilson, N.C.), 12 Feb. 1921, quoted in clipping from *Record* (Hickory, N.C.), file Suffrage—Woman—Clippings, 21 Jan.–3 Dec. 1921, C 407, all in ibid.

92. Clipping from *New York Times*, 7 May 1921, file Voting Newsclippings, 1921, C 285; Mary White Ovington to Isaac Siegel, chairman of the Committee on Census, file 1–9 Nov. 1920, C 284; and clipping on Congressman George H. Tinkham, file Voting, Dec. 1920, C 284, all in ibid. Ovington called for reapportionment in the South since "colored voters have experienced open and flagrant disfranchisement." The investigation would have focused on the entire South since reports such as Mann's came from almost every southern state.

93. This is a very conservative estimate based on figures given above in this chapter; it omits the number of registered black women in cities where no figures existed, including the two cities with the highest percentage of African Americans—Durham and Winston-Salem—and Raleigh. In Winston-Salem, for example, Ward 3 was 68 percent African American and reports emerged of "heavy new registration" in that ward, but no totals were reported. Because such rhetoric was used as a white supremacy scare tactic, I have included in the tally only those places where actual numbers were given by the registrars. See *Western Sentinel*, 29 Oct. 1920.

94. In addition to the books in Salisbury, the Mecklenburg County Voter Registration Books are available beginning in the mid-1920s at the Board of Elections, Charlotte, N.C. The Charlotte books follow the same pattern as the Salisbury books, revealing growing numbers of black voters each year, male and female, some of whom registered as Democrats. See also Lewinson, *Race, Class, and Party*, and Wilbur J. Cash, *Mind of the South*, 316. Others have found that the same pattern occurred in Virginia. See Robert E. Martin, *Negro Disfranchisement*, 158.

95. Marjorie Mann Stuart, telephone interview with author, 10 Apr. 1990.

96. "Civility" is the term William H. Chafe used to characterize race relations in Greensboro on the eve of the civil rights movement. See Chafe, *Civilities and Civil Rights*.

EPILOGUE

1. Chafe, *Civilities and Civil Rights*, 83–93. Brown died in 1961.

2. N. C. Newbold, "Some Achievements in the Equalization of Educational Opportunities in North Carolina," *Educational Forum*, offprint in folder 1045, box 115, and J. C. Dixon to All State Agents, 7 July 1950, folder 1041, box 115, both in series 1, subseries 1, General Education Board Collection, RAC.

3. "Declares the Republican Party in North Carolina Does Not Want the Negro," file Voting, 21–31 Oct. 1920, C 284, NAACP Papers. Kenneth Goings, in *NAACP Comes of Age*, argues persuasively that Parker's racial comment was a deciding factor in the vote not to confirm him, which was an important milestone for the NAACP. See also Richard L. Watson, "Political Leader Bolts" and "Southern Democratic Primary," and Rippy, *F. M. Simmons*.

4. A. R. Kelsey, interview with author, Salisbury, N.C., 14 May 1991.

5. Mary McCrorey, "Political Scene of 1940," quoted in "The Passing of Our Pioneers," *Aframerican Woman's Journal* 3 (Spring 1944): 21.

6. On McCrorey's race, see Glenda E. Gilmore, "Black Women and Ballots in a 'Progressive' Southern State: North Carolina, 1898–1937," paper presented at the Southern Historical Association meeting, Lexington, Ky., Nov. 1989, in author's possession.

7. Corine Pettey, telephone interview with author, 7 Mar. 1990.

8. Election poster, "Toward a New Democratic Coalition," in author's possession.

BIBLIOGRAPHY

PRIMARY SOURCES

Manuscript Collections

Asheville, North Carolina
  Buncombe County Public Library
    Asheville Young Men's Institute File
Athens, Georgia
  Hargrett Rare Book and Manuscript Library, University of Georgia
    Rebecca Latimer Felton Collection
Atlanta, Georgia
  Atlanta History Center
    Atlanta Lung Association Collection
  Special Collections, Robert Woodruff Library, Atlanta University
    John Hope and Lugenia Burns Hope Papers
    Neighborhood Union Papers
Cambridge, Massachusetts
  Arthur and Elizabeth Schlesinger Library on the History of Women in America, Radcliffe College
    Charlotte Hawkins Brown Collection
Chapel Hill, North Carolina
  North Carolina Collection, Wilson Library, University of North Carolina
    Thomas W. Clawson manuscript
    Clipping File
    J. Allen Kirk manuscript
    Alfred Moore Waddell manuscript
  Southern Historical Collection, Wilson Library, University of North Carolina
    Jessie Daniel Ames Papers
    Marion Butler Papers
    Thomas Clawson Papers
    Henry Groves Connor Papers
    Charles L. Coon Papers
    De Rosset Family Papers
    Elvira Evelyna Moffitt Papers
    North Carolina Commission on Interracial Cooperation Papers
    Matthew W. Ransom Papers
    Daniel Lindsay Russell Papers
    Alfred Moore Waddell Papers
Charlotte, North Carolina
  Administrative Records, Johnson C. Smith University
  Board of Elections
    Mecklenburg County Voter Registration Books

Robinson-Spangler Room, Charlotte Public Library
  Charlotte Colleges and Universities File
  Charlotte Young Women's Christian Association File
  Good Samaritan Hospital for Colored People File
  Rose Leary Love, "Plum Thickets and Field Daisies," [1981]
  McCrorey File
  Jane Renwick Wilkes Papers
Special Collections, Atkins Library, University of North Carolina
  Charlotte Woman's Club Papers
Durham, North Carolina
  Manuscript Department, Perkins Library, Duke University
    Josiah Williams Bailey Collection
    Bryan Family Papers
    Cronly Family Papers
    Marmaduke Hawkins Collection
    Charles N. Hunter Collection
    Romulus A. Nunn Collection
    Edwin A. Oldham Collection
    Furnifold M. Simmons Papers
Evanston, Illinois
  Frances E. Willard Memorial Library for Alcohol Research
    Frances Willard Scrapbook
Greensboro, North Carolina
  University Archives, Walter Clinton Jackson Library, University of North Carolina
    Julius I. Foust Collection
    Charles D. McIver Collection
    Lula Martin McIver Collection
New Bern, North Carolina
  William J. Clarke Papers, in the possession of Mary Moulton Barden
  Craven-Pamlico-Carteret Regional Library
    Dudley Family Scrapbook, compiled by Elizabeth Marsh
    New Bern Female Benevolent Society Minute Book
  Dudley Family Scrapbook, in the possession of Allene Dudley Bundy
New Orleans, Louisiana
  Amistad Research Center, Tilton Hall, Tulane University
    American Missionary Association Archives
    Mary McLeod Bethune Papers
    Lincoln Academy Papers
    Uncataloged North Carolina material
New York, New York
  Dudley and Pettey Family Papers, in the possession of Corine Pettey
  Schomburg Center for Research in Black Culture, New York Public Library
    John E. Bruce Collection
Northampton, Massachusetts
  Smith College
    Young Women's Christian Association Papers, Sophia Smith Collection

North Tarrytown, New York
  Rockefeller Archive Center
    General Education Board Collection
    Laura Spelman Rockefeller Collection
    Rockefeller Sanitary Commission Collection
Philadelphia, Pennsylvania
  Medical College of Pennsylvania
    Archives and Special Collections on Women in Medicine
Raleigh, North Carolina
  American Lung Association of North Carolina Records, American Lung Association of North Carolina Headquarters
  Richard B. Harrison Public Library
    Mollie Lee Collection
  North Carolina Division of Archives and History
    Charles Brantley Aycock, Governor's Papers and Letter Books
    Charles Brantley Aycock, Private Collection
    John Herritage Bryan Collection
    Craven County Court of Pleas and Quarter Sessions Minutes
    Craven County Deed Books
    Craven County Estates Records
    Craven County Marriage Bonds
    Craven County Minutes of the Wardens of the Poor
    Craven County Miscellaneous Records, Slaves and Free Negroes, 1775–1861
    Good Samaritan Hospital Collection
    Jane S. McKimmon Papers
    Mille Christine Collection
    Romulus A. Nunn Papers, Private Collection
    William Blount Rodman Papers
    Gertrude Weil Papers, Private Collection
    Wilkes County Marriage Bonds
    World War I Papers, Military Collection
Salisbury, North Carolina
  Aggrey Family Papers, in the possession of Abna Aggrey Lancaster
  Carnegie Library, Livingstone College
    African Methodist Episcopal Zion Church Records and Conference Minutes
    John C. Dancy Collection
    Sylvia G. L. Dannett Collection
    Livingstone College Records, Memorabilia, and Faculty Files
    Minutes of the Salisbury Colored [Negro] Women's Civic League
    John B. Small Diaries
    William Trent Collection
  Edith M. Clark History and Genealogical Room, Rowan County Public Library
    McCubbins Collection
    Rowan County Voter Registration Books

Heritage Hall, Livingstone College
    African Methodist Episcopal Zion Church Records
Taylorsville, North Carolina
    Annie Watts Eckerd Scrapbook, in the possession of Opal Watts Harrington
Washington, D.C.
    Manuscript Division, Library of Congress
        National Association for the Advancement of Colored People Papers
    Moorland-Spingarn Research Center, Howard University
        J. E. Kweygir Aggrey Papers
        Anna Julia Cooper Papers
        Arthur B. Spingarn Papers
        Washington Conservatory of Music Records
    National Archives
        Department of Justice, Record Group R660
Collections on Microfilm
    Hampton University Newspaper Clipping Files
    National Woman's Party Papers
    Records of the National Association of Colored Women's Clubs, 1895–1992
    Woman's Christian Temperance Union Papers

Interviews

Blackwell, George Lincoln. Telephone interview with author, 13 January 1991.
Bundy, Allene Dudley. Interview with author, New Bern, N.C., 12 October 1990.
Crosby, Kathleen. Telephone interview with author, 8 September 1989.
Dudley, Edward Richard, III. Telephone interview with author, 13 January 1990, and subsequent telephone conversations; private correspondence in author's possession.
Harrington, Opal Watts. Telephone interview with author, 13 January 1990.
Kelsey, A. R. Interview with author, Salisbury, N.C., 14 May 1991.
Lancaster, Abna Aggrey. Interview with author, Salisbury, N.C., 25 June 1991, 13 July 1993.
Pettey, Corine. Interview with author, New York, N.Y., 14 June 1990, and subsequent telephone conversations.
Stuart, Marjorie Mann. Telephone interview with author, 10 April 1990; private correspondence in author's possession.
Williams, Hazel. Telephone interview with author, 7 March 1990.

Newspapers and Periodicals

Africo-American Presbyterian (Charlotte, N.C.)
Afro-American (Baltimore, Md.)
A.M.E. Zion Quarterly Review (Salisbury, N.C.)
The Anchor (Greensboro, N.C.)
Asheville Citizen
Carolina Watchman (Salisbury, N.C.)
Charlotte News
Daily Charlotte Observer
Daily Nut Shell (New Bern, N.C.)

The Educator (Fayetteville, N.C.)
Greensboro Daily News
Greensboro Patriot
The Living-stone (Salisbury, N.C.)
The Messenger (Charlotte, N.C.)
The Missionary Seer (Salisbury, N.C.)
New Berne Journal
News and Observer (Raleigh, N.C.)
North Carolina White Ribbon
The People's Paper (Charlotte, N.C.)
Progressive Farmer
The Radical (New Bern, N.C.)
Raleigh Gazette
Salisbury Evening Post
Southern Workman (Hampton, Va.)
Star of Zion (Charlotte, N.C.)
Temperance Herald (Concord, N.C.)
Union Signal (Evanston, Ill.)
Western Sentinel (Winston-Salem, N.C.)
Wilmington Messenger
Wilmington Morning Star
Woman's Era (Boston, Mass.)

Published Works

Acceptance and Unveiling of the Statue of Charles Brantley Aycock. Washington, D.C.: Government Printing Office, 1932.

Alderman, Edwin A., IV. "Charles Brantley Aycock: Southern Pioneers in Social Interpretation." *Journal of Social Forces* 2 (November 1923–September 1924): 487–91.

———. "Education for White and Black." *Independent* 53 (7 November 1901): 2467.

Alexander, Julia. *Charlotte in Picture and Prose*. Charlotte: J. Alexander, 1906.

Annual Report of the Board of Public Charities of North Carolina. Various publishers, various dates.

Annual Report of the Lindley Training School, Asheville, N.C., for the Year Ending March 31, 1900. N.p., [1900].

Annual Report of the North Carolina Bureau of Labor and Printing. Raleigh: various publishers, 1889–1922.

Ansley, Lulu Barnes. *History of the Georgia Woman's Christian Temperance Union from Its Organization, 1883–1907*. Columbus, Ga.: Gilbert, 1914.

Ashmore, Harry S. *The Negro and the Schools*. Chapel Hill, n.d.

Atkins, Simon. *Livingstone College Quarto-Centennial*. [Salisbury, N.C.], 1910.

Bailey, Josiah W. "Popular Education and the Race Problem in North Carolina." *Outlook* 68 (11 May 1901): 114–16.

———. "Thomas Dixon, Junior." In *Library of Southern Literature*, ed. Edwin Anderson Alderman and Joel Chandler Harris, 4:1405–8. Atlanta: Martin and Hoyt, 1907.

Bailey, Thomas. *Race Orthodoxy in the South and Other Aspects of the Negro Question.* New York: Neale Publishing Company, 1914.

Baker, Ray Stannard. *Following the Color Line: An Account of Negro Citizenship in the American Democracy.* New York: Doubleday, Page, 1908.

Baker, Thomas Nelson. "The Negro Woman." *Alexander's Magazine* 2 (15 December 1906): 71–85.

Baldwin, Maria L. "Votes for Teachers." *Crisis* 10 (August 1915): 189.

Baldwin, William H., Jr. "The Present Problem of Negro Education in the South." *Proceedings of the Second Capon Springs Conference for Education in the South.* Raleigh: Edwards and Broughton, 1899.

Barringer, P. B. *The American Negro: His Past and Future.* Raleigh: Edwards and Broughton, 1900.

Bassett, John Spencer. "Stirring Up the Fires of Race Antipathy." *South Atlantic Quarterly* 2 (October 1903): 297–305.

Beasley, Delilah. *The Negro Trail-Blazers of California.* 1919. Reprint, San Francisco: R & E Research Associates, 1968.

Beveridge and Co.'s North Carolina State Directory, 1877–1878, Containing a Business Directory of Merchants, Manufacturers, Mills, Physicians, Lawyers, Etc., and a List of Principal Farmers. Raleigh: News Publishing Company, 1878.

Biennial Report of the Attorney-General of the State of North Carolina. Various publishers, 1894–1900.

Biennial Report of the Superintendent of Public Instruction of North Carolina. Various publishers, 1884–1920.

Bishop, Charles M. "The Causes, Consequences, and Cure of Mob Violence." In *Democracy in Earnest: The Southern Sociological Congress, 1916–1918,* ed. James McCulloch, 191–200. Washington, D.C.: Southern Sociological Congress, 1918.

Boris, Joseph J., ed. *Who's Who in Colored America.* New York: Who's Who in Colored America Publishers, 1927.

Branson's North Carolina Business Directory for 1884. Raleigh: Levi Branson, 1884.

Branson's North Carolina Business Directory, 1896. Raleigh: Levi Branson, 1896.

Brawley, Benjamin. *Negro Builders and Heroes.* Chapel Hill: University of North Carolina Press, 1937.

——. *The Negro Genius.* Chapel Hill: University of North Carolina Press, 1930.

——. *A Short History of the American Negro.* New York: Macmillan, 1922.

——. *Women of Achievement.* Chicago: Women's American Baptist Home Mission Society, 1919.

Breckinridge, Sophonisba. *Women in the Twentieth Century.* New York: McGraw-Hill, 1933.

Brooks, Eugene Clyde. "Women Improving School Houses." *World's Work* 12 (September 1906): 7937–38.

Brown, C. S. "Negro Baptists of North Carolina and Education." *Home Mission College Review,* November 1928, 13–20.

Brown, Charlotte Hawkins. *Mammy.* Boston: Pilgrim Press, 1919.

——. *The Negro and the Social Graces.* Atlanta: Commission on Interracial Cooperation, n.d.

Brown, John M. "The Ordination of Women." *A.M.E. Church Review* 2 (April 1886): 354–61.

Brown, Lucy Hughes. "Minutes of the Hospital Association." *Hospital Herald*, 25 January 1899.

Brownlee, Fred Leslie. "She Did It." *American Missionary*, July 1927, 711.

Business Directory of New Berne, N.C. Raleigh: Edwards and Broughton, 1893.

Butler, Marion. "Election in North Carolina." *Independent* 52 (April 1900): 1953–55.

Caldwell, A. B. *History of the American Negro.* Atlanta: A. B. Caldwell, 1921.

Catalogue of Livingstone College. Salisbury, N.C.: Livingstone College, various dates.

Catt, C. C., and Nettie Shuler. *Woman Suffrage and Politics: The Inner Story of the Suffrage Movement.* New York: Scribner's, 1926.

Centennial Year, Woman's Baptist Home and Foreign Missionary Convention of North Carolina. Raleigh, 1984.

Charles Emerson and Co.'s New Bern Directory, 1880–'81. Raleigh: Edwards and Broughton, 1880.

Charlotte City Directory. Charlotte: Ernest & Miller, 1920.

Chataigne's North Carolina State Directory and Gazetteer, 1883–1884. Raleigh: J. H. Chataigne, 1883.

Chesnutt, Charles W. *The Marrow of Tradition.* 1901. Reprint, Ann Arbor: University of Michigan Press, 1969.

——. *"The Wife of His Youth" and Other Stories of the Color Line.* New York: Houghton, Mifflin, 1899.

——. "Women's Rights." *Crisis* 10 (August 1915): 182–83.

Clark, Walter. "Legal Status of Women in North Carolina, Past, Present, and Prospective." Address delivered to the Federation of Women's Clubs, New Bern, N.C., May 1913.

——. "Negro Soldiers." *North Carolina Booklet* 18 (July 1918): 57–62.

"Class Distinctions among Southern Negroes." *Southern Workman* 27 (October 1899): 371.

Clement, Rufus E. "The Church School as a Social Factor in Negro Life." *Journal of Negro History* 12 (January 1927): 5–12.

Clinton, Bishop George W. "What Can the Church Do to Promote Good Will between the Races?" In *Democracy in Earnest: The Southern Sociological Congress, 1916–1918,* ed. James McCulloch, 366–71. Washington, D.C.: Southern Sociological Congress, 1918.

Coffey, Francis B. "Suffrage Limitations at the South." *Political Science Quarterly* 20 (May 1905): 52–67.

Collins, Winfield. *The Truth about Lynching and the Negro in the South.* New York: Neale Publishing Company, 1918.

The Colored Woman of the South: Her Own Story, by One of Their Number. Boston: Women's American Baptist Home Mission Society, n.d.

Colton, Elizabeth. "Improvement in Standards of Southern Colleges since 1900." Reprinted from *Proceedings of the Tenth Annual Meeting of the Southern Association of College Women.* [Richmond?], 1913.

——. "Southern Colleges for White Women." In *Proceedings of the Seventeenth Annual Meeting of the Association of Colleges and Preparatory Schools of the Southern States,* 46–58. Nashville: Publishing House of the Methodist Episcopal Church, South, 1910.

——. "Standards of Southern Colleges for Women." *School Review* 20 (September 1912): 458–75.

Comments by the State Democratic Committee on the Hand Book Issued by the People's Party State Executive Committee. N.p., [1898].

Connor, R. D. W., and Clarence Poe, eds. *The Life and Speeches of Charles B. Aycock.* New York: Doubleday, Page, 1912.

Coon, Charles L. "The Beginnings of North Carolina City Schools, 1867–1887." *South Atlantic Quarterly* 12 (July 1913): 235–47.

——. *Facts about Southern Educational Progress.* Durham: Campaign Committee of the Southern Educational Board, 1905.

——. *Public Taxation and Negro Schools.* Cheyney, Pa.: Committee of Twelve for the Advancement of the Interests of the Negro Race, 1909.

——. "School Support and Our North Carolina Courts." *North Carolina Historical Review* 3 (July 1926): 399–438.

——. *A Statistical Record of the Progress of Public Education in North Carolina, 1870–1906.* Raleigh: Office of the Superintendent of Public Instruction, 1907.

——. "Where Negroes May Not Go." *Harper's Weekly* 48 (16 January 1904): 102.

Cooper, Anna Julia. *A Voice from the South.* 1892. Reprint, New York: Oxford University Press, 1988.

Cooper, George M. "Medical Inspections of Schools in North Carolina." *Southern Medical Journal* 2 (February 1918): 112–15.

Coppin, Fannie J. *Reminiscences of School Life and Hints on Teaching.* Philadelphia: African Methodist Episcopal Church, 1913.

Coston, W. Hilary. *The Spanish-American War Volunteer.* Middletown, Pa.: Mount Pleasant Printery, 1899.

Cotten, Sallie. *To the Women of North Carolina.* Raleigh, n.d.

"A Crime against the Ballot." *Independent* 50 (November 1898): 1433–34.

Crouch, John. *Historical Sketches of Wilkes County.* Wilkesboro, N.C.: Chronicle Job Office, 1902.

Culp, D. W., ed. *Twentieth Century Negro Literature: Or, A Cyclopedia of Thought on the Vital Topics Relating to the American Negro.* Toronto: J. L. Nichols, 1902.

Cutler, James Elbert. *Lynch Law: An Investigation into the History of Lynching in the United States.* New York: Longmans, Green, 1905.

Daily Journal of the Sixteenth Quadrennial Session of the General Conference of the A.M.E. Zion Church of America Held at Montgomery, Alabama, May 1880. N.p., [1880].

Daily Proceedings of the Eighteenth Quadrennial Session of the General Conference of the A.M.E. Zion Church of America Held in St. Peter's A.M.E. Zion Church, New Berne, N.C., May 2nd, 1888. N.p., [1888].

Daniels, Josephus. *Editor in Politics.* Chapel Hill: University of North Carolina Press, 1941.

——. *Tar Heel Editor.* Chapel Hill: University of North Carolina Press, 1939.

Davis, Daniel Webster. "The Black Woman's Burden." *Voice of the Negro* 1 (July 1904): 308.

Dellinger, J. Elmer. "Hospital Work for Negro Women." *Spelman Messenger* 18 (March 1902): 1–7.

Dickerson, C. Hatfield. "Woman Suffrage." *A.M.E. Church Review* 4 (October 1887): 196–99.

Dillard, James Hardy. "County Machinery for Colored Schools in the South." *School and Society* 6 (8 September 1917): 293–95.

The Directory of Charlotte, N.C., for 1893–1894. Charlotte: J. S. Drakeford, 1893.

Dixon, Thomas, Jr. *The Clansman: An Historical Romance of the Ku Klux Klan*. New York: Doubleday, Page, 1905.

———. *The Leopard's Spots: A Romance of the White Man's Burden, 1865–1900*. New York: Doubleday, Page, 1902.

———. *The Sins of the Father: A Romance of the South*. New York: Appleton, 1912.

———. *Southern Horizons: The Autobiography of Thomas Dixon*. Edited by Karen M. Crowe. Ann Arbor: UMI, 1984.

Dowd, Jerome. "Art in Negro Homes." *Southern Workman*, February 1901, 90–95.

———. "Colored Men as Cotton Manufacturers." *Gunton's Magazine*, 1902, 254–56.

———. *The Negro in American Life*. New York: Century, 1926.

———. *The Negro Race: A Sociological Study*. New York: Macmillan, 1914.

Du Bois, W. E. B. "The Black Mother." *Crisis* 5 (December 1912): 78.

———. *Darkwater: Voices from within the Veil*. 1920. Reprint, New York: AMS Press, 1969.

———. *The Souls of Black Folk*. 1903. Reprint, New York: Signet Classic, 1982.

———. "Votes for Women." *Crisis* 4 (November 1912): 234.

———. "The Woman Voter." *Crisis* 21 (March 1921): 200.

———, ed. *The College-Bred Negro: Report of a Social Study Made under the Direction of Atlanta University*. Atlanta: Atlanta University Press, 1900.

———. *The Negro Artisan: Report of a Social Study Made under the Direction of Atlanta University*. Atlanta: Atlanta University Press, 1902.

———. *The Negro Church: Report of a Social Study Made under the Direction of Atlanta University*. Atlanta: Atlanta University Press, 1903.

———. *The Negro Common School: Report of a Social Study Made under the Direction of Atlanta University*. Atlanta: Atlanta University Press, 1901.

———. *The Negro in Business: Report of a Social Study Made under the Direction of Atlanta University*. Atlanta: Atlanta University Press, 1899.

Dunbar, Paul Lawrence. *Representative Negroes: The Negro Problem*. New York: James Pott, 1903.

Dunn, Mary Noreen. *Women and Home Missions*. Nashville: Cokesbury, 1936.

"Editorial Comment in Memoriam Henry Lawrence McCrorey, 1863–1951." *Quarterly Review of Higher Education among Negroes* 19 (July 1951): 171–73.

Edwards, Richard, ed. *Statistical Gazetteer of the States of Virginia and North Carolina*. Richmond, 1856.

Eleventh Annual Report of the National Association for the Advancement of Colored People for the Year 1920. New York: National Association for the Advancement of Colored People, 1921.

"Experiences of the Race Problem." *Independent* 56 (17 March 1904): 590–94.

Federal Writers' Project. *These Are Our Lives*. Chapel Hill: University of North Carolina Press, 1939.

Fifth Annual Report of the Bureau of Labor Statistics of the State of North Carolina for the Year 1891. Raleigh: Edwards and Broughton, 1892.

Fisher, Samuel J. "Biographical Sketch of Henry Lawrence McCrorey, Sr." *Johnson C. Smith University Bulletin* 11 (30 May 1935).

Fonvielle, William Frank. *Some Reminiscences of College Days*. Raleigh: Privately published, 1904.

——. "The South As I Saw It." *A.M.E. Zion Church Quarterly* 4 (July 1894): 419–58.

"Freedom of Opinion in the South." *Nation* 83 (4 January 1906): 6.

Fulton, David B. [Jack Thorne]. *Eagle Clippings*. New York: D. B. Fulton, n.d.

——. *Hanover; Or, The Persecution of the Lowly: A Story of the Wilmington Massacre*. [New York]: M. C. L. Hill, n.d.

——. "A Plea for Social Justice for the Negro Woman." Occasional Paper no. 2, Negro Society for Historical Research, Lincoln Press Association, Yonkers, N.Y., 1912.

Gaines, Bishop W. J. *The Negro and the White Man*. Philadelphia: African Methodist Episcopal Publishing House, 1897.

Gale, Zona. "N.A. Colored Women's Biennial." *Life and Labor*, September 1914, 264–68.

General Education Board. *Annual Report of the General Education Board, 1918–1919*. New York, n.d.

——. *Annual Report of the General Education Board, 1920–1921*. New York, 1922.

——. *Report of the Secretary, 1914–1915*. New York, n.d.

——. *Report of the Secretary, 1916–1917*. New York, n.d.

——. *Report of the Secretary, 1917–1918*. New York, n.d.

Grimké, Archibald H. "The Sex Question and Race Segregation." Occasional Paper nos. 18 and 19, American Negro Academy, Washington, D.C., 1916.

Gwyn, Elsie. "Uncle Remus and His Son." *State Normal Magazine* 3 (December 1898): 329–34.

Hammond, Lily Hardy. *In Black and White: An Interpretation of Southern Life*. New York: Fleming H. Revell, 1914.

——. *In the Vanguard of a Race*. New York: Council of Women for Home Missions and Missionary Education Movement of the United States and Canada, 1922.

——. *Southern Women and Racial Adjustment*. Lynchburg, Va.: J. P. Bell, 1917.

——. "The White Man's Debt to the Negro." *Annals of the American Academy of Political and Social Science* 49 (September 1913): 67–73.

Harper, Frances Ellen Watkins. "National Woman's Christian Temperance Union." *A.M.E. Church Review* 5 (July 1888): 2442–45.

Harris, Mrs. L. H. "A Southern Woman's View." *Independent* 51 (18 May 1899): 1354–55.

Hartshorn, W. N. *An Era of Progress and Promise*. Boston: Priscilla Publishing Company, 1910.

Haskin, Sara Estelle. *Women and Missions in the Methodist Episcopal Church, South*. Nashville: Methodist Publishing House, 1925.

Havens, Jonathan. *The New Bern and Pamlico Section of North Carolina*. New Bern: N. S. Richardson and Son, 1886.

Hayden, Harry. *The Story of the Wilmington Rebellion*. Wilmington, N.C.: Privately published, 1936.

Helm, Mary. *From Darkness to Light*. New York: Fleming H. Revell, 1909.

——. *The Upward Path: The Evolution of a Race*. New York: Young People's Missionary Movement of the United States and Canada, 1909.

Henry, Josephine K. "The New Woman of the New South." *Arena* 11 (February 1895): 353–62.

Hicks, Frank A. "Negro Business in Raleigh." *Home Mission College Review* 4 (May 1930): 18–19.

Hobson, Mrs. E. C., and Mrs. C. E. Hopkins. *A Report Concerning the Colored Women of the South*. Baltimore: Trustees of the John F. Slater Fund, 1896.

Hoge, Sara A. "Organization and Accomplishments of the W.C.T.U. in Virginia." *Annals of the American Academy of Political and Social Science* 32 (December 1908): 527–30.

Hood, J. W. "The Enfranchisement of the Negro Race a Benefit to the State." *A.M.E. Zion Quarterly Review* 12 (July–September 1902).

——. *One Hundred Years of the African Methodist Episcopal Zion Church*. New York: African Methodist Episcopal Zion Publishing House, 1895.

House and Senate Journal, Extra Session. Raleigh: Mitchell Printing, 1920.

Howell, Gertrude Jenkins. *The Women's Auxiliary of the Synod of North Carolina, 1912–1937*. Wilmington, N.C.: Wilmington Stamp and Printing Company, 1938.

Hunton, Addie. "Negro Womanhood Defended." *Voice of the Negro* 1 (July 1904): 280–81.

——. "Women's Clubs." *Crisis* 2 (September 1911): 210–12.

"In Memoriam." In *76th Annual Commencement, Johnson C. Smith University*. Charlotte: Johnson C. Smith University, 1944.

"Is It Negro Rule?" *Independent* 50 (November 1898): 1514–16.

Jackson, Mary E. "The Self-Supporting Woman and the Ballot." *Crisis* 10 (August 1915): 187–88.

Jefferson, Olive Ruth. "The Southern Negro Woman." *The Chautauquan* 8 (1893): 91.

Jemand, Amanda Smith. "A Southern Woman's Appeal for Justice." *Independent* 53 (January–April 1902): 438–40.

Johnson, Edward A. *A History of Negro Soldiers in the Spanish-American War and Other Items of Interest*. Raleigh: Capital Printing Company, 1899.

——. *Light Ahead for the Negro*. New York: Grafton Press, [1904?].

——. *A School History of the Negro Race in America*. Raleigh: Privately published, 1890.

Johnson, James Weldon. "About Aunties." *Crisis* 10 (August 1915): 180–81.

——. "The Black Mammy." *Crisis* 10 (August 1915): 171.

Johnson, William H. *History of the Colored Volunteer Infantry of Virginia, 1871–1899*. Richmond, 1923.

Johnston, Kate Burr, and Nell Battle Lewis. "A Decade of Social Progress in North Carolina." *Journal of Social Forces* 1 (May 1923): 400–403.

Jones, Anna H. "The American Colored Woman." *Voice of the Negro* 2 (October 1905): 692–94.

——. "A Century's Progress for the American Colored Woman." *Voice of the Negro* 2 (September 1905): 631–33.

Jones, Harry H. "The Crisis in Negro Leadership." *Crisis* 19 (March 1920): 256–59.

Jones, M. Ashby. "The Approach to the South's Race Question." *Journal of Social Forces* 1 (November 1922): 40–41.

Journal of the Senate of the General Assembly of the State of North Carolina. Winston, N.C.: M. I. and J. C. Stewart, 1897.

Journal of the Senate of the General Assembly of the State of North Carolina, Session 1899. Raleigh: Edwards and Broughton and E. M. Uzzell, 1899.

Joyner, James Yadkin. *A Decade of Educational Progress in North Carolina, 1901–1910*. Raleigh: Office of the Superintendent of Public Instruction, 1912.

Kearney, Belle. *A Slaveholder's Daughter*. New York: Abbey Press, 1900.

Kerlin, Robert T., ed. *The Voice of the Negro, 1919*. New York: Dutton, 1920.

Kilgo, John Carlisle. "An Inquiry Concerning Lynchings." *South Atlantic Quarterly* 1 (January 1902): 4–13.

Kimball, Annie. "Signs of Negro Elevation." *Living-stone* 8 (May 1891): 3.

King, Willie J. *The Negro in American Life*. New York: Methodist Book Concern, 1926.

King, Willie Mae. "Suffrage and Our Women." *Competitor*, June 1920, 60–61.

Kletzing, H. F., and W. H. Crogman. *Progress of a Race, Or, The Remarkable Advancement of the Afro American*. Atlanta: J. L. Nichols, 1897.

Knight, Edgar W. *Education in the South*. Chapel Hill: University of North Carolina Press, 1924.

———. *Notes on Education*. Durham: Seeman Press, 1927.

———. "The Peabody Fund and Its Early Operation in North Carolina." *South Atlantic Quarterly* 14 (April 1915): 171.

———. *Public School Education in North Carolina*. 1916. Reprint, New York: Negro Universities Press, 1969.

Laney, Lucy. "The Burden of the Educated Colored Woman." Paper presented at the Hampton Negro Conference, Report III, Hampton, Va., July 1899.

Latta, Morgan London. *History of My Life and Work*. Raleigh, 1903.

Leavell, Ullin W. "Trends of Philanthropy in Negro Education: A Survey." *Journal of Negro Education* 2 (January 1933): 38–52.

Locke, Alain Le Roy. *The New Negro: An Interpretation*. New York: Albert Charles, 1925.

Logan, Adella Hunt. "Colored Women as Voters." *Crisis* 4 (September 1912): 242–43.

Ludington, Arthur. "Ballot Laws in the Southern States." *South Atlantic Quarterly* 9 (January 1910): 12–34.

Lumpkin, Katharine Du Pre. *The Making of a Southerner*. 1946. Reprint, Athens: University of Georgia Press, 1991.

Lynk, Miles V. *The Black Troopers, Or, The Daring Heroism of the Negro Soldiers in the Spanish-American War*. Jackson, Tenn.: Lynk Publishing Company, 1899.

McAfee, Mrs. L. D. [Sarah Jane]. *History of the Woman's Missionary Society in the Colored Methodist Episcopal Church*. Jackson, Tenn.: Publishing House of the Colored Methodist Episcopal Church, 1934.

MacBrady, John E., ed. *A New Negro for a New Century*. Chicago: American Publishing House, 1900.

McCord, Charles H. *The American Negro as a Dependent, Defective, and Delinquent*. Nashville: Benson Printing Company, 1914.

McCrorey, Mary Jackson. "Lucy Laney." *Crisis* 41 (June 1934): 161.

McCuistion, Fred. *The South's Negro Teaching Force*. Nashville: Julius Rosenwald Fund, 1931.

McIver, Charles Duncan. "Disfranchisement and Education." *Southern Workman*, February 1901, 189–90.

McIver, Mrs. Charles D. "The Betterment of Public Schoolhouses in North Carolina." *State Normal Magazine* 7 (October 1902): 56–60.

McKelway, A. J. "The Cause of the Troubles in North Carolina." *Independent* 50 (November 1898): 1488–92.

———. "The North Carolina Suffrage Amendment." *Independent* 52 (August 1900): 1955–57.

———. "The Race Problem in the South: The North Carolina Revolution Justified." *Outlook* 60 (31 December 1898): 1057–59.

Majors, Monroe A. *Noted Negro Women: Their Triumphs and Activities*. Chicago: Donahue and Hennesbery, 1893.

Massey, Mable Parker. "Vital Statistics in North Carolina." *South Atlantic Quarterly* 13 (April 1914): 129–33.

Mayo, A. D. "The Woman's Movement in the South." *New England Magazine* 5 (October 1894): 249–60.

Mebane, C. H. *The Woman's Association for the Betterment of Public Schoolhouses in North Carolina*. Raleigh: Office of the State Superintendent of Public Instruction, 1908.

Mercantile Association of Carolinas Reference Book. Wilmington, N.C.: Jackson and Bell, 1890.

Meserve, Charles F. "Shaw University." *American Baptist Home Mission Monthly* 21 (August 1889): 316.

Miller, Kelly. "As to *The Leopard's Spots*: An Open Letter to Thomas Dixon, Jr." In *Race Adjustment: Essays on the Negro in America*, ed. Kelly Miller, 28–56. New York: Neale Publishing Company, 1908.

———. "The Race Problem in the South II: A Negro's View." *Outlook* 60 (31 December 1898): 1059–63.

———. "The Risk of Woman Suffrage." *Crisis* 11 (November 1915): 37–38.

Minutes of the Fifteenth Annual Meeting of the Woman's Missionary Societies. Raleigh, 1905.

[Minutes of the] First Convention of the Woman's Christian Temperance Union of the State of North Carolina. Greensboro: Thomas, Reece, 1883.

[Minutes of the] Second Convention of the Woman's Christian Temperance Union of the State of North Carolina. Greensboro: Thomas, Reece, 1884.

Minutes of the Woman's Christian Temperance Union of North Carolina at the [Third] Annual Meeting. Greensboro: Thomas, Reece, 1885.

Minutes of the Fourth Annual Convention of the Woman's Christian Temperance Union of North Carolina. Greensboro: Thomas, Reece, 1886.

Minutes of the Fifth Annual Convention of the Woman's Christian Temperance Union of North Carolina. Greensboro: Thomas, Reece, 1887.

Minutes of the Sixth Annual Convention of the Woman's Christian Temperance Union of North Carolina. Greensboro: Thomas Brothers, 1888.

Minutes of the Seventh Annual Convention of the Woman's Christian Temperance Union. Greensboro: Thomas Brothers, 1889.

Minutes of the Eighth Annual Convention of the Woman's Christian Temperance Union of North Carolina. Greensboro: Thomas Brothers, 1890.

Minutes of the Ninth Annual Convention of the Woman's Christian Temperance Union of North Carolina. Greensboro: Thomas Brothers, 1891.

Minutes of the Tenth Annual Convention of the Woman's Christian Temperance Union of North Carolina. Greensboro: Thomas Brothers, 1892.

Minutes of the Eleventh Annual Convention of the Woman's Christian Temperance Union of North Carolina. Greensboro: C. F. Thomas, 1893.

Minutes of the Twelfth Annual Convention of the Woman's Christian Temperance Union of North Carolina. Greensboro: C. F. Thomas, 1894.

Minutes of the Thirteenth Annual Convention of the Woman's Christian Temperance Union of North Carolina. Greensboro: C. F. Thomas, 1895.

Minutes of the Fourteenth Annual Convention of the Woman's Christian Temperance Union of North Carolina. High Point: Enterprise Book and Job Print, 1896.

Minutes of the Fifteenth Annual Convention of the Woman's Christian Temperance Union. N.p., n.d.

Minutes of the Sixteenth Annual Convention of the Woman's Christian Temperance Union of North Carolina. High Point: Enterprise Job Print, 1898.

Minutes of the Thirty-first Annual Session of the Halifax County Sunday School Convention. Weldon, N.C.: Harrell's Printing House, 1909.

Minutes of the Twenty-second Annual Session of the Women's Baptist Home Mission Convention of North Carolina Held at St. James Church, Rocky Mount. Henderson, N.C.: Pryce T. Jones, 1907.

Minutes of the Twenty-third Annual Session of the Women's Baptist Home Mission Convention of North Carolina. Raleigh: Edwards and Broughton, 1908.

Moore, Fred. "How to Keep Women at Home." *Colored American Magazine* 14 (January 1908): 7–8.

Morgan, Thomas J. "The Higher Education of Colored Women." *American Baptist Home Mission Monthly* 18 (May 1896): 160.

———. "Negro Preparation for Citizenship." *American Baptist Home Mission Monthly* 22 (December 1900): 334–37.

Morris, Charles S. "The Wilmington Massacre, 1898." In *A Documentary History of the Negro People in the United States*, ed. Herbert Aptheker, 1:813–15. New York: Citadel Press, 1969.

Morris, Joseph, and St. Clair Adams, eds. *It Can Be Done: Poems of Inspiration*. New York: George Sully, 1921.

Mossell, Mrs. N. F. [Gertrude]. *The Work of the Afro-American Woman*. 1908. Reprint, New York: Oxford University Press, 1988.

"Mrs. Mary Jackson McCrorey." *Quarterly Review of Higher Education among Negroes* 12 (January 1944): 53–54.

Murphy, Edgar Gardner. *The Problems of the Present South*. New York: Macmillan, 1904.

Murray, Anna E. "The Negro Woman." *Southern Workman* 33 (April 1904): 232–40.

Murray, Ella Rush. "The Woman's Party and the Violation of the Nineteenth Amendment." *Crisis* 21 (April 1921): 259–61.

"Negro and White Labor." *Outlook* 59 (14 August 1897): 980.

"The Negro Common School in North Carolina." *Crisis* 34 (June 1927): 117–18.

"The Negro Problem: How It Appears to a Southern Colored Woman." *Independent* 54 (18 September 1902): 2221–28.

New Bern, N.C., Directory. Richmond: Hill Directory Company, 1907.

Newbold, Nathan C. "Common Schools for Negroes in the South." *Annals of the American Academy of Political and Social Science* 140 (November 1928): 209–23.

——. "Conference for Negro Education in Raleigh." *Journal of Social Forces* 1 (November 1922–September 1923): 145–47.

——. "Negro County School Commencements." *Southern Workman*, December 1916, 662–67.

Nichols, J. L., and W. H. Crogman, eds. *Progress of a Race*. Naperville, Ill.: J. L. Nichols, 1920.

North Carolina Federation of Women's Clubs. *Yearbook*. Various publishers, 1902–31.

"North Carolina Race Conflict." *Outlook* 60 (19 November 1898): 707–9.

"North Carolina Race Riots." *Collier's Weekly* 22 (November 1898): 4–16.

Official Journal of the Twenty-second Quadrennial Session of the General Conference of the African Methodist Episcopal Zion Church, May 4–May 19, 1904. N.p., [1904].

Page, Thomas Nelson. *The Negro: The Southerner's Problem*. New York: Scribner's, 1904.

Page, Walter Hines. "Booker T. Washington: The Characteristics of the Colored Leader Who Has Shown the Way to Solve the Hardest Problems of Our National Life." *Everybody's Magazine* 6 (April 1902): 393–98.

——. "The Forgotten Man." *State Normal Magazine* 1 (June 1897): 74–89.

——. "The Only Way to Allay Race Friction." *World's Work* 6 (August 1903): 320–21.

Peele, Rennie. "Charles L. Coon." *North Carolina Teacher* 4 (February 1928): 179.

Penn, I. Garland. *The Afro-American Press and Its Editors*. 1891. Reprint, New York: Arno Press, 1969.

Pickens, William. "The Woman Voter Hits the Color Line." *Nation* 111 (6 October 1920): 372–73.

Pocket Manual of North Carolina for the Use of Members of the General Assembly. Raleigh: North Carolina Historical Commission, 1911.

Poe, Clarence. "Rural Land Segregation between Whites and Negroes: A Reply to Mr. Stephenson." *South Atlantic Quarterly* 13 (July 1914): 207–12.

Poland, C. Beauregard. *North Carolina's Glorious Victory*. Raleigh: Privately published, 1898.

Powell, Jacob W. *Bird's Eye View of the General Conference of the African Methodist Episcopal Zion Church*. Boston: Lavalle Press, 1918.

Presentation and Unveiling of Memorial Tablet, Charles Brantley Aycock, Goldsboro, North Carolina, November 1, 1929. N.p., n.d.

Price, Joseph C. "The Negro in the Last Decade of the Century." *Independent* 41 (January 1891): 5.

——. "Temperance Mission Work among the Colored People of the South." *A.M.E. Zion Church Quarterly* 4 (April 1894): 288–96.

Proceedings of the Third Annual Session of the Union Baptist State Convention of North Carolina. N.p., [1917].

Proceedings of the Thirty-first Annual Session of the Baptist Educational and Missionary Convention of North Carolina. Raleigh: Capital Printing Company, 1898.

Proceedings of the Thirty-second Annual Session of the Baptist State Educational and Missionary Convention of North Carolina. Raleigh: Edwards and Broughton, 1900.

Proceedings of the Thirty-sixth Annual Session of the Baptist Educational and Missionary Convention of North Carolina. Raleigh: Baptist Sentinel Print, 1904.

Proceedings of the Thirty-seventh Annual Session of the Baptist Educational and Missionary Convention of North Carolina. Fayetteville: N.C. Baptist Publishing Company, 1905.

Proceedings of the Thirty-ninth Annual Session of the Baptist Educational and Missionary Convention of North Carolina. Fayetteville, N.C.: G. H. Thomson, [1907].

"Race Troubles in the Carolinas." *Literary Digest* 17 (26 November 1898): 623–27.

Raper, Charles L. *The Church and Private Schools of North Carolina: A Historical Study.* Greensboro: Joseph J. Stone, 1898.

Reference List of Private and Denominational Southern Colored Schools. John F. Slater Fund Occasional Papers, no. 20. Lynchburg, Va.: J. P. Bell, 1918.

Richings, F. G. *Evidences of Progress among Colored People.* Philadelphia: George S. Ferguson Company, 1903.

Roster of the North Carolina Volunteers in the Spanish-American War, 1898–1899. Raleigh: Edwards and Broughton and E. M. Uzzell, 1900.

Ruffin, Josephine St. Pierre. "Trust the Women." *Crisis* 10 (August 1915): 188.

Salisbury-Spencer, North Carolina, City Directory II. Asheville, N.C.: Hackney and Moale, 1910.

Scomp, Henry Anselm. *King Alcohol in the Realm of King Cotton.* Chicago: Blakely, 1888.

Scruggs, Lawson Andrew. "Medical Education as a Factor in the Elevation of the Colored Race." *African Expositor* 9 (April 1886): 3.

———. *Women of Distinction: Remarkable in Works and Invincible in Character.* Raleigh: L. A. Scruggs, 1893.

Shaw, Easdale. *History of the North Carolina Branch of the International Order of the King's Daughters and Sons.* Raleigh: Capital Printing Company, 1929.

Shotwell, Captain R. A. *Shotwell's New Bern Mercantile and Manufacturer's Directory, 1866.* New Bern: Vestal, 1866.

Simmons, Enoch Spencer. *A Solution of the Race Problem in the South.* Raleigh: Edwards and Broughton, 1898.

Simmons, William J. *Men of Mark: Eminent, Progressive, and Rising.* Cleveland: George M. Rewell, 1887.

Sketch Book of Livingstone College and East Tennessee Industrial School. Salisbury, N.C.: East Tennessee Industrial School Print, 1903.

Souvenir and Official Program: The Negro Young People's Christian and Educational Congress. Nashville: National Baptist Publishing Board, [1902].

Stephenson, Gilbert. "Education and Crime among Negroes." *South Atlantic Quarterly* 16 (January 1917): 14–20.

———. "The North Carolina Race Conflict." *Outlook* 60 (November 1898): 707–9.

———. "The North Carolina Troubles." *Independent* 50 (December 1898): 1794–97.

———. "Race Distinctions in American Law." *American Law Review* 43 (January–February 1909): 29–52.

——. "The Race Issue in the South." *Literary Digest* 17 (November 1898): 538–40.

——. "The Race Problem: An Autobiography. . . ." *Independent* 54 (17 March 1904): 586–89.

——. "The Segregation of the White and Negro Races in the Cities." *South Atlantic Quarterly* 13 (January 1914): 1–18.

——. "The Segregation of the White and Negro Races in the Rural Communities of North Carolina." *South Atlantic Quarterly* 13 (April 1914): 107–17.

Steward, T. S. *The Colored Regulars in the United States Army*. 1904. Reprint, New York: Arno Press, 1969.

Stowell, Jay S. *Methodist Adventures in Negro Education*. New York: Methodist Book Concern, 1922.

Tayleur, Eleanor. "The Negro Woman: Social and Moral Decadence." *Outlook* 76 (30 January 1904): 266–71.

Terrell, Mary Church. *A Colored Woman in a White World*. Washington, D.C.: Ransdell Publishing Company, 1940.

——. "The Justice of Woman Suffrage." *Crisis* 4 (September 1912): 243–45.

——. "A Plea for the White South by a Colored Woman." *Nineteenth Century* 60 (July 1906): 70–84.

——. "The Progress of Colored Women." *Voice of the Negro* 1 (July 1904): 291–94.

——. "Woman Suffrage and the Fifteenth Amendment." *Crisis* 10 (August 1915): 191.

Terrell, Robert H. "Our Debt to Suffragists." *Crisis* 10 (August 1915): 181.

Thomas, William Hannibal. *The American Negro: What He Was, What He Is, and What He May Become*. New York: Macmillan, 1901.

Thompson, Holland. *The New South: A Chronicle of Society and Industrial Evolution*. New Haven: Yale University Press, 1921.

Tompkins, Daniel Augustus. *Cotton Mill, Commercial Features*. Charlotte: Privately published, 1899.

Tourgee, Albion W. *A Fool's Errand*. 1879. Reprint, New York: Harper and Row, 1966.

Traywick, A. W. "The Play Life of Negro Boys and Girls." In *Democracy in Earnest: The Southern Sociological Congress, 1916–1918*, ed. James McCulloch, 354–62. Washington, D.C.: Southern Sociological Congress, 1918.

Turner's North Carolina Almanac, 1873. Raleigh: Edwards and Broughton, 1873.

U.S. Bureau of the Census. Manuscript Census, 1850, 1870, 1880, 1900, and 1910.

——. *Negro Population in the United States, 1790–1915*. Reprint, New York: Arno Press, 1968.

——. *Occupations at the Twelfth Census*. Washington, D.C.: Government Printing Office, 1904.

——. *Population of the United States in 1860*. Washington, D.C.: Government Printing Office, 1864.

——. *Religious Bodies, 1916, Part II*. Washington, D.C.: Government Printing Office, 1919.

——. *Special Reports: Religious Bodies, 1906, Part II*. Washington, D.C.: Government Printing Office, 1910.

———. *Thirteenth Census of the United States Taken in the Year 1910*. Vols. 3 and 4. Washington, D.C.: Government Printing Office, 1914.

U.S. Department of the Interior. *Negro Education: A Study of the Private and Higher Schools for Colored People in the United States*. Bulletin no. 38. Washington, D.C.: Government Printing Office, 1917.

Vass, L. C. *History of the Presbyterian Church in New Bern, N.C.: A Resume of Early Ecclesiastical Affairs in Eastern North Carolina and a Sketch of the Early Days of New Bern*. Richmond: Whittel and Shepperson, 1886.

Waddell, Alfred Moore. *Some Memories of My Life*. Raleigh: Privately published, 1908.

———. "The Story of the Wilmington, N.C., Race Riots." *Collier's Weekly* 22 (26 November 1898): 4–16.

Waldron, J. Milton, and J. D. Harkless. *The Political Situation in a Nut-Shell: Some Uncolored Truths for Colored Voters*. Washington, D.C.: Trades Allied Printing Council, 1912.

Walters, Alexander. *My Life and My Work*. New York: Fleming H. Revell, 1917.

Washington, Booker T. "Durham, North Carolina: A City of Negro Enterprise." *Independent* 70 (30 March 1911): 642–50.

———. "Education and Suffrage of Negroes." *Education* 19 (September 1898): 49–50.

———. *The Future of the American Negro*. Boston: Small, Maynard, 1902.

———. *My Larger Education: Being Chapters from My Experience*. Garden City, N.Y.: Doubleday, Page, 1911.

———. "The New Negro Woman." *Lend a Hand* 15 (October 1895): 254.

———. *The Story of the Negro*. New York: Doubleday, Page, 1909.

———. *Up from Slavery: An Autobiography*. New York: Doubleday, Page, 1902.

Washington, Mrs. Booker T. "The Gain in the Life of the Negro Woman." *Outlook* 76 (30 January 1904): 271–74.

———. "The Negro Home and the Future of the Race." In *Democracy in Earnest: The Southern Sociological Congress, 1916–1918*, ed. James McCulloch, 334–41. Washington, D.C.: Southern Sociological Congress, 1918.

———. "Social Improvement of the Plantation Woman." *Voice of the Negro* 1 (July 1904): 288–90.

Watson, C. H., ed. *Colored Charlotte*. Charlotte, [1915].

Weatherford, W. D. "Lynching: Removing Its Causes." Address delivered to the Southern Sociological Congress, New Orleans, La., 14 April 1916.

———. *Negro Life in the South: Present Conditions and Needs*. New York: Association Press, 1918.

Weeks, A. L. E. *Victims of Circumstances and Heroes of the Truth*. New Bern: Weeks, Principal of the New Bern Collegiate Industrial Institute, 1909.

Weldon, Frank. "The North Carolina Race Conflict." *Outlook* 60 (19 November 1898): 707.

Wells-Barnett, Ida B. "Lynching: Our National Crime." In *Proceedings of the National Negro Conference, 1909*, 174–79. Reprint, New York: Arno Press, 1969.

———. *On Lynchings: Southern Horrors, a Red Record, and Mob Rule in New Orleans*. 1892, 1895, 1900. Reprint, New York: Arno Press, 1969.

West, Henry L. "The Race War in North Carolina." *Forum* 26 (September 1898–February 1899): 578–91.

White, George H. *Defense of the Negro Race: Charges Answered.* Washington, D.C.: [Government Printing Office], 1901.

———. "The Injustice to the Colored Voter." *Independent* 52 (January 1900): 176–77.

"The White Woman's Burden." *Nation* 112 (16 February 1921): 257–58.

Whitted, J. A. *History of Negro Baptists of North Carolina.* Raleigh: Edwards and Broughton, 1908.

Willard, Frances E. *Glimpses of Fifty Years: The Autobiography of an American Woman.* 1889. Reprint, New York: Source Book Press, 1970.

———. *Woman and Temperance, Or, The Work and Workers of the W.C.T.U.* Hartford, Conn.: Park Publishing, 1883.

Williams, Fannie Barrier. "The Club Movement among Colored Women of America." In *A New Negro for a New Century*, ed. John E. McBrady. Chicago: American Publishing House, 1900.

———. "The Club Movement among the Colored Women." *Voice of the Negro* 1 (March 1904): 99–102.

———. "The Intellectual Progress of the Colored Women of the United States since the Emancipation Proclamation." In *The World Congress of Representative Women*, ed. May Wright Sewell. Chicago: Rand, McNally, 1898.

———. "The Need of Organized Womanhood." *Colored American Magazine* 15 (January 1909): 653.

Williams, Sylvania F. "The Social Status of the Negro Woman." *Voice of the Negro* 1 (July 1904): 198–200.

Williams, W. T. B. *Report on Negro Universities and Colleges.* John F. Slater Fund Occasional Papers, no. 21. N.p.: Trustees of the John F. Slater Fund, 1922.

———. *Report on Negro Universities in the South.* John F. Slater Fund Occasional Papers, no. 13. N.p.: Trustees of the John F. Slater Fund, 1913.

Winston, George T. "The Higher Education of Women." *State Normal Magazine* 3 (April 1899): 433–41.

———. "Industrial Training in Relation to the Negro Problem." In *Proceedings of the Fourth Conference for Education in the South*, 103–7. New York: Committee on Publication, 1901.

———. "The Relation of the Whites to the Negroes." *Annals of the American Academy of Political and Social Science* 18 (July 1901): 105–18.

Winston, Robert W. "Aycock: His People's Genius." Founder's Day Address, 12 October 1922, University of North Carolina. *Alumni Review* 22 (November 1933): 24.

———. *It's a Far Cry.* New York: Henry Holt, 1937.

———. "An Unconsidered Aspect of the Negro Question." *South Atlantic Quarterly* 1 (July 1902): 265–68.

Woman's Association for the Betterment of Public School Houses in North Carolina. *Constitution and By-Laws.* Greensboro, 1902.

"Woman Suffrage and the *Messenger*." *Messenger* 2 (January 1918): 9.

"Woman Suffrage and the Negro." *Messenger* 1 (November 1917): 6.

Woodson, Carter G. *A Century of Negro Migration*. Washington, D.C.: Association for the Study of Negro Life and History, 1918.

Work, Monroe N. *Negro Yearbook: An Annual Encyclopedia of the Negro, 1921–1922*. Tuskegee, Ala.: Negro Yearbook Publishing Company, 1922.

——. "Self-Help among Negroes." *Survey* 22 (7 August 1909): 606–18.

Yates, Josephine Silone. "The National Association of Colored Women." *Voice of the Negro* 1 (July 1904): 283–87.

Yearbook of the East Cedar Grove Missionary Baptist Association. [Creedmoor, N.C.], 1913.

Yenser, Thomas. *Who's Who in Colored America*. 6th ed. New York: Thomas Yenser, 1944.

The Young Women's Christian Association among Colored Women in Cities. New York: National Board of the Young Women's Christian Association, 1915.

SECONDARY SOURCES

Abelove, Henry, ed. *Visions of History*. New York: Pantheon, 1984.

"Abolish the White Race—By Any Means Necessary." *Race Traitor* 1 (Winter 1993): 1–8.

Absher, Mrs. W. O. *Wilkes County, N.C., Will Abstracts, Books One and Two, 1778–1811*. Easley, S.C.: Southern Historical Press, 1989.

——, ed. *The Heritage of Wilkes County*. Winston-Salem: Wilkes County Genealogical Society and Hunter Publishing, 1982.

Alexander, Adele Logan. "Adella Hunt Logan and the Tuskegee Woman's Clubs: Building a Foundation for Suffrage." In *Stepping out of the Shadows: Alabama Women, 1819–1990*, ed. Mary Martha Thomas, 96–113. Tuscaloosa: University of Alabama Press, 1995.

——. *Ambiguous Lives: Free Women of Color in Rural Georgia, 1789–1879*. Fayetteville: University of Arkansas Press, 1991.

——. "How I Discovered My Grandmother: And the Truth about Black Women and the Suffrage Movement." *Ms.*, November 1983, 29–33.

Alexander, Ann Field. "Black Protest in the New South: John Mitchell, Jr. (1863–1929), and the Richmond *Planet*." Ph.D. dissertation, Duke University, 1973.

Alexander, Roberta Sue. "Hostility and Hope: Black Education in North Carolina during Presidential Reconstruction, 1865–1867." *North Carolina Historical Review* 53 (April 1976): 113–32.

——. *North Carolina Faces the Freedmen: Race Relations during Presidential Reconstruction, 1865–1867*. Durham: Duke University Press, 1985.

Almond, Gabriel. "Separate Tables." *Political Science and Politics* 21 (Fall 1988): 828.

Anderson, Eric. *Race and Politics in North Carolina, 1872–1901: The Black Second*. Baton Rouge: Louisiana State University Press, 1981.

Anderson, James D. *The Education of Blacks in the South, 1860–1935*. Chapel Hill: University of North Carolina Press, 1988.

Anderson, Jervis. *This Was Harlem: A Cultural Portrait, 1900–1950*. New York: Farrar Straus Giroux, 1982.

Andolsen, Barbara Hilkert. *"Daughters of Jefferson, Daughters of Bootblacks": Racism and American Feminism*. Macon, Ga.: Mercer University Press, 1986.

Andrews, William L. *The Literary Career of Charles W. Chesnutt*. Baton Rouge: Louisiana State University Press, 1980.

——. *Sisters of the Spirit: Three Black Women's Autobiographies of the Nineteenth Century*. Bloomington: Indiana University Press, 1986.

Antone, George P. "Willis Duke Weatherford: An Interpretation of His Work in Race Relations, 1906–1946." Ph.D. dissertation, Vanderbilt University, 1969.

Aptheker, Bettina. *Woman's Legacy: Essays on Race, Sex, and Class in American History*. Amherst: University of Massachusetts Press, 1982.

Aptheker, Herbert. "The Negro College Student in the 1920s—Years of Preparation and Protest: An Introduction." *Science and Society* 33 (Spring 1969): 150–67.

——. "The Washington–Du Bois Conference of 1904." *Science and Society* 13 (Fall 1949): 344–51.

Argersinger, Peter H. "The Southern Search for Order." *Reviews in American History* 3 (June 1975): 236–41.

Armstrong, Nancy, and Leonard Tennenhouse. "History, Poststructuralism, and the Question of Narrative." *Narrative* 1 (January 1993): 45–58.

Ashe, Samuel A. *History of North Carolina*. Raleigh: Edwards and Broughton, 1925.

Ashmore, Nancy Vance. "The Development of the African Methodist Episcopal Church in South Carolina, 1865–1965." Master's thesis, University of South Carolina, 1969.

Atkinson, Ray M. "*Our Living and Our Dead*: A Post-Bellum North Carolina Magazine of Literature and History." *North Carolina Historical Review* 40 (Autumn 1963): 423–33.

Ayers, Edward L. *The Promise of the New South: Life after Reconstruction*. New York: Oxford University Press, 1992.

——. *Vengeance and Justice: Crime and Punishment in the Nineteenth Century South*. New York: Oxford University Press, 1984.

Badger, Henry C. "Negro Colleges and Universities, 1900–1950." *Journal of Negro Education* 21 (Winter 1952): 89–93.

Baer, Hans, and Merrill Singer, eds. *African-American Religion in the Twentieth Century: Varieties of Protest and Accommodation*. Knoxville: University of Tennessee Press, 1992.

Baker, Paula. "The Domestication of Politics: Women and American Political Society, 1780–1920." *American Historical Review* 89 (June 1984): 620–47.

Balanoff, Elizabeth. "Negro Legislators in the North Carolina General Assembly, July 1868–February 1872." *North Carolina Historical Review* 49 (Winter 1972): 22–55.

Bardaglio, Peter W. "Rape and Law in the Old South: 'Calculated to Excite Indignation in Every Heart.'" *Journal of Southern History* 60 (November 1994): 749–72.

Baughman, Laurence Alan. *Southern Rape Complex: Hundred Year Psychosis*. Atlanta: Pendulum Books, 1966.

Bederman, Gail. "'Civilization,' the Decline of Middle-Class Manliness, and

Ida B. Wells's Antilynching Campaign." *Radical History Review* 52 (Winter 1992): 5–30.

Beede, Benjamin R., ed. *The War of 1898 and U.S. Interventions, 1898–1934: An Encyclopedia*. New York: Garland, 1994.

Bell, John L., Jr. "Baptists and the Negro in North Carolina during Reconstruction." *North Carolina Historical Review* 42 (October 1965): 391–409.

Benn, S. I., and G. F. Gaus, eds. *Public and Private in Social Life*. New York: St. Martin's Press, 1983.

Berkeley, Kathleen. " 'Colored Ladies Also Contributed': Black Women's Activities from Benevolence to Social Welfare, 1866–1896." In *The Web of Southern Social Relations: Women, Family, and Education*, ed. Walter J. Fraser, Jr., R. Frank Saunders, Jr., and Jon L. Wakelyn, 181–203. Athens: University of Georgia Press, 1985.

———. " 'The Ladies Want to Bring Reform to the Public Schools': Public Education and Women's Rights in the Post Civil War South." *History of Education Quarterly* 44 (Spring 1984): 45–58.

Bernhard, Virginia, Betty Brandon, Elizabeth Fox-Genovese, Theda Perdue, and Elizabeth H. Turner, eds. *Hidden Histories of Women in the New South*. Columbia: University of Missouri Press, 1994.

Berry, Mary Frances. "Judging Morality: Sexual Behavior and Legal Consequences in the Late Nineteenth-Century South." *Journal of American History* 78 (December 1991): 835–56.

———. "Twentieth-Century Black Women in Education." *Journal of Negro Education* 51 (Summer 1982): 288–300.

Billings, Dwight B., Jr. *Planters and the Making of a "New South": Class, Politics, and Development in North Carolina, 1865–1900*. Chapel Hill: University of North Carolina Press, 1979.

Birmingham, Stephen. *Certain People: America's Black Elite*. Boston: Little, Brown, 1977.

Bishir, Catherine W. "Landmarks of Power: Building a Southern Past, 1885–1915." *Southern Cultures*, Inaugural issue [Fall 1993]: 5–45.

———. *North Carolina Architecture*. Chapel Hill: University of North Carolina Press, 1990.

Blair, Karen J. *The Clubwoman as Feminist: True Womanhood Redefined, 1868–1914*. New York: Holmes and Meier, 1980.

Blanchard, Mary W. "Boundaries and the Victorian Body: Aesthetic Fashion in Gilded Age America." *American Historical Review* 100 (February 1995): 21–50.

Blassingame, John. *The Slave Community: Plantation Life in the Antebellum South*. New York: Oxford University Press, 1972.

Blee, Kathleen M. *Women of the Klan: Racism and Gender in the 1920s*. Berkeley: University of California Press, 1991.

Bleser, Carol, ed. *In Joy and in Sorrow: Women, Family, and Marriage in the Victorian South, 1830–1900*. New York: Oxford University Press, 1991.

Blocker, Jack S. *American Temperance Movements: Cycles of Reform*. Boston: Twayne, 1989.

———. *"Give to the Winds Thy Fears": The Women's Temperance Crusade, 1873–1874*. Westport, Conn.: Greenwood Press, 1985.

Bloomfield, Maxwell. "Dixon's *The Leopard's Spots*: A Study in Popular Racism." *American Quarterly* 16 (1964): 387–401.

Blumin, Stuart M. *The Emergence of the Middle Class: Social Experience in the American City, 1760–1900*. New York: Cambridge University Press, 1989.

Bode, Frederick A. "The Formation of Evangelical Communities in Middle Georgia: Twiggs County, 1820–1861." *Journal of Southern History* 60 (November 1994): 711–48.

Boles, John B. *Black Southerners, 1619–1869*. Lexington: University Press of Kentucky, 1983.

———. *The Great Revival, 1787–1805: The Origins of the Southern Evangelical Mind*. Lexington: University Press of Kentucky, 1972.

Boles, John B., and Evelyn Thomas Nolen. *Interpreting Southern History: Historiographical Essays in Honor of Sanford W. Higginbotham*. Baton Rouge: Louisiana State University Press, 1987.

Bond, Horace Mann. "The Negro in the Armed Forces of the United States Prior to World War I." *Journal of Negro Education* 12 (Summer 1943): 263–87.

Bordin, Ruth. *Alice Freeman Palmer: The Evolution of a New Woman*. Ann Arbor: University of Michigan Press, 1993.

———. *Frances Willard: A Biography*. Chapel Hill: University of North Carolina Press, 1986.

———. *Woman and Temperance: The Quest for Power and Liberty, 1873–1900*. Philadelphia: Temple University Press, 1981.

Boris, Eileen. "From Parlor to Politics: Women and Reform in America, 1890–1925." *Radical History Review* 5 (Spring 1991): 191–203.

———. "The Power of Motherhood: Black and White Activist Women Redefine the 'Political.'" In *Mothers of a New World: Maternalist Politics and the Origins of the Welfare State*, ed. Sonya Michel and Seth Koven, 213–45. New York: Routledge, 1993.

Bowles, Elizabeth Ann. *Good Beginnings: The First Four Decades of the University of North Carolina at Greensboro*. Chapel Hill: University of North Carolina Press, 1967.

Boykin, James H. *The Negro in North Carolina Prior to 1861*. New York: Pageant Press, 1958.

Bradley, David Henry, Sr. *A History of the A.M.E. Zion Church, Part II, 1872–1968*. Nashville: Parthenon Press, 1970.

Brandon, Betty Jane. "Alexander Jeffrey McKelway: Statesman of the New Order." Ph.D. dissertation, University of North Carolina at Chapel Hill, 1969.

Brawley, James S. *Rowan County . . . A Brief History*. Raleigh: North Carolina Division of Archives and History, 1974.

Breen, William J. "Black Women and the Great War: Mobilization and Reform in the South." *Journal of Southern History* 44 (August 1974): 421–40.

———. "Southern Women in the War: The North Carolina Women's Committee, 1917–1919." *North Carolina Historical Review* 55 (July 1978): 251–81.

Brett, Sally. *Awakenings: Writings and Recollections of Eastern North Carolina Women*. Greenville, N.C.: National Printing Company, 1978.

Brod, Harry, ed. *The Making of Masculinities*. Boston: Allen and Unwin, 1987.

Brodhead, Richard, ed. *The Journals of Charles W. Chesnutt*. Durham: Duke University Press, 1993.

Bromberg, Alan B. "Pure Democracy and White Supremacy: The Redeemer Period in North Carolina, 1876–1894." Ph.D. dissertation, University of Virginia, 1977.

Brooks, Aubrey Lee. *A Southern Lawyer: Fifty Years at the Bar*. Chapel Hill: University of North Carolina Press, 1950.

Brown, Elsa Barkley. "African-American Women's Quilting: A Framework for Conceptualizing and Teaching African-American Women's History." *Signs* 14 (Summer 1989): 928–29.

——. "Mothers of Mind." *Sage* 6 (Summer 1989): 3–10.

——. "Negotiating and Transforming the Public Sphere: African American Political Life in the Transition from Slavery to Freedom." *Public Culture* 7 (1994): 107–46.

——. "Polyrhythms and Improvisation: Lessons for Women's History." *History Workshop Journal* 31 (1991): 85–90.

——. "To Catch the Vision of Freedom: Reconstructing Southern Black Women's Political History, 1865–1895." Unpublished paper in author's possession.

——. "Uncle Ned's Children: Negotiating Community and Freedom in Post-emancipation Richmond, Virginia." Ph.D. dissertation, Kent State University, 1994.

——. " 'What Has Happened Here': The Politics of Difference in Women's History and Feminist Politics." *Feminist Studies* 18 (Summer 1992): 295–312.

——. "Womanist Consciousness: Maggie Lena Walker and the Independent Order of Saint Luke." *Signs* 14 (Spring 1989): 610–33.

Brown, Hugh Victor. *E-Qual-ity Education in North Carolina among Negroes*. Raleigh: Irving-Swain Press, 1964.

——. *A History of the Education of Negroes in North Carolina*. Raleigh: Irving-Swain Press, 1961.

Brownell, Blaine A. "The Urban Mind of the South: The Growth of Urban Consciousness." Ph.D. dissertation, University of North Carolina at Chapel Hill, 1969.

Brownell, Blaine A., and David Goldfield. *The City in Southern History: The Growth of Urban Civilization in the South*. Port Washington, N.Y.: Kennikat Press, 1977.

Brundage, Fitzhugh W. *Lynching in the New South: Georgia and Virginia, 1880–1930*. Urbana: University of Illinois Press, 1993.

Buenker, John D. *Urban Liberalism and Progressive Reform*. New York: Scribner, 1973.

Buhle, Mari Jo, and Paul Buhle, eds. *The Concise History of Woman Suffrage: Selections from the Classic Work of Stanton, Anthony, Gage, and Harper*. Urbana: University of Illinois Press, 1978.

Bullock, Henry Allen. *A History of Negro Education in the South: From 1619 to the Present*. Cambridge: Harvard University Press, 1967.

Burgess, Allen E. "Tar Heel Blacks and the New South Dream: The Coleman Manufacturing Company, 1896–1904." Ph.D. dissertation, Duke University, 1977.

Burke, De Grandial. *The Brooklyn Story*. Charlotte: Afro-American Cultural Center, 1978.

Burkett, Randall K., and Richard Newman. *Black Apostles: Afro-American Clergy Confront the Twentieth Century*. Boston: G. K. Hall, 1978.

Busby, Michelle D. "The Effect of Race and Class on the Development of the Charlotte Young Women's Christian Association, 1902–1966." Master's thesis, University of North Carolina at Charlotte, 1994.

Butchart, Ronald E. *Northern Schools, Southern Blacks, and Reconstruction: Freedmen's Education, 1862–1875*. Westport, Conn.: Greenwood Press, 1980.

Butler, Jon. *Awash in a Sea of Faith: Christianizing the American People*. Cambridge: Harvard University Press, 1990.

Butler, Judith, and Joan W. Scott. *Feminists Theorize the Political*. New York: Routledge, 1992.

Byerly, Victoria Morris. *Hard Times Cotton Mill Girls: Personal Histories of Womanhood and Poverty in the South*. Ithaca, N.Y.: ILR Press, 1986.

Bynum, Victoria E. *Unruly Women: The Politics of Social and Sexual Control in the Old South*. Chapel Hill: University of North Carolina Press, 1992.

Calhoun, Craig, ed. *Habermas and the Public Sphere*. Cambridge: Massachusetts Institute of Technology Press, 1992.

Camp, Cordelia. *Some Pioneer Women Teachers of North Carolina*. N.p.: Delta Kappa Gamma Society, 1955.

Campbell, Walter Elijah. "The Corporate Hand in the Jim Crow Journey." Ph.D. dissertation, University of North Carolina at Chapel Hill, 1991.

Carby, Hazel V. *Reconstructing Womanhood: The Emergence of the Afro-American Woman Novelist*. New York: Oxford University Press, 1987.

Carlson, Shirley. "Black Ideals of Womanhood in the Victorian Era." *Journal of Negro History* 77 (Spring 1992): 61–73.

Carnes, Mark, and Clyde Griffen. *Meanings for Manhood*. Chicago: University of Chicago Press, 1990.

Carraway, Gertrude S. *Carolina Crusaders: History of the North Carolina Federation of Women's Clubs*. New Bern: Owen G. Dunn, 1941.

Carter, Wilmoth Annette. *The New Negro of the South: A Portrait of Movements and Leadership*. New York: Exposition Press, 1967.

———. *Shaw's Universe: A Monument to Educational Innovation*. Raleigh: Shaw University, 1973.

———. *The Urban Negro in the South*. New York: Russell and Russell, 1962.

Casdorph, Paul D. *Republicans, Negroes, and Progressives in the South, 1912–1916*. Tuscaloosa: University of Alabama Press, 1981.

Cash, Loretta Barnett Floris. "Womanhood and Protest: The Club Movement among Black Women, 1892–1922." Ph.D. dissertation, State University of New York–Stony Brook, 1986.

Cash, Wilbur J. *The Mind of the South*. New York: Vintage Books, 1969.

Cavallo, Dominick. *Muscles and Morals: Organized Playgrounds and Urban Reform, 1880–1920*. Philadelphia: University of Pennsylvania Press, 1981.

Cecelski, David S. "The Shores of Freedom: The Maritime Underground Railroad in North Carolina, 1800–1861." *North Carolina Historical Review* 71 (April 1994): 174–206.

Cell, John W. *The Highest Stage of White Supremacy: The Origins of Segregation in South Africa and the American South*. Cambridge: Cambridge University Press, 1982.

Chadbourn, James H. *Lynching and the Law*. Chapel Hill: University of North Carolina Press, 1933.

Chafe, William H. *Civilities and Civil Rights: Greensboro, North Carolina, and the Black Struggle for Equality*. New York: Oxford University Press, 1980.

——. "Women's History and Political History: Some Thoughts on Progressivism and the New Deal." In *Visible Women: New Essays on American Activism*, ed. Nancy A. Hewitt and Suzanne Lebsock, 101–18. Urbana: University of Illinois Press, 1993.

Chambers, Clarke. "Women in the Creation of the Profession of Social Work." *Social Science Review* 60 (March 1986): 1–33.

Charlotte City Directory. Charlotte: Ernest and Miller, 1920.

Cheney, John L., Jr., ed. *North Carolina Government, 1585–1979: A Narrative and Statistical History*. Raleigh: North Carolina Department of the Secretary of State, 1981.

Chesnutt, Helen. *Charles Waddell Chesnutt, Pioneer of the Color Line*. Chapel Hill: University of North Carolina Press, 1952.

Childs, J. B. "Concepts of Culture in Afro-American Thought, 1890–1920." *Social Text* 4 (Fall 1981): 28–43.

Claiborne, Jack. *The Charlotte Observer: Its Time and Place, 1869–1986*. Chapel Hill: University of North Carolina Press, 1986.

Clement, Rufus Early. "A History of Negro Education in North Carolina, 1865–1928." Ph.D. dissertation, Northwestern University, 1930.

Cohen, William. *At Freedom's Edge: Black Mobility and the Southern Quest for Racial Control, 1861–1915*. Baton Rouge: Louisiana State University Press, 1991.

Coleman, Willie Mae. "Keeping the Faith and Disturbing the Peace—Black Women: From Anti-Slavery to Woman Suffrage." Ph.D. dissertation, University of California, Irvine, 1982.

Collins, Patricia Hill. *Black Feminist Thought: Knowledge, Consciousness, and the Politics of Empowerment*. Boston: Unwin Hyman, 1990.

——. "Learning from the Outsider Within: The Sociological Significance of Black Feminist Thought." *Social Problems* 33, no. 6 (1986): 14–32.

——. "The Social Construction of Black Feminist Thought." *Signs* 14 (Summer 1989): 745–73.

Collins, Patricia Hill, and Margaret L. Anderson, comps. *Race, Class, and Gender: An Anthology*. Belmont, Calif.: Wadsworth, 1992.

Connor, R. D. W. *North Carolina: Rebuilding an Ancient Commonwealth, 1584–1925*. Chicago: American Historical Society, 1929.

Conway, Jill. "Women Reformers and American Culture, 1870–1939." *Journal of Social History* 5 (Winter 1971–72): 164–77.

Cook, Raymond Allen. *Fire from the Flint: The Amazing Careers of Thomas Dixon*. Winston-Salem, N.C.: John F. Blair, 1968.

Cooper, John Milton. *Walter Hines Page: The Southerner as American, 1855–1918*. Chapel Hill: University of North Carolina Press, 1977.

Correll, Emily Clare Newby. "Woman's Work for Woman: The Methodist and Baptist Woman's Missionary Societies in North Carolina, 1878–1930." Master's thesis, University of North Carolina at Chapel Hill, 1977.

Cott, Nancy F. "Across the Great Divide: Women in Politics before and after 1920." In *Women, Politics, and Change*, ed. Louise A. Tilly and Patricia Gurin, 153–86. New York: Russell Sage Foundation, 1990.

———. *The Bonds of Womanhood: "Woman's Sphere" in New England, 1780–1835*. New Haven: Yale University Press, 1977.

———. "Feminist Politics in the 1920s: The National Woman's Party." *Journal of American History* 71 (June 1984): 43–68.

———. *The Grounding of Modern Feminism*. New Haven: Yale University Press, 1987.

———. "On Men's History and Women's History." In *Meanings for Manhood*, ed. Mark Carnes and Clyde Griffen, pp. 153–76. Chicago: University of Chicago Press, 1990.

———. "What's in a Name?: The Limits of 'Social Feminism,' Or, Expanding the Vocabulary of Women's History." *Journal of American History* 76 (December 1989): 809–29.

Cotten, Sallie Southall. *History of the North Carolina Federation of Women's Clubs, 1901–1915*. N.p.: North Carolina Federation of Women's Clubs, 1925.

Cox, Oliver Cromwell. *Caste, Class, and Race: A Study in Social Dynamics*. Garden City, N.Y.: Doubleday, 1948.

Cozart, L. S. *A Venture of Faith: Barber Scotia College, 1867–1967*. Charlotte: Heritage Printers, 1976.

Cripps, Thomas R. "African Americans on the Silver Screen." In *Hollywood's America: United States History through Its Films*, ed. Steven Mintz and Randy Roberts, 112–23. St. James, N.Y.: Brandywine Press, 1993.

———. "The Reaction of the Negro to the Motion Picture *Birth of a Nation*." *Historian* 25 (Spring 1963): 344–62.

Crow, Jeffrey J. " 'Fusion, Confusion, and Negroism': Schism among Negro Republicans in the North Carolina Election of 1896." *North Carolina Historical Review* 53 (October 1976): 365–84.

Crow, Jeffrey J., and Robert F. Durden. *Maverick Republican in the Old North State: A Political Biography of Daniel L. Russell*. Baton Rouge: Louisiana State University Press, 1977.

Crow, Jeffrey J., and Flora J. Hatley, eds. *Black Americans in North Carolina and the South*. Chapel Hill: University of North Carolina Press, 1984.

Crow, Jeffrey J., and Robert Winters, Jr., eds. *The Black Presence in North Carolina*. Raleigh: North Carolina Museum of History, 1978.

Curtis, Susan A. *A Consuming Faith: The Social Gospel and Modern American Culture*. Baltimore: Johns Hopkins University Press, 1991.

Cuthbert, Marion V. *Education and Marginality: A Study of the Negro Woman College Graduate*. New York: Garland, 1987.

Dabney, Virginius. *Liberalism in the South*. Chapel Hill: University of North Carolina Press, 1932.

Dailey, Jane. "Race, Sex, and Citizenship: Biracial Democracy in Readjuster Virginia, 1879–1883." Ph.D. dissertation, Princeton University, 1995.

Dancy, John C. *Sands against the Wind: Memoirs of John C. Dancy*. Detroit: Wayne State University Press, 1966.

Daniel, Sadie Iola. *Women Builders*. Washington, D.C.: Associated Publishers, 1970.

Dannett, Sylvia G. L. *Profiles of Negro Womanhood*. New York: M. W. Lads, 1964–66.

Da Point, Durant. "The Greatest Play of the South." *Tennessee Studies in Literature* 2 (1957): 15–24.

Davenport, F. Garvin, Jr. "Thomas Dixon's Mythology of Southern History." *Journal of Southern History* 36 (August 1970): 350–67.

Davis, Allen F. *Spearheads for Reform: The Social Settlements and the Progressive Movement, 1890–1914*. New York: Oxford University Press, 1967.

Davis, Angela Y. *Women, Race, and Class*. New York: Random House, 1981.

Davis, Denoral. "Toward a Socio-Historical and Demographic Portrait of Twentieth-Century African-Americans." In *Black Exodus: The Great Migration from the American South*, ed. Alferdteen Harrison, 1–19. Jackson: University Press of Mississippi, 1991.

Davis, Elizabeth L. *Lifting As They Climb: The National Association of Colored Women*. Washington, D.C.: National Association of Colored Women, 1933.

Davis, Marianna W., ed. *Contributions of Black Women to America*. Columbia, S.C.: Kenday Press, 1981.

Davis, Mollie C. "Southern Women, Social Reconstruction, and the Church in the 1920s." *Louisiana Studies* 13 (Winter 1974): 307–11.

Dean, Pamela. "Covert Curriculum: Class and Gender in a New South Woman's College." Ph.D. dissertation, University of North Carolina at Chapel Hill, 1995.

——. "Learning to Be New Women: Campus Culture at the North Carolina Normal and Industrial College." *North Carolina Historical Review* 67 (July 1991): 286–306.

——. *Women on the Hill: A History of Women at the University of North Carolina*. Chapel Hill: Division of Student Affairs, University of North Carolina, 1987.

Deaton, Thomas. "Atlanta during the Progressive Era." Ph.D. dissertation, University of Georgia, 1969.

Delany, Sarah, and A. Elizabeth Delany, with Amy Hill Hearth. *Having Our Say: The Delany Sisters' First 100 Years*. New York: Kodansha International, 1993.

Delap[p], Simon. "The Populist Party in North Carolina." *Trinity Archive* 14 (1922): 40–74.

Deutsch, Sarah. "Learning to Talk More Like a Man: Boston Women's Class-Bridging Organizations, 1870–1940." *American Historical Review* 97 (April 1992): 379–404.

Dill, Bonnie Thornton. "The Dialectics of Black Womanhood." *Signs* 4 (Spring 1979): 543–55.

Dittmer, John. *Black Georgia in the Progressive Era, 1900–1920*. Urbana: University of Illinois Press, 1977.

Dodson, Jualynne E. "Power and Surrogate Leadership: Black Women and Organized Religion." *Sage* 2 (Fall 1988): 40.

Dollard, John. *Caste and Class in a Southern Town*. 3d ed. Garden City, N.Y.: Doubleday, 1957.

Doss, Harriet E. Amos. "White and Black Female Missionaries to Former Slaves during Reconstruction." In *Stepping out of the Shadows: Alabama Women, 1819–1990*, ed. Mary Martha Thomas, 43–56. Tuscaloosa: University of Alabama Press, 1995.

Doyle, Don H. *New Men, New Cities, New South: Atlanta, Nashville, Charleston, and Mobile, 1860–1910*. Chapel Hill: University of North Carolina Press, 1990.

Dubbert, Joe L. *A Man's Place: Masculinity in Transition*. Englewood Cliffs, N.J.: Prentice Hall, 1979.

——. "Progressivism and the Masculinity Crisis." In *The American Man*, ed. Elizabeth H. Pleck and Joseph H. Pleck, 303–20. Englewood Cliffs, N.J.: Prentice Hall, 1980.

Du Bois, Ellen Carol. "The Radicalism of the Woman Suffrage Movement." *Feminist Studies* 3 (Fall 1975): 63–71.

——. "Working Women, Class Relations, and Suffrage Militance: Harriot Stanton Blatch and the New York Woman Suffrage Movement." *Journal of American History* 74 (June 1987): 1894–1909.

Du Bois, W. E. B. *The Autobiography of W. E. B. Du Bois: A Soliloquy on Viewing My Life from the Last Decade of Its First Century*. New York: International Publishers, 1968.

——. *Black Reconstruction: An Essay toward a History of the Part Which Black Folk Played in the Attempt to Reconstruct Democracy in America, 1860–1880*. New York: Harcourt, Brace, 1935.

Duster, Alfreda, ed. *Crusade for Justice: The Autobiography of Ida B. Wells*. Chicago: University of Chicago Press, 1970.

Dyer, Thomas G. "Higher Education in the South since the Civil War." In *The Web of Southern Social Relations: Women, Family, and Education*, ed. Walter J. Fraser, Jr., R. Frank Saunders, Jr., and Jon L. Wakelyn, 127–45. Athens: University of Georgia Press, 1985.

——. *Theodore Roosevelt and the Idea of Race*. Baton Rouge: Louisiana State University Press, 1980.

Dykeman, Wilma. *Prophet of Plenty: The First Ninety Years of W. D. Weatherford*. Knoxville: University of Tennessee Press, 1966.

Dykeman, Wilma, and James Stokely. *Seeds of Southern Change*. Chicago: University of Chicago Press, 1962.

Eagles, Charles W. *Jonathan Daniels and Race Relations: The Evolution of a Southern Liberal*. Knoxville: University of Tennessee Press, 1982.

Edmonds, Helen G. *The Negro and Fusion Politics in North Carolina, 1894–1901*. Chapel Hill: University of North Carolina Press, 1951.

Edwards, Laura. "Defiance and Protection: The Reconstruction-Era Struggle over Concepts of Womanhood in Granville County, North Carolina." Unpublished paper in author's possession.

——. *"Gendered Strife and Confusion": The Politics of Reconstruction*. Urbana: University of Illinois Press, forthcoming.

——. "The Politics of Manhood and Womanhood: Reconstruction in Granville County, North Carolina." Ph.D. dissertation, University of North Carolina at Chapel Hill, 1991.

——. "Sexual Violence, Gender, Reconstruction, and the Extension of Patriarchy in Granville County, North Carolina." *North Carolina Historical Review* 68 (July 1991): 237–60.

——. "'To Act Like Men': The Collapse of Radical Politics in a North Carolina County." Unpublished paper in author's possession.

Ellis, Richard J. *American Political Cultures*. New York: Oxford University Press, 1993.

Elmore, Joseph Elliot. "North Carolina Negro Congressmen, 1875–1901." Master's thesis, University of North Carolina at Chapel Hill, 1964.

Elshtain, Jean Bethke. *Public Man, Private Woman: Women and Social and Political Thought*. Princeton: Princeton University Press, 1981.

Enstam, Elizabeth York. "They Called It 'Motherhood': Dallas Women and Public Life, 1895–1918." In *Hidden Histories of Women in the New South*, ed. Virginia Bernhard, Betty Brandon, Elizabeth Fox-Genovese, Theda Perdue, and Elizabeth H. Turner, 71–95. Columbia: University of Missouri Press, 1994.

Epstein, Barbara Leslie. *The Politics of Domesticity: Women, Evangelism, and Temperance in Nineteenth-Century America*. Middletown, Conn.: Wesleyan University Press, 1981.

Escott, Paul D. *Many Excellent People: Power and Privilege in North Carolina, 1850–1900*. Chapel Hill: University of North Carolina Press, 1985.

Evans, Mercer Griffin. "A History of the Organized Labor Movement in Georgia." Ph.D. dissertation, University of Chicago, 1929.

Evans, Sarah M. "Women's History and Political Theory." In *Visible Women: New Essays on American Activism*, ed. Nancy A. Hewitt and Suzanne Lebsock, 119–39. Urbana: University of Illinois Press, 1993.

Evans, W. McKee. *Ballots and Fence Rails: Reconstruction on the Lower Cape Fear*. Chapel Hill: University of North Carolina Press, 1967.

Fahey, David M., ed. *The Collected Writings of Jessie Forsyth, 1847–1937: The Good Templars and Temperance Reform on Three Continents*. Lewiston, N.Y.: Edwin Mellen Press, 1988.

Farnham, Christie. *The Education of the Southern Belle: Higher Education and Student Socialization in the Antebellum South*. New York: New York University Press, 1994.

Fen, Sing Nan. "Notes on the Education of Negroes in North Carolina during the Civil War." *Journal of Negro Education* 36 (Winter 1967): 24–31.

Fields, Barbara Jeanne. "The Advent of Capitalist Agriculture: The New South in a Bourgeois World." In *Essays on the Postbellum Southern Economy*, ed. Thavolia Glymph and John J. Kushma, 73–94. College Station: Texas A & M University Press, 1985.

——. "Ideology and Race in American History." In *Region, Race, and Reconstruction: Essays in Honor of C. Vann Woodward*, ed. J. Morgan Kousser and James M. McPherson, 143–77. New York: Oxford University Press, 1992.

——. "Slavery, Race, and Ideology in the United States of America." *New Left Review* 181 (May–June 1990): 95–118.

Fields, Mamie Garvin, with Karen Fields. *Lemon Swamp and Other Places: A Carolina Memoir*. New York: Free Press, 1983.

Filene, Peter G. *Him/Her/Self: Sex Roles in Modern America*. Baltimore: Johns Hopkins University Press, 1986.

——. "An Obituary for the Progressive Movement." *American Quarterly* 22 (Spring 1970): 20–34.

Fink, Gary M. *The Fulton Bag and Cotton Mills Strike of 1914–1915: Espionage, Labor Conflict, and New South Industrial Relations*. Ithaca, N.Y.: ILR Press, 1993.

Firestone, Shulamith. *The Dialectic of Sex: The Case for Feminist Revolution*. New York: William Morrow, 1970.

Fisher, Cynthia Griggs. "The Effect of Higher Education on Black Tennesseans after the Civil War." *Phylon* 44 (September 1983): 204–16.

———. "A Survey of the Beginnings of Tennessee's Black Colleges and Universities, 1865–1920." *Tennessee Historical Quarterly* 39 (Summer 1980): 195–207.

Fisher, John E. *The John F. Slater Fund: A Nineteenth Century Affirmative Action for Negro Education*. Lanham, Md.: University Press of America, 1986.

Fitzpatrick, Ellen. *Endless Crusade: Women Social Scientists and Progressive Reform*. New York: Oxford University Press, 1990.

Flanagan, Maureen A. "Gender and Urban Political Reform: The City Club and the Woman's City Club of Chicago in the Progressive Era." *American Historical Review* 95 (October 1990): 1032–50.

Fleming, G. James, and Christian E. Burckel, eds. *Who's Who in Colored America*. Yonkers, N.Y.: Christian E. Burckel and Associates, 1950.

Flexnor, Eleanor. *Century of Struggle: The Woman's Rights Movement in the United States*. New York: Antheneum Press, 1973.

Fligstein, Neil. *Going North: Migration of Blacks and Whites from the South, 1900–1950*. New York: Academic Press, 1981.

Floyd, Josephine Bone. "Rebecca Latimer Felton, Champion of Women's Rights." *Georgia Historical Quarterly* 30 (June 1946): 81–104.

———. "Rebecca Latimer Felton, Political Independent." *Georgia Historical Quarterly* 30 (March 1946): 14–34.

Flusche, Michael. "On the Color Line: Charles Waddell Chesnutt." *North Carolina Historical Review* 53 (January 1976): 1–24.

Flynn, Joyce. "Melting Plots: Patterns of Racial and Ethnic Amalgamation in American Drama before Eugene O'Neill." *American Quarterly* 38 (1986): 417–38.

Foner, Eric. "The Meaning of Freedom in the Age of Emancipation." *Journal of American History* 81 (September 1994): 435–60.

Foner, Jack D. *Blacks and the Military in American History: A New Perspective*. New York: Praeger, 1974.

Foner, Philip. *Major Speeches by Negroes in the United States, 1797–1971*. New York: Simon and Schuster, 1972.

———. *Organized Labor and the Black Worker, 1619–1973*. New York: International Publishers, 1982.

Foster, Gaines M. *Ghosts of the Confederacy: Defeat, the Lost Cause, and the Emergence of the New South, 1865–1913*. New York: Oxford University Press, 1987.

Foucault, Michel. *Discipline and Punish*. New York: Vintage Books, 1979.

———. *The History of Sexuality*. New York: Pantheon, 1978.

Fowler, Robert Booth. *Carrie Catt: Feminist Politician*. Boston: Northeastern University Press, 1986.

Frankel, Nora Lee, and Nancy S. Dye. *Gender, Class, Race, and Reform in the Progressive Era*. Lexington: University Press of Kentucky, 1991.

Frankenburg, Ruth. *White Women, Race Matters: The Social Construction of Whiteness*. Minneapolis: University of Minnesota Press, 1993.

Franklin, Jimmy Lewis. "Black Southerners, Shared Experience, and Place: A Reflection." *Journal of Southern History* 60 (February 1994): 3–18.

Franklin, John Hope. "*The Birth of a Nation*: Propaganda as History." In *Race and History: Selected Essays, 1938–1988*, ed. John Hope Franklin, 10–23. Baton Rouge: Louisiana State University Press, 1989.

———. *The Free Negro in North Carolina, 1790–1860*. Chapel Hill: University of North Carolina Press, 1943.

———. *From Slavery to Freedom: A History of Negro Americans*. New York: Alfred A. Knopf, 1967.

———. "Slaves Virtually Free in Antebellum North Carolina." In *Race and History: Selected Essays, 1938–1988*, ed. John Hope Franklin, 73–91. Baton Rouge: Louisiana State University Press, 1989.

Franklin, John Hope, and August Meier, eds. *Black Leaders of the Twentieth Century*. Urbana: University of Illinois Press, 1982.

Franklin, Vincent P. "Whatever Happened to the College-Bred Negro?" *History of Education Quarterly* 24 (Fall 1984): 411–18.

Franklin, Vincent P., and James D. Anderson, eds. *New Perspectives on Black Educational History*. Boston: G. K. Hall, 1978.

Fraser, Nancy. "Rethinking the Public Sphere: A Contribution to the Critique of an Actually Existing Democracy." In *Habermas and the Public Sphere*, ed. Craig Calhoun, 109–42. Cambridge: Massachusetts Institute of Technology Press, 1992.

———. *Unruly Practices: Power, Discourse, and Gender in Contemporary Social Theory*. Minneapolis: University of Minnesota Press, 1989.

Fraser, Walter J., Jr., R. Frank Saunders, Jr., and Jon L. Wakelyn, eds. *The Web of Southern Social Relations: Women, Family, and Education*. Athens: University of Georgia Press, 1985.

Frazier, E. Franklin. *Black Bourgeoisie*. New York: Free Press, 1957.

———. *The Negro Church in America*. 1964. Reprint, New York: Schocken Books, 1974.

———. "The Negro in the Industrial South." *Nation* 125 (27 July 1927): 83–84.

Frederickson, Mary. "'Each One Is Dependent on the Other': Southern Churchwomen, Racial Reform, and the Process of Transformation, 1880–1940." In *Visible Women: New Essays on American Activism*, ed. Nancy A. Hewitt and Suzanne Lebsock, 296–324. Urbana: University of Illinois Press, 1993.

Fredrickson, George M. *The Arrogance of Race: Historical Perspectives on Slavery, Racism, and Social Inequality*. Middletown, Conn.: Wesleyan University Press, 1988.

———. *The Black Image in the White Mind: The Debate on Afro-American Character and Destiny, 1817–1914*. New York: Harper and Row, 1971.

Freedman, Estelle. "Separatism as Strategy: Female Institution Building and American Feminism, 1870–1930." *Feminist Studies* 5 (Fall 1979): 512–29.

Friedman, Jean E. *The Enclosed Garden: Women and Community in the Evangelical South, 1830–1900*. Chapel Hill: University of North Carolina Press, 1985.

Friedman, Lawrence Jacob. *The White Savage: Racial Fantasies in the Post-Bellum South*. Englewood Cliffs, N.J.: Prentice Hall, 1970.

Fuller, Paul E. *Laura Clay and the Woman's Rights Movement*. Lexington: University Press of Kentucky, 1975.

Gaston, Paul Morton. *The New South Creed: A Study in Southern Mythmaking*. New York: Alfred A. Knopf, 1970.

Gatewood, Willard B. "Alabama's Negro Soldier Experiment, 1898–1899." *Journal of Negro History* 57 (October 1972): 333–51.

———. *Aristocrats of Color: The Black Elite, 1880–1920*. Bloomington: Indiana University Press, 1990.

———. "Black Americans and the Quest for Empire, 1898–1903." *Journal of Southern History* 38 (November 1972): 545–66.

———. "Kansas Negroes and the Spanish-American War." *Kansas Historical Quarterly* 37 (Autumn 1971): 300–313.

———. "Negro Troops in Florida, 1898." *Florida Historical Quarterly* 49 (July 1970): 1–15.

———. "North Carolina's Negro Regiment in the Spanish-American War." *North Carolina Historical Review* 47 (October 1971): 370–87.

———. *"Smoked Yankees" and the Struggle for Empire: Letters from Negro Soldiers, 1898–1902*. Urbana: University of Illinois Press, 1971.

Gavins, Raymond. "Black Leadership in North Carolina to 1900." In *The Black Presence in North Carolina*, ed. Jeffrey J. Crow and Robert Winter, Jr., 1–8. Raleigh: North Carolina Museum of History, 1978.

———. "A Sin of Omission: Black Historiography in North Carolina." In *Black Americans in North Carolina and the South*, ed. Jeffrey J. Crow and Flora J. Hatley, 3–51. Chapel Hill: University of North Carolina Press, 1984.

Gay, Dorothy A. "Crisis of Identity: The Negro Community in Raleigh, 1890–1900." *North Carolina Historical Review* 50 (April 1973): 121–40.

Genovese, Eugene. *Roll, Jordan, Roll: The World the Slaves Made*. New York: Pantheon, 1974.

Gerard, Philip. *Cape Fear Rising*. Winston-Salem, N.C.: J. F. Blair, 1994.

Gibbs, Warmoth T. *History of North Carolina Agricultural and Technical College, Greensboro, North Carolina*. Dubuque, Iowa: William C. Brown, 1966.

Giddings, Paula. *When and Where I Enter: The Impact of Black Women on Race and Sex in America*. New York: William Morrow, 1984.

Gilbert, Dorothy L. *Guilford: A Quaker College*. Greensboro: Trustees of Guilford College, 1937.

Gilkes, Cheryl Townsend. "From Slavery to Social Welfare: Racism and the Control of Black Women." In *Class, Race, and Sex: The Dynamics of Control*, ed. Amy Swerdlow and Hanna Lessinger, 288–300. Boston: G. K. Hall, 1983.

———. " 'Holding Back the Ocean with a Broom': Black Women and Community Work." In *The Black Woman*, ed. LaFrances Rodgers-Rose. Beverly Hills, Calif.: Sage, 1980.

———. " 'Together and in Harness': Women's Traditions in the Sanctified Church." *Signs* 10 (Summer 1985): 678–99.

Gilmore, David D. *Manhood in the Making: Cultural Concepts of Masculinity*. New Haven: Yale University Press, 1990.

Gilmore, Glenda E. "Black Militia in the Spanish-American/Cuban War." In *The War of 1898 and U.S. Interventions, 1898–1934: An Encyclopedia*, ed. Benjamin R. Beede, 2:53–54. New York: Garland, 1994.

———. " 'We Can Go Where You Cannot Afford to Go': Intersections of Gender and Race in New South Political Praxis." In *New Viewpoints in Women's History: Working Papers from the Schlesinger Library Fiftieth Anniversary Conference, March 4–5, 1994*, ed. Susan Ware, 158–79. Cambridge: Arthur and Elizabeth Schlesinger Library on the History of Women in America, 1994.

Ginzburg, Lori. *Women and the Work of Benevolence: Morality, Politics, and Class in the Nineteenth-Century United States*. New Haven: Yale University Press, 1990.

Gleason, William. "Voices at the Nadir: Charles Chesnutt and David Bryant Fulton." *American Literary Realism* 24 (Spring 1992): 22–41.

Glenn, Joanne. "The Winston-Salem Riot of 1918." Master's thesis, University of North Carolina at Chapel Hill, 1979.

Glymph, Thavolia, and John J. Kushma, eds. *Essays on the Postbellum Southern Economy*. College Station: Texas A & M University Press, 1985.

Goings, Kenneth W. *The NAACP Comes of Age: The Defeat of Judge John J. Parker*. Bloomington: Indiana University Press, 1990.

Goldhaber, Michael. "A Mission Unfulfilled: Freedman's Education in North Carolina, 1865–1870." *Journal of Negro History* 77 (Fall 1992): 199–210.

Goodwyn, Lawrence. "Populist Dreams and Negro Rights: East Texas as a Case Study." *American Historical Review* 76 (December 1971): 1435–56.

———. *The Populist Moment: A Short History of the Agrarian Revolt in America*. New York: Oxford University Press, 1978.

Gordon, Elizabeth Putnam. *Women Torch-Bearers: The Story of the Woman's Christian Temperance Union*. Evanston, Ill.: National Woman's Christian Temperance Union Publishing House, 1924.

Gordon, Linda. "Black and White Visions of Welfare: Women's Welfare Activism, 1890–1945." *Journal of American History* 78 (September 1991): 559–90.

———, ed. *Women, the State, and Welfare*. Madison: University of Wisconsin Press, 1990.

Gordon, Lynn D. *Gender and Higher Education in the Progressive Era*. New Haven: Yale University Press, 1990.

Gorn, Elliot J. "'Gouge and Bite, Pull Hair and Scratch': The Social Significance of Fighting in the Southern Backcountry." *American Historical Review* 90 (February 1985): 18–43.

Grantham, Dewey W. "The Progressive Movement and the Negro." *South Atlantic Quarterly* 54 (October 1955): 461–77.

———. *Southern Progressivism: The Reconciliation of Progress and Tradition*. Knoxville: University of Tennessee Press, 1983.

Graves, John William. "Jim Crow in Arkansas: A Reconsideration of Urban Race Relations in the Post-Reconstruction South." *Journal of Southern History* 55 (August 1989): 421–48.

———. *Town and Country: Race Relations in an Urban-Rural Context, Arkansas, 1865–1905*. Fayetteville: University of Arkansas Press, 1990.

Green, Dan S., and Earl Smith. "W. E. B. Du Bois and the Concepts of Race and Class." *Phylon* 44 (December 1983): 262–72.

Green, Elna. "'Ideals of Government, of Home, and of Women': The Ideology of Southern White Antisuffragism." In *Hidden Histories of Women in the New South*, ed. Virginia Bernhard, Betty Brandon, Elizabeth Fox-Genovese, Theda Perdue, and Elizabeth H. Turner, 96–113. Columbia: University of Missouri Press, 1994.

————. "Those Opposed: Southern Antisuffragism, 1890–1920." Ph.D. dissertation, Tulane University, 1992.

————. "Those Opposed: The Antisuffragists in North Carolina, 1900–1920." *North Carolina Historical Review* 67 (July 1990): 315–33.

Green, Fletcher M., ed. *Essays in Southern History*. Chapel Hill: University of North Carolina Press, 1949.

Green, John B., III. *A New Bern Album: Old Photographs of New Bern, North Carolina, and Surrounding Countryside*. New Bern: Tryon Palace Commission, 1985.

Greenberg, Kenneth S. "The Nose, the Lie, and the Duel in the Antebellum South." *American Historical Review* 95 (February 1990): 57–74.

Greenwood, Janette Thomas. *Bittersweet Legacy: The Black and White "Better Classes" in Charlotte, 1850–1910*. Chapel Hill: University of North Carolina Press, 1994.

Griggs, A. C. "Lucy Craft Laney." *Journal of Negro History* 19 (January 1934): 97–102.

Gross, Seymour, and John Edward Hardy, eds. *Images of the Negro in American Literature*. Chicago: University of Chicago Press, 1966.

Grossman, James R. *Land of Hope: Chicago, Black Southerners, and the Great Migration*. Chicago: University of Chicago Press, 1989.

Gusfield, Joseph R. *Symbolic Crusade: Status Politics and the American Temperance Movement*. Urbana: University of Illinois Press, 1963.

Gutman, Herbert G. *The Black Family in Slavery and Freedom, 1750–1925*. New York: Pantheon, 1976.

————. *Work, Culture, and Society in Industrializing America*. New York: Vintage Books, 1976.

Guy-Sheftall, Beverly. "Black Women and Higher Education: Spelman and Bennett Colleges Revisited." *Journal of Negro Education* 51 (Summer 1982): 278–87.

————. *"Daughters of Sorrow": Attitudes toward Black Women, 1880–1920*. New York: Carlson, 1990.

Habermas, Jurgen. *The Structural Transformation of the Public Sphere: An Inquiry into a Category of Bourgeois Society*. Cambridge: Massachusetts Institute of Technology Press, 1989.

Hahn, Steven. "Class and State in Postemancipation Societies: Southern Planters in Comparative Perspective." *American Historical Review* 95 (February 1990): 99–123.

————. *The Roots of Southern Populism: Yeoman Farmers and the Transformation of the Georgia Upcountry, 1850–1890*. New York: Oxford University Press, 1983.

Haley, John. *Charles N. Hunter and Race Relations in North Carolina*. Chapel Hill: University of North Carolina Press, 1987.

Hall, Jacquelyn Dowd. "Disorderly Women: Gender and Labor Militancy in the Appalachian South." *Journal of American History* 73 (September 1986): 354–82.

————. "Location, Location, Location." In *New Viewpoints in Women's History: Working Papers from the Schlesinger Library Fiftieth Anniversary Conference, March 4–5, 1994*, ed. Susan Ware, 40–52. Cambridge: Arthur and Elizabeth Schlesinger Library on the History of Women in America, 1994.

————. "'The Mind That Burns in Each Body': Women, Rape, and Racial Violence." In *Powers of Desire: The Politics of Sexuality*, ed. Ann Snitow, Christine

Stansell, and Sharon Thompson, 328–49. New York: Monthly Review Press, 1983.

———. "O. Delight Smith's Progressive Era: Labor, Feminism, and Reform in the Urban South—Atlanta, Georgia, 1907–1915." In *Visible Women: New Essays on American Activism*, ed. Nancy Hewitt and Suzanne Lebsock, 166–98. Urbana: University of Illinois Press, 1993.

———. *Revolt against Chivalry: Jessie Daniel Ames and the Women's Campaign against Lynching*. Rev. ed. New York: Columbia University Press, 1993.

Hall, Jacquelyn Dowd, James L. Leloudis, Robert R. Korstad, Mary Murphy, Lu Ann Jones, and Christopher B. Daly. *Like a Family: The Making of a Southern Cotton Mill World*. Chapel Hill: University of North Carolina Press, 1987.

Hall, Jacquelyn Dowd, and Anne Firor Scott. "Women in the South." In *Interpreting Southern History: Historiographical Essays in Honor of Sanford W. Higginbotham*, ed. John B. Boles and Evelyn Thomas Nolen, 454–509. Baton Rouge: Louisiana State University Press, 1987.

Halliburton, Cecil D. *A History of Saint Augustine's College, 1867–1937*. Raleigh: Saint Augustine's College, 1937.

Hamilton, J. G. De Roulhac. *Reconstruction in North Carolina*. New York: Columbia University, 1914.

Hanchett, Thomas W. "The Rosenwald Schools and Black Education in North Carolina." *North Carolina Historical Review* 64 (October 1988): 387–427.

Harding, Vincent. *There Is a River: The Black Struggle for Freedom in America*. New York: Harcourt Brace Jovanovich, 1981.

Harlan, Louis R. *Booker T. Washington: The Making of a Black Leader, 1856–1901*. New York: Oxford University Press, 1972.

———. *Booker T. Washington: The Wizard of Tuskegee, 1901–1915*. New York: Oxford University Press, 1983.

———. *Separate and Unequal: Public School Campaigns in the Southern Seaboard States, 1901–1915*. New York: Atheneum, 1968.

Harley, Sharon. "Anna J. Cooper." In *The Afro-American Woman: Struggles and Images*, ed. Sharon Harley and Rosalyn Terborg-Penn, 87–96. Port Washington, N.Y.: National University Publications, 1978.

———. "For the Good of Family and Race: Gender, Work, and Domestic Roles in the Black Community, 1880–1930." *Signs* 15 (Winter 1990): 336–49.

———. " 'When Your Work Is Not Who You Are': The Development of a Working-Class Consciousness among Afro-American Women." In *Gender, Class, Race, and Reform in the Progressive Era*, ed. Noralee Frankel and Nancy S. Dye, 42–55. Lexington: University Press of Kentucky, 1991.

Harley, Sharon, and Rosalyn Terborg-Penn. *The Afro-American Woman: Struggles and Images*. Port Washington, N.Y.: National University Publications, 1978.

Harris, Fredrick C. "Something Within: Religion as a Mobilizer of African-American Political Activism." *Journal of Politics* 56 (February 1994): 42–68.

Hart, James D. *A Companion to California*. New York: Oxford University Press, 1978.

Harvey, Claire. "The Black Woman: Keepers of the Faith." *Church Woman* 35 (November 1969): 15–18.

Hauck, Thomas H. "A Newspaper History of Race Relations in Durham, 1910–1940." Master's thesis, Duke University, 1941.

Haws, Robert, ed. *The Age of Segregation: Race Relations in the South, 1890–1945.* Jackson: University Press of Mississippi, 1978.

Hays, Samuel P. "The Politics of Reform in Municipal Government in the Progressive Era." *Pacific Northwest Quarterly* 55 (October 1964): 157–69.

——. *The Response to Industrialism, 1885–1914.* Chicago: University of Chicago Press, 1957.

Hendrick, Burton J. *The Life and Letters of Walter H. Page.* Garden City, N.Y.: Doubleday, Page, 1925.

Herndon, Jane Walker. "The Phasing Out of the Savannah Negro Militia." *Atlanta Historical Bulletin* 19, no. 3 (1975): 42–49.

Hewitt, Nancy A. "Beyond the Search for Sisterhood: American Women's History in the 1980s." *Social History* 10 (October 1985): 299–321.

——. "Compounding Differences." *Feminist Studies* 18 (Summer 1992): 313–26.

——. "In Pursuit of Power: The Political Economy of Women's Activism in Twentieth-Century Tampa." In *Visible Women: New Essays on American Activism*, ed. Nancy A. Hewitt and Suzanne Lebsock, 199–222. Urbana: University of Illinois Press, 1993.

——. "Politicizing Domesticity: Anglo, Black, and Latin Women in Tampa's Progressive Movements." In *Gender, Class, Race, and Reform in the Progressive Era*, ed. Noralee Frankel and Nancy S. Dye, 24–41. Lexington: University Press of Kentucky, 1991.

——. "Varieties of Voluntarism: Class, Ethnicity, and Women's Politics in Tampa, Florida." In *Women, Politics, and Change*, ed. Louise A. Tilly and Patricia Gurin, 63–86. New York: Russell Sage Foundation, 1990.

——. *Women's Activism and Social Change: Rochester, New York, 1822–1872.* Ithaca, N.Y.: Cornell University Press, 1984.

Hewitt, Nancy A., and Suzanne Lebsock, eds. *Visible Women: New Essays on American Activism.* Urbana: University of Illinois Press, 1993.

Hickerson, Thomas Felix. *Happy Valley: History and Genealogy.* Chapel Hill: Privately published, 1940.

Hicks, John D. "The Farmers' Alliance in North Carolina." *North Carolina Historical Review* 2 (April 1925): 162–87.

Higginbotham, Evelyn Brooks. "African-American Women's History and the Metalanguage of Race." *Signs* 17 (Winter 1992): 251–74.

——. "Beyond the Sound of Silence: Afro-American Women's History." *Gender and History* 1 (Spring 1989): 50–67.

——. "The Feminist Theology of the Black Baptist Church, 1880–1900." In *Class, Race, and Sex: The Dynamics of Control*, ed. Amy Swerdlow and Hanna Lessinger. Boston: G. K. Hall, 1983.

——. "Rethinking the Subject of African American Women's History." In *New Viewpoints in Women's History: Working Papers from the Schlesinger Library Fiftieth Anniversary Conference, March 4–5, 1994*, ed. Susan Ware, 64–69. Cambridge: Arthur and Elizabeth Schlesinger Library on the History of Women in America, 1994.

———. *Righteous Discontent: The Women's Movement in the Black Baptist Church, 1880–1920*. Cambridge: Harvard University Press, 1993.

———. "The Women's Movement in the Black Baptist Church, 1880–1920." Ph.D. dissertation, University of Rochester, 1984.

Higuchi, Hayumi. "White Supremacy on the Cape Fear: The Wilmington Affair of 1898." Master's thesis, University of North Carolina at Chapel Hill, 1980.

Hill, Kenneth. "Politics and Participation in the Black Church." *Western Journal of Black Studies* 14 (Summer 1990): 123–35.

Hill, Samuel S., Jr. *Religion and the Solid South*. Nashville: Abingdon Press, 1972.

Hine, Darlene Clark. *Black Women in White: Racial Conflict in the Nursing Profession, 1890–1950*. Bloomington: Indiana University Press, 1989.

———. "Rape and the Inner Lives of Black Women in the Middle West: Preliminary Thoughts on the Culture of Dissemblance." *Signs* 14 (Summer 1989): 912–20.

———. "'We Specialize in the Wholly Impossible': The Philanthropic Work of Black Women." In *Lady Bountiful Revisited: Women, Philanthropy, and Power*, ed. Kathleen McCarthy, 70–93. New Brunswick, N.J.: Rutgers University Press, 1990.

———, ed. *Black Women in America: An Historical Encyclopedia*. New York: Carlson, 1993.

Hodes, Martha. "Romantic Love across the Color Line: White Women and Black Men in Nineteenth Century America." In *New Viewpoints in Women's History: Working Papers from the Schlesinger Library Fiftieth Anniversary Conference, March 4–5, 1994*, ed. Susan Ware, 81–98. Cambridge: Arthur and Elizabeth Schlesinger Library on the History of Women in America, 1994.

———. "Sex across the Color Line: White Women and Black Men in the Nineteenth-Century South." Ph.D. dissertation, Princeton University, 1991.

———. "The Sexualization of Reconstruction Politics: White Women and Black Men in the South after the Civil War." *Journal of the History of Sexuality* 3 (January 1993): 402–17.

Hofstadter, Richard. *The Age of Reform: From Bryan to F.D.R.* New York: Alfred A. Knopf, 1955.

———. *The American Political Tradition and the Men Who Made It*. New York: Alfred A. Knopf, 1948.

Holder, Rose Howell. *McIver of North Carolina*. Chapel Hill: University of North Carolina Press, 1957.

Holt, Rackham. *Mary McLeod Bethune: A Biography*. Garden City, N.Y.: Doubleday, 1964.

Holt, Sharon Ann. "Making Freedom Pay: Freedpeople Working for Themselves—North Carolina, 1865–1900." *Journal of Southern History* 60 (May 1994): 229–62.

Holt, Thomas C. "'An Empire over the Mind': Emancipation, Race, and Ideology in the British West Indies and the American South." In *Region, Race, and Reconstruction*, ed. J. Morgan Kousser and James M. McPherson, 283–313. New York: Oxford University Press, 1982.

———. "Marking: Race, Race-making, and the Writing of History." *American Historical Review* 100 (February 1995): 1–20.

———. "The Political Uses of Alienation: W. E. B. Du Bois on Politics, Race, and Culture." *American Quarterly* 42 (June 1990): 301–23.

———. *The Problem of Freedom: Race, Labor, and Politics in Jamaica and Britain, 1832–1938*. Baltimore: Johns Hopkins University Press, 1992.

hooks, bell. *Ain't I a Woman?: Black Women and Feminism*. Boston: South End Press, 1981.

———. *Feminist Theory from Margin to Center*. Boston: South End Press, 1984.

———. *Talking Back: Thinking Feminist, Thinking Black*. Boston: South End Press, 1989.

Horowitz, Helen Lefkowitz. *Alma Mater: Design and Experience in the Women's Colleges from Their Nineteenth-Century Beginnings to the 1930s*. New York: Alfred A. Knopf, 1984.

Horton, Paul. "Testing the Limits of Class Politics in Postbellum Alabama: Agrarian Radicalism in Lawrence County." *Journal of Southern History* 57 (February 1991): 63–84.

Howe, Florence. *Myths of Coeducation: Selected Essays, 1964–1983*. Bloomington: Indiana University Press, 1984.

Hudson, Gossie Harold. "North Carolina Blacks and the Professions." In *Paths toward Freedom*, ed. Doris Lucas, Tom Parramore, and Earlie Thorpe, 53–68. Raleigh: Center for Urban Affairs, North Carolina State University, 1976.

Hughes, Ruth Anita Hawkins. *Contributions of Vance County People of Color*. Raleigh: Sparks Press, 1988.

Hughes, William Hardin, and Frederick D. Patterson, eds. *Robert Russa Moton of Hampton and Tuskegee*. Chapel Hill: University of North Carolina Press, 1956.

Hull, Gloria T., ed. *Give Us Each Day: The Diary of Alice Dunbar-Nelson*. New York: W. W. Norton, 1984.

Hull, Gloria T., Patricia Bell Scott, and Barbara Smith, eds. *All the Women Are White, All the Blacks Are Men, but Some of Us Are Brave: Black Women's Studies*. Old Westbury, N.Y.: Feminist Press, 1982.

Humphreys, Margaret. *Yellow Fever and the South*. New Brunswick, N.J.: Rutgers University Press, 1992.

Hunt, James L. "The Making of a Populist: Marion Butler, 1863–1895." *North Carolina Historical Review* 62 (January 1985): 53–77, (April 1985): 170–202, (July 1985): 317–43.

Hunt, Michael H. *Ideology and U.S. Foreign Policy*. New Haven: Yale University Press, 1987.

Hunter, Tera W. " 'The Correct Thing': Charlotte Hawkins Brown and the Palmer Institute." *Southern Exposure* 11 (September/October 1983): 37–43.

———. "Domination and Resistance: The Politics of Wage Household Labor in New South Atlanta." *Labor History* 34 (Spring/Summer 1993): 205–20.

———. "Household Laborers and Work in the Making: Afro-American Women in Atlanta and the Urban South, 1861–1920." Ph.D. dissertation, Yale University, 1991.

Hurtado, Aida. "Relating to Privilege: Seduction and Rejection in the Subordination of White Women and Women of Color." *Signs* 14 (Summer 1989): 833–55.

Hutchinson, Louise Daniel. *Anna J. Cooper: A Voice from the South*. Washington, D.C.: Smithsonian Institution Press, 1981.

Huthmacher, J. Joseph. "Urban Liberalism and the Age of Reform." *Mississippi Valley Historical Review* 44 (September 1962): 231–41.

Ingalls, Robert P. *Urban Vigilantes in the New South, 1882–1936*. Knoxville: University of Tennessee Press, 1988.

Ingle, H. Larry. "A Southern Democrat at Large: William H. Kitchen and the Populist Party." *North Carolina Historical Review* 48 (April 1968): 178–94.

Inscoe, John. "*The Clansman* on Stage and Screen." *North Carolina Historical Review* 64 (April 1987): 139–61.

Irwin, Inez Haynes. *The Story of the Woman's Party*. New York: Harcourt, Brace, 1921.

Jagger, Alison M. *Feminist Politics and Human Nature*. Totowa, N.J.: Rowman and Allanheld, 1983.

Janiewski, Dolores. *Sisterhood Denied: Race, Gender, and Class in a New South Community*. Philadelphia: Temple University Press, 1985.

Jaynes, Gerald David. *Branches without Roots: Genesis of the Black Working Class in the American South, 1862–1882*. New York: Oxford University Press, 1986.

Jenkins, Clara Barnes. "An Historical Study of Shaw University, 1865–1963." Ed.D. dissertation, University of Pittsburgh, 1965.

Jenkins, Maude Thomas. "The History of the Black Woman's Club Movement in America." Ed.D. dissertation, Columbia University Teachers College, 1984.

———. "She Issued the Call: Josephine St. Pierre Ruffin." *Sage* 5 (Fall 1988): 75.

Johnson, Charles S. *The Negro College Graduate*. Chapel Hill: University of North Carolina Press, 1938.

Johnson, Daniel M., and Rex R. Campbell. *Black Migration in America: A Social Demographic History*. Durham: Duke University Press, 1981.

Johnson, Guion Griffis. "The Ideology of White Supremacy, 1876–1910." In *Essays in Southern History*, ed. Fletcher M. Green, 124–56. Chapel Hill: University of North Carolina Press, 1949.

———. "Southern Paternalism toward Negroes after Emancipation." *Journal of Southern History* 23 (November 1957): 483–509.

Johnson, Kenneth R. "Kate Gordon and the Woman Suffrage Movement in the South." *Journal of Southern History* 38 (August 1972): 365–92.

———. "White Racial Attitudes as a Factor in the Arguments against the Nineteenth Amendment." *Phylon* 31 (Spring 1970): 31–37.

Johnston, James Hugo. "Miscegenation in the Ante-Bellum South." Ph.D. dissertation, University of Chicago, 1937.

———. *Race Relations in Virginia and Miscegenation in the South, 1776–1860*. Amherst: University of Massachusetts Press, 1970.

Jones, Adrienne Lash. *Jane Edna Hunter: A Case Study of Black Leadership, 1910–1950*. New York: Carlson, 1990.

Jones, Jacqueline. *The Dispossessed: America's Underclasses from the Civil War to the Present*. New York: Basic Books, 1992.

———. "Encounters, Likely and Unlikely, between Blacks and Poor White Women in the Rural South, 1865–1940." *Georgia Historical Quarterly* 76 (Summer 1992): 333–53.

———. *Labor of Love, Labor of Sorrow: Black Women, Work, and the Family from Slavery to the Present*. New York: Basic Books, 1985.

——. *Soldiers of Light and Love: Northern Teachers and Georgia Blacks, 1865–1873*. Chapel Hill: University of North Carolina Press, 1980.

——. "Women Who Were More Than Men: Sex and Status in Freedman's Teaching." *History of Education Quarterly* 19 (Spring 1979): 476–95.

Jones, Lance G. E. *The Jeanes Teacher in the United States, 1908–1933*. Chapel Hill: University of North Carolina Press, 1937.

Jones, Marcus E. *Black Migration in the United States with Emphasis on Selected Central Cities*. Saratoga, Calif.: Century Twenty-One Publications, 1980.

Jones, Maxine Deloris. "'A Glorious Work': The American Missionary Association and Black North Carolinians, 1863–1990." Ph.D. dissertation, Florida State University, 1982.

Jones, Theron P. "The Gubernatorial Election of 1892 in North Carolina." Master's thesis, University of North Carolina at Chapel Hill, 1949.

Joyner, Charles W. *Down by the Riverside: A South Carolina Slave Community*. Urbana: University of Illinois Press, 1984.

Kantrowitz, Steven D. "'No Middle Ground': Gender-Protection and the Wilmington 'Riot' of 1898." Unpublished paper in author's possession.

Karina, Stephen Joseph. "'With Flaming Sword': The Reactionary Rhetoric of Thomas Dixon." Ph.D. dissertation, University of Georgia, 1978.

Kars, Marjolein. "Limelight and Lily White: Female Woman Suffragists in N.C., 1913–1920." Honors thesis, Duke University, 1982.

Kasson, John F. *Amusing the Million: Coney Island at the Turn of the Century*. New York: Hill and Wang, 1978.

Keller, Frances Richardson. *An American Crusade: The Life of Charles Waddell Chesnutt*. Provo, Utah: Brigham Young University Press, 1978.

Keller, Rosemary Skinner, Louise L. Queen, and Hilah F. Thomas, eds. *Women in New Worlds: Historical Perspectives on the Wesleyan Tradition*. Nashville: Abingdon Press, 1981.

Kelley, Robin D. G. *Hammer and Hoe: Alabama Communists during the Great Depression*. Chapel Hill: University of North Carolina Press, 1990.

——. "Notes on Deconstructing 'The Folk.'" *American Historical Review* 97 (December 1992): 1400.

——. *Race Rebels: Culture, Politics, and the Black Working Class*. New York: Free Press, 1994.

——. "The Riddle of the Zoot: Malcolm Little and Black Cultural Politics during World War II." In *Malcolm X: In Our Own Image*, ed. Joe Wood, 155–82. New York: St. Martin's Press, 1992.

——. "'We Are Not What We Seem': Rethinking Black Working-Class Opposition in the Jim Crow South." *Journal of American History* 80 (June 1993): 75–112.

Kenzer, Robert. "The Black Businessman in the Postwar South: North Carolina, 1865–1880." *Business History Review* 63 (Spring 1989): 61–87.

Kerber, Linda. "The Republican Mother: Women and the Enlightenment—An American Perspective." *American Quarterly* 28 (1976): 187–205.

Kessler-Harris, Alice. *Out to Work: A History of Wage-Earning Women in the United States*. New York: Oxford University Press, 1982.

Kett, Joseph F. "Women and the Progressive Impulse in Southern Education."

In *The Web of Southern Social Relations: Women, Family, and Education*, ed. Walter J. Fraser, Jr., R. Frank Saunders, Jr., and Jon L. Wakelyn, 166–80. Athens: University of Georgia Press, 1985.

Key, V. O. *Southern Politics in State and Nation*. New York: Alfred A. Knopf, 1949.

King, Deborah K. "Multiple Jeopardy, Multiple Consciousness: The Context of a Black Feminist Ideology." *Signs* 14 (Winter 1988): 42–72.

King, William Eskridge. "The Era of Progressive Reform in Southern Education: The Growth of Public Schools in North Carolina, 1885–1910." Ph.D. dissertation, Duke University, 1969.

Kinney, James. *Amalgamation!: Race, Sex, and Rhetoric in the Nineteenth-Century American Novel*. Westport, Conn.: Greenwood Press, 1985.

Kirby, Jack Temple. *Darkness at the Dawning: Race and Reform in the Progressive South*. Philadelphia: Lippincott, 1972.

———. "The Southern Exodus, 1910–1960." *Journal of Southern History* 49 (November 1983): 585–600.

Kloppenberg, James T. *Uncertain Victory: Social Democracy and Progressivism in European and American Thought, 1870–1920*. New York: Oxford University Press, 1986.

Knotts, Alice. "Race Relations in the 1920s: A Challenge to Southern Methodist Women." *Methodist History* 26 (July 1990): 212.

Kolko, Gabriel. *The Triumph of Conservatism: A Re-Interpretation of American History, 1900–1916*. New York: Free Press, 1963.

Kousser, J. Morgan. "Progressivism—For Middle-Class Whites Only: North Carolina Education, 1880–1910." *Journal of Southern History* 46 (May 1980): 168–94.

———. *The Shaping of Southern Politics and the Establishment of the One-Party South, 1880–1910*. New Haven: Yale University Press, 1974.

Kousser, J. Morgan, and James M. McPherson. *Region, Race, and Reconstruction: Essays in Honor of C. Vann Woodward*. New York: Oxford University Press, 1982.

Kraditor, Aileen S. *The Ideas of the Woman Suffrage Movement, 1890–1920*. New York: Columbia University Press, 1965.

———. "Tactical Problems of the Woman Suffrage Movement in the South." *Louisiana Studies* 5 (Winter 1966): 289–307.

———. *Up from the Pedestal: Selected Writings in the History of American Feminism*. Chicago: Quadrangle Books, 1968.

Krause, Paul. *The Battle for Homestead: Politics, Culture, and Steel*. Pittsburgh: University of Pittsburgh Press, 1992.

Lamon, Lester C. *Black Tennesseans, 1900–1930*. Knoxville: University of Tennessee Press, 1977.

Landes, Joan. *Women and the Public Sphere in the Age of the French Revolution*. Ithaca, N.Y.: Cornell University Press, 1988.

Larsen, Lawrence H. *The Rise of the Urban South*. Lexington: University Press of Kentucky, 1985.

Larson, Karl. "A Separate Reality: The Development of Racial Segregation in Raleigh, North Carolina, 1865–1915." Master's thesis, University of North Carolina at Greensboro, 1983.

Lasch-Quinn, Elisabeth. *Black Neighbors: Race and the Limits of Reform in the Ameri-*

can *Settlement House Movement, 1890–1945*. Chapel Hill: University of North Carolina Press, 1993.

Lassiter, Mrs. J. J. *Mount Zion Woman's Missionary Union History, 1906–1956*. N.p., [1956].

Lawson, Ellen N. "Sarah Woodson Early: Nineteenth Century Black Nationalist 'Sister.'" *UMOJA* 2 (Summer 1981): 22–23.

Lebsock, Suzanne. *The Free Women of Petersburg: Status and Culture in a Southern Town, 1784–1860*. New York: W. W. Norton, 1984.

———. "Woman Suffrage and White Supremacy: A Virginia Case Study." In *Visible Women: New Essays on American Activism*, ed. Nancy A. Hewitt and Suzanne Lebsock, 62–100. Urbana: University of Illinois Press, 1993.

———. "Women and American Politics, 1880–1920." In *Women, Politics, and Change*, ed. Louise A. Tilly and Patricia Gurin, 35–62. New York: Russell Sage Foundation, 1990.

Lee, Lauranette. "More Than an Image: Black Women Reformers in Richmond, Virginia, 1910–1928." Master's thesis, Virginia State University, 1993.

Lefler, Hugh T. *North Carolina History as Told by Contemporaries*. Chapel Hill: University of North Carolina Press, 1965.

Lefler, Hugh T., and Albert Ray Newsome. *North Carolina: The History of a Southern State*. Chapel Hill: University of North Carolina Press, 1973.

Leloudis, James. "'A More Certain Means of Grace': Pedagogy, Self, and Society in North Carolina, 1880–1920." Ph.D. dissertation, University of North Carolina at Chapel Hill, 1989.

———. "School Reform in the New South: The Woman's Association for the Betterment of Public School Houses in North Carolina, 1902–1919." *Journal of American History* 69 (March 1983): 886–909.

Lemons, J. Stanley. *The Woman Citizen: Social Feminism in the 1920s*. Urbana: University of Illinois Press, 1973.

Lerner, Gerda. "Community Work of Black Club Women." *Journal of Negro History* 59 (1974): 158–67.

———. "The Lady and the Mill Girl: Changes in the Social Status of Women in the Age of Jackson." In *A Heritage of Her Own: Toward a New Social History of American Women*, ed. Nancy F. Cott and Elizabeth Pleck, 182–96. New York: Simon and Schuster, 1979.

———, ed. *Black Women in White America: A Documentary History*. New York: Vintage Books, 1972.

———. *The Majority Finds Its Past*. New York: Oxford University Press, 1979.

Levine, Lawrence. *Black Culture and Black Consciousness: Afro-American Folk Thought from Slavery to Freedom*. New York: Oxford University Press, 1977.

Lewinson, Paul. *Race, Class, and Party: A History of Negro Suffrage and White Politics in the South*. New York: Grosset and Dunlap, 1959.

Lewis, Daniel Levering. *W. E. B. Du Bois: Biography of a Race, 1868–1919*. New York: Henry Holt, 1993.

Lewis, Earl. *In Their Own Interests: Race, Class, and Power in Twentieth-Century Norfolk, Virginia*. Berkeley: University of California Press, 1991.

Lincoln, C. Eric. *The Black Church since Frazier*. New York: Schocken Books, 1974.

Lincoln, C. Eric, and Lawrence H. Mamiya. *The Black Church in the African-American Experience*. Durham: Duke University Press, 1990.

Link, Arthur S. "Correspondence Relating to the Progressive Party's 'Lily White' Policy in 1912." *Journal of Southern History* 10 (November 1944): 480–90.

———. "The Progressive Movement in the South, 1870–1914." *North Carolina Historical Review* 23 (April 1946): 172–95.

———. "What Happened to the Progressive Movement in the 1920s?" *American Historical Review* 64 (July 1959): 833–51.

Link, William A. *A Hard Country and a Lonely Place: Schooling, Society, and Reform in Rural Virginia, 1870–1920*. Chapel Hill: University of North Carolina Press, 1986.

———. *The Paradox of Southern Progressivism, 1880–1930*. Chapel Hill: University of North Carolina Press, 1992.

———. "Privies, Progressivism, and Public Schools: Health Reform and Education in the Rural South, 1909–1920." *Journal of Southern History* 54 (November 1988): 623–42.

Little, Monroe. "Extra-Curricular Activities of Black College Students, 1868–1940." *Journal of Negro History* 65 (Spring 1980): 135–48.

Littlefield, Valinda Rogers. "After Teacher Training, What?" Unpublished paper in author's possession.

———. " 'What I Ought to Do, by the Grace of God, I Will Do': Southern Black Female School Teachers, 1884–1954." Ph.D. dissertation, University of Illinois at Urbana, forthcoming.

Litwak, Leon F. *Been in the Storm So Long: The Aftermath of Slavery*. New York: Alfred A. Knopf, 1979.

Litwak, Leon F., and August Meier. *Black Leaders of the Nineteenth Century*. Urbana: University of Illinois Press, 1988.

Lockhart, Walter Samuel, III. "Lynching in North Carolina, 1888–1906." Master's thesis, University of North Carolina at Chapel Hill, 1972.

Loewenberg, Bert James, and Ruth Bogin, eds. *Black Women in Nineteenth-Century American Life: Their Words, Their Thoughts, Their Feelings*. University Park: Pennsylvania State University Press, 1976.

Logan, Frenise A. "Black and Republican: Vicissitudes of a Minority Twice Over in the North Carolina House of Representatives, 1876–1877." *North Carolina Historical Review* 61 (July 1984): 311–46.

———. "The Economic Status of the Town Negro in Post-Reconstruction North Carolina." *North Carolina Historical Review* 35 (October 1958): 448–60.

———. "The Legal Status of Public School Education for Negroes in North Carolina, 1877–1894." *North Carolina Historical Review* 32 (July 1955): 346–57.

———. "The Movement in North Carolina to Establish a State Supported College for Negroes." *North Carolina Historical Review* 35 (April 1958): 167–80.

———. "The Movement of Negroes from North Carolina, 1876–1894." *North Carolina Historical Review* 35 (January 1958): 45–65.

———. *The Negro in North Carolina, 1876–1894*. Chapel Hill: University of North Carolina Press, 1964.

Logan, Rayford W. *The Betrayal of the Negro, from Rutherford B. Hayes to Woodrow Wilson*. New York: Macmillan, 1965.

Loveland, Anne C. *Southern Evangelicals and the Social Order, 1800–1860*. Baton Rouge: Louisiana State University Press, 1980.

Lucas, Doris, Tom Parramore, and Earlie Thorpe, eds. *Paths toward Freedom*. Raleigh: Center for Urban Affairs, North Carolina State University, 1976.

Luker, Paul. *The Social Gospel in Black and White: American Racial Reform, 1885–1912*. Chapel Hill: University of North Carolina Press, 1991.

Lynn, Susan. *Progressive Women in Conservative Times: Racial Justice, Peace, and Feminism*. New Brunswick, N.J.: Rutgers University Press, 1992.

Mabry, William Alexander. "Disfranchisement of the Negro in Mississippi." *Journal of Southern History* 4 (August 1938): 318–33.

———. *The Negro in North Carolina Politics since Reconstruction*. New York: A.M.S. Press, 1940.

———. "Negro Suffrage and Fusion Rule in North Carolina." *North Carolina Historical Review* 12 (April 1935): 70–102.

———. "White Supremacy and the North Carolina Suffrage Amendment." *North Carolina Historical Review* 13 (January 1936): 1–24.

McAdam, Doug. *Political Process and the Development of Black Insurgency, 1930–1970*. Chicago: University of Chicago Press, 1982.

McCandless, Amy Thompson. "Progressivism and the Higher Education of Southern Women." *North Carolina Historical Review* 70 (July 1993): 302–25.

McCarthy, Kathleen D., ed. *Lady Bountiful Revisited: Women, Philanthropy, and Power*. New Brunswick, N.J.: Rutgers University Press, 1990.

McCormick, Richard L. "The Discovery That 'Business Corrupts Politics': A Reappraisal of the Origins of Progressivism." *American Historical Review* 86 (April 1981): 247–74.

McCurry, Stephanie. *Masters of Small Worlds: Yeoman Households, Gender Relations, and the Political Culture of the Antebellum South Carolina Low Country*. New York: Oxford University Press, 1995.

———. "The Two Faces of Republicanism: Gender and Proslavery Politics in Antebellum South Carolina." *Journal of American History* 78 (March 1992): 1245–64.

McDowell, John Patrick. *The Social Gospel in the South: The Woman's Movement in the Methodist Episcopal Church, South, 1886–1939*. Baton Rouge: Louisiana State University Press, 1982.

McDuffie, Jerome A. "Politics in Wilmington and New Hanover County, N.C., 1865–1900: The Genesis of a Race Riot." Ph.D. dissertation, Kent State University, 1979.

McGerr, Michael. "Political Style and Women's Power, 1830–1930." *Journal of American History* 77 (December 1990): 864–85.

McGovern, James. "The American Woman's Pre–World War I Freedom in Manners and Morals." *Journal of American History* 55 (September 1968): 315–33.

McIlwaine, Shields. *The Southern Poor-White, from Lubberland to Tobacco Road*. New York: Cooper Square Publishers, 1970.

McKinney, Gordon B. "Southern Mountain Republicans and the Negro, 1865–1900." *Journal of Southern History* 41 (November 1975): 493–516.

McKinney, Richard I. *Religion in Higher Education among Negroes*. New Haven: Yale University Press, 1945.

MacLean, Nancy. *Behind the Mask of Chivalry: The Making of the Second Ku Klux Klan*. New York: Oxford University Press, 1994.

McMath, Robert C. *Populist Vanguard: A History of the Southern Farmers' Alliance*. Chapel Hill: University of North Carolina Press, 1975.

McMillen, Neil R. *Dark Journey: Black Mississippians in the Age of Jim Crow*. Urbana: University of Illinois Press, 1989.

McMurray, Linda O. *Recorder of the Black Experience: A Biography of Monroe Nathan Work*. Baton Rouge: Louisiana State University Press, 1985.

McNeill, Rosalie F. "The First Fifteen Months of Governor Daniel Lindsay Russell's Administration." Master's thesis, University of North Carolina at Chapel Hill, 1939.

Malson, Micheline R., Elisabeth Mudimbe-Boyi, Jean F. O'Barr, and Mary Wyer, eds. *Black Women in America: Social Science Perspectives*. Chicago: University of Chicago Press, 1990.

Marable, Manning. *How Capitalism Underdeveloped Black America: Problems in Race, Political Economy, and Society*. Boston: South End Press, 1983.

———. "Religion and Black Protest Thought in African American History." In *African American Religious Studies: An Interdisciplinary Anthology*, ed. Gayraud S. Wilmore, 330–31. Durham: Duke University Press, 1989.

Margo, Robert A. *Disenfranchisement, School Finance, and the Economics of Segregated Schools in the United States South, 1890–1910*. New York: Garland, 1985.

———. "Teacher Salaries in Black and White: The South in 1910." *Explorations in Economic History* 21 (July 1984): 306–26.

Marks, Carole. *Farewell—We're Good and Gone: The Great Black Migration*. Bloomington: Indiana University Press, 1989.

Marsh, Margaret. "Suburban Men and Masculine Domesticity." *American Quarterly* 40 (June 1988): 165–86.

Marteena, Constance Hill. *The Lengthening Shadow of a Woman*. Hicksville, N.Y.: Exposition Press, 1977.

Martin, Robert E. *Negro Disfranchisement in Virginia*. Washington, D.C.: Howard University Studies in the Social Sciences, 1938.

Marx, Gary. "Religion: Opiate or Inspiration of Civil Rights Militancy among Negroes?" *American Sociological Review* 32 (1969): 64–72.

Maslowski, James Joseph. "North Carolina Migration, 1870–1915." Ph.D. dissertation, University of North Carolina at Chapel Hill, 1953.

Massengill, Stephen E. " 'Portraits by the Sunlight Made': Daguerrean Artists in North Carolina, 1842–1861." *Carolina Comments* 41 (September 1993): 137–49.

Massey, Douglas, and Nancy A. Denton. *American Apartheid: Segregation and the Making of the Underclass*. Cambridge: Harvard University Press, 1993.

Mathews, Donald G. *Religion in the Old South*. Chicago: University of Chicago Press, 1977.

Matthews, Donald. *North Carolina Votes*. Chapel Hill: University of North Carolina Press, 1962.

Mattison, Richard. "The Evolution of Raleigh's Black Neighborhoods in the Nineteenth and Twentieth Centuries." Unpublished paper, Raleigh Historic Properties Commission.

Mays, Benjamin E., and Joseph W. Nicholson. *The Negroes' Church*. New York: Russell and Russell, 1933.

Meier, August. "The Boycott against Jim Crow Streetcars in the South, 1900–1906." *Journal of American History* 55 (March 1969): 756–75.

——. "History of the Negro Upper Class in Atlanta, Georgia, 1890–1958." *Journal of Negro Education* 28 (Spring 1959): 128–39.

——. "Negro Class Structure and Ideology in the Age of Booker T. Washington." *Phylon* 23 (Fall 1962): 258–66.

——. *Negro Thought in America, 1880–1915: Racial Ideologies in the Age of Booker T. Washington*. Ann Arbor: University of Michigan Press, 1963.

Meier, August, and Elliott Rudwick. *Along the Color Line: Explorations in the Black Experience*. Urbana: University of Illinois Press, 1976.

——. *From Plantation to Ghetto: An Interpretive History of American Negroes*. New York: Hill and Wang, 1966.

Mendenhall, Marjorie Stratford. "Southern Women of a Lost Generation." *South Atlantic Quarterly* 33 (January 1935): 343–53.

Meyerowitz, Joanne. *Women Adrift: Independent Wage Earners in Chicago, 1880–1930*. Chicago: University of Chicago Press, 1988.

Michel, Sonya, and Seth Koven. "Womanly Duties: Maternalist Politics and the Origins of Welfare States in France, Germany, Great Britain, and the United States, 1880–1920." *American Historical Review* 94 (October 1990): 1076–1108.

Milkman, Ruth. *Gender at Work: The Dynamics of Job Segregation by Sex during World War II*. Urbana: University of Illinois Press, 1987.

Miller, Bertha H. "Blacks in Winston-Salem, N.C., 1895–1920: Community Development in an Era of Benevolent Paternalism." Ph.D. dissertation, Duke University, 1981.

Miller, George M. "The Social Mission of Bishop Alexander Walters." In *Black Apostles: Afro-American Clergy Confront the Twentieth Century*, ed. Randall K. Burkett and Richard Newman, 247–52. Boston: G. K. Hall, 1978.

Mitchell, Broadus. *The Rise of Cotton Mills in the South*. Studies in Historical and Political Science. Baltimore: Johns Hopkins University Press, 1921.

Mitchell, Mark. "A History of the Black Population of New Bern, North Carolina, 1852–1872." Master's thesis, East Carolina University, 1980.

Mitchell, Memory F. "Freedom Brings Problems: Letters from the McKays and Nelsons in Liberia." *North Carolina Historical Review* 70 (October 1993): 430–65.

Mitchell, Theodore. *Political Education in the Southern Farmers' Alliance*. Madison: University of Wisconsin Press, 1987.

Mobley, Joe A. *James City: A Black Community in North Carolina*. Raleigh: North Carolina Department of Cultural Resources, 1981.

Montgomery, William Edward. "Negro Churches in the South, 1865–1915." Ph.D. dissertation, University of Texas at Austin, 1975.

——. *Under Their Own Vine and Fig Tree: The African-American Church in the South, 1865–1900*. Baton Rouge: Louisiana State University Press, 1993.

Moore, John Hammond. "The Negro and Prohibition in Atlanta, 1885–1887." *South Atlantic Quarterly* 68 (1970): 38–57.

Morgan, David. *Suffragists and Democrats: The Politics of Woman Suffrage in America*. Lansing: Michigan State University Press, 1972.

Morrison, Joseph L. *Governor O. Max Gardner: A Power in North Carolina and New Deal Washington*. Chapel Hill: University of North Carolina Press, 1971.

——. *Josephus Daniels: Small-d Democrat*. Chapel Hill: University of North Carolina Press, 1966.

——. *Josephus Daniels Says . . . : An Editor's Political Odyssey from Bryan to Wilson and F.D.R., 1894–1933*. Chapel Hill: University of North Carolina Press, 1962.

Morton, Patricia. *Disfigured Images: The Historical Assault on Afro-American Women*. Westport, Conn.: Greenwood Press, 1991.

Mowry, George. *The California Progressives*. Berkeley: University of California Press, 1951.

Muller, Philip Roy. "New Populism: North Carolina, 1884–1900." Ph.D. dissertation, University of North Carolina at Chapel Hill, 1949.

Mullins, Jack Simpson. "Lynching in South Carolina, 1900–1914." Master's thesis, University of South Carolina, 1961.

Mullis, Sharon M. "Extravaganza of the New South: The Cotton States, An Industrial Exposition, 1895." *Atlanta History Bulletin* 2 (Fall 1976): 17–29.

Muncy, Robin. *Creating a Female Dominion in American Reform, 1890–1935*. New York: Oxford University Press, 1991.

Murray, Pauli. *Proud Shoes: The Story of an American Family*. New York: Harper and Row, 1956.

Murray, Percy. *History of the North Carolina Teachers Association*. [Washington, D.C.]: National Education Association, [1984].

Myrdal, Gunnar. *An American Dilemma: The Negro Problem and Modern Democracy*. 2 vols. New York: Harper and Brothers, 1944.

Nalty, Bernard C. *Strength for the Fight: A History of Black Americans in the Military*. New York: Free Press, 1986.

NASC Interim History Writing Committee. *The Jeanes Story: A Chapter in the History of American Education, 1908–1968*. Atlanta: Southern Education Foundation, 1979.

Nathans, Sydney. *The Quest for Progress: The Way We Lived in North Carolina, 1870–1920*. Chapel Hill: University of North Carolina Press, 1983.

Neverdon-Morton, Cynthia. *Afro-American Women of the South and the Advancement of the Race, 1895–1925*. Knoxville: University of Tennessee Press, 1989.

——. "The Black Woman's Struggle for Equality in the South, 1895–1925." In *The Afro-American Woman: Struggles and Images*, ed. Sharon Harley and Rosalyn Terborg-Penn, 43–57. Port Washington, N.Y.: National University Publications, 1978.

——. "Self Help Programs as Educative Activities for Black Women in the South, 1895–1925." *Journal of Negro Education* 51 (Summer 1982): 207–21.

Newbold, N. C. *Five North Carolina Negro Educators*. Chapel Hill: University of North Carolina Press, 1939.

Newby, I. A. *Black Carolinians: A History of Blacks in South Carolina from 1895 to 1968*. Columbia: University of South Carolina Press, 1973.

——. *Jim Crow's Defense: Anti-Negro Thought in America, 1900–1930*. Baton Rouge: Louisiana State University Press, 1965.

Newsome, Clarence Genu. "Mary McLeod Bethune in Religious Perspective: A Seminal Essay." Ph.D. dissertation, Duke University, 1982.

Noble, David W. *The Progressive Mind, 1890–1917*. Minneapolis: Burgess Publishing Company, 1981.

Noble, Jeanne L. *Beautiful Also Are the Souls of My Black Sisters: A History of the Black Woman in America*. Englewood Cliffs, N.J.: Prentice Hall, 1978.

———. *The Negro Woman's College Education*. New York: Columbia University Press, 1956.

Noble, M. C. S. *A History of the Public Schools in North Carolina*. Chapel Hill: University of North Carolina Press, 1930.

Noblin, Stuart. *Leonidas LaFayette Polk: Agrarian Crusader*. Chapel Hill: University of North Carolina Press, 1949.

Nolen, Claude H. *The Negro's Image in the South: The Anatomy of White Supremacy*. Lexington: University Press of Kentucky, 1967.

Norton, Mary Beth. *Liberty's Daughters: The Revolutionary Experience of American Women, 1750–1800*. Glenview, Ill.: Scott, Foresman, 1980.

Novick, Peter. *That Noble Dream: The "Objectivity Question" and the American Historical Profession*. Cambridge: Cambridge University Press, 1988.

Nowaczk, Elaine Joan. "The North Carolina Negro in Politics, 1865–1876." Master's thesis, University of North Carolina at Chapel Hill, 1957.

O'Neill, William L. *Everyone Was Brave: A History of Feminism in America*. Chicago: Quadrangle, 1969.

Orr, Oliver. *Charles Brantley Aycock*. Chapel Hill: University of North Carolina Press, 1961.

Osborne, Heather A. "Widening the Sphere: The Response of Upper-Class Southern Women to Their Post–Civil War Role." Honors thesis, University of North Carolina at Chapel Hill, 1987.

Osterweis, Rollin G. *The Myth of the Lost Cause, 1865–1900*. Hamden, Conn.: Archon Books, 1973.

Ownby, Ted. *Subduing Satan: Religion, Recreation, and Manhood in the Rural South, 1865–1920*. Chapel Hill: University of North Carolina Press, 1990.

Padgug, Robert A. "Sexual Matters: On Conceptualizing Sexuality in History." In *Passion and Power: Sexuality in History*, ed. Kathy Peiss and Christina Simmons with Robert Padgug, 14–31. Philadelphia: Temple University Press, 1989.

Painter, Nell Irvin. *Exodusters: Black Migration to Kansas after Reconstruction*. New York: Alfred A. Knopf, 1976.

———. "The Journal of Ella Gertrude Clanton Thomas: An Educated White Woman in the Eras of Slavery, War, and Reconstruction." In *The Secret Eye: The Journal of Ella Gertrude Clanton Thomas, 1848–1889*, ed. Virginia Ingraham Burr, 1–67. Chapel Hill: University of North Carolina Press, 1990.

———. " 'Social Equality,' Miscegenation, and the Maintenance of Power." In *The Evolution of Southern Culture*, ed. Numan B. Bartley, 47–67. Athens: University of Georgia Press, 1988.

———. *Standing at Armageddon: The United States, 1877–1919*. New York: W. W. Norton, 1987.

Palmer, Bruce. *Man over Money: The Southern Populist Critique of American Capitalism*. Chapel Hill: University of North Carolina Press, 1980.

Palmer Memorial Institute: The Mission and the Legacy. Greensboro: Women of Greensboro, [1981].

Pankey, George E. "Life Histories of Rural Negro Teachers in the South." Master's thesis, University of North Carolina at Chapel Hill, 1927.

Paoli, Donna Jeanne. "Marion Butler's View of the Negro, 1889–1901." Master's thesis, University of North Carolina at Chapel Hill, 1969.

Paris, Peter J. *The Social Teaching of the Black Churches*. Philadelphia: Fortress Press, 1985.

Parker, Inez Moore. *The Biddle–Johnson C. Smith University Story*. Charlotte: Charlotte Publishing, 1975.

Parsons, Margaret Ellen Kidd. "White Plague and the Double-Barred Cross in Atlanta, 1895–1945." Ph.D. dissertation, Emory University, 1985.

Pascoe, Peggy. "Race, Gender, and the Privileges of Property: On the Significance of Miscegenation Law in United States History." In *New Viewpoints in Women's History: Working Papers from the Schlesinger Library Fiftieth Anniversary Conference, March 4–5, 1994*, ed. Susan Ware, 99–122. Cambridge: Arthur and Elizabeth Schlesinger Library on the History of Women in America, 1994.

———. *Relations of Rescue: The Search for Female Moral Authority in the American West, 1874–1939*. New York: Oxford University Press, 1990.

"The Passing of Our Pioneers." *Aframerican Woman's Journal* 3 (Spring 1944): 21.

Pateman, Carole. "Feminist Critiques of the Public/Private Dichotomy." In *Public and Private in Social Life*, ed. S. I. Benn and G. F. Gaus, 281–303. New York: St. Martin's Press, 1983.

Patterson, Orlando. *Slavery and Social Death*. Cambridge: Harvard University Press, 1982.

Patton, June O. "Lucy Craft Laney." In *Black Women in America: An Historical Encyclopedia*, ed. Darlene Clark Hine, 693–95. New York: Carlson, 1994.

Paulson, Ross E. *Women's Suffrage and Prohibition: A Comparative Study of Equality and Social Control*. Glenview, Ill.: Scott, Foresman, 1973.

Peare, Catherine Owens. *Mary McLeod Bethune*. New York: Vanguard Press, 1951.

Pearson, Charles C., and J. Edwin Hendricks. *Liquor and Anti-Liquor in Virginia, 1619–1919*. Durham: Duke University Press, 1967.

Peek, William W. *The History of Education in North Carolina*. Raleigh: North Carolina Department of Public Instruction, [1993].

Peiss, Kathy, and Christian Simmons, eds., with Robert A. Padgug. *Passion and Power: Sexuality in History*. Philadelphia: Temple University Press, 1989.

Perkins, Carol O. "Pragmatic Idealism: Industrial Training, Liberal Education, and Women's Special Needs—Conflict and Continuity in the Experience of Mary McLeod Bethune and Other Black Women Educators, 1900–1930." Ph.D. dissertation, Claremont Graduate School and San Diego University, 1987.

Perkins, Linda. "The Impact of the 'Cult of True Womanhood' on the Education of Black Women." *Journal of Social Issues* 39, no. 3 (1983): 17–28.

Perman, Michael. *The Road to Redemption: Southern Politics, 1869–1879*. Chapel Hill: University of North Carolina Press, 1984.

Pettis, Joyce. "The Literary Imagination and the Historic Event: Chesnutt's Use of History in *The Marrow of Tradition*." *South Atlantic Review* 55 (1990): 37–48.

———. "*The Marrow of Tradition*: Charles Chesnutt's Novel of the South." *North Carolina Literary Review* 2 (Spring 1994): 108–18.

Phelps-Stokes Fund. *Negro Status and Race Relations in the United States, 1911–1946*. New York, 1948.

Pickens, Ernestine Williams. *Charles W. Chesnutt and the Progressive Movement*. New York: Pace University Press, 1994.

Pinckney, Darryl. "Aristocrats." *New York Review of Books*, 11 May 1995, 27–34.

Pleck, Elizabeth H., and Joseph H. Pleck, eds. *The American Man*. Englewood Cliffs, N.J.: Prentice Hall, 1979.

Poe, Clarence. *My First Eighty Years*. Chapel Hill: University of North Carolina Press, 1963.

Poole, Thomas G. "'What Country Have I?': Nineteenth-Century African-American Ideological Critiques of the Nation's Birth and Destiny." *Journal of Religion* 72 (October 1992): 533–48.

Pope, Christie Farnham. "Preparation for Pedestals: North Carolina Antebellum Female Seminaries." Ph.D. dissertation, University of Chicago, 1977.

Poppenheim, Mary B. *The History of the United Daughters of the Confederacy*. Richmond: Garrett and Massey, 1938.

Potwin, Marjorie A. *Cotton Mill People of the Piedmont: A Study in Social Change*. New York: Columbia University Press, 1927.

Powdermaker, Hortense. *After Freedom: A Cultural Study of the Deep South*. New York: Viking Press, 1939.

Powell, Ruth Gilliam. "History of the Southern Commission on Interracial Cooperation." Master's thesis, University of South Carolina, 1936.

Powell, William S. *North Carolina through Four Centuries*. Chapel Hill: University of North Carolina Press, 1989.

——, ed. *Dictionary of North Carolina Biography*. 5 vols. to date. Chapel Hill: University of North Carolina Press, 1979–.

Prather, Henry Leon. "The Red Shirt Movement in North Carolina, 1898–1900." *Journal of Negro History* 62 (April 1977): 174–84.

——. *Resurgent Politics and Educational Progressivism in the New South: North Carolina, 1890–1913*. Rutherford, N.J.: Associated Universities Press, 1979.

——. *We Have Taken a City: Wilmington Racial Massacre and Coup of 1898*. Rutherford, N.J.: Associated Universities Press, 1984.

Pratt, Minnie Bruce. "Identity: Skin Blood Heart." In *Yours in Struggle: Three Feminist Perspectives on Anti-Semitism and Racism*, ed. Elly Bulkin, Minnie Bruce Pratt, and Barbara Smith, 9–64. Ithaca, N.Y.: Firebrand Books, 1984.

Rabinowitz, Howard N. *The First New South, 1865–1920*. Arlington Heights, Ill.: Harlan Davidson, 1992.

——. "Half a Loaf: The Shift from White to Black Teachers in the Negro Schools of the Urban South, 1865–1890." *Journal of Southern History* 40 (November 1974): 565–94.

——. *Race Relations in the Urban South, 1865–1890*. New York: Oxford University Press, 1978.

Raboteau, Albert J. "Martin Luther King, Jr., and the Tradition of Black Religious Protest." In *Religion and the Life of the Nation: American Recoveries*, ed. Rowland A. Sherril, 46–63. Urbana: University of Illinois Press, 1990.

——. *Slave Religion: The "Invisible Institution" in the Antebellum South*. New York: Oxford University Press, 1978.

Rachleff, Peter J. *Black Labor in the South: Richmond, Virginia, 1865–1890*. Philadelphia: Temple University Press, 1984.

Rae, Nicol. "Class and Culture: American Political Cleavages in the Twentieth Century." *Western Political Quarterly* 45 (September 1992): 629–50.

Ransom, Roger L., and Richard Sutch. *One Kind of Freedom: The Economic Consequences of Emancipation*. Cambridge: Cambridge University Press, 1977.

Raper, Arthur F. *Preface to Peasantry*. Chapel Hill: University of North Carolina Press, 1936.

———. *The Tragedy of Lynching*. Chapel Hill: University of North Carolina Press, 1933.

Rawick, George P. *From Sundown to Sunup: The Making of the Black Community*. Westport, Conn.: Greenwood Press, 1972.

Raynor, George. *Rebels and Yankees in Rowan County*. Salisbury, N.C.: Salisbury Post, 1991.

Redkey, Edwin S. *Black Exodus: Black Nationalist and Back-to-Africa Movement, 1890–1910*. New Haven: Yale University Press, 1969.

Reichley, A. James. *Religion in American Public Life*. Washington, D.C.: Brookings Institution, 1985.

Reid, George W. "A Biography of George H. White, 1852–1918." Ph.D. dissertation, Howard University, 1974.

Richardson, Harry Van Buren. *Dark Salvation: The Story of Methodism As It Developed among Blacks in America*. Garden City, N.Y.: Anchor Press, 1976.

Richardson, Joe M. *Christian Reconstruction: The American Missionary Association and Southern Blacks, 1861–1890*. Athens: University of Georgia Press, 1986.

Richardson, Marilyn. *Black Women and Religion: A Bibliography*. Boston: G. K. Hall, 1980.

Rieff, Lynne A. " 'Go Ahead and Do All You Can': Southern Progressives and Alabama Home Demonstration Clubs, 1914–1940." In *Hidden Histories of Women in the New South*, ed. Virginia Bernhard, Betty Brandon, Elizabeth Fox-Genovese, Theda Perdue, and Elizabeth H. Turner, 134–52. Columbia: University of Missouri Press, 1994.

Riley, Denise. *Am I That Name?: Feminism and the Category of "Women" in History*. Minneapolis: University of Minnesota Press, 1988.

Rippy, James Fred, ed. *F. M. Simmons, Statesman of the New South: Memoirs and Speeches*. Durham: Duke University Press, 1936.

Robbins, Richard. "Blacks and Business." In *Paths toward Freedom*, ed. Doris Lucas, Tom Parramore, and Earlie Thorpe, 75–79. Raleigh: Center for Urban Affairs, North Carolina State University, 1976.

Rodgers, Daniel T. "In Search of Progressivism." *Reviews in American History* 10 (December 1982): 113–32.

Rodgers-Rose, LaFrances, ed. *The Black Woman*. Beverly Hills, Calif.: Sage, 1980.

Roediger, David R. *Towards the Abolition of Whiteness*. London: Verso, 1994.

———. *The Wages of Whiteness: Race and the Making of the American Working Class*. London: Verso, 1991.

Rogers, Lou. "Dr. Delia Dixon-Carroll: A Woman Whose Dreams Came True." *We the People* 1 (August 1943): 12.

———. *Tar Heel Women*. Raleigh: Warren Publishing Company, 1949.

———. "The W.C.T.U. in North Carolina." *We the People* 3 (August 1945): 22–23.

Rogin, Michael. "'The Sword Became a Flashing Vision': D. W. Griffith's *The Birth of a Nation*." In *Ronald Reagan, The Movie*, 190–235. Berkeley: University of California Press, 1987.

Roller, David C. "The Republican Party of North Carolina, 1900–1916." Ph.D. dissertation, Duke University, 1965.

Roper, John Herbert. "Charles Brantley Aycock: A Study in Limitation and Possibility." *Southern Studies* 16 (Fall 1977): 277–91.

Rosenstone, Robert A. "Experiments in Writing the Past: Is Anybody Interested?" *Perspectives*, December 1992, 10, 12, 20.

Ross, Edyth L., ed. *Black Heritage in Social Welfare, 1860–1930*. Metuchen, N.J.: Scarecrow Press, 1987.

Roth, Darlene Rebecca. "Matronage: Patterns in Women's Organizations—Atlanta, Georgia, 1890–1940." Ph.D. dissertation, George Washington University, 1978.

Rothman, Sheila M. *Woman's Proper Place: A History of Changing Ideals and Practices, 1870 to the Present*. New York: Basic Books, 1978.

Rountree, Louise Marie, comp. *A Brief Chronology of Black Salisbury-Rowan*. [Salisbury, N.C.], 1976.

Rouse, J. K. *The Noble Experiment of Warren C. Coleman*. Charlotte: Crabtree Press, 1972.

Rouse, Jacqueline Anne. "Atlanta's African-American Women's Attack on Segregation, 1900–1920." In *Gender, Class, Race, and Reform in the Progressive Era*, ed. Noralee Frankel and Nancy S. Dye, 10–23. Lexington: University Press of Kentucky, 1991.

———. *Lugenia Burns Hope: Black Southern Reformer*. Athens: University of Georgia Press, 1989.

Rowland, Sue. "Frances Joseph Gaudet: Independent Black Reformer." Unpublished paper in author's possession.

Roydhouse, Marion W. "Bridging Chasms: Community and the Southern YWCA." In *Visible Women: New Essays on American Activism*, ed. Nancy A. Hewitt and Suzanne Lebsock, 270–95. Urbana: University of Illinois Press, 1993.

———. "The 'Universal Sisterhood of Women': Women and Labor Reform in North Carolina, 1900–1932." Ph.D. dissertation, Duke University, 1980.

Ryan, Mary P. *The Cradle of the Middle Class: The Family in Oneida County, New York, 1790–1865*. New York: Cambridge University Press, 1981.

———. "Gender and Public Access: Women's Politics in Nineteenth-Century America." In *Habermas and the Public Sphere*, ed. Craig Calhoun, 259–88. Cambridge: Massachusetts Institute of Technology Press, 1992.

———. *Women in Public: Between Banners and Ballots, 1825–1880*. Baltimore: Johns Hopkins University Press, 1990.

Salem, Dorothy. *To Better Our World: Black Women in Organized Reform, 1890–1920*. New York: Carlson, 1990.

Savitt, Todd L. "The Education of Black Physicians at Shaw University, 1882–1918." In *Black Americans in North Carolina and the South*, ed. Jeffrey J. Crow and Flora Hatley, 160–88. Chapel Hill: University of North Carolina Press, 1984.

Saxton, Alexander. *The Rise and Fall of the White Republic: Class Politics and Mass Culture in Nineteenth-Century America*. New York: Verso, 1990.

Schechter, Patricia. "Feminism and the Color Line: Black Women, Temperance, and Suffrage." Unpublished paper in author's possession.

Schlesinger, Arthur M. "Biography of a Nation of Joiners." *American Historical Review* 50 (October 1944): 1–25.

Schwalm, Leslie Ann. "The Meaning of Freedom: African-American Women and Their Transition from Slavery to Freedom in Lowcountry South Carolina." Ph.D. dissertation, University of Wisconsin-Madison, 1991.

Schwartz, Michael. "An Estimate of the Size of the Southern Farmers' Alliance, 1884–1890." *Agricultural History* 51 (October 1977): 759–69.

Schweninger, Loren. "The Anomaly of Black Slaveholding." *North Carolina Historical Review* 67 (April 1990): 159–92.

——. *Black Property Owners in the South, 1790–1915*. Urbana: University of Illinois Press, 1990.

——. "Prosperous Blacks in the South, 1790–1880." *American Historical Review* 95 (February 1990): 31–56.

Scott, Anne Firor. "After Suffrage: Southern Women in the 1920s." In *Making the Invisible Woman Visible*, ed. Anne Firor Scott, 222–43. Urbana: University of Illinois Press, 1984.

——. "Historians Construct the Southern Woman." In *Sex, Race, and the Role of Women in the South*, ed. Joanne V. Hawks and Sheila L. Skemp, 95–110. Jackson: University Press of Mississippi, 1983.

——. "A Historian's Odyssey." In *Making the Invisible Woman Visible*, ed. Anne Firor Scott, xviii–xix. Urbana: University of Illinois Press, 1984.

——. "Most Invisible of All: Black Women's Voluntary Associations." *Journal of Southern History* 56 (February 1990): 3–22.

——. *Natural Allies: Women's Associations in American History*. Urbana: University of Illinois Press, 1991.

——. "The 'New Woman' in the New South." *South Atlantic Quarterly* 61 (August 1962): 473–83.

——. "On Seeing and Not Seeing: A Case of Historical Invisibility." *Journal of American History* 71 (June 1984): 7–21.

——. "A Progressive Wind from the South, 1906–1913." *Journal of Southern History* 29 (February 1963): 51–70.

——. *The Southern Lady: From Pedestal to Politics, 1830–1930*. Chicago: University of Chicago Press, 1970.

——. "Women, Religion, and Social Change in the South, 1830–1930." In *Religion and the Solid South*, ed. Samuel S. Hill, Jr., 92–121. Nashville: Abingdon Press, 1972.

——, ed. *Making the Invisible Woman Visible*. Urbana: University of Illinois Press, 1984.

Scott, Anne Firor, and Andrew M. Scott. *One Half the People: The Fight for Woman Suffrage*. Philadelphia: J. B. Lippincott, 1975.

Scott, James C. *Domination and the Arts of Resistance: Hidden Transcripts*. New Haven: Yale University Press, 1990.

———. *Weapons of the Weak: Everyday Forms of Peasant Resistance*. New Haven: Yale University Press, 1985.

Scott, Joan Wallach. "Experience." In *Feminists Theorize the Political*, ed. Judith Butler and Joan W. Scott, 22–40. New York: Routledge, 1992.

———. *Gender and the Politics of History*. New York: Columbia University Press, 1988.

Segal, Lynne. *Slow Motion: Changing Masculinities, Changing Men*. New Brunswick, N.J.: Rutgers University Press, 1990.

Seidman, Steven, ed. *Jurgen Habermas on Society and Politics: A Reader*. Boston: Beacon Press, 1989.

Sellers, James Benson. *The Prohibition Movement in Alabama, 1702–1943*. Chapel Hill: University of North Carolina Press, 1943.

Shadron, Virginia. "Out of Our Homes: The Woman's Rights Movement in the Methodist Episcopal Church, South, 1890–1918." Master's thesis, Emory University, 1976.

Shadron, Virginia, Eleanor Hinton Hoytt, Margaret Parsons, Barbara B. Reitt, Beverly Guy-Sheftall, Jacqueline Zalumas, and Darlene R. Roth, eds. *Stepping off the Pedestal: Academic Women in the South*. New York: Modern Language Association of America, 1982.

Shapiro, Herbert. *White Violence and Black Response, from Reconstruction to Montgomery*. Amherst: University of Massachusetts Press, 1988.

Sharf, Lois, and Joan M. Jensen, eds. *Decades of Discontent: The Women's Movement, 1920–1940*. Westport, Conn.: Greenwood Press, 1983.

Shaw, J. Beverly. *The Negro in the History of Methodism*. Nashville: Parthenon Press, 1954.

Shaw, Stephanie J. "Black Club Women and the Creation of the National Association of Colored Women." *Journal of Women's History* 3 (Fall 1991): 10–25.

Shivery, Louise. "The History of Organized Social Work among Atlanta Negroes, 1890–1935." Master's thesis, Atlanta University, 1946.

Silber, Nina. *The Romance of Reunion: Northerners and the South, 1865–1900*. Chapel Hill: University of North Carolina Press, 1993.

Simmons, Linda, ed. *The Heritage of Blacks in North Carolina*. Charlotte: North Carolina African American Heritage Foundation with the Cooperation of the Delmar Company, 1990.

Simpson, Nancy W. *Heritage of Wilkes County, North Carolina*. Vol. 2. Charlotte: Delmar Publishing, 1990.

Sims, Anastatia. "The Power of Feminism and Femininity in the New South." Ph.D. dissertation, University of North Carolina at Chapel Hill, 1985.

———. "Sallie Southall Cotten and the North Carolina Federation of Women's Clubs." Master's thesis, University of North Carolina, 1976.

———. "Sisterhoods of Service: Women's Clubs and Methodist Women's Missionary Societies in North Carolina, 1890–1930." In *Women in New Worlds: Historical Perspectives on the Wesleyan Tradition*, ed. Rosemary Skinner Keller, Louise L. Queen, and Hilah F. Thomas, 2:196–210. Nashville: Abingdon Press, 1982.

———. " 'The Sword of the Spirit': The W.C.T.U. and Moral Reform in North Carolina, 1883–1933." *North Carolina Historical Review* 64 (October 1987): 394–415.

Sklar, Kathryn Kish. "The Historical Foundations of Women's Power in the Creation of the American Welfare State, 1830–1930." In *Mothers of a New World: Maternalist Politics and the Origins of the Welfare State*, ed. Sonya Michel and Seth Koven, 43–93. New York: Routledge, 1993.

Slagell, Amy Rose. "A Good Woman Speaking Well: The Oratory of Frances E. Willard." Ph.D. dissertation, University of Wisconsin-Madison, 1992.

Smith, Edwin W. *Aggrey of Africa: A Study in Black and White*. New York: Doubleday, Doran, 1929.

Smith, Rogers M. "Beyond Tocqueville, Myrdal, and Hartz: The Multiple Traditions in America." *American Political Science Review* 87 (September 1993): 549–66.

Smith, Samuel L. *Builders of Goodwill: The Story of the State Agents of Negro Education in the South, 1910–1950*. Nashville: Tennessee Book Company, 1950.

Smith, T. Lynn. "The Redistribution of the Negro Population of the United States, 1910–1960." *Journal of Negro History* 51 (July 1966): 155–73.

Smith-Rosenberg, Carol. "Beauty, the Beast, and the Militant Woman: A Case Study in Sex Roles and Social Stress in Victorian America." *American Quarterly* 23 (October 1971): 562–84.

———. *Disorderly Conduct: Visions of Gender in Victorian America*. New York: Alfred A. Knopf, 1985.

Snitow, Ann, Christine Stansell, and Sharon Thompson, eds. *Powers of Desire: The Politics of Sexuality*. New York: Monthly Review Press, 1983.

Solomon, Barbara Miller. *In the Company of Educated Women*. New Haven: Yale University Press, 1985.

Soloutos, Theodore. *Farmer Movements in the South, 1865–1933*. Berkeley: University of California Press, 1960.

Spero, Sterling D., and Abram L. Harris. *Black Worker: The Negro and the Labor Movement*. New York: Columbia University Press, 1931.

Spruill, Albert W. *Great Recollections from Aggieland*. [Wilmington, N.C.]: Whitehead Printing, 1964.

Stansell, Christine. *City of Women: Sex and Class in New York, 1789–1860*. New York: Alfred A. Knopf, 1986.

Stanton, Elizabeth Cady, ed., and Susan B. Anthony, Matilda J. Gage, and Ida H. Harper, joint eds. *History of Woman Suffrage*. 1881–1922. Reprint, New York: Source Book Press, 1970.

Stearns, Peter N. *Be a Man!: Males in Modern Society*. New York: Holmes and Meier, 1979.

Steelman, Joseph Flake. *North Carolina's Role in the Spanish-American War*. Raleigh: North Carolina Division of Archives and History, 1975.

———. "The Progressive Era in North Carolina, 1884–1917." Ph.D. dissertation, University of North Carolina at Chapel Hill, 1955.

———. "Republican Party Strategists and the Issue of Fusion with Populists in North Carolina, 1893–1894." *North Carolina Historical Review* 47 (July 1970): 244–69.

Sterling, Dorothy. *Black Foremothers: Three Lives*. New York: Feminist Press, 1988.

———. *We Are Your Sisters: Black Women in the Nineteenth Century*. New York: W. W. Norton, 1984.

Stewart, Ruth Ann. "Charlotte Eugenia Hawkins Brown." In *Notable American Women: The Modern Period*, ed. Barbara Sicherman and Carol Hurd Green, 111–13. Cambridge: Belknap Press, 1980.

Stoler, Ann L. "Making Empire Respectable: The Politics of Race and Sexual Morality in Twentieth-Century Colonial Cultures." *American Ethnologist* 18 (November 1989): 634–60.

Stowe, Steven M. *Intimacy and Power in the Old South: Ritual in the Lives of the Planters*. Baltimore: Johns Hopkins University Press, 1987.

Stowell, Jay S. *Methodist Adventures in Negro Education*. New York: Methodist Book Concern, 1922.

Stringer, Patricia A., and Irene Thompson, eds. *Stepping off the Pedestal: Academic Women in the South*. New York: Modern Language Association of America, 1982.

Strong, Charles M. *History of Mecklenburg County Medicine*. Charlotte: News Printing House, 1929.

Stuckey, Sterling. *Slave Culture: Nationalist Theory and the Foundations of Black America*. New York: Oxford University Press, 1987.

Swerdlow, Amy, and Hanna Lessinger, eds. *Class, Race, and Sex: The Dynamics of Control*. Boston: G. K. Hall, 1983.

Szuberla, Guy. "Ladies, Gentlemen, Flirts, Mashers, Snoozers, and the Breaking of Etiquette's Code." In *Prospects: An Annual of American Cultural Studies*, ed. Jack Salzman, 169–96. New York: Cambridge University Press, 1990.

Talmadge, John E. *Rebecca Latimer Felton: Nine Stormy Decades*. Athens: University of Georgia Press, 1960.

Tate, Claudia. *Domestic Allegories of Political Desire: The Black Heroine's Text at the Turn of the Century*. New York: Oxford University Press, 1992.

Tatum, Noreen. *A Crown of Service: A Story of Woman's Work in the Methodist Episcopal Church, South, from 1878–1940*. Nashville: Parthenon Press, 1960.

Taylor, Arnold H. *Travail and Triumph: Black Life and Culture in the South since the Civil War*. Westport, Conn.: Greenwood Press, 1976.

Taylor, Elizabeth A. "The Woman Suffrage Movement in North Carolina." *North Carolina Historical Review* 37 (January 1961): 45–61, (April 1961): 173–89.

Taylor, Frances Saunders. " 'On the Edge of Tomorrow': Southern Women, the Student YWCA, and Race, 1920–1944." Ph.D. dissertation, Stanford University, 1984.

Taylor, Mark T. "Seiners and Tongers: North Carolina Fisheries in the Old and New South." *North Carolina Historical Review* 69 (January 1992): 1–36.

Taylor, Mattie W., ed. *Celebrating One Hundred Ten Years of Winning "The World for Christ," 1880–1990*. New York: Mission Education Committee, [1990].

Taylor, Rosser H. *Carolina Crossroads: A Study of Rural Life at the Horse-and-Buggy Era*. Murfreesboro, N.C.: Johnson Publishing, [1966].

———. *The Free Negro in North Carolina*. Chapel Hill: University of North Carolina Press, 1920.

Terborg-Penn, Rosalyn. "African-American Women's Networks in the Anti-Lynching Crusade." In *Gender, Class, Race, and Reform in the Progressive Era*, ed. Noralee Frankel and Nancy S. Dye, 148–61. Lexington: University Press of Kentucky, 1991.

——. "Afro-Americans in the Struggle for Woman Suffrage." Ph.D. dissertation, Howard University, 1977.

——. "Discontented Black Feminists: Prelude and Postscript to the Passage of the Nineteenth Amendment." In *Decades of Discontent: The Women's Movement, 1920–1940*, ed. Lois Sharf and Joan M. Jensen, 261–78. Westport, Conn.: Greenwood Press, 1983.

——. "Discrimination against Afro-American Women in the Woman's Movement, 1830–1920." In *The Afro-American Woman: Struggles and Images*, ed. Sharon Harley and Rosalyn Terborg-Penn, 17–27. Port Washington, N.Y.: Kennikat Press, 1978.

——. "The Historical Treatment of the Afro-American in the Woman Suffrage Movement, 1900–1920: A Bibliographical Essay." *Current Bibliography on African Affairs* 7 (1974): 245–59.

Thelen, David. "Social Tensions and the Origins of Progressivism." *Journal of American History* 56 (September 1969): 323–41.

Thelen, David, Howard N. Rabinowitz, and C. Vann Woodward. "Perspectives: The Strange Career of Jim Crow." *Journal of American History* 75 (December 1988): 841–68.

Thomas, Mary Martha. *Stepping out of the Shadows: Alabama Women, 1819–1990*. Tuscaloosa: University of Alabama Press, 1995.

Thompson, E. P. *The Making of the English Working Class*. New York: Vintage Books, 1966.

Thompson, Holland. *From Cotton Field to Cotton Mill*. New York: Macmillan, 1906.

Thompson, Kathleen. "Charlotte Hawkins Brown." In *Black Women in America: An Historical Encyclopedia*, ed. Darlene Clark Hine, 172–74. New York: Carlson, 1993.

Thornbrough, Emma Lou. "American Negro Newspapers, 1880–1908." *Business History Review* 40 (Winter 1966): 467–90.

——. "The National Afro-American League, 1887–1908." *Journal of Southern History* 27 (November 1961): 494–512.

Tilly, Louise A., and Patricia Gurin, eds. *Women, Politics, and Change*. New York: Russell Sage Foundation, 1990.

Timberlake, James H. *Prohibition and the Progressive Movement, 1900–1920*. Cambridge: Harvard University Press, 1966.

Tindall, George Brown. "Business Progressivism: Southern Politics in the Twenties." *South Atlantic Quarterly* 62 (Winter 1963): 92–106.

——. "The Campaign for the Disfranchisement of Negroes in South Carolina." *Journal of Southern History* 15 (May 1949): 212–34.

——. *The Emergence of the New South, 1913–1945*. Baton Rouge: Louisiana State University Press, 1967.

——. *The Persistent Tradition in New South Politics*. Baton Rouge: Louisiana State University Press, 1975.

——. *South Carolina Negroes, 1877–1900*. Columbia: University of South Carolina Press, 1952.

Tolnay, Stewart E., and E. M. Beck. "Rethinking the Role of Racial Violence in the Great Migration." In *Black Exodus: The Great Migration from the American*

South, ed. Alferdteen Harrison, 20–35. Jackson: University Press of Mississippi, 1991.

Trattner, Walter I. *Crusade for the Children*. Chicago: Quadrangle Books, 1970.

Trelease, Allen W. "The Fusion Legislatures of 1895 and 1897: A Roll-Call Analysis of the North Carolina House of Representatives." *North Carolina Historical Review* 57 (July 1980): 280–309.

Trotter, Joe W. "African-American History: Origins, Development, and Current State of the Field." *OAH Magazine of History* (Summer 1993): 12–18.

——. *Coal, Class, and Color: Blacks in Southern West Virginia, 1915–1932*. Urbana: University of Illinois Press, 1990.

——. "Introduction: Black Migration in Historical Perspective." In *The Great Migration in Historical Perspective: New Dimensions of Race, Class, and Gender*, ed. Joe W. Trotter, 1–21. Bloomington: Indiana University Press, 1991.

——, ed. *The Great Migration in Historical Perspective: New Dimensions of Race, Class, and Gender*. Bloomington: Indiana University Press, 1991.

Turner, Elizabeth Hayes. "Benevolent Ladies, Club Women, and Suffragists: Galveston Women's Organizations, 1880–1920." Ph.D. dissertation, Rice University, 1990.

——. "Women, Religion, and Reform in Galveston, 1880–1920." In *Urban Texas: Politics and Development*, ed. Char Miller and Heywood T. Sanders, 75–95. College Station: Texas A & M University Press, 1990.

Turner, Grace, and Miles S. Philback, comps. *Wilkes County, North Carolina, Will Abstracts, 1777–1910*. N.p., 1988.

Tyack, David, and Elisabeth Hansot. *Learning Together: A History of Coeducation in American Schools*. New Haven: Yale University Press and the Russell Sage Foundation, 1990.

Tyler, Helen E. *Where Prayer and Purpose Meet: The W.C.T.U. Story*. Evanston, Ill.: Signal Press, 1949.

Tyrrell, Ian. *Woman's World/Woman's Empire: The Woman's Christian Temperance Union in International Perspective*. Chapel Hill: University of North Carolina Press, 1991.

Underwood, Evelyn. "The Struggle for White Supremacy in North Carolina, 1880–1930." Master's thesis, University of North Carolina at Chapel Hill, 1943.

Urban, Wayne J. "History of Education: A Southern Exposure." *History of Education Quarterly* 21 (Summer 1981): 131–45.

Vance, Norman. *The Sinews of the Spirit: The Ideal of Christian Manliness in Victorian Literature and Religious Thought*. Cambridge: Cambridge University Press, 1985.

Vickers, Gregory. "Southern Baptist Women and Social Concerns, 1910–1929." *Baptist History and Heritage* 23 (October 1988): 3–13.

Wactor, Hildred Henry. *Miscellany: A Manual for the Young Woman's Home and Foreign Missionary Society*. Fayetteville, N.C.: Worth Printing Company, 1975.

Walker, Alice. *In Search of Our Mothers' Gardens: Womanist Prose*. New York: Harcourt Brace Jovanovich, 1983.

Walker, Clarence Earl. *A Rock in a Weary Land: The African Methodist Episcopal Church during the Civil War and Reconstruction*. Baton Rouge: Louisiana State University Press, 1982.

Walkowitz, Daniel J. "The Making of a Feminine Professional Identity: Social Workers in the 1920s." *American Historical Review* 95 (October 1990): 1051–75.

Walls, William Jacob. *The African Methodist Episcopal Zion Church: The Reality of the Black Church*. Charlotte: African Methodist Episcopal Zion Publishing House, 1974.

———. *Joseph Charles Price: Educator and Race Leader*. Boston: Christopher Publishing House, 1943.

Walton, Hanes, Jr. "Another Force for Disfranchisement: Blacks and the Prohibitionists in Tennessee." *Journal of Human Relations* 18 (First Quarter 1970): 728–38.

Walton, Hanes, Jr., and James E. Taylor. "Blacks and the Southern Prohibition Movement." *Phylon* 32 (Fall 1971): 247–59.

Ware, Susan, ed. *New Viewpoints in Women's History: Working Papers from the Schlesinger Library Fiftieth Anniversary Conference, March 4–5, 1994*. Cambridge: Arthur and Elizabeth Schlesinger Library on the History of Women in America, 1994.

Ware, Vron. *Beyond the Pale: White Women, Racism, and History*. London: Verso, 1992.

Waring, Joseph Ioor. *A History of Medicine in South Carolina, 1825–1900*. N.p.: South Carolina Medical Association, 1967.

Warlick, Kenneth Ray. "Practical Education and the Negro College in North Carolina, 1880–1930." Ph.D. dissertation, University of North Carolina at Chapel Hill, 1980.

Washington, Harold R. "History and Role of Black Law Schools." *North Carolina Central Law Journal* 5 (Spring 1974): 158–89.

Washington, Mary Helen. "Introduction." In *Anna Julia Haywood Cooper: A Voice from the South by a Black Woman of the South*. 1892. Reprint. New York: Oxford University Press, 1988.

Waskow, Arthur. *From Race Riot to Sit In, 1919 to the 1960s*. Garden City, N.Y.: Anchor Press, 1966.

Watson, Alan. *A History of New Bern and Craven County*. New Bern: Tryon Palace Commission, 1987.

Watson, Richard L. "From Populism through the New Deal." In *Interpreting Southern History: Essays in Honor of Sanford W. Higginbotham*, ed. John Boles and Evelyn Thomas Nolen, 329–56. Baton Rouge: Louisiana State University Press, 1987.

———. "Furnifold M. Simmons: Jehovah of the Tar Heels." *North Carolina Historical Review* 44 (April 1967): 166–87.

———. "A Political Leader Bolts: F. M. Simmons in the Presidential Election of 1928." *North Carolina Historical Review* 37 (October 1960): 516–43.

———. "A Southern Democratic Primary: Simmons versus Bailey in 1930." *North Carolina Historical Review* 42 (January 1965): 21–46.

Weare, Walter B. *Black Business in the New South: A Social History of the North Carolina Mutual Life Insurance Company*. Urbana: University of Illinois Press, 1973.

Weaver, Garrett F. "The Politics of Local Democratic-Populist Fusion in the Election of 1896 in North Carolina." Master's thesis, University of North Carolina at Chapel Hill, 1968.

Weaver, Phillip J. "The Gubernatorial Election of 1896 in North Carolina." Master's thesis, University of North Carolina at Chapel Hill, 1937.

Webber, Thomas L. *Deep Like the Rivers: Education in the Slave Quarter Community, 1831–1865.* New York: W. W. Norton, 1978.

Wedell, Marsha. *Elite Women and the Reform Impulse in Memphis, 1875–1915.* Knoxville: University of Tennessee Press, 1991.

Weiner, Jonathan. "AHR Forum: Class Structure and Economic Development in the American South, 1865–1955." *American Historical Review* 84 (October 1979): 970–1006.

——. *Social Origins of the New South, 1860–1885.* Baton Rouge: Louisiana State University Press, 1978.

Weisenfeld, Judith. " 'Who Is Sufficient for These Things?': Sara G. Stanley and the American Missionary Association, 1864–1868." *Church History* 60 (December 1991): 493–507.

Welter, Barbara. *Dimity Convictions: The American Woman in the Nineteenth Century.* Athens: Ohio State University Press, 1976.

Wesley, Charles Harris. *The History of the National Association of Colored Women's Clubs: A Legacy of Service.* Washington, D.C.: The Association, 1984.

West, Cornel. *Prophecy Deliverance!: An Afro-American Revolutionary Christianity.* Philadelphia: Westminster Press, 1982.

Westin, Richard B. "The State and Segregated Schools: Negro Public Education in North Carolina, 1863–1923." Ph.D. dissertation, Duke University, 1966.

Whatley, Warren C. "African American Strikebreakers from the Civil War to the New Deal." *Social Science History* 17 (Winter 1993): 525–58.

Wheeler, Edward L. *Uplifting the Race: The Black Minister in the New South, 1865–1902.* Washington, D.C.: University Press of America, 1986.

Wheeler, Marjorie Spruill. "Mary Johnston, Suffragist." *Virginia Magazine of History and Biography* 100 (January 1992): 99–118.

——. *New Women of the New South: The Leaders of the Woman Suffrage Movement in the Southern States.* New York: Oxford University Press, 1993.

——, ed. *Votes for Women: The Woman Suffrage Movement in Tennessee, the South, and the Nation.* Knoxville: University of Tennessee Press, forthcoming.

White, Deborah Gray. "The Cost of Club Work, the Price of Black Feminism." In *Visible Women: New Essays on American Activism,* ed. Nancy A. Hewitt and Suzanne Lebsock, 247–69. Urbana: University of Illinois Press, 1993.

——. "The Slippery Slope of Class in Black America: The National Council of Negro Women and the International Ladies' Auxiliary to the Brotherhood of Sleeping Car Porters—A Case Study." In *New Viewpoints in Women's History: Working Papers from the Schlesinger Library Fiftieth Anniversary Conference, March 4–5, 1994,* ed. Susan Ware, 180–95. Cambridge: Arthur and Elizabeth Schlesinger Library on the History of Women in America, 1994.

White, Frank H. "The Economic and Social Development of Negroes in North Carolina since 1900." Ph.D. dissertation, New York University, 1960.

White, Shane. " 'It Was a Proud Day': African Americans, Festivals, and Parades in the North, 1741–1834." *Journal of American History* 81 (June 1994): 13–50.

Whitener, Daniel Jay. *Prohibition in North Carolina, 1715–1945.* Chapel Hill: University of North Carolina Press, 1945.

Whites, LeeAnn. "The Charitable and the Poor: The Emergence of Domestic Politics in Augusta, Georgia, 1860–1880." *Journal of Social History* 17 (Summer 1984): 601–15.

———. "The De Graffenreid Controversy: Class, Race, and Gender in the New South." *Journal of Southern History* 54 (August 1988): 449–78.

———. "Rebecca Latimer Felton and the Problem of 'Protection' in the New South." In *Visible Women: New Essays on American Activism*, ed. Nancy A. Hewitt and Suzanne Lebsock, 41–61. Urbana: University of Illinois Press, 1993.

———. "Rebecca Latimer Felton and the Wife's Farm: The Class and Racial Politics of Gender Reform." *Georgia Historical Quarterly* 76 (Summer 1992): 354–72.

Wiebe, Robert H. *The Search for Order, 1877–1920.* New York: Hill and Wang, 1967.

Wilkerson-Freeman, Sarah. "The Emerging Political Consciousness of Gertrude Weil: Education and Women's Clubs, 1879–1914." Master's thesis, University of North Carolina at Chapel Hill, 1985.

———. "Women and the Transformation of American Politics: North Carolina, 1898–1940." Ph.D. dissertation, University of North Carolina at Chapel Hill, 1995.

Willard, George-Anne. "Charles L. Coon: Crusader for Educational Reform." Ph.D. dissertation, University of North Carolina at Chapel Hill, 1974.

———. "Charles Lee Coon, Negro Education, and the Atlanta Speech Controversy." *East Carolina College Publications in History* 3 (1966): 151–74.

Williams, Felicia McLellan. "The History of Negro Education in New Hanover County, North Carolina, to 1953." Master's thesis, North Carolina Agricultural and Technical College, 1954.

Williams, Gilbert Anthony. "The A.M.E. Christian Recorder: A Forum for the Social Ideas of Black Americans, 1854–1902." Ph.D. dissertation, University of Illinois at Urbana-Champaign, 1979.

Williamson, Joel. *After Slavery: The Negro in South Carolina during Reconstruction.* Chapel Hill: University of North Carolina Press, 1965.

———. *The Crucible of Race: Black-White Relations in the American South since Emancipation.* New York: Oxford University Press, 1984.

———. *New People: Miscegenation and Mulattoes in the United States.* New York: Free Press, 1980.

Wilmore, Gayraud S. *African American Religious Studies: An Interdisciplinary Anthology.* Durham: Duke University Press, 1989.

———. *Black Religion and Black Radicalism: An Interpretation of the Religious History of Afro-American People.* 1973. Reprint. Maryknoll, N.Y.: Orbis Books, 1983.

Wilson, Charles Reagan. *Baptized in Blood: The Religion of the Lost Cause, 1865–1920.* Athens: University of Georgia Press, 1980.

———, ed. *Religion in the South.* Jackson: University Press of Mississippi, 1985.

Wilson, Emily Herring. *Hope and Dignity: Older Black Women of the South.* Philadelphia: Temple University Press, 1983.

Wilson, Richard W. *Compliance Ideologies: Rethinking Political Culture.* Cambridge: Cambridge University Press, 1992.

Winston, George T. *A Builder of the New South: Daniel Augustus Tompkins.* Garden City, N.Y.: Doubleday, Page, 1920.

Wolfe, Thomas. *Look Homeward, Angel.* 1929. Reprint. New York: Charles Scribner's Sons, 1957.

Wolgemuth, Kathleen Long. "Woodrow Wilson's Appointment Policy and the Negro." *Journal of Southern History* 24 (November 1958): 457–72.

Wolters, Raymond. "Personal Connections and the Growth of NAACP." *Reviews in American History* 2 (March 1974): 138–45.

Wood, Phillip J. *Southern Capitalism and the Political Economy of North Carolina, 1880–1980*. Durham: Duke University Press, 1986.

Woodman, Harold D. "Sequel to Slavery: The New History Views the Postbellum South." *Journal of Southern History* 43 (November 1977): 523–54.

Woodson, Carter G. *The History of the Negro Church*. Washington, D.C.: Associated Publishers, 1945.

Woodward, C. Vann. *The Burden of Southern History*. Rev. ed. Baton Rouge: Louisiana State University Press, 1968.

——. *Origins of the New South, 1877–1913*. Baton Rouge: Louisiana State University Press, 1951.

——. *The Strange Career of Jim Crow*. 3d ed., rev. New York: Oxford University Press, 1974.

Woody, Thomas. *A History of Women's Education in the United States*. New York: Octagon Books, 1966.

Wooley, Robert Howard. "Race and Politics: The Evolution of the White Supremacy Campaign of 1898 in North Carolina." Ph.D. dissertation, University of North Carolina at Chapel Hill, 1977.

Workers of the Writers' Project of the Works Progress Administration. *The Negro in Virginia*. New York: Hastings House, 1940.

Wright, Arthur D. *The Negro Rural School Fund, Inc. (Anna T. Jeanes Foundation), 1907–1933*. Washington, D.C.: Negro Rural School Fund, 1933.

Wright, Gavin. *Old South, New South: Revolutions in the Southern Economy since the Civil War*. New York: Basic Books, 1986.

Wright, George C. *Life behind a Veil: Blacks in Louisville, Kentucky, 1865–1930*. Baton Rouge: Louisiana State University Press, 1985.

Wyatt-Brown, Bertram. *Southern Honor: Ethics and Behavior in the Old South*. New York: Oxford University Press, 1982.

Wynes, Charles E. *Race Relations in Virginia, 1870–1902*. Charlottesville: University Press of Virginia, 1961.

——, ed. *The Negro in the South since 1865: Selected Essays in American Negro History*. Tuscaloosa: University of Alabama Press, 1965.

Yandle, Paul. "Joseph Charles Price and His 'Peculiar Work.'" *North Carolina Historical Review* 70 (January 1993): 40–56, (April 1993): 130–52.

Yates, Walter L. *He Spoke, Now They Speak: A Collection of Speeches and Writings on the Life and Works of Joseph C. Price*. Salisbury, N.C.: Hood Theological Seminary, 1952.

Yenser, Thomas, ed. *Who's Who in Colored America, 1933–1937*. 4th ed. New York: Thomas Yenser Publisher, 1937.

——. *Who's Who in Colored America, 1941–1944*. New York: Thomas Yenser Publisher, 1944.

Young, Henry. *Major Black Religious Leaders, 1755–1940*. Nashville: Abingdon Press, 1977.

Zimmerman, Loretta Ellen. "Alice Paul and the National Woman's Party, 1912–1920." Ph.D. dissertation, Tulane University, 1964.

Palmer Memorial Institute, 180; funding, 183–84, 187–89, 297–98 (n. 48); curriculum, 184; designation as historic site, 294 (n. 5); converted to prep school, 296 (n. 26)

Parent Unions, 162, 164, 165

Parker, John J., 215, 226

Pasteur, Dinah, 5

Pasteur, Edmund, 5–6, 232–33 (n. 19)

Pasteur, Richard, 5

Pasteur, Sarah, 6–7, 232 (n. 15); descendants, 232 (n. 16)

Pettey, Charles Calvin, 11–12, 16–20, 22–23, 29, 80, 83, 87, 117, 236 (n. 50), 237 (n. 53); views on education, 26; illness and death, 126, 128, 278 (n. 50)

Pettey, Corine, 227–28, 235 (n. 38)

Pettey, Sarah Dudley. See Dudley Pettey, Sarah

Petteyville, Calif., 12, 237 (n. 53)

Philanthropists, 138–40

Physicians, black, 21, 240 (n. 94)

Pickenpack, Lula, 11–12

Piedmont, 2, 64

Place, sense of, 3–4, 183–84

Plessy v. Ferguson, 20

Policemen, black, 97

Political office, African Americans in, 7–9, 78, 122, 234 (n. 27)

Politics: black women and, 18, 93, 99–105, 107–8, 147–50, 172–73, 201–2, 203–4, 211–15, 218–24; white women and, 93–99, 110, 117, 203–10, 215–18, 268 (n. 55)

Polk, Leonidus, 66, 77

Polling places. See Voter registration *and specific elections*

Poll taxes, 120

Populist Party, 77–78, 85; and 1898 election, 98; and disfranchisement, 121–22; racial views of, 267 (n. 35)

Presbyterian Church, 11, 41

Price, Joseph, 14, 40, 140, 182

Pritchard, Jeter C., 78, 123, 129–30, 276 (n. 23)

Procrustes, 2

Progressive Era, 147–50, 152, 156, 173–75

Progressivism: role of women in, 147–48; role of white women in, 149; role of black women in, 149–50, 152, 173–75

Prohibition, 46, 50, 55, 58–59, 249–50 (n. 74). See also Independent Order of Good Templars; Woman's Christian Temperance Union

Propaganda, 88–89; Thomas Dixon, Jr.'s, works as, 69–70, 135–38; African Americans' response to, 142–43; use of image of African Americans wearing eyeglasses as, 275 (n. 15). See also Rape; White supremacy campaign

Property ownership, 15–16

Prostitutes, 72

Public health, 292 (n. 113); Modern Health Clubs, 163–64; community cleanup days, 168–73

Public life: integration in, 73–74; white women and, 95–96; black women and, 102–5, 147–48, 151, 172

Purity: of white women, 23, 47, 72–73, 94–95, 106; of black women, 36, 104, 140–41

Railroads: segregation on, 2, 126, 185, 201, 242–43 (n. 133); lawyers for, 257 (n. 22)

Raleigh, N.C., 66

Raleigh *News and Observer*, 66, 88, 98, 125

Ransom, Matthew, 77

Rape: as explanation for biracial people, 68–69; in propaganda campaign, 82–89, 91–92; linked to fusion rule, 84–85; statistics on, 86, 262–63 (nn. 134–35); black men's condemnation of, 87–88; by whites, 266 (n. 27)

Reconstruction, 7, 62; Thomas Dixon, Jr.'s, account of, 67, 136–38

Red Shirt rallies, 98–99

Gender and Jim Crow: Women and the Politics of White Supremacy in North Carolina, 1896–1920, by Glenda Elizabeth Gilmore (1996)

Delinquent Daughters: Protecting and Policing Adolescent Female Sexuality in the United States, 1885–1920, by Mary E. Odem (1995)

U.S. History as Women's History: New Feminist Essays, edited by Linda K. Kerber, Alice Kessler-Harris, and Kathryn Kish Sklar (1995)

Common Sense and a Little Fire: Women and Working-Class Politics in the United States, 1900–1965, by Annelise Orleck (1995)

How Am I to Be Heard?: Letters of Lillian Smith, edited by Margaret Rose Gladney (1993)

Entitled to Power: Farm Women and Technology, 1913–1963, by Katherine Jellison (1993)

Revising Life: Sylvia Plath's Ariel Poems, by Susan R. Van Dyne (1993)

Made From This Earth: American Women and Nature, by Vera Norwood (1993)

Unruly Women: The Politics of Social and Sexual Control in the Old South, by Victoria E. Bynum (1992)

The Work of Self-Representation: Lyric Poetry in Colonial New England, by Ivy Schweitzer (1991)

Labor and Desire: Women's Revolutionary Fiction in Depression America, by Paula Rabinowitz (1991)

Community of Suffering and Struggle: Women, Men, and the Labor Movement in Minneapolis, 1915–1945, by Elizabeth Faue (1991)

All That Hollywood Allows: Re-reading Gender in 1950s Melodrama, by Jackie Byars (1991)

Doing Literary Business: American Women Writers in the Nineteenth Century, by Susan Coultrap-McQuin (1990)

Ladies, Women, and Wenches: Choice and Constraint in Antebellum Charleston and Boston, by Jane H. Pease and William H. Pease (1990)

The Secret Eye: The Journal of Ella Gertrude Clanton Thomas, 1848–1889, edited by Virginia Ingraham Burr, with an introduction by Nell Irvin Painter (1990)

Second Stories: The Politics of Language, Form, and Gender in Early American Fictions, by Cynthia S. Jordan (1989)

Within the Plantation Household: Black and White Women of the Old South, by Elizabeth Fox-Genovese (1988)

The Limits of Sisterhood: The Beecher Sisters on Women's Rights and Woman's Sphere, by Jeanne Boydston, Mary Kelley, and Anne Margolis (1988)